Books by Burton J. Hendrick

Life and Letters of Walter H. Page, 3 vols.

The Education of an American

The Lees of Virginia

Bulwark of the Republic

Statesmen of the Lost Cause

Life of Andrew Carnegie, 2 vols.

Lincoln's War Cabinet

The Age of Big Business (*Yale Chronicles of America*)

The Victory at Sea (*With William S. Sims*)

William Crawford Gorgas: His Life and Work
(*With Marie Doughty Gorgas*)

Letters of Andrew Carnegie, 2 vols. (*Editor*)

Books by *Burton J. Hendrick*

Life and Letters of Walter H. Page, *3 vols.*

The Education of an American

The Lees of Virginia

Bulwark of the Republic

Statesmen of the Lost Cause

Life of Andrew Carnegie, *2 vols.*

Lincoln's War Cabinet

The Age of Big Business (*Yale Chronicles of America*)

The Victory at Sea (*With William S. Sims*)

William Crawford Gorgas: His Life and Work
(*With Marie Doughty Gorgas*)

Letters of Andrew Carnegie, *2 vols.* (*Editor*)

LINCOLN'S WAR CABINET

Reproduced by courtesy of Mr. Newcomb Carlton of New York

Evening Reception at the White House

From a painting probably by Francis B. Carpenter. The date was March 1, 1864, when General Grant, coming to Washington to receive his commission as Lieutenant General, was the hero of the occasion. Grant stands next to Lincoln, who is greeting Mrs. Grant. At the extreme left is William H. Seward, Secretary of State. In the center is secretary of the Treasury Salmon Chase, with his daughter Kate. To the immediate right of Lincoln is Edwin Stanton, Secretary of War, and still further to the right (profile with white whiskers) is Gideon Welles, Secretary of the Navy. The second figure to the right of Welles is Simon Cameron, ex-Secretary of War, and next to him Montgomery Blair, Postmaster General. In the right foreground is Mrs. Lincoln sitting with General Scott

LINCOLN'S
War Cabinet

by Burton J. Hendrick

WITH ILLUSTRATIONS

AN ATLANTIC MONTHLY PRESS BOOK

LITTLE, BROWN AND COMPANY · BOSTON
1946

FIRST EDITION

Published November 1946

ATLANTIC–LITTLE, BROWN BOOKS
ARE PUBLISHED BY
LITTLE, BROWN AND COMPANY
IN ASSOCIATION WITH
THE ATLANTIC MONTHLY PRESS

PRINTED IN THE UNITED STATES OF AMERICA

CONTENTS

ILLUSTRATIONS

BOOK ONE

A Ministry of All the Talents

I

IT WAS a matter of frequent remark with Abraham Lincoln that the cabinet which, in completed form, he submitted to the Senate on March 5, 1861, was essentially the same as the one he had selected on November 7, 1860, the day following his election. In the construction of his official family Lincoln displayed the qualities that were to distinguish his administration. Independence of opinion, absolute reliance on his own judgment, a willingness to listen to advice, a readiness to compromise, so long as the main object was achieved, and a logically thought out scheme of action – all these well-known Lincoln characteristics were ultimately brought to bear in making this, his first great decision. The original choice of counselors was made on Lincoln's own initiative, with no broader outlook on the national field than could be obtained from the window of his little shabby law office in Springfield. In after years Lincoln liked to relate the story to his favorite intimates. One of them, Gideon Welles, has left an account in Lincoln's own words, incidentally giving the first close-up picture we have of Lincoln after his election to the Presidency. He spent the evening of that fateful November 6, 1860, in the telegraph office at Springfield, the superintendent having placed the room at his exclusive disposal. "I was there without leaving, after the returns began to come in until we had enough to satisfy us as to how the election had gone. I went home, but not to get much sleep, for I felt then, as I never had before, the responsibility that was upon me. I began to feel at once that I needed support – others to share with me the burden. This was on Wednesday morning, and, before the sun went down, I had made up my cabinet. It was almost the same that I finally appointed." [1]

True as was this statement of the case, the selection of the cabinet was not the simple process that Lincoln's words imply. Probably no President underwent such anguish in organizing an administration as

[1] Welles, Gideon, *Diary*. Boston, Houghton Mifflin Co., 1925. I, 82. The selections from this book are used by permission of the publishers, Houghton Mifflin Company.

the one elected on the eve of the Civil War. Though the new department heads had been chosen before the sun went down November 7, the cabinet, in definite form, was not complete even on the day of inauguration. When Lincoln, on February 11, 1861, began his journey to Washington, only two cabinet members had been offered appointments and had accepted them. While the somewhat drab inaugural procession was advancing on March 4 from the White House to the ceremonies in front of the domeless Capitol, the most important post, that of Secretary of State, was still hanging in suspense. When the completed list reached the Senate the following day, five nervous expectant statesmen obtained the first official news of their selection.

The reasons for this deliberation are found both in the critical state of public affairs at the moment and in the complex character of the party placed in Lincoln's hand for their solution. By March 4, 1861, seven states had seceded from the Federal government and established what they persisted in calling a new and independent Republic. Lincoln's task was to bring this so-called Confederacy to an end and re-establish the Union. The means which had been allotted for this purpose was the political organization known as the Republican Party. Wise statesmanship called upon the new leader to transform this agency into a harmonious and compact mass, using it as a powerful, homogeneous unit for the achievement of the great purpose. Had the party, in 1860, been a solid, well-established entity, strengthened by decades of tradition and loyalty, the objective would have been a difficult one. But the aggregation of which Lincoln had suddenly found himself the captain was something new – only four years old; and had never before won a national election. Moreover, it was by no means united or composed of sympathetic elements. In fact, hardly any such unit as a Republican Party existed on the day of Lincoln's election. An organization bearing that official title, it is true, had assembled in Chicago in early May 1860, and launched the campaign for the control of Federal affairs that had now proved successful. But it was not a coherent nor, except on one issue, a congenial, smoothly working association. The so-called party comprised several groups, under chieftains personally hostile and full of jealousy and rivalry, who had come together upon one question only. The determination of Southern cotton planters to extend slavery into the territories, and the appalling success their program had achieved in the preceding fifteen years, formed the danger that had brought under one standard many otherwise conflicting forces, resolved to check the aggression by political action. In 1860 no certainty existed that the Republican Party represented a permanent movement. Failure to achieve its announced intention would have meant its speedy end. In 1840 and 1844 the Liberty Party, pledged to the abolition of slavery in every region where it prevailed, had unsuccessfully contested for the Presidency. It had promptly disappeared as a political power. In 1848 the Free-Soil Party, committed against the extension of slavery into the new territory recently acquired from Mexico, had similarly gone down to defeat, and had similarly vanished as an organized force. The Republican Party of 1860 had carried the country on the platform of no new slave territories and no more slave states, but it contained so many various and antagonistic elements, and so many jealous aspiring leaders, that even the most hopeful did not confidently predict a long existence. Old-line Whigs, old-line Democrats, Abolitionists, Free-Soilers, Know-Nothings, and other factions had for the time united, but how long they could be kept enrolled under a single leadership and how successful they could be in achieving their aims, no man was bold enough to prophesy.

The Chicago Convention of May 1860 has been described as "a loose aggregation of free thinkers," and it was indeed a collection of independent, stubborn men, holding no general orthodox creed, agreeing only in opposition to slavery, and even on that topic entertaining a variety of opinions. Nothing more suggestively emphasized discord than the unpopularity of the word "Republican." In the minds of most Americans the term signified the same thing as abolitionism, yet the majority of the new party members, including Lincoln himself, repudiated that sect. From 1856 to 1860, there was a general shrinking from the name. The hosts assembled in the Chicago Wigwam had been organized under several designations. In Missouri they called themselves simply the Opposition. In that locality several of the factions which made up the anti-Democratic forces refused to enter state and county conventions that had enrolled under the "Republican" banner. In Ohio and Pennsylvania the same forces chose to be known as the "People's" or the "Popular" Party. Union Party, Anti-Nebraska Party, Antislavery Party, Free-Soil Party, were a few of the other denominations which the enemies of slavery extension preferred to the newfangled standard. Even in 1864, when the clans assembled in Baltimore to nominate Lincoln for a second term, the gathering adopted the name of National Union Party. Not until 1868 did the word "Republican" definitely fix itself in the political glossary of the nation. Slavery had then been extinguished, new issues were claiming attention, and no fear any longer prevailed that to be called a Republican was to write oneself down as another John Brown or William Lloyd Garrison.

Thus the organization whose members came to refer to it as the Grand Old Party was certainly not old, and perhaps not "grand," in

1860, but something entirely new. The mere lust for public office had led a considerable number into the new amalgamation, especially those Whig politicians who, after the disappearance of that party, could find no other refuge. Most of the famished cormorants who followed the rail splitter to Washington in February 1861 had never tasted the spoils of office. Not a well-co-ordinated army of conquest, but a disharmonious potpourri of factions, each demanding "recognition"—such was the Joseph's coat of a party which an inexperienced stranger from the prairie was expected to transform into a well-articulated machine for solving mighty problems. To the extent that this fact gave Lincoln a free hand, it was an advantage. In the main, however, it added to the difficulties of the problem, for to create a happy family of discordant rivals, most of them having their own personal ambitions and their own favorite plan for solving the nation's ills, could tax the ablest diplomatic skill. Nor did the attitude of the party leaders towards Lincoln make the problem easier. Few conventions have left such bitterness as that held in Chicago in May 1860. Of all the candidates presented to the noisy congregation the one that seemed to be the least promising had carried off the prize. Great Senators like William H. Seward and Salmon P. Chase, for thirty years the nation's leaders in the antislavery crusade, and old war horses like Edward Bates, Simon Cameron, and William L. Dayton, had gone down to defeat before a man whose national prominence, such as it was, had been the development of two or three years. Of the seven men whom Lincoln finally gathered around his council table there was probably not one who did not regard himself, in experience, intellect, and capacity to lead, superior to the nominal chieftain.

For a President to appoint a rival for nomination to his cabinet was not unprecedented, but to collect under his wing nearly all the disappointed men whom he had defeated in the convention represented a new experiment in party conciliation. The fact that Lincoln successfully performed this feat indicates traits of character not suspected at the time, though they were to become evident enough in the trying times ahead. In this the man displayed supreme self-reliance and a conscious sense of leadership. Lincoln was not one of those Presidents who hesitate to surround themselves with men as strong as or stronger than themselves. He deliberately sought the most commanding associates he could find, not at all fearful that they would gain the upper hand, entirely confident of his own ability to control and direct and to retain complete authority in his own hands. Personal likes and dislikes had nothing to do with Lincoln's choice of advisers. He seriously put himself to what he regarded as his supreme task, that of organizing a compact working force that could best destroy the Confederate States of America and preserve the Union. The only instrument available to his hand was that discordant congeries of men and principles which called itself, almost half-ashamed, the Republican Party.

Once having formed this general plan, certain choices for the cabinet became almost automatic. From the day of nomination, Lincoln had fixed upon the men for the two most important posts. Excepting the new President himself – and probably neither of these two statesmen would have granted the exception – William H. Seward and Salmon Portland Chase outranked all Republican statesmen of the day, in the brilliancy of their careers, in the predominant leadership evinced in the antislavery crusade, in their intellectual attainments, in gifts of oratory, capacity as legislators, and strength of character. Their courses in public life had followed similar lines. Both had gained national fame by opposing the growing power of slavery, both had served their states as governors for two terms, Seward in New York and Chase in Ohio, and as Senators of the United States. The fame of the two men stood so high that Lincoln in the early days felt for them a kind of awe. That the new Republican Party should have turned to him for leadership, and ignored the claims of his most prominent rivals, was something that he had found it hard to understand. "What's the use of talking of me for President," Lincoln had said to Jesse W. Fell, when that enterprising presidential boomer[2] had held up the splendid prospect of the White House, "when we have such men as Seward, Chase, and others, who are so much better known and whose names are so intimately associated with the principles of the Republican party? Everybody knows them. No one, scarcely, outside of Illinois, knows me. Besides, is it not, as a matter of justice, due to such men, who have carried this movement forward to its present status, in spite of fearful opposition, personal abuse and bad names? I think so." Lincoln coupled Seward and Chase in this comparison, but there is little doubt that Seward was the man who had first claim upon his respect, and not many Americans of the time would have disagreed with this preference.

Seward entered the Senate in 1849 at the time when Webster, Clay, and Calhoun were fighting their last battles on the slavery issue. The illustrious trio all died in the next two or three years, and thus left a vacant space for new leaders. Of the group that quickly sprang into

[2] Fell was an active member of the Illinois group who had Lincoln's candidacy in hand. He is famous as the correspondent to whom Lincoln addressed his letter of December 20, 1859, giving a three-page biographical sketch. See *Works*, V, 286.

fame, Seward, Chase, Sumner, from the North, Judah P. Benjamin, Jefferson Davis, and John Slidell from the South, the New Yorker probably found the greatest favor with the public. For Seward was then a forceful, hard-hitting debater and party leader; he was an intense human being, and like that exotic figure in the English House of Commons, Benjamin Disraeli, had an unusualness in manner and appearance which made him the most interesting member of the assembly. Certainly the man whom visitors to Washington in the late fifties most wished to see and hear was the senior Senator from New York. The sight itself justified a visit to Washington. By 1860 the "redheaded upstart" who had sought to be governor of the largest state in the Union at the age of thirty-three had considerably aged; but the gangling body moved among his colleagues with all its youthful swiftness. Seward's stature, only five feet four, and his clothes, old-fashioned even then – oaken-colored trousers, popularly known as pantaloons, long-tailed coat whose skirts hung listlessly from his chair, lofty collar, encircled by a black stock with huge expanse of white shirt bosom below – always attracted the fixed gaze of the visitors' gallery. The feature that most impressed the same observers was the nose, large, elongated, beaklike, subtended by thick lips, the under one protruding, and a weak recessive chin. In one respect this face departed from the favored type of the sixties and clung to the Clay-Webster pattern, for Seward never fell victim to the Civil War passion for a beard; his countenance, always scrupulously shaved, high cheekboned, in his latter years slightly shriveled, was long and narrow; the head, compared by a contemporary to a haystack, was crowned by a mass of tousled hair – red in Seward's youth, rather straw-colored in middle age, practically white in the final years. Huge ears, heavy brows, blue-gray eyes that were at the same time shrewd and dreamy, neck as small as a woman's, slender shoulders that sloped at an angle of at least forty-five degrees, long, dangling arms, spindly legs, gracefully contracted waistline – when this Dickensian figure disentangled itself and rose to address the Senate the torrent of powerful though slightly husky eloquence came as a surprise. A speech by Seward was an experience, not only for the address itself, but for the ritual that accompanied it. Inevitably when the orator finished and sat down, he would reach for his snuffbox, take a pinch, emit a tremendous sneeze, and conclude the ceremony by the application to his hawklike nose of a huge yellow silk handkerchief.

In speech Seward possessed few old-fashioned qualities. He represented the transition that was taking place from resounding declamation to restrained lawyer-like arguments. His voice had little carrying power, and the gestures were awkward; the intellectual content, the wide reading and grasp of principles, and the persuasive reasoning, gave Seward's deliverances far more influence when read than when spoken. A certain Disraelian cynicism, sometimes at the expense of the Southern states, added to their literary value. An occasional biting aside did not increase his popularity south of the Potomac. Once a Virginia statesman interrupted to declare that the "pestilent" agitation of slavery was depreciating the value of that type of "property." "No," gently replied the New Yorker, hitting the South in one of its most sensitive spots, "I think youth and beauty still bring the accustomed high prices." That Seward was more of a scholarly than a popular speaker is evident in the fact that his *Works*, in five large volumes, were published in his own lifetime. His most famous speeches circulated in printed form like popular novels, one of them, made on the meeting of the Congress in 1861, reaching a distribution of more than a million copies.

To the prevailing petty vice of American statesmen of the time, especially that of the South – tobacco chewing – Seward was not addicted, but he was a continuous smoker of cigars. In conversation his disorganized frame usually sat hunched up in an armchair, one yellow-sheathed leg thrown over the other, the rest of the person concealed by mighty eruptions of smoke. Since he was pre-eminently the social man, solitary smoking did not accord with Seward's taste. "The Secretary lit his cigar, then gave me one" – so William Howard Russell, correspondent of the London *Times*, begins his account of a famous interview with Seward, in the early days of the war. This liberality indicated a side of Seward almost as important as his statesmanship. Association with human beings was a necessity of his nature. He was on easy terms, not only with his party associates and the diplomatic body, but with his political foes. Jefferson Davis was one of his closest friends and remained such up to the time he became President of the Confederate states. Men of as divergent opinions as Charles Sumner and Pierre Soulé, little as they frequently sympathized with Seward's opinions, found him a delightful companion. Conversation, constant, unrestrained, frequently reckless, gave him more pleasure than the finest senatorial debate. Seward was one member of the cabinet who was not shocked by Lincoln's "undignified" yarns, for he was an irreclaimable storyteller himself. Dining, wining, table gossip, personal discussion, were the gifts that made the New York statesman the most affable of the cabinet group. Though well versed in more difficult literature – for Seward was a student of Burke, Bacon, Bolingbroke, and other political philosophers, as well as of the classics, Tacitus and

Cicero being particular favorites – he had also a fondness for light literature, frequently passing whole evenings reading aloud with his wife, and his addiction to the theater startled his more somber associates, such as Chase and Bates, who held the conventional attitude of the day towards that Satanic diversion. Seward never missed performances of the Booths, of James H. Hackett, Edmund Kean, Edwin Forrest, Sheridan Knowles, and other favorite contemporaries. Charlotte Cushman, whenever she came to Washington, was usually a guest in the Seward home, and the Senator once caused a minor scandal by calling upon the lustrous Adah Isaacs Menken, in her dressing room, to express the pleasure derived from her performance.

Seward had the charming, but not too common talent of revealing his inmost self in his letters. His wife was too much of an invalid to stand the hard life of Washington and almost daily letters to her, lover-like in devotion, reveal the Senator in a variety of moods. In these and other letters it appears that Seward's real home was not the house he maintained in Washington so many years, but the considerable estate acquired as a young man in Auburn, New York, whose development was the delight of his existence. The flowers, the vegetables, the dogs, cats, chipmunks, and birds, the days passed with his friends in the garden, the long drives with Mrs. Seward in the beautiful country of the Finger Lakes – hardly any letters give so pleasant a view of American rural life. "The advance of spring in the country," he writes one April morning, "was always interesting to me; and this is the first time I have enjoyed it in four years. I watch the development of vegetables with a lover's interest. I have my hot bed in delightful success. My cucumbers are commencing their ramblings. The radishes begin to gather roughness upon the leaf. The saps start from my grapes, and the polyanthus is in full bloom. . . . The crocus has flourished in bright yellow flowers, and is drooping beneath the gaudy rivalry of the daffodils which burst upon us in full splendor with the rising sun this morning. The little border flower, with the pretty name that I cannot remember, disclosed its petals at the same time. The lilac buds are bursting and the gooseberries almost in leaf. . . . I am writing with my window open into the shrubbery and the air is redolent of sweets and the birds are in full chorus." Seward would write pages about "Bob," his mockingbird, and describe at length the antics of other animals. On his return from Europe in 1859, of all the honors received, the one that apparently gave him most satisfaction was that his cat – an animal not usually responsive to the softer virtues – displayed the utmost joy and insisted on sitting on his shoulder for the larger part of the first day.

Evidently in William Henry Seward we have a public man who was also very much of a human being; and this attractive personality formed the background of one of the most influential and puzzling careers of his time. With that literary gift which provided the chief stock in trade for his public work, Seward, in his *Autobiography*,[3] has pictured his early days – an important contribution, though unfortunately the narrative stops at the year 1834, when the author's political days had hardly begun. The foundation, however, had been laid. The village of Florida in which Seward was born in 1801 was only about seventy-five miles from the city of New York. Seward's father, a successful farmer, physician, banker, politician, and judge, rich enough to endow the Seward Institute, an educational foundation which had a long and prosperous existence, owned three Negro slaves, two women and a boy, whom the childish Seward found the most entertaining part of the household. They were the boy's perpetual delight; he reveled in their ghost stories, their familiarity with witches and the devil, with the criminal history of the region – the men who had been hanged, and the disreputable and drunken Negroes who periodically ran away, and were usually brought back with iron yokes about their necks. "What wonder that I felt their apartment more attractive than the parlor, and their conversation a relief from the severe decorum that prevailed there?" New York did not abolish slavery until 1827; so most of the families in Seward's region had as many bondmen as his own father, or even more. Seward's personal experience with the institution as boy and young man "determined me, at that early age, to be an abolitionist." By 1820, at the age of nineteen, however, an even more arresting discovery was made. "I found that, after all, politics was the important and engrossing business of the country." By this time his education was complete. Diffident and awkward as a child, not over-robust, a red-haired boy not pugnacious in disposition, Seward spent most of his early time in study and reading. Books gave his mind a turn that remained to the end, influencing even his course on the crisis preceding Sumter.

Addison's *Cato*, which Seward as a child witnessed at a school exhibition, "made me a hater of military and imperial usurpation for life. I think it is a misfortune that that great drama has lost its place on the modern stage."[4] Prepared by local academies, Seward received his bachelor's degree at Union College, Schenectady, in 1820 – an institution which, with characteristic loyalty and affection, remained close to

[3] Seward, William Henry, *Autobiography of William Henry Seward 1801–1834 with a memoir of his life and selections from his letters from 1831–1846*. Ed. by Frederick Seward. D. Appleton Co., 1877.

[4] *Ibid.*, p. 23.

his heart all his life. At Union his rustic clothes, strange appearance, and drawling speech at first provoked undergraduate ridicule, but Seward quickly won popularity by his wit, his genial adaptability and leadership, particularly in intellectual pursuits. The obvious career was law; this Seward studied, after the practice of the time, in a lawyer's office, finally determining, after a few skirmishes in Orange County, to begin life in a new country – in other words, to go "West." The particular "West" selected was the still log-cabin frontier lying between Lake Cayuga and Owasco in New York. Perhaps the natural beauty of the region enticed the young man; but there was an even more romantic explanation. Seward had fallen deeply in love with Frances Miller, daughter of Judge Elijah Miller, the foremost lawyer of Auburn. The girl was a schoolmate of Seward's sister at Miss Willard's Academy in Troy and, about 1822, came to Florida for a visit at the Seward home. Seward believed that he could make better progress with the widowed father – the girl was quickly committed – if the prospective son-in-law planned to live permanently near the paternal home. The plan succeeded perfectly; Judge Miller made his son-in-law his partner, and the trio, Judge Miller, Frances, and "Henry," lived a most harmonious life, for many years, under the same roof. Mrs. Seward was an educated girl, intelligent and charming, with a moral fervor on certain questions, especially slavery, that strongly influenced her husband at critical times. She became his closest adviser in every important decision. And Seward's rapid success as a lawyer, the political honors that in rapid succession came his way, and his genial companionship naturally made him a favorite with his father-in-law.

At about the same time that Seward fixed upon politics as the most entertaining phase of American life, he decided on two other desirable spheres of conduct. A citizen having any regard for salvation, in this world or the next, should join one of the two major political parties and also some well-established church. He had no taste for innovation in either mundane or spiritual concerns. In fulfillment of the latter resolve, he allied with the Episcopal communion – an allegiance which was maintained steadily, though not demonstratively or fanatically, to the end of his days. A choice in the more worldly field did not prove so easy. For the first twenty-five years of Seward's life, only one political party really prevailed in the United States. Seward was born a few months after Thomas Jefferson hitched his horse and ostentatiously walked, unescorted by military and civil pomp, to the new Capitol, still smelling of fresh mortar, where John Marshall administered the presidential oath. The Federal Party had disappeared under a blizzard of adverse ballots, never to rise again, and the next twenty-four years of

Jefferson-Madison-Munroe supremacy offered a spectacle of one-party rule almost as complete as that which Nazi Germany and Fascist Italy attained a century afterward. Seward attached himself as a stripling to this Jeffersonian phalanx, then known as the "Republican" Party. He had had the traditional young American's admiration for the Declaration of Independence. Still, certain things in Jefferson's creed he could not accept. For example, he did not like those Virginia and Kentucky Resolutions, setting forth the doctrines of Nullification and Secession, ultimately doomed to cause such universal havoc. But about the time that Seward cast his first presidential vote, in 1824, a new light was dawning in the east. The United States, like its political parent England, is by nature a two-party country with plentiful family quarrels and factional eviscerations, and by the time Andrew Jackson, Henry Clay, and John Quincy Adams were engaged in a death grapple for the great prize in 1824, signs of an inevitable bifurcation had appeared. The long-entrenched Jeffersonian cohorts had split into two fairly defined groups – one tracing descent to the still living patriarch, known as Democratic-Republicans, the other calling themselves National Republicans. When the latter body succeeded, in 1824, in placing in the White House that acrid Puritan, John Quincy Adams, it really assumed the proportions of a second great political party. Young Seward became an eager follower of the righteous New Englander. He stumped for Adams in Cayuga County, prepared an address for De Witt Clinton, the National Republican candidate for governor of New York – still printed in Seward's *Works* – and also won his first laurels in an occupation that soon made him indispensable – that of ghost writer of speeches and resolutions for less literate defenders of correct principles. One of these efforts gave him fame – an address denouncing the Albany regency, a group of insiders who controlled the Democratic-Republican stronghold, which in 1824 and for several years afterward constituted a political machine whose main mission was the advancement of the presidential aspirations – ultimately successful – of Martin Van Buren. Seward had every reason to feel content with this, his first participation in state and national politics. Both his candidate for governor of New York and his candidate for President of the United States, John Quincy Adams, were projected into office as the outcome of what a historian of New York calls a "political tornado." By 1832, the National Republicans, solidified as a great and strong second party, proudly took to themselves the old cognomen of English Liberals, and, as Whigs, for the next twenty years divided the allegiance of the American electorate.

Seward joined the Whig Party and remained with it as long as the party itself endured. Herein he illustrated, in his own course, the second of his tenaciously held principles. Seward remained all his days an unswerving partisan. Anyone desiring to influence public life and to advance great causes, he insisted, must do it as a member of one of the two majority parties. Select the aggregation in which you believe, and stick to it through thick and thin. Never attempt the promotion of reforms by organizing or joining third parties; that was the one sure way of getting nowhere and defeating any purpose dear to your heart. "My duty," he said afterward in the time of his political maturity, "is to promote the welfare, interest and happiness of the people of the United States, and I hold that I can do so in no effectual way by going alone and independently. That is always the error of schismatics." Herein we are brought face to face with the question that constantly arises in reviewing Seward's career: to what extent was it directed by an unselfish idealism, and to what by personal ambition? For while it is true that he could set forth, ably enough, this philosophy of party loyalty, it is also true that advancement in public office could be most expeditiously achieved by keeping strictly within the purlieus of the machine. Seward shocked his admirers once by an address to young men, advising them all "to join a political party — it doesn't much matter which" — an impartial attitude which at first smacks of cynicism, but was certainly not so intended, for Seward meant that causes in which one believed could be accomplished by a great popular political organization and that either of them, if dominated by the right kind of citizens, could be welded into a compact citizenry working for the public good. At the time of Seward's remark, for example, the antislavery elements were struggling for the control of both the Democratic and the Whig Party, an effort which failed in both quarters, but the result was the ultimate coming together of all antislavery followings in one earnest amalgamation that did accomplish the reform.

Perhaps Seward's allegiance to this belief reflected his own experience. In his political adolescence Seward did work as a third-party man — and this as participant in one of the most absurd partisan developments in American history. In September 1826, one William Morgan was abducted from a jail in Canandaigua, New York, in which he had been confined on a trumped-up charge, and surreptitiously carried to parts unknown. That he had been drowned in the Niagara River was the common belief; the mystery of his disappearance, however, has never been solved. "Where is Morgan?" was the question that for years stirred the state of New York — a question always addressed to members of the various Masonic orders. Morgan had for years belonged to this secret society, but a short time before his exit had repudiated his old-time fraternal associates, and had written a book – published some time after his vanishing – "exposing" the whole Masonic brotherhood as an organization which, unless it were checked, would undermine and destroy the American nation. The hysterical excitement this proceeding gave rise to can hardly be imagined. Beginning in western New York, the anti-Masonic fury extended to the eastern section, then moved into Vermont, Massachusetts, and Pennsylvania; the thunderous denunciation with which most pulpits raged against this ancient institution resembled somewhat the ecclesiastical crusade a century afterward against the liquor trade. A political party that quickly came into existence for the purpose of exterminating Freemasonry made astonishing progress. In 1827 it elected five senators and seventeen assemblymen in New York. A year or two afterward, it elected a governor and a majority of the legislature in Vermont; it achieved marked successes in other states, and in 1830 the new party held a national convention in Philadelphia, nominating for President William Wirt, one of the most eminent Americans of the time.

Seward, despite his antagonism to third parties, joined this one, at first rather surreptitiously, acting as its secret penman in the production of platforms and addresses, beginning in 1828, when he attended the Antimasonic state convention at Albany; and became a delegate from western New York to the national assemblage in Philadelphia. To just what extent his allegiance represented fervent opposition to Freemasonry, and to what extent he was tempted by it as a quick road to public office, students of his career are not agreed. His brief association with the party – it virtually passed from the scene in 1832 – is mainly interesting for the two public men with which it brought the young man in close communion. For the Antimasonic agitation made Seward the friend of the two public characters whom he revered above all others in American public life. Both Thurlow Weed and John Quincy Adams became Antimasons of a sort, and Seward, on this digression from a straight political path, found them most congenial fellows. The fact that Seward had a conscience so flexible that it could adopt Thurlow Weed and Quincy Adams as the two gods of his political idolatry tells much of the man. To the respectable citizen of that time it would seem like bowing down simultaneously to Satan and the angel Gabriel. No two men more unlike have figured upon the American stage. Adams was a man of fine intellect, dour temperament and manners, unselfish principle, and idealistic purpose; Thurlow Weed was a leader of nimble wit, genial, lovable personality, and utter unscrupulousness, so far as politics were concerned, in aim and method. In the pursuits of party ends, Weed saw only one issue at stake – public office for his henchmen; other matters, such as the public interest, occupied a minor place in his purview. New York had known political bosses before Weed's ascendancy, but hardly one who had constructed a machine so selfish in its purpose and so well oiled in its articulation. By all accounts he was the ablest spoilsman who had thus far appeared in the state whose politics, in the words of Seward's other guardian angel, John Quincy Adams, were "the devil's own incomprehensibles."

The son of a shiftless farmer who occasionally spent periods in the debtors' prison, Weed grew up with almost no schooling, starting to earn his living as a child of eight as assistant to a blacksmith and rising, at eleven, to an apprenticeship as printer's devil; at thirty-three he was a full-fledged editor, proprietor of the *Albany Evening Journal.* This paper – still in existence – he established as an organ of the Antimasonic movement, serving as reporter, editor, frequently proofreader and pressman, incidentally finding time to perform his duties as a member of the New York legislature – almost the only public responsibility which Weed ever assumed. All this time he was a sprightly party worker – rapidly building up a machine of officeholders, large and small, with which for the next thirty years he dominated the Antimasonic and subsequently the Whig and Republican Parties. The spoils system incarnate, Weed cared nothing for official gold braid himself, leaving such gewgaws to faithful followers who really coveted them, as did Seward; at a time when his autocratic control gave him the pick of all the jobs in the state, Weed accepted only that of state printer – the least ornamental, but the one that yielded the largest money return. There are no indications that Weed used his power to accumulate fortune for himself, but for party and friends his lack of scruple knew no bounds. Bribery at the polls, the purchase and sale of legislators, were things he regarded as normal and, indeed, inescapable in the conduct of public affairs. Almost any trick that would advance his partisan purpose he unhesitatingly put to work. Just before the election of 1828, at the height of the Antimasonic fury, a drowned body appeared on the surface of the Niagara River, not far from the accepted scene of Morgan's disappearance. Naturally this macabre object developed into a campaign issue, the Antimasons insisting that it was the murdered Morgan, the other side just as fiercely scorning such an identification. "It's a good enough Morgan until after the election" – such was the comment attributed to Weed, an observation that followed the great Boss to the end of his days, despite his denials. The words seemed so perfectly to express Weed's politics that he never lived them down.

What can be thought of the principles of a young man – Seward was in his middle twenties when the association began – who picked out Thurlow Weed as his lodestar in politics and followed him for the next fifty years? Affection explains, in part, this useful loyalty. For the intimacy that began in Antimasonic days was as much personal as political. Only four years separated the two in age, Weed being the elder; both liked fishing and the out-of-doors, both were given to travel, and both had a passion for political intrigue. Thus they became good companions, went on journeys and vacations together; when Seward was in Albany they dined together constantly and usually spent their evenings in converse and smoke. In popular speech the dominant faction in New York State was always described as the "Seward-Weed" or "Weed-Seward" machine. Perhaps one reason for Seward's admiration was that, at any rate in the earlier time, his political conceptions did not differ particularly from those of this, his other self. No one ever accused Seward of dishonesty or corruption in the grosser sense, but he accepted readily enough the pursuit of office, and the division of spoils exclusively among party workers, as indispensable to party politics. He also admired Weed's brain power and managerial genius. That supreme talent impressed many of the foremost men of the day. According to Horace Greeley, Thurlow Weed was "the greatest man we have left, Seward not excepted." Even Samuel Bowles, in 1860, described his fellow journalist as "a great man – one of the most remarkable men of our time. . . . He is cool, calculating, a man of expedients, who boasts that for thirty years he has not in political affairs let his heart outweigh his judgment." Still another reason impelled Seward to attach his fortunes to this consummate cavalier. Despite Mr. Bowles's qualification, an element of selflessness entered into Weed's relations with Seward. From the day of their first meeting the brilliant young man's advancement in public life seemed to have become his chief reason for existence. Weed guarded the Seward career as a hen does its chicks. Hardly had he landed him in one office before he began laying plans for another. To Weed political intrigue was the finest of the fine arts, and in this spirit he deliberately molded the man of Auburn, designing him to be his ultimate masterpiece. He made Seward state legislator, then governor, then United States Senator, all these offices being merely gradations in what Weed planned for many years as the splendid climax. His failure to place the crown of the Presidency on his protégé's head broke the old man's heart – for by 1860 Weed had become a tall, stately, white-haired, venerable figure, one of the handsomest and most distinguished, at least to outward view, of the politicians of this time.

The first attempt to make Seward governor failed, as noted above, but in 1838, at the age of thirty-seven, Seward drove William L. Marcy from that commanding post and remained in it for the next four years. This quadrennium forms an important one in the history of state and nation. On the issue for which his predecessor, Marcy, has become so notorious – "To the victors belong the spoils" – Seward's administration was quite as ravenous as the preceding one, Thurlow Weed standing constantly at the young governor's elbow to assist in the noble business. To find fault with Seward on this ground may be rather captious, for few men, even the most politically devout, saw any sin in the Roman proscriptions that accompanied each rotation in party control. Reform of the Spoils System was an emotion of a later, more squeamish era. Two public issues figured largely in the new administration; these two may be taken as a portrait of Seward in his two antagonistic phases – in his Thurlow Weed and his John Quincy Adams characters. Both questions had much to do with shaping the Seward career in the national field.

In the eighteen-thirties and -forties, the foreign-born, especially Irish and German immigrants, were every day making their influence felt in politics. The antagonisms that were, in a few years, to give rise to the American, or Know-Nothing Party, were already stirring in the breasts of many of the "old American" element. A large proportion of immigrants belonged to the Roman Catholic Church, and this fact particularly frightened those conservatives who stood in mortal terror of popish aggression. The school question in New York now for the first time raised its head. In those days, as now, the Catholic hierarchy insisted that education, above all in the primary grades, should be its exclusive province, and resented the fact that children of Catholic families, when they received any religious instruction at all in the public schools, were subjected to Protestant ways of thought. The demand that money for public education be distributed to schools conducted by various religious denominations was the practical form the controversy assumed then, as it has ever since. The story, so far as it affects Seward, cannot be related in detail; it is enough to say that, in general, the new governor officially sympathized with the Catholic contention. He and Archbishop Hughes of New York became good friends. Seward's first message to the legislature contained one sentence that blew the smoldering fire of religious controversy into a blaze. Speaking of the inadequate instruction given children of the foreign born, the new governor wrote: "I do not hesitate to recommend the establishment of schools in which they may be instructed by teachers speaking the same language and professing the same faith." Probably no single sentence in all the several volumes of Seward's *Works* had a more fatal influence – justly or unjustly – upon his career. In the opinion of a diagnostician so expert as Alexander K. McClure, these few words prevented Seward from becoming President of the United States. That they aroused to fury citizens of old native origin who regarded the American English-speaking public schools, in which religion was not taught but reserved for the institution — the Church — especially established for that purpose, as the one solid foundation stone of the American fabric may be taken for granted. Seward increased the unpopularity he had aroused in these conservative quarters by further demonstrations. He manifested an intense hostility to England; as governor he became the favorite orator on St. Patrick's Day and other anti-John Bull demonstrations. The time was one of what the English insisted on calling "Irish agitation," and in gatherings assembled in the interests of Irish reform Seward also took a leading part. However sincere the brilliant young governor may have been in all this — and at least in his dislike of England he was sincere — no public man could take such a stand without being accused of political motives. There were too many votes to be cultivated for him to escape charges of expediency. From the day of his governorship to his death Seward was the great hero of the foreign-born — a fact that caused one part of the population to regard him as the most enlightened of statesmen and another to assail him as a demagogue who was betraying American institutions to advance his political fortunes.

The other conspicuous event in Seward's four years at Albany also aroused excited controversy, but this followed sectional and not religious lines. Slavery, in the late eighteen-thirties, was daily assuming greater importance as the one pressing question of the time. Seward's early association with the institution in his father's home had displayed it in its benign aspects, but in the summer of 1835, Seward and his wife took one of those long carriage drives which formed their chief outdoor diversion — this time through Pennsylvania and Virginia. Four years before the man who was to prove his successful political rival, at that time an elongated flatboatman of New Salem, Illinois, had made his celebrated trip down the Sangamon and Mississippi Rivers, finally landing his cargo of hogs and produce in the market place of New Orleans. On these voyages, near enough in time to give point to their observation, the two future statesmen had their first intimate view of that labor system which was to shape the careers of both. Certain recorded impressions reflect fundamental traits in the two men. The Shenandoah Valley disclosed the darker phase of slavery on every hand, but it was mainly the degenerate *Kultur* of the country — the run-down farms, the unpainted, ramshackle homesteads, the poorly clad and hungry-looking white gentry — that chiefly impressed Seward as the economic fruits of an outworn institution. "An exhausted soil," he wrote, "old and decaying towns, wretchedly neglected roads, and, in every respect, an absence of enterprise and improvement, distinguish the region through which we have come, in contrast to that in which we live. Such has been the effect of slavery. And yet the people are unconscious, not merely of the cause of the evil, but are in a great degree ignorant that other portions of the country enjoy greater prosperity." Contrast this observation, which emphasized the economic wrong in slavery, with the familiar description of Lincoln's visit to New Orleans as set forth in Herndon. The sight of a slave auction, especially the exhibition of a young, comely mulatto girl to a crowd of coarse and brutal bidders, aroused all the wrath of the young man's fiery soul – Lincoln was only twenty-two at the time. "By God, boys," Herndon quotes him as saying to his companions, "let's get away from this. If I ever get a chance to hit at this, I'll hit it hard." [5] The emotion attributed to Lincoln was adequately felt on this Shenandoah drive by Frances Seward, whose nerves were unstrung by the sight of Negroes chained in gangs like criminals, of naked Negro boys tied together like puppies and driven to a horse trough for watering. Things like these aroused in Seward's wife, the gentlest of human beings, a burning hatred of the evil, and from that moment she was an influence at his side, constantly stimulating his hostility to the encroachments of the slave power.

It is therefore not strange that Seward's several face-to-face conflicts with the South on this issue gave him national reputation. As a candidate for governor, however, his attitude proved far from satisfactory to the growing abolition sentiment in New York State. His replies to three questions addressed to him by Gerrit Smith and Judge William Jay, leaders of the antislavery forces, again illustrated the Seward habit of expediency, rather than disinterested frankness, in meeting public problems. Was the Whig candidate for governor – such was the first item in the questionnaire – in favor of jury trial for Negroes charged with being fugitive slaves? Seward replied to this directly and satisfactorily: Yes, he was. In those days, New York permitted slaveholders to bring their "servants" into the state and keep them as slaves, provided the sojourn did not exceed nine months. Thus this great commonwealth, to the disgust of advanced abolitionists, was, with a limitation, itself a protector of the hated thing. New York was a favorite vacation ground of Southern cotton planters and their families, especially such watering

[5] Herndon, W. H., and Weik, J. W., *Abraham Lincoln.* D. Appleton & Co., 1892. I, 67. Herndon says that he obtained the story from John Hanks and Lincoln himself but most Lincoln scholars dismiss it as legendary. For a discussion of its doubtful authenticity see Paul Angle's edition of Herndon and Weik, *Life of Lincoln.* Albert and Charles Boni, 1930, p. 64.

places as Niagara Falls and Saratoga Springs; Southern women always brought their Negro maids and their husbands their Negro body servants. Was Seward in favor of repealing that law? The candidate did not seem to be; such a repeal, he insisted, would be an act of "inhospitality" to the Southern brethren. At that time New York, and practically all Northern states, excluded – this was the practical effect of the election laws – free Negroes from the franchise. Would Seward, as governor, work for the repeal of all disqualifications based on "complexion"? The reply seemed ambiguous and hedging. Seward, victorious at the polls, thus entered office with no approval from antislavery forces but after a few months became their favorite public character.

In September 1839, Virginia demanded by requisition three black men, at the time safe from its clutches in New York, who had promoted the escape of a slave. Seward refused to surrender the culprits, on the ground that the "felony" of which they had been accused was not recognized as a crime by the laws of New York, and for two years a lively, ill-natured correspondence followed between the astute governor of New York and several executives of Virginia, in which the constitutional rights involved were discussed to exhaustion. Virginia passed retaliatory laws against New York – offering to repeal them when the accused black men were given up; other Southern states, especially Mississippi and South Carolina, participated in something resembling a sympathetic strike against the Empire State. Seward remained adamant. It was not only his firmness, but the brilliancy of his letters that aroused general enthusiasm in the North. "I cannot," he wrote, "to save the commerce of the state, or even the peace of the country, subscribe to the faith prescribed to me. I cannot believe that a being of human substance, form and image – endowed with the faculties, propensities and passions common to our race, and having the same ultimate destiny, can, by the force of any human constitution and laws, be converted into a chattel or a thing, in which another being like himself can have property." In these words appears the first trace of that "law higher than the constitution" for which Seward subsequently became famous; on strict, constitutional interpretation probably Virginia had the right in the argument, but the outcome of the matter was that Seward, perhaps a little to his own surprise, found himself an antislavery leader in the national field. The abolitionists even tried to nominate him for President in 1840 – an offer Seward tactfully put aside.

Thus Seward remained true to his expressed dislike of third parties; he preferred the private life that was his portion from 1842, when his governorship expired, until 1848, when his career as Senator began, to leadership of any such assortment of "schismatics." In this interim, however, his fame steadily grew, both as a lawyer and as a political influence. He made a superb jury pleader; his defense of the Negro Freeman, unquestionably guilty of murder, but just as certainly a hopeless imbecile, aroused interest abroad, especially in England; Gladstone told Charles Sumner that Seward's defense of Freeman was "the finest forensic effort in the English language." [6] He also defended – without fee – several fugitive slaves and added to his reputation by speeches, usually published and distributed in great quantities, on the slavery issue, every day becoming more intense. When the Democratic ascendancy of the forties came to an end in 1848, and the New York legislature again elected a Whig majority, there was no doubt as to who would be chosen to the vacant seat in the United States Senate. By this time Seward-Weed had gained such power in national politics that the choice of Zachary Taylor as presidential candidate was laid at their doors. The Whigs of New York really decided the question – and Seward and Weed ruled the New York organization. The selection of Taylor illustrates again Seward's twofold political character. "You made General Harrison President," John Quincy Adams said to Seward at their last interview in 1847. "You can make the next President. Will you give us a man who is not for slavery? Tell me that. Assure me of that, and I shall be prepared to make my testament." The slavery issue had reached a new crisis in 1848, as a result of the new domain added to the United States as spoils of the Mexican War – hence Mr. Adams's almost deathbed injunction. Instead of the antislavery man Adams demanded, Seward and Weed, by their control of the New York delegation, awarded the nomination to a man who knew nothing of public affairs, had belonged to no political party, was a Southerner and a slaveholder, and had never shown anything but orthodox Southern views on the prevailing question. In the Mexican War he had led the armies to victory, and had become a popular hero. Taylor was thus the most available vote-catcher in sight, the presidential candidate who could carry New York State for the Whigs and elect a legislature which would send William H. Seward to the United States Senate and to this expedient end he unquestionably owed his nomination and election.

In the ten years that followed – the turbulent period of the 1850 Compromise measures, of the Kansas-Nebraska Act, the Repeal of the Missouri Compromise, the struggles in bleeding Kansas, the Dred Scott

[6] Despite Seward's plea, Freeman was convicted by the jury. The Supreme Court, however, granted a new trial, but the maniac died in prison before it was held.

decision, and the organization of the Republican Party – Seward grew to be one of the leaders of the antislavery cause, but again in a somewhat zigzag fashion, now making a speech that would set the nation aflame, then again trimming his course to the political winds, always having in view the ultimate prize of the White House. Seward was a man of fine, even exalted instincts, who at first naturally put himself on the right, unselfish course; after this had once been done, and the adverse effects on his political ambitions appeared, he was too inclined to modify, and qualify, and seek to accommodate his views to both sides. Perhaps it was the malign influence of Thurlow Weed which explained this tendency to face both ways. Certainly that decade from 1850 to 1860 tested a man's idealism. The fact that such subservient double-dealers as Franklin Pierce and James Buchanan reached the White House would seem to indicate that any open defiance of the South on slavery extension meant political extinction. In Weed's mind the attitude that gathered in the most votes was the one that Seward should pursue. The outspokenness of many of his favorite's addresses alarmed the veteran campaigner. Seward's speech on the Compromise measures of 1850 might be hailed even by the Garrisonians, but it aroused Weed's misgivings. When Seward climaxed his first Senate speech by a declaration that there was a "higher law" than the Constitution to which the enemies of slavery could appeal, the supreme manipulator of caucuses and elections took genuine fright. Seward was perhaps winning fame in antislavery circles, but was he not destroying his chances for the Presidency? A certain amount of negrophilism to please a few cranks in New England and the Middle West would be quite desirable, but to attack Daniel Webster to his face – as this reckless new Senator had done, for Seward's eleventh of March speech was intended as a direct reply to the more gentle handling of the fugitive slave question with which Webster had delighted the South and enraged the North four days previously – to challenge the scowling John C. Calhoun on what was almost the dying South Carolinian's last appearance in the upper chamber – "a dangerous young man," he called Seward – this was a little more independence of thought and rather more moral courage than the nicely balancing Weed thought appropriate in a statesman already favorably looked upon as a promising candidate for the highest office. Perhaps Weed's moderating influence explains Seward's vacillating career for the next ten years, though that Senator himself cannot be entirely acquitted, for ambition marched side by side with moral enthusiasm in marking out his pathway. Thus Seward stayed faithful to the Whig Party as long as any signs of vitality remained in that discredited body, although the one apparent fact from

1840 until the end, in 1856, was that that timid aggregation would never meet flatly the overwhelming issue of the day, but with eyes fixed upon the election booths would year after year follow a temporizing program. The searcher of Seward's record in that period will find plenty of things to admire, and plenty of things to condemn. Strong antislavery man as he appeared to be, Seward left to Salmon Chase the main burden of opposing the Kansas-Nebraska Act; on the other hand, he made a vigorous speech denouncing the specific repeal of the Missouri Compromise. There were other outgivings in which the course of Southern statesmen was denounced in phrases that resounded in all sections of the country.

The most famous was the "irrepressible conflict" address of October 25, 1858. It is interesting, however, that Abraham Lincoln, just four months before in Springfield, on his nomination for the Illinois senatorship, had made a speech expressing the same ideas; one wonders whether the national acclaim raised by Lincoln's declaration did not inspire Seward's emulation, perhaps unconscious plagiarism.

The two orations have an interest for the student of literary style; no comparison could more eloquently bring out the difference in these two men. "A house divided against itself cannot stand. I believe that this government cannot endure permanently, half slave and half free. I do not expect the Union to be dissolved – I do not expect the house to fall – but I do expect it will cease to be divided. It will become all one thing or all the other. Either the opponents of slavery will arrest the further spread of it and place it where the public mind shall rest in the belief that it is in course of ultimate extinction; or its advocates will push it forward until it shall become alike lawful in all the states, old as well as new, North as well as South." Compare this with Seward's four months afterward: "It is an irrepressible conflict between opposing and enduring forces and it means that the United States must and will, sooner or later, become either entirely a slave holding nation or entirely a free-labor nation. Either the cotton and rice fields of South Carolina and the sugar plantations of Louisiana will ultimately be tilled by free labor, or else the rye fields and wheat fields of Massachusetts and New York must again be surrendered by their farmers to slave culture and to the products of slaves and Boston and New York become once more markets for trade in the bodies and souls of men." From the standpoint of literature there is little comparison between the quiet majesty of Lincoln's homely words and the more bookish, more labored phraseology of Seward, but it is significant that in this address Seward boldly cast his fortunes on the side of slavery restriction and that, in doing so, he followed the lead of a previously disregarded new antagonist already looming in the public mind as the possible Republican candidate in 1860.

Seward's backing and filling all through this decade caused him to experience the usual fate of trimmers, and to become unpopular with both sides. The South, still smarting from his tilt with Virginia some years before, was roused to fury by the "irrepressible conflict" speech, though it had not been particularly disturbed by Lincoln's milder, and even more forcible, expression of the same idea. The great Seward, of course, was looked upon as the more important man, and therefore the one to be feared. A humorous, but still instructive incident of a feverish time was an advertisement published in a Richmond newspaper a few months after the "irrepressible conflict" speech, offering a reward of twenty-five dollars for "the heads of the following traitors" – among them being Charles Sumner, Horace Greeley, Wendell Phillips, Henry Ward Beecher, Joshua Giddings, and many other notorious antislavery leaders. "For the head of William H. Seward," however, this Virginian would raise the emolument to five hundred dollars. It is significant of the little hostility – or perhaps the little notice – aroused in the South by Lincoln that his name did not appear, even in the twenty-five-dollar appraisement of "traitors," although the list was a long and inclusive one. Unpopular as the genial, kindly Seward had become with slave-owners, he was almost as obnoxious to the more extreme slavery restrictionists north of the Ohio and the Potomac. The bloc of senatorial and cabinet allies who were destined to make miserable his life in Lincoln's cabinet – Sumner, Hale, Fessenden, Wade, Chase, George W. Julian, and others – was formed in the few years preceding the Civil War. These men, extremists on the slavery issue – they figured in much subsequent history as "radicals" – regarded Seward as opportunistic, as completely under the thumb of one of the shrewdest and most unprincipled politicians of the day, and as a candidate whose views were uniformly tempered to accord with the political breezes. Seward's strange behavior in the few weeks following the murderous bludgeoning of Sumner by Bully Brooks of South Carolina made a bad impression – for, unlike most Northerners, Seward did not seem particularly outraged and almost held aloof from the attempts of his Republican colleagues to obtain something resembling redress.

After the proslavery Democrats, with Whig support, had triumphed in their Kansas-Nebraska legislation, the eyes of all antislavery elements were turned towards Seward as the leader in the organization of a new antislavery party. But there was no response. Seward would take no part in the Republican Party that was coming into being in his own New York State. When old man Blair in 1855, sent him an invitation to join in a meeting at his Maryland home, Silver Spring, to discuss the formation of a new party, Seward sent a courteous refusal. When the meeting came together in Pittsburgh, in February 1856, for definite organization, Seward declined to be a delegate. That the New Yorker always offered plausible reasons for his coyness is true; still his hesitating mood did not enhance his standing as an unselfish champion of the antislavery cause. When, as the time approached for the Philadelphia convention of 1856, it became evident that the Whig Party was dead, past all hope of resurrection, Seward not only joined the new organization scrambled together under the title "Republican," but looked forth longingly to being its first candidate for the Presidency. Weed, however, held him back; the candidate of 1856, that wise old gentleman insisted, was sure to be defeated; he was holding Seward in reserve for 1860, and did not wish his candidacy to be tainted with a great failure. That Seward was profoundly disappointed when John C. Frémont received that honor his letters to his most confidential friend – his wife – make clear. "Greeley has struck hands with enemies of mine and sacrificed me for the good of the cause, to be obtained by the nomination of a more available candidate and Weed has concurred and demanded my acquiescence. . . . I shall submit with better grace than others would." He thought that the proper course for him now was "withdrawal from public and political life, at the close of the present session of Congress." Nearly twenty years afterward Seward and Weed, both old men, were driving up Broadway, New York, past Union Square. "If it hadn't been for you, Weed," Seward remarked, pointing to a bronze statue, "I would be up on that pedestal, instead of Abraham Lincoln"; this was a reference to Weed's blocking his nomination in 1856, for Seward always declared – a conviction in which few agreed with him – that, had he received the prize instead of the unhappy Frémont, he would have been elected, with consequences very different to the history of his country.

Disappointed as Seward was in 1856, his chagrin was slight compared to that which overwhelmed him four years afterward. That he was to be the destined leader of his party in 1860 was not only his own conviction and that of Weed, but of nine out of ten Americans. What other Republican compared with him in eminence in statesmanship and world-wide reputation? Salmon Portland Chase, it is true, towered above most Republican leaders; there was Edward Bates, of Missouri, Simon Cameron of Pennsylvania, a certain Caleb B. Smith of Indiana, William L. Dayton of New Jersey, and several other "favorite sons" – the expression was already in use – each with his own noisy company of boomers. None of these had anything except a professional following of state politicians. The news from Illinois, where several newspapers and local leaders were talking of the ungainly creature who, in a series of debates, had lain low Stephen A. Douglas, the man up to that time regarded as the ablest platform antagonist in the nation, was not especially disturbing. Even when Lincoln, in February 1860, accepted an invitation of New York Brahmins and appeared at Cooper Union, in ill-fitting clothes, with hair askew, and delivered a speech which at once marked him as the most forcible champion of the antislavery cause, Seward still maintained his serenity. The only emotion the new portent inspired was that of irritation. One day in late February 1860, Seward called into his senatorial office Joseph Medill, Washington correspondent of the *Chicago News and Tribune*, who had most audaciously written an article extolling Lincoln as a presidential candidate, incidentally pointing out why Seward would not be an ideal selection. "The article irritated Seward," wrote Medill afterward,[7] "and he took occasion to see me immediately after, and 'blew me up' tremendously for having disappointed him – 'gone back on him' – and preferring 'that prairie statesman' as he called Lincoln. He then proceeded to declare, with much heat of temper and expression, that if he was not nominated as the Republican candidate for President at the ensuing convention he would shake the dust off his shoes, and retire from the service of an ungrateful party for the remainder of his days. He gave me to understand that he was the chief teacher of the principles of the Republican party before Lincoln was known other than as a county lawyer of Illinois. . . . He dismissed me from his presence, saying that hereafter he and I would no longer be friends, but would each go his own way in the future." There was at least one other Republican who would have assented to this uncomplimentary tirade, and that was Lincoln himself. At this time, the coming man did not take seriously his boom, launched by his parochial admirers in Illinois; he really aspired to represent Illinois in the United States Senate, and was enough of a politician to understand that the association of his name with the White House would be excellent publicity in his campaign for that office.

The summer of 1859 Seward spent in Europe, and the reception received in all countries and from all orders of society testified to the world-wide distinction his antislavery activities had brought. The almost daily letters to Mrs. Seward disclosed that the statesman was human enough to relish this acclaim. "Nor can I omit to say, for this once, and to yourself, and to yourself alone, that there is a recompense for long years of endurance of contumely at home, in the universal respect and sympathy which my poor efforts for freedom and human-

[7] Bancroft, Frederick, *Life of William H. Seward*. Harper & Bros., 1900. I, 531.

ity there, have won for me here." The interest in American slavery was active in all the enlightened nations of Europe; Seward's personal qualities, his wit and social adaptability, soon made him a general favorite. Incidentally, the experience proved an educational preparation for the office which, although he did not realize it at the time, was soon to fall to his lot; for most of the European diplomats with whom he was to come to grips as foreign secretary of Lincoln's cabinet showed him cordial attention. In England, Lord Palmerston entertained him at his Piccadilly home, Lord Lansdowne at Lansdowne House, Lord Granville at Chiswick, the Duke of Sutherland at Stafford House, and Lord John Russell at Pembroke Lodge. Here were several present and future Prime Ministers, two in particular – Palmerston and Russell – who were to cause a good deal of trouble in the few years ahead. Queen Victoria was not celebrated for her interest in the heroes of democracy, but Seward proved an exception. When she was informed that etiquette prevented Mr. Seward from being invited to a great royal function, because he had not been introduced at court, no courts having been held during his visit, the gracious lady arranged for a private presentation. Louis Napoleon, Eugénie, King Victor Emmanuel, Count Cavour, the Pope – Pio Nono taking this opportunity to thank Seward for a helping hand in the matter of New York parochial schools, and requesting that he continue the good work – there was hardly a crowned head, a statesman, or a literary light who failed to do the famous American honor. There was another reason besides the slavery question for this interest. Everyone apparently took it for granted that this affable guest was the destined next President of the United States. The reception accorded the returning traveler, in disembarking in New York, formed a fitting climax. A salute of one hundred guns greeted his arrival. An imposing public reception was tendered by the mayor and common council, and Seward's journey north to Albany and west to Auburn was one long ovation. Crowds gathered at every railway station, and, as Seward landed in his home town, all the main streets were decorated, a multitude of inscribed banners were waving in the breeze, and even the school children were given a holiday to march in the procession that escorted their hero to his home. Few towns ever loved a fellow citizen as Auburn loved Seward and its pride rose high that morning, for it was confident that the nation was reaching out to this little western New York community for the man who was to succeed James Buchanan in the White House.

On May 16, 1860, the day of the Chicago Convention, the citizens once more assembled almost en masse. Great crowds gathered before the Seward home, as many as could get in crowded the grounds, cordially received and entertained by the affable and confident statesman. A large cannon had been placed at the gateway to boom the salute of triumph when the expected news, announcing Seward's nomination, came over the wire. Materials for bonfires, bunting for decorations, had been prepared for celebrating fittingly the greatest day in Auburn's history. How could that possibly fail to come to pass? Great sections of the nation, parts of New England, all of New York, nearly all the Northwest – excepting those states which, like Pennsylvania, New Jersey, Ohio, Indiana, Illinois, and Missouri, had instructed their delegates for eminent citizens of their own – had already spoken for William H. Seward. Weed was in Chicago in charge of operations; the program, as he and most other observers saw it, was evident and simple. On the first ballot Seward would so outdistance all competitors that most of the delegates would switch from local candidates, and cast their ballots for the New Yorker. That it would be Seward on the second ballot was the confident expectation. That certain forces were arrayed in deadly opposition was no secret. In particular it was known that Horace Greeley, in low-crowned, wide-brimmed hat and linen duster, was in Chicago as a delegate from Oregon, industriously canvassing all the delegations, telling them that Seward would not carry New York and certainly not Pennsylvania, Indiana, and Illinois; but it was believed that not much consideration would be shown him, for his intense enmity to Seward, springing from no higher motive than revenge against the "governor" and Weed for failing to satisfy his unquenchable thirst for public office, was understood. Any fears of Seward admirers that Greeley's hostility would influence the Convention were silenced when the *Tribune* appeared on the morning of May 18, with Greeley's own statement that the opposition to Seward had not been able to concentrate on any candidate and that he would therefore be the nominee. The newspapers, full of accounts of the tremendous cheering that greeted Seward's name, of the crowds of "irrepressibles," as Seward's supporters were called, everywhere stirring up enthusiasm for their favorite, increased the confidence. The first telegram, handed to Seward as he was surrounded by friends, lowered no one's spirits. On the first ballot Seward had received 173½ votes – it required 234 to nominate – Lincoln 102, Cameron 50½, Chase 49, Bates 48, and other candidates "scattering." In a short time the telegraph messenger handed Seward another envelope, containing the results of the second ballot – Seward 184½, Lincoln 181, while most of the other contestants lost ground. That tally was an ominous piece of news; it really spelled Seward's doom. He had gained, but only slightly, whereas Lincoln had ascended to a point where his support nearly equalled that of the leading competitor. But Seward was smiling and assured. "I shall be nominated on the next ballot," he told the assembled neighbors.

Soon the messenger came running toward Seward again, handing him another slip of paper. After Seward opened it and read, his face turned ashen. Abraham Lincoln of Illinois had been unanimously nominated for President of the United States. The third ballot had given Seward 180, Lincoln 231½; as soon as that result was announced, the five Ohio delegates had changed their votes, thus giving the rail splitter the needed majority. The usual scramble for the bandstand followed, delegation after delegation changing its votes from Seward to Lincoln, until finally William M. Evarts, the great New York lawyer who had placed Seward's name in nomination, advanced to the platform and, in a graceful speech, moved that the nomination of Abraham Lincoln be made unanimous. The yells of men, the screams of women, the salvos of cannon, the throngs of frenzied enthusiasts, inside the Convention Hall and out, were something different from the deathlike quiet that fell on Seward and the gathering on his lawn. His neighbors silently dispersed, the field piece that was to boom on the expected triumph was dragged away, its powder unburnt, and Auburn was like a graveyard. This condition of stunned sorrow lasted for several days. "I had the rare experience," Seward wrote a friend, describing the atmosphere, "of a man walking about town, after he is dead, and hearing what people would say of him. I confess I was not prepared for so much real grief as I heard expressed on every corner." When Seward returned to Washington to resume his duties in the Senate, his friends gathered around him to console, and to speak of "ingratitude" and "vindication"; even those Southern Democrats with whom he had so frequently clashed on the slavery question – Jefferson Davis and John Murray Mason – showed friendly sympathy. To the outward world, Seward maintained a dignified serenity – "He's the only cheerful person in Auburn," his neighbors said – but his letters to Mrs. Seward show that the iron had bitten deep. "The journey and the re-appearance," he wrote her from Washington, May 30, 1860, "in the character of a leader deposed by my own party, in the hour of organization for decisive battle, thank God are passed – and so the last of the humiliations has been endured."

Thurlow Weed, after the failure of his life's ambition, retired alone to his room in the Richmond House and there burst into tears. Judge David Davis and Leonard Swett, who had had charge of Lincoln's campaign, sought him out. After the nomination, the Lincolnians had approached the Seward forces and offered to let them name the candidate for Vice-President, but had met with a contemptuous refusal.

They evidently wanted nothing further to do with the campaign. Weed received Davis and Swett courteously, but coldly; the visitors invited the disheartened man to call upon Mr. Lincoln on his return to New York, and he agreed to consider the matter. But to representatives of the state of Pennsylvania, whose swing to Lincoln on the second ballot did more than anything else to determine the outcome, Weed showed his disgust. "I called on Weed during the evening after the nomination," wrote Alexander K. McClure, chairman of the State Committee, "expecting that, with all his disappointment, he would be ready to co-operate for the success of the ticket. . . . I found him sullen and offensive in both manner and expression. He refused even to talk about the contest, and intimated very broadly that Pennsylvania, having defeated Seward, could now elect Curtin and Lincoln." The Mr. Curtin in question was the Republican candidate for governor of Pennsylvania, who, as a delegate to Chicago, had been most outspoken in opposition to Seward; McClure insisted that he, above all others, was responsible for Lincoln's nomination. Curtin, also, on this same evening, made a propitiatory visit to Weed. "He was very rude indeed," said Curtin afterward. "You have defeated a man," said Weed, "who of all others was most revered by the people and wanted as President. You and Lane [candidate for governor in Indiana] want to be elected, and to elect Lincoln you must elect yourselves." Curtin subsequently made a brilliant record as war governor of Pennsylvania, but Seward, all through the four years, treated him, whenever the two met, with frigid formality. Several times, in the course of the presidential campaign, Curtin had occasion to write to Weed, but Weed never answered his letters. A few days after the convention, Henry J. Raymond, editor of the *New York Times*, paid a visit to Seward in Auburn. He reported to his readers that there was no possibility that Seward would accept a post in Lincoln's cabinet in the event of success.

II

IF SEWARD suggested in several ways Benjamin Disraeli, his chief rival for ascendancy in the Republican Party might be compared to Gladstone. Salmon P. Chase, like his British contemporary, was a man of fine, even majestic, presence – tall, straight, massive in figure, with a finely shaped head and piercing blue eyes, with features of a classic regularity, and a kind of imperious manner that demanded, and usually received, universal attention. This impressive outward man clothed a spirit as austere and unbending as Gladstone's own. Like his British exemplar, Chase was profoundly religious, and religious in ways that appeal least to the modern mind. He was sanctimonious and ritualistic, addicted to theology and distinctions fairly Byzantine in character, and to a daily routine of prayer, sermon reading, and soul-searching introspection. Like Gladstone, he had also intellectual tastes, facility with foreign languages, ancient and modern, and was extensively read in the more serious branches of literature. Similar motives inspired both men in their public careers. Rigid morality, the advocacy of great principles rather than the desire for high office, are virtues which their admirers have attributed to both men. On the other hand, their detractors have assailed them as not altogether sincere, as casuists who could always persuade themselves that what they personally desired represented the best interests of the state, and as proud, vain, selfish, and ambitious for distinction. In another quality attributed to Gladstone, that of changing political convictions with changing times, Chase far outdistanced the great English liberal.

Gladstone started life, in Macaulay's words, as the "rising hope of the unbending tories" and ended as the advocate of most of the things they detested, but the career of Chase discloses far more vacillations. As a young man of twenty, he drafted for Quaker friends an appeal requesting Congress to abolish slavery in the District of Columbia. His first view of the democracy of Andrew Jackson filled him with disgust for its "savage spirit." The Whig Party that came into existence in 1832 proved more attractive; Chase supported Harrison in 1836 and 1840, but in 1841 made his first switch in allegiance, becoming one of the organizers of the Liberty, or Abolition, Party, stumping for its candidate, James G. Birney, in 1844. Four years afterward, Chase again changed, going over to the Free-Soilers, supporting for President that Martin Van Buren whom he had previously assailed as "cold, selfish, base, and faithless." The next year, 1849, found Chase enrolled as a Democrat, having been elected to the United States Senate from Ohio by a Democratic–Free-Soil coalition. In 1852 he went back to the Free-Soilers, endorsing for President that forlornest of all forlorn hopes, the Abolitionist John P. Hale. In 1855, the resilient gentleman accepted a nomination for governor of Ohio from the American, or "Know-Nothing" convention, thus joining that antiforeign element of the fifties against which Seward had so fiercely protested. In 1856 Chase entered that new catch-all, the Republican Party, and was disappointed, like Seward, in not becoming its presidential nominee. A canvass of Chase's affiliations after 1860 would show the same disposition to change. That he sedulously solicited the Republican nomination in 1864, in opposition to Lincoln, was one of the scandals of the time. In 1868, though Chief Justice of the United States, Chase was openly seeking it. Even in 1872, though desperately ill – he died in May 1873 – the poor man was receptive for the nomination of the new Liberal Party that went to the unfortunate Horace Greeley. Thus, in the forty years from 1832 to 1872, Chase belonged to at least nine parties or groups of parties. Two facts must not be overlooked in connection with these fluctuating allegiances. One is that Chase could always find most plausible reasons, based on good citizenship and the public interest, for every change. The other is that his personal political fortunes were involved in each transition.

From these and other circumstances it would be a simple matter to draw the portrait of a hypocritical self-seeker, a man with no convictions that could not be changed when self-advantage pointed the more expedient way. The same hasty criticism was made of Gladstone. Such a sweeping condemnation would be unjust to both men, for Chase's career discloses the truth that a man may be eaten by ambition and led by it into what seem dishonorable compromises, and yet at the same time pursue throughout his life one lofty purpose. Whatever may be thought of the man's divagations in the pursuit of the unattainable – the Presidency – there is no question that his championship of the black man was sincere, even fanatical.

The fundamental spring of action throughout Chase's sixty-five years of life was religion, and religion of theological type. Chase, like Gladstone, was not only a twenty-four-hour-a-day Christian and pietist, but a rigid churchman. Born in 1808, in a particularly puritanical section of New Hampshire, he was marked, as a boy, for good behavior, scholarly tastes, and sobriety in conduct and religious observance. As such he fell into the good opinion of his uncle, Bishop Philander Chase, one of the great names in the history of the American Episcopal Church. Here was a hopeful, that dignitary concluded, divinely set apart for the ministry. So Uncle Philander, a harsh, autocratic, determined man of God, removed the promising novitiate, at the age of twelve, from his mother's farm, carried him off to Worthington, Ohio – afterward to Cincinnati – and proceeded to give him that severe training in books and theology necessary in preparation for the destined career. Chase's father – Ithamar – never a very successful man, but one of high standing for character and public spirit, had died three years before, financially ruined by the War of 1812, leaving his widow with eleven children. Probably therefore the uncle's offer to take Salmon into his family and educate him had come as something of a relief. Chase himself afterward wrote that he was regarded as "quite a prodigy," for, although only twelve, he had already read most of Virgil, had gone through a large part of the Greek testament, and resolved many propositions of Euclid. Though he was given to the usual diversions of a New England boyhood – fishing in the Connecticut in summer, sleigh riding and bobsledding in winter, and the like – the religious instinct was strong in Chase, even then. "It shocked me greatly," he reminisced afterward, "to hear boys swear, and I obeyed my mother's injunctions to keep away from them as much as I could."

Despite these favorable early signs, the plan to make an Episcopal minister out of Philander's nephew did not succeed. After three years under the Bishop's forbidding roof, increasing his stock of learning, he gained admittance into the junior class of Dartmouth College in 1824. Yet Chase's years under the Bishop's guardianship exercised the profoundest influence upon his life and character. They made even more intense his personal relation to God and the Church and gave him his first experience with slavery. Cincinnati and the surrounding region, as Mrs. Stowe was learning at almost the same time, formed an ideal school for the study of this institution. Not only were fugitive slaves constantly crossing the river that formed the only barrier between them and liberty, but from his uncle's Cincinnati farm, Chase, while milking the cows or pitching hay – for Uncle Philander believed in making the boy work for his keep – could obtain a fair view of Kentucky and its black helots toiling in tobacco fields. It is suggestive that, after having completed his law studies and been admitted to the bar, the young man went back to Cincinnati and made it his permanent home.

The interim between Dartmouth and this renewed residence in the West, however, gave Chase an opportunity to develop in other ways. He spent three years in Washington, from 1826 to 1829, opening, as a means of livelihood, a "select classical seminary"; his real purpose in Washington, however, was to prepare himself in law. It speaks much for a personality that afterward impressed friends and foes alike that the young man – he was only eighteen on arrival in the Capital – at once began to make influential friends. That Chase had a tropism for the "best people" is true – all his life he was to be accused of being a snob – yet it must be said that his inclination was not for the merely ostentatious, but for men and women of solid qualities and intellectual interests. For the new rich, indeed, destitute of "culture," absorbed mainly in the "mechanical" rewards of self-seeking, his letters breathe contempt. His "select classical seminary" attracted the children of leading citizens. One of them – the son of William Wirt – at once introduced the young pedagogue to perhaps the most distinguished family in Washington. William Wirt was a leader of the American bar – in several cases that gave definitive interpretations to the Constitution, such as *McCulloch* v. *Maryland* and *Ogden* v. *Gibbons*, he had been chief counsel for the government – and was at the time of Chase's arrival, Attorney General in the cabinet of John Quincy Adams. He was also one of the most popular authors of the day. Chase became almost a member of the Wirt family, and a delightful family it was, the two daughters in particular, Agnes and Alice, adding to the amenity of the young man's days. He became their escort to presidential and other functions, and in their honor he composed a long poem in blank verse, the "Sisters," as well as other verses, some of which the fickle rhymster afterward warmed over for a girl with whom he had genuinely fallen in love. The Wirt association had more than a social and sentimental interest. Mr. Wirt gladly accepted Chase as a student in his office. After a few months reading of Blackstone, he gained an easy admission to the bar, packed his bag, and returned to that Cincinnati, where, under Uncle Philander's wing, he had passed the critical years of boyhood.

Chase was now twenty-one, and though in appearance not the really splendid figure of a man that subsequently awed all beholders, he already had a presence and an intelligence that again paved his way into the best life of the town. He was quickly on familiar terms with the Longworths, the Burnetts, the Caswells, and other rich and enlightened clans. Though Chase had attained the more than six feet of stature, with the massive shoulders, the Jovelike head, the expansive round face, with pink complexion and gray-blue eyes, and the firm aggressive jaw that made him look like the sculptor's ideal of a President of the United States, a certain tinge of New England rusticity still clung to his person. When his friendship with Katherine Garniss grew to be a matter of sentimental gossip, some of the girl's companions bewailed a certain awkwardness in Chase's manners, as contrasted with what one of her admirers described as "the superb carriage and bearing of Katherine, one of the most beautiful and brilliant women of the West." Even Kitty herself occasionally ridiculed the stark Puritan. "He is so uncouth and has such an unmanageable mouth. Wait till I polish him up a little!" Chase's character, or at least certain phases of it, can best be studied in his relations with women, especially the three whom he married – for it was his tragic fate to become a widower three times in seventeen years. The man's religiosity comes out in its least attractive side. His Diary records most solemnly the reason why he failed to fall in love with another promising girl. "Every word and tone of hers is sweet music" – so runs the entry for January 7, 1830, when Chase was twenty-two – "sweeter because, like the tones of the wind through the harp, they are unsubjected to the rules of art. . . . Her face is beautiful in feature and still more beautiful in expression. Even her looks of anger and scorn have a pretty gracefulness which half disarms them. Her form is light and frail, but exquisitely molded. Her motion is free as the summer's breeze, and, like it, soft and gentle, or animated and unreserved." Evidently Chase could appreciate feminine charms, but the outcome is disappointing. "I was very near falling in love with this lady – nay, I would certainly have done so, had not our tastes been, in one particular, wholly dissimilar. She is fond of the gay world – I have no desire to partake in its vanities. She is disinclined to religion and its duties. I value them more than any earthly possession."

One could easily point out other traits in the young man that placed him in a class apart from Seward. He cared nothing for the theater and shrank from cards, his one game being chess; early in life he took the vow of temperance so popular at the time, and even looked kindly upon its political manifestations. Afterward that pitiless analyst of cabinet comrades, Gideon Welles, liked to point out that his fellow New Englander had not a particle of humor. "Chase's jokes are always clumsy; he is destitute of wit." But religion took precedence over everything, even love affairs. The story of that first marriage, to Katherine Garniss, is heart-rending. The girl – she was only twenty at the time of her death – was dominated by two men, her father and her husband, both of whom regarded this earthly life as important mainly as preparation for the next. A year after the marriage, on the birth of a daughter, Kitty fell desperately ill of childbed fever. In these times her life could easily have been saved, but the crude medical procedure of the early eighteen-thirties – especially profuse bleeding of the patient – resulted in what was little less than murder. In Kitty's last moments, her father hung over the bed, fiercely catechizing her as to the state of her soul, her willingness to die, and her hope of salvation. Chase himself was in Philadelphia, having been called away on a law case. For this absence he was hardly blameworthy; the physician had informed him that the crisis had been passed, that his wife was rapidly recovering, and that his refusal to meet an important legal engagement would have a bad effect upon her. But the husband's remorse, as set forth in page after page of his Diary, was terrible. Entire days spent in prayer and Bible reading offered little relief. That Kitty had died without "the opportunity of publicly testifying to her faith in Christ" tormented Chase the rest of his life. For months he haunted the grave, and the three remaining members of the household – father, mother, and Chase – began and ended every day on their knees. "I rose this morning with a heavy heart" – so reads one of countless entries of the kind in Chase's journal – "I had been dreaming of accompanying my dear wife to the church, and I awoke to the mournful conviction that never more would we walk in the House of God or take sweet counsel together. The day was very fine and it pained my heart to think that never more would my dear wife be gladdened by the brightness of the sun. At length I endeavored to seek God in prayer. I read the last chapter in the first Epistle of John, in which he sets forth so strongly the pre-eminent necessity and excellence of Christian love, and I went downstairs, where I was soon joined by my mother-in-law and father-in-law, and we united in family prayer. Oh! that God would give me a deeper sense of my own sinfulness and destitution, that I might pray with more earnestness and humility; greater love for others, that I might pray for them more heartily. . . . What grieves me most is that I was not, while my dear wife lived, so faithful with her on the subject of religion as I should have been; and I have now no certain assurance that she died in the faith. I am not, blessed be God, without strong hope; but I have not that clear evidence of her salvation which might reasonably have been expected to result from more faithful and diligent efforts on my part for her conversion. Oh! if I had not contented myself with a few conversations on the subject of religion, with a few recommendations of religious books, with faint prayers; if I had incessantly followed her with kind and earnest persuasion; if I had ceaselessly brought God's blessing upon my efforts; if I had even exhibited before her an example of the Christian life, she might have been, before her death, enrolled among the professed followers of the Lamb. But I procrastinated and now she is gone."

To add to Chase's tragedy, the child, named Katherine, died about four years after the mother. Soon afterward, Chase married Eliza Ann Smith, who survived the wedding only six years, and, in November 1846, Sarah Dunlop Ludlow, who also remained with the now distinguished man six years. In these ten years of married life Chase became the father of six children, of whom only two girls grew to womanhood. To the daughter of his second wife Chase gave in memoriam the name of his first – the vivacious child who grew up to be the famous Kate Chase Sprague, the most dazzling social leader of the Lincoln administration, as celebrated for beauty and brains as for the assiduity with which she worked for her father's political advancement. The death of three wives and four children in a comparatively short time naturally increased the somber phases of Chase's character. "What a vale of misery this world is!" he wrote Charles Sumner, January 28, 1850, on the death of a favorite sister. "To me it has been emphatically so. . . . Death has pursued me incessantly ever since I was twenty-five. My path has been – how terribly true it is – through the region of his shadow. Sometimes I feel as if I could give up – as if I must give up. And then after all I rise and press on." Two things forced him to renewed desire to live – an ambition that knew no limit and a zealot's devotion to the cause. For in this period of domestic sorrow, with brief intervals of happiness, Chase's stature was growing, both as lawyer and as public man.

The times ideally suited a man of his rigid moral conviction. In him was concentrated all the essential material of the Abolitionist. At moments Chase would deny his membership in this uncompromising school; by this disclaimer evidently meaning that he did not accept the Garrisonian attitude in all its wild insistencies – that is, he did not believe in tearing up the Constitution, in secession by the North from the "hellish" Federal Union; nor was he opposed to political action, as were the Garrisonians, as a means of ridding the nation of a great evil. Lincoln, however, in forming his cabinet, turned to Chase as representing the Abolitionists, and the Ohioan's thirty years' activity as an antislavery man justified the choice. And certainly the leaders of the radical wing, such as Charles Sumner, Ben Wade, Joshua R. Giddings, and George W. Julian, regarded Chase as one of themselves. Chase's ideal of a public man, indeed, was Sumner. The close co-operation between these two contentious zealots that was to endure all through the Lincoln administration – frequently to its embarrassment – began as far back as 1847. The correspondence started at that time continued until Chase's death in 1873. The basis for this alliance Chase set forth in a letter to Sumner, using the language in which both men were completely at ease: "*Idem velle et idem nolle.*" [1] One of the points on which these extremists agreed, several years before the Civil War, was in giving the franchise to Negroes. That definitely fixed the standing of both men as die-hards on the slavery issue. "*Laus Deo!*" Chase writes Sumner on the latter's election to the Senate in 1851. "Now, I feel as if I had a brother-colleague – one with whom I shall sympathize and be able fully to act." "We all remember you," he writes some years afterward, "with love and admiration. Your picture hangs alone in my library over a framed autograph of Charles Carroll. It hangs with others, all of earnest men, in my dining room. I put them up as a defiance to the pro-slavery men – as symbols of my faith and purpose." The correspondence betrays a distrust of a contemporary Senator, a dislike which boded ill for the future. "I don't know what Seward will do. I have never been able to establish much sympathy between us. He is too much of a politician for me. It is said that he is disinclined to agitation. . . . Seward, though meaning to maintain his own position as an anti-slavery man, means to maintain it in the Whig party and only in the Whig party."

Yet Chase had made his most famous appearance as "attorney general for fugitive slaves" in association with Seward. The two men appeared in 1842, before the Supreme Court of the United States as unpaid lawyers for John Vanzanda, charged with harboring runaways. Both men in this suit not only won wide fame for eloquence and legal skill but gave Mrs. Stowe material for the Van Trompe incident in *Uncle Tom's Cabin.* Seward and Chase at this time were facing the crisis of their careers. Political parties and political leaders could no longer evade the slavery question. The years that Chase spent with these extremists, 1841–1848, probably represent the sincerest period of his public life. He was fighting with all the earnestness of his evangelistic spirit, on the stump, in the courts, and on the platform, for the cause in which he devoutly believed, and it was this championship that made his name one of the best known in the nation.

But Chase had one failing that made him also sometimes an object of execration: an insatiable lust for public office. In 1850 he announced boldly, anticipating a similar boast made nearly forty years afterward by the egregious David B. Hill of New York: "I am a democrat." As the Democratic Party was the one most subservient to the South and its proslavery interests, this announcement scandalized many. As a result of

[1] To wish the same things and to dislike the same things.

a three-cornered fight in the senatorship contest in Ohio in 1849, a struggle that lasted several months and demoralized the state, Chase had been elected to the United States Senate. The legislature, in addition to its Democratic and Whig members, contained thirteen Free-Soilers, the party in which Chase had been one of the chief pillars in 1848. These Free-Soilers, by combining with the Democrats, had mustered the majority that won the coveted honor for the distinguished antislavery leader. The story is a most complicated one – of deals, intrigues, disputed elections, trading of jobs and out of it all Chase emerged as Senator, but with a clouded title. Though he now proclaimed himself a Democrat, his new party associates in the United States Senate did not acclaim him as a brother. He was not invited into the Democratic caucus and his committee assignments were inconsequential. He was also treated at times cavalierly on the Senate floor. More than once his new-found fellows expatiated on the circumstances of his election, one of the most biting critics being that noble scion of Louisiana, Judah P. Benjamin. Chase justified his change of party on two grounds. The old Jacksonian organization, he insisted, comprised an element he called the "old line democrats," and this would ultimately prevail and win the party for the antislavery cause – an optimistic view of the future that made the cynics smile. Again, on all questions except slavery, Chase accepted Democratic principles, especially the high tariff – an item in his creed which caused still more confusion when, in 1860, he aspired to the presidential nomination of the Republican Party, strongly pledged to protection.

Even Warden, Chase's worshipful official biographer, can find no excuse for his "hero" when he accepted a nomination for governor of Ohio in 1855, from what was virtually a Know-Nothing Convention – with a small sprinkling of Whigs. "I do not attempt to vindicate his coalition with the Know-Nothings. Then he seemed to me most dangerously wrong; and now I find no reason for supposing that my judgment, then, did him an injustice." But Chase, unlike the man to whom he entrusted all his papers for biographical use, had no such difficulty. He did not call the body which nominated him a Know-Nothing Convention, as everybody else did, but an "Anti-Nebraska Convention, in which the Americans [Know-Nothings] so called, had a decided majority." The party was more interested, he explained, in opposing slavery than in promoting its antiforeign program – was this not reason enough why he should accept a nomination at its hands? His various party affiliations did not lower him in the eyes of Sumner and other "radicals," and it must be said that Chase survived a chameleon-like career of thirty years with his standing as an impassioned anti-slavery leader unimpaired. Perhaps the best that can be said for Chase in these disputed episodes he said himself. In a letter written soon after that first dubious election as Senator, he reviews the political maneuverings that culminated in success: "I will not say that in the counsels I gave last winter I was not uninfluenced by personal considerations; but I can say I do believe that I was not influenced by such considerations to any extraordinary degree. Certainly I neither modified nor compromised in any way my political principles." The same double motive can be found in most of his critical decisions – an inordinate desire for office caused a certain myopia as to ways and means of attaining it. Yet through all his life Chase did stand as an effective leader in the cause to which he had devoted his splendid talents from youth.

And this fact made him one of the leading candidates for the great prize in 1860. Chase, however, was never a formidable contestant. Prominent as he had been, eloquent as he had shown himself to be in the great senatorial debates of the fifties – that on the Compromise measures of 1850 and the Nebraska Act of 1854 – the man had none of the necessary qualities of a commanding party leader. In this respect he does not resemble Gladstone. He was too austere and too humorless in bearing, too averse to human companionship, too theological and too ostentatiously moral, to be ever liked, not to say loved; no crowds and brass bands ever spontaneously gathered to greet Chase as they did Seward; nor did his neighbors ever weep over his political misfortunes. Thus Chase never built up a real political following, and, above all, never attached to his fortunes an adroit, personally devoted manager, like Thurlow Weed. He was always a distant, lonely figure, regarding public office, even the highest, as a right, and believing that it should come to him as a kind of law of nature. When Chase's ambition became manifest in the Chicago Convention of May 1860, there was really no man, except Chase himself, inordinately attached to his interests. The Ohio State Convention did adopt him as the favorite son, but that convention controlled only four delegates-at-large, and Chase could not get all of the remaining forty-two. This ruined his chances at the start, for a favorite son who does not command the undivided allegiance of his own state can hardly hope for support outside. Thus, on the first ballot, Chase obtained only 34 of Ohio's 46 votes, eight of them ominously going to Lincoln. On the third ballot, when Lincoln needed only two and one-half more votes to attain the needed majority of 234, they came with a tremendous shout from Ohio. Chase always attributed his failure to get the nomination to this lack of unanimity in his own state. "It may be," he wrote soon after Lincoln's nomination, "that I had no chance at Chicago, but I suppose that nobody doubts that had the Ohio delegates manifested the same disregard of personal preferences, which was exhibited by the New York, Illinois and Missouri delegations, and given to me, as the nominee of Ohio, the same earnest and genuine support which was given to Mr. Seward, Mr. Lincoln and Mr. Bates by those delegations respectively, that my vote on the first ballot would have largely exceeded Mr. Lincoln's." Had that happened, the embittered man reasoned, the candidate on whom the anti-Sewardites finally united would have been himself. Though he spoke pleasantly enough of Lincoln at that time, Chase really never forgave him for his own presidential collapse. That this failure to obtain the unanimous support of his homeland represented any criticism of himself or his career, the self-righteous statesman never apparently suspected.

III

THUS SEWARD, in the political amalgamation which came into power March 4, 1861, represented the steady old-line Whig turned Republican, and Chase the Democratic element which had abandoned the party of Jackson and Buchanan, and joined the new party solely on the question of slavery. Edward Bates, the third member of the trio which loomed large as the first inevitable cabinet choices, typified a different following. This lifelong "old fogy" Whig, as Bates described himself, rather took pride in the fact that he had never been a Republican and never intended to become one. A mild opponent of the slavery extensionists who, by 1856, had gained absolute control of the Federal government in all three departments – the Presidency, Congress, and the Supreme Court – Bates still had declined to follow Seward and other Whig leaders into the Republican Party, supporting in 1856 the candidate of the Americans, or Know-Nothings, Millard Fillmore. The old gentleman tenaciously retained his favorite Whig allegiance long after the party having that name had ceased to exist, presiding over the last convention held in Baltimore in 1856. When Bates's admirers in the Southwest, under the leadership of the Blair family, proposed him as a presidential leader for 1860, they did not press him specifically as a Republican, but as the candidate of the "Opposition" – opposition, that is, to the Buchanan and Douglas Democrats and all their works. To nominate as a Republican candidate a man who had rejected Frémont in 1856, and who, in short, had enlisted in a cause so discredited as that of the Know-Nothings, put a severe strain on the groups who had decided that the time had finally come to fight a straight antislavery issue. Bates's nomination and election, however, seemed to a more compromising element to be the one way of preventing Civil War. Long after Lee's surrender, his admirers bewailed Bates's failure to head the Republican ticket in 1860; had he been the standard-bearer, they always insisted, the dangerous controversy would have been peacefully and equitably adjusted. For Bates was perhaps the leading man in the great Southwest, the region that formed the connecting link between North and South, and with him in the White House all that debatable land – Missouri, Arkansas, Kentucky, Tennessee, Maryland, perhaps even Virginia and North Carolina – could have been kept within the Union. Bates's unquestioning loyalty to the Federal compact no one ever questioned. A similar reason made almost inevitable his inclusion in the Lincoln cabinet. The great problem facing the administration in March 1861 was that of keeping the Border states in the Union. At that time, Maryland, Kentucky, and Missouri were tottering on the brink of secession; in each state a powerful minority was working night and day to accomplish its withdrawal from the Union. Had these disrupting efforts not failed, the new Confederacy would have had more than even chances of success. As an essential part of Lincoln's statesmanship, two cabinet members were selected from these critical commonwealths – Edward Bates from Missouri and Montgomery Blair from Maryland.

Bates was an ideal choice for this purpose, not only because of his high personal character, his prominence as a lawyer, his widespread reputation in the Southwest for sagacity and public spirit, but because he was, in birth, training, and to a large extent in sympathy, a Southerner. He was born in Virginia, of a long line of "old" Virginia ancestors, had spent the first twenty-eight years of his life in the Old Dominion, and was, despite an active career in his adopted Missouri, throughout life Southern in manner and feeling. His wife was a South Carolinian of ancient stock; one of his sons, to Bates's grief, served as a Confederate officer in the Civil War. Not inappropriately did Bates take the conservative side on all questions, for he was born in 1793, in the administration of George Washington, and, despite Quaker antecedents, had served as a soldier in the War of 1812. His opposition to slavery could probably be explained on the same grounds, for Bates came of that Virginia stock, and was indeed not far removed from that Virginia generation – the generation of Washington himself, Jefferson, Madison, the Lees, George Mason – who regarded slavery as an evil which it was the duty of the coming century to correct. Soon after leaving this paternal soil and starting life anew in St. Louis – then a straggling trading post, not far advanced from the log-cabin stage – Bates, just under thirty, took part in framing Missouri's constitution. That famous enactment known as the Missouri Compromise – which excluded slavery forever from all that part of the Louisiana Purchase lying north of 36° 30′ degree of latitude – was as sacred in Bates's mind as the articles of the Christian creed in which he so devoutly believed. From 1820, Missouri's two leading citizens were Thomas Hart Benton and Edward Bates, and as Benton, being United States Senator, was absent practically all the time in Washington, priority undoubtedly belonged to the ex-Virginian. Always more Hamiltonian than Jeffersonian in political conceptions, he broke away from the Jacksonian wing in the late eighteen-twenties and joined that Whig Party, from which he could never be dissociated. This allegiance in itself made impossible any great political career in Missouri, for the new state became overwhelmingly Democratic and has remained so up to the present writing.

Bates unsuccessfully contested the United States Senatorship with Benton in 1828, a failure that confined his career on the national stage to a single session in the lower house. But his law practice and his lifelong position as "sage" – what today would be called elder statesman – caused President Fillmore, in 1850, to select him as Secretary of War – an offer which Bates declined. He preferred, so the President was informed, to devote his energies to his profession, to the affairs of his community, and to his domestic concerns. The last item catalogued in this renunciation would seem adequate in itself. In 1823, Bates had married Julia Davenport Coalter, a union that had been blessed with a family of seventeen children, of whom eight were living in 1860. Bates all his life displayed a patriarchal devotion to his section. St. Louis, not Chicago, he believed, would grow to be the great entrepôt of the Middle West; river transportation would make inevitable the flow of traffic north and south; even the newfangled railroad would never divert it east and west. This conviction he insisted made impossible an independent Southern Confederacy; would the powerful and rapidly growing Middle West ever permit the control of this vast river system to rest in the hands of an "alien" nation? On this issue Bates became what is usually described as a "national figure." His speech as president of the Rivers and Harbors Convention in 1844 produced an effect not unlike that of William Jennings Bryan's cross-of-gold oration in Chicago in 1896. The present generation can hardly imagine a great crowd going wild on a topic so little suggestive of the higher life as that of dredging rivers and harbors, but on this theme Bates's oratory waxed really Demosthenic.

After that address Edward Bates remained for years the leading citizen of the Southwest – a position which Harvard recognized in 1858 by making him an honorary doctor of laws. His separation from the ferocious battles of the fifties added to his usefulness as the possible peacemaker of 1860. Not that his attitude on the issues had ever been concealed. Benton's opposition to the Compromise of 1850 shocked his onetime rival, who joined in the movement that led to "Old Bullion's" defeat for re-election to the Senate. The repeal of the

Missouri Compromise in 1854 – a measure which Bates, like all loyal Whigs, had always regarded as the final solution of the slave question, at least in the Louisiana country – proved an even greater disillusionment. Yet in the main, on slavery and other matters, Bates still remained faithful to his Virginian tradition. In him there was nothing of the radical; Seward and Chase, closely identified with the antislavery cause, Bates regarded as politicians guilty of using an inflammatory issue for personal ends; "abolitionists," such as Garrison, Sumner, and Wendell Phillips, represented an accursed tribe. The views he entertained on the Negro to the end of his days were those of the traditional Southerner – the black man belonged to an inferior race, unfitted for the higher civilization, and any suggestion of endowing him with civic obligations, above all the franchise, was a wild proposal originating in the brains of those whom Bates stigmatized as "Jacobins." Still slavery, he agreed, was an evil, barbarous and unchristian, which might be tolerated for a time in the old slave states but which must not be permitted to extend into the new national domain. Quite naturally, therefore, Bates, when the Whig Party disappeared, joined the "opposition" – never the "Republicans" – and when Missouri became the recruiting ground of "border ruffians," stampeding into Kansas in the mad chase to make it another slave state, Bates took his stand with the comrades in the North and West who were determined that it should be free. During this tumultuous decade, however, the old Missourian held no office and served in no lawmaking bodies; he was simply the influential citizen whose words, in press and platform, acquired a nationwide audience.

A prevailing contemporary estimate of Bates is echoed in a characterization by Joseph Medill, who described him as "a fossil of the Silurian era – red sandstone at least – who should never have been quarried out of the rocks in which he was embedded." The Missourian's old-fashioned exterior justified somewhat this irreverent classification. Bates, in his Missouri home, with an unending cavalcade of sons and daughters and grandchildren, really did suggest another geologic period. Even in the Lincoln cabinet a kind of classic antiquity enveloped him; he was its oldest member, sixty-eight when the administration began, seventy-two on his voluntary retirement in 1864. A certain quiet sobriety in appearance and behavior harked back to the country's prime. In a cabinet which, in the main, was as closely shaved as Julius Caesar, Bates shared honors with Welles for a shrubby white beard – though, in strange contrast, his hair retained its dark and ruddy aspect almost to the end. "That's because Bates uses his chin more than his head," Lincoln, personally very fond of his friend, would remark. The joke, however, was one of those which depend for effect upon misrepresentation, for cerebral labor, not idle conversation, had been Bates's main characteristic all his life. A man of slight build – in Carpenter's stodgy picture of the Emancipation reading Bates seems almost the smallest and certainly the most retiring figure – with thin shoulders and a neck which appears hardly separate from the head, Bates's gentle but rugged face, vigorous nose, heavy brows, pensive and questioning eyes, faithfully indicate the man – the literal logician, utterly lacking in imagination, the conservative whose sole reliances in his earthly course were God, the law, and the Constitution.

Bates was another of the statesmen of that time given to diary keeping. His output, in five bulky volumes, now reposing in the Library of Congress,[1] offers a queer mélange of manuscript entries, newspaper clippings, letters, speeches, broadsides, election handbills, and printed pamphlets – all grouped by himself under the general heading of "Notes." One feature is an amazing disregard of spelling – for the man who gained such eminence at the American bar preferred "gits" to "gets," usually insisted on "Byrnside" and "Farrigat" as designations of certain military and naval chieftains, and constantly treated the most commonplace words in a similarly cavalier fashion. Yet at the same time Bates was deeply immersed in classic lore; when analyzing what he regarded as fallacies in Jefferson's Preamble to the Declaration, he falls back on Aristotle's *Politics*, and when contemplating the excesses of the democratic system, he turns to Cicero's *Letters*, which, in his view, in their account of the declining days of the Roman Republic, contained valuable lessons for his own age. As a diarist, Bates falls far behind the standards of John Quincy Adams and Gideon Welles, for his crabbed pen did not flow readily and his insight into men and actions was not keen. Yet the self-portrait, unconsciously set forth, does survive. As the picture of a philosophic farmer, living in rural elegance not far from St. Louis, whose interest in the minutiae of life is fairly Washingtonian, the volume is a precious document. The progress of his beans, corn, wheat, and also of the animals, is devoutly set down from day to day, as well as the appearance of the "first crocus of the season"; the morning when "the earlier trees, such as maple, box elder, etc. are in full leaf – almost," and one when "the elms have been shedding seed and the oaks are in full tassel" and the "flowers, Hyacinthe, Johnquils [*sic*] are gone," are religiously noted. When it comes to larger things, Bates's occasional grief over the excesses of the time, the frequently unflattering comments passed upon

[1] It was published as Vol. II in the *Annual Report* of the American Historical Association for 1933.

cabinet associates, the loyalty always evident towards Lincoln himself, make his Diary a permanent social and political record.

The Diary also gives perhaps the best inside picture we have of that psychological phenomenon in American politics – the expectant presidential candidate. The infection, once instilled into the human system, acts apparently somewhat like the poet's oft-quoted description of vice – at first hated and ignored, but by the gradual process of familiarity, ultimately endured and finally embraced. Bates was honestly astonished when his name was first broached. "I must try," he writes on July 5, 1859, "to resist the temptation and not allow my thoughts to be drawn off from the common channels of business and domestic cares. Ambition is a poison, at once strong and insidious, and is very apt to cheet [*sic*] a man out of his happiness and his true respectability of character." Yet soon the chronicler is noting with eagerness indications that appear in several sections in his favor. Connecticut seems to incline in his direction – in fact, seven of its twelve delegates did vote at Chicago for the Missourian on the first ballot. Greeley, of the *Tribune*, is loudly advocating Bates – but the victim does not appraise that support at its true worth, for Greeley, a venomous enemy of Seward, is scanning the horizon for some promising candidate with whom to effect his "irrepressible's" ruin. Newspaper editorials, endorsing Bates or speaking kindly of him, are excised and carefully pasted in the bulky record, and resolutions passed by political groups, to the same effect, are similarly enshrined. Soon Bates is not only completely reconciled to this dazzling future but is confident that he will be the man. "Without some great change before next spring," he ventures to predict, "my nomination for the Presidency is more probable than that of any other man, but I will not set my heart upon it, so as to be painfully disappointed in the event of failure." But as convention time draws near, he really has set his heart upon it. "I think now," he writes on December 1, 1859, "that the probabilities of my nomination are strengthening every day. In the present state of public feelings the Republican party (even if they desire it which I think they do not) will hardly venture to nominate Mr. Seward. And I have many and strong assurances that I stand second – first in the northwest and in some states in the northeast, and second in New York, and Pa. In the latter (Pa.) Mr. Cameron for local reasons shows first but he has not strength elsewhere."

The contest, the diarist is confident, lies between Seward of New York and Bates of Missouri. Is there any likelihood of Chase? Seward, in case he fails of the nomination, will never accept the Ohioan. Lincoln's name does not appear in the Diary until April 20, 1860 – less than a month before the convention meets. "As a matter of state pride" Illinois will support Lincoln on the first ballot, and, after that, "there is a good feeling for me." By this time Bates, who at first was flabbergasted that anyone should think of him for the Presidency, is not only convinced that he will be nominated but believes that he should be. He is by all odds the best man "they" – this is the distant way in which he refers to the Republicans from whom he expects this honor – could put forward. The chief argument for his selection by the Republicans is, paradoxically enough, that he is not a Republican. He kept away from that miasma, even in 1856, when practically all "old fogy Whigs" like himself had succumbed to the taint. That will make him popular in the Border states and other regions where Republican "abolitionists" are anathema. Again Bates had been identified with the "Know-Nothing" Party in 1856, when what was left of the Whigs put forth Fillmore as their candidate; that will reinforce him greatly in Pennsylvania, Indiana, and other states where the feeling against immigrants and Catholics is becoming more bitter every day.

Bates appeared openly the candidate – though he denied the allegation – when, in reply to certain admirers in New York, he wrote a letter setting forth his views on the state of the Union. In this he strongly opposed fighting the election of 1860 on the slavery issue. It was time that that pestilential "agitation" should come to an end. What were the really burning questions at stake? The Pacific railroad, the tariff, the improvement of harbors and rivers, the homestead laws, immigration, and many questions of internal improvement. This pronouncement somewhat disheartened the Blairs, Greeley, Charles A. Dana, and other Bates boomers, but that canny gentleman looked upon it as the acme of wisdom. A great point, he noted, was that "it keeps me separated from the Republican party and yet not so far removed as to prevent their support." Verily the antique Cato of the Missouri farm was now behaving much like a presidential candidate. Unremitting efforts of friends to detach him from this position and to say something to the point about slavery had little effect. When Henry J. Raymond, editor of the *New York Times*, called on Bates February 4, 1860 – three months before the convention – and attempted to get a more satisfactory expression of views, the same discretion of the receptive candidate was evident. "Doubtless a most intelligent man," Bates confided to his Diary, "but he seemed reserved and rather watching me than displaying himself. *I* talked freely and I supposed he thought imponderably. But, knowing his political Status, I talked so on purpose. Seeming to be very open and bold, I took care to say nothing that I had not said and published often before."

Obviously the body which Bates insisted on calling "The National Union Convention" could not select as its candidate in 1860 a man who thought that antislavery was a "pestilential agitation" and that the campaign should be waged on the Pacific railroad and the Homestead Law. Bates, however, unlike Seward and Chase, showed no bitterness over the outcome. He was nearing his seventieth year, and had no intention of wasting his few remaining days in self-pity and recrimination. He still believed that "they" – the new Republican Party – were a temporary apparition that would disappear after the manner of all previous antislavery groups. "The party will henceforth subside into weakness and then break into pieces, its fragments seeking each its own safety in new affiliations and other organizations." He did not like the Chicago platform: it was "exclusive and defiant. . . . To please the Germans especially it galls (not to say insults) the Americans [that is, the Know-Nothings] and all the Republicans who came in through the American party – such as Gov. Banks, Mr. Colfax and the like." It also needlessly exposed "the party to the specious charge of favoring negro equality – and this only to gratify a handful of extreme Abolitionists, led on by Mr. Giddings." Mr. Lincoln "personally is unexceptionable but politically is as fully committed as Mr. Seward is to the extremist doctrines of the Republican party." When the Lincolnites appealed to the Missourian to take the stump, he declined on the valid ground of old age; but he promised to write a letter endorsing the candidate in the strongest terms – a letter that was most gratefully received and had a powerful effect. For Bates, despite his reservations on abolitionism, still continued to be a strong Union man. His comment on the situation, however, shows how far he was removed from the spirit of the time. Even as late as the secession of South Carolina he refused to take seriously the threat of national disruption. "I think that, except for a few demented fanatics, it is all brag and bluster"; Jefferson Davis and his like "were only hoping to make a better compromise with the timid patriotism of their opponents. In playing this dangerous game they may go further than they now intend and actually commit their states to open rebellion and civil war."

IV

ALL THAT I am in the world," Lincoln remarked to a friend, in a moment of despondency over his cabinet situation, "the Presidency and all else, I owe to the opinion of me which people express when they call me 'honest old Abe.' Now, what would they think of their 'honest old Abe' if he should make such an appointment as the one proposed?" The President-elect was referring to Simon Cameron of Pennsylvania, who aspired to be his Secretary of the Treasury. Lincoln was not the only President who had entertained an unfavorable view of this lithe Pennsylvanian. Cameron had been closely associated with three Presidents, Jackson, Polk, and Buchanan – all of whom have left on record most unflattering views of his character. Jackson described him as a man "not to be trusted by anyone in any way, and as a renegade politician who got elected Senator by selling himself to the Whiggs [*sic*]."[1] James K. Polk, to whose party – at that time – Cameron belonged, regarded him not more kindly, confiding to his Diary an inability to express his "contempt for a Senator capable of such coarseness and vulgarity. . . . Cameron is a managing tricky man in whom no reliance is to be placed. He professes to be a Democrat but he has his own personal and sinister purposes to serve."[2] In the first half of his political life Cameron's closest associate in the Democratic ranks had been James Buchanan, President from 1857 to 1861, and after twenty years of the most intimate companionship this eminent authority referred to his one-time manager as "a scamp," "an unprincipled rascal," and as always a "disorganizer" when his "personal interest came into conflict with the success of the party." Certain celebrated anecdotes have given Cameron his own niche in the national portrait gallery. To him is usually ascribed that immortal definition of an "honest politician" as one who, "when bought, stays bought."

[1] Jackson, Andrew, *Correspondence*. Ed. by John Spencer Bassett. Carnegie Institute, 1926–1927. VI, 395.

[2] *Diary of James K. Polk*, Quaife, Milo M., ed. A. C. McClurg & Co., 1910. I, 426.

Another Lincoln story – one of his favorites – the world will never willingly let die. "Is Cameron an honest man?" the President asked Thaddeus Stevens, whose opinion, as a contemporary Pennsylvanian, should certainly have had value. "I don't think he would steal a red hot stove," Stevens replied. The aphorism having reached Cameron's ears, that gentleman demanded an apology. "Oh, well," Stevens retorted, "I apologize. I said Cameron would not steal a red hot stove. I withdraw that statement."

Most of the epithets directed at Cameron, it will be observed, imply a certain untrustworthiness of character – a lack of faithfulness to the spoken word, a tendency to betray friends and to sacrifice parties and principles in the pursuit of personal aims. To the present generation it probably comes as a surprise that Simon Cameron ever occupied a high position in the political party founded by Thomas Jefferson. Ever since the Civil War, Simon and his son and co-worker James Donald – more colloquially "Don" – have enjoyed national fame as creators of the Republican imperium of Pennsylvania, a despotism which, under them and their successors, Matthew S. Quay and Boies Penrose, kept the land of William Penn securely in the Republican ranks for seventy-five years, until it met destruction in the Roosevelt debacle of 1932. Yet the historic truth is that, from about 1844 to 1856, Simon Cameron held lofty place as party chieftain in the Jeffersonian – or Jacksonian – stronghold. This domination became so strong that on two occasions Cameron wrested from unwilling associates election to the United States Senate. Not until 1856 did he enroll in the Republican Party, and then he did so halfheartedly, for no public reason, least of all because of a moral revolt against slavery, but simply because this transition would best promote the purposes of the moment. Like Chase, Cameron also cultivated the Know-Nothings, but unlike Chase, he never troubled himself about finding a reason for the change based on principle. That politics was the exclusive end of his public life Cameron would have been the last man to deny, and by politics he did not mean the use of parties for advancing great causes but for furthering personal and business advantage.

The offices, great and small, and legislation that would enhance private business, even at the expense of the body politic – to Cameron public life meant these things and these things only. Almost any methods that would bring such desirable results were their own justification. For the twenty-four years preceding 1860 one great cause had monopolized the attention of Americans in both public and private station, yet in all that time Cameron's voice was practically never raised on the slavery issue. One can read his letters, so far as they are available, and study his legislative performances without ever suspecting that the nation was being rocked by the most disturbing public question in its history. No speeches from Pennsylvania's Senator can be quoted for or against the Mexican War, the Wilmot Proviso, and related issues. Only one address of more than trifling consequence graces the Cameronian record in his two senatorial terms and that was devoted to the protective tariff. This subject began to assume importance in the early forties, with the dawn of Pennsylvania's industrial age, and Cameron, now a manufacturer, mine owner and railroad operator himself – already launched on his progress to millionairedom – made it his chosen legislative child. In this he perhaps faithfully represented his state, for Pennsylvania, though the problems rising out of the extension of slavery were not entirely ignored, gave chief emphasis to a high tariff as the real question of the time. This absorption in the tariff and kindred business legislation provided the ruling motif of Cameron's career. Many candidates are forthcoming when an attempt is made to point to some one man as the founder of the Boss system in politics, but a good case can be made for Simon Cameron as the man who, above all others, laid the basis of that alliance of business and politics which has reached its finest development in his native state. The beginnings of this system Cameron laid in the two decades preceding Sumter, and brought to its present perfection in the great industrial expansion that followed Appomattox. His influence did not end with the war. His last two terms in the Senate followed that event, and then came three for his son.

That two such seasoned veterans as Thurlow Weed and Simon Cameron should join hands in something resembling a conspiracy against the rustic Lincoln was natural enough. Both in their experiences and in their conceptions, the two men had much in common, though, on the human side, Weed unquestionably had the greater appeal. Like Weed, Cameron was born in poverty, obtained little schooling, and was cast out at a tender age to earn his living. The printer's office attracted this boy, as it had Weed; he became a printer's devil in a newspaper office, and rose by stages to be proprietor and editor of prosperous weekly and daily journals. Cameron could never have been a real editor even to the degree that Weed became, for his New York exemplar did have a taste for reading, with considerable interest in public questions, whereas Cameron cared nothing for books or ideas. The Pennsylvanian's journalism, from all accounts, had the same practical quality as his politics; soon dropping active work in that field – although he remained a newspaper proprietor all his days – Cameron gave his time to more mundane concerns. Prosperity in business, as intimated above, soon crowned his efforts. Political activity had contributed largely to this result. The man's real education may be said to have begun about 1822, the year that found him in Washington, working in the printing office of Gales & Seaton, publishers of the *National Intelligencer*, and of the *Annals of Congress* – the *Congressional Record* of the day. In this employment the twenty-two-year-old apprentice evidently made the same discovery that took possession of Seward at about the same time – that, after all, the most absorbing business of a rapidly developing democracy was politics.

It was an excellent period to gain schooling of the kind. The long Jeffersonian era was coming to a close in the last years of James Monroe, and the splitting of the Jeffersonian amalgam into two groups had already begun. In this division Seward and Weed joined the Whigs, but Cameron remained faithful to the Jacksonian Democrats. Cameron spent much time in the halls of the Capitol, making friends with politicians – two years that definitely fixed his career. Returning to Harrisburg about 1824, Cameron started work on the *Republican*, to such good purpose that in a year or two he owned the paper. Appointed to the governor's staff in 1826, he acquired that title of "General" which followed him all his life. Like Weed in New York, Cameron obtained the lucrative post of state printer, and his yeoman service in Pennsylvania for Martin Van Buren resulted in his appointment as agent for the settlement of the claims of the Winnebago Indians. This proved an unhappy stroke of fortune, for it involved Cameron in a mercenary scandal which he never lived down. Even while Lincoln was struggling with the man as a cabinet problem certain embarrassing cartoons appeared in the comic press, picturing the tall, lank Cameron dressed up in full Indian regalia, and labeled the great "Winnebago Chief." The story is too long and tedious for repetition in this place. Briefly the scandal charged that Cameron, through third parties, had acquired at ridiculously low figures the claims of these half-breeds and had sought to collect at face value for his own benefit. Despite Cameron's spirited denials for the rest of his days, the truth remained that the Indian Commissioner had refused to honor his warrant for payment on the ground of fraud, that Cameron was dismissed from his post, and that a new man was sent west to do his work all over again.

The events that made Cameron so odious to Democrats and Republicans alike were his two elections to the United States Senate, one in 1844 and the other in 1857. Scandal in plenty involved both these triumphs. In 1844, the Democrats, having won a majority of the legislature, supposedly controlled the election of the new Senator. The Democratic caucus had nominated for this post George W. Woodward, a man of ability and character; under the circumstances a caucus nomination amounted to an election. When the votes of the assembled legislators were counted, however, Simon Cameron, whose name had hardly been mentioned in connection with the honor, had a majority. It was Cameron's first exploit in that field of political legerdemain for which he was to become so celebrated. How had he performed the miracle? In part his handling of the tariff issue gives the explanation. Woodward, an orthodox Democrat, was a low-tariff man – he was even accused of being a free trader; the large business interests of Pennsylvania, outraged by the tariff of 1842, were already exercising a strong influence in politics. With their aid, Cameron manipulated a combination of high-tariff Democrats and Whigs – the "Whiggs" who so aroused the anger of Andrew Jackson – and walked away with the seat. Popular resentment proved so strong that Cameron stood no chance of reelection in 1849 and was forced to spend some years in retirement – very profitably, for his business and fortune increased in the interval. In 1855, having made arrangements with the Know-Nothings, Cameron tried again for the Senate, but succeeded only in deadlocking the legislature, Pennsylvania being forced, thanks to his activities, to rest content with only one United States Senator for about a year. In 1857 – Cameron was now a Republican – better luck attended his efforts. The situation that existed in the state legislature that year would have discouraged a man of inferior ability, but it furnished precisely the medium in which Cameron felt most at home. Again the legislature was Democratic, but by a small majority, and again it would naturally have chosen the new Senator. Cameron, who became the accepted Republican candidate, needed three Democratic votes to win – and he obtained exactly the three required. How? Such a question would have caused a smile in any group of Pennsylvanians of the time. It would have been a hard task to persuade any of them that the votes had not been bought for cash.

So deeply entrenched at the head of affairs was Cameron in 1860 that he actually became Pennsylvania's official candidate for the Republican nomination at Chicago. Of course no one, not Cameron himself, took this seriously; it was merely the usual method of consolidating the Pennsylvania delegation to use for trading purposes. One reason that Cameron could not really aspire to the highest office was that, like Chase in Ohio, he did not command the wholehearted support of his own state. Powerful as Cameron seemed, another man had recently come to the front and was challenging his dictatorship. Young Andrew Curtin had not only much of Cameron's skill as a tactician, but many desirable qualities which the older man lacked. Curtin was brilliant, magnetic, honest, and popular, so popular that, in 1860, he gained the Republican nomination for governor, against the fiercest opposition of Cameron himself. Since 1857, when Curtin led the forces attempting to defeat Cameron's election to the Senate, the two men had been locked in deadly feud – a feud that reached the floor of the Chicago presidential convention with historical results. At one time Cameron sought a compromise: he would accept Curtin as candidate for the governor's chair, if Curtin would accept him seriously as Pennsylvania's candidate for the successorship to James Buchanan in the White House. Nothing indicates more clearly Curtin's rising power than his success in winning the gubernatorial nomination without definitely committing himself to Cameron's aspiration. The latter secured Pennsylvania's endorsement, it is true, but everyone knew that this commitment would endure only for one ballot and that after that the delegation would swing to another man. That the man on whom Pennsylvania finally fixed approval would become the nominee seemed fairly certain. Who, then, would be Pennsylvania's second choice? Up to the time the convention came to order, Curtin's position was not generally known, but everybody believed that Cameron's favorite – next to himself of course – would be William H. Seward. Seward and Weed apparently had every reason to count upon these fifty and one-half votes. In fact, Seward believed they had been definitely pledged. In the latter part of March 1860, Seward had visited Cameron at Harrisburg, for a general discussion. "He took me to his house," Seward reported to Weed, "told me all was right. He was for me and Pennsylvania would be. It might happen that they would cast the first ballot for him, but he was not in, etc. He brought the whole legislature of both parties to see me, feasted them gloriously, and they were in the main so generous as to embarrass me." [3]

Today, as we scan the proceedings of that Chicago Convention, the fact stands forth clearly that the nomination of Abraham Lincoln was inevitable from the start. After that first ballot, when Seward obtained only 173½ votes of a needed majority of 234, there could have been no other outcome. With Seward eliminated, as he had been eliminated by this unsatisfactory showing, the choice narrowed to three men – Lincoln, Chase, and Bates. Nobody wanted Chase except, of course, Chase himself and his ambitious daughter Kate. Bates quickly dropped out for causes set forth above. Had Cameron been able to deliver Pennsylvania's delegation to Seward on the second ballot, as, according to Seward's understanding, he had promised to do, then Seward would probably have attained his great objective. But Andrew Curtin

[3] Crippen, Lee F., *Simon Cameron: Ante Bellum Years*. Mississippi Valley Press, 1942. P. 209.

stood in the way. Curtin spent a large part of Wednesday and Thursday visiting important delegations, pounding into their heads endlessly the one pre-eminent fact: Seward, he declared, could never carry Pennsylvania. Seward's extreme antislavery record did not constitute the chief argument against him. In Pennsylvania, antiforeign and anti-Catholic sentiment raged more fiercely than in any other state. In the land of William Penn the Know-Nothings had displaced the Whigs as the second political party; their votes could easily turn the election, and to them Seward was the most odious of public men. His association with Archbishop Hughes of New York, and his attempt to obtain public money for parochial schools, would prove impossible hurdles in November – so Curtin insisted. That Curtin was sincere in this belief – and correct in his contention – no one questioned. He had every reason for sincerity. He was a candidate for governor at the coming election; he could not win, the delegates were informed, with Seward on the same ticket. In struggling to keep Seward off the Pennsylvania ballot, Curtin was thus promoting his own election as well as that of the nominee for President. Thus the fact that his motives were in part selfish added to the impressiveness of his arguments.

Another anti-Seward advocate, Henry S. Lane of Indiana, put up a similar plea. Lane was candidate for governor in Indiana just as Curtin was in Pennsylvania. He too would lose, he declared, if Seward ran upon the same ticket; for the New Yorker was just as unpopular in Indiana as in Pennsylvania, and for the same reasons. Any Republican who could not carry Illinois, Indiana, and Pennsylvania would lose the election; had Frémont been victorious in these states in 1856, he would have won. Another fact added to the strength of the Curtin-Lane demonstration: both Pennsylvania and Indiana were "October states" – that is, elections took place there a month before the nationwide assize in November; for the Republicans to lose these states at this critical time would have a demoralizing effect upon the presidential contest. Curtin and Lane were eloquent, persuasive talkers, and by the time the sun went down Thursday evening, they had convinced the brethren that to nominate Seward was to insure Republican defeat. Thus Seward was really dead as a candidate before the balloting began.

Such a situation gave a rare opportunity to a politician of Cameron's skill. He had promised Seward his delegation on the second ballot, it is true, but such commitments did not disturb this leader. Besides, Cameron could not have delivered a unanimous delegation had that been his desire, for Curtin's large contingent would not have obeyed his instructions. Yet, though Cameron certainly could not nominate himself, and almost as certainly could not nominate Seward, there still remained an ample field for pickings of another kind. Cameron had played a dominating part in several presidential conventions and understood their most labyrinthine workings. The two bucolic statesmen acting as Lincoln's captains lacked this experience. Could not the adroit Pennsylvanian manipulate these two backwoods politicians in ways to serve his own ends? It may safely be assumed that Cameron, by Thursday evening, after the convention had been in session for two days, clearly saw that Lincoln was the coming man. That other less shrewd observers had not grasped this was true; Horace Greeley, as noted above, had failed to gauge events – but that was only one of countless occasions when Greeley displayed his unparalleled talent for guessing wrong.

Neither had the truth apparently penetrated the obtuseness of David Davis and Leonard Swett, in charge of Lincoln's interests. That these two nervous and perspiring gentlemen would go to almost any extremes to gain the Pennsylvania delegation Cameron understood. What happened has been told – though not completely – in a letter written years afterward by Leonard Swett.[4] "In the small hours of Friday morning" – the day of balloting – "two of Lincoln's friends" – the writer did not name them, but they were, of course, Swett himself and David Davis – "and two of Cameron's friends" – also not named, but they were John P. Sanderson and Alexander Cummings – met in a room of the Tremont House and made the deal. "Our arguments prevailed," says Swett, "and the Cameron men agreed to come to us on the second ballot. They did so most nobly and gave us forty-eight votes." Among the details Swett omitted in this relation were the nature of "our arguments." From abundant sources, we know precisely what they were. Only definite "practical" arguments would bring over a veteran like Simon Cameron. Swett and Davis promised, in so many words, that if Pennsylvania's forty-eight votes went to Lincoln on the second ballot, Cameron would become a member of his cabinet. Swett forgot another important detail in his revelation. In making what proved to be a most embarrassing bargain, he had acted not only without the consent of Lincoln, but in defiance of Lincoln's explicit instructions. Before this Tremont Hotel conclave, Davis had telegraphed Lincoln that the offer of a cabinet post for Cameron might secure the Pennsylvania delegation. "I authorize no bargain and will be bound by none," was Lincoln's emphatic reply; it certainly could not have been made stronger. It was followed by another message, scribbled in Lincoln's handwrit-

[4] Weed, Thurlow, *Autobiography of Thurlow Weed.* Ed. by H. A. Weed. Boston, 1884. II, 291.

ing on the margin of a newspaper, and sent to Davis by William H. Herndon, Lincoln's law partner: "Make no contracts that will bind me" – the words having been underscored for good measure. The corpulent Davis, said to be losing almost a pound of flesh a minute in his excitement and anxiety, was furious at Lincoln's injunctions. "Lincoln ain't here," he shouted, "and don't know what we have to meet. So we will go ahead as if we hadn't heard from him, and he must ratify it."

Essentially the same situation prevailed in the Indiana delegation, that other "doubtful" state without which no Republican candidate could succeed at the polls. The name of Caleb Blood Smith does not fill a large space in American history though some perhaps vaguely remember that a man of that name occupied an inconspicuous place in Lincoln's cabinet for a short time. In the Chicago Convention of 1860, however, Caleb Smith became an important character. His record up to that time had not been particularly distinguished. An inflexible Whig, as hostile to third-party movements as Seward himself, a one-time newspaper editor, lawyer, and railroad man, Smith had served two or three times in Congress creditably enough, but had attained no eminence. He enjoyed a political reputation as a stump speaker – at which he was fluent and persuasive. In 1860 he became a delegate at large to Chicago, and chairman of the Indiana delegation, in which capacity he had seconded the nomination of Abraham Lincoln. A good deal of backstairs work had preceded this open pronouncement for the Illinois candidate. In the main it had followed the Pennsylvania pattern. Indiana's twenty-six votes would go for Lincoln – and on the first ballot – in case Caleb B. Smith could obtain a cabinet position. To sit in a presidential council had long been Mr. Smith's ruling ambition; he had unsuccessfully tried to become Postmaster General under Zachary Taylor, but now David Davis and Leonard Swett, again in utter disregard of Lincoln's command against "bargains," promised him such a post. And the parallel with Pennsylvania held good in another particular.

Smith, as clever as Cameron himself, promised a delegation to the Lincoln managers which he did not control. The feeling against Seward among the Indiana delegates was even greater than among the Pennsylvanians. "The Indianans," wrote Murat Halstead, "were heart-sick" at the probability of Seward's nomination. "They look heart-broken at the suggestion that Seward has the inside track and throw up their hands in despair. They say that Lane will be beaten, the legislature pass entirely into the hands of the Democrats and the two Republican senators hoped for heard of no more." The delegation was thinking of Seward at no time; its choice, from the first day at Chicago, lay between Lincoln and Bates, and such interest as the latter inspired quickly disappeared. Thus Indiana would have gone for Lincoln irrespective of the foolish pledges made by Davis and Swett. "I have frequently heard," writes Matilda Gresham, in the *Life* of her father, Walter Q. Gresham, "Judge Otto tell how Caleb B. Smith imposed on Judge David Davis and Joseph Medill when the latter, during the Convention, was pledging everything in sight to insure Mr. Lincoln's nomination. 'Mr. Smith,' Judge Otto said, 'made Judge Davis believe that the Indiana delegation would go to Seward unless Smith was promised a place in the cabinet; when the truth was that none of us cared for Smith and after we got to Chicago and looked over the ground all were for Lincoln.' That the pledge was made I have heard from Judge Davis. That it was kept everybody knows." [5]

[5] Gresham, M., *Life of Walter Quintin Gresham.* Rand, McNally & Co., 1919. I, 110.

V

MEANWHILE claims persistently put forth from another source – claims as obnoxious to Seward and Cameron as those of Chase himself – could not be ignored. Two houses in Washington and adjoining Maryland had for the previous fifteen years wielded powerful influence in the early tentative days of the Republican Party. Today the stately brick "mansion" at 1651 Pennsylvania Avenue, diagonally opposite the White House, is a cherished possession of the Federal government. Yellow-stuccoed, green-shuttered, white-linteled, it is half museum and half official residence, held in reserve for distinguished guests of Uncle Sam. Visitors today usually pause to read the tablet that gives the tale of its eventful history – high light of all being the information that within its walls Robert E. Lee was offered the post of commander-in-chief of the Union Army in 1861, a few days before reaching the decision that made him serve under the Confederate flag. Built in 1810, it passed in 1836 into the hands of Francis Preston Blair, to a large extent the brains of the Jackson Administration, and for the eight years preceding Lincoln's accession had been the home of his son Montgomery. As such, it was for years one of the most cultivated social centers of Washington, and at the same time a vital meeting place for the nation's political and intellectual life. Here had been the favorite headquarters of Jackson's kitchen cabinet, and to this same niche of wisdom, perhaps of intrigue, Martin Van Buren had for many years turned for inspiration.

When the elder Blair gave this residence to Montgomery in 1853, he himself withdrew to his new country estate in Maryland, about seven miles from the Capitol – itself visible from certain elevations of ground – at Silver Spring. Few country homes have formed the background of so much political history as this secluded retreat. Even before Lincoln, in the harried days of civil war, sought privacy and comfort under its friendly chestnuts, pines, and poplars, Silver Spring had been intimately associated with all the great Americans since Jackson's day. Buchanan, Thomas Hart Benton, Van Buren, Thomas

Ritchie, Jefferson Davis, Seward, William C. Rives, Chase – these were men of discordant convictions and inharmonious allegiances but all liked to get away from official duties, bask in the coolness of their old friend's "grottoes," drink his wines, eat his well-cooked food, loiter in the shrubbery-lined walks, enjoy the hospitality of his wife, Violet Gist, granddaughter of Washington's famous friend Christopher Gist – and of the lovely daughter, Betty, whose portrait by Sully, hanging today in the drawing room of the still well-preserved family home, substantiates all the agreeable things said of her in her lifetime. Silver Spring was more than a house of genial and cultured entertainment. Historians point to Francis Preston Blair as the man more responsible than any other for the founding of the Republican Party, and it was at Silver Spring that the consultations were held which led to the Philadelphia Convention of 1856.

Naturally Silver Spring could not escape comparison with Horace's Sabine Farm, and in this case the resemblance had merit, for, in addition to the essential ingredients of a rustic villa – gardens for both vegetables and flowers, orchards, graperies, herds, dairies, mills, and the like – its *fons Bandusiae* formed the center of the scene, the sparkling vantage point about which the whole place had been created. It was the discovery of this crystal water, in a section of Maryland utterly primeval, never turned to use by tobacco planters or cultivators of any sort, which led the Blair family to settle in these woods in 1845. A true son of Kentucky, Blair was an expert horseman, and his wife and daughter displayed a similar proficiency in the saddle. Cantering one day along the old Seventh Street road, his mount, a spirited Arab, disengaged his rider and started on a wild run into the forest. Blair followed in pursuit; the animal's bridle was caught by a branch of a tree, and his master overtook him in a dense growth of pines and chestnuts. It was not the beauty of the richly overundulating ground that first fascinated Blair. He was brought to a halt near a gently rising, gently falling fountain of the clearest water; the visible bottom of white sand, in which small pieces of sparkling mica were embedded, gave a diamond-like effect. Blair was entranced. At that time the editor-statesman was suffering a temporary eclipse of influence. James K. Polk, who had come to the Presidency in 1845, did not favorably regard this Southern man who had no zeal for the extension of slavery, and was lukewarm on the Mexican aggression. But Blair, in Polk's eyes, had committed a more positive sin: he had worked hard for Van Buren's renomination in 1844, and had written disrespectfully of Polk in his *Globe*. The new President had no use for Jacksonians, of whom Blair, next to the old warrior himself, was the most conspicuous, and proceeded to reorganize the Democrats on an extreme State rights, proslavery and pro-Southern basis. There could be only one fate for malcontents like Blair. Polk summoned the unwilling Thomas Ritchie from Richmond, forced Blair to sell the *Globe*, the party organ, made Ritchie editor, and attempted meanwhile to ease Blair's descent by offering him the mission to Madrid – which the stranded editor declined. Simon Cameron played a part – as usual an underhanded one – in this transaction, thereby starting the Blair-Cameron feud that boded ill for harmony in 1860.

Though Blair, in 1845, was a rich man, the *Globe* and government printing having recouped his fortunes, his spirits were naturally depressed. A lodge in some vast political wilderness fitted well into the veteran's mood. As a result he purchased several hundred acres surrounding this unfailing gush of water, built a large frame house a considerable distance away – still standing in excellent preservation and in use by his descendants – laid out his walks and "grottoes" and summerhouses, planted his shrubs and ivies, and moved his household treasures into the country. The house at 1651 Pennsylvania Avenue was leased to a number of tenants – the most distinguished being George Bancroft, his turgid *History* already three volumes complete, who gave to its further prosecution in the Blair House such time as he could spare from his duties as Secretary of the Navy in Polk's administration – and Blair, although only a little more than fifty, established himself as a "sage," a gentleman supposed to be above the hurly-burly of contention, but to be full of recollection and wisdom which would be useful to those more actively engaged. And such proved to be the case. The most frequented shrine at Silver Spring was a wooden construction called, from its shape, the "Acorn," a sequestered nook in which Blair's friends gathered to discuss problems of state and politics, and lay plans for the triumph of correct causes. Twenty or thirty visitors a day were not unusual; a visitor's book of the Acorn, had one been kept, would be rarely prized by autograph hunters today. The memories of its walls would give far more knowledge of the events of 1850–1860 – and after – than thousands of "documents" and manuscripts gathering dust in great libraries. For this information would be alive, full of the hates, jealousies, loyalties, friendships, and ambitions that constitute the flesh and blood of history. Not all the visitors came to plot stratagems or to promote noble principles. Some came for rest and surcease. One of these was Charles Sumner, who, after the assault of Bully Brooks, was brought by Blair to Silver Spring in the hope that its quiet would aid his restoration. Nor did Blair's retirement to his Alban Hills lessen the bond between him and his son Montgomery.

Not only did the younger man build a home of his own, called Falkland, on the same estate – it was burnt in 1864 by Jubal Early in his raid on Washington – but the father made frequent trips on horseback, usually accompanied by Betty, to his old home opposite the White House. William Lyon Mackenzie, the Canadian revolutionist, wrote of Montgomery's splendid Washington mansion in which he "gave dinners and suppers to presidents, foreign ambassadors, cabinet ministers and congressmen in a style of oriental magnificence." The sight which old Washingtonians chiefly loved to recall was that of Francis Blair and son Montgomery standing with bared heads before the equestrian statue of Andrew Jackson in Lafayette Square. They admired this, not only as an appropriate memorial to their idol, but as a work of art – a judgment on which less reverential Americans today are not unanimous.

The servants who served Francis Blair's cool vintages and much prized food to an avalanche of friends were Negro slaves – and they remained such until the Fourteenth Amendment set them free. Silver Spring, indeed, had many characteristics of a Southern plantation – though the profit motive was absent; it had its "quarters" for the black folk, its outdoor kitchens, its mills, blacksmith and carpenter's shops, and other appurtenances of a self-sufficient economy. These facts fix Blair's position amid the disturbing complications of the time. For Blair was a Southerner, born in Kentucky, of Virginia forebears, in 1791 – thus being another of the Lincoln group who dated back to Washington's administration – and until the crisis demanded new alignments in 1848 and 1856, a lifelong Democrat. When Amos Kendall, who had been his personal crony and newspaper partner in Frankfort, Kentucky, called the hard-up young journalist – he appeared in the Capital in threadbare garments that aroused the pity or consternation of his new associate – to Washington in 1830, to assume the editorship of the new Jacksonian mouthpiece, the *Globe*, he launched one of the greatest of American journalists on a long, profitable career. Impartial, independent journalism is an ideal of a modern age; in that time newspapers were all organs and editors partisan spokesmen whose business it was to see only good in their friends and only evil in their foes. Thus the White House had its generally recognized papers, to which loyal party followers were expected to subscribe; any financial shortcomings the party usually provided for by awards of government printing; in Blair's case he became publisher of the *Congressional Globe*, successor to the *Annals of Congress* that had been the province of Joseph Gales, and predecessor of the present *Congressional Record*. These party editors were not looked upon, in Bismarck's phrase, as a "reptile press";

they were usually close to the party chiefs, and frequently powers in public affairs.

Of these Blair became the most influential. He performed his duties so eloquently that Jackson took him closely to his bosom, not only in an official but in a personal sense. He was soon elevated into that position of presidential penman – the irreverent call this character "ghost writer" – not unfamiliar in more recent times. Some of Jackson's most important state papers were the work of Francis P. Blair. He also became the President's most confidential adviser: practically no important decision, in politics or statecraft, was decided on without his approval. Jackson's warfare on the United States Bank is commonly attributed to this at times ferocious scribe. "Take it to Bla'r," Jackson would exclaim, when a particularly knotty problem fell on his desk. The grizzled old lonely bereaved man all but adopted the Blair children; Betty, as a little girl, lived a large part of the time in the White House, and, as she advanced in her teens, became his favorite amanuensis; it was noted that the backwoods statesman never smoked in the presence of his "little Democrat," as he called her, and was never known to use his favorite oath, "by the Eternal." Montgomery, a much more staid youngster, but brilliant in mind and persistent in industry, Jackson always regarded as a son. Readers of Jackson's letters do not need to be told of Blair's importance; more are written to him than to any other man; those phrases expressing his views on Simon Cameron, quoted above, appear in letters to this favorite correspondent. Jackson willed all his papers and literary effects to the former editor of the *Globe*, "a bequest I esteem higher," remarked the appreciative legatee, "than the fortunes of John Jacob Astor."

This association gave Blair the one undeviating principle of his life. The Federal Union became Blair's lodestar as it had been Jackson's. Southerner and slaveholder that he was, the central government had enlisted no more devout adherent. Someone has said that Lincoln's feeling for the Union had a tinge of the mystical, and the same could be said of Blair. His attitude towards slavery was not unlike Lincoln's own – it was an outmoded evil, and must in course of time disappear, but it should be tolerated for the present in the old states, for the sake of the preservation of the Union, but must not be permitted to extend its power into new fields. As long as he could Blair fought the encroachment of slavery behind the Democratic bulwarks, but in 1848 he joined the Free-Soilers, chiefly because his repudiated friend, Van Buren, was the candidate. However, he dropped back into the regular fold in 1852, on the nomination of Pierce. That new proslavery regime so affronted Blair that in 1856 he again abandoned his lifelong organization and, as already noted, played a leading role in the movement for Frémont. From 1845 onward, however, Blair was an influence, and a powerful one; he held no public office, resting content with his powerful position as philosopher of Silver Spring. More lively participation in public affairs he left to his two famous sons, the calm, intellectual Montgomery and the energetic and sparkling Frank Preston, Jr. The senior Blair had long entertained ambitions for both these young men: Montgomery he had set aside for cabinet office, while for Frank his aspirations rose higher; some day he expected to see his namesake – unquestionably the old man's favorite – installed in the White House. The first plan succeeded, but the nearest Frank came to accomplishing his father's dream was a nomination for Vice-President on the Democratic ticket in 1868 – and that ended in defeat.

By 1860 the senior member of the family – then nearing seventy – had become "old man" Blair; the Blair political activity at that time was embodied chiefly in the two "Blair boys," Monty, forty-seven, and Frank, forty-one. Both had had conspicuous careers, in politics and in professional life. Devoted as the brothers were, no two men could have been more unlike. Montgomery was stolid, dignified, learned – according to Noah Brooks the best-read man in the Lincoln cabinet, and Seward, Chase, Bates, and Welles were by no means illiterate. His father and a few intimates called him "Monty" but most followed the example of his own wife – daughter of Levi Woodbury, of New Hampshire – who always referred to him as "the Judge." Surviving pictures make him look stiff and ministerial; in fact, he was deeply religious and a lay reader in St. John's Church; his six feet of slender body always stood erect – possibly the result of military training, for President Jackson had insisted on sending him to West Point, a career in which he was certainly miscast. His blue, steadily gazing eye, smoothly shaven face, high forehead, strong chin, signified a reposeful spirit, and portrayed the man for precisely what he was – an able, well-documented lawyer, at his best in his frequent appearances before the United States Supreme Court. He had great financial ability, too, as became evident when he took charge of the affairs of his brother James, who died in 1852, managing them so skillfully that the widow was assured of a large competence for life.

This James, like Frank, Jr., represented the more adventurous strain in the Blair blood. As young men James and Frank came into romantic conflict, both having fallen in love with the same Kentucky girl; neither brother, however, would pursue his suit in rivalry with the other, and, to forget their disappointment, both departed to distant lands. Frank settled in St. Louis, Missouri, to build up a law practice and embark on a turbulent political career, while James took to the sea. Through Jackson's influence, James was commissioned a lieutenant in the navy, and joined in the famous Wilkes South Polar expedition, in the course of which he suffered frostbites that caused his premature death some years afterward. He served in the Mexican War, and on the outbreak of the California gold mania in 1848 hastened to the Pacific Coast, leading a kind of Mark Twain existence in mining camps and as steamboat pilot, accumulating in a reasonably short time, by virtue of the $1000 boat trip exacted from the eager competition of passengers to the gold fields, a considerable sum of money, which, sent to brother Frank, was invested in St. Louis real estate and – as noted above – ultimately brought the widow a substantial fortune. When James died, Montgomery went to California and brought the body home; it was buried at Silver Spring, the father Blair helping to build with his own hands the mound over the grave.

Though the Blair mansion opposite the White House and the Maryland country estate figure conspicuously in the family annals, the state of Missouri claims the Blairs – at least the two sons – as its own. Two statues stand today in the rotunda of the Capitol at Washington, as Missouri's most illustrious citizens – one that of Thomas Hart Benton, the other that of Frank Blair. No fitter companion in marble could have been found for Frank than "old Bullion"; the lives – professional and political – of both the "Blair boys" revolved about this famous Democratic Senator. In 1837 Montgomery – surrendering his commission in the United States Army – went to St. Louis, studied law in Benton's office, and soon started practice as his partner. A few years afterward Frank joined his brother in the same firm. Both made rapid progress. Montgomery quickly acquired a profitable practice as lawyer for railroads and other corporations, and became mayor of St. Louis and judge of the Court of Common Pleas. Frank, after undermining his health by too close application to books, suddenly took to the wild country along the Santa Fe Trail, and spent a considerable time in friendly association with Indians, half-breeds, Mexicans, and miscellaneous traders and outlaws, sometimes even thumping his banjo for their all-night dances and carousings. Delightful as all this was, and beneficial as it proved to Frank's health, it did not satisfy his ambitions for a career – and all Blairs, of course, must have a career; in 1847 Frank returned to St. Louis, married Appoline Alexander – his lifelong beloved "Apo" who, plain-featured but charming, proved more than a satisfactory substitute for the Kentucky maiden whom he had refused to court in fraternal competition – and presently became a rival to

Montgomery in a more prosaic field – the practice of law. Something of the frontier clung to Frank in the more polite existence he lived henceforth; his drooping mustache, for example, seemed to offer horrendous defiance to the smooth, ecclesiastical visage of brother Monty. The ruddy complexion acquired in the Cimarron country Frank never lost, nor the powerful, lithe, slender, muscular frame, six feet high, which had come as an inheritance of the same outdoors. A capacious appetite for hard liquor also remained a lifelong possession.

Frank was the only one of the Blairs who could be described as "magnetic," his honest hazel eyes, light hair, long, typically Saxon face, high forehead suggestive of brains, making him as welcome in the social circles of Montgomery's Washington home as in the rough-and-tumble political Missouri rostrums of the fifties. In politics, indeed, Frank Blair was something of a sagacious firebrand – a fierce orator, a sledgehammer rhetorician. Yet he had an intellectual basis for his polemics, and a moral purpose, unselfish and determined. His gift for repartee made Frank the terror of hecklers, yet on quieter occasions his humor – usually accompanied by strokings of that bristling upper lip – had a subtle quality. Frank needed all these traits – especially his most conspicuous one, unflinching courage – in the struggle on which he presently embarked. Despite his Southern inheritance, the man abominated slavery with a hate deep and ineradicable and the struggle of the cotton planters to extend their system into new countries fairly set him aflame. It was one thing to fight this battle from the sympathetic breastworks of New England, and quite another to take up the challenge in Missouri. That was the great border of contention where pistol shots and bowie knives often turned out to be the final arbiters.

When Frank took the stump for Lincoln in 1860, friends and enemies alike warned that these popular instruments of discussion in Missouri might bring his campaign to a sudden end. To settle matters at once he issued a general challenge to all whom it might concern, offering to meet them at any time and in any spot and with any kind of firearms they might select. There were no takers. Frank had never hesitated to oppose current opinion. He even broke away from his venerated Benton in 1848 and became the great Free-Soiler of Missouri, and in 1856, when Benton refused to support Frémont, despite the fact that that candidate was the husband of his darling daughter Jessie, Frank went over to the new Republican Party. Nothing brings out better the difference in the two brothers than the part they played in the antislavery crisis. Frank upheld the fiery cross in the open field, on the stump in Missouri and other states, slave and free, in his newspaper writings and in the halls of Congress – to which he was elected in

1858 – while Montgomery's fame as an antislavery man rests chiefly on his work as counsel for Dred Scott in one of the most fateful proceedings of the United States Supreme Court. Montgomery did not win that case – no man could have won it before the pro-Southern and proslavery Supreme Court as constituted in 1856 – but his argument was an intellectual performance that, in itself, laid the ground for his membership in Lincoln's cabinet. Frank Blair's work as an "agitator" produced more affirmative results. His speeches and writings and political campaigns laid a foundation in Missouri of understanding and influence which enabled him, in 1860, to prevent the state from joining the Confederacy. For to Frank Blair, Jr., historians attribute the "saving" of Missouri for the Union.

In the political sense the Blairs had no personal claims on Lincoln. All three attended the Chicago Convention as delegates, but their candidate was Edward Bates. The Bates boom, indeed, was largely a Blair performance. The Blairs favored him first as a Missouri man, and as the one man of those suggested who might heal the widening breach in party and nation. But for several years the Blairs and Lincoln had been on understanding terms. After Frémont's lamentable showing in the campaign of 1856, and after, old man Blair, rather weary of his protégé and with his eye searching for more promising material, went to Springfield, in order to get acquainted, as he said, with "this new man Lincoln." Their talks disclosed an identity of opinion; both believed in gradual emancipation; both opposed slavery extension; and both leaned to colonization of Negroes as the only permanent solution of the problem. Frank Junior also visited Lincoln just before the "new man" began his battle for the Illinois senatorship in 1858. Frank Blair took the stump and his paper, the *Missouri Democrat,* supported Lincoln in that contest. A young man then studying law – or pretending to – in Lincoln's office, John Hay, became Blair's Springfield correspondent and wrote descriptions of the debates which naturally did not minimize Lincoln's part in them. After the battle ended, Hay continued his sprightly letters, frequently writing with Lincoln at his elbow; tradition says that Lincoln would occasionally seize the pen himself, indite certain paragraphs or black out others. And so, although the Blairs remained faithful to Bates throughout the convention, Missouri's eighteen votes going to the "pre-Adamite" on all three ballots, the transition to Lincoln as a candidate proved an easy one. After all, was not Lincoln a denizen of the great Mississippi Valley so dear to the Blair following? Were not Illinois and Missouri bordering states, and Springfield and St. Louis close neighbors as cities? Certainly few campaign speakers did more effective work for Lincoln than Frank

Blair. After the election Frank wrote Lincoln several times, keeping the President-elect authentically informed about the position of the Border states and undoubtedly now and then putting in a word for brother Monty in the new administration.

Lincoln had no illusions about the Blairs. He knew that they always acted as a unit, at times a selfish unit, and that, zealous as they might be for the triumph of the cause, the political advancement of the family was never far in the background. "The Blairs," wrote John Hay in his Diary, in a passage that reflects Lincoln's own view, "have to an unusual degree the spirit of a clan. Their family is a closed corporation. Frank is their hope and pride. They have a way of going with a rush for anything they undertake; especially have Montgomery and the old gentleman." That they would "go with a rush" for Montgomery in the Lincoln cabinet the new President expected; Frank's ambition in the war took a different turn, and a natural one, for he donned a uniform and fought in the Federal army. Old man Blair had labored with Franklin Pierce to make Montgomery Attorney General; and this failure, it was believed, did not diminish his enthusiasm when he championed the new Republican Party. On the whole, the Blairs were not popular in political circles, and in any really partisan allotment in distributing plums would not have had many backers. Judge David Davis, Lincoln's good angel and also his evil one, never suspended his opposition to Blair, or his advocacy of his cousin, Henry Winter Davis. But this hostility was largely personal and political. Lincoln's interest in Montgomery rested on more public grounds. He regarded old man Blair as one of the most masterful politicians of the age, a man who could be of infinite use to him as counselor and friend. With Frank, Lincoln was at the moment formulating plans for keeping Missouri in the Union. The whole future of the nation depended on saving all the Border states. No human agencies could be so useful in this task as the Blair triumvirate. Their influence was paramount in two of the most critical Border states – Maryland and Missouri – the combined existence of which as members of the Federal Union would be worth a large army to the Federal cause. This is the chief reason why the clamorous protests of Blair enemies – of which the years had accumulated a goodly supply – did not cause Lincoln to change the decision he had formed, on that day following the election, of putting the Blair family into his cabinet. For to name one of the three, so far as influence in the Border states was concerned, amounted to the same thing as naming all three. The main key to the Border-state problem, Lincoln well understood, would be found at Silver Spring.

VI

NEW ENGLAND, a section that had gone unanimously for Lincoln in the electoral college, and had contributed many of the ideas on which the campaign had been fought, could not be ignored in forming the new cabinet. The necessities of party balance required the selection of a former Democrat as its representative. This consideration eliminated two men who were early pressed upon the President-elect. Charles Francis Adams and Seward were friends of long standing; their intimacy was personal as well as political; together they had stumped the Northwest for the Lincoln and Hamlin ticket, and they were also both advocates of compromise in face of secession. Naturally, Adams was Seward's first choice as New England's cabinet member. But Mr. Adams, like Seward himself, was a Whig of Whigs, and his presence in the cabinet would, Lincoln thought, unduly emphasize the predominance of that element in the Republican Party. A similar objection held, with even greater force, against the other New Englander who was moving heaven and earth for a seat at the new council table. Nathaniel P. Banks had started his opportunistic career in 1848 by election to the Massachusetts legislature as the coalition candidate of Democratic and antislavery forces; since then any party or faction that would promote his political ambitions had been indiscriminately adopted. His greatest triumphs, an election to Congress in 1853 – a success that made him ultimately speaker of that body – and his elevation to the governorship of Massachusetts in 1857, were achieved as favorite of the Know-Nothings. Whatever political attribution could be made for Banks in 1861, he was emphatically not the old-line Democrat for whom Lincoln was looking to uphold the dignity of Yankeedom at his official board. Despite the man's reputation as a trimmer, he had obtained impressive backing. Samuel Bowles, editor of the *Springfield Republican*, and George S. Boutwell, governor of Massachusetts 1851–1852, afterward Secretary of the Treasury, supported him in his native state. Seward, if his favorite Adams proved impossible, was willing to accept Banks as a fairly satisfactory substitute.

Seward's acquiescence in Banks was probably not inspired by any undue admiration for that kaleidoscopic statesman, but by the hostility with which he regarded the candidate who held first place in Lincoln's mind. For on the original Springfield list of cabinet officers had appeared the name of Gideon Welles. For him Seward and Weed felt a loathing almost as deep as that aroused by Salmon P. Chase. In the pre-convention angling for New England delegates, the Sewardites had met not only opposition at the hands of this Hartford editor, but an iciness of revulsion of which only the Puritan temperament is capable. Seward indeed regarded Welles as one of the chief architects of his humiliation at Chicago, and almost any other man in the whole expanse of New England would have been more acceptable as a colleague in the new administration. Yet Welles unquestionably possessed the two attributes which, in addition to character and ability, Lincoln regarded as indispensable in the New England member. So far as New England was concerned, Welles was a veritable autochthon of the soil. The farm on which he had been born in Glastonbury, Connecticut, in 1802, was the land which his American ancestor, Thomas Welles, an early governor of Connecticut, had purchased from the Indians in 1632, and which had remained in uninterrupted possession of his descendants ever since. Again there was no question about Welles's democratic antecedents. He had joined the Jeffersonian wing of that party as a young man, and had remained faithful to it until the great issue of slavery extension, and the subserviency of the Pierce administration to proslavery dominance, had compelled him to transfer his allegiance to the Republicans in 1856. He had not made this transition, as had Seward and others, reluctantly, almost hoping for a new turn in the political whirligig that would restore both the name and the power of the old party allegiance, but with all the zeal for a holy cause one would expect from his upbringing. In an activity that, by 1860, had absorbed his chief energies for nearly forty years, Welles had manifested qualities that had attracted respect, if not much personal popularity. He was honest, sincere, fearless and just, never a timeserver, and never agitating a cause in which he did not believe. He was also shy, averse to close association with his fellow humans, severely critical of their faults, with the Puritan's talent for detecting their failings rather than their virtues. He was equally gifted in looking into his own motives, and laying them bare to his conscience, and in analyzing the characters of all with whom he was thrown into association. This gift, which was to have historic consequences in the Lincoln cabinet, Welles had displayed from his earliest days. Nothing ever interested him quite so much as men, and his ability to appraise them, and to phrase that appreciation in words

Bates Welles Blair Seward Chase Lincoln. Scott. Smith. Cameron.

From a painting by Christian Schuessele

The Original Lincoln Cabinet

At this time Simon Cameron was Secretary of War. The picture shows General Scott, head of the army, who occasionally attended cabinet meetings to advise on the military situation. Through the window on the left is seen the Washington Monument in its unfinished condition

Gideon Welles (1802–1878)
Secretary of the Navy

that at times fairly became literature, is perhaps his greatest claim to immortality. He describes himself in an early Diary as one "with feelings easily given to irritation and a man that is often lost in gloomy melancholy." Probably his constant dissatisfaction with human nature as it unfolded before his eyes was the chief reason for this pessimism. Yet he found an artist's delight in observing these phenomena and conveying his impressions to paper. "I like to catch people in the suds," was the way he described this diversion, "to fall upon them by surprise, when it is washing day, not only with their hands, but with their temper." [1] It is perhaps not strange that the debonair and mercurial Seward, who sometimes boasted of his lack of fixed principles, and Thurlow Weed, whom Welles dismissed angrily as a "lobby jobber," did not survive this "suds" treatment in any too immaculate a fashion.

The rise of Jacksonian democracy presented two incongruous personal spectacles in New England. In Massachusetts and Connecticut, the most conservative of New England states, the leaders of this movement belonged to old traditional Federalist and Brahmin families. In Massachusetts George Bancroft, member of the clan which looked upon Jackson as Antichrist, as it had upon Jefferson in an earlier day, emerged as virtual "boss" of the Jacksonian party, and in Connecticut, Gideon Welles, inheritor of a similar attitude, occupied a corresponding position of vantage. The two men had certain things in common: the main interest of the two, outside politics, was literature and writing. Welles never achieved a literary fame comparable to that of the first important American historian – unless his great Diary elevates him to that class – but, from his earliest days, no career appeared to him worth while except one carved out by his pen. A writer of "poetry" and romances in his days at the Cheshire Academy in Connecticut, Welles, as a young man, enjoyed some fame as a man of letters. He had written a good many sketches and stories which had been accepted by one of the fugitive magazines of the day, an initial success which determined his profession. A more sordid field than tales of lovelorn Indian maidens and shipwrecked adventurers was to enlist Welles's maturing talents. Newspaper writing was not looked upon by his family and friends as an entirely reputable, not to say lucrative, occupation; indeed, when Welles fell in love with his cousin, Mary Ann Hale – and with an ardor and persistent pursuit surprising in one of his stolid temperament – the girl's mother seriously objected to the match on the ground that he was editor of the *Hartford Times*, a position hardly in keeping with the girl's social standing. Welles had started on this paper writing ro-

[1] West, Richard S., Jr., *Gideon Welles, Lincoln's Navy Department.* Bobbs Merrill, 1943. P. 28.

mantic trifles that could be printed among the advertisements as a decoy to readers; but about 1826 he purchased an interest in the paper, and settled down solemnly as a journalistic eulogist of the Jackson administration. His vigorous editorial style and unbridled championship soon made the *Times* one of the leading Democratic organs. Perhaps the fervor of Welles's pen was excited by the prospect facing him, for, from the third-floor window at which he sat preparing his copy, a good view could be obtained of the old red brick Connecticut capitol, the building in which had met the Hartford Convention, symbol of everything odious in a Federalism which the youthful scribe was denouncing in most uncompromising style. At moments Welles had aspirations for a life of action. This led him, in 1826, to write Henry Clay, Secretary of State in Adams's administration, asking for an appointment as Secretary of Legation in London; Clay turned down the application on the ground that Welles's "credentials" were not in proper form; if this snub did not accentuate the fluency of Welles's detractions of the regime in power, it certainly did not mollify it. At another time Welles sought – this time successfully – election as a member of the Connecticut General Assembly. His main performance in this capacity gave him a black mark forever in the estimate of the most pious people of the state. At that time a man could not qualify as a witness in court unless he professed belief in God and in a future life. Welles was a steady churchgoer and a deeply religious man, but he denounced this law as contrary to religious liberty and freedom of thought and pushed through a "witness bill" which drastically modified the prevailing court procedure. What better could be expected, exclaimed every Presbyterian pulpit, from a devotee of the pagan Jefferson and the barbarian Jackson? The episode well illustrates Welles's courage and honesty, but in itself it blocked any political career in Connecticut. He therefore became reconciled to a future as observer and polemic, not an active participant in the political hurly-burly. Indeed no pride Welles may have felt in his native state blinded him to the evils of its public affairs. With a frankness worthy of his best days in Washington he remarked – as usual in writing – after this brief sojourn in its legislative chamber, "I am ashamed to say of the civil and political complexion of my state, that a degraded, bigoted, hidebound, aristocratic, proud, arrogant, and contemptible policy governs her, through designing hypocrites, and artful and unprincipled knaves." [2] He also put a sacrilegious finger on the fountain of corruption. "Every measure that is agitated in our legislature and generally in

[2] West, *op. cit.*, p. 32, quoted from Gideon Welles's Copy Book, p. 96. Library of Congress.

our state, has a political spice from old Yale College." Thus early had Welles developed the gift for depreciation for which he was to find so promising a field in the Lincoln cabinet.

Jackson appointed Welles postmaster at Hartford, a position held in greater estimation in those days than now; it made him virtually leader of the Jacksonian forces in Connecticut. In 1845 Polk called him to Washington as Chief of the Bureau of Provisions and Clothing in the Navy Department. This assignment did not impress Welles as a particularly brilliant one; indeed, he underwent some humiliation in accepting it, but the experience had important results not appreciated at the time. Among the many naval officers whom he met frequently one above all the rest left an indelible memory. A certain Lieutenant David Glasgow Farragut, who at that time was struggling for some important duty in the Mexican War, and attracting little attention, seemed to Welles keen, resourceful, energetic, the plans he had formulated for an attack on Vera Cruz especially enlisting Welles's admiration. Sixteen years after when Welles, as Secretary of the Navy, was seeking the right man to command an expedition against New Orleans, his mind immediately reverted to this young man. This again illustrates Welles's most valuable talent, his insight into men. It was this quality that gave him, in the twenty years preceding the Civil War, a wide acquaintance with influential Americans. His political career, if such it can be called, was an unusual one; outside of his own parish few of the American rank and file had ever heard his name, but he enjoyed a kind of confidential reputation in high circles. This he owed, as he did most things that came his way, to his literary gifts. Welles early learned that his lack of geniality and forensic talents would preclude him from political activity of the usual sort. As a young man he began writing letters, on subjects of current interest, with a variety of correspondents, great and small. The practice was a useful one for the editor of a live newspaper, for in this way Welles obtained opinions and facts that served him profitably in framing his daily editorials. His letters also must have contained a good deal of meat, for several of the most powerful Jacksonians of the day, especially Amos Kendall, Duff Green, and above all, Francis P. Blair, came to depend upon him as the most reliable source of information on matters in the Eastern states. These men invited him to Washington for additional enlightenment; the visits became an annual event in Welles's life, with the result that he became, so far as a man of his unsocial manners could, a friend and confidant of many of the men who were making history. Especially did his friendship with Francis P. Blair serve as appropriate prologue to Welles's work in the Lincoln cabinet. Welles was Blair's sympathizer in one of the great political disturbances of the time. In 1830, Duff Green, editor of the *United States Telegraph*, the mouthpiece of Andrew Jackson, fell under suspicion as a "traitor" to his chief, who had not only made him newspaper spokesman of the administration organ, but had given him vast largess in the shape of government printing, pap without which no Washington journalist could attain virility. The ungrateful Duff Green was supposed to be working secretly in behalf of Jackson's chief enemy – the one whom Hickory threatened to hang as "high as Haman" – John C. Calhoun, for the presidential nomination in 1832. When Green began mousing around Gideon Welles, in the hope of winning the Connecticut delegates for Calhoun, Welles at once reported the facts to Francis P. Blair – who himself aspired to Green's job, especially to the government printing that accompanied it – and a terrific explosion ensued. As a result, Duff Green was thrown into the abyss. Blair became administration editor and began the career that led to wealth, power, and the estate at Silver Spring. The friendship thus cemented with Blair – and with "the Blairs" – lasted unbroken until the end. Welles, on his annual visits to Washington, became one of the most favored habitués of the Acorn on the Maryland estate and deep in the confidence of all the bigwigs in the new Republican Party.

When the time approached for the Chicago Convention, Welles had really become a political force, not to be overlooked by any aspirant for the Republican nomination. He was Connecticut member of the national committee, member of its executive committee, and chairman of the Connecticut delegates at the Wigwam. Though few citizens in the broad country knew of his existence, there were two men who rated at its true value his influence and laid plans to conciliate it. William H. Seward and Thurlow Weed believed they had a natural claim upon the allegiance of New England. What interest had this province contiguous to New York in such outlanders as Edward Bates, Salmon P. Chase, and Abraham Lincoln? Naturally this steady area fell into the Knickerbocker sphere of influence. Thurlow Weed, making a preliminary survey in the spring of 1860, found a good deal of encouragement in Massachusetts, New Hampshire, even in Maine. Connecticut, however, the political satrapy of Gideon, proved a harder nut to crack. There was more than one reason for his recalcitrance. In the first place, Welles hated political corruption. A few years previously, he had resigned the presidency of Charter Oak Life Insurance Company, to which he had been recently elected, when certain bills were placed before him for approval – bills awarding compensation to particular gentry for "legislative services." He would not be concerned in such dirty business, he exclaimed, leaving the office in dudgeon. It was this phase of public life, he believed, that Thurlow Weed, if not William H. Seward, had made a specialty. In recent years Welles had been drawn within the orbit of William Cullen Bryant, editor of the *Evening Post* of New York; from Hartford he sent editorials and political correspondence to Bryant, who eagerly sought and published them. Welles's newspaper style, he wrote at the time, "is much better than that of any newspaper correspondent we have." In consequence Welles was drawn into the confidence of the Bryant-George Opdyke-David Dudley Field-Hiram Barney coterie in New York, whose chief reason for existence was to oppose the Seward-Weed machine. These men kept Welles up to date on Weed's obliquities, laying particular emphasis on the "railroad grab" which Weed had just jammed through the Albany legislature. Welles believed also that the nomination of Seward would be a serious tactical mistake. It was the split in the Democratic Party in 1860 that made certain Republican success. Seward was so detested in the South that the Democrats would very likely put aside their internal quarrels, close ranks, and unite on a single candidate in its zeal for his defeat. Welles's favorite candidate was Salmon P. Chase – perhaps Chase's New England origin had something to do with the preference. Thus Weed's attempt to win over the saturnine publicist in Hartford got nowhere. At the Chicago Convention this distant attitude became open warfare. Largely owing to Welles's assiduous buttonholing of the New England delegates, Seward's showing in that region, on the first ballot, fairly appalled his friends. Connecticut and Rhode Island did not give him a single vote. Neither did Vermont, its ten going to a favorite son, Jacob Collamer. Maine, which was expected to be all-Seward, cast ten for the New Yorker and six for Lincoln. New Hampshire stood one for Seward and seven for Lincoln. Even Massachusetts, which Weed thought unanimous for his candidate, threw four votes for Lincoln. This poor showing – especially the manifest leaning to Lincoln, who, at the start of proceedings, was dismissed as having no strength in New England – proved a crushing blow to the Seward boom. Both Seward and Weed attributed it to Welles's campaigning, and never forgave him.

Though Welles did not support the Lincoln candidacy at Chicago – even on the fateful third ballot the Illinoisan secured only four of Connecticut's twelve votes – the final choice afforded him great satisfaction. In Lincoln's tall, gaunt form he detected a resemblance to the idol of his youth, Andrew Jackson, and the rail splitter's insistence on the preservation of the Union as the one great question of the time seemed to Welles's appreciative ears an echo of the stirring events of 1832. In February of 1860, the Hartford editor had had an opportunity for one of those searching analyses of character of which he was so fond. And never had he exercised his pre-eminent talent so incisively. After the Cooper Union speech Lincoln made a rapid tour of New England, reaching Hartford on the evening of March 5. Weary and travel-stained – and the grime of railroads was a more disfiguring blemish then than now – Lincoln was rushed from the station to a large meeting awaiting him; his speech, largely a repetition of the same ideas that had entranced the New York gathering a few nights before, made the audience quickly forget his unpressed garments and his bedraggled collar. Next morning Lincoln spent an hour with Welles in the office of the *Hartford Evening Press*, of which he was one of the proprietors, elaborating his remarks of the previous evening, and entertaining the not too humorous Welles with the usual jokes and stories. Next day, in the *Evening Press*, Welles gave his impressions of his visitor. "This orator and lawyer has been caricatured. He is not Apollo, but he is not Caliban. He was made where the material for strong men is plenty; and his loose, tall frame is loosely thrown together. He is in every way large – brain included, but his countenance shows intellect, generosity, great good nature, and keen discrimination. . . . He is an effective speaker, because he is earnest, strong, honest, simple in style, and clear as crystal in his logic." One can almost sense Welles, as he wrote these lines, judiciously weighing each adjective. One must keep in mind that this characterization was committed to paper two months before Lincoln's nomination, almost exactly a year before he took up his duties in the White House. Yet the portrait sketched by Welles, after an hour's confidential chat, differs little with that upon which history is now agreed. Thus Gideon Welles, of all the seven men whom Lincoln called to his council, was the only one who had anything approaching an accurate appreciation of his caliber. Not one of them, except this Connecticut Yankee, saw in him any possibilities of greatness. Most of them looked upon Lincoln with contempt, sometimes not too carefully concealed, as a kind of Christopher Sly, who had gone to bed one night a ragged tinker, and had awakened the next morning to find himself clothed in magnificent finery and chief lord of his region. In fact, some such conception remained with most of the cabinet members until the end. It is one of Welles's greatest claims to respect that to him alone, in four years of close association, was Lincoln, to use Welles's favorite expression, "that illustrious man."

VII

SUCH WERE the names that loomed largest for the cabinet in the last months of this presidential year. Five of them – Seward, Chase, Welles, Bates, and Blair – were, in Lincoln's mind, practically selected; the two others – Cameron and Smith – were presenting difficult problems. Two of them, Seward and Bates, represented the old Whig element in the Republican Party; two, Bates and Blair, as definitely represented old-line Democrats; one, Chase, if not technically an abolitionist, was acceptable as an extreme antislavery man to that usually uncompromising group; if Cameron and Smith should succeed in forcing themselves upon the hesitating President-elect, one would probably go in as a Democrat, the other as an unquestionable Whig. Thus would Lincoln gather together the many groups that had combined to curb the aggressions of the South and form an impregnable political power for enforcing the people's will. He believed that a new political era had dawned; that the Whig Party was as dead as the Federalist; that a new organization, destined to permanence, had come into being, of which he had been chosen the head, and with which, discarding all past affiliations, he was prepared to face the future.

His most powerful rival for the nomination, and the man he had assigned for first place in his cabinet, did not accept this simple reading of events. It was as a Whig that Seward contemplated the organization of the new regime. The party that had contributed the largest number of votes to Lincoln's election – perhaps two thirds – should dominate the administration. The cabinet should be an all-Whig cabinet. Antislavery Democrats, Free-Soilers, Abolitionists, "Americans," and the rest should have no representatives in that sacred society. These groups, it was true, had rallied to Lincoln's support at the ballot box; without their votes, indeed, he could not have succeeded – this Seward grudgingly admitted; they were therefore entitled to "recognition" of a minor kind – a foreign legation of secondary rank here and there, perhaps an occasional collectorship, more postmasterships, but they should never hope to enter the inner shrine. The cabinet that Seward had previsioned would contain four or five old-line Whigs from the Northern and Western states and two or three from the South. Thus would the old Whig Party be born again. That party had been national in scope; the inclusion in the new formation of old-time Southern Whigs like John A. Gilmer of North Carolina, John M. Botts of Virginia, Emerson Etheridge of Tennessee—and there were plenty of others who could be called upon if necessary – would not only symbolize the restoration of the ancient regime, but give the so-called Republicans something they desperately needed, a national character. Such a cabinet would also strengthen Seward's hands in his plans for healing the breach that was widening between North and South, for the example of his great former chieftain, Henry Clay, seemed to Seward to indicate the one safe road open to the nation in the crisis of 1860. To put into the cabinet Democrats like Blair and Welles and Free-Soilers like Chase would not only destroy the harmony Seward regarded as essential to his plan of conciliation, but would amount to little less than a challenge hurled at the seceding states.

Thus there was a certain flavor of statesmanship in Seward's insistence on an all-Whig cabinet – visionary as was his solution of a crisis infinitely greater than those that Henry Clay had failed to settle with his "compromises" – but, as was usually the case with Seward, personal ambition as well as principle was involved. For his cabinet was to be not only "all-Whig" but "all-Seward." The leadership of the Whig Party which had been his dearest possession in its prosperous days he was determined to maintain. The strange behavior of the Chicago Convention had not changed this leadership. Seward declined to admit that the election of Abraham Lincoln had in any way deposed him from his political throne. Let Lincoln live in the White House and ostensibly perform the functions of his office; the real seat of authority would be wherever Seward saw fit to establish himself. A new conception of the American Constitution now began to take shape in his resourceful mind. His imagination evolved a kind of British cabinet system in the place of the one handed down by the fathers. One of the most popular diplomats at Washington in those days was Baron Schleiden, Minister from the Republic of Bremen. Seward especially was likely to unbosom himself at times to this companionable gentleman. On February 18, 1861, Baron Schleiden reported to his government a conversation in which Seward had set forth his recently improvised theory of the presidential office. "Seward consoled himself with the clever remark that there is no great difference between an elected President of the United States and an hereditary monarch. The latter is called to the throne through the accident of birth, the former through the chances which make his election possible. The actual direction of public affairs belongs to the leader of the ruling party, here as well as in any hereditary principality."[1] Properly understood, Lincoln could have accepted this constitutional theory, only he would have added that the President, merely by the fact of having been elected, becomes the "leader of the ruling party," but Seward – although he was of course really too wise and experienced a man to believe his own interpretation – meant it in a different sense. He meant that Lincoln was to be sovereign on the British model, while he was destined Prime Minister. Just as the British Prime Minister had almost autocratic power in naming the members of the cabinet, so Seward believed that, as Secretary of State and head of the party, he should select the men who were to form the presidential council. At least he was convinced Lincoln should take counsel with him and appoint no one to whom he was opposed. All Seward's references to the political crisis in the winter of 1860–1861 imply that the coming regime was to be a Seward administration and that the supreme task of saving the Union rested on his shoulders. How could he accomplish this huge task unless he had sympathetic associates around the council board, men of his own selection identified with Seward principles and ready to support him in all important decisions? All this seems grotesque today, yet the fact remained that in 1861 most thoughtful citizens entertained practically the same view of Seward's role in the counsels of Abraham Lincoln. Everyone took it for granted that Seward would be the brains and engine of the new dispensation.

Lincoln himself, however, was one of the minority who entertained radically different ideas. The election of 1860, he believed, had marked a turning point in American history. A national crisis had called into existence a new party, made him its head, and elected him President; he intended to accept the mandate and the responsibility thus conferred. With the plan for an all-Whig cabinet, still less an all-Seward one, he had not the slightest sympathy, and he certainly had no intention of abdicating the Presidency and transferring it to a political clique dominated by Seward and Thurlow Weed. He sincerely desired to give Seward first place in the cabinet; that formed an indispensable part of his plan of a composite administration; to leave out the Whigs, the most numerous branch of the new alignment, were to leave out Hamlet indeed. But Lincoln intended to have Seward on his own terms, not on Seward's. Intimations had come in in plenty that it would be difficult to accomplish this. Immediately after the triumph at the polls the news was conveyed to Lincoln in several ways that Seward did not wish to

[1] Adams, Ephraim D., *Great Britain and the American Civil War*. Longmans Green, 1925. I, 116.

enter the cabinet; but that, as recognition of his personal eminence and his influential following, he was entitled to an offer of the Secretaryship of State – an offer that would be declined. It was more than broadly hinted that Seward expected to be consulted on the selection of the cabinet as a whole: his own decision as to accepting Lincoln's proffer would depend largely on whether he was to have a voice in choosing his colleagues. This came pretty close to being an ultimatum. The cabinet must be a Seward, and a Whig, cabinet, or he would have no part in the new era. Lincoln afterward explained the situation to Gideon Welles, who made a written memorandum of the conversation, which he placed among his papers.[2] It had seemed proper, Lincoln told Welles on this occasion, that Seward be offered first place "in view of his admitted talents and great public services." For the same reason he should take into his administration "Chase and Bates, men of undoubted ability though less conspicuous. . . . But he did not think it came within the scope of his duty or courtesy to turn over to either of them the selection of the men with whom he was to be associated as advisers, and who were to compose his official family. He was willing to hear suggestions from any of them, or their friends, and to give their opinions for or against any individual all the weight and consideration to which they were entitled, but he reserved to himself the appointment of the men whose assistance he needed, with whom he was to confer, and to whom he was to give his confidence. . . ." Lincoln desired each of the "parties of the past" to be represented in his cabinet. "His administration was not to be Whig or Democratic or Abolitionist or so-called American [Know-Nothing] but a Republican administration. . . . To select representative men of each of the old parties, Democratic and Whig, but who nevertheless were recognized and earnest Republicans, was a primary starting point, a basis on which to build." Lincoln gave Welles the names of the men he had selected as cabinet timber the day following the election. They were Seward, Chase, Welles, Bates, and Dayton; two others that were favorably regarded were Blair and N. B. Judd.

Dayton, for whom Lincoln had high regard, had been one of his minor competitors at Chicago – he was reconciled for his exclusion by a handsome appointment as minister to France. Judd had been a friend for many years, and one of the managers of the Lincoln nomination campaign; his name was dropped, because he came from Illinois, a state which Lincoln decided had been sufficiently recognized by having the Presidency, because he was pushed aside to make room for Caleb B. Smith, and because Mrs. Lincoln, who hated him with real feminine

[2] This was not published until 1925, in the *Magazine of History*. Extra number 105, Vol. XXVII.

intensity, would give her distracted husband no peace until he was cast into outer darkness — in other words, the legation in Berlin. To three names on this list, Lincoln told Welles, the Seward party showed tenacious hostility. These were Chase, Welles, and Blair. Chase, they argued, could not be regarded as an appropriate representative of the Democratic Party; he was really an Abolitionist; that the Liberty Party man of 1844, the Free-Soiler of 1848, and the Know-Nothing of 1855 did fall somewhat short of Democratic orthodoxy Lincoln was forced to admit. But the Democrat the Sewardites preferred as Secretary of the Treasury afforded Lincoln little comfort: for Simon Cameron's record as a consistent Democrat was also clouded, to say nothing of his not too savory personal standing. Welles the Seward crowd hated for the part he had played in turning New England against their favorite in Chicago; besides he was a disagreeable person and a hidebound State rights man; in comparison with Charles Francis Adams, ex-Governor Banks, or Governor Andrew he had little to recommend him. "The name of Mr. Montgomery Blair was quite as distasteful to the representatives of the Albany policy as that of Mr. Welles. Two such men, it was asserted, would give the administration undue Democratic bearing and their association with the Secretary of State would be so uncomfortable that it was represented that Mr. Seward would hardly consent to go into the cabinet with them. His [Seward's] voice, it was claimed, ought to be so potential as to exclude men who were not acceptable to him." With Lincoln's purpose of including Blair as a friendly gesture to the Border states Seward was sympathetic, but "others from the same locality might be substituted, Mr. Gilmer, of North Carolina, or Mr. Emerson Etheridge, of Tennessee" — both old-line Southern Whigs — "were named as preferable to Mr. Blair."

This same distrust of Seward and his monopolistic ambitions was manifest when Lincoln met Edward Bates and offered him a cabinet post. The urbane Missourian was one of the few men on Lincoln's list who aroused no opposition in the Seward camp. The reasons for this friendly disposition are evident. Mr. Bates was an old-line Whig — an even more persistent one than Seward himself; for he had not gone through even the form of joining the Republicans; he had not been identified with active politics for years and had no ambitions that would run afoul of Seward's; he was sixty-seven years old in 1860, and could probably — at least so the New Yorker fancied — be brought within the Seward sphere of influence. About a month after the election, Bates received a message from Springfield: the President-elect was contemplating a visit soon to St. Louis, and wished to talk with its most distinguished citizen on future plans. The old-fashioned nature of Bates is well illustrated by his response to this invitation; to say that he was shocked puts it mildly: a prospective Sovereign taking a long river trip to call upon him, a private citizen! The proposal argued ill for the new standard of official dignity and manners about to be installed in the White House. Did not the rail-splitting statesman understand that he was now the future ruler of his people, and that it was his duty to summon to the presence such ordinary mortals as he deigned to consult? Evidently the punctilious Bates did not understand Lincoln's practical reason for disregarding etiquette. Lincoln's official headquarters in the Springfield capitol and his home were so crowded with rapacious visitors that his only chance of a quiet talk was in some secluded spot. But Bates at once telegraphed that he would appear in Springfield the following Saturday and place himself at executive disposal. On the appointed morning the grizzled veteran informed John Nicolay, Mr. Lincoln's secretary, that he could not think of permitting the President-elect to come to St. Louis, but that he esteemed it a great honor "to wait upon" his chief. Lincoln did his best to secure privacy by calling upon Bates at his hotel, and secreted in his bedroom they had a fairly satisfactory talk. "He is not of impressive exterior," Nicolay noted of Bates in his Diary, but his first unfavorable impression changed when Bates began to talk. "His flow of words in conversation is very genial and easy, seeming at first to verge upon extreme politeness, but soon becoming very attractive." Afterwards, in serious conversation with Mr. Lincoln, Mr. Bates became "earnest and spoke his thoughts in clear, concise language, indicating a very definite and intellectual grasp of ideas and a great facility in their expression."

Bates wrote in his Diary, after the interview with Lincoln, "I found him free in his communications and candid in his manner." Lincoln was especially candid on the question which, he admitted to the Missourian, was causing him much trouble – what to do about Mr. Seward? From the beginning, it had been his wish to tender Bates a position in his cabinet; if he had been free to do so, he would have offered him the prime place – that of Secretary of State. But there was Seward; Lincoln regarded himself "as under moral, or at least party duress" to offer the New Yorker that distinguished office. Mr. Seward, said Lincoln, was a man of great ability and integrity, and his fitness for the post was commanding. Not to make Mr. Seward Secretary of State would probably cause a rupture in the Republican Party at the start of the new administration; his large and influential following was insistently demanding such an appointment. Yet, said the President-elect, such a decision would invite dangers of another kind. The South regarded Mr. Seward "as the embodiment of all that they hold odious in the Republican party," and with Seward at the head of the cabinet would stiffen its resistance to conciliation. Again, though a large element in the party was demanding the New Yorker's elevation, another large and weighty group was opposed. These factions had defeated Seward for the presidential nomination and they feared that, should this enemy succeed to this powerful office, he might use it for purposes of revenge. Lincoln was evidently referring to the factions in New York State led by Hiram Barney, David Dudley Field, and William Cullen Bryant, who were determined to keep Seward out of the cabinet. The impression Bates apparently gathered from Mr. Lincoln's disturbed state of mind was that he would offer Seward the State Department, but that he hoped the offer would be declined. That this represented Lincoln's real desire is not likely, but there were undoubtedly times, such as the morning of this talk with Bates, when such a solution of his problem would have been not unwelcome. Under these circumstances, Lincoln said that he could not appoint Mr. Bates to the "Premiership," but would be most grateful if he would accept the post of Attorney General. Should he consult his own inclinations, Bates replied, he would decline this opportunity, as he had a similar one proposed by President Fillmore in 1850; but in view of the critical state of affairs he would accept any office in which the President-elect thought he might be useful. This disclaimer, this call to duty, in most cases would have been merely perfunctory, but not in the case of so sincere a patriot as Edward Bates. Though Virginia born, with views on the Negro and his future far less radical than were acceptable to some of his future colleagues, Bates's loyalty to the Union was steadfast, as he showed when discussing the dangers then facing the country. The South, he thought, could not really secede, but if it did, he saw his duty clear. "I am a man of peace," Bates said to the President-elect, "and will defer fighting as long as possible, but, if forced to do so against my will, I have made it a rule never to fire blank cartridges." [3]

A few days after this visit an item appeared in the *Missouri Democrat*, as follows: "We have the permission of both Mr. Lincoln and Mr. Bates to say that the latter will be offered, and accept, a place in the new cabinet, subject, of course, to the action of the Senate. It is not yet definitely settled which department will be assigned to Mr. Bates." Lincoln himself wrote these lines, which were printed as an editorial. It shows his uncertainty at the time over Seward as Secretary of State – a post that he was possibly holding in reserve for Bates, should the New Yorker decline appointment.

[3] Bates, *Diary*, pp. 164–166.

VIII

According to Gideon Welles, Thurlow Weed was "chief engineer of the Albany plan" – the plan, that is, of sidetracking a constitutionally elected President and elevating his foremost competitor to the supreme control of the party. This "Albany plan" evidently took form in Weed's mind as soon as the shouts had subsided in the Chicago Wigwam. As soon as Weed's grief over the collapse of a life ambition died down, like a good politician he began to take stock; perhaps, after all, some salvage could be gathered from the wreck. The propitiatory visit of Andrew Curtin, who had dealt such a deathblow to Seward in helping the transfer of Pennsylvania's delegates to Lincoln on the second ballot, has already been noted. David Davis and Leonard Swett similarly paid a call on the disgruntled Titan. Davis and Swett recognized the need of harmony in the approaching campaign, and were willing to go to almost any extreme to soothe the feelings of the New York delegation. Their olive branch was received more politely than the friendly advances of Curtin. They were met with sorrowful reproaches indeed, but not with ferocious discourtesy. The reason is plain. Swett and David Davis of all men stood closest to Lincoln's ear, and no wise politician would antagonize such ascendant luminaries on the Republican horizon.

Swett invited Weed to visit the new nominee on his way back to New York. The suggestion was eagerly accepted. He was about to go to Iowa for a week or two, Weed replied, and on his return would take pleasure in dropping off for a few hours at Springfield. This trip to Iowa was probably a fiction. That a vast deluge of visitors would overwhelm Lincoln's home immediately after the nomination Weed well knew; he did not wish to be one of a crowd, but preferred to have his session with Lincoln after the rush had quieted, and all rival bigwigs had left. Gideon Welles, one of the committee sent to Springfield to notify Lincoln officially of his nomination, also spent a few days after the excitement had died down, in western and southern Illinois. One evening, a few days after leaving Springfield, he boarded what he called an "irregular" boat at Rock Island, on the way to Quincy. The Connecticut Yankee, who seemed to have the habit of turning up unexpectedly on embarrassing occasions, was astonished to find Thurlow Weed a fellow passenger. "I had supposed he was at that time in Minnesota, and he probably believed me in Connecticut when we found ourselves face to face on the Mississippi steamer." Welles was no more rejoiced than Weed over the accidental rencontre. "I at once saw," Welles adds, "that the meeting afforded him no gratification," and the interchange of recognition was perfunctory on both sides. Evidently Weed had been spending several days sailing up and down the Mississippi, killing time and thus giving his competitors for future favor at Springfield a chance to visit Mr. Lincoln and depart. In Welles's own words, Weed "performed a circuit of many hundred miles to obtain a private interview with Mr. Lincoln."

So far as reaching any understanding with Lincoln, Weed's visit, when he finished his roundabout journey and landed in Springfield, was not fruitful. "As the representative of his friend in Auburn," says Welles, Weed was "somewhat presuming and officious yet he was treated with considerate courtesy. He accomplished, however, nothing that was decisive or satisfactory in regard to the influence which Mr. Seward might be allowed to exercise in forming the cabinet or shaping the policy of Mr. Lincoln. The comments of the self-appointed ambassador on individuals and their relation to the Albany policy were "listened to kindly but without any satisfactory answering response. No commitments for or against anyone were obtained from Mr. Lincoln and Weed returned in a not very complacent state of mind to Albany."[1] But twenty-five years afterward, Weed, in his *Autobiography*, recalled this preliminary visit as a happy one – a rosy remembrance perhaps enhanced by the lapse of time and Lincoln's unanticipated immortality. "I found Mr. Lincoln sagacious and practical. He displayed throughout the conversation so much good sense, such intuitive knowledge of human nature, and such familiarity with the virtues and infirmities of politicians that I became impressed very favorably with his fitness for the duties which he was not unlikely to be called upon to perform."

In one respect, however, Weed's Springfield visit did have important results. David Davis and Leonard Swett came down from Bloomington and were present at the interview. At this time the basis was laid for an alliance of the three leaders that was to embarrass Lincoln seriously at the outset of his administration. In political ideals, the trio had much in common. Both Davis and Swett embodied all those conceptions of

[1] Memorandum previously cited. See p. 82.

partisanship and spoils which Weed had practiced so successfully and so long in New York. For many years the two had been on the closest terms with Lincoln. On the famous Eighth Circuit in Illinois, the triumvirate of Lincoln, Davis, and Swett had for years enjoyed a fame all their own. Together they had "ridden" the circuit; had eaten their meals at the same table; had slept in the same room and, when pinched for accommodations, in the same bed. Their arrival was always eagerly anticipated by the rustics who gathered nightly around the stove in the common room, and their conversation and stories afforded far more entertainment than the occasional theatrical troups that played the frontier towns. While Lincoln outranked his fellows in anecdote and humor, Davis in those days easily held first place in dignity and position. He had already embarked on that career as speculator in public lands that was to make him a millionaire; besides, he was generally looked upon as a man of education, having spent four years at Kenyon College, Ohio, under the supervision of Philander Chase. Indeed Davis enjoyed considerable prestige in that rough country as an "aristocrat." The Davis family, old Federalists and Episcopalians, had for generations held high state in Maryland; in the early nineteenth century, Dr. David Davis was an esteemed physician in Cecil County, while his brother, Reverend Henry Lyon Davis, was President of St. John's College at Annapolis. Both these men had sons who, for good or ill, were to figure large in the new Republican Party. The first was the father of David Davis, Lincoln's friend, the second of Henry Winter Davis, who was to become one of the most brilliant orators of his time and one of Lincoln's most implacable foes. Henry Winter Davis remained in Maryland, rose high in Maryland politics, fought with the Blairs a lifelong battle for the control of the Republican Party in the state, and at this very moment was an aspirant for the seat in Lincoln's cabinet which his enemy obtained.

His cousin David was one of the many "southern aristocrats" who had left the ancestral home to carve out a career in the western wilderness. In due course he arrived at Bloomington, Illinois, and began the practice of law with a capital, as he was always proud to remember, of "two bits." Davis's rise was not due to any profound knowledge of the law. Neither in his Illinois period nor in after years when, by grace of Abraham Lincoln, he sat on the Supreme Court of the United States, did he impress his observers as a learned jurist. But he was able to find opportunities in foreclosed sales to pick up farms and other properties at a nominal investment, and these, increasing in value with the years, made him more than prosperous. Previously to this judgeship he served one term in the Illinois legislature as an uncompromising

Whig; and the taste for politics this engendered never left him, not even after he donned his judicial robes on the nation's highest court. All his life Davis exemplified that doubtful character in American public life, the politician-judge; even when sitting on the supreme tribunal in Washington, he spent much of his time angling for a presidential nomination, and in 1872 he actually received ninety-two votes at the Liberal convention, ultimately losing the dubious prize to Horace Greeley.

Great public questions never much interested Davis; the slavery issue aroused only perfunctory attention, and he hated abolitionists with a fervor worthy of his Southern origin. Politics, in his view, amounted simply to spoils. Davis had the personal qualities essential to success in this field. He was jovial, interested in people, Lincolnian in his love of laughter and yarn-swapping. In court one day, one of the ornaments of the bar burst out into a loud guffaw – Lincoln had just told him in whispers a side-splitting story. His Honor promptly fined the offender for contempt of court. After adjournment he called the disrespectful person to the bar. "What was the story Lincoln told you?" he asked. On hearing it Davis himself doubled up with mirth. "Fine remitted!" he shouted in appreciation. The episode suggests the rollicking qualities of the man. Another thing that contributed to his fame was his "physical enormity." Davis weighed, at his peak, three hundred pounds; it was a matter of common remark that he was never measured for his clothes, but "surveyed." At Chicago, in May 1860, his wallowing form, his long black coat and round white hat became almost as familiar a sight as the wind-blown, undulating garments of Horace Greeley. At Lincoln headquarters in the Tremont House – for which Davis paid the rent out of his own pocket – he majestically presided, issuing orders right and left.

This occasion represented the supreme moment in the judge's life. Lincoln had been an object of admiration for several years. Fond of talking himself, Davis would always keep silence when Lincoln was discoursing. Nor would he permit any interruptions. If, in the tavern symposiums which formed the chief diversion of circuit riding, some third person tried to get in a word, Davis would quiet him with a wave of his hand. "Be still! Lincoln is speaking!" He liked his companion both in his droll and in his serious moments. "Lincoln," he said, "is the best speaker in the state. He shows the want of early education, but he has great power on the stump." Among the many claimants as "original Lincoln man," Davis naturally took high rank. Though Davis had strong support from Leonard Swett and Joseph Medill, he was generalissimo of the Lincoln campaign, but scored his triumph on terms that made Lincoln himself mourn. "They have gambled on me all around," said the successful candidate. "Bought and sold me a hundred times. I cannot begin to fill the pledges made in my name." [2] That Davis should offer Simon Cameron and Caleb B. Smith seats in Lincoln's cabinet in exchange for the Pennsylvania and Indiana delegates accorded with the kind of politics he had practiced all his life.

Leonard Swett participated in this unhappy bargain, but he was of considerably finer strain than the Maryland blueblood. A man of benign presence, with white chin beard and long, meditative face, this gentle promoter of Lincolnian ambitions might easily have been mistaken for a Methodist bishop. He too was a man college trained, an able lawyer, with a personal charm that from the first made him one of Lincoln's favorites on the circuit. Lincoln always liked to have Swett as associate in a case, especially a murder trial, for his magnetic qualities had an almost irresistible effect upon juries. These same talents served him well as politician, a career in which he more skillfully advanced others' interests than his own, for, though Swett made a large fortune in practice, his two life ambitions, to represent his district in Congress and to become governor of his state, were not realized. Though much closer in affection to Lincoln than Davis, he sought no appointment at his hands, resigning all claims to "recognition" in favor of Davis. For he held to the prevailing custom of the time and regarded Davis's elevation to the Supreme Bench as an appropriate reward for the labors the two had performed in Lincoln's nomination.

Like Seward and Weed, Davis and Swett were old-line Whigs, and accepted the Albany plan as the appropriate basis for the new cabinet. They had a personal interest too; for they had made the bargain with Cameron and Caleb B. Smith, and were bound in honor, as they thought, to secure its fulfillment. Thus, unfortunately for the new President, the all-Whig, all-Seward program found troublesome recruits at his own political fireside. Weed completely won over these allies at that first interview in the Richmond House, Chicago, in May 1860. "Mr. Weed did not talk angrily as to the result," Swett afterwards wrote, "nor did he complain of anyone. I remember the substance of his words, as with much feeling, and confessing to the great disappointment of his life, he said, 'I hoped to make my friend, Mr. Seward, President and I thought I could serve my country in so doing.' He was a larger man intellectually than I anticipated and of finer fibre. There was in him an element of gentleness and a large humanity which won me and I was pleased no less than surprised." This admiration for Weed increased as time went on. "We all feel," Swett wrote Weed Decem-

[2] Hollister, O. J., *Life of Schuyler Colfax.* Funk and Wagnalls, 1887. P. 147.

ber 26, 1860, after the election and when cabinet plans were taking shape, "that New York and the friends of Seward have acted nobly. They have not only done their whole duty to the party, but they have been most generous and magnanimous. We should be exceedingly glad to know your wishes and your views and to serve you in any way in our power."

Despite this good understanding, the Seward-Weed wing of the Republican Party in New York had shown no undiplomatic haste in supporting the Lincoln-Hamlin ticket. Up to late August, Seward remained secluded in Auburn and Weed in Albany, giving a certain amount of lip service to the candidates of their party, but postponing any energetic action in their behalf until fall. Because of the rivalries that were rending the party in twain in the Empire State, Lincoln felt great anxiety as to the outcome in November – for without New York's electoral vote, success, even with a divided Democratic Party, was by no means assured. In August, a kind of Lincolnian embassy of Davis and Swett therefore started east, to survey the troubled waters and discover, if possible, some way of calming the storm. Naturally, as designated emissaries of the presidential candidate, they met all the big men in the Republican high command and received most encouraging reports on the outlook for November.

The chief purpose of the Davis-Swett eastern pilgrimage was to obtain the whole-souled support of Seward in the election of the man who had humiliated him at Chicago. This Seward was disposed to grant, but on a *quid pro quo*. Weed invited Davis and Swett to meet him at Saratoga, where a kind of Potsdam Conference was to be held of this "Big Three" to discuss the future of the party and to apportion the spoils of expected victory. That certain changes in personal relations had been accomplished since the national convention was evident from the fact that two other men, not New Yorkers, had been invited to this secret confabulation. Simon Cameron had left his country estate at Lochiel in the Pennsylvania mountains, and had brought with him one of his favorite henchmen – just which one is not specified, but the probability is that it was either Alexander Cummings or John P. Sanderson, the men who, at Chicago, had managed the great deal that transferred Pennsylvania's votes to Lincoln. Seward and Weed, at the end of the Chicago battle, had entertained about as revengeful emotions towards Cameron as towards Curtin, his rival in the Pennsylvania domain. Cameron, Seward insisted, had personally guaranteed him the fifty-four Pennsylvania delegates, on the second ballot, and then had shamelessly turned them over to the gentleman from Illinois. In the three months' interval, however, certain practical considerations had drawn Cameron and Seward closer together. In the new administration Pennsylvania would have to be represented and Seward, much as he resented Cameron's "treason," preferred him in the cabinet to any adherent of the Curtin phalanx. As a practical politician, Seward regarded Lincoln as already committed; Lincoln's agents had promised Cameron a post, and how could any honorable man refuse to indorse such an obligation?

"Cameron's desire for relief from his awkward position," Seward wrote Weed on January 26, 1861, when that statesman's fortunes were still hanging in the balance, "seems so reasonable and the consequences of a feud if it is not obtained so fearful" that he could not understand Lincoln's hesitation. Seward disliked the suggestion of any Democrat in the new cabinet, but if a Democrat could not be avoided he preferred one of the Cameron type – a practical politician, like himself, a man fond of combinations and intrigue, who would naturally form one of the Seward party. The one thing above all which Seward had determined to prevent was the appointment of Chase to the Treasury. Chase was the one man who could presume to rival the Auburn statesman. There could never be two MacGregors sitting at the Lincoln table.

Such was the background of the "Saratoga Conference," a meeting between the friends of Lincoln and Seward to fix the terms on which the Sewardites would join heartily the Lincolnian ranks. The fact that there is no record of the conversation is one of the most tragic lapses in Lincoln literature. On the main results, however, there seems little question. Seward was to be Secretary of State in the new administration and Simon Cameron Secretary of the Treasury. These were the main points settled in the Saratoga pact, and with these as a foundation, involving as they did Chase's banishment into limbo, Seward felt secure of the future. "As the representative of Mr. Seward," Welles remarks, "the great object of Weed was to exclude Mr. Chase from the cabinet, if possible, and failing in this, to secure, at all events, the Treasury for Mr. Cameron. This was the Saratoga arrangement, but Mr. Lincoln did not consummate it." Intimations – perhaps more than intimations – were forthcoming that Mr. Seward also expected to be consulted about his colleagues, and the first hint was conveyed of the ultimatum-like position of Seward in the coming months – that only if he were permitted to influence these selections would he himself consent to serve. However, there was nothing irritating or menacing in the attitude of Weed or Cameron or the latter's so-far-anonymous henchman. The five men parted with the friendliest of feelings and Davis and Swett departed for Springfield, entirely complacent over the results. It is not likely that Lincoln regarded the embassy as an unqualified success. With certain details – Seward as Secretary of State – he was content, but the proposal of Cameron for the Treasury did not accord with his intentions. However, the time – the middle of a presidential campaign – was not a favorable one for stirring up dissensions, and Lincoln decided to play a little politics himself. After all, Davis and Swett had no right to commit the potential President on such important matters and his decision could wait until after the election. The Saratoga "arrangement," commented Gideon Welles, was "for the time apparently acquiesced in by Mr. Lincoln or at least was not emphatically repelled." So far as taking an active part in the campaign Seward certainly kept his side of what he apparently regarded as a definite bargain. In an October stumping campaign through the Northwest, he threw all the weight of his oratory into the Lincoln cause. On the passage through Illinois, his train passed by Springfield; Lincoln met him at the station, the two men shook hands most cordially in the face of an applauding multitude, and this sign of reconciliation between the great contenders at Chicago was hailed by loyal Republicans as an omen of a November triumph. The same cannot be said of Cameron, whose listless behavior in the most critical political campaign the nation had engaged in up to that time augured ill for his loyal support of the administration in war.

Immediately after the electoral triumph in November, the Sewardites kept up their pressure. Thurlow Weed suggested that Lincoln pay a visit to Seward at Auburn to discuss the policy of the new administration and the selection of the cabinet. As a precedent for this remarkable proposal, Weed called to mind that William Henry Harrison, after his election to the Presidency in 1840, had gone to Frankfort, Kentucky, for a "conference" with Henry Clay. The historical parallel probably did not impress Lincoln as an auspicious one. That Seward should have detected a vivid resemblance between his position in 1860 and Clay's in 1840 was natural enough. In the former time Clay, like Seward in 1860, was the leader of the Whig Party – and that party, in 1840, was as much a coalition as the Republicans in the year preceding the Civil War. In 1840 Clay was the leading candidate for the presidential nomination; indeed he entered the convention with the necessary votes in hand, and was maneuvered out of it by the machinations of an adroit intriguer from New York – none other than Thurlow Weed himself, even then boss of the Whigs in his own state. Clay was embittered when the prize, his by personal pre-eminence and party strength, went to an obscure aspirant whom practically all his countrymen regarded – and he regarded himself – as utterly unfit for the office. Clay was as determined to dominate the first Whig administration – to name the cabinet, or most of it, and control policy – as was Seward after the accession of Abraham Lincoln. Hence his imperious summons to Harrison for a party consultation at his own home – a command which Harrison did his best to avoid, but which, fearing the power of his haughty rival, he did not dare disregard. Out of this meeting, as Lincoln of course knew, for he was active in politics then himself, emerged practically an all-Clay cabinet; Daniel Webster, a Clay foe, became Secretary of State, it is true, but four of the other five members of Harrison's council were Clay men.

Lincoln showed more backbone than had Harrison on the former occasion. He understood what the invitation meant – and was intended to mean. It was Seward's rather crude way of displaying his predominance. To force the recently elected President to take a long journey from his western home to Auburn, New York, there spend several days in consultation with Seward and Weed, would almost amount to giving up the Presidency and making Seward regent. The spectacle would be a public one, too, held in full view of the nation, the central item of news in several thousand newspapers. "But no argument or urging," notes Welles, "could persuade him to such a step. He had too much self-respect and self-reliance to listen to those who approached him on the subject . . . to put himself in training in the keeping of any man or men." Then Weed made another approach. He suggested that Lincoln and Seward meet at a neutral spot – say Chicago. This also the President-elect flatly declined. On November 21, two weeks after the election, he had gone to Chicago to discuss cabinet appointments with Hannibal Hamlin and other friends, and this widely publicized visit probably led Seward and Weed to believe that a similar opportunity would be extended to them. But again Lincoln refused.

There was thus left only one way of obtaining an understanding with Lincoln. Weed must go to Springfield himself. His eagerness to receive an invitation rather belied the reports that were constantly forthcoming from Seward's friends and the Seward press. Seward desired no place in the Lincoln administration, it was said, and would accept no cabinet post. But Weed's sudden appearance in Springfield on December 20 was evidence that Seward did desire a cabinet post, and hoped to force Lincoln at the same time to accept his conditions. The probability was that Lincoln did not welcome this visit. By December 10 a whole month had passed since election, and no invitation to an audience had come to Seward or Weed. And no spontaneous invitation came even then. To get even an indirect summons Weed was obliged to enlist as intermediaries his friends David Davis and Leonard Swett. On December 10 Weed received a letter from Swett informing him that "Mr. Lincoln would be very glad to see you. He asks me to tell you so. . . . Mr. Lincoln wants your advice about his cabinet and the general policy of his administration and I would greatly like to have him have it." In the same mail came a letter from David Davis, also conveying Lincoln's pseudo-invitation. "I would advise you, inasmuch as Mr. Lincoln requests it, to go to Springfield at once." When Lincoln had really wished to see Bates and Chase he wrote them cordial letters in his own hand.

Before Weed could reach Springfield, an important development had taken place. All this time Lincoln had not departed from his original intention of making Seward Secretary of State. But he wanted him as Secretary of State only, not as generalissimo of his administration. That step had been definitely determined at his consultation with Vice-President-elect Hamlin in Chicago. At this session, Lincoln informed the gentleman from Maine that he intended to offer first place in his cabinet to Seward, and, according to Hamlin's biographer, seemed somewhat disturbed about the reports constantly appearing in the press that Seward would decline.[3] The discussion ended by Hamlin's becoming Lincoln's go-between in approaching the difficult Auburn statesman. Lyman Trumbull, Senator from Illinois, was a third party to the negotiation. Hamlin, in carrying out Lincoln's mission to "sound" Seward, at first approached the task indirectly, through Preston King, Seward's colleague as Senator from New York. On King's obvious and wise suggestion that Seward be approached in person, Hamlin wrote Lincoln for further instructions. "Shall I confer with the Governor directly, and ask him what are his wishes and desires?" Hamlin wrote Lincoln on December 4. "My impression is that he will not desire a place in your cabinet, but he may." Probably the conviction rankled in Seward's breast that the Lincolnian offer, when it came, would be intended merely as a compliment, and that self-respect would demand a declination. To settle the question, Lincoln, in answering Hamlin's questions, sent him two letters sealed in one envelope addressed to William H. Seward, and, in another envelope, unsealed copies for Hamlin's personal inspection. "Consult with Judge Trumbull," Lincoln wrote, "and if you and he see no reason to the contrary, deliver the letter to Governor Seward at once."[4] As soon as Senator Trumbull read the Lincoln letters, he advised that Hamlin present them immediately to the gentleman most concerned.

[3] Hamlin, Charles Eugene, *Life and Times of Hannibal Hamlin.* Riverside Press, 1899. P. 371.

[4] *Ibid.*, p. 272.

The scene between Hamlin and Seward that now took place can be reconstructed from several sources. Hamlin gave some of the details to Senator George Fogg of New Hampshire, who passed them on to Gideon Welles [5] for incorporation in that catch-all of a Diary. Other items appear in the account given in the official life of Hamlin by his grandson.[6] One afternoon, soon after the arrival of Lincoln's letter, Seward and Hamlin, the Senate having adjourned, found themselves in each other's company, walking down Pennsylvania Avenue in most friendly fashion. When they reached Hamlin's hotel, the latter invited Seward to his rooms for a private talk. The New Yorker seemed to be – perhaps affected to be – in a despondent frame of mind; he was tired of public life – so he said – intended soon to resign his seat in the Senate and retire for the rest of his days to his home at Auburn. Again Seward insisted that there was no place in Mr. Lincoln's gift that he would accept; over and over again he repeated that he would not go into the cabinet. "If that is what you have come to talk to me about, Hamlin, we might as well stop here. I don't want the place, and, if I did, I have reason to know that I could not get it. Let us have no more talk about it." This was really good news to Hamlin, who from the first believed that Seward in the cabinet would be a constant embarrassment and irritation to the President. Very well, he replied, he would not pursue the matter further; Mr. Lincoln, however, had sent him a letter for Mr. Seward, and he suggested that the New Yorker read it before his refusal was made explicit. Hamlin related that Seward, "pale with excitement," opened the communication with trembling hands. The first of Lincoln's two letters would have chilled any man. "My dear Sir: With your permission I shall at the proper time nominate you to the Senate for confirmation as Secretary of State for the United States. Please let me hear from you at your own earliest convenience. Your friend and obedient servant, A. Lincoln." Such a cold, concise offer, standing by itself, would have justified Seward's worst apprehensions and would certainly have invited a declination; but there was a second missive, and when Seward read this, he became a changed man. He reached forth and grasped Hamlin's hand. "This is remarkable," he said. "I will consider the matter, and, in accordance with Mr. Lincoln's request, give him my decision at the earliest practicable moment."

Lincoln's letter was about as gracious and dignified as any he ever penned. "In addition to the accompanying and more formal note, inviting you to take charge of the State Department," wrote the Presi-

[5] Welles, *op. cit.*, II, 389.
[6] Hamlin, *op. cit.*, pp. 372–373.

dent-elect, "I deem it proper to address you this. Rumors have got into the newspapers to the effect that the department named above would be tendered you as a compliment, and with the expectation that you would decline it. I beg you to be assured that I have said nothing to justify these rumors. On the contrary, it has been my purpose, from the day of the nomination at Chicago, to assign you, by your leave, this place in the administration. I have delayed so long to communicate that purpose in deference to what appeared to me a proper caution in the case. Nothing has developed to change my view in the premises; and I now offer you the place in the hope that you will accept it, and with the belief that your position in the public eye, your integrity, ability, learning, and great experience, all combine to render it an appointment pre-eminently fit to be made. One word more. In regard to the patronage sought with so much eagerness and jealousy I have prescribed for myself the maxim, 'Justice for all'; and I earnestly beseech your co-operation in keeping the maxim good. Your friend and obedient servant, A. Lincoln." [7]

Seward at once acknowledged Lincoln's letter, thanking him for the proffer, and saying that he would definitely reply as soon as he could consult his friends. There were only two intimates whose advice was desired – Thurlow Weed and Mrs. Seward. Seward received Lincoln's letters on December 13 – almost the same time that Lincoln's "invitation" to Weed, via Davis and Swett, reached its destination. He at once left Washington for Albany for a talk with Weed. Then Weed took the train for Springfield.

[7] Lincoln, Abraham, *Complete Works, Comprising His Speeches, Letters, State Papers, and Miscellaneous Writings*. Ed. by John G. Nicolay and John Hay. Century Company, 1894. VI, 192–220.

IX

WEED HAD several purposes in making this wintry pilgrimage. Really, he was seeking to learn the terms on which Seward was to enter the cabinet. To what extent was Lincoln disposed to accept the Albany plan, as formulated at the Saratoga Conference? Would it be an all-Seward, all-Whig cabinet? Would the Southern Whigs whom Seward favored form part of the new administration? Or would Lincoln persist in his determination to include those odious outsiders, Chase, Blair, and Welles, in what would certainly be a disharmonious family? There were other questions also to be settled. Seward desired control of the administration, not only from motives of ambition, but to enforce his favorite policy of dealing with the seceding South. Would Seward be permitted to play the role of Henry Clay and come forth, at the critical moment, with another compromise that would conciliate the South and at least postpone the "irrepressible" conflict? It was known that Lincoln was "inflexible" against any new legislation that contemplated any extension of slavery. Would he abandon this attitude as part of his price for Seward's acceptance of the State Department?

Weed's first stopping place on this voyage of exploration was not Springfield, but Bloomington. Here he met the two men who had become his partisan intimates, Leonard Swett and David Davis, and the trio proceeded to Lincoln's home. In the conversations that lasted for the better part of two days, Davis and Swett were always present though their contributions to the discussions were not important. Unfortunately no stenographic report of the sessions is at hand, though hardly any record could have shed such light upon the inner political workings of the time. Two participants have indeed left accounts, Weed himself and Leonard Swett[1]—both of them embodied in the *Life of Thurlow Weed*, published by that statesman's family; these transcripts, however, are not contemporary, having been written

[1] Weed gave his version of the talks in his *Autobiography*, I, 603–614. Leonard Swett's appears in the same work, pp. 293–296.

several years after Lincoln's death, and are colored by a consciousness of subsequent events, above all by Lincoln's fame, and by the understandable desire of their authors to make the best possible showing in history. Thus Weed's memorandum seems to evince more concern for the great public issues involved in the new aspect of affairs than for such egoistic matters as the assignment of patronage. Yet his recollections have considerable vividness and, in a measure, make possible the reliving of what must have been a picturesque scene. For gathered there in the rococo parlor of the Lincoln home, with its haircloth furniture and whatnots, ornamented with sea shells and other genteel bric-a-brac of the day, Lincoln and Weed – Davis and Swett putting in an occasional word – discussed the new administration. Both Lincoln and Weed made striking human figures. Both were more than six feet high, both spare of frame, both bearing in a rugged exterior signs of that hard fight each had had with poverty. Weed, twelve years Lincoln's elder, seemed the less worldly looking object and indeed the more venerable. His nimbus of white hair, surmounting a finely shaped head, and accentuating the innocent impression conveyed by a cherubic face, large-featured and pink, contrasted strikingly with the rough-hewn, deeply seared, dry, parchment-like countenance of Lincoln. Weed's gentle voice, enticing smile, and friendly blue eyes enhanced the general benignity which the man radiated at every pore. If the purpose of his visit was to put a collar about Lincoln's neck, and lead him captive into the Seward-Weed compound, there was nothing in his benevolent behavior indicating any such intention. Weed was no longer the crushed, beaten, angry stalwart of the last hours of the Chicago Convention, but the accommodating, ingratiating politician, determined to manipulate such advantage as he could from an unfortunate turn of fortune. Weed knew precisely what he wanted from Lincoln. Equally important was the fact that the President-elect also knew, so that the talks resembled something in the nature of a sparring match, disguised as they might be by good temper, happy turns of speech, breakfast of sausages and cakes at the Lincoln house, and an always pertinent flow of anecdotes and jokes from the prospective head of the nation.

Lincoln showed his firmness too, and his determination in certain prime matters. His first statement must have disconcerted Weed, especially as it was made unequivocally, as a matter absolutely fixed in Lincoln's mind. Long before November, he told his visitor, he had decided, in case of success at the polls, to make William H. Seward Secretary of State and Salmon P. Chase Secretary of the Treasury. Lincoln could at times say things with a discouraging finality – indeed almost arrogance. He evidently wished Weed to understand at the start that Chase was to be a member of the cabinet, and soon said so with a directness that left no room for argument. And Weed attempted no rejoinder. That was that, and the discussion at once went on to candidates for other seats in the council. What was Mr. Weed's opinion of Edward Bates for Attorney General? Was there any objection to him? "None," replied Weed, with real cordiality. "Not a shadow or a shade of an objection. That is a selection, as Mr. Webster might have said, eminently fit to be made." Lincoln's proposal of Gideon Welles as Secretary of the Navy was not so amiably received. New England, said Lincoln, should have a place in the cabinet; its representative should be a former Democrat, and Welles by all odds seemed to be the best choice. Not at all, Weed replied; he thought that several men would be more acceptable to New England than this old Jacksonian editor. In discussing Mr. Welles, just before leaving Springfield, Weed became entertaining and contemptuous. He suggested that Mr. Lincoln, when on his way to the inauguration, get off at New York long enough to select a wooden ship figurehead. He should take this to Washington, adorn it with whiskers and a wig, and place it over the entrance to the Navy Department. This would, said Weed, prove quite as serviceable a secretary as Gideon Welles – and less expensive. Lincoln was amused – or pretended to be – but said that, after all, he would have to have "a live Secretary of the Navy."

Another appointment Lincoln was seriously considering aroused even more anguish. Judge Blair had been suggested, he said.

"What Judge Blair?"

"Judge Montgomery Blair."

"Has he," asked Weed, "been suggested by anyone except his father, Francis P. Blair, Sr.?" That remark, Lincoln said, reminded him of a story, which he told – though Weed, in his account, does not repeat the anecdote, fearing that "its spirit and effect would be lost." But Montgomery Blair he was sure would never do. These Blairs – father and two sons – were an impossible lot. Wherever they might be they always made trouble. They would make trouble for the new President if he removed them from Maryland and put them at his council table. Everybody, like Weed, always referred to any member of the Blair family as "they," for there was little doubt that, in putting one Blair into the cabinet, Lincoln would really put in the trio – for they always acted as a unit. Lincoln said that he felt it necessary to include one or two men from the Border states, for keeping them in the Union was really a matter of life and death. Weed endorsed this idea – but anyone except a Blair! Whom would he propose? "If we were legislating on this question," said Weed, "I would move to strike out the name of Montgomery Blair and insert that of Henry Winter Davis."

Judge David Davis, present at the conclave in all his sublime rotundity, must have beamed satisfaction at this proposed substitution. From the beginning he had been pestering Lincoln to take his distinguished cousin into the presidential circle. He had no more use for the tribe of Silver Spring than had Seward and Weed. Perhaps David Davis also foresaw – what came to be the fact – that Henry Winter, if rebuffed by Lincoln and passed over in favor of his bitterest political opponent, Montgomery Blair, would be a dangerous thorn in Lincoln's side. If the Maryland Davis had been present at this interview, his fierce, excitable nature would certainly have had something to work upon, for Lincoln refused to regard him seriously as a cabinet candidate and passed the whole thing off as a joke. "Davis has been posting you up on this question," he replied with a laugh, turning to his friend from Bloomington. "He has got Davis on the brain. Maryland must be, I think, a good place to come from." This was a pleasant thrust at the politician-judge who had left his native state to seek better opportunities in Illinois. Weed's suggestion reminded Lincoln of the witness in court who gave his age as sixty, only to be called to account by the judge, who happened to know that he was seventy-five. "Oh, you are thinking about that fifteen years that I lived down by the eastern shore of Maryland; that was so much time lost and don't count." Weed did not greatly relish the anecdote; he thought the President-elect was injecting it into the discussion to ease what was getting to be a tense situation. It was evident that the selection of Montgomery Blair was a fixed fact, and it was a disturbing fact to Weed; "and, although I subsequently ascertained the reasons and influences that controlled the selection of other members of the cabinet I never did find out how Mr. Blair got there."

Now came the most difficult question of all. How about the redoubtable Simon Cameron? In the conversation on that subject, both Lincoln and Weed were clearly trying to feel each other out. Neither was frankly committal. It was only on the subject of Cameron, Leonard Swett says in his paragraphs devoted to this meeting, "upon which Mr. Weed, as it seemed to me, did not speak with entire freedom." Good reasons existed for this hesitation. Lincoln, in declaring his intention of making Chase Secretary of the Treasury, had spiked Weed's guns, for that was the post the Albany plan had assigned to Simon Cameron. Pennsylvania, Lincoln argued, was the second largest state in the Union, and could not be ignored in assembling the cabinet. If it were recognized, it was difficult to see how Cameron could be passed by. What did Weed think of Cameron for such a post? His relations with Cameron, Weed replied, had always been pleasant; he had known him for twenty-five years, and had towards him a most friendly feeling.

"But you do not say what you think of him for the cabinet," persisted Lincoln.

Lincoln of course knew very well that Weed favored him as Secretary of the Treasury, but Weed continued to evade the question. Lincoln's pronouncement on Chase had clearly tied the New Yorker's tongue. No flat statement on the subject could the President-elect elicit. Presently, therefore, all parties to the discussion dropped Cameron and took up other questions. Weed particularly desired that one or two places be given to loyal Union men in certain slave states – Virginia, North Carolina, or Tennessee.

"Could you rely upon such men if their states should secede?" asked Lincoln.

"Yes, sir; the men whom I have in mind can always be relied on."

"Well," said Lincoln, "let us have the names of your white crows, such ones as you think are fit for the cabinet." Weed mentioned again Henry Winter Davis, of Maryland, and he thought that John M. Botts of Virginia, John A. Gilmer of North Carolina, and Bailey Payton of Tennessee would also fit into the situation. The only one of these names which much interested Lincoln was Gilmer of North Carolina, with whom he did enter into negotiation, but the impending secession of North Carolina made it impossible for Lincoln to offer him a place, or for Mr. Gilmer to accept.

Weed pointed out the most serious mistake Lincoln was making. The cabinet, as outlined in this tentative fashion, would contain more former Democrats than Whigs. Was that fair to the element that contributed the largest number of voters to the Republican Party? Lincoln replied that, as a Whig, he thought he could afford to be liberal to a section of the Republican Party without whose votes he could never have been elected. It might be all right to have Democrats in the cabinet, argued Weed, but after all, why not recognize the preponderance of Whigs? Four Democrats and three Whigs – was that the right representation? Why not reverse the formula? That would more equitably represent the situation. "You seem to forget," replied Lincoln, "that I expect to be there; and counting me as a Whig, you see how nicely the cabinet would be balanced and ballasted."

Though the two men spent the better part of two days together in the friendliest fashion, Weed left Springfield a disgusted man. He had failed in every object aimed at. Seward was to have a place in the cabinet, but was to have little influence in selecting the other members.

Lincoln clearly intended to be the head of the administration. It was not to be all-Whig, but a coalition. The three men whom, as cabinet associates, Seward most abhorred – Chase, Welles, and Blair – stood high in Lincoln's favor. About including some distinguished Southerner Lincoln was more acquiescent, but he still apparently thought that the Border states were adequately represented by Bates and Blair.

Seward was defeated. Yet as soon as Weed had reported the facts, he wrote Lincoln, accepting the Secretaryship of State. "I have after due reflection and with much self-distrust, concluded that, if I should be nominated to the Senate for the office of Secretary of State, and the nomination should be confirmed, it would be my duty to accept the appointment." But in his own heart he accepted no position subordinate to Lincoln. He had failed in his first attempt to dictate terms, but he did not look upon the loss of this preliminary skirmish as final. "I have advised Mr. Lincoln," he wrote his wife on the same day as his letter to the President-elect, "that I will not decline. It is inevitable. I will try to save freedom and my country."

Thus Seward took for granted, even after Weed's failure, that national salvation rested in his hands, not Lincoln's.

X

EVIDENTLY THE Seward problem had been settled, at least for the time being, but that of Cameron and Chase still remained. In early January another deputation started for Springfield, representing the influential wing of New York politicians who for years had been daggers drawn against the Seward-Weed machine. These gentlemen, George Opdyke, Judge Hogebloom, and Hiram Barney, came primarily to protest against Seward in the cabinet, but they were equally emphatic in denouncing Cameron and in advocating Chase. They had also an appreciative word for Gideon Welles.

The two most powerful Republican papers in New York City, the *Tribune* and the *Evening Post*, had joined hands in this twofold campaign to keep Seward and Cameron out of the administration and to get Chase and Welles in. "Now I am even with Seward," Horace Greeley had exclaimed after the defeat of his enemy at the Chicago Convention, but his appetite for revenge had not been satiated. The motives of William Cullen Bryant, of the *Evening Post*, possibly had a more elevated character. The *Evening Post* represented the views of a faction which for years had been fighting the Seward-Weed machine as a corrupting force in the state. Cameron ranked second as an odious public character while their admiration for Chase knew no bounds. Already the Bryant faction had approached Lyman Trumbull, Senator from Illinois, and close to Lincoln in cabinet consultations, to save the country from the Albany "plunderers." Replying to Trumbull's letter conveying this information, Lincoln declared that the New Yorkers, who had so loyally supported Seward at Chicago, "ought not and must not be snubbed as they would be by the omission to offer Governor Seward a place in the cabinet. I will myself take care of the question of 'corrupt jobs' and see that justice is done to all our friends of whom you wrote as well as others."

The newest delegation stopped off at Columbus, Ohio, for consultation with Chase, then occupying the governor's chair, and resumed their journey, apparently reinforced in enthusiasm for that statesman as head of the Treasury Department. Up to this time, opposition to Seward had always been accompanied by eager endorsement of Chase and Welles, and by similarly eager antagonism to Cameron. "There is no more truly upright man and few men in public life are so intelligent," Bryant had written Lincoln concerning Welles, but of Cameron his opinion was not so complimentary: "The general sensation aroused by the suggestion of Cameron in the cabinet," wrote Mr. Bryant, "is one of consternation. Mr. Cameron has the reputation of being concerned in some of the worst intrigues of the Democratic party. Those who favor his appointment in this state are the men who last winter so shamefully corrupted our Legislature" [1] – another slap at Weed, and through him, at Seward. Thus Lincoln had been well prepared for the visit of the protesting New Yorkers, to whom he listened patiently but to whom he refused to make any commitments. By this time – early January – the weary man at Springfield was rather tired of these importunate delegations, and had reached a conclusion which he now imparted to the Opdyke-Barney mission. The whole matter, he said, of cabinet selections would be postponed until his arrival in Washington. Lincoln evidently did not impart to these two anti-Seward guests that about a week before he had received a letter from Seward, accepting the offer of the State Department.

The friends of Cameron displayed the same persistence. They constantly prodded at Lincoln's elbow, making his days and nights miserable. Seward pressed Weed to make another trip to Springfield, for the express purpose of pushing Cameron's pretensions, but Weed, probably still smarting under his not too successful efforts with Lincoln in late December, declined. David Davis, the man chiefly responsible for the Cameron predicament, left his home in Bloomington and camped in Springfield, sticking to Lincoln, in the words of Horace White, "like a burr." Lincoln's hesitation in honoring the unholy bargain Davis had concluded at Chicago irritated this judicial Warwick, and his insistence frequently aroused Lincoln's anger. An avalanche of letters from Pennsylvania were also demanding Cameron's preferment, Lincoln remarking in a letter to Lyman Trumbull that for some strange reason the Pennsylvania boss was "more amply recommended for a place in the cabinet than any other man." Lincoln's use of the word "strange" was probably ironical, for the most pressing of these recommendations came from gentlemen – like David Wilmot of the famous Proviso – who were ambitious of succeeding to Cameron's seat in the Senate, and this fact was not likely to elude a student of human nature

[1] Godwin, Parke, *A Biography of William Cullen Bryant.* D. Appleton & Co., 1883. II, 152.

and politics so acute as the distracted President-elect. And influential voices in plenty were lifted up on the opposing side. Lincoln asked the opinion of Henry C. Carey, of Philadelphia, and obtained a quick response. "There exists throughout the state," wrote Mr. Carey, "an almost universal belief that his fortune has been acquired by means that are forbidden to the man of honor. There stand upon the records of the courts and but a very few years old charges that would, if proved, involve the commission of serious crime. Most of all well disposed fellow citizens look upon him as the very incarnation of corruption. . . . His appointment would be a signal to all the vultures of the Union to flock around the Treasury." [2]

Charles Sumner, uttering vivid phrases, as always, was storming around Washington. Cameron, he declared, was "reeking with the stench of a thousand political battles." He was "this political Judas from Pennsylvania, whom Providence had marked with the capillary sign of his character and who might have sat to Leonardo da Vinci for the picture in the Milanese refectory." [3] Other anti-Cameronians were sending elegant extracts from Congressional documents detailing the sorrows of the swindled Winnebagos. Chase was attacking his future cabinet associate in a Columbus paper he controlled; Lyman Trumbull and other powerful anti-Sewardites were doubling the effort to prevent the impending scandal. "Another very serious objection to Cameron," wrote Trumbull, "is his connection with Gov. Seward. The latter is a man who acts through others, and men believe that Cameron would be his instrument in the cabinet." [4] One anecdote tells how Lincoln, in desperation, burst into the office of his Springfield friend, Gustave Koerner. "I am in a quandary," he said. "Pennsylvania is entitled to a cabinet office. But whom shall I appoint?" "Not Cameron!" shouted Koerner and others present in chorus. He was a "tricky and corrupt politician." "I know, I know," said Lincoln, "but can I get along if that state should oppose my administration?" "Lincoln is in a fix," wrote his sympathetic law partner, William H. Herndon, to Lyman Trumbull. "Cameron's appointment to an office in his cabinet bothers him. If Lincoln do appoint Cameron, he gets a fight on his hands, and if he do not, he gets a quarrel deep abiding and lasting. Poor Lincoln! God help him."

[2] Carman, Harry J., and Luthin, Reinhard H., *Lincoln and the Patronage.* Columbia University Press, 1943. P. 39.

[3] *Diary of a Public Man; an intimate view of the national administration, Dec. 28, 1860 to March 15, 1861.* Privately printed. Abraham Lincoln Bookshop. Chicago, 1945. P. 64.

[4] White, Horace, *Life of Lyman Trumbull.* Houghton Mifflin Co., 1913. Pp. 146–147

How deep a "fix" had engulfed the new President perhaps even Herndon did not understand, and certainly few of those besieging Springfield had all the facts. In the weeks following the selection, Cameron, determined on the redemption of his bond, had been angling for an invitation to Springfield, and the mere fact that Lincoln showed no disposition to extend hospitality did not daunt his intrepid spirit. Of all aspirants for presidential favor, indeed, Cameron was the one whom Lincoln least desired to meet face to face. Gideon Welles sheds light on this matter, as on so many others. Cameron, he says,[5] summoned Leonard Swett to Lochiel and, plying him with entertainment, expressed an ambition to visit the new seat of political power. Swett himself, knowing that the initiative would not be forthcoming from Springfield, extended the sign of welcome in Lincoln's name. On almost the last day of that epochal year, 1860, Simon Cameron presented himself at Lincoln's door. Another guest reached Springfield simultaneously – this one, Edward Bates, in response to a personal invitation from Lincoln. Bates's attitude towards public office differed from Cameron's; when Lincoln told him of his cabinet troubles, the Missourian at once offered to retire, thinking that another great office at his disposal might assist Lincoln in satisfying the voracious party appetite. Lincoln immediately brushed aside the suggestion.

Bates met Cameron and was apparently somewhat puzzled by him. "After Mr. Lincoln retired," Bates wrote in his Diary, "I remained in company with Mr. Cameron and a Mr. Sanderson, of Philadelphia (who tells me that he was a member of the Whig Convention of Baltimore of 1856). I did not find out what brought Senator Cameron to Springfield. It is generally surmised, however, that he is a strong candidate for Secretary of the Treasury. I found him pleasant enough in conversation, but rather reticent about politics or parties. There was nothing private or confidential between us, and I suppose he did not wish me to know the object of his visit – our meeting there was accidental."[6] The most significant feature of this meeting Bates clearly did not understand. That was the presence with Cameron of John P. Sanderson, the same Sanderson who, in the back-room meeting at the Chicago Convention, had pledged the Pennsylvania delegation to David Davis for Lincoln, in exchange for the "recognition" of Cameron in Lincoln's cabinet. He had now come to Springfield with his party chief to exact the payment of that debt.

No account has been preserved of the interview or interviewers; all that we know is the result. After discussing the matter at length

[5] Welles, *op. cit.*, II, 390.
[6] Bates, *op. cit.*, p. 171.

with Cameron and his companions – for others than Sanderson had joined in the attack – Lincoln gave Cameron a letter, now duly printed in all editions of his works. "I think fit to notify you, now" – the date is December 31, 1860 – "that, by your permission I shall at the proper time nominate you to the United States Senate for confirmation as Secretary of the Treasury or as Secretary of War – which of the two I have not yet definitely decided. Please answer at your own convenience." That Lincoln had permitted himself to be browbeaten – almost blackmailed – by the Cameronian onslaught seems a fair conclusion; yet certain extenuating circumstances must be set down on the other side. Lincoln would have been the last man to deny that he was a practical man, even a practical politician. And an extremely practical question confronted the Republican Party and the nation at that moment. One Southern state was following another in secession; only a great opposition, strong and united, could successfully deal with the crisis. To ignore Cameron, Lincoln sincerely believed, would split the Republican administration in two. Not only would Pennsylvania, the most powerful state in the Union next to New York – in many ways more powerful – be hopelessly divided. The strongest element in the national organization, Seward-Weed, was besieging Lincoln in the interest of Cameron. To have sent Cameron away from Springfield unsatisfied might have been a slap in the face of the New Yorker whose support was regarded as indispensable.

This compromise, however, did not solve the problem, but really brought a new sea of troubles. Cameron, usually the most discreet and silent of men, could not restrain his satisfaction over this turn of fortune. Returning to Harrisburg, he proudly exhibited Lincoln's letter, confidential as it was, to his intimates, and in a few hours the news had spread all over the state. A terrific explosion resulted, the reverberations reaching as far as Springfield. In the feud that had been rocking Republican Pennsylvania for several years, the new President, the anti-Cameronians declared, had gone over to the enemy! With Cameron in the cabinet, and with a vast patronage at his disposal, what would become of Curtin and his friends? Clearly, nothing remained for them but political death. These sentiments presently began speeding over the telegraph wires to Lincoln's home. The regular Republican organization, led by the state chairman, Alexander K. McClure, telegraphed a most energetic protest. Cameron's appointment to the Treasury, Colonel McClure informed the President, would destroy the Republican Party in Pennsylvania – in other words, the very calamity that nomination was intended to prevent would come to pass. Lincoln, startled, summoned McClure to Springfield for further elucidation.

Colonel McClure, in his reminiscences of Lincoln, tells the story of this visit, but only in general outline.[7] For three hours, in the "parlor" of Lincoln's home, the two men discussed Cameron and Pennsylvania politics; yet just what were the charges against Cameron laid before the President by McClure has never been disclosed. They evidently were more serious than those that had been associated with Cameron's name since the days of Andrew Jackson, for when Lincoln asked McClure to put his accusations in writing, with the evidence supporting them, that cautious politician declined to do so. He did not care to appear as "an individual prosecutor of Cameron" – such was McClure's somewhat unsatisfactory reply to this request. McClure's review of Cameron's career and his account of the distracted state of Pennsylvania politics, and the further demoralization that would result from Cameron's elevation, however, had the desired effect. McClure left Lincoln's home at eleven o'clock on the night of January 3, and, inasmuch as Lincoln's second letter to Cameron carried this same date, it was evidently written immediately after the interview. "Since seeing you," Lincoln wrote Cameron, "things have developed which make it impossible to take you into the cabinet. You will say this comes from an interview with McClure; and this is partly, but not wholly true. The more potent matter is wholly outside Pennsylvania, and yet I am not at liberty to specify it. Enough that it appears to me to be sufficient. And now I suggest that you write me declining the appointment, in which case I do not object to its being known that it was tendered you. Better do this at once, before things so change that you cannot honorably decline, and I be compelled to openly recall the tender. No person living knows or has an intimation that I write this letter. Yours truly, A. Lincoln. P. S. Telegraph me instantly on receipt of this, saying 'All right.' "

That "all right" message, which Lincoln anxiously awaited the next few days, never came. This information that his presence in the cabinet was not desired apparently did not affect Cameron as it would have a man of ordinarily sensitive nature. It seemed rather to stimulate his determination to attain the goal. The fact is that, with a man of Cameron's ideals, this cabinet seat was not an honor, not a summons to serve the nation in the impending crisis, but something in the nature of a vested right, for which he had given his consideration, and intended to demand payment. Instead, therefore, of accepting the situation as Lincoln urged, Cameron kept pounding on the Lincolnian door. All the time-honored machinery of insistence and persuasion was pressed into service. The Pennsylvania legislature passed resolutions

[7] McClure, Alexander K., *Abraham Lincoln and War Time*. Times Publishing Company, 1892. Pp. 48, 151–154.

eulogizing Cameron and urging his claims to a cabinet seat. Leonard Swett and David Davis renewed their campaign in Cameron's behalf. Swett especially objected to the abrupt English used by Lincoln in ejecting Cameron from his forthcoming council table. Cameron was pictured as grieving over this insult to his dignity, and surely Lincoln, the kindest of men, could not have intended to wound so sorely the feelings of this loyal supporter! Telegrams and letters again began inundating the Lincoln home. On January 11 John P. Sanderson, Cameron's other self, left for another uninvited visit to Springfield. With him came Edgar Cowan, recently, by Cameron's favor, elected United States Senator from Pennsylvania. They protested against the "bluntness" of Lincoln's letter and asked for a reconsideration. On the main point Lincoln refused to change his mind but he granted two concessions. One was another letter to Cameron, expressing regret that the previous one, written under "great anxiety," was "not so guarded in terms" as it should have been and disclaiming "any intention of giving offense." It was suggested that Cameron destroy this letter and substitute another – which Lincoln now sent – containing the same request that Cameron withdraw from the cabinet contest, but expressed in gentler terms. The second request was expected to mollify still further Cameron's perturbed spirit. "If I should make a cabinet appointment for Pennsylvania before I reach Washington, I will not do so without consulting you and giving all the weight to your wishes which I consistently can. This I have always intended."

On the very day of the Sanderson-Cowan visit Lincoln wrote Seward that he was "being teased to insanity" over cabinet matters and saying that no more appointments would be made for the present. Another problem was now causing anxiety – that of Salmon Portland Chase. From the beginning Chase had been Lincoln's almost automatic choice for the Treasury Department, but, as set forth above, both the Seward and the Cameron elements disliked this prospect. That January 3, the date of Lincoln's evening talk with Colonel McClure, and his "blunt" letter to Cameron had been a busy one in other ways. In reply to Lincoln's written request to Chase, that "in these troublous times I should like a conference with you. Please visit me here at once," Chase came to Springfield, arriving on January 4.

Chase, like Cameron, though for different reasons, was suffering from wounded vanity, to which Lincoln's letter had come somewhat as a balm. Two months had passed since the election, and not a word had reached him from Springfield as to any plans Lincoln might have for his future. The well-advertised visit of Weed and the certainty that

Seward would receive – or at least be offered – first place in the administration did not tend to soothe the feelings of the haughty Ohioan. Why should Seward be regarded as the first man in the Republican Party? Did not Chase's long record of service to the cause, and his eminence as an individual, entitle him to that distinction? From the beginning of the new era Chase had made no secret of his ambition; though he felt no particular yearning for a cabinet seat – so he informed his friends – still, if he was to become an inner member of the administration, he looked upon the first place as his due. For diplomacy and the general conduct of foreign affairs Chase fancied that he had particular talents – and perhaps he had – but Lincoln had already set aside that supreme post for Seward, and this meant that Chase, if he went into the cabinet at all, must do so in a secondary position. Yet there is no doubt that, despite his deprecating attitude, Chase really desired an appointment. It was true he frequently said, in letters and conversations, that his work as Senator from Ohio – to which he had been recently chosen for a second term – was preferable to administration routine, but he always expressed a willingness to serve wherever he might be most useful. Perhaps Seward's preferment itself stimulated his desire for a cabinet place – such a position would enable him to keep an eye upon his rival and counteract his influence with the head of state. "It would be rather superfluous to decline what has not been offered," Chase wrote Charles A. Dana, November 10, 1860. "Neither do I say that I would accept it: – but only this: – that is, that if the offer were made . . . I should be bound to consider it honestly and carefully, with the help of the best advisers I could consult and should be governed in my decision, not so much by my personal inclination as by my obligations to the cause and its true and faithful friend."

Chase had several talks with Lincoln in the two days following his arrival in Springfield. Lincoln went to extremes to show cordiality and respect; took him to church; called upon him at his hotel, and, at the beginning of the discussion, thanked him for the support he had brought Lincoln in his contest with Douglas in 1858, and for the effective assistance in the campaign just closed. For all Lincoln's attempts to be agreeable and conciliatory, the consultation proved awkward and embarrassing to both men. Lincoln referred to the expectation of Chase's friends that first place in the cabinet should be his by right, and, as tactfully as he could, expressed his dissent. The Department of State, he said, had from the first been assigned to Mr. Seward; had the New Yorker declined, then, Lincoln added, it had been his intention to offer it to Mr. Chase. However, this remark was not to be misconstrued. Lincoln did not wish Mr. Seward to refuse; in fact, in Chase's own words, he was glad that Seward "had accepted" for Seward "was the generally recognized leader of the Republican party." One can imagine how these frank words must have made the vain and haughty Ohioan writhe. As Lincoln went to the next point the tension became more acute. "I have done with you," said Lincoln, "what I perhaps would not have ventured to do with any other man in the country – sent for you to ask you whether you will accept the appointment of Secretary of the Treasury, without, however, being exactly prepared to offer it to you." The difficulty with Cameron explained in part, but only in part, this unflattering invitation to a cabinet post. Still back in Lincoln's mind lay the troublous question of Seward. The New Yorker had definitely accepted, but at the same time his friends were conducting a campaign against Chase. With Chase in the Treasury would Seward remain faithful to his promise? Would he serve in any cabinet that included this rival? That Lincoln's misgivings on this subject were amply justified subsequent events disclosed, and the way in which he put the question would indicate that, in this particular stage of cabinetmaking, he might have sacrificed Chase rather than have lost "the recognized leader of the Republican party." Chase replied that he desired no appointment, "certainly not a subordinate one," and that Mr. Lincoln's question had placed him in an "unpleasant position." However, the two men talked long and agreeably, Chase making no direct reply to the conditional offer, and Lincoln insisting on no commitment of a definite kind. "I replied," said Chase afterward in a written memorandum, "that I did not wish and was not prepared to accept that place if offered. A good deal of conversation followed in reference to other possible members of the cabinet but everything was left open when we parted and I returned to Columbus." [8] And the question remained in this uncertain state until the fifth of March.

In spite of this unpromising beginning to their relation, Chase's visit to Springfield left no bitterness in his mind. "Mr. Lincoln conversed frankly and fully," he wrote a friend on January 9, immediately after returning to Columbus. "*He is a man to be depended on.* [Italics Chase's own.] He may, as all men may, make mistakes; but the cause will be want of sufficient information, not of unsoundness of judgment or of devotion to principle." This was a somewhat higher estimate of Lincoln than Chase expressed after nearly four years' association in his cabinet.

[8] Warden, Robert Bruce, *An Account of the Private Life and Public Services of Salmon Portland Chase*. Wilstoch, Baldwin & Co., 1874. P. 365.

XI

THOUGH BY THE time Lincoln reached Washington for the inauguration only two men, Bates and Seward, had definitely received and accepted cabinet appointments, the likelihood is that most of the remaining posts had been assigned. Lincoln, however, was holding them *in petto* after the fashion of the Pope of Rome, who sometimes keeps hidden in his own breast the cardinals whom he expects to name at some future consistory. And probably Lincoln's choices were about as secret as those of the Supreme Pontiff in similar circumstances. The persistent Seward-Weed attempts to exclude Chase from the Treasury Department had not deflected the President-elect from his determination on that point. Cameron had probably been settled on for the War Department as an unsatisfactory compromise in the Pennsylvania impasse. Similarly the "all-Whig" campaign against Gideon Welles had not changed Lincoln's prepossessions in favor of that gentleman. In fact, a few days after reaching Washington a message was sent to the Hartford journalist enjoining him to repair to the National Capital – a command which Welles not illogically regarded as confirming current reports as to his selection. Caleb B. Smith for the Interior was another compromise Lincoln was obliged to make with his conscience; the man was unworthy of any appointment, but the simple fact remained that Davis had guaranteed a tricky and vapid politician this place in exchange for Indiana's forty-eight (?) votes in the Chicago Convention, and that Lincoln, although he had warned his agents against making such unholy bargains, felt under party duress to redeem the promise. Two other candidates, Norman B. Judd of Illinois and Schuyler Colfax of Indiana, were still negotiating for this place; Lincoln reimbursed Judd by sending him as minister to Prussia and made a lifelong enemy of Colfax by ignoring his solicitations. The third member of the trio who had aroused the unrestrained opposition of Weed and Seward, Montgomery Blair, of Maryland, was also practically assured of an appointment. The alternative candidate from this Border state, Henry Winter Davis, had from the first met little favor at Lincoln's hands. Had the Seward proposal for some Southern statesman – say Gilmer of North Carolina, Botts of Maryland, Etheridge of Tennessee – proved feasible, probably Blair would have been dropped in the interest of this attempt at conciliation. An exchange of letters between Gilmer and Lincoln, however, had showed the futility of the plan. States on the verge of secession could hardly be represented in a cabinet pledged, first of all, to preserving the Union, and Gilmer's subsequent election to the Confederate Congress showed where his final sympathies lay.

The nine-day interval between the President-elect's arrival in Washington and the inauguration witnessed a renewal of the cabinet intrigues that had driven Lincoln almost to distraction for three months in Springfield. The pro-Seward forces, headed by the burr-like David Davis, had clung closely to Lincoln since his departure from Springfield. Another recruit, Orville H. Browning, whom Lincoln held in much higher regard than Davis, had joined the calvalcade at Indianapolis. When Lincoln made his unhappy entrance into Washington early in the morning of February 22, Seward appeared as a reception committee of one and took Lincoln in tow. He did not disassociate himself from his destined chief for the next few days. He entertained him at breakfast in the morning and at dinner in the evening of that first Saturday, escorted him to church the next day, called with him for a courtesy visit on President Buchanan, who received his elected successor most graciously and introduced him to his cabinet.

Hannibal Hamlin and Lyman Trumbull, both anti-Seward and pro-Chase, had attempted to secure a favored position in Lincoln's entourage, but had been outwitted. To protect the next President from too much contamination by the enemy they had secured interim headquarters for Mr. and Mrs. Lincoln and their two sons in a private house on a quiet Washington street. Here their charges could pass the nine days before inauguration undisturbed by the armies of suppliants already congregated in the Capital and be accessible only to those Illinois friends who had been Lincoln's companions and co-workers for years. Thurlow Weed had successfully protested against this domicile. The ever-faithful David Davis rallied to his side. "It will never do," Weed wrote Davis, "to allow him to go to a private house. He is now public property and ought to be where he can be reached until he is inaugurated." In a brief period Davis had persuaded William E. Dodge, the millionaire, to vacate temporarily the finest suite in Willard's Hotel, Parlor No. 6, and place it at Lincoln's disposal. David Davis himself took up quarters only a few doors away from the presidential apartment. Salmon Portland Chase also established himself on the same second floor, and soon a kind of theatrical queue, of the great and small, had joined the procession to the new seat of power. One of the earliest callers was old man Blair from Silver Spring, who had many chats with the President-elect in the course of the next week, in which it may be assumed that the elevation of his son Montgomery was not forgotten. Lincoln received as many men of less importance as time allowed, listened to as many pleas for foreign missions, postmasterships, collectorships, and the like as was humanly possible – making, however, few commitments – and shook hands with thousands of self-invited greeters, men and women, with all the good nature and patience that were to be manifest during the coming four years. Everyone who met the President-elect remarked upon his worried, melancholy appearance. "He is not a great man, certainly," observed one of his visitors at this time, "and, but for something almost woman-like in the look of his eyes, I should say the most ill-favored son of Adam that I ever saw." "He owned to me that he was more troubled by the outlook than he thought it discreet to show. . . . Half an hour with Mr. Lincoln confirmed my worst fears. I should say he is at his wit's end if he did not seem to me to be so thoroughly aware of the fact that some other people are in that condition." "I was struck and pained by the haggard, worn look of his face, which scarcely left it during the whole time of our visit." [1]

The most vivid view of Washington for those nine tumultuous days is derived from that *Diary of a Public Man* from which these quotations, describing Lincoln's melancholic state of mind, are taken. This is one of the most valuable and most mysterious documents in Lincoln's literature. Ever since the *North American Review*, in 1879, published extracts from this Diary, the identity of the author has baffled all students of the Lincoln era. Extensive searches for the complete Diary have failed; if found, this would be an inestimable treasure, for it is written with forceful literary grace, and in its abundance of detail and its pictures of personalities it rivals even Gideon Welles himself. This fact has led certain scholars to regard the memoirs as unauthentic. In despair at their failure to discover the rest of the record or of finding any person on whom to fix the authorship suspicions have arisen that the whole thing is a superb forgery. Internal evidence rather refutes this conclusion. The writer reveals such an intimate knowledge of the Washington panorama as it was unfolding before his eyes, his descriptions of persons and incidents are so detailed, familiar, and lifelike – in a word, the whole story conveys such a complete impression of firsthand knowledge that the Diary, if a literary concoction, must be, as F. Lauriston Bullard says in his introduction to the recently

[1] *Diary of a Public Man*, 44.

published edition, "the perfect crime." In fact it bears the evidence of reality in every line. In the opinion of Frank Maloy Anderson, for many years Professor of American History at Dartmouth College, the scholar who has investigated the problem most exhaustively, the "highly probable" author was Amos Kendall.[2] This famous member of Andrew Jackson's kitchen cabinet, having made a comfortable fortune with Samuel F. B. Morse in exploiting the telegraph, was then spending his last years in Washington, and was probably in closer touch than any man, except old man Blair, with the leaders of that era. This would explain not only the energy of the literary style, and the intimate information revealed, but also the disappearance of the complete Diary itself, for most of Kendall's papers were destroyed in a warehouse fire in Washington.

If Kendall wrote this Diary, he had certainly outgrown one of the enthusiasms of his youth. It was this versatile journalist and statesman and young Francis Blair who had edited jointly the *Argus* of Frankfort, Kentucky, and it was Kendall who had brought his companion, in 1830, to Washington to edit the Jacksonian *Globe*. But "Public Man," in 1861, regarded Blair as a dangerous influence and resented the almost certain prospect of Montgomery in the Lincoln cabinet. The elder Blair's frequent appearances in the Willard Hotel during that fateful winter aroused Public Man's worst fears. He quotes with apparent approval Stephen A. Douglas's characterization of the Blairs as "those born conspirators and makers of mischief." "I do not like the Blairs," wrote the author of this Diary, "and indeed I know nobody who does. But of them all I like Montgomery least; and I can imagine nothing less to be desired than his entrance into the cabinet, which Senator Douglas regards as inevitable. He goes further than I do in his views as to the policy which he thinks the Blairs are bent on cajoling or compelling Mr. Lincoln to adopt. They are co-operating now, for the moment, he thinks, with the extreme anti-Seward men both here and in New York. 'What they really want,' said Senator Douglas, 'is a civil war. They are determined, first, on seeing slavery abolished by force, and then on expelling the whole negro race from the continent. That was old Blair's doctrine, sir.' " It was the elder Blair's attitude on the great pending problem – what to do about Fort Sumter – that particularly aroused this Public Man, as it did Douglas, for the Blairs believed that the Federal government should hold and reinforce that bastion, whereas Douglas and Kendall – if it was Kendall – believed with Sew-

[2] See Professor Anderson's article on Amos Kendall in the *Dictionary of American Biography*, X, 325–327. Since writing this article, Professor Anderson is said not to be so sure of the conclusion expressed in it.

ard that the place should be abandoned to South Carolina, as the best means of averting civil war.

Public Man's view of Lincoln was that of most intellectuals of the day; he was as startled as Charles Francis Adams himself at the President's ungainly appearance, his ill-fitting clothes, his lack of Bostonian manners, and his apparent failure to realize the enormity of the crisis. Though in fleeting moments the diarist catches glimpses of another Lincoln concealed within this strange exterior, he is appalled by the prospect of entrusting the nation's destinies to his care. That Lincoln could never direct his own administration, and that the real power must be delegated to a stronger, abler brain – the prevailing opinion appears vividly in this memoir. Who then is the real ruler of the nation to be? Seward is evidently the indicated man, yet this likelihood is not entirely reassuring. Public Man distrusts the man's sincerity. Relating an anecdote that reveals the New Yorker's cynicism, he comments: "It is a serious misfortune at such a time as this that such stories are told and believed of the man who apparently is to control the first Republican administration in the face of the greatest difficulties any American administration has ever been called upon to encounter." Yet he sees no one except Seward who can possibly take up the reins of state. "From what Mr. Seward tells me, it is plain that he has more weight with Mr. Lincoln than any other public man, or than all public men put together, and I confess that I grow hourly more anxious as to the use that will be made of it." Presently, however, the writer's judgment is more qualified. Several interviews with Lincoln himself, though they did not change Public Man's dislike of the President-elect's log-cabin demeanor and at times apparently carefree view of things, called forth a new note. After his first talk with Lincoln, "I gathered for myself that he is not so much in the hands of Mr. Seward as I had been led to think and I incline to believe that Mr. Barney [Hiram Barney, anti-Sewardite of New York] is nearer the truth than I like to think." That Lincoln may not virtually abdicate to the New Yorker Public Man evidently looks upon as an impending danger. "There can be no doubt about it any longer. This man from Illinois is not in the hands of Mr. Seward. Heaven grant that he may not be in other hands – not to be thought of without patience!" – probably another hit at "the Blairs." That Lincoln must be in someone's "hands" and, indeed, ought to be is clearly assumed. "I can not feel even sure now that Mr. Seward will be nominated at all on Tuesday; and certainly he neither is nor after this can be the real head of the administration, even if his name is on the list of the cabinet."

This entry accurately conveys the uncertain atmosphere that

shrouded cabinetmaking on the date it was made – March 2. The preceding week had been one of tension and strain. The fact is that Seward, the most important of the cabinet possibilities, had not for a moment abandoned the Albany plan. He and Weed – and Davis – were working hard for the fulfillment of the Saratoga pact, which meant the exclusion of Chase, Blair, and Welles from the presidential council. Hardly had Lincoln been deposited in Willard's Hotel when the intrigue started afresh. The anxiety of the New Yorkers had probably been heightened by a sharp letter dispatched by Lincoln to Weed before the departure of the train from Springfield. Disturbed by current reports of the dominant part the new Albany regency expected to play in the new dispensation, the President-elect administered a rebuff to Weed which must have been as unwelcome as it was unprecedented in that dominant gentleman's career. "As to the matter of dispensing patronage," Lincoln had written Weed, "it perhaps will surprise you to learn that I have information that you claim to have my authority to arrange that matter in New York. I do not believe that you have so claimed; but still so some men say. On that subject you know all I have said to you is 'Justice to all,' and I have said nothing more particular to any one. I say this to reassure you that I have not changed my position."

Public Man's comments on Seward's declining position as boss of the Lincoln administration were made on the day that marked a crisis in the relations of the two men. Of certain details Public Man apparently knew nothing; on one of the most important he is almost our only authority. This diarist did not know, for example, that Seward the day before had called upon Lincoln and filed a complaint that he was not being consulted in cabinetmaking. Lincoln had indeed yielded, with sour face, in the matter of Cameron and Smith, but evidently that had not been concession enough. That Cameron was to become Secretary of War, not of the Treasury, did not accord strictly with the Saratoga demand, and this was resented especially because it left second post open to the detested Chase. The man who was selected for "Premier" was usually consulted about the other members; Seward now insisted on this personal talk with Lincoln. He was grieved that Lincoln had ignored this precedent. The large Democratic representation – especially Blair, Chase, and Welles – was unfair to the old Whigs who made up the great majority of the new party. Seward quoted President Jackson, who insisted that a cabinet should be a "unit"; certainly the one that Lincoln had put together would possess little unity. Welles and Blair were bad enough, but the main point of contention was Chase. Seward flatly told Lincoln that Chase must be excluded, if he himself were to remain. He and the Ohio Puritan could never sit at ease at the same table. "Mr. Lincoln expressed his surprise that after all that had taken place and with the great trouble on his hands, he should be met with such a demand at this late day. He requested Mr. S. to further consider the subject." Gideon Welles, who provides this account of what must have been an embarrassing interview,[3] does not quote a remark made at this time, reported by Nicolay and Hay. Late one night Norman B. Judd gained access to Lincoln, and asked in some excitement whether he intended to drop Montgomery Blair and award the Postmaster Generalship to Henry Winter Davis. "Judd," said Lincoln, "when that slate breaks again, it will break at the top."[4] If this remark reached Seward's ears – and, in the gossip wildly flying around Washington at the time, it most likely did – it could hardly have assuaged that statesman's resentment at the turn matters were taking.

The next day, March 2, two days before inauguration, the situation moved to a real crisis. For some time a group of New Yorkers, headed by Simeon Draper, a rich and politically influential merchant, long one of Seward's most valiant champions in New York, subsequently by Seward's favor Collector of the Port, had been waiting on the outskirts, seeking an interview with the President-elect. All these gentlemen were Sewardites, particularly interested in eliminating Salmon P. Chase from the Lincoln council table. Their hostility reflected not only loyalty to Seward, but apprehension about the tariff views of the Ohio Senator. What would become of the United States, if a free trader, as Chase was accused of being, should be placed at the head of the Treasury Department? The day following Seward's protesting talk with Lincoln, the promised audience was granted. Lincoln received the delegates in his usual friendly way and listened patiently as, one after another, they set forth their belief that Chase in the administration would be a prime mistake. He was an abolitionist, they urged, a man who sympathized with the Garrisonian view that a Union with slave states was an abomination, and that a northern republic, perhaps including Canada, would be an ideal way out of the present impasse; let the South, with its slaves and its State rights, go to the devil – so loyal Garrisonians held – in any way it pleased. Lincoln watched each speaker carefully, and, after all had had their say, asked them just what they wanted him to do, or to forbear to do. "Do not name Chase for the Cabinet!" the opposition chorused. "He cannot sit around the same table with Seward. He wouldn't wish it, and his following and his state would not tolerate it – couldn't tolerate it – it must not be." Lincoln

[3] Welles, *op. cit.*, p. 391.
[4] Nicolay and Hay, *Abraham Lincoln.* Century Company, 1917. III, 370.

seemed much depressed, and sat – as he usually did in such awkward moments – for a considerable time, saying nothing. Then, speaking in a low voice, he said that it was very hard to reconcile conflicting claims and interests; the only hope was to form an administration that would inspire general confidence; he had the deepest respect for Mr. Seward, but Chase had great claims, too, which could not be disregarded. Lincoln granted that Chase's pretensions did not equal Seward's; still he ranked second to the New Yorker as a national leader. Then Lincoln opened a table drawer, took out a piece of paper, and contemplated it for a time. "I had written out my choice of secretaries in the cabinet after a great deal of pains and trouble; and now you tell me that I must break the slate and begin all over."

Something in the President-elect's unaggressive manner made the delegation think that they were gaining their desire, and when Lincoln went on to say that he had at times thought he might have to revise his cabinet, the visitors really thought that victory was at hand. The fact was, continued Lincoln, that he had drawn up an alternative list, should that need become imperative. He did not like this second cabinet nearly so well as the old one, which had Mr. Seward as Secretary of State and Mr. Chase as Secretary of the Treasury, "but he could not expect to have things exactly as he liked them; and much more to the same effect, which set the listeners quite agog with suppressed expectations of carrying their point. "This being the case, gentlemen," Lincoln continued, "how would it be for us to agree upon a change like this? How would it be to ask Mr. Chase to take the Treasury and to offer the State Department to Mr. William L. Dayton?" Mr. Dayton was from New Jersey, which "is next door to New York." He was an old-line Whig, like Seward and himself. He had been candidate for Vice-President on the Frémont ticket, and was "a most conservative, able, and sensible man." Mr. Seward could go as minister to Great Britain, where he was well known and would find abundant scope for his talents in keeping Europeans from mixing in American troubles.

At this suggestion the New York delegation was literally speechless. Here was a sad outcome of their warfare on Chase; the net result of their reconnaissance in force was likely to be the exclusion of Seward altogether and his exile to London. One of Lincoln's visitors finally found voice enough to thank their host for his kindness in receiving them, and then all noiselessly withdrew. "Whether this prefigures an exclusion of Mr. Seward from the cabinet, who can tell?" writes Public Man, after describing the scene in the above terms. "Nor does that possibility alone make it alarming. It does not prefigure – it proves that the new administration will be piloted on a dangerous and not a safe key. It makes what was dark enough before, midnight black. What is to come of it all?"

Lincoln, of course, understood that this last-minute attempt to keep Chase out of his administration had been instigated by Seward and Weed – certainly acquiesced in. The reply that he had made to the New York delegation had really been addressed to Seward. He had carried out the threat confided to Judd the night before – that, if the cabinet slate broke again, it would "break at the top." The "top" was Seward, and Lincoln's remarks to the protestants merely informed Seward, without any beating about the bush, that if he desired to come into the cabinet on the President's terms he would be gladly received, but if he persisted in saying who should be his associates, then his services would be dispensed with. Of course the New Yorkers at once reported the result of their mission to their chief. Seward was angry and bitter. He at once seized his pen and addressed the following curt note to the President-elect, two days before the inauguration: "My dear Sir: Circumstances which have occurred since I expressed to you in December last my willingness to accept the office of Secretary of State seem to me to render it my duty to ask leave to withdraw that consent. Tendering you my best wishes for the success of your administration, with my sincere and grateful acknowledgment of all your acts of confidence and kindness towards me, I remain, very respectfully and sincerely, your obedient servant, William H. Seward."

And so it came about that when the inaugural procession, on March 4, started up Pennsylvania Avenue to the Capitol Edward Bates was the one man definitely agreed upon for the cabinet. Lincoln pondered the situation all day Saturday and Sunday. He knew he could still have Seward if he would accept Seward's terms. In view of events of the preceding twenty-four hours – Seward's visit to Lincoln, the Draper delegation at Willard's – the letter was simply an ultimatum. If Lincoln would exclude Chase – and probably Blair and Welles – he would head the cabinet; otherwise, the Lincoln administration must get along without "the leader of the Republican party" at the council board. Seward and other cabinet ministers, in the course of the next four years, were to learn of Lincoln's most positive trait – an iron will and determination when his mind, after reflection and apparent yielding and even doubting, had fixed upon a course of action. Seward was to become aware of this characteristic now. Lincoln thought that the best time to fix the issue definitely of who was to head the government was at the beginning of his term. To have yielded to Seward would have been almost to abdicate the Presidency, and make Seward virtually chief of state. Not to yield might be to lose the man then generally regarded as the ablest in matters of state in the nation, and probably convert him and his large following into enemies working at cross-purposes with the White House. Lincoln, so far as is known, said nothing to anyone about this letter – except to his secretaries – but thought out the problem, as was his custom, then and afterward, alone. Monday morning, while the inaugural procession was forming in the streets, he wrote his reply, handing it to his secretary to copy, remarking – a remark that summed up in real Lincolnian language the great principle at stake – "I can't afford to let Seward take the first trick."[5] Lincoln dated the letter "Executive Mansion, March 4, 1861" – though it was actually written in his apartment at the Willard. "My dear sir: Your note of the 2nd instant, asking to withdraw your acceptance of my invitation to take charge of the State Department, was duly received. It is the subject of the most painful solicitude with me; and I feel constrained to beg that you will countermand the withdrawal. The public interest, I think, demands that you should; and my personal feelings are deeply enlisted in the same direction. Please consider and answer by nine o'clock A.M. tomorrow. Your obedient servant, A. Lincoln."

And so the President-elect did not yield a jot. His letter in turn was an ultimatum – and an ultimatum with a date limitation. Seward was given until nine o'clock, March the fifth, to say whether he would accept a cabinet post on Lincoln's own terms. Lincoln put the argument on high grounds: the interest of the nation required Seward's presence in the cabinet; he also added to his previous statement that this was his personal wish. But he made none of the concessions that Seward had been insisting on. If Seward had not rescinded his letter then William L. Dayton would have been Secretary of State during the Civil War. But Seward made a complete capitulation – at least to outward view. After the inaugural he called on Lincoln at the White House and the two had a long and amiable talk, as a result of which Seward withdrew his withdrawal. "The President," Seward wrote his wife, "is determined to have a compound cabinet and that it shall be peaceful, and even permanent. I was at one time on the point of refusing – nay, I did refuse for a time, to hazard myself in the experiment. But a distracted country appeared before me, and I withdrew from that position. I believe I can endure as much as anyone; and maybe I can endure enough to make the experiment successful. At all events, I did not dare to go home, or to England, and leave the country to chance." And "leave the country to chance"! Here again Seward assumes that

[5] Nicolay and Hay, *op. cit.* III, 371.

the fate of the nation rested on him, not on the President-elect. It is doubtful if he ever really outgrew this conviction.

Lincoln, however, completely understood. That evening, at the inaugural ball, the correspondent of the *New York Herald* approached the President, and asked if he had any message for his editor, James Gordon Bennett. "Yes," replied Lincoln, "you may tell him that Thurlow Weed has discovered that Seward was not nominated at Chicago." If there was a certain note of exultation and anger in this retort, the tension of the hour, and the way in which Seward, by his demands and intransigence, had added to them, were sufficient excuse.

The next day, March 5, Lincoln sent to the Senate his cabinet and it was immediately confirmed: –

For Secretary of State: *William H. Seward*, of New York.
For Secretary of the Treasury: *Salmon P. Chase*, of Ohio.
For Secretary of War: *Simon Cameron*, of Pennsylvania.
For Secretary of the Navy: *Gideon Welles*, of Connecticut.
For Secretary of the Interior: *Caleb B. Smith*, of Indiana.
For Attorney General: *Edward Bates*, of Missouri.
For Postmaster General: *Montgomery Blair*, of Maryland.

And so, after many tribulations, Lincoln obtained the cabinet – with one or two exceptions – that he had fixed upon, with the help of no advisers, the day following his election.

BOOK TWO

William Henry Seward: "Prime Minister"

I

AT NIGHT. President Lincoln's first cabinet meeting," Edward Bates noted in his Diary for March 6, "Intended, I suppose, to be formal and introductory only. In fact, uninteresting." Inevitably this group of ill-assorted statesmen must have felt some awkwardness at their first assembling. They were far from being a mutual-admiration society. Three of them, Chase, Blair, and Welles, were confronting a "Premier" who, for the preceding four months, had used all his resources of intrigue, and even of intimidation, to keep them out of the intimate White House circle. And of his maneuverings all three were well aware. But even Chase, Blair, and Welles, although they had a common bond of accord in hostility to the Secretary of State, were not entirely companionable themselves. Welles and Blair, it is true, could rub elbows on congenial terms; Welles's friendship with the Blair family, beginning in the Jacksonian era, and cemented afterward by cordial association at Silver Spring, had laid the basis of a co-operation that survived the Lincoln administration. They were almost the only friendly couple in the cabinet. Both men, however, had little regard for Chase. All three had another aversion in common – the lanky Pennsylvanian who had finally succeeded, with the help of Seward and David Davis, in slithering into the Secretaryship of War. To Edward Bates, who found that first evening's proceedings so "uninteresting," not one of his associates embodied his ideal of a statesman. Welles was probably the only one for whom he felt any personal attraction. Cameron himself did not find a single friend at Lincoln's board unless his marriage of convenience with Seward – soon to be dissolved – put the Secretary of State in that class. Caleb B. Smith was isolated, both by his own unimportance and by the methods he had used to obtain his seat. Seward, from the first, refused to take any of his fellow members seriously. Not one of them, in his view, was to play any figure in the general conduct of affairs. His failure to dominate Lincoln in cabinetmaking had taught him nothing. Perhaps Thurlow Weed had learned, in Lincoln's phrase, that Seward had not been nominated at Chicago, but that statesman's behavior, in the very first business that faced the administration, showed that Seward had not taken the lesson deeply to heart.

This first question awaiting decision was critical indeed. Immediately after inauguration a telegram from Major Anderson, commanding Fort Sumter, had been handed the new President. The little garrison of less than a hundred men could hold out for only a brief time unless resupplied and reinforced. The matter that had kept the United States in a turmoil for three months – whether to attempt to retain the bastion by force, or to evacuate it in the face of superior numbers and dwindling supplies – could not much longer be postponed.

Seldom has the nation passed through such a period of anxiety and disquiet as the quarter year that preceded Lincoln's accession. The Buchanan administration, though repudiated at the polls, still held possession of the government. Not until March 4 would the new regime be installed in office. The aging President himself, irresolute, inert, without courage or initiative, extremely partisan and hidebound to the South, did nothing when confronted with national dissolution. While state after state had been leaving the Union, each appropriating to itself such Federal property as could be seized within its limits, Buchanan spent his days and nights weeping, praying, and proclaiming his inability to cope with disaster. Though he was feebly loyal himself, his cabinet, until reorganized in late December, contained at least three members – Cobb of Georgia, Secretary of the Treasury, Floyd of Virginia, Secretary of War, and Thompson of Mississippi, Secretary of the Interior – who were arch secessionists and who were suspected, how justly is still a moot question, of using their Federal positions to strengthen the seceding states. With the Federal army of only sixteen thousand men scattered in distant posts on the western frontier, from which it could not be reassembled for months, and with the fighting ships of the navy lying in foreign ports, the central government had scant means of defending itself against the threat of attack that every day grew more formidable. The state of affairs in Washington led the young Henry Adams to compare the National Capital to ancient Rome in the days of Cataline. Expressions of sympathy for the Southern cause were daily events. Jefferson Davis and his associates were holding secession meetings in the Capitol building itself, rumors of oath-bound organizations said to be sworn to prevent Lincoln's inauguration filled every street and home, and fears of an attempt to seize the city and government in the interest of the Confederacy distracted the patriotic mind.

If conditions did indeed recall to a classic-minded Bostonian the time of Cataline, who was there in all this welter to perform the part of Cicero? Though Seward was much more mild-mannered and less vituperative than his ancient exemplar, he was a man of comparable vanity and assurance, and clearly regarded himself as the one statesman who could save a dissolving nation from its domestic foes. The vacillating statesman in the White House was clearly not the man for the occasion. The rustic President-elect in Springfield was untried in large concerns, and was still a private citizen.

In his letters to Lincoln, Seward had shown little modesty. Even toward the leader most concerned, he did not hesitate to assume a superior attitude. "I, my dear sir," he wrote Lincoln on February 24, "have devoted myself singly to the study of the case here with advantage of access and free communication with all parties of all sections. I have a common responsibility and interest with you and I shall adhere to you faithfully in every case." Only a few days before, in suggesting changes in the inaugural address, Seward had expressed similar ideas to his nominal chief. "Only the soothing words which I have spoken have saved us and carried us along thus far. Every loyal man and indeed, every disloyal man in the South, will tell you this." To others, Seward's letters were written in the same strain. Those to Mrs. Seward portray himself as the one man pursuing a steady, definite purpose amid the accumulating ruins. "All parties, north and south, cast themselves upon me." "My future responsibilities have already begun." "I have assumed a sort of dictatorship for defense, and am laboring night and day." "It seems to me that, if I am absent only three days, this administration" – the letter was written in January 1861, so the reference is to the Buchanan regime – "the Congress and the District would fall into consternation and despair. I am the only hopeful, calm, conciliating person here." "Mad men North and mad men South are working together to produce a dissolution of the Union by civil war. The present [Buchanan] administration and the incoming [Lincoln] are united in devolving on me the responsibility of diverting these disasters."

If Lincoln felt chagrin at Seward's statement that he had an equal responsibility with him in "saving" the Union, and that his course during the interim from election to inauguration had succeeded in turning over to the new President a government still secure, there is no record to indicate the fact. But that he seriously differed with Seward in his proposals for counteracting secession there is abundant evidence. The gulf between their fundamental conceptions of duty in the crisis had been widening for a considerable period. The best index to their conflicting views can be obtained from the speeches each delivered in

February 1860, about three months before the Chicago Convention. Lincoln's address was the one made in Cooper Union February 27, and Seward's was spoken in the Senate two days afterward. Both men probably had in view the forthcoming Chicago Convention, and intended their respective orations to be regarded more or less as personal platforms in rivalry for the nomination. The important fact about Lincoln's statement of the case was that it differed hardly at all from the judgments he had expressed in the debates with Douglas two years before. Slavery in the states in which it already existed he had no disposition to disturb; that the Constitution recognized and protected it was granted; thus the Federal government had no right to interfere. But to the creation of new slave territories and ultimately new slave states in the national domain west of the Mississippi River Lincoln declared himself inexorably opposed. That had been his stand from the time he began to study and discuss the question and that continued to be his position during the campaign of 1860 and afterward.

Seward's Senate speech of February 29, 1860, however, had completely reversed his previous attitude. Where before he had been unyielding towards the Southern claim, he now displayed a more acquiescent mood. Where in earlier speeches Seward had declared that slavery and free labor could not exist permanently side by side in the same nation, he now saw a harmonious fraternal relationship between the two sections, irrespective of their different labor systems. Even obnoxious words were avoided; instead of "slave states," the Southern commonwealths were described in this speech as "capital states." The North had no desire "to force or even intrude" its labor system upon the Southern brethren. The Republicans, said Seward, were now planning to play a national role, thus virtually admitting the claim of the South that they had formed a sectional party. By mentioning only incidentally slavery in the territories, and by talking much of the homestead laws and Pacific railroads, Seward almost echoed the plea of Edward Bates for a moratorium on the "agitation." It was the duty of the hour to get down to "practical" issues, and "leave metaphysical speculation to those whose duty it is to cultivate the ennobling science of political philosophy."[1] This thrust may have drawn a laugh from his Southern associates, but it could not have pleased those at whom the satire was aimed – the crusading antislavery men who had formerly regarded Seward as their intrepid champion.

Of course in this speech Seward was again playing politics – the Republican National Convention was only ten weeks in the future – and this conciliatory attitude he continued to express in the next few

[1] Seward, William Henry, *Works*. Redfield, 1853–1884. Vol. IV, 619–643.

months. He did not desert it even after Lincoln's nomination and election. That this policy satisfied a considerable section of the Whig Party, especially that element representing business and finance, soon became evident. Seward and Weed had always been spokesmen of what today would be called "Big Business." In Wall Street and in the industrial sections of New England and Pennsylvania, support was found in plenty for the pressure which these two leaders now began to exert on Lincoln. Northern manufacturers did an extensive trade with the South and had large outstanding accounts; and this talk of secession and war was "bad for business." Politicians of the victorious party, eager for temporary advantage, more interested in spoils than in saving the Union, similarly gave Seward their acclaim. His plan for "soothing" the South and in this way averting war found many followers among those less affected by personal interests. They soon began to besiege the President-elect. That avalanche of letters which inundated Lincoln's humble home and that procession of visitors which converged on the same point did not consist exclusively of office seekers. A good-sized proportion came to beg the President-elect to issue a "statement of his views." They asked for something which would mollify the South and check its determination to secede. Only such a "proclamation," as some of the visitors called it, could quiet the turmoil and save the Union. Many of the nation's leading citizens, especially in business and financial circles, took part in this bombardment. August Belmont, A. T. Stewart, William B. Astor, Jay Gould, William H. Aspinwall, Moses H. Grinnell, Abbott Lawrence, and other money kings joined in the demand. But these appeals for a "statement" were not precisely what they purported to be. Lincoln's views on the Southern question had been set forth frequently and in detail; they had been expressed many times in the preceding two years, in most public fashion. They existed in printed form, readily accessible to anyone really interested in ascertaining his attitude. In reply to personal and written requests, Lincoln appropriately called attention to these discussions, and declared that they still continued to be his opinions on current problems. In doing this, he frequently made direct citations, giving dates and pages of his published speeches. There were, for example, his debates with Douglas in the senatorial contest of 1858; on page so and so the questioner would find a specific answer to his specific question. There was the Cooper Union speech of February 27, 1860 – his position, Lincoln would write, had not changed from the one expressed in that utterance. Above all, there was the Chicago platform on which he had been elected; the sections in that document concerning slavery in the territories accurately defined the program he still upheld. But such rejoinders, apt as they might be, did not satisfy those besieging the Springfield statesman. It was, indeed, precisely because Lincoln's ideas had been so widely disseminated and were so well known that a new "statement" was demanded. What the politicians and business leaders really desired was not a "proclamation" of Lincoln's well-known articles of faith, but an entirely new creed. They demanded that Lincoln abandon his long-cherished convictions and adopt their own. They insisted that he violate the pledges on which he had been nominated and elected and make a complete surrender to the South. The word that had already played so calamitous a role in the slavery dispute was again pressed upon the forthcoming Chief Magistrate. The quarrel had been "compromised" in 1820 and 1850; why should Lincoln not assume the role of Henry Clay and compromise it again?

The demand took definite form about three weeks after the election, under the leadership of a powerful wing of the Republican Party. On November 24, 1860, an editorial on the state of the Union appeared in the *Albany Evening Journal*. Ordinarily, an article in a small-town partisan newspaper would not have attracted national attention. But Thurlow Weed, editor of this organ, was Republican Boss of New York State and an aspirant for an extension of his power throughout the nation. Any discussion of his on such a vital subject would therefore arouse wide interest. In this pronouncement Weed, after picturing in melancholy colors the condition of public affairs, made a definite proposal, which, in his view, would settle all pending troubles. Only one concession, he suggested, would keep the cotton states in the Union. This was the proposal advanced in the recent debate in the Georgia Legislature by Robert Toombs and Alexander H. Stephens, who had said that the enactment of Federal laws that would protect slavery in the territories would keep Georgia from seceding. There, Weed proclaimed in the *Journal* article, is "something to go upon." In two sentences, he propounded his solution: "Why not restore the Missouri Compromise line? That secured to the South all the territory adapted by soil and climate to its peculiar institution."

For thirty years Thurlow Weed and William H. Seward had been the closest personal friends and political co-workers. So intimate was this relationship that the popular mind had long bracketed the two almost as a single person. Seward openly proclaimed this close partnership and seemed almost to glory in it. "Seward is Weed and Weed is Seward," he once informed his colleagues in the Lincoln cabinet. "What I do Weed approves. What he says, I endorse. We are one." [2] In an association now extending over thirty years they had never

[2] Welles, Gideon, *Lincoln and Seward*. Shelden & Co., 1874. P. 25.

William Henry Seward (1801–1872)
Secretary of State

Thurlow Weed (1797–1882)

Republican Boss of New York State and intimate associate of William H. Seward

Reproduced by courtesy of the Harvard College Library

Caleb Blood Smith (1808–1864)

Secretary of the Interior

taken opposite stands on any public policy or party program; their association represented probably the closest co-operation that had ever existed in American politics. Moreover, Weed's assistant editor on the *Albany Journal* was Frederick W. Seward, son of the future Secretary of State. It was this lifelong companionship that gave such importance to Weed's editorial. The public at once assumed, in the words of Charles A. Dana, then Greeley's chief co-worker on the *Tribune*, that "the voice was the voice of Seward, though the hand was the hand of Weed"; an impression that was strengthened when, a few days afterward, the *New York Times*, then under the editorship of Henry J. Raymond, another confidential associate of Seward, endorsed the *Albany Journal's* plan. When the *New York Courier and Enquirer*, edited by James Watson Webb, another member of the Seward-Weed group, added its voice of approval, this impression became a fixed conviction. Seward's denials – or semi-denials – the public refused to accept at face value. Evidently the general belief that he had inspired Weed's outgiving caused him some uneasiness. "Mr. Weed's articles have brought perplexities about me," Seward wrote his wife, "which he, with all his astuteness, did not foresee. But you need not expect, or rather fear, that I will act unwisely or wrong." In one or two newspaper publications he repudiated Weed as his mouthpiece, though in none of them did he express disagreement with his proposals. Not even in his letter to his wife did he reject his friend's main thesis – an assurance that Mrs. Seward, not always a follower of her husband in slavery questions, would have been glad to receive. The nationwide commotion produced by this sensational suggestion, however, compelled both Weed and Seward to issue disclaimers. Six days after the original publication Weed, replying to its unfavorable reception, remarked, "We think and speak only for ourself." On December 5, the *New York Tribune* contained a brief paragraph that bore signs of having been officially inspired. "Mr. Seward will make no speech immediately and will submit no proposition. . . . He is in no manner or form responsible for the various suggestions recently put forward in certain newspapers, which have been supposed to reflect his views, and was not consulted concerning, or in any way privy to their publication. His policy is to watch the development of events and to direct them wisely at the proper time for peace and the preservation of the Union." This last sentence, again emphasizing Seward's conviction that in him rested the salvation of the Union, gives the cue to his behavior, at this critical moment. The same idea had been expressed in a recent letter to Weed; in the present picture of affairs, Seward wrote, he intended to be "silent but not sullen." In maintaining this extreme caution he had two persons, or groups of persons, in view. To have championed publicly Compromise on the Weed pattern would have brought about his ears the slavery radicals – men like Sumner, John P. Hale, Ben Wade, Wendell Phillips, long his enemies in public life and destined to make his career miserable in the next four years: the hullabaloo from this source would have made any attempt at conciliation, however moderate, out of the question. Seward perhaps felt even more concerned about the response that might come from a thoughtful and patient man then watching his every move from his home in Springfield, Illinois. Seward, despite his somewhat offish attitude at the time, clearly yearned to occupy the chief cabinet post in the new administration. To take publicly a position on slavery opposed to that of his prospective chief would make impossible his appointment. One pointed sentence in Lincoln's letter offering Seward the State Department may be repeated. The new President had delayed so long in filling the post, he wrote, "in deference to what appeared to me a proper caution in the case." Why was such "caution" necessary? Not improbably Seward's conciliatory speeches, his remark that he "would make any sacrifice to save the Union," had aroused doubts in Lincoln's mind. The Weed editorial, published at the time Lincoln was deeply concerned with his Seward problem, must have inspired misgivings. It is not too much to assume that Seward's repudiation, published in the *Tribune* on December 5, was intended, above all, to quiet any apprehensions Lincoln may have felt. Significantly, Lincoln did not write his letters, offering Seward the Secretaryship of State, until three days after that statesman's rejection of Thurlow Weed as his spokesman had been published.

The fact of course is that Weed's *démarche* was merely a feeler – an instance of that most familiar device of the practical statesman, a trial balloon. Its purpose was to test public sentiment, to discover how press and public would regard the plan for quieting the national excitement on which Seward had set his heart. If this had been the Seward-Weed purpose, the answer they received removed all doubts. A tornado of disapproval fell on Weed, and also on Seward, for the public refused to accept his denial of co-authorship. So strong was this in Republican circles, even in New York itself, where Weed was supposed to be supreme, that a movement started to deprive him of that contract for state printing which he had profitably enjoyed for many years. No single person had been shocked more than the President-elect. Lincoln had just fought successfully a presidential campaign on an issue which Weed now proposed that he surrender to the South. The Republican platform had denounced, as a "dangerous heresy," the doctrine that "the Constitution, of its own force, carries slavery into any and all the territories of the United States"; and had denied "the authority of Congress, of a territorial legislature, or of any individual to give legal assistance to slavery in" any part of the unsettled domain. It was for the maintenance of this principle that the Republican Party had come into existence. On this declaration of intention it had won the election. To repudiate the Chicago platform was to reverse the result of the election and give victory to the South. Such a change would mean the abandonment of everything that Lincoln had stood for since he had joined the ranks in 1856. It would have made meaningless his political career for it was a career which had been based on opposition to slavery in the territories. Lincoln, in a letter to Seward, written some time after these events, explained his position on this question with his usual clarity. "I say now, as I have all the while said," he wrote, "that on the territorial question – that is, the question of extending slavery under the national auspices, – I am inflexible. I am for no compromise which assists or permits the extension of the institution on soil owned by the nation. And any trick by which it is to acquire territory, and then allow some local authority to spread slavery over it, is as obnoxious as any other. I take it that to effect some such result as this, and to put us again in the high road to a slave empire, is the object of all these proposed compromises. I am against it."

This Weed-Seward definite suggestion of extending the Missouri line, Lincoln insisted, was another attempt to build up a "new slave empire." Such was the scarcely concealed purpose of the so-called Crittenden Compromise then enjoying the distracted attention of Congress – a compromise which, as its main item, embraced the suggestion Weed had put forth. This drew an imaginary line of latitude 36° 30′, extending from the southern boundary of Missouri to California, north of which slavery was to be forever excluded, but south of which – territory now including Oklahoma, New Mexico, Arizona – it was to be permitted. The phraseology of the proposed constitutional amendment – for this principle, as well as other concessions favorable to the slave interest, was to be imbedded in the fundamental law – comprised more than this. Slavery was to become legal not only in all territories "now held" by the United States south of this line, but in all "hereafter acquired" south of the same parallel. It was that "hereafter acquired" that made Lincoln, and most other orthodox Republicans, look upon the Crittenden Compromise as a plan to create a "new slave empire." Southerners of the Davis and Yancey school had never concealed their plan to secure territory in Mexico, Central America, and the Caribbean and create new slave states in this region. In this ambition, the Buchanan administration had been a sympathetic co-worker. Buchanan's pet idea was the annexation by purchase, or force of arms, of Cuba – a fruitful island out of which more than one slave state could be created. Filibustering expeditions into Central America, for the purpose of seizing territory that could be incorporated into the Union and ultimately become slave states, had been a feature of American history for the preceding ten years. So, as Lincoln saw it, this compromise would merely start the old slave cycle to a new evolution. The very word "compromise" aroused sad memories. The question had been already several times "compromised" and "settled" – but to what effect. In 1820, 1850, 1854 – the story was now an old and familiar one, and the repeated violations of the several compromises gave little ground for hope that another one would lead to any other result. The politicians, North and South, on the outlook for temporary advantage, had proved false to all the compromises that had previously been entered into, and could be depended on to do so again.

The Weed publication was not necessary to show in what direction Weed and Seward were working in 1860. The story of Weed's visit to Lincoln in December has been told in preceding pages. Cabinet appointments – the plan to secure an all-Whig and all-Seward cabinet – perhaps formed the main quest of that pilgrimage, but the policy of the coming administration on the great issue was not disregarded. Had Seward and Weed succeeded in obtaining an all-Whig cabinet they would also have succeeded in bringing Lincoln to their compromise plans, for the strength of this territorial plan consisted chiefly in its old-time Whig supporters, especially in the propertied class. All those Southern Whigs whom Seward had pressed for places in the cabinet – John A. Gilmer of North Carolina, John M. Botts of Virginia, Emerson Etheridge of Tennessee, James Barbour of Virginia, Randall Hunt of Louisiana – were compromisers in 1860, while the former Democrats to whom he had been so hostile, Gideon Welles, Montgomery Blair, and Salmon P. Chase, were against making terms with the South that would have reversed the result of the election in its favor.

Just before Weed's visit to Lincoln, his *Albany Journal*, in the face of the hostility its earlier article had stirred up, came out with another advocating the same proposal. That Seward had not been consulted on this renewal of the demand is too much to believe. In fact he had spent several days in Albany with Weed preceding the publication and was present in that town the day it appeared. That it was written largely with the President-elect in view may also be assumed. In forewarning Lincoln of his friend's arrival, Seward wrote that he "would remain at home until his return, and then, in further conference with him [Weed] would have the advantage of a knowledge of the effect of public events." Thus, he virtually notified Lincoln that Weed went to Springfield as his ambassador, and the implication seemed to be that Seward's acceptance of a cabinet post would depend upon the outcome of the interview. Weed's latest journalistic effort appeared in Springfield almost simultaneously with his own arrival. Lincoln read it but did not appear to be greatly moved. "This is a heavy broadside," he remarked to Weed. "You have opened your fire at a critical moment. It will do some good or much mischief."[3] Then he changed the subject and took up the cabinet. Weed returned East, met Seward on the train at Syracuse, and the two men spent two hours discussing the unsatisfactory interview. Lincoln had given Weed a written memorandum suggesting certain concessions he was prepared to make and requesting that Seward present them to the Crittenden Committee. The extension of the Missouri Compromise line was not among them. Seward accepted his defeat in his usual philosophic spirit and wrote Lincoln, accepting the offer of the Secretaryship of State.

Having agreed to go into the cabinet, Seward could hardly vote for the Crittenden Compromise. Had he done so, the likelihood is that he would have received a letter from Lincoln, similar to the one sent Simon Cameron, withdrawing the cabinet tender. Lincoln would hardly have tolerated, as "Premier," a man who publicly endorsed a policy diametrically opposed to his own. When the amendments came up in the sessions of the Crittenden Committee, Seward seemed to Southern members to be the most difficult and unbending of all. Robert Toombs, the Georgia representative, subsequently paid tribute to Seward as the irreconcilable foe of adjustment in the Senate. "At length I saw that the compromise measures must fail," Toombs recorded years after the war. "With a persistent obstinacy that I have never yet seen surpassed, Seward and his backers refused every overture. I then telegraphed to Atlanta: 'All is at an end. North determined. Seward will not budge an inch. Am in favor of Secession.' "

Toombs did not understand, what now seems apparent enough, that Seward's opposition to the compromise was not genuine. Through Weed he had aired that proposal in the public prints, with little success, so far as popular opinion was concerned; he had sent Weed to Springfield to exert pressure on the President-elect and had almost seemed to make his entrance into the cabinet depend upon the acceptance of his peace program. Failing in all these efforts, he vigorously opposed the compromise in committee and was given chief credit by the Southern leaders for its defeat. Yet the fact is that, despite this outward show of hostility, he was as much of a compromiser as ever, and he did not cease his efforts to make this an administration issue.

[3] Weed, *op. cit.* I, 604.

II

JUST WHAT proposals for meeting the crisis were forming in Lincoln's mind from December 20, 1860, when South Carolina seceded, to March 4, 1861, when he assumed the presidential office? On this point historians apparently find little but confusion. A picture has been drawn of the President-elect, wavering from day to day, with no definite plan of operation – inscrutable, silent, aimless, melancholy. Probably Lincoln's complete self-reliance – seldom seeking advice, keeping his inmost thoughts to himself, listening willingly enough to all comers but taking none into his confidence, and making his own decisions – explains the lack of an adequate written record of his mind in the pre-inauguration period. "He was the most secretive, reticent, shut-mouthed man that ever lived," wrote William H. Herndon, his daily companion for twenty years. Judge David Davis uses almost the same words in describing his former companion and roommate on the Eighth Circuit.

The fact that Lincoln did not boldly proclaim from the housetops the plans he was contemplating for dealing with the South does not mean that his mind was a blank on this subject. As to the main questions involved, the preservation of the Union, the constitutional aspects of Secession, reclaiming, even "retaking" by force the arsenals, navy yards, customhouses, forts, and "places" which had been seized, the futility of compromise as a method of assuring the future – Lincoln left neither his friends, nor the public, in any doubt. In this interim, he wrote several letters, and in his progress from Springfield to Washington from February 11 to the twenty-third made several speeches, which clearly set forth his views on all these matters. Lincoln's much admired first inaugural, as originally written – before, on the plea of Seward and Orville H. Browning, certain crucial revisions were introduced – gives a fairly clear view of his mind at this crisis. According to Herndon, the President-elect started writing on this paper "late in January"; it was finished and secretly printed by February 11, the day

Lincoln left Springfield for Washington. This document, as it originally came from Lincoln's hands, together with certain important letters, written with great care and scrupulous phrasing, gives at least in outline the new President's plans for immediate action.

Not only the inaugural itself, but the circumstances of its writing, show what was going on in Lincoln's mind. Herndon tells how the lonely statesman, seeking asylum from visitors and office seekers who made concentration impossible in that governor's room of the state capitol which had served as headquarters since election, retired to a dingy room over a store in a near-by building and here began work on one of the most famous state papers of all time. No ghost writers and "research assistants" helped in the incubation; four pieces of literature only served as Lincoln's companions. Nothing could more eloquently portray his mental state than the classics to which the President-elect now went for inspiration. The Constitution of the United States, Andrew Jackson's Proclamation of 1832 against Nullification, Webster's Reply to Hayne, and Henry Clay's speech on the Compromise measures of 1850 – in these four political testaments Lincoln looked not only for the principles that should guide his administration, but in some instances for the policies that should carry them into effect. By the time Lincoln settled down to this literary task, seven states had gone through the form of separating from the Union; no more appropriate aids to composition could be imagined than those with which Lincoln now went into a kind of monastic seclusion. The note all these prophets most confidently sounded was union, one and indivisible. In the next few months the words of the Constitution were constantly on Lincoln's lips – this fundamental instrument that knew no such thing as secession or the right of the state to overrule the Federal legislature, whose very reason for existence, as recorded in the preamble, was "to form a more perfect Union." Lincoln took this admonition closely to heart, and insisted on it, then and in the next few years, as his pre-eminent duty. To keep that Union intact, as set forth in this Constitution, against all subversive onslaughts, to maintain the integrity of the Federal domain against all attempts to split it into sections – here was the cardinal task confronting the new regime. "My opinion," Lincoln had written to Thurlow Weed a month previously, "is that no state can in any way lawfully get out of the Union without the consent of the others; and that it is the duty of the President and other government functionaries to run the machine as it is." This latter phrase became a favorite of Lincoln's, sometimes varied by an even more homely expression of the same idea – "to keep house" – and the kindred duty laid on the President in the inaugural oath, to "take care that the laws be faithfully executed," was another injunction he regarded with solemnity.

The Union must be preserved, even at the cost of armed conflict – such was the lesson of the documents that supplied the "source materials" for the first inaugural. The Seward-Weed approaches were rejected, not only because Lincoln knew that they would be as ineffectual in the future as they had been in the past, but because they would not provide even a temporary solution. This important fact Seward did not perceive, or, if he did, proceeded, with his splendid faculty for self-deception, to ignore. Lincoln's clearer mind understood it from the first. Both men, in shaping their divergent policies, had in view the same object. The great prizes for which all devotees of the Union struggled in 1861 were the upper Southern and the Border states. With them, both Lincoln and Seward maintained, the Union could be salvaged; without them, or at least some of them, the task would be almost insurmountable. In Maryland, Virginia, North Carolina, Tennessee, Kentucky, Missouri, and Arkansas, the Union feeling up to Sumter was strong; the masses of the people, and many of the leading men, had little sympathy with the Cotton Confederacy. Certain Senators and Representatives, like Mason and Hunter in Virginia, Clingman in North Carolina, approached, in hatred of the Union, the worst of the fire-eaters of the Gulf; but they did not embody the real public sentiment of their region. With both the moderate and the irreconcilable elements Seward remained on friendly terms.

Virginia and Maryland became the chief objects of his attention. With these commonwealths, Seward believed, the fate of the Union chiefly rested. Virginia, though by no means the commanding figure it had been in earlier days, still, in historic prestige, led the South; its decision on whether to join the new Confederacy or to remain faithful to the Union would greatly influence all the Border states, especially North Carolina and Tennessee, as yet undecided between two loyalties. That Maryland would follow Virginia's leadership was a fair assumption, though it proved to be unjustified. The possibility that these two states would cross the Rubicon and march south appalled Seward, as it did Lincoln. Such a departure would leave Washington within the limits of the new Confederacy – and make its retention as the Federal capital difficult, if not impossible. Seward opposed Montgomery Blair for the cabinet in part because he believed, as Thurlow Weed had explained to Lincoln, that he had "no following in his own State," and therefore could do little in keeping Maryland in the Union; Henry Winter Davis, whom he had urged instead, was the dapper, aristocratic boss of the Baltimore "plug-uglies," as the Tammanyites of that city were styled; because of his patrician birth and his skill in practical politics, he was believed to wield great power, which he proclaimed his desire to use for the benefit of the Union. In Virginia Seward's chief reliances were James Barbour and John Minor Botts – both of whom had been included among the "White Crows" whom he had suggested for the cabinet. That Botts was a white crow events made clear, for he remained loyal to the Union after Virginia's secession, but Mr. Barbour was a Unionist of less pronounced type though Seward called him the "master spirit of the Union cause" in Virginia.

In early February, Virginia, after a spirited campaign, elected delegates to a state convention – a convention which was called to settle the question of secession. At this assize, non-seceders won a smashing victory. The returns disclosed that the people, by a vote of six to one, had turned their backs on Jefferson Davis and stretched out the friendliest hand to Abraham Lincoln. Seward and others hailed the event as almost settling the great question, on a national scale. When North Carolina and Tennessee soon afterward followed, with similar result, the Union cause indeed seemed to be triumphant. Yet the outcome in these Border states did not settle the matter at all. The election returns did not portray the real state of the public mind. The respective fates at the polls of James Barbour and John M. Botts in Virginia tell the story. Mr. Barbour was elected a delegate, while Mr. Botts was defeated. The reason for these different fates was that the Barbour loyalty to the Union was conditional, while that of Mr. Botts was unconditional. Mr. Barbour would keep Virginia faithful to the Union, provided certain "guarantees" were granted, while Mr. Botts was a Unionist through thick and thin. And what were the Barbour conditions? The Crittenden Compromise again! A letter written by James Barbour to William H. Seward, just after the convention election, warns the prospective Secretary of State not to take this victory too seriously. The election merely meant that Virginia was for the Union, provided "guarantees for slavery" were given; otherwise it would go with the lower South. Not only would Virginia insist on the new Missouri line and other concessions, but Mr. Barbour thought she was right in doing so. But the unconditional Union men – those candidates who would hold fast to the Federal government even without these Crittenden amendments – like John M. Botts – failed to obtain seats in the approaching convention. This was not all that the conditional Unionists in Virginia and the other Border states demanded as the price of their allegiance to the Union. That there should be no "coercion" of the Cotton Confederacy – no attempt to relieve Fort Sumter and Fort Pickens, or to "retake" the "places" which Jefferson Davis and his companions had seized from the Federal government, and no use of force to bring the seceded communities back under the Federal flag – was the second item in these demands. Such "coercion" would be the signal for immediate secession of the states now wavering between the two sections. Thus the once compact United States, in the spring of 1861, really consisted of three almost independent units. The free Northern and Western states comprised one part; the Border and upper Southern states – Maryland, Virginia, Kentucky, North Carolina, Tennessee, Arkansas – formed another entity attached to the Union by a tenuous thread; and the seven states already joined in a so-called Confederate Republic constituted the third. Seward planned to retain the Middle Kingdom in the Union by making almost any concession necessary to that end. Not only was he prepared to give Virginia and her sister states the "guarantees for slavery" which they insisted on, but to meet the other demands – to evacuate Fort Sumter, and to refrain from military action to regain Federal property which the states already had seized. In accomplishing this latter result, the Border states, he believed, would serve as intermediaries. Once the Border states were definitely secured, and the excitement had died down – after the passing of a few months or a few years – they would act as good angels, and persuade their "erring sisters" further south to rejoin the great Republic of the Fathers.

In the essential devotion of this difficult cotton country to the Union Seward constantly expressed his belief. At a dinner of the New England Society in the Astor House, New York, on December 24, 1860, he had phrased this conviction in words that shocked the nation by their levity – so lighthearted were they, indeed, that Seward, in the version of the speech afterward published in his *Works*, omitted certain passages. South Carolina had passed its ordinance four days previously. "They do not humbug me," he said, "with their secession. I do not believe they will humbug you and I do not believe that if they do not humbug you or me, they will succeed very long in humbugging themselves." Let no one doubt the loyalty of South Carolina to their beloved Union! That state would rise as one man if New York were attacked by a foreign foe; if South Carolina were similarly assailed, every state in the North would simultaneously spring to its defense. This latter sentiment, though thrown off extempore the same evening to his cheering and laughing auditors, afterward took such complete possession of Seward that, as will appear, it became the central point in the policy he in time submitted to Lincoln as the one way of reuniting the severed Union.

Lincoln did not share Seward's optimism. He did not believe in the innate loyalty of the seceded states. He believed – and there are few historians today who do not agree with him – that the Confederate States, organized at Montgomery in early February, 1861, represented a determined and long-planned scheme for independence. In his opinion, no concessions made to the Border states, not even the new Missouri Compromise line, would persuade South Carolina and the others to return to Federal allegiance. The Seward concessions would be interpreted by the Cotton South merely as a sign of weakness and fear and lead to further demands that would inevitably culminate in armed conflict. Civil war or submission – such was the issue of 1861, reduced to its simplest terms. The alternative was not a new one in human history; the American nation had faced it before, and would be called upon to face it again, especially in 1917 and 1941. Just when Lincoln accepted this stark conclusion cannot be said, for, as always, he kept his own counsel, but it probably antedated his election to the Presidency. Should the North agree to a dissolution of the Union, recognize the theory of secession, or resort to war? Thus the fundamental difference between Lincoln and Seward as statesmen was that the "prairie lawyer" saw these alternatives and made no effort to deceive himself and evade the truth, while the accomplished Senator from New York would not accept the situation and make his choice. Eighty years afterward, John Morley, English historian and biographer, as well as perhaps the most outspoken pacifist of his time, said the final word on this subject. The American Civil War was "the only war in modern times as to which we can be sure, first, that no skill or patience of diplomacy would have avoided it; and second, that preservation of the American Union and abolition of negro slavery were two vast triumphs by which even the inferno of war was justified."[1]

And so while Lincoln, in his dingy sanctum over a store in Springfield, was working at the inaugural which recognized the logic of circumstances, Seward, in his Auburn home and in Washington, was writing letters and making speeches intended to accomplish what, in Morley's words, was impossible – avert war by diplomacy. The most impressive effort of this kind was an address delivered in the Senate on January 12, 1861. The news that Seward was to speak drew great crowds to the Capitol. For anything resembling the eagerness with which his words were awaited one must go back thirty years, when Daniel Webster rose to make his reply to the South Carolinian Hayne. That Seward was to head the cabinet had now become public property, and he was naturally looked upon as the spokesman of the new administration. Men and women poured into the Senate Chamber, and filled

[1] Morley, John, Viscount, *Recollections*. Macmillan, 1917. I, 20.

all corridors and halls. By this time four states had seceded, but several of the figures that had been familiar sights in the days of the great slavery arguments still held their seats. Toombs had uttered his angry harangue and departed for Georgia, but Jefferson Davis, Seward's personal friend but political foe, was an attentive listener; Mason and Slidell, who in a few months were to confront Seward with his most dangerous diplomatic impasse, Judah P. Benjamin, destined to become Seward's opposite member in the Confederacy, were still Senators and gave a respectful hearing to his proposals. Crittenden, author of the Compromise – a Kentuckian who stayed loyal to the Union despite the failure of his attempted conciliation – sat directly in front of Seward, and wept during a considerable part of the discourse. For nearly two hours Seward pleaded for peace and union; an oration that was restrained but deeply moving, even impassioned, recalling the splendid past of a united nation, its greatness, the lofty position it had obtained in the respect of mankind, and the happiness it had brought to millions. How could this Union be saved? The speaker repelled the suggestion of armed force. "I dread, in my innermost soul, I abhor, civil war. I do not know what the Union would be worth, if saved by the use of the sword." To prevent such a calamity Seward could "afford to meet prejudice with conciliation, exaction with concession that surrenders no principle, and violence with the right hand of peace." As to slavery as an institution, the speech of January 12 departs a long distance from Seward's "irrepressible conflict" dogma of two years before. According to that famous declaration, the two conflicting systems, slave labor and free labor, could not exist indefinitely side by side. The conviction which had made Seward's name so odious in the South and so celebrated in the North he now cast aside. The different forms of labor, he now asserted, "if slavery were not perverted to purposes of political ambition need not constitute an element of strife." Few practical or definite proposals for resolving the issue were suggested. A constitutional amendment guaranteeing perpetual slavery in the states where it existed; the division of the remaining national domain into two states, one to remain free and the other slave – provided this could be done constitutionally – summed up the main recommendations now put forth. Seward proposed also that a new national convention be assembled, two or three years hence, "when calmness once more shall have resumed its accustomed sway over the public mind," for the revision of the Constitution and the final settlement of pending disputes. Two Pacific railroads, one with its terminus in the South and one in the North, would assist in cementing the Union.

III

SEWARD READ this speech to Charles Sumner four days before its delivery. "I protested," Sumner wrote Samuel G. Howe, "with my whole soul, for the sake of our cause, our country and his own good name, and I supplicated him to say no such thing."[1] Whittier sent Seward a poem, praising him for extending the olive branch to the South, but qualifying the eulogy by hinting that too much subserviency had been shown the slave power. Sumner and Whittier, of course, stood for the Abolitionist standpoint – a tribe for which Seward had little respect, but the response forthcoming from his fellow Republicans proved hardly more consoling. Lincoln indeed did write Seward that the speech "is well received here, and, I think, is doing good all over the country," but this faint praise to a prospective colleague did not include any approval of the sentiments expressed, and Lincoln, two weeks afterward, penned his letter to Seward expressing his explicit opinion of the slavery question, saying, "I am for no compromise which assists or permits the extension of the institution on soil owned by the nation," and, about the same time, sat down to the composition of his inaugural, the tone of which hardly echoed that of Seward's oration.

Chase, a future colleague, paid the speech a characteristically doubtful compliment: it was "not so wrong as I feared . . . not so good as I hoped." The Republican members of Congress almost unanimously condemned the Seward program, and were barely restrained from calling a caucus and passing resolutions repudiating its proposals, while elections presently held in New England and Ohio showed decreased Republican majorities – a loss generally attributed to a belief that the leaders of the party were surrendering to the South. Perhaps James Buchanan, in the apology for a misspent Presidency which he began writing on retirement, expressed as well as anybody the essential quality of Seward's forensics, on this and other occasions: "Without strong

[1] Pierce, Edward L., *Memoir and Letters of Charles Sumner*. Roberts Bros., 1877–1893. IV, 9.

convictions he understood the art of preparing in his closet and uttering before the public antithetical sentences well calculated to influence the ardor of his anti-slavery friends and to exasperate his pro-slavery opponents." But criticism fell upon Seward from a source that probably cut deeper than that of these political friends and foes. His wife did not like his speech and wrote more than once telling him so. Mrs. Seward, as ever profoundly moved by slavery, watched the progress of affairs with concern and emotion. Weed's editorials proposing a new Missouri Compromise had already disturbed her, and Seward's assurances that "you need not expect, or rather fear, that I will act unwisely or wrong" did not carry conviction. "I am not surprised you do not like the 'concessions' of my speech," Seward wrote his wife, January 18. "You will soon enough come to see that they are not compromises, but explanations." One of the "concessions" Mrs. Seward did not like was the proposal, soon framed in a definite bill, to admit New Mexico – which territory then included Arizona – as a slave state. "Three thousand square miles of God's earth," Mrs. Seward protested to her "Henry," "is a high price for the questionable advantage of a Union with the slave states." Seward kept insisting that he was no compromiser, that he could not "compromise a principle," but the person who knew him most intimately remained unpersuaded and disconsolate.

Seward himself, however, regarded this speech as having historic importance; it was a powerful influence, he thought, in tranquilizing public excitement and "saving the Union," in that dangerous interim extending from late December until inauguration. His son Frederick relates that, in all his father's letters and conversation during this period, the same expression constantly recurred: "The Government can be saved, if not betrayed before the Fourth of March." [2] At other times Seward described himself as a bridge builder, engaged in guiding public affairs so that the gulf stretching between these two fateful dates could be safely spanned. Certain historians have estimated highly his services in this interval. Henry and Charles Francis Adams, sons of Seward's minister to Great Britain, always insisted that their favorite statesman saved the nation from dissolution in these three months, and gave him credit for handing to Lincoln, on his assumption of power, a country still at peace. Perhaps the most graphic view, if not the most accurate one, of Washington in the last days of Buchanan can be obtained from the writings of Henry Adams – the *Letters*, the *Education*, and especially a brochure, *The Secession Winter, 1861–62*, written at the time,

[2] Seward's *Seward*. II, 501.

but not published until 1910.[3] Certainly no one has given a more lively picture of Seward the man than Adams, in his *Education:* "A slouching, slender figure; a head like a wise macaw's; a beaked nose; shaggy eyebrows; unorderly hair and clothes; hoarse voice; offhand manner; free talk and perpetual cigar – offered a new type – of western New York – to fathom; a type in one way simple because it was only double – political and personal; but complex because the political had become nature, and no one could tell which was the mask and which the features. At table, among friends, Mr. Seward threw off restraint, or seemed to throw it off in reality, while in the world he threw it off like a politician for effect. In both cases he chose to appear as a free talker, who loathed pomposity and enjoyed a joke; but how much was nature and how much was mask, he was himself too simple a nature to know. Underneath the surface he was conventional after the conventions of western New York and Albany. Politicians thought it unconventionality. Bostonians thought it provincial. Henry Adams thought it charming." [4]

Seward, a constant diner at the Adams board, indeed almost a member of the family, appears in his several guises in the Adams letters of the period. "Seward is great, a perfect giant in his howling"; the "wily old scarecrow" insinuates his advice, "talks slowly and watches one so hard, under those grey eyebrows of his"; he "sprawls about and snorts and belches and does all sorts of outrageous things" – such as removing his boots in the parlor, to dry his feet before the fire, undeterred by the presence of his hostess; or consuming the Adams superfine cigars in vast aureoles of smoke, and stuffing his pockets with them as he leaves the house; or patting the grandiose Mrs. Charles Francis Adams on the head, like a little girl – "from any other man this would make our dear mother furious, but he is so hopelessly lawless that she submits and feels rather flattered." It is an unforgettable picture capped by the young man's conclusion that "I have excited immense delight among some young ladies here by a very brilliant proposition which I made, to dye the old sinner's hair bright crimson, paint his face the most brilliant green, his nose yellow and then to make an exhibition of him as the sage parrot; a bird he wonderfully resembles in manner and profile." [5] But the chief impression gained from these glimpses of what

[3] In Proceedings of the Massachusetts Historical Society. XLIII, 655.

[4] Adams, Henry, *The Education of Henry Adams*. Houghton Mifflin Co., 1918. P. 104. The selections from this book are used by permission of the publishers, Houghton Mifflin Company.

[5] Adams, Henry, *Letters of Henry Adams*, 1858–1891. Ed. Worthington Chauncey Ford. Houghton Mifflin Co., 1930. Ch. 11.

many regarded as the leading statesman of his time is that of lightheartedness and gaiety. Though most contemporaries stressed the tragic aspects of the hour, young Henry Adams portrayed a man undisturbed, almost unconcerned, by the national danger, completely satisfied with the state of affairs and apparently troubled by no doubts concerning the outcome. At one of Seward's own dinner parties – apparently in early December, 1860, on the eve of the Charleston secession – the host presented a picture far from despair. Reinforced by a superior champagne, he "was chipper as a lark and swore by yea and nay that everything was going on admirably." Senator Anthony of Rhode Island remarked, "Things look pretty bad, Governor, don't you think so?" "No," growled Seward, "I don't see why they look bad." Seward at whist; Seward playing with the children; Seward sipping the Moselle of Baron Gerolt, the Russian Minister, "and we managed to be pretty jolly"; Seward entertaining everybody with a discourse on good clothes, especially amusing because his own were always so ill-fitting and unkempt; Seward convulsing the whole table with his stories, and then entrancing all present with his conversation – "I sat and watched the old fellow with his big nose and his wire hair and grizzly eyebrows and miserable dress, and listened to him rolling out his grand, broad ideas that would inspire a crow with statesmanship if she understood our language" – the picture is not that of a man overburdened by a chaotic, dissolving nation. Perhaps this was the "mask" that Seward assumed, or perhaps he was not confiding his inmost secrets to a young man of twenty-three, recently out of Harvard. Not improbably, Seward looked upon this attitude of optimism and nonchalance as the proper one to assume; it was part of the essential stage business of a prospective Secretary of State whose duty it would be to harmonize the contending sections. Seward showed the same outward aspect on other occasions. His toast at a dinner given this winter by Stephen A. Douglas to the French Minister – "Away with all parties, all platforms of previous committals and whatever else will stand in the way of a restoration of the American Union" – would have shocked Lincoln, had it been reported to him.

Yet that Seward was the "ruler" of the nation in the three months preceding inauguration not only young Adams, but his more experienced father, believed. The younger man wrote of Seward's "reign" of two months and of the "triumph of his dictatorship." Both these appraisals lacked specific details, and certain historians accepting them have similarly failed to make out a clear, consecutive story. No period in our history, indeed, seems more confused than that from the secession of South Carolina to the inauguration of Abraham Lincoln. There will be no attempt in the present instance to explore the long, involved situation again. So far as Seward's policy was concerned – of offering concessions, even extreme ones, to the Border states, and in that way keeping them in the Union, and using them as agents for persuading the lower South to see its mistake, and ultimately come back under the old flag – nothing, it is now understood, could have been more fallacious. If any good came from these efforts, it is that they may have caused hesitation and delay in such regions as Virginia and North Carolina, and thus tended to postpone hostilities before the Lincolnian advent. Had war broken out when Buchanan was in the White House – and this might have taken place, except for the hopes held out to the Border states of a satisfactory compromise – the result might have been deplorable. So far as Seward's speeches and acts in these two months helped to delay the crisis, and thus insured the setting up of a new regime, they served a genuine public end.

The famous Peace Convention of Virginia, for example, seems to have been called on Seward's prompting. Most of the states still in the Union sent delegates, but none of the states already in the Confederacy were represented; it met in Washington early in February and remained intermittently in session for three weeks. It offered no practical plan for reuniting the severed Union; all it could do was to propose again the Crittenden Compromise, with its extension of the Missouri line. But the convention may have served a valuable purpose in preventing the secession of Virginia and certain sister Border states until Lincoln had been solidly seated in power. In mature life, Charles Francis Adams, Jr., in a more accurate summary of Seward's services than the contemporary estimate of his father, and his brother Henry, said Seward "had formulated a policy based on the careful avoidance of collision and bloodshed until there had been ample time allowed for reflection and the saving second thought. The course of subsequent events showed that he was wholly wrong in basing any hopes on this misconception of the real attitude and feelings of the South; but, on the other hand, they also showed that the day of compromise was over, and that the attitude of conciliation, while it might gain valuable time, endangered nothing."[6] Seward, said the younger Charles Francis, was dwelling in his " 'Southern-Unionist' dreamland" – an experience that produced little of value in settling the question, but did have considerable value in keeping the government intact until the fourth of March.

That Sunday, February 24, the day following Lincoln's arrival in

[6] Adams, Charles Francis, *Autobiography*. Houghton Mifflin Co., 1916. P. 74. The selections from this book are used by permission of the publishers, Houghton Mifflin Company.

Washington, proved to be an engrossing one for the prospective Secretary of State. Lincoln had given Seward a copy of his inaugural soon after reaching the Capital. Secluded in his library for the greater part of the day, Seward went over the document line by line and word for word, jotting memoranda in the margin, here and there excising a phrase and substituting one of his own, finally writing a long letter to his future chief proposing many changes, and giving reasons for each suggestion. That Seward approached this task with trepidation was not surprising. Lincoln, he knew, differed diametrically from him on vital questions. In impromptu speeches on his long progress to Washington, the new leader had uttered certain sentences, even paragraphs, that offered little encouragement to that policy of extreme appeasement on which Seward had set his heart. For certain passages in the inaugural, therefore, the Secretary-to-be was well prepared, but the document as a whole lifted a great weight from his mind. A week afterwards, on another Sunday, March 3, the day before inauguration, Charles Francis Adams, the younger, dined at Seward's house in company with a number of Auburn friends. "He was comparatively quiet, and seemed less exuberant than usual; but almost the only thing he did say caused with me a long breath of relief. Referring to the coming inaugural, he remarked that he had been reading it, and that while it would satisfy the whole country, it more than covered all of his heresies." [7] Apparently Seward did not confide to his guests the chief reason for contentment. He had proposed many changes, most of them trivial, one or two of considerable importance, and Lincoln, in a friendly spirit of co-operation, had adopted a good many of his emendations.

Most of them, as he wrote Lincoln that evening of February 24, had "little importance severally," but were intended "in their general effect to soothe the public mind." Sometimes he offered a gentler word in place of Lincoln's more downright one, occasionally he gave a little easier variation to one of the President's more direct statements. Thus at the beginning Lincoln had referred to his fifteen distinguished predecessors in the Presidency who had conducted the government "on the whole, with great success." Seward's innocuous proposal that "generally" be substituted for "on the whole" Lincoln cheerfully accepted. "A disruption of the Federal government," the original address read, "is menaced, and, so far as it can be on paper, is already effected," but this plain statement of a most evident fact was changed to Seward's softer – but not so accurate – phrase: "A disruption of the Federal Union, heretofore only menaced, is now formidably attempted." If the states, one by one, could destroy the Federal Union, wrote Lincoln

[7] Adams, Charles Francis, *op. cit.* P. 95.

in his original draft, "the Union is less perfect than before, which contradicts the Constitution and therefore is absurd." That "absurd" rather startled the cautious Auburn statesman, and Lincoln, in deference to his protest, struck out the offending syllables. One clause of that Federal Constitution which Lincoln had kept close at hand while penning his address, and which he took with the utmost seriousness, was that the President "shall take care that the laws be faithfully executed." He incorporated this familiar quotation in his inaugural, thus plainly intimating an intention of living up to the obligation. Seward desired that the new President should point out that that duty was "expressly enjoined upon me" by the Constitution, and so it stands in the famous document today. When Lincoln declared that "there are persons who seek to destroy the Union," Seward asked him to add, "I am sure they must be few in number and of little influence when their pernicious principles are understood," but Lincoln refused to add a clause which was utterly at variance with the facts. "My countrymen, take time and think well on this subject," the original inaugural admonished the American people, facing a great disaster; "think calmly and think well," Seward amended: and Lincoln compromised on "think calmly and well."

Revised readings like these, of which there were many, signified little, but one passage fairly brought Seward to his feet. "All the power at my disposal will be used to reclaim the public property and places which have fallen; to hold, occupy and possess these and all other property and places belonging to the Government and to collect the duties and imposts; but beyond what may be necessary for these objects, there will be no invasion of any state." Up to this time seven states, in seceding from the Union, had seized all the customhouses, mints, arsenals, and forts within their boundaries; only Fort Sumter, in Charleston Harbor, Fort Pickens in Pensacola, Fort Taylor at Key West, and Fort Jefferson in the Dry Tortugas remained in the hands of the Federal government. These "places" could not be "reclaimed" except by force of arms; and such action meant war. This paragraph, Seward perceived, immediately destroyed his policy; it was little less than a presidential proclamation in an inaugural address, that he intended to resort to military pressure and bloodshed to bring the South to terms. Seward ran his pen through the alarming paragraph, and wrote one of his own – long, rambling in thought, almost meaningless in its qualifications – which he asked Lincoln to substitute. As a piece of English and as a piece of shuffling sophistry, it was Seward at his worst and Lincoln did not accept the two-faced disquisition.

Lincoln had shown the address to a friend of many years' standing,

Judge Orville H. Browning, for whose judicial discretion he probably entertained a higher regard than for Seward's. Judge Browning had also thought the passage little less than dynamite. The policy itself Browning approved, but this bold announcement in an inaugural struck him as unnecessary and unwise. All efforts were then being made to keep Virginia and the other Middle and Border states in the Union; and would not this "threat or menace," as Browning characterized it, be inexpedient in view of that attempt? He suggested that the sentence be changed to read: "All the power at my disposal will be used to hold, occupy, and possess the property and places belonging to the government and to collect the duties and imposts, etc." The suggested change was a radical one. Instead of informing the South that the new President intended to move an army into the Confederacy to "retake" Federal property already seized, Judge Browning's revision merely announced the intention to "hold" or "occupy" the forts that were still flying the Stars and Stripes – Forts Sumter, Taylor, Jefferson, and Pickens. Of course Lincoln, although he acquiesced in the Browning phraseology, did not intend to change his real purpose; but, not wishing to put any obstacles in the way of those still laboring for a peaceful settlement, he temporarily refrained from issuing what was little less than defiance.

From the same motive Lincoln adopted a vital request of his conciliatory Secretary of State. At the beginning of the original inaugural Lincoln had said that he would follow the declaration of the Chicago platform, upon which he had been elected. "By no other course could I meet the reasonable expectations of this country." For several months an influential section of the party, led by Weed and by Seward himself, had been urging Lincoln to abandon the Chicago platform and champion a program directly opposed to it. The Chicago platform – it may be repeated – had declared in effect that there should be no further encroachment of slavery in the territories – that is, that no more slave states should be added to the Union. Lincoln, on March 4, as well as on the day of his nomination, was "inflexible" on this point. As Seward read this reiteration in the inaugural, all his hopes of compromise seemed to have been pulled from under him. "I declare to you my conviction," he now wrote Lincoln, "that the second and third paragraphs, even if modified as I propose in my amendments, will give such advantage to the Disunionists that Virginia and Maryland will secede, and we shall within ninety, perhaps within sixty days, be obliged to fight the South for this capital, with a divided North for our reliance, and we shall not have one loyal magistrate or ministerial officer South of the Potomac. In that case, the dismemberment of the Republic would date from the inauguration of a Republican administration. I therefore most respectfully counsel the omission of these paragraphs." Again Lincoln excised the passage. But not for a moment had he abandoned his determination to shape his presidential course on the Chicago platform.

In the change Seward proposed for concluding the inaugural, he proved supremely happy. Lincoln's final paragraph has been quoted on a preceding page – the one in which he informed his "dissatisfied friends" that, come what might, he intended to enforce the Constitution and defend the Union, and that with the Secessionists lay the choice of "peace or the sword." To Seward the words sounded too much like a gauntlet thrown down to the South. The inaugural, he believed, should end on a note of fraternal affection, not of defiance. "The argument is strong and conclusive," he wrote Lincoln, "and ought not to be in any way abridged or modified. But something besides or in addition to argument is needful – to meet and remove prejudice and passion in the South and despondency and fear in the East. Some words of affection – some of calm and cheerful confidence." He submitted two paragraphs as containing at least a suggestion of what he had in mind. One was platitudinous and badly expressed, but the other had a finer quality. Why not conclude the inaugural somewhat in this fashion? "I close. We are not, we must not be, aliens or enemies, but fellow countrymen and brethren. Although passion has strained our bonds of affection too hardly, they must not, I am sure they will not, be broken. The mystic chords which, proceeding from so many battlefields and so many patriot graves, pass through all the hearts and all hearths in this broad continent of ours, will yet again harmonize in their ancient music when breathed upon by the guardian angel of the nation." Lincoln's quick literary sense leaped upon this paragraph, but also perceived that it could be improved. When it had passed through his more sensitive mind, it emerged as follows: "I am loath to close. We are not enemies, but friends. We must not be enemies. Though passion may have strained, it must not break our bonds of affection. The mystic chords of memory, stretching from every battlefield and patriot grave, to every living heart and hearthstone, all over this broad land, will yet swell the chorus of the Union, when again touched, as they surely will be, by the better angels of our nature."

Though the Lincolnian touch gave the lines a gentle dignity that Seward's version lacked, it must be granted that the New Yorker was more than half the author of one of the most admired passages in Lincoln literature. If the collaboration of President and "Premier" could produce such brilliant and harmonious results as this, the outcome for the future looked bright indeed.

IV

MAJOR ANDERSON'S message to General Scott was not the only pressing business forced on the administration at this time. On February 28, Jefferson Davis appointed a commission of three men, Martin J. Crawford of Georgia, John Forsyth of South Carolina, and André B. Roman, ex-governor of Louisiana, to come to Washington as "ambassadors" and settle questions arising out of the division of the one-time Federal Union into two parts. Mr. Crawford, the head of this delegation, reached the Capital on March 3, and, not waiting for the arrival of his associates – who, however, in due course appeared – applied to the new Secretary of State for an official reception, at which he could present his "credentials" and enter upon the business of the embassy. This business, the State Department was informed, comprised "the speedy adjustment of all the questions growing out of separation, as the respective interests, geographical contiguity and future welfare of the two nations may render necessary." Naturally the part in this letter that made Seward pause was the reference to "two nations." The Confederate States, assuming that they comprised a sovereignty as independent as Great Britain or France, had sent a commission to that foreign power, the United States of America, to set up the relations that commonly existed between civilized countries.

Mr. Jefferson Davis's appointees were instructed to demand from Washington recognition to negotiate treaties of amity and commerce, and to determine certain pressing questions. The mere fact that the two republics had spent the preceding seventy years as one government now presented the "two nations" with many knotty problems to disentangle. Together they had accumulated a national debt; how was that to be apportioned? Together they had acquired a vast territorial domain; inevitably the Confederacy would assert a right to a good-sized portion of this. Just how was this rich country west of the Mississippi to be divided? The cotton states, in secession, had seized great quantities of property belonging to the Federal Union; Washington still held certain "places" which were now included within the limits of the Confederate States; clearly – such was the Confederate view – the adjustment of final ownership called for negotiation. That the solution of the many questions proposed would be difficult – assuming that Lincoln and Seward would consent to treat with the Confederate "ambassadors" – appeared on the surface. Almost every one of the points in dispute – and many more that would arise – involved the possibility of war. Indeed, had the envoys been accredited and discussion begun, the impossibility of severing the ligament that bound these disharmonious Siamese twins would in itself have presented an unanswerable argument for Union.

The complacent pretension, in the letter to Mr. Seward, that North and South constituted "two nations" aroused popular wrath. With one bland parenthetical movement of the pen, the all-important point in the pending argument was thus swept aside. The North had steadily denied that the Constitution was a loose compact from which any state could withdraw at will, and rested its whole case upon the assertion that it formed "an indissoluble Union of indissoluble states" – that is, that secession was unconstitutional. If that principle were justified, the Confederacy did not form a separate "nation"; and if not, then its claim to independent sovereignty must be allowed and diplomatic relations established with the North. If, however, this thesis were granted, all the excitement of the preceding months was mere sound and fury. Should the Lincoln administration receive these "ambassadors," it would abandon the constitutional ground on which its whole policy depended. In the eyes of the Federal government, the recent gathering at Montgomery, resulting in the formation of the so-called Confederate States, merely represented the proceedings of disorderly private persons engaged in "rebellion"; and to those who held this view the appearance of certain emissaries in Washington, insisting on negotiations with their lawful sovereign, amounted to monstrous impudence. Imagine, it was urged, that, after the signing of the Declaration of Independence, a trio of gentlemen from Philadelphia had arrived in London, representing a new "nation" overseas, and had demanded an audience of King George to obtain recognition and negotiate treaties; what would have been their fate? They would have been thrown into the Tower, and there kept in durance awaiting trial on a charge of treason. Many fiery spirits north of the Potomac demanded that Mr. Crawford and his companions should be treated in this fashion. On March 16 another pseudo-diplomatic mission from the Confederacy, consisting of Yancey, Rost, and Mann, had been dispatched to London on essentially the same errand entrusted to the Confederate commissioners in Washington. Seward had written the American Minister instructing him to sever diplomatic relations with the Queen if this Confederate embassy were officially received. Could it be expected that the same Secretary who was to take this attitude on the matter of Confederate "ambassadors" at a foreign court could consistently have dealings with a commission engaged in an identical enterprise in his own country?

The flexibility of Seward's methods – his native tendency to opportunism in meeting drastic situations – is illustrated again in his treatment of the Crawford mission. The Secretary of State never received these deputies, even unofficially, never extended to them anything suggesting recognition, yet he did enter into negotiations with them through third parties and did seek to use them in furtherance of his conciliatory policy. Nor was this the first time that he had shown a negotiating spirit towards Southern commissioners sent to Washington. A previous delegation from South Carolina, headed by John L. Orr, arrived in the Federal Capital in late December, 1860, to settle certain questions rising out of the recent secession of that state. The great problem, then, as it remained for several months afterward, was the retention in Federal hands of the forts of Charleston Harbor, especially Moultrie and Sumter. On Christmas evening, Major Robert Anderson, in command of Federal forces at Charleston, feeling insecure in his position in Fort Moultrie, secretly moved his forces into the far stronger Fort Sumter, an act that instantaneously made him a hero in the Northern states. The rejoicing that followed in the North, the great acclaim his farsightedness and bravery brought to Major Anderson, is a long familiar story. There was one citizen, however, who did not take part in this patriotic outburst. Seward, not yet Secretary of State, though already designated for that post, was appalled at a daring step which seemed to him to destroy his whole policy. Naturally the South Carolina commissioners took the same stand, and brought pressure to bear upon President Buchanan to undo that act of Major Anderson which had made his name resound all over the country. If the *Diary of a Public Man* can be credited – and corroborative evidence from other sources exists – Seward sympathized with this effort. Mr. Orr discussed the matter with Seward on December 28; the Senator agreed with the South Carolinian that Major Anderson's movement had been "most unfortunate" and discussed a plan according to which that hardy cavalier might be ordered to return to Fort Moultrie. This plan was the occupation of Fort Sumter by forces neither of South Carolina nor of the Federal government, and its segregation as a kind of no-man's land until differences between the two sections should be placed on a more satisfactory basis.

Perhaps these discussions with the South Carolina diplomat in late December and early January involved no impropriety, for the Buchanan administration still had charge of public affairs, and Seward, of course, had no official responsibility. Such importance as he held in the eyes of the South Carolinian was derived from his position as a distinguished Republican Senator, and as "Premier" in the approaching administration. In March, however, Seward's status was very different. He was now Secretary of State; any dealings he might have with "rebel emissaries" therefore would commit the Lincoln government. Clearly he could not receive the Crawford Commission, or negotiate with it directly or indirectly; even an "unofficial" reception – such as the one interview which Lord John Russell in England had given Yancey and Mann – would not accord with the dignity of the United States. Though outwardly Seward observed the proprieties, the evidence is clear enough that he personally yearned to make use of these Southern envoys. So scrupulous was the Secretary in observing an official restraint that Mr. Crawford's letter, asking for an appointment at the State Department, was not even acknowledged; to enter into correspondence with these self-styled ministers, even to the extent of refusing an audience, would, in Seward's punctilious eyes, have had a taint of recognition.

Yet the facts disclose that this careful attention to the proprieties did not represent the Secretary's personal attitude. This was evident in a conversation with Senator R. M. T. Hunter, on March 11. Hunter, for years Senator from Virginia, afterward Secretary of State for the Confederacy, and as strong a secessionist in this March of 1861 as James M. Mason himself, had called in an effort to persuade the government to communicate in some way with Mr. Crawford. Seward, as Hunter afterward said, seemed unhappy and embarrassed; he gave his erstwhile senatorial colleague no definite reply, saying that he could do nothing without consulting the President. Whether this was merely Seward's method of avoiding a direct commitment, or whether he entertained some hope that Lincoln might give his assent, cannot be said; if the latter were the case, the Secretary received a decided veto from the White House. Next day he informed Hunter – in most courteous terms – that the request for an interview could not be granted. When, a few days afterward, Judge John A. Campbell of Alabama, then a member of the United States Supreme Court, made the same plea for a reception, Seward said flatly: "I wish I could do it. See Montgomery Blair, see Mr. Bates, see Mr. Lincoln himself! I wish you would; they are all Southern men; convince them! No, there is not a member of the cabinet who would consent to it."

An even more positive evidence of Seward's real desire appears in the account of a meeting with the Russian Minister, Baron Stoeckl, as reported by A. B. Roman, in his official dispatch to Robert Toombs, Confederate Secretary of State. In this conversation Seward evidently laid bare his deepest soul. The Russian Minister was one of Seward's closest friends in Washington; he was also personally devoted to the Federal cause, so that the Secretary of State evidently felt free to unburden himself. No coercion, Seward told Baron Stoeckl, would be resorted to against the Confederate States. Lincoln, in his inaugural, had discussed the question of collecting Federal customs dues at Southern seceded ports; though the President announced his determination to make such collections, Seward, in this informal talk with a foreign envoy, said that the seceded states would be permitted to collect the dues themselves. Seward, Baron Stoeckl reported to Mr. Roman, hoped and believed that the cotton states, if treated with consideration, would ultimately return to their old allegiance; if not, they would not be forced, but permitted to depart in peace. In his struggle for accommodation, Seward said he had to fight the "ultra-Republicans" – meaning, by that term, those who still stood by the Chicago platform – but he was gaining ground and his policy would prevail. And then came the somewhat wearied and discouraged Secretary's astonishing proposal: could not the Russian Minister arrange a meeting between himself and Mr. Roman at the Russian Legation? Two evenings later he might casually drop in for a cup of tea; perhaps the Confederate commissioner would do the same, and, if they should thus meet accidentally, opportunity would be offered for a friendly chat. Naturally, Roman wrote Toombs, he gladly fell in with this suggestion. But next day Seward sent his regrets. After all, the consultation would involve dangers; the newspapers might learn that the Secretary of State and the "rebel" commissioner had met and the scandal would injure the cause. The fact that Horace Greeley, Seward's inveterate enemy, had just arrived in Washington perhaps had something to do with this abrupt change of plan. Such a confabulation would certainly have made startling news in the *New York Tribune*, and the excitement aroused in the "ultra-Republican" camp could only be faintly imagined.

Another reason for breaking the appointment was that no need for a private discussion between Seward and one of the Confederate ambassadors existed even at a surreptitious tea party, for the Secretary, at this very moment, was negotiating with all three through other men. The one point on which that commission showed irreconcilable persistence was the situation in Charleston Harbor. Fort Sumter had by this time assumed a symbolic importance far more significant than its value for strategic purposes. Standing as it did at the entrance to Charleston Harbor, occupied by a tiny and already hungry army of Federal troops, the South regarded it as little less than an insult. So long as Lincoln held this battlement, situated in the heart of the Confederacy, its claims to being an independent "nation" seemed absurd. Its possession was essential to complete the work of the Montgomery Convocation. In the same sense it was a symbol to the North; to hold this fort was notification to the "rebels" that they were engaged, not in nation-building, but in insurrection. Other "places," still in Federal hands, embodied the same issue. But Fort Jefferson, in the Dry Tortugas, and Fort Taylor, at Key West, were not practically so important; the Washington government retained these firmly, and there was no possibility of the Confederacy securing them, for they could be captured only by a naval force, which the Montgomery forces did not possess. Fort Pickens, on Santa Rosa Island, off Pensacola, Florida, the Southerners placed in the same class as Sumter. This stronghold was easier to defend than Sumter, and for that reason perhaps did not figure so largely in the discussions, but the Confederacy was just as determined to get Pickens as Sumter.

From the day of South Carolina's secession, Seward's attitude on the Sumter question had not been concealed. Its evacuation by Federal troops he thought necessary in the interest of conciliation. A kind of truce had existed between the South and the Buchanan administration on this point. Buchanan agreed, at least tacitly, not to reinforce or resupply the forts and the South agreed not to attack them. It was probably because Major Anderson's spectacular transference of his forces from Moultrie to Sumter, on Christmas, seemed to be a violation of this "truce" that Seward believed that his coup should be undone. In this Sumter and Pickens business the new President did not agree with his Secretary. Though Lincoln, in the pre-inauguration period, had not responded to the clamorous demand for a "statement" on general issues, he was willing to take a public position on the new issue created by the secession of South Carolina. In a letter to Lyman Trumbull, four days after that event, he wrote: "Despatches have come here two days in succession, that the Forts in South Carolina will be surrendered by the order, or consent at least, of the President [Buchanan]. I can scarcely believe this; but if it prove true, I will, if our friends at Washington concur, announce publicly at once that these are to be retaken after the inauguration." [1] At about the same time

[1] Tracy, Gilbert A., Ed., *Uncollected Letters of Abraham Lincoln.* Houghton Mifflin Co., 1917. P. 173. The selections from this book are used by permission of the publishers, Houghton Mifflin Company.

he wrote to David Hunter: "If the forts fall my judgment is that they should be retaken." That this determination was not a temporary one, caused by the prevailing excitement, is evident from Lincoln's announced intention to "reclaim the public property and places which have fallen." In making the evacuation of Sumter – and probably of Pickens also, though the evidence on this latter point is not so clear – the cardinal point of his conciliatory program, Seward was thus taking a stand directly opposed to that of his chief.

Nor did Seward stand alone. The entire cabinet, on March 15, with the exception of Montgomery Blair and possibly Chase, opposed any attempt to reinforce, or even to resupply, the ominous "Gibraltar" at the entrance to Charleston Harbor. At that time it was known that Major Anderson could hold out only two weeks longer; his food was running low, and starvation itself would soon compel a surrender. On March 15, therefore, Lincoln submitted the following question to his cabinet: "Assuming it to be possible to now provision Fort Sumter, under all the circumstances is it wise to attempt it? Please give me your opinion in writing on this question." Seward's reply, sent to the President on March 16, was the longest and most detailed of the seven submitted. The answer was an emphatic negative. The Secretary of State declared himself in favor of evacuating Sumter, and surrendering it to the Confederate authorities, at the earliest possible moment. "If it were possible to peacefully provision Fort Sumter," Seward wrote, "I should answer that it would be both unwise and inhuman not to attempt it." That is, if food boats could be quietly moved to the docks, and supplies unloaded for a garrison that was nearing starvation, without any interference from the Confederate armies that were now beleaguring the fortress, the Secretary was willing that the provisioning take place. Everybody knew, however, that such orderly relief would be impossible. Any expedition to Sumter, even one attempting merely to land food supplies, would be regarded by the South as a hostile act. Armed forces, both military and naval, would be needed to effect a landing. A clash of arms and the shedding of fraternal blood would follow, and this would be the first blow in a long and terrible civil war. Seward rehearsed again all his arguments for appeasement. The secession of seven states and the organization of a Confederate government were brushed aside as a "temporary" excitement, a disturbance that had arisen merely "out of a simple and harmless disappointment in a Presidential election." Again Seward expressed his confidence in an unquenchable loyalty to the Union in the Southern states. Even in South Carolina itself "devotion to the Union is a profound and permanent national sentiment." Again the influence of the Border states, in bringing their sister communities back to their national fealty, received its by now time-honored emphasis. If the Federal government should show patience in face of the appalling crisis "we should have the spirit of the country and the approval of mankind upon our side. In the other, we should imperil peace and union, because we had not the courage to practice prudence and moderation at the cost of temporary misapprehension. If this counsel seems to be impassive and even unpatriotic, I console myself by the reflection that it is such as Chatham gave to his country under circumstances not widely different." [2]

Four other cabinet members – Cameron, Welles, Bates, and Smith – cast their votes on Seward's side, though not all for the same reasons. Chase and Blair were in favor of making the attempt. Chase's written opinion illustrated again the man's tendency to hedge. "If the attempt will so inflame civil war as to involve an immediate necessity for the enlistment of armies and the expenditure of millions" he would not favor it; but as such an outcome was "highly improbable" he was in favor of dispatching food supplies to the hungry soldiers. The only straightforward and unconditional statement in favor of an immediate expedition came from Montgomery Blair. In several ways Blair had a better right to speak with authority on this subject than any of his colleagues. He was himself of a Southern family and had a clearer insight into Southern ambitions and the Southern temperament than any man surrounding Lincoln. He himself had started life under the tutelage of Andrew Jackson, historic foe of such subversive movements as this Southern Confederacy. His father – old man Blair – still alive and an absorbed watcher of events from his retreat at Silver Spring – had stood at Jackson's elbow in 1832 when this same South Carolina had made its first attempt to lead the slave states in rebellion. If there were any principles for which the Blair family stood they were anti-Nullification and anti-Secession. Moreover, the family in this very March of 1861 was rendering services to the Union cause that in themselves justified Lincoln's determination to include one of the Blairs in his cabinet.

In Missouri, Frank Blair, Montgomery's brother, was showing that at least one Border state could stand firmly for the Union – and showing it not by argument or appeasement diplomacy, but by sledgehammer action. Few slave states were more important to the Union cause than Missouri. Its loss would not only exert strong influence upon the Border commonwealths, such as Kentucky, Tennessee, and Arkansas, but would have weakened the North in a military sense, for it commanded a long stretch of the Mississippi River and furnished the

[2] For opinions of the cabinet members see Lincoln, *op. cit.* VI, 192–220.

main gateway to the Northwest – a vast reservoir of supplies. Despite the fact that the state had been settled largely from the South, events soon disclosed that the people of Missouri were overwhelmingly Unionist in sympathy. But the politicians controlling the Democratic legislature, headed by a recently elected governor, Claiborne Jackson, were determined to carry Missouri into the Confederacy. Even after a convention, called to determine Missouri's course, had overwhelmingly voted against secession, the Southern sympathizers persisted in their secession campaign. In this tense situation Frank Blair became the leader of the Union forces. His judgment on the nature of the impending conflict differed greatly from the hesitations that clouded many minds. "It is useless," he said, "to talk further about Compromise. It is useless to expect anything from the Border slave states, the Peace Convention, or the Crittenden Compromise. I think I know the sentiments and intentions of the pro-slavery leaders. The condition means war, and nothing but war, fierce and desperate war. We might all just as well understand it and prepare accordingly; our safety is to organize and drill our people as soldiers, and the sooner we go about it the better." He suited his act to the word. The "Wide-Awakes" whom he had organized and directed in the Lincoln campaign were now called forth again and transformed into so-called Union clubs. On the surface merely patriotic organizations created to arouse enthusiasm for the Federal government, they were really military companies, regularly drilled and equipped with arms. Their business was to resist by force any efforts which the governor and his sympathizers might make to carry the state into the Confederacy – a duty which, under the skillful leadership of Frank Blair, they afterward brilliantly performed. All this preparation had preceded Lincoln's inauguration; but young Blair kept in close touch with the President-elect, who encouraged the far-sighted labors which, in April and May of '61, enabled Frank Blair to save Missouri for the Union.

Frank's brother Montgomery, in Lincoln's cabinet, entertained the same views as to the inevitable war, and from the first meeting of that body stiffened in opposition to Seward's peaceful plans. The choice of Blair, wrote the youthful Henry Adams, "was decisive of the policy of the government and the death blow to the policy of Mr. Seward." What a chasm of opinion separated the two men appeared in Montgomery's reply to the President's question on Fort Sumter. There was nothing ambiguous or halfhearted in this document; to the casuistry of Seward, the expediency of Cameron, and the hesitating assent of Chase, it stood out in brilliant contrast. Like his brother Frank in St. Louis, Montgomery immediately went to the heart of the discussion.

The Cotton South had decided on separation, even at the cost of civil war; the administration could commit no greater mistake than to display anything resembling a white feather in the face of this intention. This Southerner found the real seat of the trouble in the Southern character, and in its misapprehension of the quality of the Yankee. "The rebels," as he invariably called the secessionists, "for the most part believe that the northern men are deficient in the courage necessary to maintain the government. It is this prevalent opinion in the South which induces so large a portion of the people there to suspect the good faith of the people of the North and enable the demagogues so successfully to inculcate the notion that the object of the northern people is to abolish slavery and make the negroes the equal of the whites. Doubting the manhood of northern men, they discredit their disclaimers of this purpose to humiliate and injure them." This conviction, an abiding one with Blair, he had expressed even more strongly in a recent letter to his brother-in-law, Gustavus Vasa Fox. "The real cause of our trouble arises from the notion generally entertained at the South that the men of the North are inferiors and the rebellion springs altogether from pride which revolts from submission to supposed inferiors. You hear these blusterers say everywhere that one southern man is equal to half a dozen Yankees. They will not submit, they say, to mere numbers, made up of the mudsills, the factory people and shop keepers of the North. . . . And I really fear that nothing short of the lesson we had to give Mexico to teach the don better manners will ever satisfy the southern gascons that the people of the north are their equals even upon the field upon which they had now chosen to test the question."

The inaction of President Buchanan, Blair told Lincoln in this formal paper, had done much to substantiate this illusion. "To the connivance of the late administration it is due alone that this rebellion has been enabled to gain its present proportions." South Carolina had started a similar rebellion in 1833 and how had that been checked? It was ended by the promptitude of President Jackson "in taking measures which made it manifest that it could not be attempted with impunity. The action of the President in 1833 inspired respect, whilst in 1860 the rebels were encouraged by the contempt they felt for the incumbent of the presidency." To surrender Fort Sumter, wrote Blair, would be the surest way to provoke civil war. Such a surrender would "convince the rebels that the administration lacks firmness, and will, therefore, tend more than any event that has happened to embolden them; and so far from tending to prevent collision, will ensure it unless all other forts are evacuated and all attempts are given up to maintain the authority of the Union." If the expedition to provision Fort Sumter should succeed – and he thought this likely – that "would completely demoralize the rebellion"; if it should fail, "it will in any event vindicate the hardy courage of the North and the determination of the people and their President to maintain the authority of the government; and this is all that is wanting, in my opinion, to restore it."

That five of the seven cabinet members advised the evacuation of Fort Sumter – and that a sixth, Chase, stood on equivocal ground – naturally distressed Blair. After the cabinet meeting, he went for advice to the source of all wisdom, his father, Francis Preston, Sr. The veteran Kentuckian, at the moment sojourning in the Blair House on Pennsylvania Avenue, immediately crossed the street to the White House and found a somewhat wistful President sitting alone in the council room. His official advisers had left only a short time before, and Lincoln was still holding in his hands their written recommendations on the controverted question. Old man Blair and Lincoln had been excellent friends for years, and the elder statesman of the Jackson regime did not hesitate to express his views with the utmost candor. Had it been decided, he asked, to withdraw Major Anderson and his little force from Fort Sumter and thus surrender completely to the rebels? For Lincoln's reply to this pointed question there is only one authority, Samuel W. Crawford, the historian of Fort Sumter, who testified that he recorded it on the authority of Mr. Blair himself.[3] "The President said the matter had not yet been fully determined, but that the cabinet was almost a unit in favor of it, all except your son," and "that he thought this would be the result." The elder Blair insisted that the American people would not endorse such action, that it would destroy the Republican Party, and that impeachment would probably follow. This was rather high talking, and naturally this account of the interview, especially as it discloses Lincoln in a far from heroic mood, has not been accepted unquestioningly by all historians. As already intimated, no one can tell precisely what was the state of Lincoln's mind from March 5 when Major Anderson's telegram presented this issue in critical form, to the latter part of the same month when Lincoln definitely decided to disregard his cabinet, and make an attempt to relieve the fort. That at moments he showed outward signs of indecision may be true – something not strange, for on the word of one lonely man rested the most terrible decision, that of civil war, ever offered to an American statesman. The strongest man would have had periods of doubt when brought face to face with such a responsibility, and perhaps the elder Blair found Lincoln, with his cabinet almost

[3] Crawford, Samuel W., *The Genesis of the Civil War*. C. L. Webster and Company, 1887. P. 363.

unanimously in favor of what, in the eyes of posterity, seems a craven course, at one of these moments of hesitation. But it is not likely that an informal remark – even if the Crawford report is accurate – addressed in one of the tensest moments of his life to an excited caller, represented a matured presidential program. Even if Lincoln hesitated for a moment, the momentary emotion quickly passed, to give place to action of a decisive kind.

V

TWO OF THE most distinguished members of the United States Supreme Court at this time were Samuel Nelson of New York and John A. Campbell of Alabama. Though citizens of widely separated states, these two men had much in common. Both were strong Union men and both were opposed to secession. That Nelson, a Northern man, should entertain such convictions was natural enough, but Campbell suffered much odium in his native Alabama and indeed throughout the whole South for his loyalty – until the final break – to the Federal cause. Certain of Nelson's opinions made him a sympathetic co-worker with his Southern colleague. He believed that Lincoln's plan of collecting customs dues by force in Southern ports was unlawful and coercion of any kind against the Confederate States he disapproved. Not unfittingly, therefore, these two venerable members of the highest court in the land now became involved in one of the strangest diplomatic negotiations in American history.

Up to the present time, all efforts to obtain a reception for the Confederate commissioners, even an unofficial one, had failed. On March 15, the very day that Lincoln demanded written opinions from his cabinet members on Fort Sumter, these two Justices appeared in Seward's office, and made another plea for such a reception. That Seward personally was inclined to grant the request has already been made plain. That Lincoln and most of the cabinet would have opposed such a proceeding, the facts disclose. All that Seward could say to the Justices, therefore, was to explain his situation and repeat his refusal. The conversation would have ended at this point had not the Secretary, in the most offhand manner – whether accidentally or by design is a mystery – let fall a remark that completely changed the issue. Up to this meeting the only question that had been discussed was that of reception for the "ambassadors." Seward now dismissed this problem and raised another.

"If Jefferson Davis had known the state of things here," he said, "he would not have sent those commissioners. The evacuation of Sumter is as much as the Administration can bear."

Justice Campbell fairly jumped at this statement. Here was a clear-cut announcement, from the head man in Lincoln's cabinet, that Fort Sumter was to be evacuated. No official intimation to this effect had previously been forthcoming. That Seward would volunteer such a piece of news without authority from his chief naturally did not occur to this judicially minded man. Yet what basis the Secretary possessed for his disclosure has puzzled historians. Not a shred of evidence has ever been produced showing that Lincoln had communicated such a purpose to Seward; the facts, of course, are all of a contrary kind. It was not until the sixteenth of March, the day following this interview, that the cabinet opinions, five for evacuation, two against, were submitted to the President; this secret plebiscite, therefore, could not justify Seward's startling declaration. Moreover, Seward understood the Constitution well enough to know that such opinions were purely advisory and that the final act rested in the discretion of one man – the President. Naturally Justice Campbell seized with avidity Seward's remark. For two weeks the Southern commissioners, and those who had interfered in their behalf, had been snubbed by the Secretary of State. The evacuation of Fort Sumter had been one of the demands they had been directed to press. Toombs's official instruction had emphasized this capitulation as a *sine qua non* of any settlement with the North. And now the head of the State Department had informed Justice Campbell that this great decision had been made in favor of the Confederacy. Naturally, in view of this concession, other demands – such as the recognition of the Confederate government, the drawing up of treaties of amity and trade – could for the moment be suspended. The Southerners regarded the surrender of Sumter as in itself a recognition of Southern independence, as in reality, if not technically, it would have been.

Justice Campbell remarked that he was about to write a letter to Jefferson Davis.

"And what shall I say to him upon the subject of Fort Sumter?" he asked.

"You may say to him," replied Seward, "that before that letter reaches him – how far is it to Montgomery?"

"Three days."

"You may say to him that before that letter reaches him, the telegraph will have informed him that Sumter will have been evacuated."

"And what shall I say to him as to the forts in the Gulf of Mexico?"

Seward avoided this issue. "We contemplate no action," he replied, "as to these; we are satisfied as to the position of things there."

Though Seward and his defenders afterward maintained that this statement did not constitute a definite commitment, the documents in the case do not support this disclaimer. There is no need to rehearse again, in all its detail, the facts in a long familiar episode. Practically all historians who have done this agree with the conclusion of James Ford Rhodes that "the assurances to Campbell were simply those of an officious Secretary of State whose vanity had grown by what it fed on until now he deluded himself with the idea that he and not another was the executive of the nation."[1]

In all the discussions pro and con one fact stands out clearly: Justice Campbell transmitted to Crawford, head of the Southern commission, Seward's promise that Sumter would be given up in five days and that "no measure changing the existing status of things prejudicially to the Confederate states is at present contemplated by the administration" – an inclusive pledge that comprehended Pickens as well as Sumter. On March 15, the day the pledge was given, Justice Campbell wrote Seward informing him that he had sent this memorandum to Crawford, thus making Seward a party to the agreement. Seward gave this identical commitment not only once, but at least three times, for, after the five-day interval had expired and Major Anderson still continued to retain the rampart, Campbell visited Seward again and again was assured that the promise would be fulfilled. He did so a third time, on March 22, and a third time was assured that there had been no change in the Federal program of evacuation. Justice Campbell made a written record of this third conversation, and submitted this paper also to Seward before sending it to the Confederate authorities. Justice Nelson was present at these three interviews with Seward, was shown his associate's written accounts before they were passed on to Montgomery, and approved them as accurate. Not only do historians and biographers agree as to the definite character of Seward's pledge, but they are also a unit in the conviction that Lincoln was not consulted in the matter, and knew nothing of his Secretary's forwardness. Not until April 1 did the President obtain any inkling of Seward's negotiation. On that day Campbell made another call on the Secretary of State – Justice Nelson had by this time withdrawn from the situation and left Washington – and protested in urgent terms against the nonfulfillment of the pledge. Seward excused himself and withdrew to the White House, for a consultation with the President. On his return, he handed Campbell a paper on which he had written: "I am satisfied the Government will not undertake to supply Fort Sumter without giving notice to Governor Pickens" – Pickens, that is, the governor of South Carolina. This undertaking, evidently agreed to by Lincoln, was naturally something entirely different from the flat promise to evacuate to which Seward

[1] Rhodes, James Ford, *History of the United States*. Macmillan. III, 339.

had committed himself several times, and Campbell could only exclaim against what he regarded — and not unwarrantably — as a breach of faith.

Certain important events had taken place in the final days of March which had put an end to Seward's personal handling of the problem. Lincoln had never accepted Seward's belief that the South, even South Carolina, was fundamentally loyal to the Union cause. But he decided to put this question to a practical test — to discover by personal investigation whether the Palmetto State, if gently dealt with, would rescind its secession. He had sent his friend, S. A. Hurlburt, to Charleston, to examine the matter on the ground. Mr. Hurlburt was himself a Charlestonian by origin, and close friend of James L. Petigru, in some ways South Carolina's most distinguished citizen and an ardent champion of the Federal cause. Ward H. Lamon, another Lincoln intimate, and Gustavus Vasa Fox, afterward Assistant Secretary of the Navy, had gone to Charleston at about the same time on a similar mission. All three envoys had returned by March 29. Gustavus Fox reported that Major Anderson, with his present supplies of bread, beans, hardtack, and salt pork, could hold out not longer than two weeks. Mr. Hurlburt had had a long conference with James L. Petigru, in which that noble Roman declared that South Carolina, irrespective of any compromises or concessions, was determined on separation from the Federal government. "I am the only Unionist in the state," Mr. Petigru had declared over and over again. Ward Lamon gave identically the same report. Evidently Seward's belief that South Carolina and its sympathizing "wayward sisters" were ready, at the first sign, to return to the paternal roof had no basis. The political situation, as Petigru explained it to Lincoln's representative, was simplicity itself; his diagnosis agreed completely with that of the President and the Blairs. Only two choices were left to the Federal authorities: peaceable secession or war. Either Lincoln must agree to the permanent withdrawal of the South from the Union, or he must suppress the Confederacy by force.

On March 29, President and Mrs. Lincoln gave their first state dinner, attended by all members of the cabinet and their wives, as well as most members of the diplomatic corps. Readers of William Howard Russell's *Diary North and South* are familiar with this sumptuous event. The tart Englishman's not overeffusive references to Mrs. Lincoln; his honest admiration for the impressive personality of Secretary Chase — to say nothing of his "very agreeable, attractive and sprightly" daughter Kate; his lack of admiration for the great white beard and spectacles of Secretary of the Navy Welles, "who does not know the stem from the stern of a ship" and who had never seen the sea in his life — a strange remark to make of the son of a New England shipbuilder; his comments on the "long, lean, shambling" President, whose clothes reminded him of an "undertaker's uniform at a funeral" — all these and other details which make the chapter a journalistic classic are familiar enough to readers of Civil War literature. With all his ability as a reporter, however, Mr. Russell did not learn of the most important incident of this evening. He tried to draw Mr. Seward on the then pressing question of forts in Southern waters, but all the Secretary would confide was that the Sumter policy had been indicated in the President's inaugural and would be adhered to as there set down.

Naturally the representative of the London *Times* was not informed that the President had requested all members of the cabinet to remain after the others had departed and meet him in the council room. The presidential advisers found their usually self-possessed and good-natured chief in a state of considerable excitement. Lincoln held in his hands a paper the contents of which he read to his dinner companions. It was a communication from General Winfield Scott, General-in-Chief of the Army of the United States, in which that officer announced that the time had come to surrender both Fort Sumter and Fort Pickens. This advice was astonishing enough in itself; even more surprising were the reasons General Scott gave for his conclusion. The martial gentleman, going outside his province, rested his argument chiefly on political grounds. "It is doubtful whether the voluntary evacuation of Fort Sumter," he wrote, "alone would have a decisive effect upon the states now wavering between adherence to the Union and Secession. It is known, indeed, that it would be charged to necessity and the holding of Fort Pickens would be induced in support of that view. Our southern friends, however, are clear that the evacuation of both the Forts would instantly soothe and give confidence to the eight remaining slaveholding states and render their cordial adherence to the Union perpetual."

The words may have been the words of Scott, though even that is doubtful for he was notoriously unready with the pen; but the argument — now well worn — was certainly that of Seward. That word "soothe" had been the one constantly on Seward's lips all through the winter and spring. For the last three months the rheumatic and bulky figure of this ancient commander had lumbered in and out of the Washington crisis, always in neighborly association with William H. Seward. The two men had been cronies since 1852, when Scott, by one of those strange escapades of fate which not infrequently happen in American politics, had been nominated for President by the Whig Party, plunging that aggregation into an abyss from which it never lifted its head. Seward not only wrote Scott's speech of acceptance for him on that occasion, but remained his constant adviser throughout the campaign. For Scott's military talents and for his character as patriot – despite the fact that he was a Virginian he remained steadfastly loyal to the Union – the nation had respect; but for the General's pretensions to statesmanship – to which he was constantly giving expression – it entertained only ridicule. In the present impasse, Scott's military advice, as head of the American Army, was of course in order, but his insistence on basing this upon political considerations was not patiently endured. His views invariably echoed those of Seward and naturally he was looked upon as the Secretary's cat's paw. This proposal of evacuating both Sumter and Pickens sounded the lowest note in national humiliation that had been heard up to that time. To throw Sumter to the wolves would not be enough. That the South expected as a matter of course – its surrender would be no concession at all. A further pledge of Federal amity and noncombativeness would be needed to win Confederate affection. Therefore Pickens, which the Federal government strongly held and which could not be subdued by the tactics subsequently used against Sumter, must be added to the sacrificial altar.

It was to discuss this recommendation that Lincoln had summoned the banqueters from the state dining room. However bland Seward might appear on this critical evening, there were probably few of his colleagues who doubted that Scott's views on Sumter and Pickens had been inspired by the Secretary of State. Montgomery Blair, in the midnight cabinet meeting, could not restrain his indignation. He burst out in a violent tirade against Scott, accusing him of deserting his proper field. "Mr. President," said Blair on this occasion, "you can now see that General Scott, in advising the surrender of Fort Sumter, is playing the part of a politician, not of a general. No one pretends that there is any military necessity for the surrender of Fort Pickens, which he now says it is equally necessary to surrender. He is governed by political considerations in both recommendations."[2] In making these remarks on the general's motives, Blair kept his eyes fixed on Seward. He might as well have named "Seward" instead of Scott in his denunciation. All his colleagues – including Seward himself – knew who was the object of his wrath. Blair never concealed, then or afterward, his conviction that, in presenting this humiliating document to Lincoln, Scott was carrying out Seward's instructions.

The President requested his cabinet to assemble on the following day, March 29. At that council he held his second session on Sumter. This disclosed a striking change of opinion from the one that had been ex-

[2] Crawford, *op. cit.*, p. 363.

pressed just two weeks before. Every member, except Seward and Caleb Smith, now advised immediate relief. Probably the President's own attitude largely explains this change. It was apparent to all that the President's determination was fixed. Irrespective of anything his cabinet might say, Fort Sumter was to be relieved. The sole constitutional responsibility rested on the President, and he was ready to assume it. Seward, in his second written statement of his position, did not again rehearse the lengthy arguments of the earlier paper, but took the same ground. "The despatch of an expedition to supply or reinforce Fort Sumter would provoke an attack and so involve a war at that point. . . . I do not think it wise to provoke a civil war beginning at Charleston, and in rescue of an untenable position. Therefore I advise against an expedition in every view. . . . I would instruct Major Anderson to retire from Fort Sumter forthwith." Seward, however, did not adopt General Scott's recommendation as to Fort Pickens. "I would at once, and at every cost, prepare for a war at Pensacola and Texas, to be taken, however, only as a consequence of maintaining the possession and authority of the United States." That is, Seward would abandon Fort Sumter as a friendly gesture to the South, but would retain Pickens as a symbol of national sovereignty.

Secretary Chase now forgot his hesitation of a fortnight previously. "I am clearly in favor of maintaining Fort Pickens," he flatly wrote the President, "and just as clearly in favor of provisioning Fort Sumter. If that attempt be resisted by military force, Fort Sumter should, in my judgment, be reinforced." "I concur in the proposition to send an armed force off Charleston with supplies of provisions and reinforcements for the garrison of Fort Sumter," proclaimed Welles, reversing his first attitude. Just what position Cameron took will never be known, for he submitted no opinion in written form. Montgomery Blair waxed more emphatic than before. "As regards General Scott, I have no confidence in his judgment on the questions of the day. His political views control his judgment and his course as remarked on by the President shows that whilst no one will question his patriotism, the results are the same as if he was in fact traitorous." Not only did Blair demand vigorously the reinforcement of Sumter, but he had already written out his resignation from the Lincoln cabinet, which he intended to submit in case an attempt to resupply and reinforce this vital spot were not made.

On that same March 29, Lincoln sent orders to Secretary of War Cameron to prepare a relief expedition to Sumter ready to sail if necessary as early as April 6.

* * *

Whatever defense can be made for Seward's plan must rest upon the assumption that the South, even the Cotton South, was not so determined on separation as its acts indicated, and that the Border states, pacified by the surrender of Fort Sumter and other concessions, would remain loyal to the Union, and serve as intermediaries for reuniting the severed sections. It was exclusively on this conviction that Seward justified his dealings with "ambassadors" whom he had refused to receive officially and whom his more fervid countrymen insisted on stigmatizing as "rebels" and "traitors." What did the so-called commissioners and their superior, Robert Toombs, Confederate Secretary of State, think of Seward's program? The correspondence between the commissioners and Robert Toombs, preserved in the Library of Congress, answers this question. If his talks with Justice Campbell, Seward believed, accomplished nothing else, they would gain time; that was precisely what the Confederate agents regarded as an advantage to themselves. While the meetings were taking place, work was pushed night and day on the fortifications and batteries encompassing Fort Sumter. "We think the policy of 'masterly inactivity,'" Crawford wrote Toombs, "was wise in every particular." For Seward's high designs the commissioners expressed contempt. "His reasons and my own are as wide apart as the poles," he wrote to Toombs; "he is fully persuaded that peace will bring about a reconstruction of the Union, while I feel confident that it will build up and cement our Confederacy and put us beyond the reach either of his aims or of his diplomacy." "It is well that he should indulge in dreams which we know are not to be realized." Toombs agreed with this sentiment. "It is a matter of no importance to us," he wrote his commissioner on April 2, "what motives may induce the adoption of Mr. Seward's policy by his government. We are satisfied that it will redound to our advantage, and therefore, care little for Mr. Seward's calculations as to its future effect upon the Confederate states." The same correspondence disposes of another illusion. At times – though on this subject, as on others, Seward's mind fluctuated – he believed that the question of Fort Pickens could be handled in a way different from Sumter. But the Confederate correspondence makes it clear that the evacuation of Sumter would have been followed by a demand for the evacuation of Pickens. It might take a little longer, but "invest the latter as Sumter was and it soon becomes a necessity." Above all, Crawford wrote Toombs, the abandonment of Sumter would give the Confederacy character, power, and influence abroad.

VI

EVIDENTLY the situation was becoming tense for the Secretary of State. All of Seward's cabinet colleagues, except Caleb B. Smith and possibly Cameron, had abandoned his cause; and Lincoln, by ordering the preparation of the expedition, had brought the discussion to a sudden end. Seward's commitment made to the Confederate Commission, through Judge Campbell, evidently could not be fulfilled and as the first of April approached, his embarrassment became portentous. In response to another urgent demand from Justice Campbell that the Fort Sumter promise be redeemed, Seward had informed the insistent person that a reply would be made on April 1. As the ships that were to sail with relief were already fitting for sea in New York, the Secretary knew that he could not make good his undertaking. What was to be done? Was there still no way of stopping this expedition? One irremovable obstacle made impossible the fulfillment of the promise, and apparently forestalled the whole plan to which Seward was by this time fanatically committed for preventing war. The inexperienced statesman in the White House, who was giving signs of determination and will that had hitherto been unsuspected, stood blocking Seward's path. So long as the President held supreme executive power, the Secretary was helpless. Obviously there was no legitimate way of removing Lincoln from office. But Seward still regarded himself as head of the Republican Party and was still resentful that the accident of politics had awarded to an ignorant backwoodsman a technical leadership that on all rightful grounds belonged to an abler statesman. Only one way remained, he was honestly convinced, by which the promises made to the South could be made good and the United States of America be preserved from civil war. The nominal President must – in effect if not in form – abdicate his office and transfer its responsibilities to himself. This change in power must be made on this very day – this April 1 when Seward must speak the word to the Confederate commissioners that would mean peace or war. And so, on the morning of that day, Lincoln found upon his desk the most astounding communication ever addressed to a President of the United States.

Some thoughts for the President's consideration, April 1, 1861.

First. We are at the end of a month's administration, and yet without a policy, domestic or foreign.

Second. This, however, is not culpable, and it has even been unavoidable. The presence of the Senate, with the need to meet applications for patronage, have prevented attention to other and more grave matters.

Third. But further delay to adopt and prosecute our policies for both domestic and foreign affairs would not only bring scandal upon the administration, but danger upon the country.

Fourth. To do this we must dismiss the applicants for office. But how? I suggest that we make the local appointments forthwith, leaving foreign or general ones for ulterior and occasional action.

Fifth. The policy at home. I am aware that my views are singular and perhaps not sufficiently explained. My system is built upon this *idea*, namely, that we must

CHANGE THE QUESTION FROM ONE UPON SLAVERY, OR ABOUT SLAVERY, FOR A QUESTION UPON UNION OR DISUNION.[1]

In other words from what would be regarded as a party question, to one of *Patriotism or Union.*

The occupation or evacuation of Fort Sumter, although not in fact a slavery or a party question, is so *regarded*. Witness the temper manifested by the Republicans in the free states, and even by the Union men in the South.

I would therefore terminate it as a safe measure for changing the issue. I deem it fortunate that the last administration created the necessity.

For the rest I would simultaneously defend and reinforce all the forts in the Gulf, and have the navy recalled from foreign nations to be prepared for a blockade. Put the island of Key West under martial law.

This will raise distinctly the question of *Union* or *Disunion.* I would maintain every fort and possession in the South.

For Foreign Nations

I would demand explanations from Spain and France, categorically, at once.

I would seek explanations from Great Britain and Russia, and send agents into Canada, Mexico and Central America, to rouse a vigorous continental spirit of independence on this continent against European intervention.

And, if satisfactory explanations are not received from Spain and France,

Would convene Congress and declare war against them.

[1] All the italics and capitals in this paper are Seward's own.

But whatever policy we adopt there must be an energetic prosecution of it.

For this purpose it must be somebody's business to pursue it and direct it incessantly.

Either the President must do it himself, and be all the while active in it, or

Devolve it on some member of the cabinet. Once adopted, debates on it must end, and all agree and abide.

It is not my especial province.

But I neither seek to evade nor assume responsibility.

In this paper Seward thus definitely proposed that Lincoln not only eliminate himself from the conduct of affairs, but the cabinet as well. The demand that supreme power be "devolved" upon some member, and that "once adopted, debates on it must end, and all agree and abide" could have no other meaning. He evidently desired no more discussions such as had recently taken place on Fort Sumter; one man – that is, Seward himself – was to settle all such problems and enforce his decisions with no interference from any other source. What Seward in fact demanded was that he be made dictator and that the administration elected the previous November be abrogated. Perhaps even more astonishing was the use the Secretary intended to make of his extraconstitutional power. He would evacuate Fort Sumter, but retain Fort Pickens, and the other strongholds in the Gulf. He would scrap Lincoln's decision to support the Federal sovereignty and substitute for it his own policy of surrender. He would insist on legislation along the lines of the Crittenden Compromise, give the South guarantees for the "protection" of slavery in the territories, and in this way, as he thought, keep Virginia and the other Border states in the Union and lay the basis for the return at a later date of those already seceded. The Secretary's proposal for shelving the slavery question and substituting that of union or disunion puzzled Lincoln at the time as it has all students of the question since, for how slavery and the question of union could be separated was past thinking.

In his scheme for reuniting the country Seward betrayed again the illusion that had haunted him ever since the sectional troubles began. In the impromptu remarks at the Astor House, on December 20, 1860, quoted on a preceding page, Seward had declared that the North, at the slightest danger to the South, would rush all its men and arms to its defense, and similarly his conviction that even South Carolina, should any Northern state be attacked by a foreign power, would come to its assistance. This conception laid the basis for the plan, now unfolded to the astonished Lincoln, for silencing the slavery issue and bringing all sections of a disharmonious nation into unity and co-operation. Seward would precipitate a war with Spain and France, and, if necessary, with Great Britain and Russia. Spain had just raised the Spanish flag in San Domingo, thus clearly flouting the Monroe Doctrine; France and Great Britain were preparing to send a debt-collecting naval force to Mexico – the first step in what developed into the Maximilian enterprise; Russia's offense was less definite, but there were rumors – utterly unfounded – that the Czar was surreptitiously negotiating with Jefferson Davis as a preliminary to recognition. Seward believed, or affected to believe, that such a great conflict with the most powerful nations would compel North and South to forget their differences and embrace each other again in common defense. We know now that the outcome would have been exactly the reverse. A declaration of war against Britain, France, Russia, or all combined would have played directly into the Confederacy's hands. The republic of Jefferson Davis had only one chance of survival – that was the assistance and co-operation of Europe, especially of Great Britain and France. Far from springing to the defense of the Union, the Confederate cabinet would have hailed such a conflagration with joy, for it would have meant the success of their attempt to found a new nation, with cotton as its "king" and slavery, in the words of Alexander H. Stephens, as its "cornerstone."

Lincoln replied to this letter the same day on which it was received. In ordinary circumstances such a communication would have meant its author's retirement from the cabinet. The reasons that had persuaded Lincoln to appoint Seward to the State Department now impelled him to overlook what was really violent insubordination and retain him among his councilors. The acute state of national affairs made the disruption of the administration something not to be thought of. Seward's dismissal would have split in two the Republican Party at the very time when harmony and teamwork were most demanded, with a result upon the fate of the nation that can hardly be imagined. Lincoln therefore replied to Seward's statement of his case with a quiet dignity that in itself amounted to a severe rebuke. All the points worth an argument were replied to with a logical restraint that should have made Seward wince. The insulting criticism that the President had been too busy distributing the offices to pay attention to matters of state was properly ignored. The charge that Lincoln had no domestic policy was met by quoting from his inaugural address: "The power confided to me will be used to hold, occupy and possess the property and places belonging to the Government and to collect the duties and imposts." "This had your distinct approval at the time," Lincoln reminded his

Secretary, "and taken in connection with the order I immediately gave General Scott, directing him to employ every means in his power to strengthen and hold the forts, comprises the exact domestic policy you now urge, with the single exception that it does not propose to abandon Fort Sumter." "Again I do not understand how the re-enforcement of Fort Sumter would be done on a slavery or party issue while that of Fort Pickens would be on a more national and patriotic one." As to the carrying out of administration policy, domestic and foreign, and Seward's demand that this be placed in his untrammeled hands, Lincoln remarked that "if this must be done, I must do it. When a general line of policy is adopted, I apprehend there is no danger of its being changed without good reason, or continuing to be a subject of unnecessary debate; still upon points arising in its progress I wish, and I suppose I am entitled to have, the advice of all the cabinet."

One might think that this response would have persuaded Seward that Lincoln intended to exercise the constitutional functions entrusted to him by the people, and would in no case set up a virtual dictatorship, with his Secretary in supreme power. Montgomery Blair liked to compare his colleague to Polonius, who sought "by indirection [to] find direction out," and the fact is that, even after receiving Lincoln's pointed rejoinder, Seward kept up his underground campaign in favor of conciliation. Even after April 1, he did not cease interfering with the President's plans. To the Fort Sumter expedition Seward was still unreconciled, and he now resorted to strange maneuvers which in some ways constitute the most inexplicable chapter in his career.

Only three warships were at hand in early April as naval escort to the ships which were to carry supplies and reinforcements to Fort Sumter. The *Powhatan*, the most important of these, a steam frigate powerfully armed, was the only vessel that could be depended upon to protect the boats and tugs that were expected to run the Confederate batteries and deposit their supplies on the Sumter landing wharf. With the broadsides of the *Powhatan* the operation might have succeeded, without them it was certainly sure to fail. The *Powhatan*, the flagship of the naval force, was itself loaded with munitions sadly needed by Major Anderson, and also with launches, boats and sailors indispensable to the operations. On April 5, Gideon Welles, Secretary of the Navy, issued orders to Captain Samuel Mercer, putting him in command of the *Powhatan*, and directing him to depart at once for sea, and take his stand at a point ten miles east of Charleston light. On the evening of April 6, just as Captain Mercer was about to leave the Brooklyn Navy Yard on his fateful mission, Lieutenant David Dixon Porter – his inferior in rank – stepped aboard the *Powhatan* and demanded that the ship be placed at his disposal. Lieutenant Porter handed the dissenting Mercer an order, issued on April 1 and signed "Lincoln," with an addendum that was something new in naval procedure – "Recommended. Wm. H. Seward." Instructions bearing the same date also came to the Commandant of the Navy Yard: "You will fit out the *Powhatan* without delay. Lieutenant Porter will relieve Captain Mercer in command of her. She is bound on secret service and under no circumstances communicate to the Navy Department the fact that she is fitting out. Abraham Lincoln." When Lieutenant Porter insisted that orders from the President, his commander-in-chief, superseded orders from the Secretary of the Navy, there was of course nothing to be said. The humiliated Mercer retired from the quarter-deck, Lieutenant Porter took command, and the *Powhatan* put out to sea. However, the sturdy, recently re-equipped frigate did not bend her course in the direction of Fort Sumter. On that same busy April 1 other instructions, also signed "Abraham Lincoln," had been issued to Lieutenant Porter, directing him "to proceed to Pensacola harbor at the extreme western end of Florida," and "at any cost or risk prevent any expedition from the mainland reaching Fort Pickens or Santa Rosa." [2]

Two features involved in these instructions deserve particular attention. The orders to Lieutenant Porter enjoined him "under no circumstances [to] communicate to the Navy Department the fact that she [the *Powhatan*] is fitting out." That is, the department which had jurisdiction over the naval forces of the United States, and which at the time was in charge of one of the most critical operations in its history, was to be kept ignorant of the fact that the ship that was essential to success had been detached and sent on an entirely different mission. The second fact was that the destination itself, Fort Pickens, which protected Pensacola and its Navy Yard, presented a very different problem from that of Fort Sumter. Its safety caused no particular anxiety to the army or navy. An adequate naval force had already been assembled in the region, to protect Fort Pickens from any possible attack. Neither were the munitions and other supplies loaded on the *Powhatan* for Sumter needed at the Florida stronghold. A force of men for reinforcement had been landed at this point before the *Powhatan* came in sight of the island – a force with which the Federal government held the position all through the Civil War. In fact, the *Powhatan*, after, with some interruptions, it had reached Pickens, found nothing to do. The commandant would not permit Lieutenant Porter to make the brilliant entrance which that gallant and impetuous officer

[2] For these instructions see Official Records of the Rebellion, Series I, I, 244; and Series II, IV, 108.

had planned; after remaining for a considerable time offshore, in the Gulf of Mexico, the crestfallen Porter – whose first performance in the Civil War gave little intimation of the laurels he was to win before its end – pulled up anchor and returned to the Brooklyn Navy Yard. His voyage had accomplished nothing – for there was nothing to be accomplished. What had taken place at Fort Sumter meanwhile the world knows only too well.

How had it happened that the sagacious Abraham Lincoln, commander-in-chief of the United States Navy, interested above all else at this time in the success of the Sumter expedition, had issued orders that superseded those of his Secretary of the Navy, and did so in such complete secrecy that even Mr. Welles was kept in the dark? A midnight scene in the White House on April 6 – the day Mercer gave up his ship to Porter – for which Welles himself supplies the details, explains the mystery. Five men participated in this meeting – the President, Seward, his son Frederick, Welles, and Commodore Stringham, head of the navy's Bureau of Detail. Both Seward and Welles had received information from New York of the unexpected detachment of the *Powhatan*. A rather excited scene had taken place between the two statesmen in consequence. Why had the President countermanded the orders of the Secretary of the Navy and kept him in ignorance of the change? What right had Seward, the Secretary of State, to interfere with the operations of the Navy Department?

Only one man could settle this dispute and so Welles and Seward, despite the lateness of the hour, proceeded side by side to the White House. Welles started the proceedings by reading his order to Captain Mercer to assume command as flag officer of the *Powhatan*, reminded the President that he had submitted this message to him before putting it into force, and had received his approval – a circumstance which Lincoln acknowledged that he remembered clearly. How he had come to sign the contradictory orders to Porter Lincoln did not at the moment explain, but the facts came out in time. For the larger part of that April 1, the day when Lincoln definitely ordered the Sumter expedition, Seward and Porter had been at work in an office adjoining the President's, preparing a mass of papers dealing with that and other matters, which in due course Seward presented for the President's signature. For a President to sign a vast number of papers daily without reading them was nothing unprecedented then nor is it now. The duties of the office could not be performed on any other basis. Merely to read this daily accumulating mass of papers was, and is, a physical impossibility. The President is obliged to trust his subordinates and accept their advice that everything is right and proper. That the April 1 in question was an extremely arduous one with Lincoln the preceding pages have made clear; on this day he had received Seward's "thoughts," asking to be made *de facto* President, had fixed his plans for relieving Sumter, and doubtless had had to give some attention to the hordes of office seekers crowding the antechambers. If a President could not trust his cabinet officers, Lincoln afterward remarked to Welles, relating to him the details of this disorderly proceeding, whom could he trust? Welles has recorded his admiration for the President's frankness and honesty at this midnight gathering. It was all a mistake, Lincoln said; it was his fault, "he ought to have been more careful and attentive."[3] Then turning squarely to Seward he said that the *Powhatan* must be restored to Mercer; "on no account must the Sumter expedition fail or be interfered with." Seward protested, but Lincoln, with that imperiousness which he could assert when the occasion demanded it, cut him short. He ordered Seward to telegraph at once to Porter to turn the *Powhatan* over to its designated commander and flag officer of the Sumter flotilla, Captain Mercer.

And now came the most puzzling episode of the whole proceeding – the one that has given Seward's biographers the greatest difficulty in explaining. The new message sent to Porter, at the President's command, can be read today in the official records of the War of the Rebellion.[4] "April 6, 1861. Give the *Powhatan* up to Captain Mercer. Seward." At first glance that looks like literal obedience to the President's instructions, yet closer examination reveals a detail that Montgomery Blair and Welles always believed to be one of those deft strokes of iniquity at which they regarded Seward as a master, but which his defenders attribute to the excitement, almost hysteria, of a momentous day and evening. Undoubtedly Lincoln, in directing Seward to send this telegram, intended to have the President's name appended to the order. But the Secretary of State, in affixing his own instead, made the message a nullity. No naval officer in his right mind would pay attention to instructions signed by the Secretary of State, any more than an ambassador in London would treat with respect a dispatch signed by the Secretary of the Navy. Lieutenant Porter held command of the *Powhatan* by virtue of a paper signed by Abraham Lincoln, and only another from that same high authority could countermand it. Of this fact Seward had just been made aware. Porter had compelled Mercer to hand the frigate over to him, because Mercer's orders bore the name of Welles, while his own bore that of the President. Was it probable that he would now give up the ship by virtue of a message simply signed

[3] Welles, *Diary*. I, 25.
[4] Official Records of the Rebellion, Series I, IV, 112.

"Seward"? Porter himself presently answered that question. He had already started for Pensacola, but a fast tug was sent to overtake him, and the new instructions reached the *Powhatan* off Staten Island. As he held the vessel by presidential fiat, he could not accept the orders of the Secretary of State without making himself liable to court-martial and dismissal from the navy. He therefore proceeded to Pensacola.

Was this all a carefully thought out design on the part of the adroit Secretary of State? Who can ever answer that question? The most unbiased student of the ethical problem involved is Frederic Bancroft, who wrote his substantial and impartial biography of Seward with the sympathy of the Seward family, who gave him complete access to all the Seward documents. Making full allowance for the distractions of April 1 and the fact that the Pickens expedition was Seward's own from the first, Mr. Bancroft reaches this conclusion: "After what has been learned of Seward's methods, it would hardly be warrantable to express confidence that his despatch to Porter was not the result of subtle calculation." [5] Others express the same doubt in more explosive terms. Montgomery Blair, Seward's cabinet colleague – with whom, even at this early stage of the administration, he was hardly on speaking terms – maintained, to his dying day, that had the *Powhatan* not been taken away from the Sumter fleet, the expedition would have succeeded, and Fort Sumter saved to the Union with incalculable effect upon history. Both Blair and Welles believed that Seward, after trying in many other ways to make good to the Crawford Commission his pledge to evacuate the fort, finally resorted to this underhanded method of making Lincoln's effort at resupply a failure. If Fort Sumter had been reinforced, insisted Blair, it would have been made impregnable. After the Confederates captured the battlement, the North, though holding undisputed command of the sea, was unable to retake it in four years of war. Lincoln, in a letter to Gustavus Fox, the originator of the plan to relieve Sumter and in charge of the whole expedition, wrote, "The practicability of your plan was not, in fact, brought to a test. By reason of a gale, well known in advance to be possible and not improbable, the tugs, an essential part of the plan, never reached the ground; while, by an accident for which you were in no way responsible, and possibly I to some extent was, you were deprived of a war vessel, with her men, which you deemed of great importance to the enterprise." Gideon Welles records scraps of a conversation with Seward on the way to the President on the evening of April 6. "Mr. Seward remarked that, old as he was, he had learned a lesson from this affair and that was, he had better attend to his own business and confine his labors to his

[5] Bancroft, *op. cit.* II, 144.

own department. To this I cordially assented."[6] Yet Welles was not so certain as Blair that the desired flagship would have saved the situation. "Had the frigate remained under Captain Mercer," he wrote, "the attempt to relieve Major Anderson probably would not have succeeded, for the rebels of Charleston were strangely prepared and warned of the intended expedition and there were other movements which precipitated Rebel action."[7]

This latter sentence refers to another incident of the Sumter proceeding even harder to explain than the diversion of the *Powhatan.* This has always been known as the "Harvey incident." After Lincoln's desire to resupply the fort had been made known, an employee of the Washington telegraph office, a Connecticut friend of Gideon Welles, brought the Secretary two telegrams that had been recently sent from the Federal Capital to Charleston. These telegrams are also preserved in the Official Records of the Rebellion.[8] One of the messages, sent to a leading Confederate in Charleston, read: "Positively determined not to withdraw Anderson. Supplies go immediately, supported by naval force under Stringham if their landing be resisted. A Friend." This "friend," it presently appeared, was James E. Harvey, a native Charlestonian, a well-known newspaper correspondent in Washington, and a man who had free access to the Secretary of State. That Seward had given the vital news in the telegrams, subsequent events clearly disclosed. At that moment, no matter was quite so confidential as the President's plan for relieving Sumter. Seward himself, in explaining why the orders transferring the *Powhatan* from Mercer to Porter had been kept from the knowledge of Welles and Cameron, the two members of the cabinet officially responsible for the success of all proceedings of the kind, had declared that absolute secrecy was essential to success. Yet this even more critical news concerning Sumter he had himself confided to a newspaper reporter of Southern sympathies who at once transmitted it to the Confederate authorities.

A few days before Harvey had been detected sending this information to Charleston, Seward caused him to be made United States Minister to Portugal. In spite of the great scandal caused when this appointment became known, the Secretary of State refused to rescind it. The only explanation of these strange – perhaps even worse than strange – transactions that has been forthcoming up to the present time is a memorandum made by John G. Nicolay and published in the Nicolay and Hay *Abraham Lincoln.* "Being a correspondent and believed to be

[6] Welles, *Diary,* I, 24.
[7] *Ibid.,* I, 33.
[8] Official Records of the Rebellion, Series I, I, 187.

trusty, the secret was imprudently imparted to him [Harvey]. . . . The affair was a gross error of judgment, and a breach of confidence, but not an act of treachery. Seward obtained knowledge of the telegram the same afternoon it was sent, and in his first indignation advised the President to revoke Harvey's commission [as Minister to Portugal]. 'But thinking it over coolly,' said Seward, 'I thought it wrong to punish a man for his stupid folly, when really he had committed no crime.' "[9]

[9] Nicolay & Hay, *op. cit.* IV, 32.

VII

WITH MOST heads of state, insubordination of this kind, to use the mildest word, would have produced a cabinet crisis. Lincoln and Seward, however, continued to maintain agreeable relations. Both personal considerations, and reasons of state and politics, kept the two men in close harmonious and effective co-operation for the succeeding four years.

The support of the largest wing of the new party probably seemed to Lincoln more indispensable to national success in April and May, 1861, than in December of the preceding year. The calamity that had then been only a threat had now become a reality. The weakness of the Union party remained the same, only in larger degree. The North was by no means of one mind on the coercion of the South. The firing on Fort Sumter had indeed roused the nation to action, but the following three years were to show that nothing like unanimity prevailed on this and plenty of other issues growing out of the war. It is hard to see how the stand Lincoln had taken for war in preference to national dissolution could have won wide support, as it did, if the fact had become popularly known that his own administration was not unanimous on this decision. That Lincoln felt the personal affront involved in Seward's tortuous proceedings may be taken for granted. But in the next four years it was to be his fate to submit to many more indignities in consideration of the public good. At base, Lincoln was conscious of his own power, completely assured of his ability to keep his hand on events and prevent such manifestations as Seward's from bringing harm to the common cause. It was all a part of that mixed humility and dominance so conspicuous in his complex character. When one of his friends remarked on the Secretary of State's presumption and advised Lincoln to drop him from the cabinet, the President quietly said, "Seward knows that I am his master." He was just as sure of this at the time of the Sumter maneuvers as some time afterward when the remark was made. The statement really summed up the situation; meanwhile Seward was an extremely useful man, both as party leader and as

Secretary of State, and Lincoln gladly availed himself of the strength he brought to the administration, overlooking, as was always his custom, any incidental trouble the man's egotism and headstrong willfulness might cause him.

From the first, Lincoln had taken a personal liking to his presumptuous underling. The administration had not been under way many weeks before the friendly relationship between the two men made other members of the cabinet grieve and writhe. Seward acquired a new home on Fifteenth Street, on the east side of Lafayette Square – the present site of the Belasco Theater – only a few steps removed from the White House. This soon became a cherished haven for a distracted President. Lincoln's habit of leaving his official headquarters and dropping in unexpectedly on his intimates formed another count against an unconventional and "undignified" ruler; but the reason was plain enough. The executive offices, corridors, and even private living quarters of the White House were so constantly swarming with an office-seeking and advice-giving rabble that the only chance for relaxation was an occasional half-surreptitious visit to friends. Seward's house in particular offered charming respite of this kind. Lincoln liked to stretch his long legs before Seward's log fire and discuss a thousand subjects – not all of them concerned with the problems of the day. The Secretary's conversational gifts made him one of the delights of Washington; he could tell stories as amusing as Lincoln's own; he had a vast experience out of which to draw reminiscence and anecdote; he liked to laugh, to poke fun at his contemporaries, and to detect the ludicrous aspects of even the most serious questions. Seward himself would have been a popular figure at those tavern symposia of the Eighth Circuit in Illinois, and Lincoln found in him some compensation for the loss of this part of his life. Against the agonies of the real world outside the companionable Secretary was thus a stimulating contrast. No other cabinet associate could offer consolation of this kind. The righteous Puritanic Welles, the self-satisfied, half-contemptuous Chase, the slow-moving, legalistic Bates, the nervous, ill-tempered Blair, cut a poor figure when compared to Seward as a human being. His nature, though not lacking in cynicism, had no taint of hypocrisy; Lincoln found in this politico-statesman a relief somewhat akin to that which he drew from the pages of Petroleum V. Nasby. On Seward's first day in office he began a diary; the volume is still preserved among his papers; it consists, however, of only a single page, for the writer never got beyond the first day. Had Seward continued the record, the accounts of his day-by-day talks with Lincoln would have given posterity its most scintillating portrait of the man.

Seward was, however, much more than a court jester; he was a man of imagination – an imagination that far outdistanced that of his more matter-of-fact colleagues – and he had a suppleness of mind that enabled him to view pressing questions in all their phases. Naturally, Lincoln would like to discuss matters of state with this agile mentality, undisturbed by the presence of the rest of the cabinet. At any rate, these personal meetings grew to be a habit. Their congeniality grew closer as events proceeded, especially when, in the cleavage between the Union forces on the great civil problem presented by the war – the conditions under which the seceded states were to be readmitted to the Union – Lincoln and Seward found themselves in agreement.

But this Lincoln-Seward companionship, especially in the early days, alarmed and enraged the administration's friends and foes. In the house of Charles Francis Adams, Charles Sumner railed so fiercely that he lost the friendship of that family. Lincoln – this was the charge – was in Seward's hands. The Secretary was leading the President on the most dangerous courses; at first merely the mutterings of cloak-room and drawing-room gossip, this presently grew to such a storm that it nearly disrupted the administration. Even at his own domestic hearth Lincoln's "subserviency" to Seward caused frequent ructions. Mrs. Lincoln hated the man she described as "a dirty abolitionist sneak" so intensely that, in her drives about Washington, she would order the coachman to avoid the street on which Seward lived. "He draws you around his little finger like a skein of thread," she would tell her husband. George Bancroft, shocked, among other things, by Seward's frequent use of the words "hell" and "damn," said that his respect for the President's wife was increased by her dislike of the Secretary of State, while Greeley's hostility to Lincoln was believed to be inspired in large degree by the President's friendship for his "Premier."

The comments of cabinet members were no more appreciative. "Strange, strange," said Montgomery Blair, "that the President, who has sterling ability, should give himself over so completely to Stanton and Seward."[1] Blair sometimes spoke more emphatically. Edward Bates, in his Diary, quotes the Postmaster General as describing the Secretary of State as an "unprincipled liar – the truth is not in him."[2] He regarded Seward as "the least of a statesman and knows less of public law and of administration than any man who ever held a seat in the cabinet." Bates, almost the only one of Lincoln's original cabinet choices whom Weed and Seward had approved, did not reciprocate

[1] The remark was made somewhat later, after Stanton had displaced Cameron as Secretary of War.

[2] Bates, *op. cit.*, p. 291.

their friendly disposition. If the "Premier" really thought that the canny Missourian would ever become part of a pro-Seward coterie, he was quickly undeceived. In his first meeting with Lincoln in Springfield, Bates had shown his distrust of his fellow Whig and the closer view obtained under Lincoln's official roof only increased it. Bates's first meeting with Seward – at Washington, at the time of the inauguration – aroused his suspicions. He found his new colleague agreeable enough, but he objected to "the urgency with which he invited me to take up my quarters at his house, as his guest, until I can make permanent arrangements." Bates had no intention, then or afterward, of becoming part of a Seward cabal. It was not only that Bates distrusted Seward's methods, he had no high regard for his statecraft. This able jurist regarded the Secretary of State as ignorant of the law, blundering in his methods, overbearing to his colleagues, disrespectful to the President, "extremely loose in practical politics," "studiously dark," and generally a man in whom he had "no confidence." He found many of Seward's papers "strange documents" and, at least in one case, could not "well determine whether its errors and ambiguities result from careless haste or cautious casuistry." Again, Seward "always shuffles around a knotty point by some trick."

That Salmon P. Chase would look with disapproving eye on Seward's constant approach to the throne was natural – especially as, in the early days, he had attempted himself, without success, to acquire precedence in Lincoln's favor. Even Simon Cameron, who had entered the cabinet as a protégé of Seward, presently turned against him. That trait, conspicuous in a career of thirty years, of forsaking the men whose assistance he had used in advancing to power played true to form in his relations with Seward. The man was enraged when he learned of his friend's performance in the Sumter expedition, and filled the corridors of his office with profane denunciations. Cameron did not take too pompously his prestige as a war minister, but the realization that the Secretary of State had usurped his functions, issued orders to the army of which he knew nothing, and had, indeed, taken pains to see that he was kept in ignorance, proved too much for Cameron's not ordinarily sensitive nature. The agreeable understanding on which the two men had entered the cabinet presently collapsed.

But the man whose acid comments have become most famous was Gideon Welles. "Father Neptune," as Lincoln called his Secretary of the Navy, not only despised Seward and his whole Albany crowd, but had – what the others lacked – literary skill in setting forth his sentiments. To reproduce all Welles's unappreciative comments would mean reprinting a considerable part of the Diary. Personal animus does not, in itself, explain this attitude, though this animus existed in plenty. Welles was fundamentally a just and honest man who could see the good points of contemporaries whom he did not like, and in his objections to Seward some public interest was usually involved. Mr. Seward "has talent and genius but he has not the profound knowledge nor the solid sense, correct views and unswerving right intentions of the President." He had "very little devotion to principle which he always subordinated to his ambition." He was a "man more of expedients than principles," "assuming," "presuming," "meddling," "not particularly scrupulous in accomplishing his ends," "a schemer," "not always truthful," and was hand-in-glove with Thurlow Weed, who, according to Welles, was "of vastly more vigor of mind, is reckless and direct, persistent and tortuous, avaricious of power and always corrupt." Seward's easygoing treatment of Lincoln, even in cabinet meetings, exasperated the navy head. The man's failure to realize Lincoln's superior intellectual ability rankled. "The President he treats with a familiarity that sometimes borders on disrespect." "With temperaments so constituted and unlike it is not surprising that the obsequious affability and ready assumption of the subordinate presumed on and to an extent influenced the really superior intellect of the President and made him in a degree the centralizing personage."

The grievances of Welles and his associates against the "Premier" were founded on more than personal antagonism. Seward not only treated each individually as a nonentity, but attempted to sweep them aside as a collective body. His plan of ruling the Republic as Prime Minister, and relegating Lincoln to a position purely ceremonial, made necessary the reduction of the other Secretaries to what, perhaps, considered constitutionally, they really were – mere heads of the executive departments. In Seward's "Thoughts" of April 1, he had admonished the President that, after appointing one of his cabinet heads virtual chief of state, "debates must end" and "all agree and abide." Not one of Seward's colleagues ever knew anything of Seward's memorandum – it did not see the light until nearly a quarter of a century after the Civil War; if they had, it would have explained certain maneuvers of the Secretary of State at the time which had aroused their resentment. For Seward, in his attitude toward his colleagues, was acting as though his recommendation to the President had been accepted. That is, he was treating the cabinet as though it did not exist. As a presidential council, he regarded it as having ceased to be a part of the American system. Since Washington's day, cabinet meetings, usually on stated days, had been part of the executive routine. Washington's precedent of consultation on general governmental matters had transformed the body into a presidential council, and all his successors had continued the custom. Cabinet meetings, usually twice a week or oftener if special occasions arose, were an immutable feature of Washington life. Readers of the diaries of John Quincy Adams and James K. Polk will recall the seriousness with which those Presidents regarded "cabinet day" and the exhaustiveness with which matters affecting the administration were laid before their assembled advisers. But Seward evidently intended to end this time-honored institution. He early decided that there should be no cabinet meetings, or at least no regular meetings on fixed days. Occasionally, of course, the cabinet, or parts of it, did come together, usually in response to invitations issued by the Secretary of State. The proceedings were not impressive in dignity or content. The informality seemed to be almost studied; no regular seats were assigned, though the Secretary of State was always careful to place himself at the President's right. "It seemed inadvisable," wrote Welles, "to the Premier – as he liked to be called and considered – that the members should meet often and they did not. Consequently there was very little concerted action. At the earlier meetings there was little or no formality; the cabinet meetings were a sort of privy council or gathering of equals, much like a senatorial caucus, where there was no recognized leader and the Secretary of State put himself in advance of the President. The Secretary of State . . . from his former position as the chief executive of the largest state in the Union, as well as from his recent place as a senator, and from his admitted experience and familiarity with affairs, assumed, and was allowed, as was proper, to take the lead in consultations and also to give tone and direction to the manner and mode of proceedings. The President, if he did not actually wish, readily acquiesced in this."

Instead of holding cabinet meetings, Seward spent a considerable part of every day with the President. The two were frequently in close consultation in his private office; they took walks and drives and lunched together. It was an intimacy which the other Secretaries regarded with a suspicious eye. Not one of them enjoyed such a familiarity with Lincoln; each was confined, for the most part, to his own department, and thus obtained little knowledge of the government as a whole. That Seward showed the utmost interest in the affairs of his colleagues, but managed to keep secret about his own, aggravated this grievance. The President, naturally, knew of the important transactions of all the departments, and was believed to discuss them freely with Seward, who in this way kept in close touch with all branches of the government. But his colleagues, having few opportunities to see Lincoln at close range, could not, in the same way, learn of the doings of the State

Department. Seward usually arrived in advance of his colleagues, and frequently remained, in confidential discussion with the President, after they had left. Lincoln would let Seward apparently dominate the meeting, listen attentively to what all his Secretaries said, and then, after a most unsystematic discussion, himself sum up the pros and cons and announce his decision. Welles admitted, however, that the President's conclusions frequently ran counter to those of his chief adviser.

Seward's colleagues grew more and more restive under this humiliation. Chase was the first to break out into open protest. At an early meeting he raised the question of regular "cabinets." Had it not always been the custom for the President's associates to assemble on stated days and act as a general council in the direction of affairs? Would not this sanctified practice make for better administration? All Chase's colleagues supported his protest with the exception of Seward, who could see no value in these periodical gatherings. Lincoln approved the suggestion, and directed that the time-honored "cabinet days" be restored. However, the improvement lasted for only a brief time; because, as the other Secretaries believed, of Seward's persistent opposition, things presently relapsed into the former easygoing state. Seward's meddling in the affairs of other departments, especially the Navy, the Army, and the Attorney General's office, caused a renewal of the demand. Bates, not easily moved to anger, was outraged when he learned that Seward was sending instructions – without the Attorney General's knowledge – to district attorneys' and marshals' offices which were exclusively under the jurisdiction of the Department of Justice. He brought up the whole question of "cabinet unity" and a more regular procedure in full cabinet meeting. He protested to the President against the lack of method, and even of dignity, in the prevailing conduct of public business. From the beginning Bates, as his Diary discloses, entertained an exalted notion of the function of the cabinet in the guidance of the nation. He always refers to it as "the Council," and the spectacle which it had presented in real life, an unorderly assembling of individuals, only one of whom seemed to be in the President's confidence, and most of whom learned of vital government decisions from the newspapers, shocked him. The administration, he declared, was not a unit; it was departmentalized, each Secretary keeping monastic-like in his own office, knowing little of what was going on in the others, not participating in the general concerns of the nation. Why, he now asked Lincoln, could not the cabinet come together on stated days, and on such special occasions as the national emergency might make desirable? All of Bates' associates echoed his demand – again excepting Seward. "The Secretary of State," records

Welles, "alone dissented, hesitated, doubted, objected, thought it inexpedient, said all had so much to do that we could not spare the time." [3] Again Lincoln overruled the Secretary of State, and ordered that regular meetings in future be held on Tuesdays and Fridays. The Secretary of the Navy intimates that Lincoln probably instigated Bates in bringing the matter up in this definite fashion; at least it was evident enough that he strongly favored the plan. This time the new scheme of things became established, and Tuesdays and Fridays, for the rest of the administration, were regular "cabinet days." However, many of the old evils continued. Ultimately, as will appear, the lack of "unity" grew to be a public grievance and, manipulated as an issue by Seward's enemies in the Senate, resulted almost in breaking up the cabinet.

Great as was Seward's influence over Lincoln, that statesman was far from exercising the despotic control his colleagues suspected. In the great early issues of the conflict, it was the will of Lincoln, not that of Seward, which prevailed. He had utterly disregarded Seward's policy of avoiding the conflict by compromising with the South. The decision to preserve the Union, even at the cost of civil war, was Lincoln's, not Seward's. He overruled Seward's policy on the relief of Sumter. He had also disregarded Seward's pet solution of domestic difficulties – war with Great Britain, France, or some other formidable enemy – though no one, least of all his cabinet councilors, knew of it at the time. The obstinacy with which Seward clung to this favorite panacea was astonishing. A letter written to his wife on May 2 shows that even then he had not recovered from his delusion. Though two months had passed since Lincoln had told him, as flatly as words could express the idea, that he proposed to run his own administration and that he intended to have no trumped-up wars with Europe, the fact had apparently not deeply penetrated the man's consciousness. "I received your letter last evening, on my birthday.[4] It seemed to me a matter of regret that I had lived to reach it, under circumstances so trying and painful. A country so largely relying on my poor efforts to save it had refused me the full measure of its confidence, needful to that end. I am a chief reduced to a subordinate position, and surrounded with a guard, to see that I do not do too much for my country, lest some advantage may revert indirectly to my own fame. . . . The tide, on this side of the Atlantic, begins to turn in our favor. They have misunderstood things fearfully in Europe. Great Britain is in great danger of sympathizing so much with the South, for the sake of peace and cotton, as to drive us to make war against her, as the ally of the traitor. If that comes it

[3] Welles, *Diary*. I, 138.
[4] Seward was now sixty.

will be a strife of the younger branch of the British stock — for freedom, against the other, for slavery. It will be dreadful, but the end will be sure and swift. My last despatches from Great Britain and France have showed that they were almost ready, on some pretext, to try and save cotton, at the expense of the Union. I am trying to get a bold remonstrance through the cabinet, before it is too late."

The reference to the cabinet is obscure, for in the "bold remonstrance" in which Seward was engaged on this twentieth of May, the cabinet certainly had not been consulted. But this same "bold remonstrance" furnishes a brilliant illustration of the extent to which Lincoln was controlling his own administration, all the more impressive from the fact that it concerned a matter of supreme importance in Seward's own department. While Lincoln was contented, in routine details, to leave Seward in control of his office, on critical occasions the rail splitter could be his own Secretary of State. The paper to which Seward referred is known in the annals of Civil War diplomacy as "Despatch No. 10." The age of Seward represents one of those primitive times in American history when secretaries of state, secluded from the world, wrote their own state papers in their own hand, and this letter to Mr. Adams, the new American Minister in London, bears in every sentence evidence of Seward's literary style. Had Gideon Welles and Edward Bates ever read the message, it would have substantiated their views of the lawlessness that prevailed in early cabinet days. One might indeed have supposed that a document which was little less than a declaration of war upon Great Britain would have been submitted to the presidential council before being committed to the mail pouch, but the truth is that only Seward, Lincoln, and perhaps Charles Sumner, chairman of the Senate Committee on Foreign Relations, had any knowledge of its existence. In the diplomatic correspondence of 1861, published in connection with Lincoln's message of that year, Despatch No. 10 indeed saw the light, but the version then given to the public differed in vital details from the original composition. Not until April 1886, a quarter century after, did the American people first learn of the defiance of John Bull which Seward had prepared in the early days of the Civil War. In that month the *North American Review* published Despatch No. 10 in facsimile form,[5] the manuscript disfigured by certain elisions, interlineations, marginal comments, all in a script which is easily recognized as that of Abraham Lincoln. The President, as Lord Lyons had confided to Lord John Russell, may have been "ignorant of foreign countries and foreign affairs," but a cursory glance at the instructions Seward had transmitted in this document to

[5] *North American Review*, Vol. 142, pp. 402–410.

Mr. Adams convinced the inexperienced diplomat that certain revisions would be necessary if his country was not to be plunged into ruin.

For the anger which certain transatlantic events had aroused in American hearts appeared in every line of Seward's paper. Certain letters from George M. Dallas, Buchanan's minister to Great Britain, who remained at his post until Mr. Adams's arrival on the thirteenth of May, had caused Seward much misgiving. On May 2 – the letter must have reached Washington in the middle of the month – Mr. Dallas reported an interview with Lord John Russell. The commissioners sent by the Confederate government to solicit British recognition were then, his lordship informed the American Ambassador, in London, and he was prepared to receive them "unofficially." Even more portentous was the news that Britain and France had concluded something in the nature of an alliance, or at least an entente, to act as a unit on the "American question." A matter under consideration of these joint powers was the recognition of the Confederacy as a belligerent – which, among other things, meant a recognition of their rights to commission privateers for the purpose of preying upon Federal commerce, despite the fact that Uncle Sam had already proclaimed that such evil emissaries would be regarded as pirates, and subjected to the punishment usually meted out to free rovers of the sea. Mr. Dallas had suggested that this last item in what Seward and most Americans regarded as an unfriendly program might properly be reserved for consideration until the arrival of his successor, Mr. Adams. Though Lord John had seemed to acquiesce in this suggestion, the Queen's Proclamation recognizing Southern belligerency had in fact been issued several days before the new minister appeared in London. In England Seward was regarded – and with considerable reason – as extremely hostile to that country! Lord Lyons's letters of the time contain passages in plenty emphasizing this dislike, extending through a long political career. That Seward was meditating plans for the annexation of Canada added to this distrust. Thus public sentiment in both countries, at the outbreak of the Civil War, was suspicious and hostile, and these emotions found expression in every line of the famous dispatch.

Lord Russell's willingness to receive "unofficially" Yancey, Rost, and Mann, Confederate "Commissioners," had aroused the Secretary's wrath. In case such receptions should take place, he now informed Adams, "you will in any event desist from all intercourse whatever, unofficial as well as official, with the British government, so long as it shall continue intercourse of either kind with the domestic enemies of this country" – an instruction which, while it may not necessarily have meant the permanent severance of diplomatic relations, suggested a status dangerously approaching such an impasse. As to what Seward called "the alliance" of France and Great Britain against the United States – an alliance into which, he intimated, these countries were attempting to draw the other nations of Europe – Seward remarked that this country had a right to expect a more independent if not a more friendly course. "Recognition of the Confederacy, either as a nation or as a belligerent," Seward wrote, will "not be borne unquestioned by the United States." The British cabinet was to be notified that recognition of Southern independence – and recognition of belligerency Seward evidently regarded as merely the first step in that direction – would mean war with the United States. "When this act of intervention is distinctly performed we from that hour shall cease to be friends and become once more, as we have twice before been forced to be, enemies of Great Britain. . . . As to southern privateers, should Great Britain choose to recognize them as lawful belligerents and give them shelter from our pursuit and punishment, the laws of nations afford proper remedy and we shall avail ourselves of it" – by which cryptic statement Seward perhaps meant that American warships would follow and seize the "privateer" in British harbors. As to the war into which the American reprisals would likely engage the United States, Seward looked upon the inevitable result without anxiety. "The dispute will be between the European and the American branches of the British race. . . . A war not unlike it between the same parties occurred at the close of the last century. Europe atoned by forty years of suffering for the error that Great Britain committed in provoking that contest. If that nation shall now repeat the same great error the social convulsions which will follow may not be so long but they will be more general. When they shall have ceased, it will, we think, be seen, whatever may have been the fortune of other nations, that it is not the United States that will have come out of them with its precious Constitution altered or its honestly obtained dominion in any degree abridged." Thus Seward was threatening Great Britain not only with overwhelming defeat on land and sea, but with a struggle which would end in the overthrowing of its monarchical constitution and reorganization of its government on democratic, republican lines. The final words evidently suggested that one result would be the acquisition of Canada by the United States, a project which had long been dear to Seward's heart.

That the ruling aristocracy of Great Britain had given the United States grounds for resentment cannot be denied, yet the situation had practical aspects which Seward ignored, but which Lincoln instantly perceived. His country, Lincoln believed, in summoning all its resources for the suppression of rebellion on so vast a scale, had assumed a task sufficiently large to enlist all its energies. The accession of Great Britain, France, and other European allies to the side of the Confederacy could, at the most favorable view, seriously complicate the problem. To throw down a challenge to the British fleet, to say nothing of the British and French armies, would play directly into the hands of Jefferson Davis and enable him to attain the great objective which was indispensable to Southern success. By one simple but fundamental change, Lincoln completely transformed the character of Seward's paper. In its original version Despatch No. 10, though in form instructions to Charles Francis Adams, Minister at the Court of St. James's, was in reality a declaration addressed to Her Majesty's government. Seward had directed Mr. Adams to take the message to the Foreign Office, read it to Lord John, and leave a copy. Such procedure seemed to Lincoln dangerously provocative. He therefore excised the direction to Adams as to reading the defiance to the British Foreign Secretary, and substituted the following paragraph: "This paper is not to be read or shown to the British Secretary of State, nor are any of its positions to be prematurely, unnecessarily, or indiscreetly made known. But its spirit will be your guide." Thus Lincoln sanctioned the policies and views on international law which Seward had set forth, and, in case Britain recognized the Confederate envoys as ambassadors of an independent state, was ready to go to the limit that Seward had presented. However, he saw no need of presenting the British with a blustering threat in advance of such action.

Even when he had thus adroitly changed Despatch No. 10 from what was virtually a threat, to be officially presented to England, to a secret paper for Adams's personal information, the President made other substantial changes in Seward's text that smoothed over many a rough passage. "Leave out," "drop all from this line to the end" – such emendations, appearing in Lincoln's handwriting on the margins of Seward's manuscript, took the sting out of many a phrase. In one place, Seward had written that intercourse of any kind with the Confederate mission in London would be "wrongful" to the United States, but Lincoln deleted this word and substituted "hurtful." Seward had asserted that recognition of the Confederacy, or acts that amounted to the same thing, would not be "borne by the United States." "No one of these proceedings" – so Lincoln softened the phrase – "will pass unquestioned by the United States." Lincoln ran his pen through the passage threatening reprisals in case Southern cruisers found refuge in British harbors and wrote in the margin, "omit." "If that nation shall now repeat the same great crime," Seward said, referring to

Britain's war against the infant United States, but Lincoln thought the word "error" an improvement. Instead of the "social calamities" which Seward prophesied for England, in the event of another war, Lincoln suggested "social convulsions"; thereby pointing out to Seward a certain confusion of thought in this passage, for the alterations in the British constitutional structure which the Secretary had foreseen – a democratic franchise, perhaps a Republican form of government – Seward himself, on reflection, would not have regarded as "calamities." Lincoln must have chuckled when he made that substitution.

But Despatch No. 10, even in its emasculated form and in its completely changed character, startled Mr. Adams when it landed on the ministerial desk. What, he asked himself, had happened to Mr. Seward? The New Yorker he greatly admired; Adams and Seward had worked together in the congressional session of 1860–1861 for a plan of conciliation with the South. On the other hand, this New Englander had never recovered from the shock of his first interview with Lincoln when that statesman, clad in shabby slippers and unpressed trousers, abruptly replied to Adams's conventional thanks for the appointment to London – "Don't thank me, thank Seward," for the selection had been made at Seward's insistence. Lincoln's own choice for the London mission, as Adams doubtless knew, had been William L. Dayton – the same New Jersey man whom he had intended to make Secretary of State, in case Seward persisted in his eleventh-hour refusal to enter the cabinet. The remembrance of things like this perhaps explains Adams's comment when the immortal No. 10 reached the legation. "The government," Charles Francis wrote in his Diary, "seems almost ready to declare war with all the powers of Europe, and almost instructs me to withdraw from communication with ministers here in a certain contingency. . . . I scarcely know how to understand Mr. Seward. The rest of the government may be demented for all I know; but he surely is calm and wise. My duty here is, in so far as I can do it honestly, to prevent the irritation from coming to a downright quarrel. It seems to me like throwing the game into the hands of the enemy." One can only imagine what would have been Mr. Adams's emotions had Seward's original message been transmitted to London.

This Lincoln version, leaving everything to the discretion of Mr. Adams himself, had a fortunate outcome. Adams was a man of great good sense and honest diplomatic skill. His mere presence in London accomplished much, for Russell early formed a high regard for his character and methods. When the time came to protest against the Confederate commissioners in London, and their unofficial reception at the Foreign Office, he did it in an urbane, yet decided manner that completely disarmed the Foreign Secretary. To receive envoys of revolution unofficially, Lord John explained, was not recognition or a preliminary to recognition – it was merely one way of obtaining desired information; he had, on other occasions, received representatives of revolutionary movements in Poland, Austria, Italy, but no objection had been made by the legitimate governments with which they were at war. Had not President Pierce, he might have added, received Louis Kossuth at the White House, when that ardent spirit was leading a rebellion for the liberation of Hungary from Habsburg rule? His Lordship, had he known the facts, might have struck even closer home, and reminded the American Minister that Mr. Seward had been recently conducting negotiations through third parties with delegates from the same Confederate government whose emissaries were then in London, and had been stopped from discussing matters with them face to face only by the orders of President Lincoln. As for Yancey, Rost, and Mann, Lord John told Adams, he had seen them informally twice but had no intention of seeing them "any more." So the interview which Adams had apprehended as one of the most difficult of his career really proved to be a triumph.

This proceeding had one other result of importance. Lincoln's shrewd modification of No. 10, and the determination he had displayed, gave his Secretary of State a new conception of his chief. That Lincoln was indeed President, and intended to remain President, now apparently dawned for the first time upon Seward's slowly perceiving mind. From late May, the time of this little drama, to the end, relations between Lincoln and Seward remained on a more satisfactory basis. The plan of regaining prestige and saving the Union by plunging into universal war no longer haunted Seward's dreams. On June 5, he wrote his wife in terms very different from those expressed in the petulant, complaining letter of May 26, quoted above. "Executive skill and vigor," he said, "are rare qualities. The President is the best of us, but he needs constant and assiduous co-operation." How completely the man's belligerent mood had changed, and how earnestly Seward was now prepared to work with Lincoln – or, to use his now far from presumptuous word "co-operate" – for a sane foreign policy appeared in the new crisis, more serious than that of the Confederate commissioners in London, which presently brought England and the United States to the very brink of war.

VIII

IT SEEMS almost as though a sardonic fate had created the *Trent* crisis for the express purpose, in poker language, of calling Seward's bluff. In late November, 1861, the golden opportunity for a war with England arrived, without any artificial stimulation from the White House or State Department. When the bumptious Captain Wilkes, in command of the sloop of war *San Jacinto*, stopped the British packet *Trent* in the Bahama Straits, forcibly removed from her deck four insurgent Americans and lodged them as prisoners of war in Fortress Monroe, Virginia, he presented Seward with that European war which several months before had been the chief item in his statesmanship. The mercurial gentleman, abruptly confronted with the fact, hesitated to seize this gift from heaven. It is the most picturesque contradiction in Seward's career that, in the *Trent* disturbance, he was almost the only member of the cabinet who kept his head. All of the seven, excepting Montgomery Blair and Seward, seemed ready to go to war with England rather than back down and surrender the prisoners. Even Lincoln, the most deliberate influence in the administration, inclined to the prevailing view that Captain Wilkes must not be disavowed.

All ingredients essential to a conflagration were aroused by his high-handed act: an infuriated English populace, demanding reparation for the "insult" to the British flag; an American public, similarly excited, insisting on supporting Captain Wilkes and retaining in American custody the Confederate envoys. In its essentials, the *Trent* affair involved no diplomatic problem. Captain Wilkes, a troublesome officer whose insubordination had already involved him in one court-martial and was to involve him in another, had acted on his own responsibility, without the slightest suggestion of instructions from his government. In doing so, he had violated certain principles of international law of which the United States had been the champion for sixty years, and had acted in accordance with certain British practices against which this country had always protested. It was for doing precisely what

Captain Wilkes had done in the *Trent* that the American government had declared war on England in 1812. Had the administration promptly disavowed Wilkes's act and restored the captives to the British guardianship from which they had been ravished, it not only would have acted in a way befitting the nation's dignity, but would have scored a diplomatic triumph. Mr. Seward would have upheld American principles, and would have compelled Great Britain to recognize interpretations of maritime law which it had been disregarding for centuries.

Not improbably Seward perceived this great opportunity, but certain demonstrations, both in England and in America, made such a course almost impossible. At no time in history, even in 1776 and 1812, had England been so unpopular in the United States. That English statesmen were deliberately planning to use American domestic troubles as an excuse for disrupting the Union, destroying its trade and merchant marine, and ending the Republic as a threat to the supremacy of the British Empire, was the conviction of most Americans. It was also shared by many distinguished Englishmen. "Three fourths of the House of Commons," wrote Richard Cobden, a strong friend of America in four years of war, "will be glad to find an excuse for voting for the dismemberment of the great Republic." In a speech at Rochdale, John Bright, another unswerving English friend of the Union, declared that the attitude of the upper strata of British society was that "the republic is too great and powerful and that it is better for us – not by us meaning you, but the governing classes and the governing policy of England – that it should be broken up." The Queen's precipitate proclamation of neutrality and the recognition of the seceded states as belligerents added fuel to American hostility. Certain comments of Lord Palmerston, Prime Minister, on Northern military reverses and the vituperative editorials of the London *Times* had not softened the American temper.

It is not strange therefore that the news of the capture of Mason and Slidell, two envoys sent by the Confederacy to England and France, to secure, among other things, recognition of Southern independence, was received with a frenzy of approbation. Captain Wilkes found himself the hero of the hour. The press, the pulpit, and public men of all parties showered him with adulation. Congress hurriedly passed a resolution thanking him for his brave, adroit, and patriotic conduct in the arrest of the traitors James M. Mason and John Slidell; international lawyers of great repute defended the legality of the performance; even men of the standing of Edward Everett, ex-President of Harvard, Richard Henry Dana, and Caleb Cushing joined in the universal chorus. In England the seizure of Mason and Slidell still further enraged the enemies of the United States and dismayed its friends. Though the *Times* and other anti-American papers had seemed to have exhausted already their resources in lampooning their transatlantic kindred, they now burst out with a new fury of execration. Naturally the name of Seward loomed large in all this excitement. That Captain Wilkes had acted under his instructions, and that Seward's purpose was to start the war with England which he had long planned, seemed as clear as daylight. Seward's steady course of hostility to England in thirty years of public life, and the many unpleasant comments he had made on the British Empire and British "rapacity," were now brought forth as part explanation of the Mason-Slidell "outrage." Of all the unflattering things the Secretary had said on this subject, one in particular rankled in the English mind. In a meeting with the Duke of Newcastle in Albany in 1860, on the occasion of the Prince of Wales's visit, Seward had remarked, referring to his forthcoming Secretaryship of State, that he would soon be in a position where it would be his duty to insult Great Britain and that he should proceed to do so. The noble lord, perhaps suffering from the traditional British lack of appreciation of American humor, took the remark in all seriousness and spread it broadcast throughout the British Empire. It now reappeared in a thousand newspaper articles and reverberating platforms; if any British heart had wondered at the meaning of the words, the *Trent* affair had now supplied the answer. All over England rose an almost unanimous demand for war. The sentiment was general that only the most abject apology could save Uncle Sam from a trouncing at the hand of the British fleet. War preparations began in every British shipyard on a scale not known since the days of Napoleon. An army of twelve thousand men was assembled for immediate transport to Canada, and fortifications were thrown up in strategic places on the long undefended Canadian frontier. Under these circumstances – the roars of approval from the American population, the threat of annihilation from what was then regarded as America's most determined enemy – the likelihood that the question of the *Trent* could be settled on the basis of justice and the principles of law seemed slight.

The attitude of the seven cabinet members on the *Trent* issue thus figured large in the public mind. In some cases individual opinions were expressed with an emphasis that subsequently proved embarrassing. That roving pictorial historian Benson J. Lossing happened to be in the War Department on the morning when the news of the *Trent* "broke" in Washington. He has left a lively picture of Simon Cameron, Secretary of War, leading a large crowd of associates in three cheers for Captain Wilkes, one of the most enthusiastic of the group being

Governor Andrew of Massachusetts. The usually placid and judicial Gideon Welles, Secretary of the Navy, indulged in extravagant praise that cost him in future years a vast amount of casuistry to explain away. "I congratulate you on your safe arrival," he wrote Wilkes – a man whom he cordially detested and afterward removed from an important command – "and especially do I congratulate you on the great public service you have rendered in the capture of the rebel emissaries. Messrs. Mason and Slidell have been conspicuous in the conspiracy to dissolve the Union and it is well known that when seized by you they were on a mission hostile to the government and the country. Your conduct in seizing these public enemies was marked by intelligence, ability, decision and firmness and has the emphatic approval of this department." Chase, though, as always somewhat nebulous in his use of words, believed "that the circumstances under which the act of Captain Wilkes was done, not only repelled the imputation of aggressive or unfriendly intent, but entitled him to commendation for the motives by which his conduct was governed, and reduced the seizure and removal from the 'Trent' of the rebel commissioners to a mere technical violation of the neutral rights of England. . . . The capture was, of course, warranted, and Captain Wilkes, in making it, performed only his plain duty to his government." The ablest lawyer in the Lincoln cabinet, and the most unimpassioned judge of administrative questions, was Edward Bates, Attorney General. From him, above all others, an earnest, impartial opinion on Wilkes might have been expected, yet we find the even-tempered Bates, in his Diary, joining in the universal acclaim. "While the fact gives great and general satisfaction, some timid persons are alarmed, lest Great Britain should take offense at the violation of her flag. There is no danger on that score. The law of nations is clear upon that point, and I have no doubt that, with a little time for examination, I will find it so settled by English authorities. . . . Not only was it legal to seize the men, but, I think, the ship itself was subject to confiscation."[1]

Only one member of the cabinet evidently believed, and so expressed himself, that the whole business was a mistake. Immediately on hearing the news Montgomery Blair declared that Wilkes had acted in violation of international law and that Mason and Slidell would have to be handed over to British custody. The proper course, he said, would be for Wilkes to take Mason and Slidell on the *Iroquois*, sail to England, and deliver them to the British government. Otherwise, resulting complications would fatally interfere with the attempt to put down rebel-

[1] Bates, *op. cit.*, p. 202. The entry is dated November 16, but no news had come of the excitement in England.

lion. The elder Blair, at Silver Spring, fulminated against Seward, whom he mistakenly regarded as responsible for the crisis. Not only should Mason and Slidell be restored to England, said old man Blair, but he suggested that "Billy Bowlegs" – he was now accustomed to refer to the Secretary of State in this unseemly fashion – should be added as a sacrificial offering on the altar of British revenge.

What was the real attitude of Seward and, an even more important matter, of his chief in the White House? According to Gideon Welles – the statement was made several years after the event – "no man was more elated or jubilant over the capture of the emissaries than Mr. Seward." This may have been true as a momentary impulse, but second sober thoughts soon gained control in Seward's mind, especially as he faced the practical issue involved – either to surrender the captives or to engage in war with England. Certainly his conduct in the six weeks of the *Trent* crisis – from November 8 to December 26 – show the man at his best. Unlike several of his cabinet colleagues, he gave no public expression of his views. Those jaunty remarks which he was too inclined to throw out at dinner tables did not confuse matters in the *Trent* dispute. Lord Lyons, the British Minister, who distrusted Seward and regarded him as England's inveterate foe, a man who wished war in order to carry out his plan of Canadian annexation, was at first disposed to hold him responsible for the *Trent* performance. But the change that soon came over the Secretary amazed the British diplomat. Instead of the suspicions and detractions of Seward he had been writing Lord John Russell, he now began to speak of the Secretary in glowing terms. The dignity and courtesy with which the Secretary handled the whole matter came in for warm commendation. "I am told confidentially," he had written Lord John Russell on November 19, "that orders were given at Washington which led to the capture of the *Trent* and that they were signed by Mr. Seward without the knowledge of the President." [2] Lord John's plan for solving the difficulty had the merit of simplicity. "The best thing would be if Seward could be turned out and a rational man put in his place." But presently a new note of appreciation appears in Lyons's letters to his chief. Mr. Seward, strangely enough, was not proving an obstacle to a harmonious settlement. "Mr. Seward," Lord Lyons writes on December 19, "is now on the peace side of the cabinet."

The Secretary of State was displaying once more that talent which had proved his salvation in other crises – the ability to shift his former position and adapt his principles to a new set of circumstances. It had

[2] Newton, Thomas Wodehouse E. Legh, Second Baron, *Lord Lyons, A Record of British Diplomacy*. London, E. Arnold, 1913. I, 55.

been his lifetime habit to view problems in their practical, not their legalistic or idealistic, aspect, and the theories advanced by many respectable sources as to the rights and wrongs of Captain Wilkes's performance interested him far less than what was likely to be the definite outcome. His once cherished plan for a European war as a means of bringing North and South together no longer represented his ideal of statesmanship. "You will perhaps be surprised," wrote Lord Lyons to Lord John on December 23, while the negotiation was still pending, "to find Mr. Seward on the side of peace. He does not like the look of the spirit he has called up. Ten months in office have dispelled many of his illusions. I presume that he no longer believes in the existence of a Union party in the South; in the return of the South to the arms of the North in case of a foreign war; in his power to frighten the nations of Europe by great words; in the ease with which the U. S. could crush rebellion with one hand and chastise Europe with the other; with the notion that the relations with England in particular are safe playthings to be used for the amusement of the American people. He sees himself in a very painful dilemma. But he knows his countrymen well enough to believe that if he can convince them that there is a real danger of war, they may forgive him for the humiliation of yielding to England, while it would be fatal to him to be the author of a disastrous foreign war. How he will act eventually I cannot say.[3] . . . I cannot say that my general opinion of Mr. Seward had undergone any change," his Lordship added later, "but without enquiry into his motives I must allow him the merit of having worked very hard and exposed his popularity to great danger. . . . Mr. Seward told me he had been through the fires of Tophet in order to get the prisoners surrendered."[4]

Lincoln's position is more obscure. The conventional version shows the President as the dominant mind in the *Trent* excitement, as the cool statesman who at once perceived the realities of the situation and who compelled Seward to modify his attitude and find good reasons for giving up the captives. The known facts do not substantiate this view. Several witnesses, it is true, have recorded glimpses of Lincoln in the crisis that lend color to the legend. One of them, Benson J. Lossing, tells of meeting Lincoln on the day when the *Trent* news reached the Capital, and he portrays the President as the one man who seemed to be keeping his poise when the rest of the government had fallen victim to the prevailing madness. "I fear," he quotes Lincoln as saying, "the traitors will prove to be white elephants. We must stick to American principles concerning the rights of neutrals. We fought Great Britain

[3] *Ibid.*, I, 69–70.
[4] *Ibid.*

for insisting, by theory and practice, on the right to do precisely what Wilkes has done. If Great Britain shall now protest against the act, and demand their release, we must give them up, apologize for the act as a violation of our doctrines and thus forever bind her over to keep the peace in relation to neutrals and so acknowledge that she has been wrong for sixty years." Gideon Welles quotes Lincoln as using this same phrase, "white elephants," in reference to the Southern gentlemen then languishing in Fort Warren, Boston Harbor (to which they had been removed), and Nicolay and Hay insist that he saw the issue correctly from the first. There are indications, however, that the idea of backing down before British threats rankled in Lincoln's breast, and that he was anxious to find some other solution. Charles Sumner proved to be a wholesome influence at this time. As chairman of the Senate Committee on Foreign Relations, Sumner had considerable claims to Lincoln's confidence, and spent a part of nearly every day with him discussing the *Trent* question. Sumner saw clearly the issues involved. From the first he was for a peaceful settlement, not only because England had justice on its side, but because he knew that a military conflict would sink his country in disaster. No American of the time understood so well Englishmen and the English character. British leaders like Cobden, John Bright, William E. Foster, the Duke of Argyle, the Duchess of Sutherland, all devoted to the Northern cause, were Sumner's close friends, and the letters interchanged through four years of war form an indispensable part of the story of British-American relations in that time.

In his almost daily talks with Lincoln, Sumner would read letters from these correspondents. All pleaded with Sumner to use his influence to induce Lincoln to surrender the captives and thus ensure a peaceful solution. The British aristocracy and governing classes – they were practically identical – secretly desired war, they urged, and for the United States to maintain an irreconcilable attitude would simply play into their hands. Though Lincoln gladly listened to Sumner, he was, as always, moving slowly, taking advice from all worth-while sources, but not committing himself. In his message, sent to Congress on December 1, the *Trent* affair was not even mentioned, greatly to the disgust of British statesmen. Sumner, like Lincoln, was seeking a way out that would not mean abject surrender, and the two men gave much consideration to arbitration. Sumner was willing to go to any extreme to avert war, but the President at first hesitated at complete acquiescence in the British viewpoint. That influences other than Seward and Blair and Sumner were working to smooth the way to American acceptance of British terms was not known then, but is known today. When Seward obtained his first view of Lord John's note, demanding the surrender of Mason and Slidell, the agreeable tone in which the message was framed gave him a pleasant surprise. Seward "told me that he was pleased to find that the despatch was courteous and friendly and not dictatorial or menacing," Lord Lyons wrote the Minister of Foreign Affairs. Had Russell's original paper been handed to the Secretary of State his satisfaction would not have been so pronounced. That the Queen and the Prince Consort had edited this curt ultimatum – for in its original form it was little less – cutting out the harsh phrases and writing in more polite ones, leaving the general implications the same yet transforming it into something that a proud nation could accept without humiliation, did not become known until long after the *Trent* had become part of history.

When the cabinet came together on Christmas Day, 1861, only Seward and Blair had taken a stand in favor of the British contention. It required the better part of two days' discussion to obtain that unanimity of decision desirable in the solution of such a momentous problem. Not improbably this session was the most fateful held in the course of the Civil War. The real issue hanging in the balance was the future of the United States. A stark alternative confronted the council: refusal to accept the British demand meant that, in addition to subduing the South, American army and naval forces would be compelled to add the British Empire to its foes. In all probability the French Empire would have joined England in hostilities, as well, for Napoleon III had from the beginning supported the British and it was no secret that the dismemberment and paralyzing of American power was regarded in the Tuileries as essential to the success of French imperial schemes in Mexico. Edward Bates, whose Diary gives the best account,[5] sketchy as it is, of this cabinet session, indicates that all seven members clearly estimated the gravity of the occasion. "All of us were impressed with the magnitude of the subject," wrote Bates, "and believed that upon our decision depended the dearest interest, probably the existence of the nation." Charles Sumner attended on Lincoln's invitation, armed with the letters of Cobden and Bright which he read with due solemnity, and letters of Thurlow Weed, who was then in England as a kind of Civil War Colonel House, also urging compliance, were laid before the gathering.

Lord John Russell's letter to Seward, polite as was the phraseology, admitted of nothing but a "yes" or "no" answer. It demanded the return of Mason and Slidell to British custody and an apology for the insult to the British flag. In private instructions to Lord Lyons, Russell

[5] Bates, *op. cit.*, pp. 213–217.

had said that Britain would probably be "easy" about the apology, in consideration of American sensitiveness. Seward's statement that Captain Wilkes had acted without instructions naturally made such an apology superfluous; no nation could be reasonably expected to apologize for an offense it had not committed. After reading Russell's note, Seward laid before his colleagues the reply which, shut up all alone in his office, he had spent two days in preparing. It was a clever political paper, and one of the most characteristic ones that ever came from Seward's pen; it was written not primarily for the attention of Her Majesty's law lords but for the ears of the American public. It was not intended to be a document that would stand the closest analysis from the standpoint of international law, but one that would show the man in the street that he was not kowtowing to the British lion when he gave up his unpopular guests. Seward's main contention was that envoys on a neutral ship, carrying dispatches, were contraband of war and subject to seizure. Captain Wilkes therefore had been within his rights in firing a shot across the bow of the *Trent*, boarding that vessel, demanding her papers, and searching for forbidden matériel and personnel of war. Seward granted, however, that Wilkes had exceeded his right when he forcibly removed the suspected envoys to an American ship. He should have seized not only the "contraband" but the ship itself, taken it into the nearest American port, and handed it over to a prize court. That had always been the American practice, and Wilkes, in disregarding it, and in adopting instead the British custom of violently removing passengers from merchant vessels, had followed a procedure which his government could not support. That is, in surrendering the Southern envoys, the United States was observing principles for which it had been contending for the best part of a century. "These principles were laid down for us in 1804, by James Madison, when Secretary of State in the administration of Thomas Jefferson, in instructions given to James Monroe, our Minister to England." How could America remain true to its own doctrines and sustain Wilkes when he had violated them? "The four persons,"[6] concluded Seward, "in question are now held in military custody at Fort Warren in the State of Massachusetts. They will be cheerfully liberated. Your lordship will please indicate a time and place for receiving them."

Adroit as Seward had shown himself to be in finding a way out of this deadlock, his colleagues were slow to be convinced. To give way to detested Albion, even when a pistol was pointed at Uncle Sam's head, came hard. "There was a reluctance on the part of some of the members of the cabinet – and even the President himself," notes Bates,

[6] In addition to Mason and Slidell, their secretaries had been seized.

"to acknowledge these obvious truths." An anecdote years afterward related by Frederick W. Seward, son of the Secretary and his assistant in the State Department, describes Lincoln's hesitation in more detail.[7] Though the cabinet discussed the matter from ten o'clock in the morning till two in the afternoon, no conclusion had been reached. It was therefore decided to adjourn and meet the following morning. After all the others had left the cabinet room, Lincoln and Seward found themselves alone. "You will go on, of course," Lincoln said to Seward, "preparing your answer, which, as I understand it, will state the reasons why they ought to be given up. Now I have a mind to try my hand at stating the reasons why they ought *not* to be given up. We will compare the points on each side." Lincoln did formulate such an argument and it is now preserved among his papers. In it he approached the plan of arbitration – in this doubtless showing the influence of Charles Sumner, who had been at his elbow for several weeks pressing this solution. When the cabinet reconvened the next morning, however, Lincoln did not present his thesis. All seven men now accepted Seward's answer. After the cabinet broke up, Lincoln and Seward again held a private session. Seward referred to their talk of the day before. "You thought you might frame an argument for the other side?" Lincoln smiled and shook his head. "I found that I could not make an argument that would satisfy my own mind," he said. "That proved to me that your ground was the right one."

[7] Seward's *Seward*, III, 25–26.

IX

THE *TRENT* EPISODE made clear that Seward had other resources of diplomacy than menacing threats against the most powerful nations of Europe. Perhaps his skillful behavior when confronted with the contingency he had apparently so long hoped for sheds a new light upon the motives which had inspired these explosive moments. Seward's great responsibility, as Secretary of State, was to prevent the recognition of the Confederacy by Great Britain and France. Such recognition, he believed – and most students of the period agree with him – would have resulted in a Confederate triumph. There is little question that Great Britain would have extended this friendly welcome to Jefferson Davis, except for one thing. That was fear of war with the United States. To fight such a war successfully, England would have had to dispatch practically her entire fleet to American waters, and in the tense situation prevailing at that time in Europe, this was too dangerous a hazard to risk. Seward perceived this last from the outset, and his genius as a diplomat consists in the ability with which he utilized it as the one possible way of forestalling British intervention. From this point of view his denunciation of England at private dinner parties in the secession winter of 1860–1861, and his declaration of war in case the Palmerston government meddled in American concerns, assume a new importance.

If we seek the real secret of Seward's diplomacy, we may safely ignore the many learned studies of which it has been the subject and turn to the estimate of one who was certainly no friend – his facile antagonist, Judah P. Benjamin, Secretary of State in the Confederate cabinet. "The most surprising infatuation of modern times," wrote Benjamin to John Slidell, the Confederate commissioner who had spent nearly two years at the Court of Napoleon III, attempting to entice that monarch into the recognition of the seceded states, "is the thorough conviction entertained by the British ministry that the United States are ready to declare war against England, and it is impossible not to admire the sagacity with which Mr. Seward penetrated into the secret feelings of the British cabinet and the success of his policy of intimidation, which the world at large supposed would be met with prompt resentment, but which he, with deeper insight into the real policy of that cabinet, foresaw would be followed by submissive acquiescence in his demands." Here is a complete explanation both of Seward's methods in foreign relations and of his accomplishments. He succeeded in preventing the recognition of the South by the great European powers, not because he was a master of international law – a field in which Seward was deficient – but because he was a master of human nature. It was his lively imagination, his insight into the minds of his fellows, his artist's skill in playing upon their weaknesses and their apprehensions, his knowledge of the precise moments when to threaten and when to conciliate, that enabled him for four years to keep his country safe from European aggression. Seward could do this because, to him, diplomacy was fundamentally not a matter of protocols, precedents, and treaties, but the underlying motives and purposes of men. Of the former he knew little, but the latter had been a lifetime study. This gift, in the hurly-burly of American practical politics, had lifted the Secretary from the obscurity of a small New York village almost to the White House, and he found it equally useful in dealing with the foremost statesmen of Europe.

The bad reputation which Seward enjoyed in Europe in itself proved to be an invaluable asset. In England no American, possibly excepting Charles Sumner, was so well known. Any American who wins fame as an enemy of the British Empire is more likely to acquire notoriety in England than one who achieves high place in literature, science, art, or even statesmanship. And Seward meant to British statesmen the pre-eminent American jingo. American destiny, in the conviction to which he frequently gave expression, was to become mistress of the entire North American Continent, from the Arctic to Panama. The existence of Canada, as a dependency of the British Empire, he looked upon as little better than a standing insult. His opinions of the several sovereignties of Europe had had free circulation in the countries most concerned. "The monarchs of Europe are to have no rest while they have a colony remaining on this continent," he declared as far back as 1846. He described Napoleon III as "the sickly successor of the Romans"; the French Empire was "a hateful usurpation"; and he denounced the "treachery by which Louis Napoleon rose to a throne on the ruins of the Republic." The United States, he said, "is, and forever must be, a living offense to Russia and to Austria, and all despotic governments. You will never, by whatever humiliations, gain one friend or secure one ally in Europe or America that wears a crown." The man's choicest bits of malediction, however, were reserved for Great Britain. The British Empire, in his view, was "the greatest, the most grasping and the most rapacious in the world." "Without a war on our part, Great Britain will wisely withdraw and disappear from this hemisphere within a century – at least within a half-century."

This kind of talk may not have been admirable or statesmanlike, but it profoundly affected Civil War diplomacy. The correspondence of Lord Lyons, British Minister at Washington, indicates the apprehension which Seward's advent as Secretary of State caused in England. He could not help fearing, Lyons wrote Russell, that "Mr. Seward will be a dangerous Foreign Minister," and his anxiety was confirmed when, at a formal dinner party at the British Legation on March 25, the new Secretary began to lay down the law to all the foreign representatives present – not only the British Minister, but the French, Russian, and other distinguished emissaries. "Mr. Seward," Lord Lyons wrote his chief, "went off into a defiance of foreign nations, in a style of braggadocio which was formerly not uncommon with him, but which I had not heard from him since he had been in office." At times the Secretary of State used more subtle methods of threat. Thus on April 8, 1861, he sent for William H. Russell, correspondent of the London *Times*, and amid huge clouds of tobacco smoke entertained his guest by confidentially reading a dispatch which he was about to send to Charles Francis Adams, recently arrived American Minister in London. Russell expressed his misgivings at the menacing attitude towards Great Britain which Mr. Adams was instructed to adopt. Naturally, Russell dutifully reported the details to the British Minister, as Seward knew he would; that was the reason he had taken him into his confidence. He could not directly lay his dispatch to Mr. Adams before the British envoy, but this roundabout method served the purpose just as effectively.

Mad as all this seems, there was method in it; the one idea which Seward was determined to implant in the minds of British and French statesmen was that the recognition of the Confederacy would spell war with the United States. He did not insinuate this as the certain outcome, but framed it in the most outspoken language. Mercier, the French Minister in Washington, who was an unabashed champion of the South and an advocate of recognition, in a long talk with the Secretary of State in October 1861 expressed his well-known views that separation of North and South was inevitable, and rather impudently added that he had advised Thouvenel, Napoleon's Foreign Secretary, to recognize Southern independence. The United States, Seward snapped back, would declare war on any power that took this step. It was possible that, in such a conflict, the United States might suffer defeat, "but

France," he said, "will know that there has been a war." Over and over again he instructed Adams to inform Russell that, if Great Britain recognized the Confederacy, she should at once make plans to become its ally, for the Queen would find herself at war. In August 1862, there were signs in plenty that Earl Russell, goaded by Gladstone, was contemplating this fatal step. McClellan's reverses in the Peninsula had persuaded that statesman of the utter hopelessness of the Union cause. Minister Adams was instructed, on August 16, that if Britain took any step that indicated an intention "to dictate, or to mediate, or even to solicit or persuade, you will answer that you are forbidden to debate, to hear, or in any way receive, entertain, or transmit, any communication of the kind." If the South were "acknowledged" Adams was "immediately to suspend his function." "You will perceive," Seward concluded, "that we have approached the contemplation of that crisis with the caution which great reluctance has inspired. But I trust that you will also have perceived that the crisis has not appalled us."

Whatever may have been the shortcomings of Seward as a diplomat, he had one virtue, whose value in that evasive profession has been recognized only in modern times. He spoke in the plainest of terms; his correspondence was, indeed, "shirt sleeves" diplomacy at its best. Mr. Judah P. Benjamin, in words quoted above, gives Seward praise for "penetrating into the secret feelings of the British cabinet" and foreseeing that this "policy of intimidation" would be successful. For the historic fact is that, though Lord Lyons and Lord John Russell were accustomed to refer to these challenges as "bluster" – the word "bluff" had not acquired diplomatic standing – they were really disturbed. They believed in their hearts that Seward desired a European war as a way out of the nation's domestic difficulties. Lyons warned that such a war would be a serious matter for Great Britain. England would have to send the "largest possible naval force and bring the war to an end before the United States could prepare." Otherwise, "the spirit, the energy and the resources of this people would be difficult to overcome." In identical dispatches to Adams in London and Dayton in Paris, dated July 28, 1862, Seward set forth the reasons why war was the last thing Britain desired. The United States, he wrote, relied "upon the practice of justice and respect for our sovereignty for foreign nations"; but "it is not necessary for me to say that if this reliance fails, this civil war will, without our fault, become a war of continents – a war of the world." The calamity that finally afflicted the world in 1914 would, according to Seward's reading of world politics, have descended upon it during the American Civil War. This was the contingency that British statesmen foresaw and feared, in case they meddled in American affairs. That such a European conflict might have incalculable, perhaps fatal consequences for the British Empire needs no demonstration.

If this was a bluff it was a magnificent one, and it was justified by success. Palmerston himself succinctly, if colloquially, summed up British policy when a delegation of British clergymen, noblemen, Members of Parliament, and other distinguished gentlemen called upon him, in July 1864, to urge mediation. "They who in quarrels interpose, Will often wipe a bloody nose," he reminded his visitors – "a quotation which," commented the *Index*, the pro-Confederate weekly published in London, "in the mouth of the Prime Minister of the British Empire, and on such an occasion, must be admitted as not unworthy of Abraham Lincoln himself."

Of all Seward's threats, his masterpiece was delivered in 1863, when the so-called "rams," under construction by the Lairds of Liverpool as Confederate raiders, were nearing completion. The *Alabama*, secretly built by the same firm a year before, was wreaking vast destruction at that time on American merchant shipping. These new ships were much more powerful, and should they be permitted to "escape" from the Liverpool docks, in the manner of the *Alabama*, the American flag would have vanished from the seas. Charles Francis Adams, under instructions from Seward, had been bringing pressure for months on Lord John Russell, presenting unmistakable evidence that the ships were Confederate property and demanding their detention by the British government. Mr. Adams, in September 1862, presented his protest, concluding an eloquent state paper with the famous words that if the rams became part of the Confederate navy, "it would be superfluous in me to point out to your Lordship that this is war." This declaration, and the apparent British backdown in face of it, have become one of the legends of the Civil War. The fact is that Russell, five days before this menacing note was received, had ordered the seizure of the ships, had stationed British war vessels in Liverpool Harbor to prevent their escape – with orders to sink them, if the attempt were made – and, soon after, purchased them and made them part of the British Navy. It was not Adams's threat, but the more subtle maneuvering of Seward that had persuaded the British government to change its policy.

In July 1862, a bill was introduced in Congress authorizing the President to issue letters of marque and reprisal – that is, to commission "privateers" – as a kind of "militia of the sea" to prey upon enemy commerce, just as Confederate "corsairs" were attacking Federal ships. There was only one defect in this otherwise desirable measure: the South had no merchant marine, and therefore there were no Southern ships to attack. Because of this absurdity, the bill was pigeonholed by both House and Senate, and lay unnoticed and unacted upon in committee until February 1863. Then Congress, prompted by Seward, took up the measure and quickly passed it, with little debate. When Charles Sumner, in the Senate, objected to the bill as senseless, since the South had no mercantile marine, Senator Grimes, who had the measure in charge, replied that that was true, but added that the administration desired the legislation to use "if need arose" and hinted that privateers might be useful against British ships that had "turned Confederate." While there was much puzzlement in the United States, and while Seward, in his statements to Lord Lyons and his instructions to Adams, was rather vague, in one quarter no doubt prevailed as to the value of the measure at this critical moment. British shipping interests quickly grasped its meaning. So did Palmerston and Russell. Both these statesmen had been in public life in 1815; Palmerston, indeed, had then held a minor post in the Liverpool government; and both had vivid memories of the terrible devastation American privateers had visited on the British mercantile marine at that time. They wanted no repetition of that experience. A vast array of British merchant ships, during the Civil War, plied between home ports and the Confederacy, bringing munitions and other necessaries to the struggling South and transporting back most marketable cargoes of cotton, tobacco, and other Southern products. They had to take the chance of seizure, of course, but blockade running, despite many captures, proved to be a most profitable risk. A cordon of privateers placed out at sea, so numerous that few vessels could escape, would be a different matter. According to American law – for the United States was not a party to the Declaration of London, outlawing such procedures – enemy property in neutral ships was legally subject to attack and confiscation. That such a "flood of privateers" operating against British ships would incite war was evident. In a word, the privateering bill was Seward's reply to the construction of Confederate commerce destroyers in British shipyards. It is the opinion of Ephraim D. Adams, the classic authority on British-American relations in the Civil War, that Seward's insinuating use of this recourse was the argument that induced the British government to seize the Laird rams and to end, for good and all, the use of British shipyards to do what the Confederacy was unable to do by itself – construct a navy.[1]

In addition to knowing when to threaten, when to bluster, when to prod, to hint, to instill suspicions and fears, Seward had another gift equally serviceable in diplomacy. He knew when to conciliate and

[1] For a complete and interesting account of the whole matter, see Adams, Ephraim D., *op. cit.* II. Ch. XIII.

when, without any loss in dignity, to yield. He made use of this talent most effectively, perhaps, in the case of the *Trent*. But he displayed it with equal patience and skill in his treatment of France. Napoleon III had taken advantage of the domestic difficulties in the United States to extend his imperialistic system to Mexico. He had dispatched a French army overseas, invaded the southern republic, seized its capital, overturned its government, and on its ruins set up a puppet regime, installing Maximilian of Austria as emperor. A more complete defiance of the Monroe Doctrine could not be imagined. One would hardly have supposed that a jingo American like Seward, the well-advertised enemy of European monarchism, would hesitate long in applying the appropriate remedy. Yet this "blustering" diplomat filed no formal protest, for a protest, if disregarded, would almost necessarily mean war. Instead, with the use of those pointed, yet unprovocative phrases of which he was such a master, he conveyed to Napoleon his disapproval of this aggression, and informed him that, when home affairs had quieted down, Mexico would receive the undivided attention of the United States. Most Americans at the time regarded his Mexican diplomacy as disgraceful and pusillanimous. The House of Representatives passed a resolution denouncing it, unanimously declaring the establishment of a monarchy by a European power in this continent as contravening American policy. Seward's "cowardice" in the face of Napoleon's encroachment was a leading item in the attacks made upon him all through the war. The newspapers flamed with angry editorials; the Democratic platforms bristled with unflattering adjectives when they touched on the Mexican question. Many intelligent and undemonstrative Americans held similar views. Even John Bigelow, in Paris, who succeeded Dayton as minister in 1864, wrote Seward that a more positive attitude would accomplish results. "I think," Seward answered Bigelow in an unofficial letter, "with deference to your opinion, which I always hold in great respect, that, with our land and naval forces in Louisiana retreating before the rebels instead of marching toward Mexico, this is not the most suitable time we could choose for offering idle menaces to the emperor of France. We have compromised nothing, surrendered nothing, and I do not propose to surrender anything. But why should we gasconade about Mexico when we are in a struggle for our own life?"

Soon after Lee's surrender, however, Seward's warnings took on a definite tone. The Maximilian enterprise, he now informed the French Foreign Office, fundamentally antagonized American policy on this continent; the United States had never recognized the new Mexican Empire, and had no intention of ever recognizing it. In December he instructed Bigelow to inform the French Emperor that his behavior in overthrowing the Mexican Republic and setting up a puppet regime endangered the friendship that had so long prevailed between France and the United States. Gently as this was expressed, it amounted to a threat. It gave France the choice of withdrawing its forces from Mexico, or crossing swords with the large and well-trained American Army which General Grant had stationed along the Mexican border, and which was now free to concentrate its undivided efforts upon a new problem. In April 1866, France officially announced its plans for withdrawing from Mexico – plans which, after a little delay, it carried out, leaving Maximilian to his tragic fate at the hands of a Mexican firing squad. The nation can never be too grateful to Seward for not plunging the country into war with the greatest military power of Europe at a time when all its strength was needed in the domestic struggle, and for preventing this without sacrifice of principle or honor. Seward would have fought France at once if it had recognized the Confederacy, for in that event immediate action would be demanded; the invasion of Mexico, however, presented an issue which could be postponed to a more favorable time.

Thus, mistaken as was Seward's policy frequently in domestic matters, he was a great foreign secretary – many believe the greatest who had ever headed the Department of State.

BOOK THREE

Exit Cameron; Enter Stanton

I

DOMESTIC as well as foreign complications were disturbing the Lincoln cabinet in this critical December of 1861. Lord Palmerston, "Johnny" Russell, and Mason and Slidell were not the only public characters who were making that an arduous Christmas season for the President. Another disturber of the peace, much nearer home, was consuming that part of Lincoln's time which was not devoted to foreign problems. The selection of Simon Cameron for Secretary of War represented one of the compromises the President was frequently compelled to make in his effort to weld together a solid, compact party organization for fighting the war. That the result would be disastrous had been the popular expectation and in this foreboding Lincoln himself had joined. Events quickly justified the worst apprehensions. Probably the ablest, most conscientious conduct of the department would not have satisfied the American public in the first hysterical months of war. With practically no regular army, with a militia system unprepared and largely in the hands of politicians, with virtually no arms or war supplies and only the most rudimentary facilities for producing them, with a public ignorant of the proportions of the task it had assumed, yet loudly clamoring for immediate results, the greatest war minister in history would have proved inadequate. But the charges that soon began accumulating against Cameron concerned other things than failure to measure up intellectually to his post. That, under Cameron, the War Department would degenerate into a political machine, abounding in graft and corruption, had been generally predicted, and this gloomy forecast Cameron, almost with malice prepense, immediately proceeded to vindicate.

Alexander K. McClure, Philadelphia editor and politician, relates one anecdote in his recollections of Cameron that gives the perfect key to the man's character. As to his purely strategic candidacy for the presidential nomination of 1860, "Cameron himself believed, in after years, that he could have been nominated and elected if he had been heartily pressed by Pennsylvania. He many times chided me for refusing to give him earnest support, saying that he could have been made a successful candidate, and then, to use his own expressive language, 'We could have had everything we wanted.' "[1] Though the War Department, in normal times, was not exactly a spoilsman's paradise, the sudden turn of history in 1861 transformed it into a sumptuous field. The duty of organizing soldiers by the hundreds of thousands, purchasing their food, their transportation, their supplies, their tents, clothing, blankets, horses, their arms, opened up a dazzling prospect. The selection of officers became as much a matter of political patronage as the expenditure of millions in money. Cameron's associates in the cabinet suffered no illusions as to the spirit in which he would approach this problem. "When the Chicago nomination was made," wrote Gideon Welles,[2] "the question with him was, how and in what way was Cameron to be benefitted?" The Pennsylvanians who protested his selection insisted that the office would be used to build up an impregnable political machine. This is precisely what the Secretary proceeded to do. His chief henchmen in Pennsylvania were Alexander Cummings and John Sanderson. In the Chicago Convention these were the agents who traded the Pennsylvania delegation – which they did not control – to Lincoln, on the promise of David Davis of a seat for Cameron in the cabinet. Cameron, on assuming the War Department, immediately gave to Sanderson his most important office – that of chief clerk, which, as there was no Assistant Secretary at the time, made him second man in the department. The other lieutenant, Cummings, was made purchasing agent of army supplies at New York. When Cameron began his labors, the War Office contained only five appointees from Pennsylvania; in short order, by the decapitation of existing incumbents, the proportion had increased to twenty-seven – all selected from political motives.

Other favors granted to Pennsylvania Republicans of the Cameron school occasioned widespread criticism. Simon Stevens, a Cameronian in high standing, early figured in the celebrated saga of the Hall carbines, arms which the War Department first sold as almost worthless at two dollars each and then, in April and May, purchased back for twenty-two dollars. No one questioned the abilities of Thomas A. Scott, another Pennsylvanian, whom Cameron appointed Assistant Secretary of War in August 1861, after Congress had passed a law creating the position, but the fact that he continued his post as vice-president of the Pennsylvania Railroad – without salary, it is true –

[1] McClure, *op. cit.*, p. 153.

[2] Welles, Gideon, *Narrative of Events*. Published in the *Magazine of History*, 1925. Extra number 105, Vol. XXVII.

a corporation with which he was constantly making contracts for transporting troops and supplies, caused much criticism. The charges exacted for moving soldiers – two cents a mile in boxcars – seemed excessive. The awarding of contracts to middlemen, the greater number of whom derived from Pennsylvania, was looked upon as another Cameronian method of rewarding friends, paying political debts, and reinforcing the machine. The number of commissions awarded to Pennsylvania politicians became a matter of current jest. "No wonder Pennsylvania has so few privates in the army," a scornful Congressman declared, "since she furnishes so many officers." John Tucker, still another Pennsylvanian, was placed by Cameron in charge of water transportation, although he had never operated a vessel in his life; the excessive prices paid for water craft for this purpose made entertaining newspaper copy. In view of the political partnership between himself and Thurlow Weed – a partnership to which Cameron in large degree owed his cabinet appointment – the appearance of that politician's name in the government's reports on frauds caused no surprise. Weed early participated as middleman in the purchase of vessels for Cameron's department. The case of the *Cataline* loomed large in these investigations. Weed himself was one of the four men who purchased – with notes – this wheezy veteran of the deep for $18,000, then chartered it to Uncle Sam for three months at $10,000 a month, with a guarantee of $50,000 in case it should sink. One of the cargoes of "supplies" loaded on the *Cataline* – purchased by a clerk recommended by Weed – proved as picturesque as the ship itself: it consisted of straw hats, linen pantaloons, pickles, and other articles not found in any army ration list. That Weed had also succeeded in collecting a 5 per cent commission on powder sold to the War Department was asserted by a congressional committee.

There is no intention of rehearsing in this place the long story of jobbery and corruption in the War Department under the regime of Simon Cameron. Material on the subject is certainly not lacking. All substantial American libraries have reposing on their shelves today the bulky volume containing about three thousand pages of testimony which Congress published in 1862. It offers an abundant storehouse to which researchers into the seamy aspects of democratic government, especially in wartime, have frequently gone for enlightenment. In December of 1861 and the early months of 1862, Congress rang with fiery speeches picturing the excesses of Cameron's department. There was "indubitable evidence," said Henry L. Dawes of Massachusetts, "that somebody has plundered the public treasury in a single year as much as the entire yearly expenses of the government, which the people hurled from power because of its corruption" – meaning the Buchanan administration. The army had its regular officers, stationed at all important points, for the purchase of supplies; despite this, Cameron appointed favored gentlemen from civil life to do the work. Such appointees, of course, were politicians and speculators, who obtained contracts without public bidding, invariably in lines of business in which they had no experience. These contracts, in turn, they would sell – pocketing fat profit in every case – to dealers who actually provided the goods. Of such transactions, the ones that most shocked the public were those for the purchase of horses. Horse breeders and traders did not get the original contracts; these were awarded to political middlemen, who sublet them to professional traders. The speculators made handsome profits, but the army frequently got very poor horses. Out of a thousand animals purchased for a cavalry regiment in Louisville, 485 were discarded as diseased and worthless – blind, spavined, ringboned, afflicted with heaves and glanders. These unhappy creatures cost Mr. Cameron's department $58,200, and $10,000 for transportation, and they were fit only for the boneyard. "Many of the horses that were sent back," said Mr. Dawes, "have been tied to posts and to trees within the District of Columbia and left there to starve to death. A guide can take you around the District of Columbia today to hundreds of carcasses of horses chained to trees where they have pined away, living on bark till they starve and die." Horse contracts became so plentiful in the District of Columbia that they circulated as a kind of currency, and were used to pay political debts and heal political feuds.

In the distribution of such contracts, Cameron again displayed his fondness for Pennsylvanians. One thousand horses were purchased at extravagant prices at Huntingdon, in that state, one third of which proved to be such sad representatives of a noble beast that the people in the town protested against the transaction. Kentucky, no mean judge of horseflesh and a considerable producer, expressed justifiable rage when several of its cavalry regiments were equipped with an inferior breed transported at great expense from the Keystone State. In late October, more than eight thousand horses were eating vast quantities of forage and rendering no military service, for there were no men to mount them. Similar details could be given – and were given in the government report mentioned above – of the purchase of guns, pistols, ammunition, uniforms, and the thousands of things needed to equip an army. Cameron favored Pennsylvania, and interfered with the war in another way. All through his career as Senator, as noted in a preceding chapter, he had shown interest in only one public question –

the protective tariff. In the early days of the war, he steadfastly refused to enter the European market for the purchase of arms and ammunition. He opposed patronizing any but home industries. That his "home industries" were not yet equipped to turn out munitions in the quantity needed, and would not be for a considerable time, did not matter. Had he at once sent agents to England and France to acquire these essential materials, two ends would have been served: the Federal army would have been properly furnished, and the guns would not have been acquired, as they were, by the Confederates. When Cameron finally woke up and began scouring the European field, prices, because of these Southern purchases, had reached a high figure, and in many cases arms could not be acquired at any price, for the agents of Jefferson Davis had cornered the supply.

If one were seeking the way a war department should not be run, especially in a time of national crisis, no better model could be found than the work of Simon Cameron in the first six months of the Civil War. The sad military history of those early months did not enhance his standing with an outraged American public. An angry press undoubtedly exaggerated his misdeeds when it held his loose and corrupt administration responsible for Bull Run and Ball's Bluff. Cameron, however, early perceived that Lincoln would not long tolerate his presence in an administration to which he was daily bringing discredit. By early summer it became apparent, especially to Cameron's observant eye, that his departure from Washington was inevitable. He had no intention of surrendering his post without a struggle. The energetic and ruthless reformation of his department might have saved his head. Had Cameron thrown out all the politicians and installed a new and effective regime the public would probably have overlooked these early excesses as the mistakes and the inevitable consequences of suddenly transferring a peaceful nation to a state of war. Such a simple solution of his problem, however, did not accord with Cameron's genius. He began to look for succor in the crisis, every day growing more intense, between himself and Lincoln. He found powerful support in the most unexpected quarters. In the early days of the cabinet, Cameron worked in close sympathy with Seward. The New Yorker, as already made clear, had promoted Cameron's appointment as essential to his plans, formed immediately after Lincoln's election for control of the administration. In April and May of '61, Cameron had fulfilled Seward's fondest expectations. In the Sumter business he had acted as Seward's close ally. He undoubtedly used his position to bring General Scott under Seward's wing. With Scott's – and Seward's – proposal to surrender not only Fort Sumter, but Fort Pickens, to the Confederates,

Cameron was in cordial agreement. The Secretary of War, though his department was the one most intimately concerned, did not attend the cabinet meeting called to consider that monstrous proposal. The probability is that he was absent by design; he did not wish to go on record as favoring this surrender, for that would have displeased Lincoln, who had already manifested his anger with Scott's recommendation; on the other hand, he did not wish to oppose it, for that would have been an unfriendly act toward Seward, in all likelihood the proponent of the plan, and working hard at least for the abandonment of Sumter. So, true to his political instinct, Cameron refrained from attending the session and made no response to Lincoln's request for his written opinion – in itself an act of insubordination.

Up to this time, therefore, and for a period afterward, Cameron fulfilled Seward's expectation, and stood loyally at his side. Cameron's nature, however, did not entirely lack pride, and his fiery Scotch spirit soon began to resent his colleague's increasing encroachment on his department. Seward's assumption that he was Secretary of War as well as Secretary of State was so unconcealed that it became a joking matter in the cabinet itself. The question of dispatching General Butler to the Virginia front came up in a meeting of Chase, Cameron, and Seward. Chase, ordinarily not given to banter, said, "Well, let's leave Seward to order him off at once." [3] Cameron joined in the laughter at the sally, but it depicted a state of affairs in his office that was no longer to his taste. Seward's letters disclose his belief that he was the real head of the army – and, in fact, of the navy as well. "I am consulting with the cabinet one hour," he wrote Mrs. Seward, "with the army officers the next, and with the navy next, and I visit all troops as fast as they come." Cameron did not participate in counsels on military plans and the disposition of the forces, but Seward was invariably at the center of things. Seward, wrote Gideon Welles in his "Narrative of Events," now in the Library of Congress,[4] "seemed to consider the war department a mere appendage to that of the State and freely issued orders, projected and sent out expeditions and did some extraordinary things, which, if to be done at all, should have been by the administration and properly belonged to the secretary of war." Cameron resented in violent language the Fort Pickens undertaking, organized by Seward and kept secret even from the War Department, and threatened to have Colonel Meigs, whom Seward had put in charge, court-martialed for absence without leave and misappropriation of government funds. In the early days Seward continued to keep control of the War Depart-

[3] Warden, *op. cit.*, p. 401.

[4] It was published in the *American Historical Review*, XXXI, 492.

ment through General Scott, now so senile and weakened by dropsy that he could not walk and had to be carried by orderlies from his carriage to his office. Scott's unhappy advice on the surrender of Fort Pickens had ended his influence with Lincoln, and the battle of Bull Run had made him most unpopular – perhaps unjustly – with the public.

Seward, with that versatility in switching allegiances for which he was famous, now turned to the rising sun and attached himself to the "young Napoleon," the brilliant, handsome McClellan whom Lincoln had brought from the West and put at the head of the Army of the Potomac. McClellan, like Scott and most other leaders of that early day, regarded Seward, and not Lincoln, as head of administration, and for a time the Secretary of State and the commanding general were almost inseparable. The situation came to a crisis in a meeting in General Scott's office in early October, 1861. An important matter came up: How many troops were then stationed near Washington? Cameron was unable to answer the question. General McClellan gave no information. General Scott said that no reports had been made to him. The President, who was present, seemed vexed and disturbed at this lack of essential knowledge in responsible quarters, but Seward came to the rescue. Drawing from his pocket a slip of paper, he read off figures showing the size of the army at that moment, and gave details of the regiments that had reported in the last few days. McClellan, appealed to, said that Seward's information was correct. General Scott turned to the President in disgust and anger. "This," he said, "is a remarkable state of things. I am in command of the armies of the United States, but have been wholly unable to get any reports, any statement of the actual forces; but here is the Secretary of State, a civilian for whom I have great respect, but who is not a military man nor conversant with military affairs, though his abilities are great, but this civilian is possessed of facts which are withheld from me. Military reports are made, not to these headquarters, but to the state department. Am I, Mr. President, to apply to the Secretary of State for the necessary military information to discharge my duties?" Seward explained that he had pieced together these statistics by keeping track of the regiments as they arrived, but Scott and the others believed that McClellan was his real source of knowledge. "Your labors are very arduous," Scott said to Seward, "but I did not before know the whole of them. If you in that way can get accurate information, the Rebels can also, though I cannot." Then the old veteran turned to McClellan in restrained but magnificent fury. "You were called here," he said, "by my advice. The times require vigilance and activity. I am not active and never shall be again. When I proposed that you should come here to aid, not supersede me, you had my friendship and confidence. You still have my confidence." [5]

That Cameron should resent this state of affairs was inevitable. His anger assumed a guise that was especially offensive to Seward. Cameron gradually transferred his somewhat doubtful affections to Seward's chief rival in the cabinet, Salmon Portland Chase. On personal grounds such an alliance was incompatible; in making the austere, self-righteous head of the Treasury his cabinet confidant, however, the shrewd Cameron acted on other than personal grounds. He had been looking for an issue that would divert public attention from the scandals in the War Department, and seeking friends who would be useful in thwarting Lincoln's well-known intention to drop him overboard. Certain early developments of the Civil War had not escaped Cameron's observation. Hostilities had hardly begun when the Republicans split into two camps on the slavery question. On one side stood the "radicals," headed by such leaders as Charles Sumner, Zachariah Chandler, William P. Fessenden, and Benjamin Wade, proclaiming as the chief purpose of the war the extirpation of slavery. On the other hand were the moderates, of whom, of course, Lincoln was chief, who insisted on the preservation of the Union as the main objective. The contention between these two groups, which was to split the party in two for the next ten years and reach an explosive state in the administration of Andrew Johnson, began as soon as the Confederate guns had silenced Fort Sumter. Certain happenings in the early military operations brought the question to notice in a practical way. When Northern armies began to advance into slave states – especially in Virginia, South Carolina, Kentucky, and Missouri – considerable numbers of slaves would flee their ancient bondage and enter the Federal lines.

What disposition was to be made of these black refugees? Should they be retained in the Northern armies and set to work in ways in which they could most usefully promote their success? Should they be employed in building fortifications, throwing up entrenchments, serving as cooks and in other capacities which would relieve white soldiers for fighting in the ranks? Should they be returned to their masters, in accordance with the provisions of the Fugitive Slave Law? Should they be given their freedom, and, as free men, be permitted to enlist in the Federal forces? Had the question concerned only the slaves of states in the Confederacy the decision would not have been so difficult, for these states, engaged in rebellion, might be regarded as having lost, for

[5] Welles, *Diary*. I, 241–242.

the time being at least, their rights under the Constitution. But in most cases the trouble involved states, or parts of states, that were still loyal to the Union, whose citizens, in considerable numbers, were enlisting in the Federal armies. To deprive citizens of South Carolina or Louisiana of their slaves would not have shocked the Northern conscience, but how about those of Maryland, western Virginia, Kentucky, and Missouri, slave states which had not seceded? In these states the Constitution still ran, and that document, and the laws made under its provisions, guaranteed the citizens their "property" in black men. Lincoln, in his inaugural, had solemnly assured these states that the Federal government would not disturb their favorite institution but would protect them in their most cherished rights. Moreover, even after Sumter, the Border states that still remained faithful to the Union continued to be one of Lincoln's constant anxieties. To lose Maryland, Kentucky, and Missouri would be, he still believed, to lose the war; and in all these states the secessionists were sleeplessly at work, attempting to force them into the Confederacy. To encroach on their slave property, even in moderation, would play into the hands of the anti-Federal forces, and very probably result in secession.

II

IN THE perspective of history Lincoln's position seems unassailable; he disliked slavery as much as the radicals themselves, but believed that prudence, in the delicate situation that prevailed in the first year and a half of war, demanded that no drastic steps be taken. Extremists, however, insisted on immediate emancipation. Slavery had brought on the war; to end that vicious institution was its sublime purpose; day by day these exhorters made the halls of Congress ring for action. In the cabinet the radicals at first had only one champion. They looked upon Salmon Portland Chase as their representative, and relied upon their favorite antislavery champion to bring a reluctant President to terms. Certain politically minded generals, particularly the raffish Ben Butler in Virginia and the still ambitious Frémont in Missouri, were quick to seize the issue. That Ben Butler should suddenly become the hero of Charles Sumner and William P. Fessenden is only one of the many humorous developments of a confusing time. The fertile genius achieved this paradox, however, when he made one of the most entertaining constitutional discoveries of the day. Taking the Virginian constitutionalists at their word, he declared slaves to be property; in that case, like all other property, they were subject to seizure and confiscation. They had precisely the same standing as cows, horses, crops, and other useful articles which armies, in their progress in enemy country, have immemorially laid hands on and converted to military use. The many slaves who "crossed" into his lines at Fortress Monroe Butler confiscated as "contraband of war," and set them to labor constructing military works. Frémont, in Missouri, went further. As his armies advanced in that state, this general issued proclamations declaring all slaves in the occupied region to be free. Other fervid military leaders in other sections took similar action, greatly to the chagrin of the harassed statesman in the White House, who issued orders nullifying their acts, and, in the case of Frémont and Hunter, removed them from command for insubordination and general military unfitness.

Lincoln's embarrassment was great, because the radicals, with Chase as their cabinet leader, applauded the proclamations and made public heroes of the disobedient generals who had issued them. A considerable part of the population in the Northern states endorsed their attitude. The favor with which Butler and Frémont were regarded by a large faction of the Republican Party and the unpopularity visited upon Lincoln for thwarting their plans were not lost upon the politically minded. One sure road to popularity was evidently to take an anti-Lincoln stand on this question. Cameron was one of the earliest of the politico-statesmen to act upon this hint. No American, in the latter half of 1861, stood so emphatically in need of a little public favor. The most available way, he reasoned, of removing from the public nostril the stench of war contracts would be to champion the rights of the black man. And so Cameron, well understanding Lincoln's predicament, swung his comradeship from Seward to Chase, and openly took a stand on the side of Frémont, Butler, Sumner, Ben Wade, and other champions of early emancipation. Chase gratefully accepted his strange disciple. Like Seward, the Treasury head had his eye on the nomination in 1864, and the accession of so powerful a politician as Cameron was not to be put aside. "While he was Secretary of War," wrote Chase in 1864, in one of his autobiographical letters to John T. Trowbridge, "General Cameron conferred much with me. I never undertook to do anything in his department, except when asked to give my help, and then I gave it willingly. In addition to certain Border state matters, the principal subjects of conference between General Cameron and myself were slavery and the employment of colored troops. We agreed very early that the necessity of arming them was inevitable; but we were alone in that opinion. At least no other member of the administration gave open support, while the President and Mr. Blair, at least, were decidedly averse to it." [1]

Lincoln had indicated to Cameron, in most pointed fashion, his opposition to action at this early day, while the Border states were still hanging in the balance. Cameron, with the co-operation of Chase, had ignored the President's admonition. The letters which Cameron sent to Butler and others giving directions at variance with the President's desires were, in the main, written by Chase. When the expedition against the coast of South Carolina was planned in October, Cameron issued instructions to the commanding general, Thomas W. Sherman, which seemed to authorize the seizure and arming of slaves. There are reasons to believe that Chase had a hand in drafting this document also – a step that went beyond the Butler and Frémont measures, for

[1] Schuckers, Jacob W., *Life and Public Services of Salmon Portland Chase.* D. Appleton and Co., 1874. P. 420.

neither of those officers had made any attempt to arm fugitive slaves and enroll them in the fighting army. At any rate, a copy of the letter reposes at present in the Chase papers in the Library of Congress. In its original form it never reached its destination, for Lincoln made changes in it that eliminated the authority to enroll a slave auxiliary to the Union Army. Despite these unmistakable evidences of Lincoln's policy – which was to keep clear of the slavery question until the fortunes of the Union, especially in the Border states, had become more assured – Cameron proceeded on his course of insolent insubordination. In November, John Cochrane, a Tammany Hall politician with a varied career, made a speech-making tour, with Cameron as his fellow traveler, which embraced the cities of New York, Springfield, Massachusetts, and Washington. Cochrane's harangues were devoted chiefly to advocating the arming of slaves. Cameron sat on the platform on all occasions, thus lending his support to this anti-Lincoln campaign. After a particularly fervid address on this subject before certain troops in Washington, Cameron, after Cochrane sat down, stepped forward and said: "I will say I heartily approve every sentiment uttered by your noble speaker. They are my sentiments – sentiments that will not only lead us to victory, but will in the end reconstruct this our glorious constitution."

Thus Lincoln's own Secretary of War, in face of repeated admonitions, was openly defying the administration on the most delicate problem of the hour. The one way of saving his official head, as Cameron diagnosed the situation, was to make himself so acceptable to Sumner, Ben Wade, Chandler, and others – for the most part, the Chase following – that they would insist on his retention in the cabinet. In accordance with this strategy, Cameron, in the latter part of the year, played his final card. His report for the year 1861, to be submitted to Congress on December 1, contained a passage recommending again that creation of a slave army to which Lincoln, at this stage of proceedings, had shown himself so inexorably opposed. "If it shall be found that the men who have been held by the rebels as slaves are capable of bearing arms," read part of his famous passage, "and performing efficient military service, it is the right, and may become the duty of the government to arm and equip them, and employ their services against the rebels under proper military regulation, discipline and command." Without consulting the President, or submitting his report, Cameron had the document printed, and sent to the postmasters of all the leading cities, with instructions to issue it to the press as soon as Lincoln's message had been delivered to Congress. The report of the Secretary of War had all the sanctity of an official document; and this pronouncement made the arming of slaves an administration policy, for no one would imagine that a cabinet officer would advocate such a revolutionary proposal in so public a manner without the approval of the head of the government. What Cameron was attempting to do by this sly procedure was to force Lincoln's hand and compel him to accept, at the dictation of the Secretary of War, a program which he was known to disfavor; the outcome would be great glory to Cameron in the eyes of the antislavery extremists and a hold on the country so great that he could not be retired from the War Department. The fact that all this involved an impropriety so great as printing his report, and distributing it to the newspapers, before the President had seen a line of it, did not embarrass the agile Secretary.

Lincoln discovered this state of affairs when he began assembling the reports of his departmental heads and other official papers for transmission to Congress with his annual message. According to the artist Carpenter, who evidently received his information from Lincoln himself while painting his portrait, the government printer was the first to call the President's attention to Cameron's irregular proceeding.[2] That conscientious official called at the White House, bringing a copy for presidential inspection, and informed Lincoln that a considerable number had already been sent to several sections of the Union. The printer thought the President "ought to look it over and see if it was satisfactory." Lincoln's quick eye, roving over the pages, soon hit upon the questionable passage. The presidential wrath was not concealed. "This will never do!" he exclaimed. "General Cameron must take no such responsibility. That is a question that belongs exclusively to me." At the next cabinet meeting the Cameron report was brought up for discussion. Lincoln, in quiet but effective terms, called Cameron to account, not only for the views expressed, but for his presumption in attempting to announce a vital administration policy, which, if proclaimed at all, should be proclaimed only by the President. Cameron made a feeble defense, but Lincoln brushed his arguments aside. In the discussion that followed, Seward conspicuously failed to rally to the side of his onetime companion. Only one member out of the seven came to Cameron's support. "In the discussion that took place Cameron found a friend and supporter in the Secretary of the Treasury . . . Mr. Chase apologized for Cameron, befriended and defended him." [3] His arguments had no influence with the President. Lincoln ordered that the obnoxious paragraph be excised, a new innocuous one

[2] Carpenter, F. B., *Six Months in the White House*. Hurd and Houghton, 1866. Pp. 135–138.

[3] Welles, *Narrative of Events*.

substituted for it, and that the entire edition be destroyed. Cameron was directed to telegraph all the favored postmasters to return their copies, and in no event to facilitate publication in the daily press. The fact that a few papers, especially the widely circulated *New York Tribune*, had obtained the unexpurgated report and published the obnoxious sections did not improve relations between Cameron and the President. When malicious critics began comparing the unrevised paragraph with the one that had been hastily inserted to replace it, the fact that something resembling a schism had taken place in the cabinet could not be concealed.

Though Lincoln took no precipitate steps at the moment, Cameron knew that his days as Secretary of War were approaching an end. His high-handed act only gave Lincoln one culminating reason for dispensing with a man who had been a humiliation from the first. For the next three or four weeks he indeed treated Cameron courteously, and this caused that statesman's cabinet colleagues to think that the long-suffering President had decided again to forget and forgive. But reasons existed in plenty for Lincoln's delay. His position, as always with Cameron, was a difficult one. To throw the man out angrily and suddenly might have fatal results. It might lose for the administration the support of the organization in Pennsylvania, and without that support, Lincoln was persuaded, the whole party structure might go to pieces. In thirty years of political life Cameron had savagely turned against every President with whom he had been associated – Jackson, Van Buren, Polk, Buchanan – and Cameron *enragé*, working with a supreme talent for intrigue against his most recent executive chief, would be capable of unlimited mischief. Again, while the electorate as a whole had not been impressed by Cameron's sudden transformation into a champion of the Negro, certain of the antislavery enthusiasts, led by Sumner, Chandler, Wade, and others, were hailing the old spoilsman as the most enlightened statesman in the cabinet. While Lincoln was fumbling and bungling, completely misunderstanding the war and its causes, here was at least one man who saw clearly the issues involved and who had the courage to defy his superior in bringing them to the front.

Since a large faction in the Republican Party took this view of the Lincoln-Cameron trouble, the President's problem was to eject Cameron from the cabinet in a way that would not make that man and his following disrupting enemies of the administration. About five weeks after the episode of the report, a kind Providence indicated the way. In Lincoln's first distribution of diplomatic rewards the post of minister to Russia had fallen to the eminent Kentuckian, Cassius M. Clay.

Simon Cameron (1799–1889)
Secretary of War from March 5, 1861, to January 13, 1862

Edwin McMasters Stanton (1814–1869)
Secretary of War

A six months' sojourn in this hyperborean climate had completely satisfied Clay's ambition for residence at the court of the Czar. He wished to come home, receive a commission in the Federal Army, and fight for the antislavery cause. Here was one way of getting rid of the Secretary of War. On Sunday, January 11, 1862, about six weeks after the unfortunate incident of the "slave-arming" report, Simon Cameron received the following letter from the "Executive Mansion": "My dear Sir: As you have more than once expressed a desire for a change in position, I can now gratify you consistently with my view of the public interest. I therefore propose nominating you to the Senate next Monday as minister to Russia. Very sincerely your friend, A. Lincoln." Accompanying this formal note was another one of those "private" letters which Lincoln was so inclined to write, expressing his "high personal regard for you and my confidence in your ability, patriotism and fidelity to public trust." In view of Cameron's record, the politeness of this final clause is a little difficult even for Lincoln's admirers to swallow; it must be accepted as only another of those compromises which Lincoln never hesitated to make in his efforts to hold together the disharmonious wings of that party whose unity was essential to Federal triumph.

So far as it appears from the public record, that is the history of Cameron's exit from Lincoln's cabinet and his supercession by Edwin M. Stanton. But these official documents, now published in Lincoln's works,[4] do not tell the complete story. Other annalists, particularly Alexander K. McClure, the greatest authority on the Pennsylvania politics of the day, Gideon Welles, and Salmon P. Chase, have provided details of the backstage scenes that culminated in this easeful cabinet death. McClure goes so far as to say that Lincoln's letter, as printed above, was not the one originally sent to the exiled Secretary of War. On the evening of that January 11, McClure has recorded, he was dining with Thomas A. Scott, and enjoying an after-dinner cigar when the distracted figure of Simon Cameron burst upon their seclusion. "Read that!" he exclaimed to both men, tossing upon the table a letter which he said had reached him that evening from the White House. The document has not been preserved, but it was so brief that McClure said he had no difficulty in remembering the precise words. "I have this day nominated the Hon. Edwin M. Stanton to be Secretary of War and you to be minister plenipotentiary to Russia." That was all – no sugared compliments conveying the President's high appreciation of Cameron's services and grief for the separation. That letter, Cameron said – and the justice of his comment could not be

[4] Lincoln, *op. cit.* VII, 79–80.

gainsaid – was a personal affront from the President. It meant his political destruction, it was an "irretrievable wrong" and other things. Cameron burst into tears, and turning to McClure begged him, political foes though they were, to intercede in his behalf. "This is not a political affair; it means personal degradation; we do not agree politically, but you know I would gladly aid you personally if it were in my power."

This was the second interview Cameron had sought that Sunday evening on this same subject. The man to whom he had first turned for help, naturally enough, was his only friend in the cabinet, Salmon P. Chase. Three times that day Cameron and Chase had been in consultation – once after church, again after dinner, and again later in the evening at Seward's house, into which Cameron burst with Lincoln's letter in his hand. "He was quite offended," writes Chase in his diary, "supposing the letter intended as a dismissal, and therefore discourteous." Both Seward and Chase tried to soothe him, making much of Lincoln's choice of Stanton as his successor; this was a compliment, they said, for Stanton, like Cameron himself, was a Pennsylvanian, and was known to be Cameron's own choice, if a successor should be necessary.[5] Colonel McClure quieted Cameron in a more effective way. The following day he saw Lincoln, persuaded him to permit Cameron to write and antedate a letter of resignation, to withdraw his curt notice of ejectment and substitute the more urbane literary effort that now appears in his collected works. Thus for the second time did Lincoln suppress a sharp notification to Cameron, and substitute a more ingratiating one; the correspondence of the preceding January, in connection with the original cabinet offer, will be recalled.

Gideon Welles knew nothing of these proceedings at the time; in fact, only two members of the cabinet, Seward and Chase, were in at the Cameron demise. "I was first informed of it," wrote Welles, "by Mr. Blair, whom I met on the street. He had just been advised of the fact by President Lincoln, who had sent, or was about to send, the nomination of Mr. Stanton to the Senate."[6] Blair had been urging the President for some time to get rid of Cameron but evidently he was not taken into Lincoln's confidence when the critical moment arrived. "Strange," mused Edward Bates in his Diary entry of January 13, "not a hint of all of this was heard last Friday, at Cabinet Council, and stranger still, I have not been sent for by the President, nor spoken to by any member. The thing, I hear, was much considered, Saturday and Sunday. Hay told the ladies at Eames that the cabinet had been

[5] Warden, *op. cit.*, pp. 400–401.
[6] Welles, *Narrative of Events.*

sitting *en permanence* and Eames himself informed me that Mr. Seward had been with the President the whole of Sunday afternoon."[7] Both Blair and Welles believed that Seward had intrigued for Cameron's deposition; and it is significant that when the Pennsylvanian was fighting for his life, he appealed to Chase, not to Seward, to intercede with the President. Cameron himself suspected that Seward had engineered his retirement. "I know, and know from his own lips," wrote Welles, "that he left the cabinet with reluctance, and that he believed if Mr. Seward had been so disposed, he could have remained."[8]

There is not much in Seward's correspondence to justify these suspicions or disprove them. "General Cameron has resigned his place, and is going to Russia," he wrote Mrs. Seward January 15, in a cryptic passage which may, or may not, hint at the part he played in the translation. "Not only was the press completely taken by surprise, but, with all its fertility of conjecture, not one newspaper has conceived the real cause. So you see public men must labor, either not understood, or misunderstood by their countrymen and mankind." Had Seward really played an influential part in Cameron's displacement, that fact would doubtless have raised him in public esteem at the time, for few of Lincoln's acts were greeted with more wholehearted applause. There was universal agreement with the editorial view of the *New York Herald* that Cameron's resignation was as good as a major military victory for the Federal cause. When his name was sent to the Senate for the Russian mission, opposition developed to confirmation; one of the grotesque anomalies of a demoralized era was that Charles Sumner, completely beguiled by Cameron's sudden conversion to the abolitionist ranks, undertook his defense, and finally succeeded, after a four days' struggle, in persuading a reluctant Senate to support the nomination. The House of Representatives expressed its opinion by passing a vote of censure on Cameron for employing his political henchman, Alexander Cummings, as purchasing agent of war supplies, declaring that act proved "highly injurious to the public service." Lincoln, again acting from his desire to keep Cameron and his followers loyal to the administration, sent a message to the House, declaring that the transactions in question were not exclusively Cameron's but were approved by himself and the cabinet.

[7] John Hay, Secretary to Lincoln: Charles Eames, international lawyer, editor, diplomat, at this time counsel for the Navy Department.
[8] Welles, *Narrative of Events.*

III

THAT Edwin McMasters Stanton should have succeeded to the cabinet post of Simon Cameron presents one of the most ironic episodes in Lincoln's career. The ejected Minister of War had signed his death warrant when he surreptitiously inserted in his annual report a recommendation for arming slaves which directly contravened Lincoln's policy at the time. Lincoln was unaware that Stanton had endorsed this act; that, as there is some reason to suppose, he had even instigated the whole transaction. Several years subsequently Cameron revealed the details. His report had been submitted, Cameron said, to several political friends, chiefly Pennsylvanians, all of whom had condemned the disloyal passage and urged its elimination. Forced to seek comfort from a Democratic leader, he had then taken the document to a "man of broad views, great courage and tremendous earnestness." This was Edward M. Stanton, at that time legal adviser to the War Department. Stanton, after making certain changes "so that the lawyers would not carp at it," gave the slavery paragraph his cordial benediction. According to his most recent biographer, Stanton himself wrote the sentences that aroused Lincoln's resentment. "Those who make war against the government justly forfeit all rights of property, privilege or security derived from the Constitution and laws against which they are in armed rebellion; and as labor and service of their slaves constitute the chief property of the rebels, such property should share the common fate of war, to which they have devoted the property of loyal citizens. . . . It is as clearly the right of the government to arm slaves, when it may become necessary, as it is to use gunpowder taken from the enemy." Thus the fateful words that caused Cameron's dismissal were penned by the confidential friend and adviser who succeeded to his position in the cabinet.

Knowing what we know of Stanton's oblique and sinuous character, his impetuous ambition and unscrupulous methods in attaining ends, the suspicion naturally rises that, in encouraging Cameron to pursue a course which would end his cabinet career, Stanton was not inspired exclusively by public motives. Few men in American history have presented such divergencies of behavior. Any attempt to estimate the man is inevitably colored by his career subsequent to Lincoln's death – his disloyalty to Johnson, his alliance with Thaddeus Stevens, Benjamin Wade, and other extreme radicals for the infliction of the heaviest punitive policy on the South, and his part in the impeachment of the President. The rehabilitation of Andrew Johnson has injured no public reputation quite so severely as Stanton's. Yet even his relations with Abraham Lincoln have elicited a variety of opinions. They range all the distance from the judgment of Nicolay and Hay that Stanton was an unselfish patriot, unfailing in devotion to Lincoln and "the greatest war minister the government had ever had," to that of Gideon Welles, who hardly ever mentions his colleague's name without expressing contempt for his character and distrust for his every action. A recent volume of grotesque depreciation even suggests – without making the deliberate charge – that Stanton may have had a hand in the plot which ultimately culminated in Lincoln's assassination.[1] To Massachusetts abolitionists like Henry Wilson and Charles Sumner, Stanton at least shared the credit with Lincoln of ending slavery and saving the Union. To Democratic leaders like Jeremiah Black, he was an "apostate," a "renegade," a "betrayer of his country," a "dastard," and a "crawling sycophant."[2]

A man who could arouse such different emotions in so many respectable bosoms must have been at least an energetic person, and it is not surprising to discover that, from childhood days to the last stormy experience in Johnson's cabinet, the positive qualities chiefly associated with Stanton's name were fierce determination, instantaneous decision and execution, remorseless concentration, and a savage capacity for labor that despite perpetual ill-health made him, in the opinion of the same Jeremiah Black whose uncomplimentary adjectives are listed above, the greatest lawyer of his time, and in the view of history the most dynamic, if not the most admirable, member of Lincoln's cabinet. But nothing in Stanton's heredity or early influences would explain so passionate a character. On his father's side he came of New England Quakers, on his mother's, of a long line of easygoing Virginia planters. Both father and mother were plodding, earnest, worthy members of society. Only one decisive moment marked the life of David Stanton: when he proclaimed his intention to his Quaker brethren of marrying out of meeting, those guardians of orthodoxy raised such a

[1] Eisenschiml, Otto, *Why Was Lincoln Murdered?* Little, Brown & Co., 1937.

[2] All these elegant expletives – and many more – appear in an article contributed by Mr. Black to the *Galaxy Magazine*, vol. II, 257.

protest that he abandoned the faith of his ancestors and joined the Methodist Church of his affianced bride. Stanton's father was a moderately successful country doctor in Steubenville, Ohio, and in a humble but comfortable home in this thriving village the oldest child, Edwin, was born in 1814. Two circumstances in Edwin's boyhood and youth had much to do in directing his career. Steubenville, situated on the Ohio River, overlooking the northern notch of Virginia, gave an educational view of the problem that was to figure so conspicuously in Stanton's mature life. Like the youthful Salmon P. Chase in Cincinnati, the boy Stanton glimpsed the black men toiling for the profit of others in the open fields. More important, perhaps, the town served as a prolific station in the underground route for fugitive slaves. Stanton's father, true to his Quaker blood, was a fervent abolitionist, and discoursed extensively on the great wrong to his son, whom he used to take as a companion on the buggy drives to visit his patients on the environing farms. An anecdote which Stanton, always alive to the dramatic possibilities of his own career, liked to relate suggests Plutarch's story of Hannibal, whose father, in the great warrior's tender years, made him take an oath of undying hatred and annihilation to Rome. Similarly the elder Stanton compelled his son, as a child, to swear everlasting warfare on the South's peculiar institution.

An obscure saddler living in Wheeling, about ten miles south of Steubenville, also subsequently played a leading role in Stanton's recollections of his childhood. This was Benjamin Lundy, as deserving perhaps as any man of the credit of starting the abolition movement. Lundy frequently visited the Stanton home, and early enlisted the head of the family in establishing a journal devoted to the abolition cause. In the founding of this paper, which bore the formidable title of the *Genius of Universal Emancipation*, the elder Stanton helped with money and became the selling agent in his district. The gentle Quaker – this was another of Stanton's favorite stories – spent many a night in the Stanton home, and seemed to detect possibilities for the cause in the black-eyed and black-haired little boy whom he would frequently take upon his knee, endowing the infant mind with one of those "fixations" – so dear to the modern psychologist – against the barbarous system. The other fact of Stanton's childhood has a less spiritual import, but perhaps exercised an even more important effect upon his outlook. It may, to a considerable degree, explain those explosive, ugly traits that afterward made him an object of terror and hatred. The asthma that became a settled part of his physical life made its first attacks in childhood. From that time until his death in 1869, Stanton was never free from the disease. Seizures of paroxysmal breathing would periodically attack the man, frequently at critical times – an impending appearance in court, an important journey or social engagement; the experience would last for a few minutes, a few hours, or a few days, the sufferer always undergoing great exhaustion and agony. Perhaps it is not strange that a lifetime victim of such torment should not have developed an angelic nature. Not improbably Stanton's frequently brutal manners, crazy outbursts of rage, and tyrannous treatment of subordinates may be explained in part by the fact that with him the mere act of breathing, which to most mortals is a matter of unconscious routine, was always difficult and frequently plain torture.

The boy and man had a strange mentality, not lacking in morbid tendencies. He was devoted to study and much given to reading but, for the usual sports of youth – hunting, fishing, outdoor or indoor games – he cared nothing. When his abolitionist father died, Stanton, aged eleven, to help in family expenses secured a job in Turnbull's bookstore at four dollars a month. The work proved more profitable to Stanton than to his employers. He was far more interested in books than in customers, and spent a considerable part of each day reading his favorite authors. In spare moments, by self-study, he found compensation for his interrupted school work. He had already determined on an education, and in a brief time, by hard evening work, had acquired enough preparation for entrance to the freshman class of Kenyon College at Gambier, Ohio. His mother, who had spent her early life as a schoolteacher, sympathized with this ambition, as she did with another of her son's plans. He had decided not to adopt his father's profession of medicine, but to study law. At Kenyon, he made one of those sudden changes in allegiance for which his career was subsequently marked: influenced perhaps by Bishop Philander Chase, then the active head of Kenyon, he gave up his membership in the Methodist Church and became an Episcopalian. Religion with Stanton, then and afterward, was an important matter; the name of God, as was the case with most Civil War leaders, was frequently on his lips, though the self-immolating piety of Chase never disturbed his waking hours. At Kenyon Stanton acquired also the one lifelong conviction whose earnestness and sincerity even his worst detractors seldom questioned. He stayed at the college only little more than a year, but the period 1831–1832 was a vital one in his country's history.

In those fateful two years, South Carolina started that onslaught on Federal authority which came to full strength in 1860. At that time the slavery question had not attained a prime importance and South Carolina precipitated the great issue of State versus Federal power by declaring null and void and unenforceable within its limits a tariff law which Congress had passed against its protests. Behind it lay the threat of secession, if hostile moves were taken against this veto. At Kenyon two camps came into being, one supporting the Nullification doctrine of Calhoun, the other sustaining Andrew Jackson, in opposition to this attack on the Union. Young Stanton, already distinguished for mental vigor, powerful will, and forceful energy, "went over to Jackson," in the phrase of the time, and led the Union phalanx in the undergraduate body. It was a loyalty which never left him, a conviction that fixed his political course for the next thirty years. At Kenyon itself, however, his days were brief. Financial troubles again called him to his mother's aid; Stanton left college, took a place again in a bookstore, again devoted his spare hours, day and night, to study, this time to the law, with the result that in 1836, at the age of twenty-one, he was admitted to the bar and began practice in the little town of Cadiz, Ohio. Success greeted his efforts from the first day; the rest of the story is that of one of the most famous and prosperous lawyers of the time; Stanton advanced, by rapid stages, from Cadiz to Steubenville to Pittsburgh – each time called to a more fruitful field by a steadily enlarging practice. In 1856 this practice, more and more requiring his appearance before the United States Supreme Court, caused Stanton to settle definitely in Washington. He had married twice; his first wife was Mary Lawson, a girl of unpretentious origin like himself, whom he loved with all the passion of his nature, and of whom he remained the widower for twelve years. His second, Ellen M. Hutchison, was the daughter of one of the richest men of Pittsburgh.

Anecdotes told of Stanton's early manhood show strange, almost macabre qualities of character and temperament. His portrait, taken at this early period, while it justifies the local legend that he was the most striking, even handsome young man in that region of Ohio, suggests also the equivocal traits that made Stanton the great puzzle of his time. In this, more than in the representations of mature life, is apparent the "little black terrier" that Montgomery Blair called him. A smooth, oval countenance, surmounted by a thin layer of black, silken hair, underlaid by a delicate beard, not yet lying, patriarch-like, on an expansive breast but closely cropped *à la* Horace Greeley, with shaven chin and upper lip; small beady eyes, peering out suspiciously; large, finely shaped, generous nose; ears so closely pressed against the skull as to be scarcely visible; thin, slightly smiling lips – the general effect is one of intellect and power, and at the same time detached, scrutinizing, possibly a little sinister. In stature he lacked the majesty of Chase or the angular picturesqueness of Seward; Carpenter's group painting of the cabinet discloses Stanton as one of the shortest of the seven, nor did his quick, jerky walk, his inability to stay long in one position, add to his personal impressiveness. Here is a man who did not instinctively draw to his fellows, or inspire great sympathy or trust in them. Stanton's behavior on certain occasions in early life indicates his uncanny side. When his emotions were deeply stirred he could act almost like a madman. At certain crises, indeed, doubts of his sanity were widespread. When news came of his brother's suicide – he opened his veins like a Roman patrician – Stanton, in a disheveled state, rushed into the woods, wandering for hours until finally carried forcibly home by a searching party. His friends set two strong guards to watch him for several days, apprehending a second suicide. This fear was enhanced by the strange habit the young man had of carrying a dagger in a beautiful sheath under his waistcoat; why, no one knew, for his way of life involved no dangers, and he was not given to brawls.

A semi-romantic attachment existed in his early days at Columbus between Stanton and Anna Howard, daughter of his landlady. One day they partook together of the midday meal; that same evening Stanton, returning for dinner, was informed that Anna had died in the afternoon from cholera, then epidemic in the region, and that she had already been buried – in those days victims of this contagion were precipitately hurried to their final resting place. Stanton, transfixed with horror, refused to believe it. The insane notion seized his mind that Anna was not dead, but had been buried alive. In a frenzy he rushed to the graveyard, exhumed the unfortunate girl, and convinced himself, by a personal inspection, that the incredible story was true. Similar outbursts took place in subsequent years. The death of his first child, a baby girl, so affected Stanton that, after she had been buried a considerable time, he had the little body disinterred, enclosed in a metal casket, and placed on the mantelpiece in his bedroom, where it was kept for several years. When Mary Lawson died, in 1844, Stanton's morbidity again aroused fears for his sanity. This was the wife with whom he had spent his early days of struggle; that the end should have come when prosperity had arrived, when Stanton had just crowned his success by taking for his home the finest house in Steubenville, seemed to make the tragedy complete. The bereaved husband sent for a dressmaker and ordered her to produce a perfect duplicate of Mary's wedding gown. "She is my bride," he moaned, "and shall be dressed and buried like a bride." The Supreme Court had to suspend sessions for a month, for Stanton, whose name appeared on every calendar, would not leave his dead wife's grave. Every night he would put her nightcap and gown on her bed, and sit beside them weeping for hours. These and other signs of an unstable nervous temperament call to mind the excitement and morbid fears that so frequently possessed Stanton in Lincoln's cabinet. Gideon Welles contemptuously described his overwrought colleague when news of the *Merrimac's* depredations reached Washington – his rushings from room to room, his jumpings up and down, his predictions of the immediate bombardment and destruction of Washington, New York, Boston, and all other coast cities, his refusals to be pacified by the assurances of the sober Puritan that this Confederate terror could never leave Norfolk Harbor, because of its deep draught, were all a part of the same morose sensibility that showed itself in such strange ways in the earlier time.

All this seems foreign to the judicial weighing of evidence, the scholarly exactness in formulating briefs, the profound searchings into precedents, the orderly presentation of facts, that soon made Stanton the most successful lawyer of his section. His undivided absorption in his work largely explains his progress. Compared to the law, all other occupations, in Stanton's view, were insignificant. Presidents, Senators, cabinet officers, were not the nation's great men. The lawyers held the destiny of America in their hands. To reach the top of his profession, a seat on the United States Supreme Court, was Stanton's ambition from the earliest days – a goal that was ultimately accomplished; but here again the fate that seemed to mock Stanton's career made the prize illusory. Appointed by President Grant in 1869, Stanton died four days after confirmation by the Senate.

No man of Stanton's prominence could escape a certain part in politics, but public office, in the early days, did not figure in his aspirations. All his energies and time were concentrated on his work at the bar. "Law, law, law was his God, his mistress, and these he never ceased to worship" – in these words a contemporary described his laborious days and nights. Not that Stanton fills a particularly lofty place in legal annals. As an interpreter of fundamental American law he was no Webster or Marshall. One great case indeed – that of *Pennsylvania* v. *Wheeling*, establishing the power of Congress to control navigable rivers and harbors – brings his name into all histories of the Constitution; and other famous litigations such as the almost endless suits involving the McCormick reaper, and the brilliant exposures of land frauds in California, made his name one of the most resounding of the time. When contemporaries eulogized his legal eminence, they were thinking not of any original contribution to jurisprudence, but of the stalwart, almost ferocious pleader, the man who could marshal his facts with persuasive artistry, wring the truth and expose the prevarications of witnesses, sway juries, and, in more sober appearances before the Supreme Court, analyze cases and set forth with supreme logic and eloquence technicalities and principles. His versatility was as celebrated as his industry. He was equally at home in the criminal court and in the supreme tribunal in Washington. He could defend a man accused of murder with the same zeal and thoroughness that was bestowed on a complicated constitutional issue. His fame rested both on his reaper and bridge cases and on his sensational arguments for Daniel E. Sickles, who shot in broad daylight, on a Washington street, a man who had stolen the marital fidelity of his wife. This proceeding held the city spellbound for days; the plea Stanton invented to fit the case – one that has done heroic service in countless similar trials since – that of temporary insanity, succeeded so well that Sickles went scot-free, subsequently lost a leg in the battle of Gettysburg, became minister to Spain, and had a long and varied career in New York politics.

In his court appearances Stanton displayed the infirmities of temper and the same strength of personality that distinguished all his activities. He was frequently called to account for rudeness to judges – on several occasions barely escaping arraignment for contempt – was most overbearing to witnesses and frequently insulting to opposing counsel. "Stop your whining," he once shouted at a learned brother representing the other side. Stanton's voice itself was rough and guttural, and in reference to this defect opposing counsel remarked, "It's no worse to whine than to bark." "Yes, it is," said Stanton, "dogs bark but puppies whine." In the ensuing hubbub, in which the offended gentleman was prevented by attendants from rushing at Stanton's throat, the judge found it necessary to suspend the session. Stanton's easygoing legal ethics would possibly shock a generation more squeamish on this subject than the one that preceded the Civil War. Whether a lawyer should defend a man obviously guilty is a favorite subject of dispute, but on this point Stanton had no qualms. One dubious client of this kind, whom Stanton had aided in avoiding a penalty he richly deserved, was shocked at the size of his bill. A thousand dollars was a great fee for the period, but Stanton demanded it. "Do you think," he said, "that I would argue the wrong side for less?" A murderer whose neck he had saved from the hangman, having no money to pay a lawyer, had made over to Stanton, before he would undertake the case, his solitary piece of property – a small house and lot. When Stanton exacted fulfillment of this bond, his client pleaded for mercy. "You are taking everything I've got, and leaving me to starve." "You deserve to starve," replied Stanton, "for you were guilty." He promptly sold the house for five hundred dollars and pocketed the money.

Men may reasonably argue the moral aspects of these proceedings, but another of Stanton's methods, related by a friendly biographer, brings up a really serious question. His sister was suing her husband for divorce, and Stanton appeared as witness in the case. The opposing lawyer was quick at making objections – a trait Stanton craftily turned to account. Before taking the stand, he instructed the examining legal light to ask him if his sister had lost four front teeth, and if he knew how she had lost them. "Yes," said Stanton, in reply to the first planted question, and to the second, he began, "She once told me how she had lost them" – but by this time the agile counsel for the defense jumped to his feet, shouting objections, which the court sustained. Stanton knew that counsel would object to these improper questions, and that the judge would not permit him to go on with his answer. But he also knew that the belief would be implanted in the mind of the jury, which nothing subsequently said or done would eradicate, that the defendant husband had played some part in her misfortune. Yet the truth was that Stanton's sister had lost the four teeth in the course of nature, with no assistance from her spouse. Probably most reputable lawyers, of that time or in the present, would regard this method of inquiry as sharp practice.

Stanton's political activities in the thirty years preceding 1860 displayed the same qualities, great and small, that marked him as a lawyer. A passion for reform was combined with personal ambition, devotion to a cause was frequently laid aside in pursuit of temporary advantage, and loyalty to persons and causes was now and then tainted by that double-dealing which his enemies insisted was Stanton's controlling characteristic. He started life, as already indicated, with two solid, idealistic convictions. He hated slavery and he worshiped the Federal Union. On occasions, these principles seemed to fix his political attachments; at other times more worldly considerations dictated his courses. In 1840 Stanton attended the Democratic Convention in Baltimore as a delegate and gave himself heartily to the cause of Van Buren. In 1844 he worked hard for a Van Buren delegation from Ohio and fiercely opposed that two-thirds rule the enemy invented to bring about his hero's downfall. He resented the "insolent" dominance of Southerners in the Democratic Party and the proslavery uses they made of their ascendancy. For the policy of annexing Texas he had no friendly word. Yet in 1846 he supported the man, James K. Polk, who was the chief exponent of this Southern pretension, and regretted that ill-health prevented his shouldering a musket and fighting in the Mexican War. In 1847, he again transferred his allegiance, indorsing the Wilmot Proviso, which was intended to prevent the introduction of slavery into any territory acquired as booty in that conflict. In 1848, Stanton finally abandoned the Democrats and became a Free-Soiler. Two motives may be offered for this departure into idealism, a genuine zeal for antislavery principles, and anger at the Democrats for their treatment of Van Buren. Stanton's subsequent behavior rather inclines the balance in favor of the latter diagnosis, for, after the disappearance of the Free-Soil Party, only one sanctuary was left for those to whom its antislavery principles comprised the one question of the day. This was the new Republican amalgamation, organized in 1856. In this all the great Free-Soil leaders of 1848, Salmon P. Chase, Charles Sumner, Gideon Welles, John P. Hale, Samuel Fessenden, Charles Francis Adams, and others found a satisfactory haven. Stanton, however, did not follow their example; instead, this onetime abolitionist joined the most extreme proslavery wing of the Democratic Party, that led by James Buchanan.

It was in 1856, the year of Buchanan's election, that Stanton moved to Washington, and perhaps the Buchanan ascendancy had something to do with this choice of a new home. Stanton built a stately house on Franklin Square, and in this he and his new, handsome, and rich wife soon became the center of an influential social circle. A close friendship had been formed with Jeremiah S. Black, the Buchanan leader in Pennsylvania, who, it is believed, had induced Stanton to align himself with the Buchanan forces, not improbably holding forth the prospect of political favor. Stanton was now in the prime of his powers, only forty-two years old, in the front rank of his profession, financially and socially strong; in other words, a point had been attained when honorable service to the state would gratify ambition. That Black would be an important figure in the administration, in case of Buchanan's election, was well known; and when that event followed, it caused no surprise that he entered the cabinet as Attorney General. Brilliant, cantankerous, rabid in belief and expression, Black hated one type of citizens above all others. For the Garrisonian abolitionist his usually resourceful vocabulary could find no denunciation sufficiently acrid. That he should select Stanton as his favorite among rising administration Democrats testifies again to the flexibility of that consummate artist in being all things to all men. Stanton, from his first arrival in Washington, began quietly consorting with the antislavery leaders. He was a frequent evening visitor to the house of Dr. Gamaliel Bailey, proprietor of the *National Era*, the uncompromising abolitionist organ, in which Mrs. Stowe's *Uncle Tom* had recently been serialized. At Dr. Bailey's home, an abolition headquarters, Stanton frequently delighted the guests by recollections of his early days in Steubenville, in which the vignettes of himself as a child sitting on Benjamin Lundy's knee did emotional service. Salmon P. Chase, one of Dr. Bailey's close friends, afterward testified to Stanton's soundness on the antislavery question, and Charles Sumner, another, afterward bore testimony to Stanton as "one of us." Yet the man's outward proceedings in this prewar period were entirely satisfactory to Black and Buchanan. He supported all Buchanan's policies. In the Kansas disputation, he stood on Buchanan's side, even eulogizing the Lecompton Constitution – a measure which, had it passed, would have made Kansas a slave state. No Buchanan follower more loyally accepted the Dred Scott decision, which opened all the territories to slavery, as forever settling that crucial question. In 1860, he did not follow Douglas, the candidate of the more moderate Democrats, but Breckinridge, whose platform demanded the complete surrender of the North to the South. It was when, some years afterward, Jeremiah Black learned, among other things, of Stanton's two-faced position – consorting at the same time with the abolitionists and the Buchanan slavery extensionists – that he applied to his former companion the epithets enumerated on a preceding page.

IV

STANTON'S COURTING of the Buchananites – or, as the irreverent enemy usually called them, the Buchaneers – made possible his political advancement. The war with Mexico had left many land entanglements in California. By the treaty of Guadalupe Uncle Sam recognized all land grants which had been made by Mexico before California passed into his hands. Such a situation naturally gave opportunities in plenty for fraud. A multitude of claimants appeared, holding titles to great tracts which, they asserted, had been assigned them by the Mexican Republic. Many of these were open to suspicion. One pretender especially, José Limantour, a Frenchman, produced so-called deeds to all of San Francisco and a considerable area of adjacent territory. In early 1858, Black sent his friend Stanton to California to look into this and other claims and to take such proceedings as circumstances might warrant. The compensation agreed upon, $25,000 and expenses, made the public gasp, for such a fee for legal services was unprecedented at the time, but the outlay proved an excellent investment, for Stanton's labors in San Francisco saved the United States a sum estimated at $150,000,000. His year's experience in this frontier country probably provides the best illustration we have of Stanton's legal talents, his exhaustive industry, his pantherlike pursuit of the evildoer, and his skill in constructing an impregnable case. Though the land records of the former Mexican regime had been scattered to the four winds, Stanton, with incredible labor and patience, succeeded in reclaiming the most important – a monumental work comprising four hundred neatly bound volumes. Limantour, it appeared, was a rascal of incredible proportions: all his so-called claims rested upon forged documents; and only his precipitate flight from the country saved him from a long term in prison. Naturally both Buchanan and Black rejoiced at this performance; it gave the Buchanan administration a lift in popular esteem.

It also paved the way for the appointment of Stanton to Buchanan's cabinet – something to which he had aspired for some time. Stanton returned from California in season to take part in the epochal campaign of 1860, and his championship on the stump of the most extreme proslavery candidates put him in line for Democratic favor. Apparently Buchanan consulted Stanton in framing his message of December 3, 1860, in which he annunciated the strange doctrine that secession was unconstitutional, but that the Federal government had no right to keep a state by force in the Union. Stanton afterwards said – though his recollection has not gone uncontradicted – that he advised the President against such an interpretation; that, as a result of his persuasion, Buchanan deleted the passage, but subsequently, on the insistence of Jefferson Davis and other Southern Senators, restored it in the document presented to Congress. This message and other events, especially Buchanan's refusal to strengthen Federal forces in Charleston Harbor, caused a split in Buchanan's cabinet. Lewis Cass, the venerable Secretary of State, resigned in disgust at the President's policy, and Jeremiah Black was transferred from the Attorney General's office to the State Department. Black consented to the change only on condition that Stanton should succeed to the cabinet post left vacant. And so, on December 20, Edwin M. Stanton became Attorney General of the United States. On that same day South Carolina passed its ordinance of secession.

He attended his first cabinet meeting on December 27. That session was enlivened by one of the several "crises" that were to make the next few months so momentous. That morning news reached the administration of Major Anderson's historic maneuver – the transfer of his tiny force from the indefensible Fort Moultrie to the far stronger Fort Sumter. At that time at least three members of Buchanan's cabinet were generally referred to in the Northern press as "traitors" – John B. Floyd of Virginia, Secretary of War; Jacob Thompson of Mississippi, Secretary of the Interior; and Isaac Toucey of Connecticut, Secretary of the Navy. Howell Cobb, Secretary of the Treasury, had already departed for his native Georgia, to be succeeded by Philip F. Thomas of Maryland, a man not regarded kindly by supporters of the Union. Buchanan had already demanded Floyd's resignation – not, however, for suspected disloyalty. He had become involved in the theft – "purloining" was the President's own word – of $870,000 worth of bonds held in trust by the Interior Department for the Indian wards of the nation. Thompson, head of the Interior Department, was concerned in the same transaction, and his dismissal from the cabinet also was only a matter of time. Toucey had been an old Jacksonian Democrat, an ex-governor of Connecticut, Attorney General in Polk's cabinet, and a consistent supporter of the Southern point of view in the tumultuous fifties; his action in dispersing the Federal fleet to foreign ports, leaving less than half a dozen ships in home waters to meet the crisis of Civil War, so outraged the people of his own extremely loyal state that his portrait as governor was removed from its niche of honor in the capitol at Hartford.[1]

Whether Floyd, Thompson, and Toucey comprised a triumvirate of "traitors" is a question on which lively controversy has raged; it is not necessary to enter into the long and tedious discussion in this place. What is evident, however, is that, in the situation precipitated by Major Anderson on December 27, the three men championed the Southern side. That the trembling President Buchanan accepted their viewpoint is also a matter of history. Whether a definite "truce" had been concluded between Buchanan and South Carolina guaranteeing the "neutrality" of the forts in Charleston Harbor is another matter over which the historians have wrangled for eighty years. One cannot read the documents, however, without concluding that, if a precise "pledge" had not been given, at least something in the nature of an entente had been agreed upon. This tacit understanding provided that the Southern "rebels" would make no attack on the forts so long as the Federal government should make no attempt to change their existing status. Floyd, Thompson, and Toucey maintained that Anderson's coup had radically changed this status. Floyd comported himself at this cabinet meeting in noisy, insulting fashion. As his resignation had been demanded, he showed considerable presumption in attending the conclave; the suspicion at the time was that he intentionally stirred up a rumpus, so that he could resign on the issue of Fort Sumter, instead of submitting to dismissal on the pending charge of dishonesty. Merely to order Major Anderson back to Fort Sumter, Floyd loudly proclaimed, would not satisfy an insulted South; the offending general and all his forces must clear out of Charleston harbor altogether. "The great contest for the Union commenced a few minutes after I parted from you here," Stanton wrote his brother-in-law, Christopher P. Wolcott, describing the historic "scene." "On reaching my office I found a summons to a cabinet council. On entering the chamber, I found treason with bold and brazen front demanding the surrender of Fort Sumter. The contest continued until dark, when dispute ran so high that we adjourned until eight o'clock in the evening."

If subsequent accounts of this "scene" put in writing by Stanton himself – not the most dependable authority when his vanity was at stake – and Joseph Holt, at that time Postmaster General and Floyd's

[1] It was subsequently restored, when, after the war, a kinder judgment of his work as Secretary of the Navy prevailed.

destined successor as Secretary of War, can be depended on, this picture to his brother-in-law is a mild description. According to Holt, "the emotions of Floyd were absolutely uncontrollable, – emotions of mingled mortification and anguish and rage and panic. His fury seemed that of some baffled fiend." [2] Stanton's own relation is enshrined in a letter written October 8, 1863, and now preserved among his papers.[3] The apparent intention of the President to accept the Southern argument, to regard the brilliant movement of Anderson – with whose praises the unanimous North was then resounding – as a violation of his tacit understanding with the rebels, and to order the undoing of his act, stirred Stanton to the depths. In the presence of Floyd and the Secretaries held in part responsible for the recent defalcation of government trust funds, he told Buchanan that a reversal of Major Anderson's act "ought certainly to be regarded as most liberal towards erring brethren, but while one member of your cabinet has fraudulent acceptances for millions of dollars afloat and while the confidential clerk of another – himself in South Carolina teaching rebellion – has just stolen $900,000 from the Indian trust fund, the experiment of ordering Major Anderson back to Fort Moultrie would be dangerous. But if you intend to try it, before it is done I beg that you will accept my resignation." This challenge is quoted from an article by Thurlow Weed in the *London Observer* for the ninth of February, 1862, which Stanton, in his account written for posterity, said was "substantially true." Joseph Holt, supporting the accuracy of the whole narrative, added even more lurid details. To give up Fort Sumter, Stanton told Buchanan, "would be a crime equal to the crime of Arnold and that all who participated in it ought to be hung like André," and the intrepid Secretary added "that a President of the United States who would make such an order would be guilty of treason." "At this point," continued Secretary Holt, "and I remember the scene as clearly as though it happened yesterday – Mr. Buchanan raised his hand deprecatingly and said, as if wounded by the intensity of Mr. Stanton's language and manner, 'Oh, no! Not so bad as that, my friend! – not so bad as that!' "

George Ticknor Curtis, whose life of James Buchanan includes several labored chapters extenuating that President's behavior in these fateful December days, entered a general denial of the truth of Stanton's statements, and Jeremiah Black, in a frenzy of vituperation against

[2] *Atlantic Monthly*, XXVI, 471.

[3] Gorham, George C., *Life and Public Services of Edwin McMasters Stanton.* Houghton Mifflin Co., 1899. Pp. 151–159. The letter was not published in Stanton's lifetime.

his onetime protégé, pronounced the whole story of criticism and defiance pure "fiction." Both these defenders of Buchanan, only one of whom possessed any value as a firsthand witness, wrote several years before Stanton's recital and the corroborative indorsement of Joseph Holt were given to the world. Therefore, so far as this particular "crisis" is concerned, we are forced to waver as to the credibility to be given four persons who were present and who have gone upon record. Stanton and Holt have testified explicitly in the affirmative, while Black and Buchanan have entered an uncompromising denial. As to another "crisis" that immediately supervened, however, there is no conflict in the evidence. This second drama, while not so explosive as the preceding "scene," involved essentially the same points of dispute. Something has already been said of the "ambassadors" sent by the "Republic of South Carolina" in late December, 1860, to that foreign nation, the United States of America. Among the demands this delegation, under the headship of James L. Orr, presented to the Buchanan government was one insisting on Major Anderson's return from Sumter to Moultrie. That precipitated action, the South Carolinians maintained, nullified the "truce" tacitly agreed upon by the insurgent state and the Buchanan regime by which the *status quo* was to be respected by both parties. Before these South Carolinians would deign to enter into negotiations with the United States that soldier, with all his forces, must be ordered not only out of Sumter, but out of Charleston Harbor itself. This demand caused another crisis in the Buchanan cabinet, and another threatened flood of resignations. For the President was disposed to yield to the insistent Southerners. At a moment when most Northern newspapers were demanding that the South Carolinians be imprisoned for high treason, Buchanan, in the quiet of his study, composed a respectful communication addressed to these emissaries.

On December 29, the President read this letter to an uncomfortable and unappreciative cabinet. Not even a copy of this missive has ever been discovered. Its contents can be reconstructed, however, from a memorandum opposing the views expressed in it, drawn up by Black with Stanton's co-operation. This would indicate that Buchanan's letter to the "ambassadors" practically recognized the right of South Carolina to be represented diplomatically "near" the Federal government. It implied a willingness to negotiate with South Carolina the possession of the forts in Charleston Harbor – forts that had always been the undisputed property of the United States. It apparently rehearsed Buchanan's famous doctrine that the Federal government had no right to compel a state by force to remain in the Union. It admitted that Major Anderson had done wrong in leaving Fort Moultrie and removing his little garrison to Sumter. Conciliatory as Buchanan and his advisers were to the Southern insurrectionists, these sentiments angered every member of his official family, except Toucey, who gave his approval. In particular Buchanan's closest confidant, Jeremiah S. Black, was deeply grieved. On the Sunday following the reading, Black called upon Isaac Toucey, requesting the Connecticut statesman to inform the President that if the letter in question were sent to the South Carolina delegation, he would resign his seat in the cabinet. Black next notified Stanton of his intention. "I shall go out with you," said the Attorney General. Joseph Holt, now Secretary of War – for Floyd had been deposed – took the same stand. In response to a hurried call from Buchanan, Black went to the White House and found the venerable President on the verge of tears. "Do you too talk of leaving me?" asked their agonized modern Caesar of his Brutus.[4]

A second dislocation of his cabinet within a month was more than Buchanan could bear. His surrender was complete. Black, he declared, could write his own response to the South Carolina gentlemen; he would leave the matter entirely to his discretion. Black and Stanton spent the rest of that Sabbath composing the letter which Buchanan signed. This document, while according to modern ideas hardly satisfactory, omitted the weak concessions of the presidential draft. It greatly angered the South Carolinian "ambassadors," who answered in a diatribe so violent that Buchanan returned it, with the endorsement that it was not "one which the President of the United States could receive." The correspondence marked a new day in Buchanan's attitude towards the rebellious South. The cabinet, now reconstructed by the elimination of Floyd, Thompson, Cobb, and Thomas, contained men who were heart and soul – with the possible exception of Toucey, who lingered on until March 4 – devoted to the Union cause. Black, the new Secretary of State, much as he detested Republicans and abolitionists, loved the Union; John A. Dix, the new Secretary of the Treasury, soon gained immortality by his terse instructions to a Treasury official at New Orleans, ordering him to take possession of a revenue cutter there – "If anyone attempts to haul down the American flag, shoot him on the spot"; Joseph Holt, Secretary of War, was one of those Kentuckians who remained superloyal to the central government; and Horatio King, the new Postmaster General, was a New Yorker of the same patriotic school as Dix. As for Stanton, he displayed

[4] Black, Jeremiah S., *Essays and Speeches*. New York, 1885. P. 14. Gorham, *op. cit.*, I, 146–147. Curtis, George Ticknor, *Life of James Buchanan Fifteenth President of the United States*. Harper & Brothers, 1883. II, 383–395.

his eagerness for the Union cause in ways that enraged Buchanan and his followers when they learned of his activities – which they did not for several years – and made him the great hero of the time in the eyes of Sumner, Henry Wilson, and the whole tribe of "radicals."

The word is an unpleasant one, but no other completely fits the situation. Stanton became a spy on the Buchanan administration in the interests of the approaching Lincoln regime. According to Nicolay and Hay, Stanton was so struck with "horror" by what he discovered in the Buchanan government – before it was reformed, and when it was virtually being controlled by Jefferson Davis – that he had only one recourse. The highly ethical New England radicals found no difficulty in justifying his conduct on the loftiest moral grounds. Stanton had taken oath to support and defend the Constitution; he immediately discovered that secessionists in the cabinet were working to annihilate that instrument, to destroy the government and erect their own improvised Confederacy in its place. Washington, in December and early January, 1860–1861, was, so Stanton averred, full of Confederate agents who were secretly organizing military units, with which, before Lincoln could be inaugurated, they had planned to seize the Federal city, with all its buildings and archives, and transform it into the capital of their new Confederacy. That Lincoln entertained some such apprehension his anxieties, before inauguration, clearly show. Seward's feverish fears have already been set forth. The Washington situation in that winter might easily have disturbed the sleep of a nation overwrought and unprotected. The city was generally Southern in population and feeling. For nearly ten years Southern Democrats had controlled all three branches of government, and filled important offices and military and naval commands with men thoroughly in sympathy with the proslavery ideal. No army or military forces were at hand to safeguard the Capital from a sudden onslaught, and almost the weakest and most vacillating of American Presidents – himself for years a timeserver to Southern aspirations – reigned in the White House.

Stanton's activities at this moment suggest not so much a matter-of-fact American as a conspirator in Ruritania or Graustark. One midnight he met Charles Sumner by prearrangement in Sumner's lodgings; in the vivid words of Jeremiah S. Black he sat "squat like a toad" at the Senator's ear, stealthily giving him full details of the new gunpowder plot. Ten years afterward Sumner related the incident in a letter to Henry Wilson, published in the *Atlantic Monthly* for October 1870. "He came at one o'clock that night, and was alone with me for an hour. During this time he described to me the determination of the southern leaders and developed particularly their plan to obtain possession of the national capital and the national archives, so that they might substitute themselves for the existing government." Sumner, however, was not Stanton's most intimate confidant. "The plot is forming to seize the capital and usurp the government," Seward wrote Thurlow Weed on December 29, 1860, "and it has abettors near the President. I am writing you not from rumors but knowledge." "Treason is at work in the states," he wrote his daughter the same day, "and even in the cabinet and Senate, to overthrow the country." And to his wife: "Treason is around and amongst us; and plots to seize the capital and usurp the government." "At length I have gotten a position," he wrote Lincoln on this same exciting December 29, "in which I can see what is going on in the councils of the President. It pains me to learn that things there are even worse than we understood. The President is debating day and night on the question whether he shall not recall Major Anderson and surrender Fort Sumter and go on arming the South. A plot is forming to seize the capital on or before the 4th of March, and this, too, has its accomplices in the public councils. I could tell you more particularly than I dare write, but you must not imagine that I am giving you suspicion and rumors. Believe me I know what I write." The date of this letter is significant. It was the day before that Buchanan had startled his cabinet by reading his letter to the South Carolina ambassadors, in which he had practically acceded to all their demands. Seward's intelligence, relayed to Lincoln, shows that he had been accurately informed of this proceeding. Another letter, written to Lincoln the next day, proves that he knew of the position Black, Stanton, and others had taken, and of the result. "The President," he wrote Springfield, "has decided to stand on his loyalty. Floyd resigned and the other seceder members will. But we are trembling today, lest he may be overborne by seceding influences and recall all. The White House is abandoned to the seceders. They eat, drink and sleep with him." [5]

The man who had worked Seward up to this state of apprehension was Edwin M. Stanton. Seward wrote confidently to Lincoln of events taking place in the Buchanan cabinet because the newest addition to that company had established personal relations with the forthcoming Secretary of State, and was giving him day-by-day bulletins of its most secret transactions. He could assure Lincoln "I know what I write," because Stanton was giving him daily reports. A certain Mr. Watson, as Seward's son has related, was making frequent visits to the Seward home, ostensibly conferring with his father in the basement on an important patent case. This Mr. Watson was a real person, a close

[5] Seward's *Seward,* II, 487–488.

friend of both Seward and Stanton, and was afterward Assistant Secretary of War in the Lincoln administration. "Immediately after Mr. Stanton took office," Seward himself wrote on June 6, 1870, to Henry Wilson, "he put himself into indirect communication with me, at my house, employing Mr. Watson for that purpose. Every day thereafter, until the inauguration had passed, I conferred either in the morning or the evening or both with Mr. Stanton through this same agency, and the question of what either of us could or ought to do at the time for the public welfare was discussed and settled. Mr. Watson often brought with him suggestions in writing from Mr. Stanton and returned to Mr. Stanton with mine." [6]

On January 9 Seward wrote Lincoln that "the alarms about the capital have passed over"; significantly on this same day Jacob Thompson, the most treacherous of the secessionists in the Buchanan regime, had retired from the cabinet. Floyd, who, in addition to his part in the defalcations in Thompson's department, had been caught red-handed, in late December, in an attempt to transfer heavy artillery from the arsenal in Pittsburgh to uncompleted forts in Texas, then preparing for secession, had disappeared from Washington into the Confederate Army in early January.

It is not likely that Stanton had much influence in this cleansing of the Buchanan cabinet. He seems, however, to have been the chief instigator of the committee of the House appointed on January 26 to investigate subterranean plots believed to be hatching for attacks on Washington. According to the chairman, William Howard of Michigan, Stanton himself unquestionably drew up the resolution creating this group of inquisitors. "It would be easier," Mr. Howard said afterward, "to persuade me that Mr. Jefferson did not write the Declaration of Independence than that Mr. Stanton did not write those resolutions." [7] According to Henry L. Dawes, a Massachusetts member of the committee, Stanton kept in constant touch with its members. Dawes gave theatrical details. Papers, some of them written in a bold handwriting "that became familiar enough after Stanton was made Secretary of War," were left in secret places, where they were recovered by members of the committee, and after being "read by the light of the street lamp at night" were "returned to the place of deposit." Information derived from these memoranda, said Mr. Dawes, frequently gave the lead for the next day's cross-examination. One of Stanton's notes warned against the suspected Toucey. "There is a northern traitor in the Cabinet. Arrest him tonight. Pensacola has been given up. Stop

[6] *Atlantic Monthly*, XXVI, 465.
[7] *Ibid.*, XXVI, 467.

him before it is too late." [8] Despite this constant stream of information from a source so near the throne, the work of the House committee proved almost barren of results. After holding sessions for something more than a week, the committee reported that no evidence had been disclosed of an organized attempt to seize the Capital and prevent Lincoln's inauguration. It did unearth one Democratic "marching club" that was drilling secretly, but the revelation that its stealth was inspired by a determination to avoid creditors proved too much for the national sense of humor. Afterward Galusha Grow, a member of the committee, said that the real reason for the appointment of this committee was to let the disloyal know that Congress was on the alert – and possibly its mere existence did accomplish something in discouraging the large army of Confederate sympathizers in Washington.

Gideon Welles, who could never see a worthy motive in any of Stanton's acts, had his own explanation for his strange activities in this difficult winter. He knew that Seward was to be Secretary of State and chief man in the Lincoln administration; he had early formed his plans for preferment under the new regime, and he deliberately "betrayed" – Welles uses this word – Buchanan for the purpose of ingratiating himself with the most powerful man in the Republican Party. There seems to be little doubt that the Seward-Stanton proceedings in January and February of 1861 laid the ground for the Ohioan's entrance into Lincoln's cabinet almost precisely a year afterward. This fact, therefore, substantiates to a degree Mr. Welles's unfriendly, but as always shrewd, explanation. The intrigues in which Stanton engaged for the succession to Simon Cameron add force to the theory. On the other hand, if Stanton, in January 1861, was preparing the way for admission into Lincoln's administration, his behavior seems to have been a strange way of accomplishing his designs. His attitude for the rest of this year portrays the man in his most unpleasant light. He was one of Washington's most outspoken and loquacious enemies of Lincoln, on both personal and public grounds. He had snubbed the prairie lawyer from the day that he reached Washington. Most public men of Stanton's prominence, on the arrival of the new President, either called or at least did him the courtesy of leaving their cards. From the beginning, Stanton avoided Lincoln and all members of the cabinet; the only one with whom he had any personal dealings was Seward.

Moreover he was vulgarly insulting in his free-and-easy comments on the new incumbent. General George B. McClellan, whom Stanton – at this time – most sedulously cultivated, has recorded one of the choicest of these remarks. "He never spoke of the President in any

[8] *Ibid.*, LXXII, 163.

other way than as 'the original gorilla' and often said that Du Chaillu was a fool to wander all the way to Africa in search of what he could so easily have found in Springfield, Illinois."[9] *The Diary of a Public Man* contains allusions similarly impolite. On February 25, two days after Lincoln's surreptitious arrival in Washington, this diarist met Stanton as he was crossing Fourteenth Street. He "stopped me to ask if I had seen the President-elect since he 'crept into Washington.' It is impossible to be more bitter and malignant than he is; every word was a suppressed or an ill-suppressed sneer, and it cost me something to keep my temper with him even for a few moments. When he found that I had met Mr. Lincoln only once, to my recollection, he launched out into a downright tirade about him, saying that 'he had met him at the bar and found him a low, cunning clown.' I could not resist telling him as we parted, that I hoped the President would take an *official* and not a *personal* view of his successor in any relations he might have with him. I think he felt the thrust, for he bowed more civilly than he is apt to, when he left me."[10] Stanton's reference to his one meeting with Lincoln "at the bar" recalls the celebrated incident that, had Lincoln been of more vindictive character, would forever have excluded the Steubenville lawyer from his society. The two men were associated, in 1855, as counsel for the Manny interests in the famous McCormick reaper infringement suit. Several versions of the episode have been published, but all agree on the rudeness of Stanton's behavior – how he elbowed Lincoln out of the case, prevented him from making his argument, and browbeat him, personally and professionally, in the accustomed Stanton fashion. "Where did that long-armed creature come from, and what can he expect to do in this case?" was a remark which, according to Herndon, Lincoln through a half-opened door, overheard the distinguished Pittsburgh lawyer make concerning himself. Yet it was said that Lincoln, though disappointed and bruised in spirit, was so entranced by the intellectual power Stanton displayed in his argument that the experience, rough as it was, exercised a good deal of influence when Lincoln decided, six years afterward, to put him in the cabinet.

Not only in conversation, with "Public Man" and others, was Stanton contemptuous towards the new tenant of the White House. He has left an imperishable written record of his mental operations for the few months following the inauguration. When James Buchanan left Washington, he asked Stanton to write him occasionally, giving his impressions of the new regime and generally keeping the ex-President

[9] McClellan, George B., *McClellan's Own Story*. C. L. Webster, 1887. P. 152.
[10] *North American Review*, Vol. 129, p. 262.

abreast of the times. Stanton scrupulously complied with this request. The portrait he draws of himself in this correspondence differs surprisingly from the one he painted in the memorandum of cabinet scenes written for the benefit of posterity and preserved among his papers. The heroic paladin, storming into the Buchanan cabinet and denouncing Floyd and Thompson, and even President Buchanan himself, as "traitors," about to deliver their country over to the South, is no longer in evidence. Instead we have a Stanton who is subdued, complimentary, even oily, comparing the new administration with the old in terms to the advantage of the latter. Reading these letters, indeed, calls to mind certain adjectives, such as "sycophantic," "hypocritical," "double-dealing," which contemporaries were inclined to apply to the Secretary. Stanton writes as a loyal Buchanan Democrat reporting all the good things said in Washington of the Buchanan administration and all the unpleasant things gossiped concerning the succeeding one. "Black Republicans," he wrote were obtaining most military commissions, and the war was being fought for party ends. Corruption and inefficiency were rapidly producing chaos. One would almost think, in reading these letters, that patriotic Americans were yearning for a return of the good old Buchanan days. "I do not think," writes Stanton in April, "there will be any serious effort to assail your administration in respect to Fort Sumter." "The first month of the [Lincoln] administration has furnished an ample vindication of your policy and has rendered all occasion of other defense unnecessary."

The regime was without public respect; indeed, little confidence prevailed that it would last long. "Every day," Stanton wrote on March 16, "affords the proof of the absence of any settled policy or harmonious concert of action. Seward, Bates and Cameron form one wing. Chase, Miller,[11] Blair the opposite wing. Smith is on both sides and Lincoln sometimes on one, sometimes on the other." And on April 11: "The feeling of loyalty to the government has greatly diminished in this city. Many persons who would have supported the government under your administration refused to be enrolled. Many who were enrolled have withdrawn and refuse to take the oath. The administration has not acquired the confidence or respect of the people here. Not one of the cabinet or principal officers has taken a house or brought his family here. Seward rented a house 'while he should continue in the cabinet' but he has not opened it nor has his family come. They all act as though they meant to be ready 'to cut and run at a minute's notice' — their tenure is like that of a Bedouin on the sands of the desert. And

[11] So it appears in *Works of James Buchanan*. Ed. by John Bassett-Moore. J. P. Lippincott, 1908–1911. P. 170. Evidently a printer's error for "Welles."

besides a strong feeling of distrust in the candor and sincerity of Lincoln personally, has sprung up. . . . No one speaks of Lincoln or any member of his cabinet with respect or regard." "The imbecility of this administration," Stanton wrote Buchanan on July 26, after Bull Run, "culminated in that catastrophe – an irretrievable misfortune and national disgrace, never to be forgotten, are to be added to the ruin of all peaceful pursuits and national bankruptcy as a result of Lincoln's 'running the machine' for five months. . . . It is not unlikely that some change in the war and navy departments may take place, but none beyond those two departments until Jeff Davis turns out the whole concern."

It seems strange that Stanton should have aspired to become a member of an administration which he so despised, but there are signs in plenty that, in the summer and fall of 1861, he was maneuvering to that end. The unpopularity of Cameron and the indications that his career as War Minister was reaching a crisis naturally did not escape Stanton's notice. Moreover, events had made this department the most important of all; any man who desired to serve his country – and this unselfish motive should not be disregarded in considering the complexities of Stanton's character – would naturally turn his thoughts in that direction. Possibly the rebuff which Stanton received in his first attempt to serve the new regime explains, in part, the venom with which he assailed it. Soon after inauguration Lincoln was called upon to appoint the District Attorney for the District of Columbia. For this important office two candidates were presented, Edwin M. Stanton and Edward C. Carrington. Seward and Chase strongly endorsed Stanton, while Attorney General Bates favored Carrington. The question came up in an early cabinet meeting. Lincoln announced that he had no personal regard for Stanton – the President was still evidently smarting under the insulting treatment received at his hands in the McCormick case; still Stanton was an able man and a Democrat, and, Lincoln added, at that critical moment he would like to bring as many influential Democrats as possible to the side of the Union. Seward spoke strongly for Stanton, emphasizing the great services he had rendered to his country while in Buchanan's cabinet. Chase also, seldom found, even at that early date, on the same side as Seward, warmly supported Stanton. Bates admitted Stanton's ability, but did not trust the man. Lincoln then appealed to Blair, who, in his appearances before the Supreme Court, had had opportunities to gauge the candidate. Blair, in his explosive manner, threw a bombshell into the discussion. No one questioned, he said, that Stanton, as a lawyer, was far abler than Carrington, but, he complained, Stanton was not an honest man; he had taken bribes, and Blair said he knew of at least one case in which the evidence was complete. The charge astonishes the present generation, for Stanton, as head of the War Department, was especially distinguished for honesty and for the ferocity with which he pursued corrupt contractors; it likewise, writes Gideon Welles, "astonished the President and disconcerted both Seward and Chase, each of whom questioned whether there might not be some mistake in this matter, but Blair said there could be none, and farther that he (Stanton) was a protégé of Black, and in feeling with him." Lincoln cut the whole discussion short by saying that the matter chiefly concerned the Attorney General and that he would therefore let Mr. Bates decide between the two men. Bates at once chose Carrington.

The fact that Stanton could enlist on his behalf the two great rivals of the cabinet, Seward and Chase, again attests his versatile talent for simultaneously winning the favor of men of the most divergent views. At that time the great issue that was to raise such havoc in Lincoln's official family – the problem of the Negro – had already been definitely drawn. Seward and Chase represented the opposite poles of this question, and both men believed that Stanton belonged to their school. That he was a strong Unionist and conservative was Seward's conviction. On the other hand Chase, the leader in the administration of an extreme pro-Negro policy, regarded Stanton as one of his own party. Stanton had given both men grounds to regard him as a follower. Unfriendly critics insist that he, like Cameron, had observed the growing power of the antislavery group, and had therefore cultivated a resurgence of the abolitionist allegiances with which he had started life. "Wily Edwin M. Stanton," is the way a recent analyst puts it, "who was snuggling up to the radicals in the hope of securing Cameron's job with their aid while at the same time holding hands with his Democratic friends." [12] Whatever the method, or whatever the motive, all the great radical leaders – Chase, Sumner, Chandler, Wade, Fessenden, Julian – became Stanton's friends and joyfully acclaimed him as one of themselves.

At the same time an influence even more powerful at the moment than any of these was tenderly cultivated. Probably no man, in the latter part of 1861, could become Secretary of War without the support of the young Napoleon of the Army of the Potomac, George B. McClellan. One of the first friends that commander made after his arrival in Washington, the day following Bull Run, was the famous lawyer. Stanton became his legal adviser, his friend, and his refuge. In politics

[12] Williams, T. Harry, *Lincoln and the Radicals*. University of Wisconsin Press, 1941. P. 84.

McClellan represented a different type from either Seward or Chase. He was a Democrat of the Breckinridge-Buchanan school. Slavery, in his view, was exclusively a Southern question, and the North should let it severely alone. If remarks said to have been dropped by McClellan in Washington can be accepted as authentic, he was not an overzealous Unionist. Gideon Welles quotes with horror the McClellan statement that Massachusetts and South Carolina were equally to blame for the war, and that he would just as willingly fight one as the other. Such opinions did not prevent Stanton and the little general from becoming intimate. McClellan's *Own Story* contains a tart record of that friendship. McClellan portrays himself as an unsuspecting fly who had been beguiled into the Stanton web. All Stanton's pretensions of friendship and support were merely plottings for the succession to Cameron. "Not many weeks after arriving I was introduced to him as a safe adviser on legal points. From that moment he did his best to ingratiate himself with me, and professed the warmest friendship and devotion. . . . His purpose was to endeavor to climb upon my shoulder and then throw me down." The sequel disclosed that, whether or not Stanton's blandishments were deliberately designed to such an end, that was certainly the outcome.

McClellan makes charges that seem pretty wild. When Cameron made "quite an abolition speech," Stanton urged McClellan to arrest him – Cameron was then Secretary of War – "for inciting to insubordination. He often advocated the propriety of my seizing the government and taking affairs into my own hands." In the early time McClellan became so close to Stanton that, seeking a peaceful retreat – even from Lincoln – he took up his headquarters at Stanton's house. Here only, McClellan wrote his wife, could he be secured from "prowling Presidents." On one critical occasion Stanton rendered McClellan a friendly service. A meeting of the radicals was being held one Sunday in the White House, to decide McClellan's fate – for his long period of preparation, or failure to take a vigorous offensive, seemed to call for action. Stanton came to McClellan, who was just recovering from a serious illness, and revealed the plot against him. "They are counting on your death," Stanton said, "and are already dividing among themselves your military goods and chattels." As a result of this warning McClellan himself, generally supposed to be lying at the point of death with typhoid fever, appeared at the solemn Sanhedrin, "where my unexpected appearance," he afterward wrote, "caused very much the effect of a shell in a powder magazine." As a result, the campaign of the radicals for McClellan's military head was frustrated. Chase, McClellan believed, working in the interest of the radical party, was the instigator of the scheme against him. Thus Stanton, by quietly informing McClellan of the "plot," had, as Gideon Welles and Jeremiah Black would have put it, "betrayed" Chase's confidence. But at this very moment Chase regarded Stanton as one of the finest characters in Washington and was working hard to make him Secretary of War.

Just through whose instrumentality Stanton did attain his goal is something that, historians are generally agreed, will never be known. Three conspicuous candidates for this honor figure in all discussions of the subject: Simon Cameron, Salmon P. Chase, and William H. Seward. That these were the only members of the cabinet who knew of the appointment before it was sent to the Senate was true. In his lifetime Cameron always pointed to himself as the creator of the new Secretary of War. He has left a record of his call on Lincoln, in which he expressed a wish to retire from the War Department, and declared his willingness to do so provided Stanton were selected as his successor.[13] This is all a part of the legend which the Cameronians diligently spread that Cameron's retirement was voluntary, and may therefore be disregarded. As always, we are forced to fall back again upon that unfailing fountain of information, who gave full credit to William H. Seward. Lincoln's first choice for the post, according to Gideon Welles, was Montgomery Blair. From the professional standpoint such an appointment would have been an excellent one. Of all the cabinet members, Blair was the only one who knew anything at first hand of military affairs. He was a graduate of West Point and had served for a time in the regular army. His knowledge of the existing army situation and the soundness of his views on military plans had impressed both Lincoln and Welles in cabinet councils. The ability with which Blair managed the Post Office Department showed that he possessed administrative capacity of a high order. But from a political standpoint the promotion would have been a mistake. No man was quite so odious to both Seward and Chase as this forthright, peppery Marylander, and the Republican Party as a whole would have resented the heightened influence of "the Blairs" that such an elevation would have made inevitable. But such spadework as Seward may have performed in excluding Blair and promoting the influence of Stanton has left no trace. So far as the record shows, he had nothing to do with the cabinet change. As he was Lincoln's closest intimate, and as he spent the larger part of the Saturday and Sunday preceding the appointment in Lincoln's company, it may be assumed that Seward's assistance was not disregarded in this crisis. Always the politician, Seward was looking not only for a capable

[13] *Atlantic Monthly*, XXVI, 473.

Secretary of War, but for a personal partisan. In advocating Cameron, he had been deluded into the belief that, in a sense, he was packing the cabinet with a man of his own. This plan having failed, he now labored to oust Cameron and install a dependable Seward man in his place. One sentence in Welles's narrative concerning this cabinet change sheds more light upon the transaction than all the contradictory accounts of which it has been made the subject. Seward himself told Welles, so the latter has recorded, that Stanton had promised, in case of attaining the War Department, that "he should maintain his [Seward's] policy, vote with him and remain with him in the cabinet, and leave whenever he did." [14]

This single sentence lifts the curtain. It discloses Stanton angling for the post, and prepared to make – or at least to promise – most humiliating commitments to obtain it. It similarly discloses Seward contriving a hard-and-fast bargain as the price of his influence. After this, Chase's own elaborate story of how he first proposed Stanton for the coveted place, acted as go-between in the negotiations, and persuaded both Lincoln and Seward of the appropriateness of the appointment, need not be taken too seriously. It is interesting to observe how Welles, preparing his memorandum in the late seventies, anticipates and explains this passage in Chase's Diary, none of which had then been published. That Seward himself should lie low, and let Chase imagine himself the active manipulator in Stanton's appointment, was all a part of the Seward technique. That Stanton had insulted Lincoln to his face, that he had abused and ridiculed the administration, Seward well knew; human nature being what it is, it would seem almost too much to expect even the most tolerant of men to take the reviler to his bosom. Seward therefore needed Chase's assistance, and the best way of obtaining it was to appeal to the man's vanity and permit him to think that he was the mainspring of the transaction. There had been nothing in Stanton's career, in the campaign of 1856 – when he supported Buchanan – or in 1860 – when he took the stump for Breckinridge – or in his activities in Buchanan's cabinet to give Chase ground for foreseeing what came to pass, that Stanton would join the Chase radical party in opposing Lincoln's reconstruction policy. On his merits one would think that almost any other man would have been preferred by Chase as Cameron's successor.

Perhaps, therefore, Welles was right in thinking that Seward, by tickling Chase's vanity, manipulated him into coming to his support in urging the Stanton appointment on Lincoln. Welles also describes, as well as it has ever been described, Lincoln's reason for overlooking the

[14] Welles, *Narrative of Events*.

Stanton past. The President "was not the man to permit his personal likes and dislikes to govern his action in cases of public necessity."

The outcome was not a happy one for Lincoln personally. Stanton was insulting at times and, even worse, he was disloyal, an intriguer against his chief. For Seward's plans, Stanton was the worst selection he could have made. Perhaps Montgomery Blair summed up the matter most neatly in his comment to Welles, a few weeks after Stanton's advent. He declared that Seward had brought Stanton into the cabinet for his own purposes "after Chase had stolen Cameron and that Chase is now stealing Stanton." The flippant phrase described accurately a transition in allegiance that proved to be one of the vexations of Lincoln's life.

BOOK FOUR

The Cabinet and McClellan

I

AS AN ADMINISTRATOR of the War Department, Stanton aided powerfully in the conduct of the war. He quickly put to flight the corrupt contractors who had reaped a profitable harvest under Cameron, introduced order and honesty into every branch of the service, and won the gratitude of his generals, such as Grant and Sherman, for the efficiency with which he enrolled and transported troops and provided munitions and supplies. But on matters of general administration policy, he proved to be only another thorn in Lincoln's side. By the time of his accession, the lines that were to split the Republican Party in two – a schism that was to continue into the explosive days of reconstruction – had been definitely drawn. What was the immediate objective of the war, the preservation of the Union or the extinction of slavery? What was to be the future of the Negro? If set free, would he become a citizen, with all civic rights, on equal grounds in political, economic, and social prerogatives, with the white man? On what terms were the seceded states to be readmitted into the Federal Union? From the first Lincoln had proclaimed the reconstitution of the central government as the great aim of the conflict. He was determined to keep all other questions subordinate. In this program he had had the support of all members of his cabinet except Chase and Cameron. But with the coming of Stanton, Chase secured a powerful and resourceful as well as unscrupulous, intriguing ally. Seward, Welles, Blair, Bates, stood strongly at Lincoln's side in his struggle for Union and for a conciliatory policy toward the South, while Chase and Stanton represented a small, but effective and persistent bloc which insisted on the future of the Negro as the great question at issue and advocated harsh treatment for the states in rebellion.

The leaders in the policy of Thorough are generally known today as "radicals"; a name under which they became even more notorious in the era of Reconstruction that followed the Civil War. Those who advocated more conciliatory methods were called, then and afterward, conservatives. But the colloquial parlance of the day had coined a new appellation for the extremists. Edward Bates, in his Diary, always refers to this faction of the Republican Party as the Jacobins, and John Hay's favorite nickname for the most aggressive group was "the Jacobin Club." The title, of course, harked back to the French Revolution and to the firebrands who held their meetings at the monastery of the Jacobins in Paris, and there plotted the schemes which ultimately led to the Reign of Terror. In character and manners, the two foremost leaders, "Bluff Ben" Wade and the frequently bibulous "Zack" Chandler, mildly suggested a Marat or a Robespierre. Wade's features, as they have been handed down in the crude photographs of the time, with his mastiff-like jaw and lips, his determined eyes, thin, skeleton-like face, protruding chin and lofty cheekbones, high forehead and unruly hair, form a fitting setting for the doctrines and performances associated with his name. The last qualities the exterior man presented were the ancient culture and education of New England. Yet Wade directly derived from several of the most distinguished families of Massachusetts. Among his formidable list of grandfathers, great-grandfathers, and the like appear the names of Dudley, Upham, Bradstreet, and Wigglesworth. Anne Bradstreet, that "tenth muse" of early Puritan literature, was an ancestor, and Michael Wigglesworth, author of the *Day of Doom* – a poem compared to which Dante's *Inferno* is a work of boisterous humor – was his great-grandfather. Wade had this lugubrious masterpiece at tongue's end, and frequently entertained his friends by repeating its choicest passages, especially the stanza which promised babies born in a state of nonelection "the easiest room in hell." The obvious analyst might see in this dark family background the relentless, bloodhound qualities which Wade displayed in the pursuit of his favorite form of evil; but the man was not a religious enthusiast, still less a theological one, and his interest in ancestral literature did not spring from awe for its gloomy precepts, but rather expressed the backwoodsman type of humor for which Wade was celebrated.

Indeed, no man ever departed further from the family norm. Most of Wade's ancestors had been educated at Harvard, but a few winter months at a red brick schoolhouse represented the height of his intellectual equipment. The ministry and schoolmastering, or substantial farming, had given sustenance to most of his predecessors; but Wade at the age of twenty, with seven dollars in his pocket, and all his mundane possessions crammed into a bag and thrown over his shoulder, abandoned the "wild Agawam hills" of western Massachusetts, plunged into the wilderness, and walked all the way to the Western Reserve of Ohio. Here he cleared a tract, built a log cabin, and settled down to the life of a pioneer. In the next few years he followed a variety of occupations. He taught school – an academic degree not being a requisite for this profession on the primitive shores of Lake Erie – drove herds of cattle over the Alleghanies into Pennsylvania, hired out as woodcutter at fifty cents a cord, and worked with pick and shovel on the proudest engineering enterprise of the day, the Erie Canal. The Western Reserve – part of the empire which Connecticut claimed by royal charter, lying within certain degrees of latitude extending from the Atlantic to the Pacific Ocean – was really a piece of New England transplanted to a new frontier. Practically all its settlers came from Connecticut, Massachusetts, and New Hampshire and not unnaturally had transplanted the institutions and the mode of life that had made them what they were at home. This may explain the new ambitions which soon diverted Wade from the jack-of-all-trades existence he had pursued in the earlier years. For a brief time he studied medicine, but abandoned that profession for the law. A few months of reading in a law office at Ashtabula qualified him, in 1827, for admission to the bar. By a lucky chance Joshua Giddings offered the promising young man a partnership. This not only guaranteed Wade a modest living, but enlarged what may possibly be called his spiritual or humanitarian outlook. This Giddings was the same man who thirty years afterward impressively walked out of the Chicago Wigwam when the convention refused – a refusal afterward rescinded – to include the "created equal" phrases of the Declaration of Independence in the party platform. Giddings thus represented that extreme type of abolitionist whom only the Western Reserve of Ohio could engender. Logically enough, therefore, his rough-and-ready protégé soon blossomed forth into an unabashed and uncompromising advocate of the black man.

Wade quickly advanced from the routine business of law into the State Senate of Ohio. Here he fought the Negro's cause so vehemently that his denunciations displeased even that antislavery district, which angrily refused to return him for a second term. The usual antislavery battle cries of the day did not suffice for Wade. Opposition to fugitive-slave laws, to the extension of slavery, to slavery in the old South, to Texas annexation, to the Mexican War, provided the main items in the abolitionist creed, but Wade went in for more sweeping denunciations. He proposed to transform the Negro, at least on the political and civic side, into a white man. In Ohio State lived a considerable population of free colored men, who, except for the fact that they were not slaves, enjoyed few more civic rights than their brethren of the plantations. Wade demanded the removal of all legal distinction between them and their Caucasian fellow citizens. The right to vote, to hold office, to sit on juries – indeed, all the privileges which, in Wade's mature days in the United States Senate, became the watchwords of Reconstruction, he proposed to give Negroes in the Ohio of the eighteen-thirties. He urged the proposal in a raucous oratory which, if it accomplished nothing else – for the program of civic equality failed in the legislature – did advertise the speaker as a bold, rough-hewn reformer, of unquestioned mental power and formidable strength in debate. When his tall, straight, broad-shouldered but supple figure arose, black locks shaking and little black eyes full of sparks, only the most courageous of his enemies cared to oppose him. Those speaking habits that afterward made Wade so familiar a figure in the Federal Senate – rising and sinking on his toes in the heat of argument, now thrusting his right hand, Napoleon-like, into his coat, again shooting it out like a rocket to rivet an argument or scornfully indicate an opponent, for Wade never hesitated at personalities – marked his early efforts in Ohio. That Wade possessed many of the qualities of a leader of men – personal courage, lightning-like repartee, strong convictions, a quick and dominating mind – soon became evident. That he lacked the humane graces which make the popular favorite was also clear. He cared little for comradely association with his kind, almost never appeared at social gatherings, and as a young man cared nothing for the companionship of women. Wade did not marry until he had passed his fortieth year.

Here was an incongruous colleague, one might think, for Salmon P. Chase, and Wade, when elected to the Senate in 1851, for a time kept aloof from his stately, intellectual companion. Wade did not entirely trust Chase on the abolition issue, and looked doubtfully at the queer compromises which had made possible Chase's election. Nor did he like him personally; the popular impression of his senior was well reflected in his remark that "Chase is all right, only his theology is wrong; he thinks there is a fourth person in the Trinity!" In fact Chase and Wade never affiliated; as time went on, they became positively hostile, Chase regarding Wade, in 1860, as the man chiefly responsible for his failure to obtain Ohio's unanimous support at the Chicago Convention. In 1851, the Senate as a whole, which had become a little weary of Chase's superior manners and Latin quotations, found it something of a relief when Wade appeared. In the fifties feeling between Northern and Southern Senators raged at white heat. Students of Reconstruction are startled by the passions that ultimately swayed the two parties – the Thad Stevens who wished to transform the Southern states into a "desert," the Southern cavaliers who regarded bowie knives and shotguns as the most persuasive of arguments. Undoubtedly a good deal of this fire was kindled when Northern and Southern lawmakers fought face to face, and sometimes literally fist to fist, in the days of the repeal of the Missouri Compromise and of bleeding Kansas. It was the time of primeval passions, and as such the Senate formed an ideal bull pen for a hard hitter like Ben Wade. Northern "dough-faces" and Southern "fire-eaters" he despised with identical fervor. Certain rustics from the middle states and New England who regarded physical brawls and duelings as unchristian sometimes took too meekly the insults and challenges hurled at them by the gentlemen of the South. Wade decided on a different course. Any brother Senator who assailed him or his state, he almost officially proclaimed, would have to answer for his rashness. Immediately a brave spirit from Virginia rose in the Senate and said that Ohio was a state of "Negro thieves." "You're a liar!" Wade, as good as his word, retorted. Presently the outraged Southerner's representatives called on the Ohioan. A retraction, even a faint apology, would satisfy their principal; otherwise Mr. Wade understood what the word "liar," applied to a son of the Old Dominion, necessarily entailed. "I take this opportunity," replied Wade, "to say what I then thought, and you will, if you please, repeat it. Your friend is a foul-mouthed old blackguard." Next day in the Senate he walked up to his seat, drew from beneath his coat two huge pistols and, in full view of his associates, placed them on his desk. Strange to say, no challenge was ever received. Wade's defiance of the redoubtable Robert Toombs gave the Ohioan high standing among sports-loving Americans. Toombs was one of the Senators who, when Bully Brooks clubbed Charles Sumner into insensibility at his Senate desk, delivered a speech applauding the assault. Wade rose in fury, "his voice thundering and his eyes shooting fire," one chronicle records. "If the principle now announced," he roared, murderously looking at Toombs, "is to prevail, let us come armed for the combat, and although you are four to one, I am here to meet you." When Wade was asked to name the weapons in the expected duel, he specified "squirrel rifles at twenty paces" and demanded that both antagonists wear pieces of white paper over their hearts. Each man was to shoot at the signal, and if the bullets miscarried was to advance, for the next volley, a yard closer to his foe; if they both misfired again, another yard, and so on, until, if the affair lasted that long, they would stand practically face to face. A few days after this specification of the terms, both Wade and Toombs, who sat near each other in the Senate, resumed their seats. Toombs bent over and put his hand on the enemy's shoulder. "Wade," he said, "what's the use of two men making damned fools of themselves?" "None at all," Wade retorted, "but it is the misfortune of some men that they can't help it." From that day he and Toombs remained excellent friends.

Not unnaturally the Southern fire-eaters, much as they abhorred Wade's principles, admired him as a man. His often happy retorts in debate added to his popularity and his growing national fame. In the discussion of the Kansas-Nebraska Bill Senator Badger, of North Carolina, plaintively asked: "You mean that when I go to settle in Nebraska, I can't take my old black mammy with me?" "We haven't the slightest objection to your taking your old black mammy to Nebraska," Wade shot back. "What we object to is selling her when you get her there."

Here were clearly the makings of one of those Jacobins who were to prove as troublesome to Lincoln and his cabinet as they had proved to the Southern comrades in the Senate of the eighteen-fifties. Similar qualities embellished Zachariah Chandler, Wade's closest associate on both fields of battle. Like Wade, Chandler was uneducated and personally unpolished. His letters, while they do not lack a certain vigor, are misspelled and jumbled in construction; an amusing fact is that Chandler never mastered the orthography of the man whom he detested above all others, that young Napoleon who frequently figures in his correspondence as "that damned McLelland." Like Wade's – and indeed, like most of the Jacobins' – Chandler's origin went back to New England; he was born in the Merrimac Valley of New Hampshire, in 1814, of Puritan stock. The elder Chandler, when Zack reached his eighteenth year, offered him the choice of college education his brothers had received, or a capital gift of one thousand dollars. Chandler took the cash and let the culture go. He, too, sought fame and fortune – especially fortune – in the dawning West, landing in the frontier settlement of Detroit in 1833. In more recent times this energetic Yankee would have found himself at home in that state of steel and automobiles; in this earlier territorial period, however, Chandler opened a general store. The man evidently possessed mercantile genius. Chandler, in the experimental period, acted as his own manager, salesman, and porter; after standing at the counter all day, he would deliver the purchases, and then, returning to his emporium, would sleep on his counter with a bale of goods for pillow. He cannily invested his earnings in real estate in an expanding community. Twenty years after this beginning the "Chandler block," an architectural masterpiece – so proud Detroiters of that day regarded it – was the most imposing building in town, housing the great retail and wholesale drygoods business that had made Zack a rich man, and consequently, when he deigned to take up politics as a side issue, a power in Republican circles. On July 6, 1854, a large host of Free-Soilers, ex-Whigs, and antislavery Democrats met in the open, under the elms in Jackson, Michigan, the men in stovepipe hats and the women in coal-scuttle bonnets, and issued the call to all antislavery forces for a new party, and, as Michiganders have always insisted, for the first time adopted the designation "Republican." On this occasion Chandler was the loudest, if not the most Ciceronian, of the orators. He had already attained the boss-ship of the new party in his state, largely owing this distinction, his detractors proclaimed, to the lavish use of money and hard liquor. When Chandler first appeared in Washington, as Senator from Michigan, he proved to be the forerunner of a senatorial type that in due course exerted vast authority. At that time the United States Senate was not a rich man's club; Chandler, however, had already reached millionairedom – an attainment he made obvious in several ways. Abolitionists for the most part were a poor, scrawny lot; but Chandler occupied one of the most pretentious houses in the Capital, entertained on a sumptuous scale, and made nothing of dropping checks of $10,000 and more into the yawning party deficit. Had Chandler been an ordinary man, manifestations like this would have made him a conspicuous light; but in addition to his wealth he was vigorously able, a master politician, and a dangerous parliamentarian, not overscrupulous in accomplishing his ends, even though the ends were, in his own opinion and that of many worthy men and women, about the most idealistic that had ever fired the American conscience.

A strange mixture of practical sense and philanthropic impulse was this Zack Chandler. Edward Bates, describing what he calls "a disgraceful scene at Willard's," gives one view of the man. "Senator Chandler of Michigan was in the lobby, drunk (a bad habit that has lately grown upon him) and abused General McClellan roundly, finally calling him a liar and a coward." [1] Bates, on political grounds, despised Chandler as cordially as he hated Wade, who, in his eyes, was a "frosty demagogue." [2] Michigan, however, so excessively admired "old Zack" that his statue stands today in the Capitol in Washington, as one of the two native sons whom it chiefly delights to honor. This, of course, is intended as a tribute to what Michigan regards as Chandler's unselfish labor for the black man. And in truth the picture suggested by the censorious Bates shows only one side of the man. Not that Chandler was ever a figure of dignity. His long, horselike face, high forehead, glaring eyes, large and close together, long, aggressive nose, thin lips, the lower one protruding above the upper, the two shaggy clusters of dark hair, one rising almost vertically from his head, the other depending from the chin, his powerful frame, awkward, gaunt, and sinewy, his manners, blunt, at times good-natured, at other times overbearing –

[1] Bates, *op. cit.*, p. 260.
[2] *Ibid.*, p. 273.

such an exterior hardly made him a fitting companion of the debonair Sumner and the pompous Chase. At least they portray one advantage that helped Chandler in his early political days. He possessed the strength of a giant and sometimes used it as a giant. In the early fifties Detroit's richest and most elegantly dressed merchant would leave his counting room and descend into the voting places, where the roughs of the opposite party were using the strong-armed methods of the time. With his brawny shoulders Zack would plow through these Democratic cohorts, as handy with his fists as the less prosperous members of the proletariat.

This same personal aggressiveness was displayed from the first day in the Senate. Southern fire-eaters frightened him no more than they did Bluff Ben. In fact, Chandler and Wade drew up a written compact, to which they solemnly put their signatures, pledging themselves to resist Southern verbal offensives in the one way that gentlemen of the South were supposed to approve. So seriously did Chandler regard the agreement that, several months before going to Washington, he daily practiced marksmanship, and engaged in regular muscular exercises so as to keep his already powerful body in the pink of condition. No record indicates, however, that Chandler came so close as did Wade to upholding this agreement by deed. However, his rough-and-ready speeches on the Negro, on Kansas, on John Brown and other disquieting themes, often roused Mason, Toombs, Davis, and the rest to verbal fury. The Michigan millionaire proved to be one of the most pestiferous declaimers for Negro rights – the same Negro rights which Wade, Garrison, and other abolitionists were demanding. On the occasion of Preston Brooks's attack on Sumner, Chandler exclaimed in face of his enraged Southern brethren: "Had I been on the floor of the Senate when that assault occurred, so help me God that ruffian's blood would have flowed!" Like Wade and the others, Chandler at this time acquired that intense hatred of Southern statesmen which inspired his every act and word during the next thirty years – for his political life was a long one, culminating as Secretary of the Interior in the cabinet of President Grant. When the catastrophic year 1861 arrived, Chandler faced the situation boldly. He turned his face against all compromise. The issue, he loudly declared, was the break-up of the Union or war. He was for war. In a Senate speech on the Crittenden Compromise, which Chandler opposed, he quoted Jefferson's letter of November 13, 1787, that the "tree of liberty must be refreshed from time to time with the blood of patriots and tyrants." "Some of the manufacturing states," said Chandler, "think a fight would be awful. Without a little blood-letting this Union will not, in my estimation, be worth a rush."

Other members of the Jacobin camp were less robustious in word and deed. Charles Sumner accepted most of the Jacobin tenets and usually spoke and voted with that faction in the Senate; but he hardly had access to the inner shrine; he served as a kind of window dressing to the movement, giving it respectability and elegance. Lyman Trumbull, a member of one of Connecticut's most distinguished families, and now Senator from Illinois, also gave the Jacobin cause a dignity which at times it conspicuously needed. Perhaps the most idealistic devotee, however, and the most intellectual, was George Washington Julian, of Indiana. This star-set noncompromiser had a personal history that placed him apart from the others. Wade, Chandler, Sumner, Trumbull, all traced their origins to Puritan New England. Julian's paternal forebears – they spelled the name Julien – had fled France after the revocation of the Edict of Nantes, while his mother's ancestors were almost exclusively German. The French Huguenot and the New England Calvinist had much in common, and certainly Julian's unselfish zeal in the cause of the Negro would have satisfied the most unbending New Englander. The name of Joshua R. Giddings recurs again and again in the annals of the Jacobins; it seems fitting enough, therefore, that Julian should have married Giddings's daughter, the lady's only dowry being the fires of that abolitionism which her father had been spreading for so many years in the Western Reserve. The motives of other leaders in the Jacobin ranks – especially Wade and Chandler – may occasionally abide our question, but Julian's fiercest opponent never doubted his selfless pursuit of an ideal, his readiness to sacrifice fame, fortune, and if necessary life itself, to achieve freedom and the rights of man for the Negro. In early days his own brother had dissolved a law partnership with George Julian, because his unrestrained advocacy of abolition was driving clients from the firm. His interest in other cranky causes, such as Maine temperance laws, woman suffrage, magnetic healing, and spiritualism added little to his standing with more conventional brethren. Julian was similarly a man of the most monastic habits; bread and milk were his favorite food, water his exclusive beverage, while tobacco in any form never polluted his lips. An intellectual and bookish man, he supported the poverty-stricken old age to which the championship of unpopular causes had doomed him chiefly by fugitive magazine writing, the *Atlantic Monthly* and the *North American Review* being favorite receptacles for his essays. His speeches in Congress, to which he was elected in 1848, still occupy a place among the classics of the abolition cause.

Someone once asked Charles Sumner if he had ever looked at the other side of the slavery question; the reply was immediately flashed back, "There is no other side." That completely set forth Julian's attitude. In early life he had taken a vow never to vote for any candidate who was even slightly tainted with the great evil. He even balked at Lincoln's nomination in 1860. Had not the rail splitter taken the stump for Taylor in 1848 – Taylor, the owner of two hundred slaves? In the winter of '61, Julian made an exploratory visit to Springfield to discuss the slavery issue with the President-elect and also to protest against Simon Cameron and Caleb B. Smith in the cabinet. He was completely won by Lincoln's personal charm, but the suspicion that the new man was not entirely sound on the Negro still troubled his conscience. Lincoln's inaugural, assuring the South that no warfare was planned on its favorite institution, added to this anxiety. When the President boldly proclaimed that the purpose of the conflict was not to destroy slavery, but to save the Union, Julian went over fervently to the Jacobin camp, becoming its most eloquent representative in the lower chamber, as Wade and Chandler were in the Senate.

This trio – Wade, Chandler, and Julian – represented the most voluble and persistent foes of the Lincoln cabinet in Congress; their hostility scarcely paused from the day the Civil War began. They gave the Jacobin cause a spectacular leadership, and, in fine, gathered about them a good-sized majority in both legislative chambers. They demanded immediate emancipation, both in the deep South and in the Border states, the enlistment of Negroes in the Northern armies, the confiscation of all rebel property – this property in the main, of course, consisted of slaves – civil and political equality for the Negro, including the right to vote and to hold office. The very day after Bull Run, Chandler and Sumner called formally upon Lincoln, demanding that he immediately proclaim emancipation and announce, as the supreme object of the war, the end of slavery. That Lincoln quietly rejected the proposal probably did not surprise them. From the beginning the radicals had expected little support from Lincoln and his cabinet. For the whole administration the Wade and Chandler group entertained no feeling but distrust and contempt. The plan on which the new President had organized his official family seemed to the Jacobins almost a betrayal of the cause. A cabinet that brought into one coalition all the several elements comprising the Republican Party to them spelled the doom of the Republic. Gather around the same table onetime Whigs who had supported the Taylor regime, old-line Democrats whose hostility to slavery was limited merely to its extension, others whose sympathy with the South was hardly concealed? In the mind of the Jacobin school there was only one type of Republican worthy of a seat at the presidential table. That was the type which, fair weather and foul, and without the slightest qualification, had vowed themselves to the destruction of what Sumner had called, in a Senate speech, "the harlot slavery."

We have seen that Seward was aggrieved because Lincoln had not assembled an "all-Whig," even an all-Seward, cabinet. The Jacobins were disgusted because he had not formed an all-abolition administration. Nor, in the months following election, had they been backward in recommending names. Lyman Trumbull had proposed to Lincoln "bluff Ben Wade" and "old Zack Chandler," but the suggestions had been silently pigeonholed. A cabinet that would have satisfied these extremists can be easily outlined. Charles Sumner, Secretary of State; Salmon P. Chase, Secretary of the Treasury; Zachariah Chandler, Secretary of War; Benjamin F. Wade, Secretary of the Navy; George W. Julian, Attorney General; William P. Fessenden, Postmaster General; John P. Hale, Secretary of the Interior – here we have the kind of administration that the Jacobins would have deemed worthy of the work in hand. Instead, Lincoln had selected a ministry which, in the words of Wade, was a disgraceful surrender to the South. "A sorry, rotten cabinet, blundering, cowardly and inefficient," is only the mildest of the brickbats leveled at the new White House regime. One Jacobin editor advocated the adoption of the parliamentary system, giving cabinet heads seats in Congress. This, he urged, would "drag them out of those corrupt rat holes, their departments, where they can slink away and defy public opinion for an entire four years." Only one member, Salmon Portland Chase, measured up to the Jacobin standard; even Simon Cameron's momentary lapse into virtue did not win their confidence, though they made as much of the doubtful convert as the facts justified. Seward the Jacobins hated as the early Christians did the Emperor Julian; he was an apostate, with his plans for appeasing the South, for guaranteeing slavery in the states, for secretly negotiating with rebel commissioners, for wishing to put Southerners in the cabinet. Chandler described Seward as an "out and out traitor" who must be destroyed. Welles was no abolitionist; he was a onetime Jacksonian Democrat of only mild "anti-slavery" views. Bates was a relic of other days, still holding largely to the Virginia prejudices on the Negro to which he had been born. Smith they regarded as a corrupt Indiana politician ready to adopt any opinions that would advance him politically.

Against the President himself the Jacobins waxed similarly ferocious and abusive. They railed at Lincoln's tenderness towards the Border states, though this policy had saved for the Union cause Delaware, Maryland, Kentucky, Missouri, and nearly one third of Virginia. Even the philosophic Julian had no better word for Lincoln's forbearance than "this sickly policy of an inoffensive war." Wade, commenting on this and other aspects of the administration, lost all sense of decency. "Only a man sprung from poor white trash," he declared, would have disavowed Frémont's proclamation freeing the slaves of Missouri. The rail splitter, he added, "lacked backbone" and "not even a galvanic battery could inspire any action in the cabinet." The courtly gentleman railed at Mrs. Lincoln as though she had been a feminine Robert Toombs. Her fondness for airing her French especially riled him. Invited, as a Senator, to a White House function, Wade replied: "Are the President and Mrs. Lincoln aware that there is a civil war? If they are not, Mr. and Mrs. Wade are, and for that reason decline to participate in feasting and dancing." This hostility the Jacobins never outgrew. A first glimpse of Lincoln shocked many party leaders and aroused doubts as to his wisdom, even his serious intentions; in the vast majority of cases, however, a closer knowledge caused this skepticism to change to affection and admiration. This was not the case with Wade, Chandler, and most of the Jacobin tribe. They worked hard to defeat Lincoln for renomination in 1864 and, when their efforts failed, supported him most ungraciously. "To save the nation," wrote Wade at the time, "I am doing all for him [Lincoln] that I possibly could do for a better man." Even the tragedy at Ford's Theater did not stir these irreconcilables as it did the rest of the world. After the assassination Wade called on the new President. "Johnson," he said, "we have faith in you. By the gods there will be no trouble now in running the government." [3] Even the milder Julian, according to Nicolay and Hay, believed that "the accession of Johnson would prove a god-send to the country." [4] The usually boisterous Chandler became solemn and pious. He "intoned that God had kept Lincoln in office as long as he was useful and then had put another and better man in his place." [5] Ultimately, of course, these same Jacobins turned against Johnson, and for the same reason that they had fought Lincoln. The new President, after veering toward radicalism in the early days, finally adopted Lincoln's plans for dealing with the South. Had that impeachment succeeded, Ben Wade would have become President of the United States. He was president pro tem of the Senate in 1868, and would have succeeded to the White House in case of a vacancy. It should also be recorded to the everlasting honor of Lyman Trumbull that, although

[3] Nicolay and Hay, *op. cit.* X, 316.
[4] *Ibid.* X, 316.
[5] Williams, T. Harry, *op. cit.* Abstraction of a letter written by Chandler to his wife, April 22, 1865. P. 374.

a radical on the slavery question, and a harsh critic of President Johnson's Reconstruction policy, he was too honest a man to submit to the final outrage and voted in favor of the badgered President's acquittal. As that President's official life was saved by one vote, Trumbull has some claim to the distinction of having preserved the nation from an eternal disgrace.

II

SINCE LINCOLN and his cabinet were apparently inadequate to the task in hand, upon whom should the duty devolve? On that point the Jacobins never entertained the slightest question. The management of the war should be the prerogative of Congress – in other words, of the Jacobins themselves. The struggle that ensued between the radicals and Lincoln, and afterward Johnson, over the powers of Congress and the Executive in Reconstruction started as early as 1861, taking the form of a struggle for the control of military operations. The constitutional clause making the President commander in chief his enemies brushed aside. In the Jacobin view the commander in chief did not reside in the White House; the only proper headquarters of preparation and strategy was Capitol Hill. Though the Jacobins were fierce for war, and hailed the enlistment of an army, they looked askance at Lincoln's call for 75,000 volunteers after Fort Sumter. The men were needed, of course; but was it the business of the President to enroll them? Should not Congress itself have issued the call? Even so learned a constitutionalist as Lyman Trumbull upheld this contention. "Our power is omnipotent over this army," he declared.

The word "faction," as frequently applied to the Wade-Chandler-Julian group, needs qualification. The Radicals were the most vociferous element in the party majority and the most powerful. Their power was displayed when, in December 1861, Congress created a committee on the conduct of the war. The proposal passed the Senate by a handsome vote and was adopted by the House without debate. One or two conservative Senators did object on the ground that such a committee would interfere unwarrantably with the Executive, but William P. Fessenden sternly rebuked the timid souls. The proposed committee, he said, would "keep an anxious watchful eye over all the executive agents who are carrying on the war at the direction of the people. . . . We are not under the command of the military of this country. They are under ours as a Congress." The main duty of the committee, that is, was military; it was to see that the right officers were appointed, that their campaigns were soundly planned and executed, and that due punishments and rewards were parceled out where deserved. That this meant a constant interference with President, cabinet, and officers in the field did not disturb the committee; to them this seemed to be the strongest argument in its favor. Wade became chairman and remained in that position for four years of war; Chandler was a member, and the chief representative from the House was Julian. One of the tenets of Jacobinism insisted that military operations were not necessarily the province of men educated for that trade. In their eyes West Point was the most odious of American seats of learning. To the leadership of West Pointers the Jacobins attributed all the early failures; the detail that West Point graduates also commanded the too frequently victorious Confederate troops was quietly ignored. Wade and his group regarded West Point not only as the headquarters of military ineptitude – as a place where ridiculous stress was laid on such technicalities as strategy, exhaustive preparations, lines of supply – but as a school for proslaveryism and therefore for treason. Unless a great civilian army should be put under the control of patriotic – for patriotic read "Jacobin" – officers drawn from civil life, the rebellion could never be crushed.

The energies of the committee, under Wade and Chandler, were thus directed largely to the selection of the men who were to lead this armed citizenry. They regarded it as their right actually to appoint officers in the army. In view of that clause in the Constitution which gave the President this power, the pretension proved difficult to maintain. The committee therefore contented itself with making suggestions, constantly interfering with generals in the performance of their duties, summoning them like ill-behaved schoolboys to its presence, catechizing them about their plans, demanding explanations for failure, and insisting on being taken into the army's confidence in all matters. And political considerations governed everything. Military leaders were discredited who did not wholeheartedly sympathize with Jacobin aims. Army chiefs, in Jacobin eyes, fell into two classifications: those who were "great generals" and those who were "fool and traitor generals." The standards by which military genius and military stupidity were gauged astonishes a generation that has learned the value of professional soldiers. A "great general" in the mind of the average citizen today is the able organizer of victory, the planner and director of successful campaigns and battles. The Jacobins set up a different standard. First and foremost a great commander should be a Republican, and not a Republican of Lincolnian breed, but of the Wade-Chandler type. Unless his "heart was in the right place" – unless, that is, a general stood for immediate emancipation of the slaves and their speedy accession to the rights of citizenship – all the genius of a Caesar would avail him nothing.

Lincoln's persistence in appointing Democrats to important commands – because, in his view, many of them were best qualified for it – enraged his congressional opponents. Henry Wilson, abolitionist from Massachusetts, made an intensive study of the one hundred and ten generals in the army of 1861, and announced in the Senate that eighty of them were Democrats. How could victories be won under such leadership? Another fellow Jacobin bewailed that the higher command did not include "more than one sincere abolitionist and emancipationist." The fact that the one exception was evidently John C. Frémont tells the story. For a considerable time the former Pathfinder was the military darling of the Jacobin group. He was esteemed a great commander not because he had displayed genius in the field, which he certainly had not, but because he had issued a proclamation freeing the slaves in his department. Another general sacrosanct in Jacobin eyes was Ben Butler; even after his grotesque display of incompetence at Fort Fisher their allegiance remained unshaken. Bull Run did not shatter their belief that McDowell was a great, born leader of men; McDowell had lost that engagement, it was true, but he was sound on the slavery issue. The blunders of Rosecrans might have had disastrous results at Chickamauga, but he was right on the Negro, and the Jacobins at one time talked of running him for President. At first the committee disapproved Burnside's appointment to command of the Army of the Potomac, not on military grounds, as they well might have done, but on the ground that he was a close friend of McClellan and wrote him letters addressed to "dear Mac" and signed "Burn." After the terrible debacle at Fredericksburg, however, they took Burnside to their bosom and defended him against his "proslavery" critics. The reason is that the politically minded general, after the battle, had gone over to the radical side. After Chancellorsville, the committee hastened to the defense of Hooker, for that mercurial gentleman, like other wire-pulling officers, had adopted abolitionist opinions.

The hero-worshiping which the Jacobins lavished upon military failures who held correct views on the Negro was exceeded only by the abuse heaped upon certain triumphant captains whose attitude was more Lincolnian. Grant was beyond the pale; was he not a Democrat and a product of "that abominable and aristocratic hole, West Point?" William Tecumseh Sherman might march his army up Peachtree Street, Atlanta, and thus make Lee's surrender inevitable, but he did not win the favor of the Wade committee, for he was "disloyal" – that is, he was not an enthusiast on emancipation. Meade might win the Battle of Gettysburg, but he, too, was a moderate on the same question; therefore the committee under Wade's chairmanship went to great pains to prove his military stupidity, and to attribute the real credit for stopping Lee to certain of his subordinates – all of whom, it appeared, belonged to the radical school of politics.

But the man above all others on whom the hostility of the Jacobins centered was the "young Napoleon" of the Army of the Potomac, George Brinton McClellan. On the day following the battle of Bull Run, Lincoln had summoned to Washington this leader of the army of western Virginia, and placed in his youthful hands – McClellan was only thirty-five years old – the disorganized mob then known as the "Division of the Potomac." The choice was an inevitable one. While the unprepared nation was groaning under ineptitude on every hand, electrifying news had flashed from the mountains of that part of the Old Dominion bordering the Ohio River. A young major general recently called from civil life, at the head of an army of less than ten thousand men, had met larger Confederate forces, defeated them at every conflict, and, at the battle of Rich Mountain, had completely cleared this section of secessionists. The political result of McClellan's exploits proved more important than the military, for he was credited with saving for the Union nearly one third of the most venerated Southern state and made possible its ultimate incorporation in the Union as the new state of West Virginia – but it was the feat of arms that drove the North fairly to frenzy with joy.

McClellan's whole career, in both military and civil life, indicated him as the one man fitted to the command to which Lincoln, amid universal applause, had called him. Born in 1826 in Philadelphia, of good Massachusetts and Connecticut stock, McClellan had been graduated from West Point at the age of twenty, second in a class of fifty-one, had served creditably in the war with Mexico – his name frequently appears in the official dispatches of that conflict – and had been sent by Jefferson Davis, Secretary of War in the cabinet of Franklin Pierce, as military observer in the Crimean War, writing a report of that conflict and the lesson it held for the American Army that is still a model of its kind. Resigning his commission in 1859, McClellan engaged in business life with a success that proved executive talents of high order. Entering the employ of the Illinois Railroad as an engineer, within a year he was elected president of the Ohio and Mississippi Railroad at a salary of $10,000 – a tremendous income in those days. As soon as Fort Sumter fell, he made preparations to drop railroading and return to his old profession. Several states, including Ohio, sought to enlist McClellan's services as general in their militia; and in April he was offered, and accepted, a Federal commission as major general commanding the Department of Ohio, Indiana, and Illinois. The success that ensued turned not only his country's head, but apparently his own. In the stormy eighteen months that followed, nothing delighted McClellan so much as the public acclaim he received and especially the love and admiration he inspired in the common soldier. Whether "Little Mac" was a great general or not makes probably the fiercest controversy in the history of the American Army. The battle between those, in this and other lands, who regard him as the genius of the Civil War, and those who look upon him as the man who delayed Federal success for at least two years, still rages. Robert E. Lee said that McClellan was the ablest of Northern soldiers. He has always been extolled by Southern writers – so excessively, indeed, that the question rises whether McClellan's well-known friendly attitude to the South and his considerable sympathy with Southern views on slavery and Reconstruction may not partially explain this admiration. That McClellan possessed one of the most valuable assets of a military chieftain is generally agreed. No other leader, not even that Napoleon with whom McClellan liked to be compared, ever so completely possessed the affection of his men. At the mere sight of McClellan, dressed in the most brilliant regalia – for he loved uniforms, epaulettes, and military sashes – astride his faithful "Kentuck" – and McClellan was a superb horseman – the whole army would break into roars, and dash into almost certain death with all the éclat of conquest.

McClellan's letters – and he wrote them daily, usually to his wife – never tire of describing the almost insane loyalty of his men. In the early months of his command he inspired the same emotions in the breast of civilians. Even the Jacobins at first joined in the general acclaim. How all this affected the young man his letters reveal. The sight of the President, cabinet ministers, Senators, generals, welcoming him as another Washington, destined to save his country from ruin, overwhelmed him. "It is an immense task that I have on my hands, but I believe I can accomplish it. When I went into the Senate today and found those old men flocking around me; when I afterwards stood in the Library looking over the capitol of our great nation and saw the crowd gathering around to stare at me, I began to feel how great was the task committed to me. Oh how sincerely I pray to God that I may be endowed with the wisdom and courage necessary to accomplish the work. Who would have thought, when we were married, that I should so soon be called upon to save my country." [1] Thus in a short time

[1] McClellan, *op. cit.*, p. 83.

General George Brinton McClellan
(1826–1885)
Commander of the Division of the Potomac
1861–1862

Francis Preston Blair, Jr.
(1821–1875)
Major General of volunteers and Member of
Congress from Missouri

Reprinted from Mr. Lincoln's Camera Man *by Roy Meredith, Charles Scribner's Sons*

War (top) and Navy Department Buildings in 1861

From original wet plates by Matthew B. Brady

one fixed belief took possession of McClellan's mind. On his shoulders alone rested the salvation of his country. If the Union were to be saved, he alone would save it. A kind of religious mysticism possessed him. How did it happen that he, a man only thirty-five years old, had been suddenly lifted from the mass of his fellow men, passed over the heads of all the older experienced men in the army, and entrusted with this supreme duty? The call, McClellan devoutly believed, had come not from Abraham Lincoln or the American people, but directly from God. "I feel sure that God will give me the strength and wisdom to preserve this great nation. . . . I feel that God has placed a great work in my hands – I have not sought it – I know how weak I am – but I know that I mean to do right and I believe that God will help me and give me the wisdom I do not possess."

In a sense this may have proved a source of strength, but it explains also, in large part, the misunderstandings and accidents that beset "Little Mac's" career. The belief in himself as the personally selected instrument of the Almighty was an expression of that vanity which was the young man's overweening characteristic. It gave support to the charges which the Jacobins hurled against him in Congress and it even sowed distrust in Lincoln's mind. On personal and political grounds the Chandler-Wade group instinctively disliked McClellan. He was precisely the type of man, in birth, breeding, and political and professional association, most displeasing to them. McClellan stood far removed from the fierce antislavery leaders in social characteristics and military convictions. All of McClellan's biographers, especially the latest, William Starr Myers,[2] have much to say – probably too much – of his standing as a "gentleman" and an "aristocrat." He came of good, but not illustrious stock. Whether highly commendable antecedents lift a simple American citizen above his fellows may be questioned, but they exerted at times a baneful effect upon McClellan himself. From youth to old age, his bearing expressed a consciousness of superiority. The words "vulgar" and "low-bred" came easily to his lips in comments on his fellow man. At West Point McClellan's favorite companions had been Southerners; the plantation "aristocrat" seemed to exercise a strong hold upon his admiration. "Somehow or other," he wrote when a plebe at West Point, "I take to the southerners. I am sorry to say the manners, feelings, and opinions of the southerners are far, far preferable to those of the majority of the northerners at this place. I may be mistaken, but I like them better." An insistence on command, an impulsive temper, a tendency to despise rustics and to feel restless

[2] Myers, William Starr, *Study in Personality: George Brinton McClellan.* Appleton-Century, 1934.

and quarrelsome in the presence of superiors, were generally esteemed Southern traits, and the young McClellan would inevitably have a fellow feeling with such manners, for these were his characteristics as boy and man. His fine personal appearance gave some basis for these pretensions. Though under average height, with his erect, slender frame, broad shoulders, bright, intelligent face, and always graceful carriage, McClellan certainly looked the soldier. He was also a highly cultivated man, perhaps the best educated scholar in the army of his time. He read deeply, especially in military science, and his acquirements as a linguist set him apart from most of his brother officers. According to his official biographer he could converse freely in German, French, Italian, and Spanish, and required no interpreter in Russian, Turkish, and several North American Indian dialects. Association with persons of birth seemed indispensable to his happiness. This sometimes, even at the high tide of war, brought reproaches on his head. The presence of French royalty on his staff – the Comte de Paris, who, except for usurping Bonapartes, would have been King of France, and his brother, the Duc de Chartres – and the pleasure the American took in this close companionship, added little to his popularity with the most rigid type of Yankee Republican.

Similarly characteristics that might charm the gentlemanly Bourbons would hardly recommend McClellan to the rough-and-tumble forces then dominant in Congress. And "Little Mac" was unsympathetic to the majority not only in temperament and personality, but in opinion and in action. His views on slavery, his war aims, and his attitude towards the South and the Rebellion, seemed to men like Wade, Chandler, Julian, and Sumner little less than a betrayal of his country. No word was in more widespread use in those intolerant days than "traitor," an epithet that McClellan did not escape. In radical estimation the head of the Army of the Potomac did not fulfill the first requirement of a commander in the field. He was not a radical Republican. He was not even an antislavery Democrat. His sympathies, before and during 1860 – so the enemy argued – had lain with those Southern politicians whose excesses had resulted in civil war. In the Lincoln-Douglas debates of 1858, McClellan had championed the Douglas side, and as vice-president of the Illinois Central Railroad had shown favors to the "Little Giant" which had been denied the rail splitter. In 1860 he had voted for Douglas, and had spoken of Lincoln with disdain. Of all human cattle, there was no breed that McClellan so despised as the abolitionist. On this subject he had been most vigorously outspoken, and confirmed his well-known opinions by his acts. McClellan's proclamation, on his invasion of western Virginia, had caused almost as much excitement as had Frémont's on the brink of his campaign in Missouri, but for contrary reasons. He had not come, McClellan declared in this pronunciamento, to interfere with the property of Virginians, especially with their property in slaves. Anyone who insisted that the government was planning to disturb this institution was a "traitor." Let Virginians have no fear of slave insurrections! Should the black men rise against their masters, his army would suppress them "with an iron hand." Runaways, who found such friendly haven in the camps of Ben Butler, Hunter, and other Northern generals, met harsh treatment at McClellan's quarters; he invariably returned them to their owners, thus becoming, in the eyes of the Jacobins, that most odious of mortals, a "slave-catching general." The "Hutchinson Singers" of the early Civil War provided the same kind of soldiers' diversion that Hollywood entertainers have given in modern times. One evening these innocent young warblers sang before the Army of the Potomac "an abolition song" composed by John Greenleaf Whittier. McClellan exiled them from the Army for the "duration." His indiscreet comments on the Negro and emancipation proved to be a more serious matter. To Charles Sumner's face he ridiculed the idea that freedom for the Negro should be one of the aims of the war. Edward Bates notes in his Diary a remark of McClellan's that "the South was right and he would never fight against it, that the southern Democracy had always governed the country and ought to govern it." [3] McClellan's choice of friends added point to these accusations. His closest associate in civilian life was the celebrated New York lawyer, Samuel M. L. Barlow, whom Welles stigmatizes as a "Copperhead leader." [4] A radical Congressman once sought an interview and was denied because McClellan was colloquing with Sunset Cox and Clement L. Vallandigham, both regarded as allies of the South.

It is not strange, when Washington and the newspapers were flooded with such anecdotes, that McClellan's behavior in the winter and spring of 1861–1862 should have given rise to the darkest suspicions. The present generation, having passed through two great world wars, understands much better than that of 1861 the need of exhaustive preparation. That McClellan, from Bull Run to December 1861, had performed a marvelous feat in organizing the Army of the Potomac, everybody granted. The unarmed, undisciplined rabble of July had become, by November, one of the most powerful, best-equipped, and best-organized armies the world had ever seen. This was McClellan's work, and everyone was praising him in extravagant terms for the

[3] Bates, *Diary*, p. 253.
[4] Welles, *Diary*. II, 28.

achievement. But why did McClellan not make some use of this new engine of warfare? A Confederate army, which we now know to have been less than half as large as the Federal – though McClellan insisted that it was much larger – stood at Manassas impudently defying him and blocking the road to Richmond. Why, everyone was asking, did not McClellan attack this force, wipe it out, and end the war in a single battle? Why, after this army succeeded in breaking camp and taking up a stronger position further south, did McClellan, against the vigorous protests of Lincoln and the cabinet, suddenly change his plans and decide to approach Richmond by way of the Peninsula between the York and the James River? There is no need of going into the merits of this dispute, one of the most famous in military annals. Though the ablest professional soldiers of the last eighty years have not answered the question to their own satisfaction, the politicians who, in 1862, detested McClellan for his political views and his personal arrogance had no difficulty in solving the problem. The man's heart was not in the war; he did not want the North to win, or at least not to win quickly. Horace Greeley thundered in the *New York Tribune* that the ambitious general was determined to prolong the strife in order to be elected President. His real design, according to this Jacobin editor, was to restore the Southern dynasty that had ruled the nation before 1860, and to re-establish on an impregnable basis its system of slave labor. Not many critics of McClellan today accept this explanation, but there were plenty who, in 1862, believed it implicitly.

McClellan's uncompromising attitude towards both the Congressional leaders and the Lincoln cabinet did not help his case. He regarded them as a lot of hopeless ignoramuses and treated them with open contempt. When Wade's committee on the Conduct of the War summoned him to the presence and began to ask questions concerning his plans, McClellan flatly refused to take the lawmakers into his confidence. What was the use of talking with men who knew absolutely nothing of the art of war? Even when the cabinet called him into consultation he again refused to discuss the forthcoming campaign. He could not talk about such confidential matters, he brusquely explained, to so large a group; anything he said would be sure to leak out, and be in the possession of the Confederates in a few hours. He would, of course, tell all his plans to the President or Secretary of War, if either asked for the information, but not the cabinet and their advisers in mass meeting assembled. The mere fact that McClellan was right in this attitude – though he might have been more tactful in expression – did not lessen the anger of the august statesmen. Had the political leaders seen the letters that McClellan was daily sending his wife their fury would not have been at all assuaged. Washington he described as a "sink of iniquity." "The hounds are after me again" was one of the gentlest references to inquisitive Jacobins. "I am daily becoming more disgusted with this administration – perfectly sick of it." "How weary I am of all this business! Care after care, blunder after blunder, trick upon trick." "I am thwarted and deceived by these incapables at every turn." "History will present a sad record of these traitors who are willing to sacrifice the country and the army for personal spite and personal aims." "Alas! poor country that it should have such rulers! I tremble for my country when I think of these things; but still can trust that God in his infinite wisdom will not punish us as we deserve."

Again and again he expresses contempt for "the dolts," "the rascals," "the scoundrels," "the fools" who make up the Lincoln administration. Even in the days when things were going well and when the young general's praises were on every lip, McClellan writes of the cabinet in scurrilous terms. "When I returned yesterday," he records on October 10, 1862, "after a long ride, I was obliged to attend a meeting of the cabinet at 8 P.M. and was bored and annoyed. There are some of the greatest geese in the cabinet I have ever seen – enough to tax the patience of Job." Again on November 17, when his popularity was still unimpaired: "It is sickening in the extreme and makes me feel heavy at heart, when I see the weakness and unfitness of the poor beings who control the destiny of this great country." "I feel that the fate of the nation depends on me and I feel that I have not one single friend at the seat of government." "They have done all that cowardice and folly can do to ruin our poor country and the blind people seem not to see it. It makes my blood boil when I think of it." As early as October 1861, McClellan descends to particulars. "I can't tell you how disgusted I am becoming with these wretched politicians – they are a most despicable set of men. I think Seward is the meanest of them all – he has done more than any other one man to bring all this misery upon the country and is one of the least competent to get us out of the scrape. The President is nothing more than a well meaning baboon. Welles is the most garrulous old woman you were ever annoyed by. Bates is a good, inoffensive old man," he writes his wife. "I went to the White House directly after tea where I found 'the original Gorilla' about as intelligent as ever. What a specimen to be at the head of our affairs now! . . . I went to Seward's where I found the Gorilla again, and was of course edified by his anecdotes un-apropos and even unworthy of one holding his high position. I spent some time there and almost organized a little quarrel with Seward. It is a terrible dispensation of Providence that so weak and cowardly a thing as that should now conduct our foreign relations. Unhappily the President is not much better, except that he is honest and means well. I suppose our country has richly merited some great punishment, else we should not now have such wretched triflers at the head of affairs."

McClellan's venom against Seward is puzzling, for the Secretary of State, at the time this letter was written, was supporting him most loyally – and McClellan knew it. The resort to Darwinian primates for purposes of comparison with Lincoln is also surprising, for in his Memoirs McClellan tells of his shocked disgust with Stanton for using such metaphors in referring to the head of state. The views that McClellan entertained of Lincoln at this early stage remained with him to the end. In 1861, McClellan regarded Lincoln as a "vulgar" person, utterly unfit for his great office, and there are no signs that he ever changed his mind. His Memoirs, published in 1887, two years after his death, enshrine the opinion and epithets quoted above, but not a line suggesting that he had perceived in the man any evidence of greatness. In the first four or five months of his command Lincoln not only gave the young general his full confidence and co-operation, but attempted to treat him as a friend. The President's habit of leaving his office, dropping in on cabinet men and government departments, brought him a good deal of criticism. Surely the sovereign should summon to his presence those whom he would honor by seeking them in consultation! McClellan, who lived at the corner of H Street and Fifteenth, only a block from the White House, was the occasional recipient of such presidential visits. But he did not always receive them graciously. John Hay, in his Diary, records the incident which, perhaps more than any other, has prejudiced McClellan's character in the eyes of posterity. "I wish here to record," the President's secretary wrote November 13, 1861, "what I consider a portent of evil to come. The President, Governor Seward, and I went over to McClellan's house tonight. The servant at the door said that the general was at the wedding of Colonel Wheaton at General Buell's and would soon return. We went in, and after we had waited about an hour McC. came in, and, without paying any particular attention to the porter, who told him the President was waiting to see him, went upstairs, passing the door of the room where the President and Secretary of State were seated. They waited about half an hour, and sent once more a servant to tell the general they were there and the answer coolly came that the general had gone to bed. I merely record this unparalleled insolence of epaulettes without comment. It is the first indication I have yet seen of the threatened supremacy of the military authorities. Coming home I spoke to the President about the matter, but he seemed not to have noticed it specially, saying it was better at this time not to be making points of etiquette and personal dignity." [5]

Soon afterward Hay noted with considerable satisfaction that the President, whenever he wished to consult the commanding general, no longer dropped in for an informal visit. He summoned McClellan to the White House.

[5] Hay, John, *Lincoln and the Civil War in the Diaries and Letters of John Hay*, selected and with an introduction by Tyler Dennett. Dodd, Mead & Co., 1939. Pp. 34–35. Reprinted by permission of Dodd, Mead & Company, Inc.

III

IT WAS THIS situation – the warfare of the irreconcilable anti-slavery men on McClellan – that brought the Lincoln cabinet, in the summer of 1862, to the brink of dissolution. Up to the time of Stanton's appointment on January 16, the Wade and Chandler group, though constantly sniping against the young Napoleon, found little popular or official support. Chase, it is true, had early embraced their side, but Chase was not an effective party intriguer and enjoyed little personal influence or prestige in the White House. He was already laying plans for the presidential succession and undoubtedly his alliance with the Jacobin leaders and his antagonism to McClellan – of whom at first he had been a warm defender – were explained, in large part, by this ambition. In Stanton, however, the radicals discovered a far more adroit and useful ally. Their exultation at his elevation knew no bounds. "He is just the man we want!" exclaimed Senator Fessenden. "We agree on every point; the duties of the Secretary of War, the conduct of the war, the negro question and everything else." "He agreed with us fully," said Julian, after a personal cross-examination of the new incumbent, "in our estimate of General McClellan, and as to the estimate of an early forward movement. We are delighted with him." Sumner, Lyman Trumbull, and other more sedate radical statesmen applauded Stanton's selection and expedited confirmation by the Senate. The radical press, led by Greeley's *Tribune*, hailed Stanton's promotion to the cabinet as the beginning of a new day. "There is a very general agreement," wrote Greeley, "that the appointment of the new secretary means business. . . . No man ever entered upon the discharge of the most momentous public duties under more favorable auspices, so far as public confidence and support can create such auspices. Here is the man who would know how to deal with the greatest danger then facing the country – treason in Washington, treason in the army itself, especially the treason which wears the garb of Unionism."

One man read these tributes from extreme radical sources with surprise. Up to this time, McClellan had regarded the new Secretary as his cordial friend and co-worker. His optimism and confidence seemed to rest on solid grounds. In his Memoirs McClellan declares that he knew nothing of Stanton's impending appointment until the day it was made. On the evening of January 13, Stanton himself dropped in at McClellan's house and informed him. The new Secretary, whose nomination had gone to the Senate that afternoon, asserted that, for personal reasons, his selection was unwelcome. Only the opportunity of working in close co-operation with McClellan for the salvation of the Union could persuade him to undergo the sacrifice involved. He would accept only if General McClellan expressed his approval. "If I wished him to accept he would do so, but only on my account; that he had come to know my wishes and determine accordingly. I told him that I hoped he would accept the position." [1] Stanton, McClellan always insisted, gave other indications of a friendly spirit. He sent messages by common friends expressing his confidence in the much criticized commander, and his desire to serve his interests.

Probably Stanton's reason for this appeal for McClellan's approval was his desire to obtain his support with influential Senators, when his name came up for confirmation. At least, that is the only plausible explanation, but even this is doubtful, for Stanton met little opposition in the upper chamber, the name being approved two days after his nomination. That the new Secretary's friendly overtures to McClellan were insincere events quickly disclosed. He hardly let pass a decent interval before assuming an almost open hostility to the man with whom, six months before, he had been on daily companionable terms. The two men had held frequent consultations before the day of Stanton's appointment. On practically all points, McClellan said, they had agreed. After January 15, the day of Stanton's confirmation by the Senate, the close association came suddenly to an end. The general of the Potomac army found himself practically denied access to his chief. Stanton's association with the Republican leaders who were bent on McClellan's destruction soon became common gossip in Washington. Wade and Chandler were almost officially members of the War Department. Stanton, in his absorption with his new duties, kept himself aloof from the public. He was the most inaccessible member of the administration. Only on certain days were callers admitted to his private office. Yet all members of the Committee on the Conduct of the War had pass cards giving them entree at any time. They came and went freely while McClellan and other military leaders were excluded. Stanton frequently visited the Capitol and held sessions with the committee on the progress of the war. In these star-chamber sessions the "treason"

[1] McClellan, *op. cit.*, p. 153.

and the unfitness of McClellan, and the desirability of a new commander, were the leading topics. In fact, the Wade-Chandler-Julian committee really existed for one purpose in the period that intervened between Stanton's appointment and the Peninsular campaign; that was to "break" McClellan and secure a new general, preferably McDowell or Frémont, or – and this proved finally to be the choice – John Pope.

That Stanton began at once his campaign against the young Napoleon the record convincingly shows. On the very evening following his appointment Simon Cameron gave a dinner party, at which Stanton himself was the guest of honor. This quickly resolved itself into an indignation meeting against the unpopular chief. Colonel John Cochrane, who was present at this banquet, relates that both Stanton and Chandler were "harmonious in censure of General McClellan's dilatory conduct of the war." The day preceding this symposium, according to McClellan, Stanton had told the general he would accept the War Department only with his approval. A week afterward, in a letter to Charles A. Dana, Stanton picturesquely described his dissatisfaction with his one-time favorite. "This army has got to fight or run away; and while men are striving nobly in the West, the champagne and oysters on the Potomac must be stopped." As one of the popular grievances against the fashionable McClellan were his almost daily elaborate dinner parties – to which Republicans and administration champions were seldom invited – the shaft was unmistakable. In Stanton's meetings with Wade's committee similar sentiments were expressed. He never went to bed nights, the Secretary once declared to this inner group, "without his cheek burning with shame upon this disgrace upon the nation" – the disgrace in question being McClellan's failure to clear the virtual blockade of the Potomac River. That subtlety which was one of Stanton's greatest gifts appeared to advantage in his praise of General Grant for his brilliant achievements in Kentucky. With artistic skill, this eulogy praised Grant for the very qualities in which McClellan seemed most deficient. "The purpose of this war," he wrote in an order of January 22, 1862, "is to attack, pursue and destroy a rebellious enemy and to deliver the country from danger menaced by traitors. Alacrity, daring, courageous spirit and patriotic zeal on all occasions, and under every circumstance, are expected from the army of the United States." At that moment the nation was ringing with criticism of McClellan for the lack of those very qualities of leadership. When Grant captured Fort Henry and Fort Donelson, at the time that the McClellan question had reached a new height of frenzy, the American public did not fail to grasp the real meaning of the words in which Stanton hailed that great performance. Greeley had written, in a fulsome editorial, that it was to "Edwin M. Stanton, more than to any other individual, that these auspicious events are now due." The Secretary, with an excess of modesty hardly in keeping with his general character, at once addressed the *Tribune*, declining to accept such commendation. "Much has been said," the letter protested, "recently of military combinations and 'organizing victory.' I hear such phrases with apprehension. They commenced in infidel France with the Italian campaign, and resulted in Waterloo. Who can organize victory? We owe our recent victories to the spirit of the Lord, that moved our soldiers to rush into battle and filled the hearts of our enemies with terror and dismay. . . . We may well rejoice at the recent victories, for they teach that battles are to be won now, and by us, in the same and only manner that they were ever won by any people, since the days of Joshua – by boldly pursuing and striking the foe. What, under the blessing of Providence, I conceive to be the true organization of victory and military combination to win this war was declared in a few words by General Grant's message to General Buckner – 'I propose to move immediately upon your works.' " All this, of course, was not primarily a tribute to Grant but a Stantonian back thrust at McClellan. The Secretary frequently vented his criticism of McClellan in less exalted and less insinuating words. One of General Rosecrans's favorite stories was of his visit in April 1862 to the Secretary of War. "I was received with profuse expressions of cordiality and sent upon a mission. I was told by the same War Secretary, 'I wish you and McDowell could get to Richmond before that damned little cuss McClellan.' "

As the "damned little cuss" became aware of what he always regarded as Stanton's duplicity – swearing eternal friendship and devotion to his face, and behind his back constantly urging Lincoln to remove him from command – his loathing for his official chief knew no restraint. One or two extracts from his letters to his wife will suffice. "Stanton is without exception the vilest man I ever knew or heard of," he confided to his beloved Nellie on May 18. Afterward, in a splendid outburst, the whole thing was summed up. "So you want to know how I feel about Stanton and what I think of him now? I will tell you with the most perfect frankness. I think he is the most unmitigated scoundrel I ever knew, heard, or read of; I think that (I do not wish to be irreverent) had he lived in the time of the Savior, Judas Iscariot would have remained a respected member of the fraternity of apostles, and that the magnificent treachery and rascality of E. M. Stanton would have caused Judas to have raised his hands in holy horror and unaffected wonder – he would certainly have claimed and exercised the right to have been the betrayer of his Lord and Master, by virtue of the same merit that raised Satan to his bad eminence. . . . I remember what you thought of Stanton when you first saw him. I thought you were wrong. I now know you were right. Enough of the creature – it makes me sick to think of him. Faugh!"[2]

In the cabinet itself McClellan found little more comfort than in Stanton. Only two members for a time supported him, Seward and Montgomery Blair. As Blair was himself a West Point graduate and the cabinet member whose opinions on military matters counted most with Lincoln, his endorsement of McClellan's policy – especially as he remained steadfast to the end – was important. Blair endorsed the Peninsular approach to Richmond as strategically correct. "If you can reach your object of reaching Richmond by a slower process than storming redoubts and batteries in earthworks, the country will applaud the achievement which gives success to its arms with greatest parsimony of the blood of its children," wrote old man Blair to McClellan on April 12, 1862, and this sentiment Montgomery upheld to the end. But the Blairs could not view any question without taking thought of its political consequences and one reason they advanced to Lincoln against deposing McClellan was that this would make him a martyr and strengthen him as a presidential candidate in 1864.

Chase's admiration for other generals than McClellan was based exclusively on political grounds. McClellan did not accept the Jacobin view on the Negro; and that seemed to be sufficient reason to condemn him as a military strategist. Chase admired McDowell and wished to see him enter Richmond. His reasons for this preference were set forth in a letter to an unknown correspondent. "He never drinks, or smokes, or chews, or indulges in any kind of licence. He is serious and earnest. He resorts to no acts of popularity. He has no political aims and perhaps not any very pronounced political opinions, except the conviction that this war sprung from the influences of slavery and that whenever slavery stands in the way of successful prosecution, slavery must get out of the way."[3] A long passage contains practically nothing about McDowell's ability in the field, except the general appraisement that he "has been unfortunate, but is a loyal, brave, truthful, capable officer." Though of military science, of course, Chase knew nothing, that did not prevent him from analyzing McClellan's strategical plans and pronouncing them unsound. He "made himself as busy in the management of the army as the Treasury," notes Gideon Welles, who gives an unforgettable picture of his colleague bending, with the President,

[2] Myers, *op. cit.*, p. 395.
[3] Warden, *op. cit.*, p. 461.

over a map of the Peninsular campaign, pointing out McClellan's mistakes and indicating the correct plan of procedure.

Welles himself and Edward Bates entertained the same unfavorable opinion of McClellan as most of their colleagues. They appreciated and acknowledged the general's strong points, but had no high regard for his qualities as a leader of assault. In this they came nearest of all their associates, except Lincoln himself, to the modern view. That talent for "organizing victory" which Stanton ridiculed in his Greeley letter they believed McClellan possessed in great measure. "McClellan is an intelligent engineer and officer, but not a commander to head a great army in the field. To attack or advance with energy and power is not in him; to fight is not his forte. . . . He has military acquirements and capacity, dash, but has not audacity, lacks decision, delays, hesitates, vacillates; will, I fear, persist in delays or inaction and do nothing affirmative." Perhaps Bates put his finger definitely on McClellan's weakest quality – his egoism and allegiance to his own convictions, simply because they were his own. "I believe the general has such a morbid ambition of originality that he will adopt no plan of action suggested by another. He must himself invent, as well as execute, every scheme of operation." Neither Welles nor Bates, who, of all cabinet members, were most inclined to discuss problems on their merits, placing aside personal prejudice and political views, accepted the Stanton-Chase judgment that the man was a Democratic "traitor," and a presidential aspirant who in his heart favored the Southern cause. Bates maintained the fantastic notion that no general in chief should be selected, but that Lincoln should exercise his constitutional prerogative as commander in chief and assume personal direction of military operations. Though a good many critics think that Lincoln, despite his incongruous appearance on horseback, with stovepipe hat and long trailing coat skirts, was an able strategist, the President himself labored under no such delusion, and was content to leave movements in the field in the hands of trained officers, always insisting, however, on certain fundamental dispositions.

A good deal of criticism has been visited on Lincoln for his tolerance of McClellan in these early days, and his seemingly vacillating treatment of the commanding general. Perhaps it is not strange that he hesitated and more than once changed his mind. For the last eighty years military authorities, on both sides of the Atlantic, have argued over McClellan's strategy, and, up to the present moment, have not reached an agreement. Lincoln may be forgiven therefore, if, in all the nervousness and excitement of the McClellan era, and the pulling and hauling from a hundred directions, he spent sleepless nights trying, not with perfect success, to reach the right conclusion. On one point his admiration for the "organizer of victory" had no limits. On weighing McClellan's capacities, Lincoln always had before his mind those two contrasting scenes — the dirty, undisciplined, and even rebellious rabble that poured into Washington after First Bull Run, and the beautifully articulated, completely equipped, perfectly behaved, and vigilant host that replaced it six months afterward. Only a genius of military organization, the President believed, could have accomplished that miracle. And McClellan was the man who had done it. Lincoln did not esteem this talent as lightly as did Stanton — indeed he did not see how the war could succeed without it. Very likely McClellan was not the captain ordained to lead in battle the magnificent army he had created, but he was at least the man who had produced this superb machine. Lincoln would have endorsed McClellan's own appraisal of his work, in a letter to his wife: "I know of no man except myself who could have built up this army." For this reason Lincoln stood steadfast — until the debacle at Harrison's Landing — against all the anti-McClellan wiles of Stanton and all the sledgehammer imprecations of the Jacobins in Congress. Even McClellan's at times insulting conduct towards himself did not cause Lincoln to forget this great service to the nation. "I would hold McClellan's horse for him if that would help to win the war," the patient President once remarked, and on occasions he came close to doing just that.

Gratified as the President was by McClellan's success as an organizer, his work as a leader in offense afforded lean satisfaction. About November 1, 1861, Lincoln believed that the time had arrived for another attempt on the enemy works near Manassas. Conditions in the late fall of 1861 seemed favorable for an attack. The weather was fine, the roads in splendid condition, the army rank and file eager to avenge Bull Run, and the forces at McClellan's disposal were at least twice those that the Confederates could bring against them. But the general delayed, setting forth the argument that, by constant repetition, fairly drove the Jacobins mad — that his preparations were not complete, that the Confederate army was at least twice in numbers that of the Federal, and that their entrenchment and armament were too formidable to make feasible a frontal approach. When, at the height of the argument, the enemy suddenly decamped from the lines McClellan had declared impregnable, and it was disclosed that only comparatively light forces had ever held the position, that the so-called fortifications were really flimsy and indefensible, and that the guns which had menaced the Federals for so many months were not guns at all, but painted counterfeits of wood, inevitably McClellan, as a field commander, did not rise in Lincoln's estimation. The South roared with laughter and the North gritted its teeth in rage. But more serious happenings presently increased Lincoln's dissatisfaction.

The Peninsular campaign is a subject that belongs to the military historian; a lay writer would not have the temerity to discuss a complex series of operations on which the experts have not yet reached agreement – and probably never will. But this great episode did have political complications which profoundly concerned the Lincoln cabinet. In his Diary of February 3, 1862, Edward Bates, recording Washington gossip of the likely retirement of Seward, Welles, and Smith, concluded, "All this is very idle talk and only shows that there is a feeling of discontent. That feeling will continue until the army takes measures active, aggressive and successful. If we fail to do something effectual in the next twenty days, the administration will be shaken to pieces – the cabinet will be remodeled and several of its members must retire."[4] McClellan and his plans – or lack of plans – were causing this commotion, both in the cabinet itself and in the public mind. Stanton was constantly at Lincoln's elbow, declaring that the general's course inevitably spelled the ruin of the nation. Wade, Chandler, and their congressional followers were not only making the Senate resound with their denunciations, but were almost daily besieging the White House, accusing McClellan both of military incapacity and of stark treason. The general's hopes of the presidential succession formed the burden of the complaint. "He is more interested in reconstructing the Democratic party than the Army of the Potomac" – Stanton's argument constantly revolved on this point. The radicals asserted that the very plans for the conquest of Richmond showed that the man was working in the interest of the South. On no question was the President so sensitive as the safety of Washington. Many a sleepless night was spent agonizing over the possibility that the National Capital would fall into the hands of the Confederates.

Such a calamity, Lincoln believed, would mean the triumph of the Davis government. Both Great Britain and France had their eager eyes fixed on the military situation, hoping to find in that plausible reasons for recognizing the Confederacy. Whatever might be the state of popular feeling in both countries, there is not the slightest question that the British government of Lord Palmerston, and the autocracy of Louis Napoleon, fervently desired the success of the Rebellion. Should Washington fall into its hands, recognition from these two unfriendly powers would automatically follow; this in turn would mean war with the United States, and Lincoln did not share Seward's optimism that the

[4] Bates, *op. cit.*, pp. 227–228.

Federal forces could successfully confront the whole European continent. When Stanton and his senatorial associates began playing assiduously and almost diabolically upon this fear, they touched Lincoln in his most apprehensive spot. McClellan's strategy, they insisted, would expose Washington to capture by Jackson's and Johnston's armies. Indeed that was its very purpose. McClellan, Southern in sympathy and politics, desired the Federal cause to fail. Here was the real explanation for his plan – to take the Union forces from their stations before Washington, put them into transports, make a sea voyage to southern Virginia, and move them from the Yorktown peninsula westward into the mud and swamps of the country around Richmond. Such a disposition, they maintained, would leave Washington unprotected, and permit Jackson's army in the Shenandoah to sweep down and seize the National Capital. In Stanton's view, the only safe way to march on Richmond was directly south from the Potomac. By this plan, the bulk of the army, as it advanced on Richmond, would always stand between the Confederate Army and Washington and thus accomplish two ends at the same time – protect the Federal Capital and conquer the Rebellion.

Lincoln did not believe that McClellan had conceived his plan for the traitorous purpose of delivering Washington to Jefferson Davis, but he did think that that was likely to be the practical outcome. From the first he had opposed the McClellan roundabout strategy and favored the direct line of approach. One morning early in March, McClellan received a summons to the White House. "An ugly story," the President informed him, was broadcast in Washington. He did not himself believe the accusation, but, as a matter of frankness, McClellan should knew about the prevailing suspicion. Then the President laid bare the charges – that the Peninsular scheme had been deliberately planned to uncover Washington to the forces of disunion. McClellan indignantly asserted that he had no intention of moving his forces to the Peninsula without leaving an army of sufficient size in northern Virginia to protect the Capital. Lincoln agreed to put the disputed question to the twelve brigadier and major generals of the Potomac army, and abide by their decision. Eight of these approved McClellan's plan as strategically correct. Four opposed it as unwise in itself and as jeopardizing the Capital. This referendum had evidently decided the argument in favor of McClellan. Stanton might protest that the majority who favored the Peninsular route were all McClellan's appointees and all members of the McClellan clique; Lincoln still believed he could not justifiably disregard the advice of his highest military authorities and reluctantly acceded to the Peninsular campaign. He stipulated, however, that a force large enough be left in the camps about Washington to make that city absolutely secure from capture.

Hardly had McClellan resumed his preparations when Stanton and the Jacobins, furious at their failure, again laid siege to the harassed President. McClellan, they urged, was not obeying the President's orders. He was moving practically all of the army to the York River, and leaving utterly inadequate forces for the safety of Washington. Again charges of "treason" filled the air. Lincoln was genuinely alarmed at the figures presented to prove McClellan's disregard of his instructions. Without consulting the general, in three successive orders the President transferred 30,000 men from the Army of the Potomac, and placed them under McDowell in northern Virginia. Lincoln's action in this crisis has given rise to the most hard-fought controversy of the Civil War. According to the anti-McClellanites, even after this weakening of his command, the Federal army greatly outnumbered the Confederates. Had McClellan, they urged, conducted a vigorous offensive campaign, instead of digging trenches and engaging in prolonged sieges, he could have reached his goal in July 1862, and ended the war. That McClellan did greatly overestimate the size of Johnston's army is a matter of record. His habit of exaggerating the size of the armies opposed to him, and underestimating his own, was his greatest fault as a soldier. We now know that Johnston, in early June, had not many more than 40,000, and that Lee, after McClellan's delay of a month in the siege of Yorktown had given time for gathering reinforcements, commanded about 98,000. There was never a time when McClellan had fewer than 100,000. This was true even after Lincoln had detached 30,000 for the defense of Washington. McClellan and his apologists always maintained that this act of Lincoln's explained all the disappointments that followed. A failure the campaign certainly proved to be. After wallowing in the fever-ridden swamps of Virginia for nearly three months and fighting many battles, in some of which the Federals administered severe punishment to the rebels, the public was stunned one morning by the news that McClellan had retreated with his whole command to Harrison's Landing on the James, determined not to resume the conflict until large reinforcements – which Lincoln did not have available – were sent him. The result was his disgrace and a Stanton triumph. The McClellan army was moved from the region of Richmond and transported overseas again to northern Virginia. The reigning favorite of Stanton and the Jacobins, John Pope, was placed in command and "Little Mac," with his staff, was sequestrated at Alexandria.

Had Lincoln by this time not lost faith in McClellan's motives, as well as in his strategy, he would probably not have deprived that general of his forces and entrusted them to such an incompetent commander as Pope. Against charges impugning McClellan's loyalty – his desire to end the war and save slavery by forming some kind of combination with the South – Lincoln was adamant. The other suspicion – that the young man was politically ambitious and laying plans for the presidential succession – could not be so easily dismissed. Certain happenings of this disastrous July gave force to the impeachment. The question which is more or less solemnly debated today – was McClellan really fixing his eyes on the White House? – seems a little absurd. The fact is that, in 1864, he did accept the Democratic nomination for the Presidency against Lincoln, and accepted it from a Copperhead convention which adopted a platform declaring the war to be a failure and demanding its immediate cessation. Just as we cannot properly appraise Stanton without keeping in mind his subsequent behavior as a member of Andrew Johnson's cabinet, so we cannot truly understand the McClellan of 1862 without taking into consideration his presidential aspirations in 1864. That this dangerous seed was early sown in McClellan's mind his always revealing letters to his wife disclose. The deference and applause showered upon the "young general" on his first arrival in Washington might easily have implanted political thoughts in a mind less egoistical than McClellan's. "I find myself in a new and strange position here: Cabinet, General Scott and all deferring to me. By some strange operation of magic I seem to have become the power in the land." Almost on the day of his appointment, McClellan's presidential boom began. What could have been more natural? The military heroes of the Revolution, of the second war with England, and of the war with Mexico, had become President, and fate itself indicated the conqueror of the South as destined to follow in the footsteps of Washington, Andrew Jackson, and Zachary Taylor. Democratic leaders of the Buchanan allegiance, who subsequently adopted McClellan as their presidential candidate, began whispering in his ear at an early day. McClellan's intimate friends were men like S. M. L. Barlow, George Ticknor Curtis, August Belmont – all Democrats lukewarm in support of the war. His chief journalistic supporters were the *New York World* and the *New York Herald* – papers whose anti-Lincolnian policy frequently aroused patriotic wrath that resulted in broken windows and on one occasion at least left their premises completely wrecked. The *World*, edited by Manton Marble, Copperhead of Copperheads, was once suppressed by the government for three days and put in charge of a military guard. Though McClellan had refused to discuss his plans with the cabinet on the ground that its discretion could not be trusted, he did take into his confidence on these extremely secret matters Malcolm Ives, Washington correspondent of the *Herald* and his chief journalistic supporter. As early as August 1861, McClellan deprecatingly refers to the political ideas these supporters were instilling in his reluctant mind. "I receive letter after letter, have conversation after conversation, calling on me to save the nation, alluding to the Presidency, dictatorship, etc. As I hope one day to be united to you [his wife] forever in heaven, I have no such aspirations. I would cheerfully take the dictatorship and agree to lay down my life when the country is saved." This talk of dictatorship need not be taken too ominously, but McClellan's avoidance of conservative Republicans — leaders who held men like Stanton, Wade, Chandler, and the other Jacobins in as great abhorrence as did McClellan himself, and who would have gladly protected him from their attacks — did betray a lack of common sense. The fact is that the Democratic chieftains early concentrated on McClellan as a rallying point for their opposition to the Lincoln administration, with an eye to 1864, and that he made the serious mistake of listening to their beguilings.

For a time Lincoln remained undisturbed over McClellan's presidential prospects. Not until McClellan himself, in his communications, began to mix war and politics, did Lincoln's attitude change. The fateful moment came in early July 1862. McClellan had retreated to Harrison's Landing on the James, with Lee undefeated and Richmond uncaptured; the Peninsular campaign, into which all the national effort for a year had been concentrated, had been the ghastliest of failures. The time seemed an inopportune one for McClellan to show interest in political questions. Yet on July 7, on the occasion of Lincoln's visit to the Union camp, McClellan handed him a letter setting forth his views on the great political controversies of the day. In a telegram he had asked Lincoln's permission to write him on certain matters pertaining to the conduct of the war. Lincoln had answered affirmatively, provided McClellan could find time from his pressing duties to do so — a rather plain intimation that the President thought Lee's army quite enough to absorb the energies of his general. On July 7, in the course of Lincoln's visit to Harrison's Landing, McClellan personally handed him the promised communication. Lincoln read it in McClellan's presence, said "All right," thrust it into his pocket, and never mentioned it to McClellan again. He regarded the paper as little less than a political manifesto. It seemed to justify the prevailing criticism that McClellan was as much concerned with politics as with the conduct of the army. The latter had little to say of the military situation, which was McClellan's only legitimate province, but dealt with pending problems affecting the Negro and emancipation. Seward's presentation to Lincoln of his "Thoughts" and his criticism of Lincoln for lack of a definite policy have properly shocked posterity as presumptuous, even insolent; but Seward, after all, was a mature public man of great skill and experience, at the time regarded as the leader of the Republican Party and the occupant of the most important office in the Lincoln cabinet. McClellan had no such basis for intruding his unasked-for thoughts upon the harassed head of the nation. He was only thirty-six years old, had had no career in public affairs, belonged to the political party opposed to the administration, and had no concern in anything except military matters.

Yet he began this letter with precisely the same complaint that Seward had uttered a year before. "The time has come," McClellan admonished the Chief Executive, "when the government must determine upon a civil and military policy covering the whole ground of our national trouble. . . . The responsibility determining and supporting such civil and military policy . . . must now be assumed and exercised by you, or our cause will be lost. The Constitution gives you power sufficient even for the present terrible emergency." Thus was the veteran President, a lifelong student of the Constitution, lectured on his civic duties by his youthful commander. And the only possible "policy," continued the writer, was a "conservative" one. The war should not be one "looking to the subjugation of the people of any state in any event. It should not be a war upon population, but against armed forces and political organizations. Neither confiscation of property, political execution of persons, territorial organization of states, or forcible abolition of slavery should be contemplated for a moment." As Lincoln had already settled his mind on the question of emancipation, and had, figuratively speaking, his famous proclamation in his pocket at this very moment, McClellan's declaration against that measure could hardly have sat lightly upon him. But McClellan proceeded to criticize the administration's methods of summary dealing with public disturbers of the peace and active workers in the interest of the Confederacy – Vallandigham was the shining example – and demanded that they be stopped. "Military arrests should not be tolerated, except in places where active hostilities exist, and oaths, not required by enactments constitutionally made, should be neither demanded nor received. Military government should be confined to the preservation of public order and the protection of political rights." One sentence comprised what might be regarded as a threat. "Unless the principles guarding the future conduct of our struggle shall be made known and approved the effort to obtain requisite forces will be almost hopeless. A declaration of radical views, especially on slavery, will rapidly disintegrate our present armies." Lincoln might well have been startled by this pronouncement of the commanding general, almost saying that an emancipation proclamation would cause his soldiers to lay down their arms and disband. McClellan's final suggestion that a commander in chief, having control of all the forces of the United States on all fronts, be appointed, and his indirect proposal that he was the man for the place, similarly fell on barren ground. "I am willing to serve in such position as you may assign me" reminds one of Seward's offer to the President a year before, of himself as *de facto* President. "This is not my especial province; but I neither seek to waive nor assume responsibility."

Lincoln and the few intimates to whom he showed this letter agreed as to its purpose. It was addressed to the President, but was really intended for the American electorate. It was a statement of the platform on which McClellan intended to run for the Presidency – and indeed he did run for that office on a platform which, in spirit, was much the same. It was to be enshrined in McClellan's record, to be given free circulation at the proper time. That also is what happened. McClellan included his letter of July 7, 1862, in his report of the Peninsular operations, which was submitted to the President in August 1863, and given to the world soon afterward. The date fitted nicely into McClellan's presidential plans. On October 12, 1863, he wrote a letter endorsing George W. Woodward, the Democratic candidate for governor of Pennsylvania, who was conducting his campaign on what was practically a Copperhead platform. This letter was generally considered – as it proved to be – McClellan's bid for the presidential nomination. His greatest admirers today regard it as the most deplorable mistake of his career.

IV

McCLELLAN'S PROPOSAL of himself as commander of all the Federal armies proved to be ill-timed. In July his status as commander of only one of these armies, that of the Potomac, was in question. Stanton and Chase in the cabinet, and their allies, the Republican radicals in Congress, now advanced in a direct attack on the general. In doing so, they took a stand that was little less than rebellion against the President. To accomplish McClellan's retirement to obscurity they were even prepared to risk the disruption of the cabinet.

On July 31, Lincoln, no longer expecting results from the army penned up at Harrison's Landing, peremptorily ordered McClellan to abandon that position, move his troops to Aquia Creek, on the Rappahannock River, and deliver them to the Army of Virginia, then under the command of General Pope. The transportation of these forces did not begin until August 14, two weeks after the order had been received. Lee seized the opening thus presented, and attacked Pope's army before a junction could be formed, with the hundred thousand men moving up from the Peninsula. The outcome was the most disastrous defeat inflicted on the Federals in four years of war. The fact that the scene of the battle was that same field of Bull Run on which the Confederates had scored their first triumph fourteen months before did not lessen the humiliation of the North.

Stanton and Chase, and their congressional cohorts, attributed the full blame to McClellan. His fortnight's delay in beginning the northward movement of his army, his failure, once this army had landed on the Potomac, to rush them to Pope's hard-pressed contingents—here, they cried (and the criticisms to which the proceedings gave rise have not yet died down), was the explanation for the Federal rout. Here was more of that proslavery "treason" which had paralyzed the Union armies for the preceding ten months. McClellan, of course, had his defenders then, as he has today. He had changed his base from southern to northern Virginia, he declared, with all possible dispatch. In fact, his skill in withdrawing from the James, in face of a hostile army, his admirers have always hailed as one of those maneuvers at which he was so great a master. To get his men to the scene of active operations in the time allotted, they declare, was beyond human power. Had McClellan been guilty of the crime of which he was accused – that of deliberately withholding his troops and thus insuring Federal defeat – only a firing squad could have meted out the appropriate penalty. That mild-mannered Christian gentleman, Salmon P. Chase, advocated this as the one desirable solution of the McClellan problem. "Chase," notes Gideon Welles, said that "he deliberately believed McClellan ought to be shot, and should, were he President, be brought to summary punishment." [1]

This conviction made Chase a willing partner in the plan which Stanton set in motion for McClellan's destruction. That the program also endangered the existence of the cabinet did not deter either man. All through August, Stanton and Chase had been bringing pressure to bear on Lincoln to this end. They did not seek merely to reduce McClellan's command. Only utter disgrace – his retirement to civil life – would be deemed adequate punishment for his crime. Stanton had gone as far as his authority warranted, to accomplish this result. Probably no military man of high rank ever received a more cutting reply than when McClellan in late August telegraphed Stanton, asking what his status was. At that time his army had been taken from him and transferred to Pope. Just what then, he asked of the Secretary, did he command? "General McClellan," came the answer, "commands that portion of the Army of the Potomac that has not been sent forward to General Pope's command." As only one hundred men, many of whom were ill, remained with McClellan at the time, this official announcement may be regarded as one of those studied insults for which Stanton had so brilliant a gift. Writing to Thaddeus Stevens, expressing his satisfaction with Stanton's reply, Chase remarked, "This is late, but well, though not well enough." [2] A more fitting disposition of McClellan Stanton and Chase had been cogitating for some time. It came to a head on Saturday, August 30. News had just arrived from Pope, telling of a great Federal victory; he had defeated and was pursuing Stonewall Jackson to his destruction. Pope's message was utterly untruthful, though possibly he believed it himself; in fact, the wily Confederate leader was luring Pope into an ambush, where in due course he entrapped and destroyed him.

Chase had heard only Pope's version, when on the afternoon of that day he came into the office of Gideon Welles and handed him a paper,

[1] Welles, *Diary*. I, 102.
[2] Warden, *op. cit.*, p. 457.

which he asked the Navy head to sign. The document was written in Stanton's familiar backhand scrawl and to it the names of Stanton and Chase, with their official titles, had been appended. Both Mr. Bates, Attorney General, and Mr. Smith, Secretary of the Interior, Chase informed Welles, had signified their willingness to add theirs. The paper was addressed to the President of the United States. "The undersigned," it read, "feel compelled by a profound sense of duty to the government and the people of the United States, and to yourself as your constitutional advisers, respectfully to recommend the immediate removal of George B. McClellan from any command in the armies of the United States. We are constrained to urge this by the conviction that after a sad and humiliating trial of twelve months and by the frightful and useless sacrifice of the lives of many thousand brave men and the waste of many millions of national means, he has proved to be incompetent for any important military command, and also because by recent disobedience of superior orders and inactivity, he has twice imperilled the fate of the army commanded by General Pope and while he continues in command will daily hazard the fate of our armies, exhibiting no sign of a disposition or capacity to restore by courage and diligence the national honor that has been so deeply tarnished in the eyes of the world by his military failures. We are unwilling to be accessory to the destruction of our armies, the protraction of the war, the waste of our national resources, and the overthrow of the government, which we believe must be the inevitable consequence of George B. McClellan being continued in command, and seek, therefore, by his prompt removal to afford an opportunity to capable officers under God's providence to preserve our national existence."

Probably American history offers no parallel to this document. In the first place, it was most undignified in substance and manner. It was not an official paper, though signed by two cabinet members and addressed to the President, but a stump speech. In the most approved Stantonian style, it assumed as true all the charges then in open and whispered circulation in Washington – that McClellan was responsible for Pope's defeat, that he had deliberately withheld forces that would have ensured his victory, that he was plotting the overthrow of the government. The unasked-for advice was also an insult to Lincoln. It informed the President, in so many words, that, if he did not at once dismiss McClellan from "any command" in the Federal army, the signers – and Stanton and Chase believed they could count on at least five of the seven cabinet members – would resign their portfolios and disrupt the administration. The declaration that they would be "unwilling to be accessory" to the national calamities that would follow McClellan's retention in any command could have no other meaning. Indeed, Chase, in discussing the subject with Gideon Welles in this and subsequent interviews, avowed such to be the purpose. Chase, writes Welles, said that the letter "was designed to tell the President that the administration must be broken up or McClellan dismissed. The method was an unusual one, but the case itself was unusual." [3] "Why not take the matter up in face to face conversation with Mr. Lincoln," Welles asked, "instead of putting the matter so uncompromisingly in writing?" Nothing could be gained, Chase replied, by discussing matters of such consequence personally with the President. "Argument was useless. It was like throwing water on a duck's back. A more decisive expression must be made and that in writing." [4] Both Stanton and Chase had in fact already used verbal persuasion without result; this letter, which was virtually an ultimatum, had therefore been prepared.

Chase insisted that "the time had arrived when the cabinet must act with energy and promptitude, for either the government or McClellan must go down." [5] In a letter written to William Cullen Bryant, another fierce anti-McClellanite, on September 1, Chase took the same stand. "I do not see how I can reconcile my duty to the country with sharing the responsibilities of the administration, if it continues to allow its military actions to be guided in any considerable degree by his [McClellan's] counsels or control." The evening of the thirtieth, Welles discussed the matter with Stanton in the War Department. Stanton, as was his custom in tense moments, hitched his chair close to Welles and began to speak in whispers. He did not particularly disagree, Welles told Stanton, with his opinion of McClellan as a commanding officer, but suggested that this abrupt manner of approach showed little consideration for the President. That comment excited Stanton. "I know of no particular obligation I am under to the President," the War Secretary replied. "He called me to a difficult position and imposed on me labors and responsibilities which no man could carry." Lincoln had fastened upon him a commander who was constantly striving to embarrass him. "I cannot and I will not submit to a continuance of this state of things." Stanton instanced one of his latest grievances against the hated general. General Pope had telegraphed to McClellan for sorely needed supplies; McClellan had replied that supplies were lying at Alexandria and that Pope could have them if he would send an escort to insure their safe delivery. "A general fighting and on the field of battle to send to a general in the rear and in repose and ask for an

[3] Welles, *Diary*. I, 102.
[4] *Ibid.*
[5] *Ibid.*, I, 94.

escort!"[6] That personal feeling entered deeply into Stanton's fury was evident. "Stanton is mad and determined to destroy McClellan," Welles wrote, and that always fair-minded critic added, "perhaps with reason."[7] Doubtless Welles had in mind that telegram which McClellan had sent his chief after his collapse on the Peninsula – a remonstrance so insubordinate and insulting both to the Secretary of War and to the President that McClellan's wife, always his worshiping admirer, rebuked him for sending it. "If I save this army now," so read the celebrated dispatch, "I tell you plainly that I owe no thanks to you or to any other person in Washington. You have done your best to sacrifice this army." Stanton was probably not unmindful of this communication when he launched this determined effort, three weeks afterward, to end McClellan's career in disgrace.

Had the ultimatum succeeded, Lincoln's whole plan of a coalition cabinet would have gone adrift. The scramble that would have taken place for the control of the administration would have endangered the whole Union cause. This revolution would have triumphed – that is, the Lincoln cabinet of August 1862 would have fallen in ruins – except for one man. The old-fashioned but shrewd gentleman then filling the post of Secretary of the Navy saw the meaning of the step at a glance and stiffened his puritanical back against it. Stanton and Chase clearly understood that Welles's accession was indispensable. Though Stanton had enrolled four members of the cabinet in his palace revolution – a majority – the demonstration was not quite so impressive as it appeared on the surface. His only really strong ally was Chase. The other two, Caleb B. Smith and Bates, exercised little influence in the administration. Smith was practically a cipher; neither by character nor by ability did he enjoy the respect of his associates or the public; his career was approaching its end, and, in fact, he retired from the cabinet four months after signing the Stanton-Chase manifesto. Edward Bates was a more important convert, though he, a man without a political party, and filling a minor cabinet place, did not add great strength to the uprising. One wonders why Bates, who was a wise, honest man, with a strong sense of official propriety, permitted himself to be drawn into the intrigue. He despised both Chase and Stanton and always bracketed them as unfaithful to the President and as selfish pursuers of their own ambitions. It is also true that Bates was not overemphatic in his admiration of Lincoln. "The President," he notes on December 31, 1861 – and this remained his view to the end – "is an excellent man, and in the main wise, but he lacks *will* and *purpose*, and, I greatly fear, has not *the power to command*."[8] He thought designing men took advantage

[6] Welles, *Diary*. I, 98. [7] *Ibid.*, I, 100. [8] Bates, *op. cit.*, p. 220.

of Lincoln's "amiable weakness," that "he lacked nerve to apply the remedy," that "if he had more *vim*" he would have dismissed Stanton from the cabinet.[9] In the matter of McClellan, Bates in particular regarded Lincoln as inept and vacillating. Yet Chase was wrong in telling Welles that Bates would sign the paper. He was too judicially minded to endorse Stanton's wild charges, though, as presently became evident, he was willing to sign an appeal couched in more appropriate language.

The Stanton-Chase proposal, if it was to have any force, would need more powerful supporters than Bates or Smith. The cabinet members who, besides the two original promoters, really mattered were Blair, Seward, and Welles. There was no hope of winning Blair. The Marylander despised Pope as heartily as the rest — all the Popes, the breezy gentleman once told Lincoln, were "flatterers, deceivers, liars and tricksters"[10] — and he still, even after August 1862, believed in McClellan's military capacity. Chase, well knowing Blair's devotion to Lincoln and his confidence in McClellan, was almost morbidly fearful that he should learn of the pending plot. While Chase and Welles were discussing the matter, in their first interview on the subject, Blair casually dropped into the Secretary's room. "Chase was alarmed," recorded Welles, "for the paper was in my hand and he evidently feared I should address Blair on the subject." In deference to Chase's agitation, Welles refrained, but after the Postmaster General had left Welles asked if Blair should not be called back and taken into their confidence. "No; not now," replied the head of the Treasury. "It was best he should for the present know nothing of it." So nervous was Chase about Blair's being let into the secret that, after he had himself left the room, he returned for a final injunction to Welles; he begged his colleague to say nothing about the proposal to Blair or anyone else.[11]

As to Seward, his position in this moment of crisis will probably never be known. Up to Second Bull Run, Seward had espoused McClellan's cause; but there is reason to believe that after this defeat his loyalty paled, and that in his heart he endorsed the Stanton-Chase declaration. An open decision, however, would have proved embarrassing. A year before Seward had attempted with his "Thoughts" to get control of the administration. He understood the President's determined spirit, and the lofty respect which Lincoln, despite his informalities and his frequently jocose behavior, entertained for the dignity of his office. Perhaps the agile Secretary of State was disinclined to invite another rebuff. He had come to have a personal regard for Lincoln, and was averse to being identified with what he knew was a hostile, disloyal act and one which, if carried into effect, might cause his own retire-

[9] *Ibid.*, p. 343. [10] Welles, *Diary*, I, 126. [11] *Ibid.*, I, 95.

ment. On the other hand, Seward was always the trimmer and did not care to oppose the two most powerful members after himself of Lincoln's official family. So he boarded a train and left for a brief vacation at his home in Auburn, New York. An energetic campaign for three hundred thousand more recruits for "father Abraham" was under way in the North and Seward believed – or so he said – that his presence and speeches in that region would stimulate enlistment. So, from late August to September 4, the period of the McClellan cabinet upheaval, Seward remained absent from the presidential councils. Gideon Welles records his conviction that Seward's sudden departure was "purposeful."

Blair and Seward evidently being unavailable as signers, the leaders in their search for influential supporters had fallen back on Welles. He was indispensable to their cause, not only as head of one of the greatest departments, but for his personal standing and influence with Lincoln. With Welles the junto would have numbered five members of the cabinet out of a possible seven, and such a majority – including three of the most powerful: Stanton, Chase, and Welles – would have been impressive. But Welles, in almost belligerent fashion, refused to have anything to do with the movement. In bluntly telling Chase that he disapproved Stanton's importunities, he dropped into a Yankee phrase subsequently made celebrated by Calvin Coolidge. After the first reading of the paper, in Chase's presence, he looked up, turned his white-whiskered Santa Claus countenance to his smooth-faced visitor, and said, "I do not choose to denounce McClellan for incapacity, or to pronounce him a traitor, as declared in this paper, but I will say, and perhaps it is my duty to say, that I believe his removal from command is demanded by public sentiment and the best interests of the country." The President, Welles continued, understood his opinion of McClellan, for in many conversations on this subject he had expressed himself frankly. The general's dilatory course had long since caused Welles to lose confidence in him and this conviction was much aggravated by what he had recently learned at the War Department. If, in cabinet council, the President should request his views on the subject, they would be given freely, and would not differ greatly from those set forth in the Stanton-Chase indictment. But this method of approaching the problem Welles regarded as irregular, improper, and disrespectful to Mr. Lincoln. He flatly refused to join any "combination" whose purpose it was to seize "control" of the administration. Of all the seven cabinet members, Welles was practically the only one who, up to this time, had accurately gauged Lincoln's character and abilities. He entertained the highest opinion of both. On moral and intellectual grounds he estimated him far above Stanton, Chase, Seward, or any other public man of his time. This attempt to wrest "control" — Welles's word, repeated several times in his narrative of the uprising — of the administration by a threat of disruption in case the unasked-for advice should not be accepted aroused Welles's anger and contempt. In the next few days Chase brought pressure several times. All he received from the Navy head were a few apparently much-needed lessons in constitutional law.

Two days after his first rebuff from Welles, Chase returned with another document. This was in the trembling but clear handwriting of Attorney General Bates. That conscientious lawyer had refused to put his name to Stanton's bludgeoning paragraphs, but he agreed with the fundamental idea, and was willing to sign one expressed in more correct terms. He had been therefore asked to rephrase the protest. The Bates version omitted the traitorous charges against McClellan and, more significantly, blue-penciled the prospect of wholesale resignations, if he were retained in command. It was merely an expression of opinion, not a threat, that, if rejected, would throw the government into chaos. "The undersigned," it read, "who have been honored with your selection, as a part of your confidential advisers, deeply impressed with our great responsibility in the present crisis, do but perform a painful duty in declaring to you our deliberate opinion that, at this time, it is not safe to entrust to Major General McClellan the command of any army of the United States. And we hold ourselves ready, any time, to explain to you in detail, the reasons upon which this opinion is founded." Appended to this redaction were the names of Edwin M. Stanton, S. P. Chase, Caleb B. Smith, and Edward Bates. A white space was left between Smith and Bates for the hoped-for signature of Gideon Welles.

This document displays the difference between the constitutional lawyer, Edward Bates, and the impulsive politician, Edwin M. Stanton. Stanton's paper had embodied a gross misstatement in constitutional interpretation. It had referred to the members of the President's cabinet as his "constitutional advisers." Bates knew better and changed the words to "confidential advisers" — and admitted that they were only "part of his confidential advisers" at that. The cabinet, as Stanton ought to have known and undoubtedly did know, has no standing under the Constitution. That fundamental law makes no provision for such an agency of government. All so-called "cabinet" members are the special creatures of acts of Congress. Not one of them had any existence at the time the Constitution went into operation. In successive pieces of legislation Congress had established the administrative departments — State, Treasury, War, and the rest of the present ten — providing for a secretary to act as executive head of each. Nothing identical with a cabinet in the real meaning of the term has ever been known in the United States. The secretaries are mere underlings of the President, appointed by him and removable at his pleasure. They become "advisers" only when the President deigns to ask their advice, and then he adopts or rejects it as his judgment approves. The Constitution did take for granted executive departments and provided that the President could demand in writing the opinion "of the principal officer in each of the executive departments upon any subject relating to the duties of their respective offices." Thus, under the Constitution, cabinet members – or rather "department heads" – are not expected to offer unsolicited admonitions to the President. Had Lincoln asked their opinions on McClellan – as he did on Fort Sumter – then each member would have been obliged to render an opinion in writing. Seward once expressed tersely the relative powers of President and cabinet. "There is only one vote in the cabinet," he said, "and that is cast by the President." Legend relates how Lincoln once called for a cabinet vote on a pending question. All seven voted "no"; Lincoln voted "aye." The "ayes have it," the President declared. The anecdote, true or not, correctly epitomizes the authority and responsibility of the Chief Executive, as compared to that of his "department heads." To frame a round robin and place it in menacing fashion under the President's nose was a proceeding not justified in law or morals.

Bates's revised declaration was a great improvement on Stanton's, but even his went too far, and it is surprising that so excellent a jurist and so fair-minded a man should have been beguiled by Stanton and Chase into writing and signing it. The Attorney General's modifications did not remove Welles's objections. He was opposed not only to the form of the demand, but to the demand itself. He complimented Chase on the improvement over Stanton's epistolary manners, but even the more correct form he regarded as irregular and disrespectful to Mr. Lincoln. "I told Chase I did not like and could not unite in the movement; that in a conference with the President, I should have no hesitation in saying or agreeing to what was there expressed. . . . Reflection had more fully satisfied me that this method of conspiring to influence or control the President was repugnant to my feelings and was not right; it was unusual, would be disrespectful, and would justly be deemed offensive; that the President had called us around him as friends and advisers, with whom he might counsel and consult on all matters affecting the public welfare, not to enter into combinations to control him. Nothing of this kind has hitherto taken place in our intercourse." [12]

[12] Bates, *op. cit.*, pp. 101–102.

Chase attempted to argue the case, but Welles proved inflexible. As a result, the whole matter was dropped. "My refusal," Welles afterward wrote, "and perhaps my remarks prevented the matter from proceeding further. The President never knew of this paper." [13]

That Lincoln would have flatly rejected the cabinet proposal, even at the cost of a cabinet resignation en masse, events made clear. Perhaps the tensest of all cabinet meetings in the Civil War assembled on the morning of September 2 – the day after Chase's first unsuccessful appeal to Welles for co-operation in the warfare on McClellan. All were present except Seward – and, as the pertinacious Welles again notes, "I think there was design in his absence." Washington had reached a state of hysteria. Authentic news had then arrived at the Capital of Pope's calamitous proceedings at Bull Run. If any emphasis were needed to give point to his defeat, the thousands of stragglers from his army, rushing almost in rout to the Washington entrenchments, would have supplied it. The city was hourly expecting the arrival of Lee's army and a battle in front of the Capital that would decide the fate of the nation. Lincoln's "department heads" assembled before his arrival and were excitedly discussing the situation. Most of them were hurling imprecations impartially at McClellan and Pope. Montgomery Blair, in references to the latter commander, was free with his usual expletives: Pope, he declared again, was a "braggart and a liar" – the latter word now had a particular application, for Pope's first message, reporting a smashing victory, had lifted Northerners everywhere in exultation, only to have their hopes dashed to a new depth when the real truth arrived.

Of all the assembled statesmen, Stanton showed the greatest emotion. As Welles records, the Secretary of War was "trembling with excitement." He was big with news, which he announced "in a suppressed voice." McClellan, he informed his colleagues, had been restored to command of the Army of the Potomac! Consternation and amazement followed the declaration. At the height of the discussion, the tall, gaunt figure of the President entered, calm and controlled, yet evidently laboring under a great strain. All the perturbed cabinet faces turned in his direction. Was it true that McClellan had been replaced in his old position? Yes, Lincoln quietly answered, it was true. His delay in reaching the cabinet meeting had been caused by his absence in consultation with that military chieftain. He and General Halleck had called at McClellan's house, routed him out before breakfast, and ordered him to take command of the Federal armies stationed about Washington. In response to the anxious expressions on every face – which, in the case of Stanton and Chase, amounted to surly glares

[13] Welles, *Lincoln and Seward*. Pp. 193–194.

– Lincoln said that he had done what seemed best under all the circumstances.

"No order to that effect," said Stanton, "has been issued from the War Department."

Lincoln turned on his insolent subordinate with that cold finality he could use at times most effectively. "The order is mine," he replied, "and I will be responsible for it to the country." He acknowledged all McClellan's shortcomings. The general had "the slows" and was not to be depended on for aggressive fighting. But he was a good engineer, a splendid organizer of armed forces; he knew, better than any man, conditions that then surrounded Washington, and no man in the nation was so competent for the immediately pressing task – that of reconstituting the demoralized hordes then pouring into the Washington forts, and whipping them expeditiously into a fighting force.

So far as his counselors gave their opinions, Lincoln received more blame than praise. Most of them accepted the information in respectful silence, though Montgomery Blair expressed approval. The attitude of Chase and Stanton approached pretty close to insulting disrespect. The Secretary of the Treasury insisted that the President's changes of commanding general would prove to be a "national calamity." When Lincoln said that McClellan was the best man to put the forts in order, Chase retorted that the engineer who had constructed them could do the job just as well. He recalled his whole attitude towards McClellan; said that he had welcomed him to Washington and had given him support as long as he could do so without proving faithless to the national cause. Even after Chase had felt compelled to withdraw that confidence, he had, in deference to the President's disinclination to appoint another commander, supported him in every possible way. He had no personal animosity against the man and devoutly wished him to succeed. But what had been the outcome? McClellan's campaigns had been a series of failures. He had shown no alacrity in forwarding assistance to Pope. His delay in hastening troops to the scene of action on the preceding Friday and Saturday had evinced a spirit which rendered him unworthy of trust. "I cannot but feel," Chase declared, "that giving the command to McClellan is equivalent to giving Washington to the rebels." "This and more I said," Chase wrote rather proudly in his Diary. Lincoln replied that he was distressed exceedingly to find himself differing in so important a matter from the Secretary of the Treasury and the Secretary of War. He saw no one who could do the work that was immediately at hand so well as McClellan. Whom would Chase suggest? The Secretary proposed Hooker, or Sumner, or Burnside. "Either of them would do the work better." Lincoln did not agree, and the long discussion finally ended, the President still determined in his plan, though most of his cabinet took stand against him.

One curious misstatement in connection with this meeting has crept into the most respectable histories, which does a great injustice to Lincoln. He has been pictured as so driven by despair that he informed his cabinet, on this occasion, that he would "gladly resign his place." "The President retained his dignity and maintained at first a calm attitude" – so reads the account of this cabinet meeting in *McClellan's Own Story*.[14] "He had been accustomed for months to the nagging policy of the Secretaries; but it now became so personal and bitter that he was at last driven to the exclamation that he would gladly resign his high office." To prove that Abraham Lincoln had reached such a low state of mind, a passage from Chase's Diary, as extracted and published by his biographer, Robert Warden, is reproduced. In this work Lincoln is indeed quoted as saying to Chase "that he would gladly resign his place." Even so careful a historian as James Ford Rhodes repeats the supposed cry of anguish as indicating the state of demoralization prevailing in Washington at that time, and other writers have dutifully copied the sentence. Seldom has a misprint done a statesman such injustice. In 1903, the American Historical Association published Chase's Diary. From this it appears that Lincoln did not inform that gentleman that he would "gladly resign his place," but that he would "gladly resign his plan."[15] It was a frequent remark of Lincoln in laying his proposals before his advisers that he would be happy to give up his plan if they could suggest something better, and it was in response to this question that Chase had indicated as "something better" any one of the three generals – Hooker, Sumner, or Burnside – all three of whom were favorites with the congressional Jacobins, all three having accepted the radical view on the Negro question.

The next day, Chase, meeting Welles on the White House lawn, upbraided him for not giving his support to his anti-McClellan demonstration. He could now see to what straits his failure to sign the pronunciamento had brought the nation. McClellan would never have been restored to a place where he would be able to accomplish unutterable mischief if that written defiance had been placed on the President's desk. But Welles knew better than that. In a private conversation Lincoln had gone further into detail with Welles on this matter. He was willing to admit that most of the criticisms lavished on his difficult general had a genuine basis. He was even prepared to believe, in a

[14] McClellan, *op. cit.*, p. 544.

[15] Page 65. The Diary formed part of the Annual Report of the American Historical Association for 1902, Vol. II.

measure, that "Little Mac" had been derelict in forwarding reinforcements to the fiercely pressed Pope. "He acted badly towards Pope, he wanted him to fail," Nicolay and Hay report the President as having remarked to them, and Welles records similar confidential criticisms made to him. Most of the recent troubles, Lincoln declared, were caused by "the quarrels of the generals"; their jealousies and personal ambitions provided the real explanation for the state to which the country had been reduced. Welles thought the same, but neither he nor Lincoln accepted the easy belief that the man was a traitor, that he deliberately planned to deliver Washington to Lee; the thing was subtler than that. It stemmed from the paralyzing effect produced on a man's actions by his conviction that he had been wronged, and that, through spite, a soldier whose character and abilities he despised had been given the work which he himself was the only one competent to do. All that, Lincoln said, should be overlooked in face of the fact that the one man in the army best fitted to stop the demoralization everywhere becoming worse and to make over the forces for the defense of the capital was the recalcitrant McClellan. The mere fact that he was recalled from obscurity to repair the injury inflicted on the nation by the hated Pope would put him on his mettle. "It was humiliating" – Welles quotes the President to this effect – "after what had transpired and all we knew, to reward McClellan and those who failed to do their whole duty in the hour of trial, but so it was. Personal considerations must be sacrificed for the public good. He had kept aloof from the discussions that prevailed and intended to, but, said he, 'I must have McClellan to reorganize the army and bring it out of chaos.' "[16] The task which McClellan must do now was almost indentically the same that he had so brilliantly performed after First Bull Run. He had created a splendid fighting force out of all that confusion and he could do so again. The nation must use the best talent available to its hand for the work that immediately needed to be done. That Lincoln was right the events proved. In less than two weeks, the restored general had repeated his former brilliant performance, and out of the scattered fragments of Pope's hordes had created the host that brought Lee to defeat at South Mountain and Antietam.

The affair increased the already profound admiration which Welles entertained for his chief. His handling of the McClellan crisis in September 1862 Welles regarded as one of the greatest moments in Lincoln's life. He expressed this view at the time, and again long after Lincoln's death. "From what I have seen and heard within the last few days," he wrote on September 7, 1862, "the more highly do I appre-

[16] Welles, *Lincoln and Seward*. P. 197.

ciate the President's judgment and sagacity in the stand he made." Probably the fact that Welles had himself done yeoman work in supporting his chief – all unknown to the man concerned – heightened his satisfaction. The President was "never unreasonably obstinate or wilful," he wrote in a brochure published in 1874,[17] "even when his intentions were defeated. . . . In the generosity of his nature, he was tolerant of acts where a more arbitrary and imperious mind would have been implacable and unforgiving. There were occasions, however, when, relying on his own convictions, and the exigencies being great, he exercised the executive will – the one-man power – with intelligent determination and effect. His promptness and energy in an emergency were displayed on one memorable occasion, when danger was imminent and immediate decision necessary. It may be mentioned as illustrative of his executive ability, promptness, and self-reliance. Gloom and national disaster were upon the country, but the President met the crisis with firmness, rose with the exigency, and independent of his cabinet and against the general sentiments of the people, and by a sacrifice of personal feeling, adopted a course which results justified and proved his ability as a chief." It was Lincoln's action in the McClellan crisis that called forth this eulogy from the most penetrating and just member of his cabinet.

Some days after this critical cabinet meeting, Welles, walking on a Sunday evening on Pennsylvania Avenue, sighted what he at first thought was a squadron of cavalry men, about thirty in number. It proved to be McClellan and his staff, caparisoned in all their old-time splendor. Welles raised his hand in salute as the dashing young general approached. McClellan, recognizing the Secretary, stopped, leaned down, and shook the old man's hand in his most friendly, charming manner. This handclasp, he said, was intended as a farewell. "Then," inquired Welles, "you go up the River?" Yes, he had started to take charge of the army for the operations above – where Lee's forces were known to be gathering. "Well," said the Secretary of the Navy, "onward, General, is now the word; the country will expect you to go forward." "That," replied McClellan, "is my intention." "Success to you, General, with all my heart!" and the men waved hands in farewell. In a few days the Army of the Potomac, in four columns, was marching along the north side of the Potomac towards the battlefield of Antietam.

[17] *Ibid.*, p. 189.

BOOK FIVE

Senate versus Cabinet

I

THE NEXT FEW weeks proved to be a period of mingled triumph and disaster. In that time McClellan justified both the favorable and the unfavorable opinions Lincoln held of his character. He had been specifically summoned to reorganize the shattered Potomac forces and re-establish them as a fighting army and the task had been accomplished with McClellan's customary speed and completeness. The army that advanced in late September to meet Lee in western Maryland was the finest, in equipment, courage, and fighting power, that this continent had known up to that time. These qualities were displayed when it came face to face with the Confederate forces, who, overconfident from their recent campaigns, now boldly attempted an invasion of the North. Lee had expected that all Maryland, including Washington and Baltimore, would quickly fall into his hands, and that this would lead to the capture of Philadelphia and Harrisburg and even of New York. But McClellan, at Antietam Creek, in one of the bloodiest battles of the war, stopped Lee's forces, threw them back, and sent them in retreat to their Virginia strongholds.

This failure taught the South that it was about as difficult to invade the North as similar misadventures had taught the Federals that it was to invade the South. After achieving this success, however, McClellan's familiar qualities of doubt and procrastination again came to the surface. Lincoln believed that Antietam had delivered the Army of Northern Virginia into McClellan's hands and that, had the success been vigorously pursued, Lee's forces would have been captured or destroyed and the back of the Rebellion broken. Day after day the distracted leader in the White House sent peremptory orders to McClellan to follow up his advantage and not let the Southerners cross the Potomac into Virginia. Instead of obeying these instructions, McClellan again set up his usual demands for reinforcements, and made his usual complaints of the lack of supplies and of the Potomac mud. His patience exhausted, Lincoln formed a resolve, not communicated to anyone until long afterward. If McClellan permitted Lee to cross the Blue

Ridge Mountains and place himself between Richmond and the Army of the Potomac, he would remove him from command.[1] On November 5 news reached Washington that Lee and Longstreet had arrived safely at Culpepper Court House; Lincoln at once sent a message to McClellan, directing him to turn over command of the Army of the Potomac to General Ambrose E. Burnside and retire to Trenton, New Jersey, and there await further orders. The days of George Brinton McClellan as a commanding officer in the United States Army had definitely come to an end.

Whatever may be thought of McClellan's dismissal – and on this, as on all episodes in his career, controversy is still raging – the selection of Burnside was one of Lincoln's greatest mistakes. This incapable officer led the Federal forces to another disaster at Fredericksburg on December 13, and in so doing, brought the cabinet to the verge of ruin. The threatened breakup of the regime in August had been a palace revolution, an uprising of an inner group of the cabinet itself, led by Stanton and Chase, who were bent on seizing control of affairs and conducting the war in accordance with their own military and political doctrines. The revolt that assailed it in December 1862 had a more dangerous origin. The cabinet crisis of August came from within the breastworks, that of December from without. It presented a spectacle practically unprecedented in American history. Quarrels between Congress and President have been common enough, but a fairly ferocious attempt of the legislature to seize the executive power, to dictate cabinet removals and appointments, was something new. Yet the senatorial onslaught on Lincoln in December of this year virtually amounted to this. It was an attempt to transfer the seat of executive power from the White House to the Capitol. Had the attempt succeeded the Jacobins would not only have usurped control of the war, they would have revolutionized the American system of constitutional government. Yet in the December attack on the Lincoln administration, the leading spirits were the same as those who led the cabinet's abortive uprising. In August, Stanton and Chase had incited their colleagues to reorganize and control the Executive. In the December crisis, their hands did not appear so conspicuously, yet neither can escape a good share of the responsibility for one of the most harassing experiences in Lincoln's official life.

It was not only the tragedy of Fredericksburg that gave the anti-administration leaders in the cabinet and in Congress their opportunity. The long, patient tolerance with which McClellan had been treated infuriated the Jacobins, and Lincoln's steadfast refusal to regard the

[1] Nicolay and Hay, *op. cit.* VI, 188.

extinction of slavery as the object of the war, his persistence in maintaining the salvation of the Union as the great end in view, added fuel to the flame. The elections of November 1862 were hailed as indicating popular sympathy with the Jacobin cause and a lowered esteem for the Executive. In several important states – Ohio, Indiana, New York, Pennsylvania, Illinois, and others – the Democrats had emerged either victorious or with a greatly increased vote. While it was not unusual in those days, as in modern times, for midterm elections to go against the party in power, public dissatisfaction with the conduct of the war had considerably affected the result. Again, in the latter part of 1862 the publication of Seward's first volume of diplomatic correspondence caused great excitement in antislavery quarters. This unhappy opus not only explained the criticisms that for some time had been hurled at the cabinet, but gave Congress a shining figure upon whom to center its hostility. Certain passages in Seward's letters to Minister Adams in London were cynical and reckless, even for Seward. They were certainly improper things to have written in the first place, and fairly outrageous when given to the world in an official document. The fact that Seward had printed them with apparent malice prepense increased the popular uproar. The volume in which they appeared was liberally sprinkled with asterisks, indicating the omission of doubtful paragraphs. Such editorial precautions could easily have been applied to the offending sentences, yet the Secretary had permitted his views on secession, emancipation, and other similarly delicate matters to stand in all their nakedness. A letter of April 10, 1861 – on the verge of Sumter – that clearly committed the administration to the Buchanan theory of secession gave particular umbrage. In this, Seward declared that the President was not disposed to "reject a cardinal dogma" of the South, "that the Federal government could not reduce the seceding States to obedience, even although he were disposed to question that proposition. But in fact the President willingly accepts it as true. Only an imperial or despotic government could subjugate thoroughly disaffected or insurrectionary members of the state." [2]

Astonishing as were these sentiments, expressed by the first member of the cabinet, the word of Seward, boldly proclaiming these obnoxious Buchanan opinions as Lincoln's, caused widespread amazement. Of course Seward's exposition of these views as Lincoln's was false. Lincoln had never held them, and certainly not when he had started a great war based on an interpretation of the Constitution directly at variance with the one Seward presumptuously set forth. Lincoln flatly denied the right of secession and maintained the duty of the Federal

[2] *Diplomatic Correspondence, 1861.* U. S. Government. P. 74.

government to use force to keep a seceded state in the Union. On any other reading of the Constitution the war on which the nation had embarked would have been as wicked as Southern spokesmen contended. Another passage in the correspondence enraged the Jacobins even more. On July 5, 1861, Seward had written Adams – and had published the passage in December 1862 – as follows: "It seems as if extreme advocates of African slavery and its most vehement opponents were acting in concert together to precipitate a servile war – the former by making the most desperate attempts to overthrow the federal union, the latter by demanding an edict of universal emancipation as a lawful and necessary, if not, as they say, the only legitimate way of saving the Union." [3] There was probably no man whom these expressions shocked more than the diplomat – a man of Boston antislavery antecedents – to whom they had been addressed. In these few casual lines Seward accused the secessionists of the South and the radicals of the North of joining hands to cause an uprising of slaves. Incidentally he had cast a slur upon the Proclamation of Emancipation which, at the time this letter was published, the President had given to the world.

Seward had already taken his place, in the estimate of the Jacobins, as "the evil genius" of the cause and the "bane of the administration," a bad eminence which these indiscretions lifted to an even more odious height. Charles Sumner, a copy of the book in hand, rushed to the White House and showed the passages to Lincoln. The President was as greatly shocked as the Boston abolitionist. He informed Sumner that this was the first time he had ever seen the paragraphs. The presidential remark, quickly circulated in the Senate lobby by Sumner, gave a new turn to the rising indignation. Evidently, it was said, the Secretary of State was accustomed to send dispatches of vital importance to the diplomatic corps without submitting them to the responsible Chief of State. Procedure like this was unknown in any well-conducted government. For a year criticism had been in circulation that Seward regarded himself as the real head of the nation and ignored the President in the most important decisions. Here, the radicals insisted, was clear proof that this gossip was true. Seward's letter to Adams outlining Lincoln's attitude on the right of secession and the wickedness of force in suppressing it, which, Seward well knew, was directly opposed to the views Lincoln held and was acting upon, indicated the really contemptuous opinion he held of the President and his conviction that the "Premier" was in fact his superior.

Could one ask – inquired the Jacobins – a more adequate explanation of the failures and humiliations of the preceding eighteen months? The

[3] *Diplomatic Correspondence, 1862.* P. 124.

power that really controlled the nation did not believe in the war! The head man felt no sympathy with its object, and had been intriguing, before and after it began, for a peace that would leave its problems unsolved and the South the virtual victor. That Seward had supported McClellan almost to the day of his deposition was common knowledge. He had opposed emancipation, and even now was attempting to dissuade Lincoln from that policy; here was another charge that his blatantly published dispatches to Mr. Adams seemed to substantiate. That he had once been hailed as a great antislavery leader was true; and thus to his other vices as a public man Seward had added those of an apostate. One need look no further, it was said, for the influence that had persuaded Lincoln, every time a patriotic general – like Frémont and Hunter – issued a proclamation freeing the slaves in his military district, to issue orders revoking the decree. The Jacobin press, led by Horace Greeley's *Tribune*, teemed with denunciations. The time had come to get rid of this incubus, once for all. A writer in the *Tribune* denounced the Secretary of State for his "shallow smartness" and for the "coldness, alienation, and almost open hostility which the incompetent cunning of our Secretary has exerted in our regard in almost every quarter." Others described Seward as "the unseen hand," "the mesmerist" who had reduced the President to hypnotic ineptitude. Joseph Medill, of the *Chicago Tribune*, expressed this latter criticism with a picturesqueness all his own. "McClellan in the field," he wrote Schuyler Colfax, "and Seward in the cabinet have brought our grand cause to the very brink of death. Seward must be got out of the cabinet. He is Lincoln's evil genius. He has been President *de facto* and has kept a sponge saturated with chloroform to Uncle Abe's nose all the while, except for one or two brief spells." The eccentric Pole, Adam Gurowski, who held a minor job in the State Department, echoed the same general view. "Lincoln," he noted in his diary, dropping into that English which made him one of the jokes of Washington, "is under the tumb of Seward, to a degree allmost ridiculous. Seward brings him out to take airing as he were Lincoln's nurse." Early in September a committee of New York Republicans waited on Lincoln, demanding Seward's dismissal. The presumption, even discourtesy, of this self-appointed board of censors irritated the calmest of Presidents. "There is not one of you," he told them flatly, "who would not see the country ruined if you could turn out Seward."

Soon, however, the anti-Seward campaign assumed more ambitious proportions. It was urged that not only Seward, but all the rest of the cabinet, with the exception of Chase and Stanton, would have to go. "Common sense, if not common honesty, has fled from the cabinet,"

William Pitt Fessenden wrote his family on December 7, 1862, "and the country has little to hope, I fear, from Mr. Lincoln or his advisers. I very much fear that there will be an outbreak in Congress." [4] An insurrection was indeed stirring in the upper chamber and Fessenden became the most aggressive leader. One of the ablest statesmen of his day, a scholar of economics and finance, a man of courage and integrity, an eloquent, if somewhat acrid speaker, Fessenden, since his entrance into the Senate in 1855, had been an uncompromising opponent of slavery, and was now an unremitting advocate of making its extirpation the cardinal issue of the Civil War. In character a higher type than Wade or Chandler – for his sincerity and his unselfish devotion to the cause were never questioned – Fessenden's accession to the radical cause, like that of Sumner, gave it a dignity not conspicuous in all its champions. His unbending manners, his frequently sharp, harsh comments on men and things, his general unsociability, reminded his admirers of the rock-bound coast of the Maine from which he hailed. It was perhaps characteristic of Fessenden's philosophic mind that the discussion of the weaknesses in Lincoln's cabinet, which stirred up a tempest in the last week of December, 1862, should have taken a constitutional turn. The remedy he proposed was revolutionary. In short, what Fessenden and his companions aimed at was to supplant the presidential system – as Walter Bagehot called it – by the parliamentary form. In Britain the House of Commons votes cabinets in and out of office. From time to time voices have been heard in the United States suggesting the adoption of the British system. They became quite audible during the Civil War. One feature of the Constitution recently adopted by the Confederate States of America was regarded by many as an improvement over that of the Federal Union. This gave cabinet members seats in Congress, and thus subjected them to the inquisition of the legislature. The Jacobins could have put such a device to profitable use in the Civil War had the fathers embodied it in the Constitution. One can imagine how Wade, Chandler, Sumner, and Julian would have rejoiced to hail their dearest foe, William Henry Seward, before either house, in full sight of the nation, and submit him to one of those questionings that are a part of the British system.

Whether Fessenden had definitely committed himself to such a procedure is not clear, but he did insist that the upper branch of Congress, the Senate, should exercise authority in executive concerns. At least his opinion in the new crisis, as reported by himself, amounted practically to such a startling pretension. That senatorial meddling in executive affairs would be extraconstitutional he granted, but he declared

[4] Fessenden, Francis, *Life and Public Services of William Pitt Fessenden.* Houghton Mifflin Company, 1907. I, 265.

that the Senate should "no longer be content with its constitutional duties." The national situation was so serious that the upper chamber would be justified in taking general control. It was the more august half of the legislative body and, as such, could properly step outside the specific duties assigned it by the fundamental law and assert supreme power in the state. Fessenden's own word for the assumption by the Senate of a kind of universal providence was to "interpose." [5] By December 1862, he was prepared to "interpose" to the extent of seizing control of the cabinet. At another time he asserted a similar right of the Senate to direct military matters. "We are not under the command of the military of this country," he said in a Senate speech. "They are under ours, as a Congress, and I stand here to maintain it." This overlordship Fessenden would have carried into all branches of the government. He had been disgruntled with Lincoln's cabinet from the first. He disliked the manner in which it had been selected as well as its personnel. Lincoln, he insisted, should not have chosen his official family until arriving in Washington, and then he should have done so in consultation with the Senators representing the party that had placed him in power. With the President's conception of a coalition cabinet, taken from the leaders of the several elements making up the new Republican Party, Fessenden completely disagreed. The cabinet, he never tired of saying – and it was an orthodox item in the Jacobin creed – should be a unit. It should include only those men who had taken the lead in fighting slavery. Instead of this what kind of administration had Lincoln created? "The simple truth," declared Fessenden, "is, there was never such a shambling half-and-half set of incapables collected in one government since the world began." The cabinet should work on equal terms with the Chief Executive in all matters. For Fessenden echoed the now familiar grievance that Lincoln never regarded his department heads as "constitutional advisers." Most vital courses he decided himself, frequently without consulting his council. Each department chieftain was secluded in a hermetically sealed compartment, transacting routine business; the cabinet as a whole seldom met in solemn assembly, settling critical matters, as Fessenden seemed to think they should be decided, by a majority vote. Instead of this council, the President leaned almost exclusively for direction on one man, and that the one who was regarded by the radicals as little better than a "traitor."

The sources from which Fessenden and his group had learned of this lack of cabinet "unity" were no secret. No men had given this criticism quite so extensive advertisement as Chase and Stanton. Since 1855, when Fessenden first came into the Senate, his closest political intimate

[5] *Ibid.*, II, 234.

had been the Ohio Senator. This intimacy had been maintained after Chase's accession to the Treasury. Fessenden's duties as chairman of the Senate Finance Committee – which he ably performed – brought him into almost daily association with the Treasury head. Together they had worked over financial legislation and decided the fiscal policy of the nation. On methods of waging the war, of re-establishing the nation and uplifting the Negro, they were at one – and their policies usually ran counter to Lincoln's. Both supported the several attempts that had been made by generals like Ben Butler, Frémont, and Hunter to emancipate in advance of presidential action the slaves in their military departments. In the most recent case – that of Hunter, in May 1862 – the Jacobins, under the leadership of Chase and Stanton, had rushed to Lincoln imploring him not to revoke the proclamation. Chase wrote the President a personal letter making the same plea. The reply received from Lincoln indicated that the President, with all his other talents, could effectively snub. "No commanding general" – his note to Chase consisted of this single sentence – "shall do such a thing, upon *my* responsibility, without consulting me." Emancipation, when it should be granted, would not be extended piecemeal by generals, but by the one officer who could legally exercise that prerogative – the President.

Stanton, when first appointed, did not enjoy Fessenden's confidence. His service as Buchanan's Attorney General did not inspire complete faith in his soundness on the Negro question. Fessenden therefore secured postponement by the Senate of Stanton's nomination as Secretary of War until he could look into his record. Chase brought Fessenden and Stanton together for a personal comparison of views, and after this meeting the Senator declared his admiration for the new appointee and obtained quick action on confirmation. "With Stanton," Fessenden said, "we shall soon see a new face on affairs and God knows we need it." From that day, this trio – Fessenden, Chase, and Stanton – had worked in the utmost harmony, and in Lincoln's cabinet Chase and Stanton were the only two members who met Fessenden's approval. These two would serve as a nucleus about which a genuine cabinet could be constructed; one that would be a "unit" and devoted to the radical cause. His brother Senators had selected Fessenden himself as Seward's successor, but the gentleman from Maine, with more delicacy than his compatriots, rejected the proposal; he could hardly step into the shoes of a man whom he had been instrumental in expelling from public life. Yet the time was to come, a year afterward, when Fessenden would enter the cabinet, as Secretary of the Treasury in succession to his friend Chase.

II

ON TUESDAY afternoon, December 16, 1862, three days after the Battle of Fredricksburg, the Republican Senators met in secret caucus on Capitol Hill. The proceedings began with a motion to the effect that "the chairman be instructed to offer in open Senate a resolution expressing a want of confidence in William H. Seward, Secretary of State," words that recall those frequently used in the British House of Commons when the opposition seeks to throw out the ministry. Perhaps the form, as well as the substance, struck the more sober Senators as incongruous. At least several raised objections and this particular resolution was dropped. However, this new mood indicated no kindly attitude toward the White House; as soon as the caucus got under way, it resolved itself into an indignation meeting, directed at the "Premier" of the cabinet. No improvement in the state of the nation, military or civil – such seemed to be the unanimous opinion – would be possible so long as this obnoxious person held sway in the State Department. All the charges that had been circulating against Seward for a year and a half received another eloquent airing. He had never believed in the war. He was constantly seeking to bring it to an end. He was determined to surrender to the South. He had no desire to see the Negro obtain his freedom. Senator Fessenden, the chief speaker, said that the meeting had been called to learn whether the Republicans in the Senate could reach unanimity on this subject. There was no use in pursuing the Seward crisis or anything else, unless all Republicans could agree. "It had been said that there was a secret influence that controlled the President. He had been told by a member of the cabinet" – Fessenden did not give the name, but everyone knew that Chase was meant – "that there was a backstairs influence which often controlled the apparent conclusions of the cabinet itself."

"Is the name of that backstairs influence," asked Howard of Michigan, "William H. Seward?"

"No name was given," replied Fessenden, "but Senators may draw their own conclusions." Both Fessenden and Wade clearly made manifest the real grievance rankling in the Jacobin heart. "Measures should be taken," said the Maine Senator, "to make the cabinet a unity and to remove from it anyone who does not coincide heartily with our views in relation to the war." Wade censured Lincoln "for placing our armies under the command of officers who did not believe in the policy of the government and had no sympathy with its purposes." By "our views," of course, Fessenden meant the negrophile policies he and his associates had been preaching since the war began and Wade's criticism meant that too many Democrats had been made generals. All high officers, Wade insisted, should be Republicans and Republicans of his own stripe.

On the issue of flatly demanding Seward's removal a certain number of Senators balked at this first meeting. They believed the question should be framed in less offensive words. Thus the unanimity that Fessenden had declared to be essential could not be obtained – though a good-sized majority was voted in its favor. At an adjourned meeting held the next day, all the thirty-two Republican Senators, except one, did agree upon the same demand when it was set forth in more general terms. The size of this vote indicated the proportions to which the Jacobin cause had grown since its attack on the administration began. It disclosed also the really formidable proportions of the hostility directed from the legislative chamber against Lincoln. Senator Preston King of New York, who had been Seward's colleague for several years, and was a loyal friend and supporter, declined to vote; he was thus the only Republican Senator who did not join in the attack. Seward's successor in the Senate, Mr. Harris, presented the resolution that met general approbation. It ran as follows: "Resolved, that in the judgment of the Republican members of the Senate, the public confidence in the present administration would be increased by a reconstruction of the cabinet." John Sherman, brother of the general, who was then beginning a public life that was to last thirty years, called attention to one misconception that might arise from this sweeping proposal. It might be taken as the opinion of the Republican majority that all members of the cabinet should "go out." He presumed that this was not desired. "No one wished Mr. Chase to leave the Treasury, which he had managed so ably." Mr. Sherman further said that he doubted whether changing the cabinet would remedy the evil. The difficulty was with the President himself. "He had neither dignity, order, nor firmness. His [Mr. Sherman's] course would be to go directly to the President and tell him his defects. It was doubtful if even that would do any good."

The particular fault which Senator Sherman found in the phrase-

Montgomery Blair (1813–1883)
Postmaster General

Zachariah Chandler
(1813–1879)
Senator from Michigan

William Pitt Fessenden
(1806–1869)
Senator from Maine; successor to Chase as Secretary of the Treasury

Benjamin Franklin Wade
(1800–1878)
Senator from Ohio

Charles Sumner
(1811–1874)
Senator from Massachusetts

Leaders of the Senatorial Opposition to the Cabinet

ology was quickly remedied. The resolution finally called, not for the elimination of everybody around Lincoln's council table, but for "a change in and partial reconstruction of the cabinet." A committee was appointed, of which the seventy-one-year-old Senator from Vermont, Jacob Collamer, was made chairman, to wait solemnly upon the President, and present this resolution. The other members were Wade, Trumbull, Sumner, Grimes, Fessenden, Harris, Pomeroy, and Howard. Good judgment had been displayed in selecting Collamer as spokesman. No member of the Senate was held in greater respect. Collamer was not a Jacobin, and was probably designated for that reason, for naturally a protest presented by one of the conservative Senators would carry greater weight than one proffered by a well-known firebrand. Senator Harris, the New Yorker who had presented the resolution – probably to forestall a more destructive one which he feared – was also a conservative. But all the other members belonged to the radical wing.[1]

While this vote was being taken, another scene was being enacted at the other end of Pennsylvania Avenue. Senator Preston King's name appears in the record as "not voting" – the only name, in fact, that was not cast in favor of the resolution. The fact is that Mr. King had hastily left the caucus room before his name had been called and betaken himself to Seward's home. Several Senators had insisted in their speeches that all the proceedings should be kept secret, but King angrily declared that he declined to observe any such injunction. Soon this corpulent and visibly very much disturbed statesman burst into the library of the Secretary of State, who was sitting nonchalantly, in his usual informal dress, before a cheery fire, immersed in a favorite volume and enjoying his customary after-dinner cigar. Seward's peace of mind was apparently not greatly upset after King had given a complete account of the senatorial proceedings of the two preceding days. The Republican Senators, he said, were "thirsty for a victim" in view of recent misfortunes, and, among others, had selected as sacrifice Mr. Lincoln's chief lieutenant. "Seeing how things were going," said Mr. King, "I did not stay for the last vote, but just slipped out of the chamber, to tell you, for I thought you ought to know. They were pledging each other to keep the proceedings secret, but I told them I was not going to be bound." Seward acted quickly on receipt of the news. "They may do as they please about me," he said, "but they shall not put the President in a false position on my account." He took a sheet of paper

[1] Senator Fessenden made at the time a long memorandum of the caucus proceedings, which forms the chief authority for the present narrative. See Fessenden, *op. cit.* I, 231–252.

and wrote the following, addressed to the President: "Sir, I hereby resign the office of Secretary of State, and beg that my resignation may be accepted immediately." He called in his son Frederick, who was assistant Secretary of State, and instructed him to write his resignation also. Then, at Seward's direction, King and the younger Seward took the resignations, crossed over to the White House, and placed them in President Lincoln's hands.

"What does this mean?" said the puzzled President, and then Senator King repeated the story he had just told Seward. Lincoln at once took his hat and crossed the White House lawn to his Secretary's house. When the President expressed regret at Seward's drastic action, the latter replied that it would be a relief to be freed from official cares. Lincoln answered: "Ah yes, Governor, that will do very well for you, but I am like the starling in Sterne's story. 'I can't get out.' "

And so, when the august senatorial committee advanced on the White House the next morning, the President was well prepared for their interview. Their main purpose – for Seward's overthrow, despite the form their formal protest had assumed, was the great objective – had apparently already been achieved. That is, Seward had freed Lincoln from all embarrassment, had the President really desired his retirement. But should Lincoln decline to accept the resignation, Seward's triumph over his enemies would be fairly overwhelming. He had practically given the President the choice between himself and the Jacobins who had been seeking, for some time, to get control of the administration.

Probably the White House had never been the scene of more tense proceedings than those that took place in the next three days. Lincoln had never before displayed his several talents – conciliation, diplomacy, manipulation of individuals, ability to center on the main point and gently turn persons and incidents to the important issue – so conspicuously as in his handling of this crisis. If he detected also in the quickly passing event materials for humor he gave no indication of the fact – unless, perhaps, when things had been finally adjusted. He quickly understood that a situation of great danger had suddenly taken form, and one that might endanger the successful outcome of the war. To hand over the government to the Wades, the Chandlers, the Julians, the Fessendens, and the Sumners of Congress would spell disaster to the nation. Yet when thirty-one out of thirty-two Republican Senators had taken a position that amounted practically to such a demand, an opposition of really portentous size had developed against the administration. A less tactful and farseeing man might have spoiled his case at the start. Gideon Welles did not quite approve the presidential acquiescence in the request of the Collamer committee for the presentation of the resolution – virtually a declaration of war. The Senate was clearly going outside its province, he said, in its attempt to dictate to the President about his cabinet, and an Executive with a more arrogant sense of the dignity of his office than Lincoln would have refused to parley with its representatives. Men like Jackson or Cleveland might likely enough have shown the intruding gentlemen the door. But Lincoln, as always, laying aside prerogatives and personal pride, took a practical view of the matter. A terrible civil war was raging; these Senators, if treated as their insolence properly deserved, could become implacable foes, capable of doing the cause infinite harm. When Senator Collamer therefore asked for an opportunity of placing their grievances before the Executive, Lincoln fixed seven in the evening of Thursday, December 18, for their reception.

The paper which this seventy-one-year-old chairman read to the President set forth, in fairly moderate terms, what he regarded as the conclusions which the Republican majority had reached in its long deliberations. The document, with some decency, refrained from mentioning Seward's name, though its phrasing pointed clearly enough to him as the chief villain of the piece. The first section, for example, emphasized the need for a vigorous and successful prosecution of the war; and the third insisted that "the cabinet should be exclusively composed of statesmen who are the cordial, resolute, unwavering supporters of the principles and purposes first above stated." Put these two declarations together and they summed up to a demand for Seward's official head. Another extract from Senator Collamer's précis – now read to the President – declared that "it is unwise and unsafe to commit the direction, conduct or execution of any important military operation or separate general command or enterprise in this war to anyone who is not a cordial believer and supporter of the same principles and purposes first above stated." Thus Lincoln was instructed to get rid of Democratic generals and put the armies exclusively under the command of those who adhered to the Jacobin creed.

Several speeches that followed Senator Collamer's presentation of the chapter of grievances made both these points clear. Wade, who spoke in his most raucous style, asserted that "the conduct of the war lay in the hands of men who had no sympathy with it or its cause." He rubbed in the recent elections, "imputing the defeat of the Republicans to the fact that the President had placed the direction of our military affairs in the hands of bitter and malignant Democrats." Fessenden indorsed this general indictment. The war, he told Lincoln, "was not sufficiently in the hands of its friends. Perhaps at the outset this was unavoidable, as the officers of the regular army had little sympathy with the Republican party. They were largely pro-slavery men and sympathized strongly with the southern feeling. It was signally unfortunate that almost every officer known as an anti-slavery man had been disgraced. He instanced General Frémont, Hunter, Mitchell, and others. It was time to change this condition of affairs. The war should be conducted by its friends. The administration should protect itself. It was evident that it had nothing to expect from the Democrats. General McClellan had been used for party purposes and was now busy in making an attack upon the government." All this was intended, among other things, as a criticism of Seward: the Secretary of State was looked upon as McClellan's chief supporter in the cabinet. Fessenden recalled the common belief "that the Secretary of State was not in accord with the majority of the cabinet and exerted an injurious influence upon the conduct of the war." [2]

The second part of Collamer's bill of complaints was the most revolutionary of all. It set forth that new theory of the cabinet to which Lincoln could not assent and which probably no student of the Constitution, in that day or this, could endorse. Collamer was a learned student of that document, as was Lincoln himself, and it seems inconceivable that he could have accepted as good law the principle which was now enunciated. "The theory of our government" – read this remarkable paragraph – "and the early and uniform construction thereof, is, that the President should be aided by a cabinet council, agreeing with him in political theories and general policy, and that all important public measures and appointments should be the result of their combined wisdom and deliberation. This most obviously necessary condition of things, without which no administration can succeed, we and the public believe does not now exist and therefore such selections and changes in its members should be made as will secure to the country unity of purpose and action, in all material and essential respects, more especially in the present crisis of public affairs." The suggestion was made that the President should make appointments only after submitting names to the cabinet and obtaining its approval. That the President and his cabinet should hold the same views on policy was another thrust at Lincoln's program of coalition government.

Lincoln said little in the course of the three hours' discussion to which this paper gave rise, though he treated the visitors with the utmost candor and courtesy, letting them expand on his errors at will. He had already fixed in his mind his method for meeting the situation.

[2] Fessenden, *op. cit.* I, 240–242.

He knew precisely where these criticisms, especially that one of ignoring his official counselors, had originated. He knew the amount of extracurricular talking on this dereliction that Chase and Stanton had indulged in, and, less openly, Bates. He also knew that to a considerable degree, this was jealousy; Lincoln's preference for Seward as his most companionable intimate had offended Chase from the first, and Stanton, great as were his obligations to Seward for his cabinet post, had been disappointed at not having secured a closer access to the presidential ear. Why not therefore, Lincoln concluded, bring these two opposing forces face to face? Why not let the Senate committee and the cabinet confront one another and debate their differences to their heart's content? Hence the day after this interview the Senate received word from the White House that the President would like to have another session with the committee that evening at seven and a half o'clock. That same morning, at a special cabinet meeting, Lincoln had informed his counselors of the senatorial demands and of Mr. Seward's resignation. The evening had been passed "in a pretty free and animated conversation"; some "not very friendly feelings" had been expressed in regard to other department heads, though no specific resignations had been demanded except that of the Secretary of State. The President had invited the committee to meet him again that evening, and he wished all members of the cabinet – except, of course, Mr. Seward – to join in the discussion.

Only two of the Secretaries objected to this plan. Chase could see no point in facing the cabinet with their senatorial accusers. "Bates knew of no good that could come of an interview." Both these statesmen, as explained above, had good reasons for opposing the President's proposal. Other cabinet members, perhaps with a little malice – for Chase was not popular with his colleagues – warmly seconded Lincoln's plan. Welles, who always liked to score on the Secretary of the Treasury, eagerly approved. Blair thought the plan an excellent one, and "finally all acquiesced." Blair and Welles understood Chase's predicament and were awaiting with equanimity his forthcoming experience on the gridiron.

Outwardly, when he met the insurgent Senators that evening, Lincoln was composed and genial, yet there are indications that inwardly he was in one of his melancholic moods. Senator Orville Browning, one of his most intimate friends, had had a few moments' talk with the President just before the session began.

"What do these men want?" Lincoln asked.

"I hardly know, Mr. President, but they are exceedingly violent towards the administration, and what we did yesterday" – he was referring to the Senate caucus – "was the gentlest thing that could be done. We had to do that or worse."

"They wish to get rid of me," Lincoln replied, "and I am sometimes half disposed to gratify them."

Browning protested against this despairing remark.

"We are now on the brink of destruction," Lincoln replied. "It appears to me the Almighty is against us, and I can hardly see a ray of hope."

Again Browning protested the pessimism. "You ought to have crushed the ultra-impracticable men last summer. You could then have done it and escaped these troubles. . . . Mr. Seward appears now to be the special object of hostility. Still I believe he has managed our foreign affairs as well as anyone could have done. Yet they are very bitter against him, and some of them very bitter upon you."

"Why should men believe a lie," Lincoln replied – referring to the charges that Seward dominated the President – "an absurd lie, that could not impose on a child, and cling to it and repeat it in defiance of all evidences to the contrary?"

"The committee is to be up to see me at seven o'clock," Lincoln concluded. "Since I heard last night of the proceedings of the caucus, I have been more distressed than by any event of my life." [3]

In the evening, the senatorial critics arrived at the appointed time. The President informed them that he had summoned his cabinet – except Seward – for a general all-around debate. The six gentlemen then marched solemnly in. This was the first intimation the statesmen from Capitol Hill had received that they were to meet face to face the body that, with one or two exceptions, had fallen under their condemnation. They were surprised and, as the subsequent proceedings disclosed, irritated. Had their frequently expressed preference for the parliamentary system been sincere, however, they should have welcomed this confrontation. Lincoln's informal gathering was, indeed, not precisely the same thing as "question time" in the House of Commons, yet it probably achieved as complete a reproduction of that phenomenon as was possible under the more rigid American system. Often in congressional speeches certain of the Jacobins had expressed a wish that cabinet members could have seats in the national legislature, where they could be submitted to "interpellation." Now, to a degree, their wishes had been gratified. "Here are the statesmen of whom you so disapprove" – Lincoln did not use these precise words, but they represented his attitude – "so let's talk things over face to

[3] Browning, Orville H., *Diary*. Illinois State Historical Library. I, 600–601.

face, as friends and equals, and see if we can reach some settlement of our differences."

The Senators, and perhaps a few members of the cabinet, may have been embarrassed, but Lincoln showed no signs of discomfort. Three of the gentlemen present have left accounts of the proceedings – Welles, Fessenden, and Bates;[4] in all, Lincoln appears as master of the situation, conciliatory but firm, patiently listening to all complaints, but leaving no one in doubt that he regarded the cabinet as his own affair, and was not in the least disposed to submit to dictation by the Senate. As always, Welles was the most admiring. "The President managed his own case, and showed great tact, shrewdness, and ability." Those accustomed to sneer at Lincoln's manners would have been ashamed could they have witnessed the restrained courtesy with which he received these belligerent guests and sought to put them at their ease. He began proceedings by reading the memorandum of grievances which Senator Collamer had put in his hands two evenings previously. He then discussed it at length, defending the Secretary of State. Special attention was paid to the charge that the cabinet was not a unit and was not sufficiently consulted. That it was not called together on all questions Lincoln granted. He instanced decisions that he had made on his sole responsibility. McClellan's reïnstatement after Second Bull Run, the appointment of Halleck as commander in chief, were among the important steps Lincoln granted had been taken without consulting his official advisers. But in the main, Lincoln insisted, the cabinet was a unit. Naturally seven men, all of them of independent thinking and positive character, did not agree on every policy. But there was general acquiescence in measures, once they were decided on. The President could have cited – though none of the records specifically say that he did so – such questions as the Fort Sumter expedition and the *Trent* affair, as matters of supreme importance on which cabinet meetings had been held. That Mr. Seward was in the habit of making vital decisions without presidential approval was denied. Seward submitted to the President practically all his dispatches before sending them to foreign parts. On mere matters of routine Lincoln admitted he was not usually advised and he saw no reason why he should be.

On the question of cabinet consultations a little sprightly debate followed between Fessenden and Blair. The Maine Senator, according to Welles, who evidently enjoyed the altercation, "was skillful, but a little tart; felt, it would seem, more than he cared to say," and harked back to John Quincy Adams. Mr. Adams, as President, apparently did

[4] Welles, *Diary*. I, 197–199. Fessenden, *op. cit.* I, 243–248. Bates, *op. cit.*, pp. 268–270.

submit important measures to cabinet vote, and accepted the judgment of the majority. Blair, who, Welles felt, "spoke earnestly and well," but in Fessenden's estimation "in a long and rambling" manner, dissented from this conception of a "plural executive"; there was only one head of the state: the President might ask opinions of his cabinet members – of one, or of as many as he pleased – but he alone was accountable to the people and all decisions rested with him alone. Blair was so offended by this senatorial interference that he even came to the support of Seward. He and the Secretary of State had differed on many questions, but he "thought him as earnest as anyone in the war" and it would be injurious to the public service to permit him to resign. Blair flatly told the Senate committee that they "had better not meddle in matters of that kind." Bates, who really admired Seward as little as Blair, defended him valiantly, and for the same reason – the Senators were mingling in something that was none of their concern.[5] In a long disquisition on constitutional interpretation, Bates supported Blair's views but in more learned phraseology. Fessenden, in his abstract of the debate, remarks that "Mr. Bates spoke of himself as 'a garrulous old man' and I think there was a general acquiescence in the correctness of the description."

But these discourses on the Constitution did not form the chief object of interest in this little assembly. As always, the personal drama concerned the observers far more than the old-time cabinet practices of John Quincy Adams or Andrew Jackson. And in this concentration of interest it was not Fessenden, or Bates, or Blair, or Sumner, or even Lincoln himself, who commanded universal attention. The man in whose plight all present displayed the liveliest curiosity was the Secretary of the Treasury, Salmon P. Chase. That he was chiefly responsible for this gathering of statesmen everybody knew. The accusations generally hurled against Seward as the "bane" and "evil genius" of Lincoln – the man, as Lincoln himself said, generally regarded as the one who, whenever the President had a decent impulse, "managed to suck it out of him" – had originated, in large part, with Chase. There was probably not a Senator in Lincoln's sanctum on this momentous evening who had not heard many times, from Chase's own lips, the commentaries on Lincoln, Seward, and his other cabinet colleagues which formed the basis of the indictment. No one understood that fact more completely than Lincoln himself. His main motive in bringing together the statesmen from the Capitol and his Secretaries was to force Chase into the open, to put Chase "on the spot." In modern parlance what the President aimed at was a "showdown." After finishing his remarks,

[5] Welles, *Diary*. I, 197–198.

insisting on the unity of the cabinet, Lincoln therefore asked for expressions of opinion on that point from the several cabinet members present. The views he particularly wished to obtain were those of the Secretary of the Treasury. That this put Chase in an awkward dilemma was true, and that was probably Lincoln's intention. Should Chase sustain the President's argument, he would stand disgraced in the eyes of the Senators, who had many times heard him express contrary views. Should he agree with the Senators, he would portray himself as disloyal to his chief and as promoter of the present uprising; such a disclosure would necessitate his withdrawal from the cabinet. Perhaps Lincoln was a little merciless in forcing his Secretary into this position, but he had a reason for doing it.

When the President put this vital question to the cabinet, therefore, Chase was greatly embarrassed. Not only embarrassed, but angry. He would not have come to the session, he replied, if he had known that he was "to be arraigned." According to Bates, he "seemed offended"; and his reply to Lincoln's question was halting and indefinite. His evidence in the case, so far as it has been preserved, was somewhat confused, but on the whole Chase did about the only possible thing in the circumstances. He certainly did not sustain the senatorial accusations, and in general supported his chief. Matters of first importance, Chase said, had usually come before the cabinet, though perhaps "not so fully as might be desired. There had been no want of unity in the cabinet, but a general acquiescence in public measures." Still "he regretted that there was not a more full and thorough consideration and canvass of every important measure in open cabinet." Though Chase's approval of Lincoln's cabinet policy was hedged about by qualifications, his concessions did not please the Senators. Fessenden, in no equable frame of mind, told Chase that he was not being "arraigned." This joint session of cabinet and Senators "had not been arranged by the Senate committee." It "was no movement of ours, nor did we suspect or come here for that purpose." That the President, under the Constitution, need not be bound by the cabinet's advice, Fessenden admitted; he still believed, however, that all important questions should be discussed in full cabinet council. The Senators had no desire to dictate to the President, or in any way to interfere with his prerogatives. The statesman from Maine did come to Chase's relief when Lincoln began to poll the Senators on their views. After this long discussion of Seward's merits, did they still think that his resignation should be accepted? "I do not think it proper to discuss the merits or demerits of a member of the cabinet in the presence of his associates," said Fessenden, ignoring the fact that that is precisely what had been going on for a considerable time, with himself as one of the most voluble disputants. Chase heartily seconded this opinion. "I think members of the cabinet should withdraw," Chase said, and in solemn procession they filed out of the room.

It had been a most unpleasant experience for the Treasury head, and he lost prestige with his brother radicals from that time forward. They regarded him as something of a renegade – as having deserted them at a critical time. He had incited, directly or indirectly, this frontal attack on the cabinet, which was also, of course, an attack on Lincoln, yet had backed down when the President called upon him to make his position known. Nicolay and Hay have recorded Lyman Trumbull's displeasure at the Secretary's conduct. "As the Senators were retiring, Mr. Trumbull paused for a moment at the door, then turning, walked directly back to the President and said to him privately, but with great vehemence, that the Secretary of the Treasury had held a very different tone the last time he had spoken with him."[6] "It struck me," Fessenden wrote in his memorandum, "that Mr. Chase seemed to have very much modified his opinions, often previously expressed to me, as to Mr. Seward's influence on the mind of the President, and the want of unity in the cabinet." In a letter to his family, the Maine statesman waxed more emphatic. "The story of the last few days will make a new point in history, for it has witnessed a new proceeding – one probably unknown to the government of the country. Had all men on whom we had a right to rely proved brave and true, and forgotten themselves in their love of country, I think it would have been productive of great good. As it is the result will be to unmask some selfish cowards and perhaps frighten them into good behavior." At least two of Chase's cabinet colleagues expressed disgust with his double attitude. Smith told Fessenden that he had been tempted to contradict Mr. Chase on the spot, but, as he expected to leave the cabinet very soon, concluded to be silent.

Stanton referred to his favorite cabinet ally in unfraternal language. At the joint session the wily Secretary of War had kept silent, neither repeating in the Senators' presence the violent criticisms of Lincoln and his associates which he had many times made to them personally, nor accepting Lincoln's invitation to confirm the President's analysis of the situation. The next day, however, in a private talk with Fessenden, he unbosomed himself freely. "He remarked," wrote the Senator, "that the interview the evening before was the most impressive scene he had ever witnessed, and that he was particularly struck by the dignity and propriety exhibited by the senators and disgusted with the cabinet; that what the senators had said about the manner of doing business in

[6] Nicolay and Hay, *op. cit.* VI, 267.

the cabinet was true, and *he* did not mean to lie about it; that he was ashamed of Chase, for he knew better." Senator Collamer was even more explicit than Stanton in his disgust at Chase. The Diary of Orville H. Browning contains a succinct passage setting forth Collamer's judgment on the Secretary of the Treasury. Browning, relating the proceedings at the senatorial caucus to Lincoln, had unhesitatingly put his finger on the instigator. "The attack in the Senate caucus upon Mr. Seward," he told the President, was by the partisans of Mr. Chase and he had reason to believe "that he had set them on." Their game was to drive all the cabinet out – then force upon him Mr. Chase as Premier, and form a cabinet of ultra men around him. Lincoln said that he was master and that they should not do that. Why had Chase, after inspiring the revolt, weakly forsaken his senatorial allies and taken refuge on the side of the President? That was the question Browning had put forth to Senator Collamer. "I asked Judge Collamer how Mr. Chase could make such a statement" – that is, that the cabinet was a harmonious body – "in the presence of senators to whom he had said that Seward exercised a back-stairs and malign influence upon the President and thwarted all measures of the cabinet. He answered: 'He lied.'"[7]

Stanton went to extremes in his attempt to keep the news of Seward's resignation out of the public prints. Though Washington, as Bates noted, was "all a-buzz" with stories, true and false, about the disturbance – some said that all the cabinet had resigned, others that the President had abdicated – and speculation as to a cabinet about to be formed was prevalent in all quarters, Stanton clamped down the censorship and prohibited the telegraph from sending the news broadcast. When, three days after the excitement had subsided and the New York papers finally published an account of the affair, Chase came in for a severe grilling. The *New York Herald* denounced him as the "Mephistopheles" of the cabinet. He "had been the prime mover in all the radical schemes and an active co-worker with his confederates in the Senate against Mr. Seward."

Despite his backwoods manner, there was an element of subtlety in Lincoln, and not improbably his real motive in unmasking Chase did not appear upon the surface. The one thing he desired to obtain, above all, was Chase's resignation. Not that Lincoln wished to separate the Secretary from the cabinet at that time. But Chase's resignation would be of the utmost value in solving the issue in a satisfactory way. To have Chase and Seward on an equality, so far as their relation to the cabinet was concerned, would greatly facilitate the negotiations. To

[7] Browning, *op. cit.* I, 603.

have the resignations of the two chief men safely in Lincoln's hand would make him master of the crisis. In that event, he could not accept one without accepting the other. Seward represented the conservatives in the Republican Party, Chase the radicals; to accept the resignation of Seward would be to hand the government over to the Jacobins; to accept that of Chase would be to take a stand exclusively on the side of the conservatives. But Lincoln had no wish for a decision that would make him adopt one wing of the party and desert the other. Internal conflicts over the conduct of the war and its aims, now extending over nearly two years, had reached a more demoralizing climax than ever. Profoundly as the radicals were displeased with the way Chase had deserted them at this evening session, they would have been outraged had the episode ended in his elimination from the cabinet and the retention of Seward. Such an outcome would have been a melancholy conclusion of all their contrivings. They would have lost the one man in Lincoln's inner circle who represented their point of view and their whole uprising would merely have rebounded against themselves. Stanton would still have remained, it is true, but, much as the Jacobins valued his adhesion to their cause, they distrusted him, as did everybody else, and regarded him as a rather slippery reliance.

Not improbably Lincoln, with that shrewdness which Welles so admired, had deliberately maneuvered Chase into a position where his resignation became inevitable. At any rate that was the result. The Secretary of the Treasury, smarting from the undignified role he had played before the Senators, went home and wrote his resignation. The next morning he entered Lincoln's office with the paper concealed in his pocket. Gideon Welles has described the scene that ensued.[8] The head of the Navy had spent a sleepless night, turning over the rights and wrongs of the two parties to the dispute. He admired Seward no more than did Blair, but no more than Blair did he believe that a senatorial cabal should force his retirement from the administration. "A senatorial combination to dictate to the President in regard to his political family in the height of a civil war which threatens the existence of the Republic cannot be permitted to succeed, even if the person to whom they object were as obnoxious as they represent; but Seward's foibles are not serious failings." The next morning Welles repaired to the White House as soon as he thought that the President had breakfasted. Lincoln, he advised, should not accept Seward's resignation. To yield to a party in the Senate on what was exclusively an executive function "would be an evil example and fraught with incalculable injury to the government and the country." Lincoln, much

[8] Welles, *Diary*. I, 199.

gratified, said that such was his view. If he let the Senators have their way, "the whole government must cave in; it could not stand, could not hold water; the bottom would be out."

Later that same morning Welles returned to the President's office, where he found Chase and Stanton. Lincoln presently came in. The four men grouped themselves around the fire, Chase and Stanton facing it, Lincoln at one side, while Welles sat on a sofa near the east window. Chase began complaining of his harrowing experience the preceding evening. It had been a total surprise to him – so he said – and had affected him most painfully. In fact, he had prepared his resignation as Secretary of the Treasury. If Chase had expected this announcement to startle the President, he was quickly undeceived. Lincoln's face lighted up with eagerness.

"Where is it?" he asked.

"I brought it with me," Chase answered, taking a paper from his pocket.

"Let me have it," said Lincoln, reaching his long arm and bony fingers in Chase's direction.

Chase half drew the paper back. Lincoln rose, and almost ripped the document from Chase's reluctant hand. Lincoln tore the envelope hastily and read: "Sir: I resign the office of Secretary of the Treasury which I have had the honor to hold under your appointment. Whatever service my successor may desire of me in making him acquainted with the conditions and operations of the department will be most cheerfully rendered. Yours truly, S. P. Chase."

Lincoln could not conceal his delight. He glanced towards Welles with what the latter described as "a triumphal laugh." "This cuts the Gordian knot. I can dispose of this subject now without difficulty. I see my way clear." Then Stanton spoke up in his most solemn manner. "Mr. President, I informed you day before yesterday that I was ready to tender you my resignation. I wish you, sir, to consider my resignation at this time in your possession." But Lincoln waved him gaily aside. "You may go to your department," he said. "I don't want yours. This" – and he held out Chase's letter – "is all I want; this relieves me; the case is clear, the trouble is ended. I will detain neither of you longer." Lincoln used several other characteristic expressions – inheritance of his pioneer days in Illinois – to express his delight at the success of his maneuver. "Now I have the biggest half of the hog," he told one friend, and to others he summed up the situation in one of the most apt metaphors of his career. "Now I can ride; I have got a pumpkin in each end of my bag." The illustration calls up one of the familiar sights of pioneer days in the West: the farmer riding horseback to market, with a bag containing pumpkins; obviously, if he had one in each end of the receptacle, the balance would be complete. A year afterward, recalling the transaction, Lincoln declared: "I do not see how it could have been done better. I am sure it was right. If I had yielded to that storm and dismissed Seward the thing would have all slumped over one way, and we should have been left with a scant handful of supporters. When Chase gave in his resignation I saw that the game was in my hands and I put it through." [9]

With these two resignations in hand the problem was quickly adjusted. Lincoln emphasized his impartiality by writing a note, jointly addressed to the two Secretaries, declining to permit them to leave the cabinet, and insisting that the services of both were needed for the successful prosecution of the war. The President sincerely believed this. Despite their temperamental differences, and the annoyances they caused the administration, Lincoln admired the way Seward and Chase were conducting the State Department and the Treasury. One of the main advantages of this amicable settlement – for both accepted Lincoln's solution and returned to the White House council table – was that it retained in the Federal service two men of great ability in their respective offices whom it would have been difficult at that time to replace. Other permanent benefits accrued. The attack that was to destroy the administration resulted in knitting it in closer harmony than it had previously known. From now forward, if the administration did not become a unit in the sense the Jacobins desired, it did become one in the Lincolnian sense. The effort to substitute an all-radical cabinet in place of the coalition had failed, and failed definitely. Though the Jacobin element did not cease its onslaughts on Lincoln for his conciliatory attitude towards the South, its failure in December 1862 proved to be a discouraging setback. If Lincoln did not remain complete master of his party, he certainly did remain the undisputed ruler of the executive department.

The incident similarly brought Seward and Chase closer together. Up to this time they had regarded themselves more or less as rivals for the presidential succession. On this ambition Seward's hopes were not so fondly set as Chase's, but the disappointment of 1860 had not been finally assuaged, and if Lincoln, as was perhaps the general belief at that time, could not survive more than one term, Seward could think of no one so entitled to the succession as himself. But any expectation Seward may have cherished up to this time was dashed when all the Republican Senators except Preston King turned against him. The discouraging lesson Seward now took to heart was that he no longer

[9] Nicolay and Hay, *op. cit.* VI, 271.

had any political following in the Republican Party. His only possible future was as second man to Lincoln. His loyalty to Lincoln acquired a new zeal, and single-minded devotion to his official duties, rather than conciliatory gestures towards the South, became his one interest. Chase did not abandon his ambitions, it is true, but the episode had greatly weakened his chances of success. He had lost caste with the radical forces who had been his main reliance.

As for Lincoln, he emerged with greatly enhanced prestige. This "prairie lawyer" had proved to be a handler-of-men of previously unsuspected power. He had confronted the rebels in his own cabinet and all the Republicans in the Senate and had defeated the machinations of both. The eulogy of his admiring secretaries, Nicolay and Hay, close inspectors of the whole proceeding, was not undeserved. "The untrained diplomatist of Illinois had thus met and conjured away, with unsurpassed courage and skill, one of the severest crises that ever threatened the integrity of his administration. He had to meet it absolutely unaided; from the nature of the case he could take no advice from those who were nearest him in the government. By his bold and original expedient of confronting the senators with the cabinet, and having them discuss their mutual understandings under his own eye, he cleared up many dangerous misconceptions, and, as usually happens when both parties are men of intelligence and good will, brought about a friendlier and more considerate feeling between his government and the Republican leaders than had ever before existed. By placing Mr. Chase in such an attitude that his resignation became necessary to his own sense of dignity, he made himself absolute master of the situation; by treating the resignations and the return to the cabinet of both ministers as one and the same transaction he saved for the nation the invaluable services of both, and preserved his own position of entire impartiality between the two wings of the party." [10]

One change in the cabinet did take place at this time, though it was unrelated to the general crisis. Caleb Blood Smith, who had obtained the Interior Department as the result of a bargain made by David Davis and Leonard Swett, had for some time been bored by his inconspicuous duties and perhaps the unimportant part he was playing in public affairs. Lincoln solved this problem in characteristic fashion. In December 1862, he appointed Smith judge of the United States District Court of Indiana, a position for which he was well fitted, being an excellent lawyer. Smith enjoyed his new duties for only a little more than a year, dying in January 1864. Lincoln promoted to the vacant cabinet

[10] Nicolay and Hay, *op. cit.* VI, 270–271.

post John Palmer Usher, who for some time had been Assistant Secretary of the Interior. Usher was an Indiana lawyer who had once ridden the eighth circuit with Lincoln. He had been an earnest Republican from the founding of the party, but up to his appointment to the cabinet had filled no important legislative or executive office.

III

ON SUNDAY, the 13th of July, 1862," wrote Gideon Welles, "President Lincoln invited me to accompany him in his carriage to the funeral of an infant child of Mr. Stanton. Secretary Seward and Mrs. Frederick Seward were also in the carriage. . . . It was on this occasion and on this ride that he first mentioned to Mr. Seward and myself the subject of emancipating the slaves by proclamation in case the Rebels did not cease to persist in their war on the government and the Union, of which he saw no evidence. He dwelt earnestly on the gravity, importance, and delicacy of the movement, said he had given it much thought and had about come to the conclusion that it was a military necessity absolutely essential for the salvation of the Union, that we must free the slaves or be ourselves subdued. This was, he said, the first occasion when he had mentioned the subject to any one, and wished us to frankly state how the proposition struck us. Mr. Seward said that the subject involved consequences so vast and momentous that he should wish to bestow on it mature reflection before giving a decisive answer, but his present opinion inclined to the measure as justifiable, and perhaps he might say, expedient and necessary. These were also my views. Two or three times on that ride the subject, which was of course an absorbing one for each and all, was reverted to, and before separating the President desired us to give the question special and deliberate attention, for he was earnest in the conviction that something must be done. It was a new departure for the President, for until this time, in all our previous interviews whenever the question of the emancipation or mitigation of slavery had been in any way alluded to, he had been prompt and emphatic in denouncing any interference by the general government with the subject. This, I think, was the sentiment of every member of the cabinet." [1]

And so the question which for a year and a half had split the Republican Party in two had at last come to a decision. Behind all the ferocious assaults of the radicals – the warfare on McClellan, the senatorial

[1] Welles, *Diary*. I, 70–71.

uprising of December, the wranglings over the army command, the angry debates in Congress, and the dissensions within the cabinet itself — had stalked the shadowy but still distinct figure of the black man. The war had found this disturbing character a slave; how was it to leave him? The patient, plaintive laborer had been the cause of the conflict; what effect would it have upon his fortunes? Lincoln settled this question, at least in part, when on July 22, amid all the gloom of military disasters, he called his cabinet, took from his pocket a carefully guarded paper, and read its fateful contents. What the startled gentlemen listened to was a document which, though it comprised less than five hundred words, was probably the most momentous state paper that had seen the light since the adoption of the Federal Constitution. The gist of it was brief and to the point: on the first day of January 1863, he, Abraham Lincoln, acting solely on his responsibility as President of the United States and Commander in Chief of the Army and Navy, would issue a proclamation, declaring that "all persons held as slaves," within any states at that time in rebellion against the Federal government, "shall then, thenceforward, and forever be free." On September 22, five days after the battle of Antietam, Lincoln made public this edict, or one that substantially resembled it, and on January 1 it duly became the law of the land. Up to the time of that first reading, on July 22, only two members of the cabinet — William H. Seward and Gideon Welles — had known anything of the President's intention. All during the contentions described in preceding pages, the Proclamation, in one form or another, had lain on Lincoln's desk, awaiting the moment when it could most effectively be given to the world.

In his masterly letter to Horace Greeley of August 22, written at a time when his course had been already decided, Lincoln reiterated that he was waging war not to destroy slavery, but to save the Union. Whatever steps he might or might not take on that question, he declared, would be taken exclusively with this great purpose in mind. His proclamation indicated no departure from that assertion. If he could save the Union by freeing all the slaves, Lincoln had said, he would do that; if he could save it by freeing none, he would adopt that program; if he could save it by freeing some and leaving the rest in bondage, he would follow this middle course. It was the third alternative that seemed the wisest in July and September. Lincoln's preliminary and final proclamation set "forever free" the slaves of the regions still in rebellion but did not free those of the Border states. There were two excellent reasons for this discrimination. In the first place, Lincoln had no constitutional power over the property of states not at war with the Union. Under the Constitution, slavery was exclusively a

Reading of the First Emancipation Proclamation, July 22, 1862

Painting by Francis B. Carpenter, now hanging in the old Supreme Court Chamber, the Capitol, Washington. This, the artist's final revision, differs in several important details from the engravings in general circulation

Left to right: Stanton, Chase, Lincoln, Welles, Smith, Seward, Blair, Bates

Edward Bates (1793–1869)
Attorney General

state prerogative over which the Federal government had no jurisdiction. Only, the military power could be invoked, and that only against the states in rebellion; it could not be used against the loyal slave states, since they were not engaged in war against the Federal government. Thus, had Lincoln desired to do so, he could not have extended emancipation over Delaware, Maryland, Kentucky, western Virginia, and Missouri; in fact he had no such desire. Such an act would have contravened his steadfast policy of conciliating these states and strengthening their loyalty to the Union. The Federal government, under military necessity, could seize the human property of citizens engaged in treason, just as it could seize their horses, cattle, pigs, and materials of war. Once having seized these chattels, it could dispose of them in the way most useful in the prosecution of the war – and it chose to transform them into freemen. Properly considered, Lincoln's historic edict was thus first an act of confiscation, and secondly of manumission.

Both the proclamations – that of July 22 and that of September 22, for the document issued on January 1, 1863, was merely an addendum to the latter – embodied Lincoln's solution for the difficult problem of slavery. They offered the areas that were in arms against the Federal government two alternatives. If they returned to their old allegiance by January 1, they would be permitted to retain their favorite domestic institution, the ultimate destiny of which was to be left to the civilizing processes of time. If they should resume "their constitutional relations" to the central power at Washington and simultaneously abolish slavery, they would be compensated for their surrendered property, presumably at the rate of $400 a head. If they declined either of these alternatives, then their 4,000,000 Negroes were to be "forever free." The cabinet meetings at which these papers were proposed and discussed have been frequently described. The surprise of the department heads at the presentation of the preliminary paper; Seward's proposal that it be postponed until a military success had crowned the Federal army; Lincoln's acceptance of the suggestion; the President's introducing the second debate on the subject by reading a chapter from Artemus Ward; Stanton's indignation and Chase's pained surprise at the apparent levity; Chase's amendment that some recognition of the favor of God should be incorporated in the Proclamation, an amendment that Lincoln accepted – all this is a long-familiar story. The cabinet had really little to do with the conception or formulation of this measure. It was, except for a few minor suggestions, exclusively Lincoln's work. None of his acts so completely embodied his conception of presidential responsibility.

The President's critics in the Senate who had complained that Lincoln made important decisions without consulting his cabinet – and that, indeed, he declined to regard that aggregation as an executive council, with authority almost equal to his own – could have found their most impressive illustration in this instance. For more than a year, the subject of emancipation had been revolving in Lincoln's mind; he had discussed it with intimates, inside the cabinet and out. He had been closely following the argument in Congress and the press and had been attentively listening to visiting delegations, urging action one way or another. But none of these several exponents of public opinion had obtained any inkling as to his decision. Before reading the momentous paper to the cabinet, Lincoln emphasized the fact that the act was his own. He had settled the question, he declared, in his own conscience and did not wish their advice as to its propriety and wisdom.

"The President states," records Gideon Welles, "that the question was finally decided, the act and the consequences were his, but that he felt it due to us to make us acquainted with the fact, and to invite criticism on the paper which he had prepared. There were, he had found, not unexpectedly, some differences in the cabinet, but he had, after ascertaining in his own way, the views of each and all, individually and collectively, formed his own conclusions and made his own decisions." [2] "I have got you together to hear what I have written down," writes Chase, quoting the President's very words in his account, which for once is much more graphic and complete than that of his fellow diarist of the Navy Department. "I do not wish your advice about the main matter – for that I have determined for myself. This I say without intending anything but respect for any of you. But I already know the views of each upon this question. They have been heretofore expressed and I have considered them as thoroughly as I can. What I have written is that which my reflections have determined me to say. If there is anything in the expressions I use, or in any other minor matter, which any one of you think had best be changed, I shall be glad to receive the suggestions. . . . I am here. I must do the best I can, and bear the responsibility of taking the course which I feel I ought to take." [3]

The precise moment when Lincoln's decision to issue the Proclamation had been made is something, of course, that cannot be determined. On the general conviction that the time must come when the slave should be liberated he had from the first completely agreed with the most ardent radical. In a theoretical sense, he knew when the moment

[2] Welles, *Diary*. I, 143

[3] American Historical Association. *Diary and Correspondence of Salmon P. Chase*. Annual Report, 1902. II, 88.

for action would arrive. That would be the time when such an extreme measure would most effectively promote the cause to which, above all, Lincoln had dedicated himself – the preservation of the Union. He had resisted all the exhortations of radicals and humanitarians for a year and more, knowing that the action they proposed was premature and premature emancipation, Lincoln had always insisted, would have defeated the purpose at which he aimed. Had the Proclamation been issued six months before it was actually given to the world, Lincoln told the artist Carpenter, it would have worked great injury to the cause. In early July 1862, however, the President concluded that the moment had come to deprive the South of its most powerful instrument of warfare. The McClellan disasters in the Peninsula had much to do with this decision. "It had got to be midsummer, 1862" – so Carpenter quotes Lincoln. "Things had gone on from bad to worse, until I had felt that we had reached the end of our rope on the plan of operations we had been pursuing; that we had played our last card, and must change our tactics or lose the game. I now determined upon the adoption of the emancipation policy; and, without consultation with, or knowledge of the cabinet, I prepared the original draft, and, after much anxious thought, called a cabinet meeting on the subject." [4]

However, the President's casual remarks to an artist engaged in painting his picture did not tell the whole story. While the military situation in Virginia might be desperate, in other parts of the embattled region things were fairly prosperous. In the pivotal Border states, for example, conditions had vastly improved. The Federal troops, by completely defeating the pro-Confederacy forces in Missouri, had removed that region from the list of states of doubtful loyalty. Missouri was now securely anchored to the Union, beyond the power of the secession elements to dislodge it. Grant's victories in Kentucky and on the Tennessee and Cumberland Rivers had sealed the Federal triumph in that strategic region. How definitely Maryland had taken its place on the side of the Union was shown two months afterward, when Lee attempted unsuccessfully to invade it. He came, the Confederate commander told Marylanders in a proclamation, to free them from the "oppressor," and he invited them to rise, flock to his arms, and join the confederacy. Fewer than one hundred men had accepted the invitation; the great mass of the people seemed perfectly content in their "subjection" to Federal rule. Thus by July 1862, and even more emphatically in September, the Border states were strongly allied to the Union cause and no fear existed that emancipation would alienate them – especially

[4] Carpenter, *op. cit.*, p. 20.

as the measure affected only the regions in rebellion, and left the institution of slavery in the loyal states precisely where it had been before.

The foreign situation, in the summer and fall of 1862, had reached a critical stage. Confederate recognition by Great Britain and France was assuming more ominous proportions every day. Lincoln's declaration to Horace Greeley that he was waging war not to end slavery, but to save the Union, gave the English supporters of the South a powerful argument. The masses in both Britain and France had sympathized with the North chiefly because they hated slavery. But, Confederate apologists in England and France urged, Lincoln, according to his own declaration, was fighting not for freedom of the black but for power — not to end an abominable social evil, but to secure the dominance of the North. Gladstone advocated, practically openly, the admission of the "nation" that Jefferson Davis had made to fellowship with Great Britain; Russell, the Foreign Secretary, as his correspondence with Palmerston shows, had settled his mind on recognition. Emancipation, Lincoln knew, would end this agitation at once and forever make its renewal impossible. Political considerations at home also had their influence. The question of the black man was threatening the integrity of the Republican Party. In both House and Senate the champions of the slave, and of his immediate freedom, had an overwhelming majority. Lincoln, the supreme politician and party manager, realized that he could not much longer preserve Republican solidarity, indispensable to success in war, without taking this forward step. The statement is sometimes made that the Jacobins had at last forced the President's hand, and to an extent this is true, but the political situation on Capitol Hill was only one of the reasons, and not the most important, that persuaded Lincoln to take decisive action.

Yet when the President, on July 22, read his first preliminary proclamation to his cabinet, only two of his advisers gave it their wholehearted assent. The septuagenarian Edward Bates, the most conservative and "fossilized" of them all, the Virginia-born jurist who for a lifetime had held, for the most part, the opinions of his native state on the Negro, expressed approval. He particularly liked Lincoln's recommendation for deportation of the ex-slaves. "He dreaded any step which should be taken to bring about social equality between the two races. The effect, he said, would be to degrade the whites without elevating the blacks. Demoralization, vice and misery would follow." [5] Stanton was the other cabinet member who showed no hesitation. From the beginning the Secretary of War had promoted the radical interest, of which emancipation was the leading item; besides, Stanton, as head of military af-

[5] Welles, *Diary*. I, 158.

fairs, understood its importance better than his colleagues. From Stanton's first day in the War Department, the strength which the Confederacy derived from its slave population had impressed and appalled him. Probably no nation had ever possessed such a powerful prop to military operations. The slaves for the larger part remained at home, cultivating the farms, raising food and caring for the wives and children left behind. This placed the entire white male population at the disposition of the recruiting officer. Slavery thus gave the Confederacy an immense advantage over the North, where a large proportion of the men must be left at home to provide for the domestic and military economy. In the Northern armies again able-bodied soldiers by the tens of thousands were necessarily set aside for nonmilitary duties such as digging entrenchments, building fortifications, acting as teamsters, cooks, and the like. In the Southern forces these essential services were performed by slaves, and all the white men could be used as combatants. If these slaves, or a considerable part of them, could be appropriated for the Northern armies, the South, to the extent of the appropriation, would be weakened in military power, and the North correspondingly strengthened. How could such a shift in resources be brought to pass? Whenever the Northern armies approached the region of serfdom, the black folk had already shown an eagerness to abandon their allegiances, leave home, and enter territories under Federal control. To stimulate this migration, emancipation would offer the two inducements that appeal most eloquently to human nature. Such *émigrés* would be assured of their freedom and be paid wages for their labor. As the Northern armies advanced into rebel territory, the newly conquered domain would become in fact, as it was under the proclamation in theory, free. Vast human resources would be lost to the Confederates and transferred to the Federals.

In his report for 1862, Stanton had given a graphic illustration of the anticipated benefits. The sea cotton islands lying off the coast of South Carolina, then in control of the Federal armies, could supply forage enough for the whole department of the South – South Carolina, Georgia, and Florida. Under prevailing conditions the Federal armies had to draw these supplies from Northern ports, entailing a serious problem of transportation. But it was very difficult to get the Negroes on the islands to supply the labor. Give these Negroes their freedom, however, and the protection of Northern troops, and the problem of labor and supplies would be solved. "By striking down this system of compulsory labor," said Stanton, "which enables the leaders of the rebellion to control the resources of the people, the rebellion would die of itself."

That Stanton would immediately assent to the new measure, which aimed to accomplish the very destruction of the labor system he had demanded, could therefore be taken for granted. Stanton himself hastily made notes of the proceedings at that first discussion of July 22 – a valuable document that still exists in his hurried backhanded scrawl among his voluminous papers. "The Attorney-General and Stanton are for its immediate promulgation," this paper says, referring to the first session on the Proclamation of July 22, but no such definite commitments are recorded for Stanton's colleagues. Welles apparently received the proposal in silence though subsequently he gave it loyal support. Blair – this fact, however, Stanton's memorandum does not record – opposed it on political grounds. Blair was not present when the session began, but came in before it was finished. He was an emancipationist from principle, he announced, but he thought the time badly taken; it would give the Democrats a club with which to beat the administration at the polls. Smith vigorously argued against the document on the same practical grounds. His Assistant Secretary, soon to be his successor, John P. Usher, quotes him as saying that if Lincoln issued such a rescript, "I will resign and go home and attack the administration." [6]

While the objections of Blair and Smith were not based on the highest grounds, they proved to be good prophets, for emancipation doubtless did exercise an important influence on the misfortunes that overwhelmed the Lincolnian party in November.

The strangest feature of this first session was the lack of enthusiasm displayed by Chase. Of all men close to Lincoln, the Secretary of the Treasury, for the last two years, had been the most outspoken apostle of freedom and enfranchisement for the African. But, according to one part of Stanton's memorandum, Chase was "silent," and in another page it says that "Chase thinks it a measure of great danger and would lead to universal emancipation. The measure goes beyond anything I [Chase] have recommended." Chase had always endorsed the proclamations of his favorite generals, but this sweeping ukase from the one man who had the authority to take such action evidently left him cold. The conclusion seems justified that Chase, although he desired emancipation, did not desire it by act of Abraham Lincoln. He wished it to be done piecemeal by military commanders in the respective districts. The precedents set by Frémont and Ben Butler this great champion of the Negro still believed to be the ideal way of approaching a momentous national problem. That the Secretary of the Treasury was already laying plans for the presidential nomination in 1864 necessarily arouses suspicion of his motives. Was Chase relying upon freedom for the Ne-

[6] Usher, John P., *President Lincoln's Cabinet.* Nelson H. Loomis, 1925. P. 17.

groes as the issue on which he hoped to win, and did this aspiration explain his unzealous reception of the document? The insinuation may seem unworthy but it is set forth in plainer terms by that merciless analyst of his colleagues' character, Gideon Welles. "The subject should not become mixed with party issues," old Neptune notes in his Diary for August 22, 1863, "but yet it can scarcely be avoided. Chase gathers it into the coming presidential election; feels that the measure of emancipation, which was decided without first consulting him, has placed the President in advance of him in a path which was his specialty."

IV

PERHAPS OTHER grounds would explain the hesitation of Chase. The Proclamation in its two separate forms – that of July 22 and of September 22 – contemplated indemnity for slaves to all states adopting emancipation, including such states then in rebellion as should return to their Federal allegiance. Chase was opposed to compensated emancipation; he agreed with the abolitionist view that this was giving malefactors payment for the restoration of stolen goods. Colonization, which Lincoln had been advocating for a long time, the Secretary also disapproved. His treatment for the Negro insisted on his elevation, so far as civil rights and citizenship were concerned, to an equality with the whites. "How much better," he said, "would be a manly protest against prejudice against color! And a wise effort to give freemen homes in America! A military officer, emancipating at least the slaves of South Carolina, Georgia, and the Gulf States" – the reference, of course, is to General Hunter, who had attempted that very thing – "would do more to terminate the war and ensure an early restoration of solid peace and prosperity than anything else that can be devised." Chase confided this view to his Diary[1] on August 15 – about a month after Lincoln had informed his cabinet of his intention; any proper scheme of emancipation, he said, should lay the basis for "ultimate enfranchisement," and he was stronger than ever for enlisting Negroes in the armies. For such extreme measure Lincoln's proclamation made no provision, nor did the President conceal his opposition to giving the Negro the vote at this time. Still, lukewarm as Chase may have been towards the decree, he still accepted it as better than nothing. After setting forth his views in a cabinet meeting on August 3,[2] he concluded that he "regarded this as so much better than inaction on the subject that I should give it my entire support," and by January, when the final document received the seal of the United States, he surveyed the completed work with satisfaction. His attitude somewhat resembled that of William Lloyd Garri-

[1] Chase, *Diary*, p. 59.
[2] *Ibid.*, p. 54.

son, who looked kindly on the Proclamation as a "step in the right direction" and perhaps even approximated the opinion expressed by Wendell Phillips when told of Garrison's faint praise. "A step!" retorted this extremist. "It's a stride!"

Gideon Welles, at first hesitant, came around slowly to cordial approbation. The edict had troubled him from the first on constitutional grounds. To him it seemed "an arbitrary and despotic measure in the cause of freedom." This doubt explained this Yankee's reluctance to give an opinion when Lincoln, at the Stanton funeral, sounded him on the subject and also the silence with which he had received the first reading in July. The Constitution gave the Executive no such autocratic power, Welles believed, the act resting solely upon Lincoln's authority as commander in chief; in other words, the Proclamation was not an executive but a military prerogative; and these considerations would naturally give pause to a thinker who, throughout his whole life as journalist and public man, had strongly supported the doctrines of State rights and strict construction. However, with Welles, this proved to be only a passing phase. At the September cabinet meeting, Stanton, after speaking in favor of immediate emancipation, with all the fervent eagerness of his nature, turned with some irritation towards Chase and Welles. Two members of the cabinet, he said, had not spoken. Then the Secretary of the Navy explained briefly the constitutional reasons for his hesitation. But, he concluded, "the Rebels themselves had invoked war on the subject of slavery, had appealed to arms and they must abide the consequences. It was an extreme exercise of war powers, and under the circumstances and in view of the condition of the country and the magnitude of the contest I was willing to resort to extreme measures and avail ourselves of military necessity, always harsh and questionable." From this attitude of moderation, as years went on, Welles went to the most heartfelt appreciation. The time came when he estimated the Proclamation as the supreme achievement of Lincoln's career, and as one of the greatest acts in modern history. In 1874, twelve years after the signing, when Welles, long after retirement from the cabinet, was spending a meditative old age in Hartford, Connecticut, pondering the great episodes of which he had been a part and committing his recollections to paper, he set forth his mature convictions on this subject. "The distinctive measure of Mr. Lincoln's administration, beyond all others, that makes it an era in our national history, is the decree of emancipation. Results have proved that there was in the measure thought, statesmanship, courage and far-seeing sagacity—consummate executive and administrative ability which was after some reverses crowned with success. The nation, emerging from gloom and disaster, and the whole civilized world, united in awarding honor and gratitude to the illustrious man who had the mind to conceive and the firmness to decree the emancipation of a race." [3]

But the most important member of the cabinet held no such exalted view of Lincoln's act. For Seward's position we are indebted again to that industrious compiler of Lincoln memoranda, the artist Francis B. Carpenter. In the course of his work on the emancipation picture, Carpenter came frequently into association with the Secretary of State. "I told the President the other day," Seward remarked at one of these meetings, "that you were painting your picture upon a false assumption." The bewildered artist asked for an explanation. "You appear to think," Seward explained, "in common with many other foolish people, that the great business of this administration is the destruction of slavery. Now allow me to say that you are much mistaken. . . . Had you consulted me on a subject to paint, I should not have given you the Cabinet Council on Emancipation, but the meeting which took place when the news came of the attack upon Sumter, when the first measures were organized for the restoration of the national authority. That was the crisis in the history of this administration – not the issue of the Emancipation Proclamation." [4] Seward's behavior at the time accords with this opinion. Again that distinguishing trait of his character comes to the surface – the tendency to hesitate, to take both sides of a question, to compromise. One would have thought that Seward, having the control of foreign affairs in his hands, would have promptly hailed the proposal. One of Lincoln's purposes was to ease the foreign situation and make impossible that recognition of the Confederacy which was imminent in the summer and fall of 1862.

Seward did indeed show interest from the standpoint of foreign relations, but in a way precisely opposed to Lincoln's intention. The Secretary of State at first deprecated emancipation on the strange ground that it would injure our standing in Europe. The universal dislike of slavery that prevailed on the Continent he disregarded. Seward believed that the one and only interest Britain and France had in the contest was a material one. In their eyes – so he insisted – the United States was important only as a source of cotton; for these nations there were no principles involved; anything that increased the supply of this essential material would receive their approval and anything that diminished it would arouse their hostility. Emancipation, in Lincoln's view, would destroy the Southern labor system, and thus would be an excellent

[3] Welles, *Lincoln and Seward*. Pp. 204–207.

[4] Gideon Welles also gives an account of this conversation, which took place at his house but not in his hearing. See *Diary*, I, 549.

thing; Seward agreed that it would handicap Southern agriculture, and for that very reason he looked upon it unfavorably. The British governing classes and their commercial and financial allies hated the North, above all, because the war, by depriving their spindles of cotton, had created vast unemployment and put millions of people on public relief; the Proclamation would make conditions worse, and still further stimulate the demand for recognition. Two days after Lincoln had submitted his original paper, Seward wrote John Lothrop Motley, minister to Austria, inquiring: "Are you sure that today, under the seductions and pressures that could be applied to some European powers, they would not rise up and resist an attempt to bestow freedom upon the laborers whose capacity to supply cotton and open a market for European fabrics depends, or is thought to depend, upon their continuance in bondage?" Motley's almost thunderous negation, "A thousand times No!" was evidently not exactly the response which Seward had hoped to elicit.

Stanton's hurried memorandum of that first discussion again makes clear Seward's scarcely concealed hostility to Lincoln's edict. "Seward argues," Stanton jotted down, "that foreign nations will intervene to prevent abolition of slavery for the sake of cotton. Argues in a long speech against its immediate promulgation. Wants to wait for troops. Wants drum and fife and public spirit. Wants Halleck here. We break up our relations with foreign nations and the production of cotton for sixty years." Did Seward sincerely believe that foreigners would oppose emancipation for the sake of cotton, or was he using this argument to defeat a measure to which he was naturally hostile? The question is a difficult one. Not improbably Seward was still adhering to his policy of settling the war by propitiation. Lincoln's bold move would certainly forever put an end to this dream. The promise to leave their sacred institution intact had formed the basis of all the conciliatory approaches Seward had made to the Secessionists; and he was still nourishing hopes that, by this and other guarantees, the erring sisters could be brought back into the Union. At times, indeed, Seward spoke approvingly of the Proclamation, particularly in the cabinet sessions called to discuss it; yet a different spirit is manifest in his private letters, written while it was under consideration. These occasionally display, if not an unfriendly disposition towards it, certainly a doubtful and cynical one. "Proclamations are *papers*," he wrote Mrs. Seward on July 29, one week after Lincoln had presented his first version to the cabinet. "It is mournful to see a great nation shrink from a war it has accepted, and insist on adopting proclamations, when it is asked for force. The Chinese do so without success." "The President's proclamation," he wrote his daughter soon after it had been given to the public press, "so long and importunately clamored for by a portion of our people, is out at last. It is now evident that the Proclamation has not been delayed too long. In a short time we shall know whether it has come too soon. I hope that this may not prove to be the case. I was fearful of prematurely giving to the people, prone to divide, occasion for organizing parties, in a crisis which demands union and harmony, in order to save the country from destruction."

At the same time Seward's bantering reference to "proclamations" frequently annoyed more serious colleagues. Thus when Lee was on the brink of invading Pennsylvania, Chase quotes in his Diary Sewards' remark that "some one had proposed that the President should issue a Proclamation . . . freeing all the apprentices of that state." "I thought the jest ill-timed," solemnly comments Chase. Orville H. Browning's Diary notes several talks with Seward, in which the Secretary's opposition to the Proclamation is recorded. Browning, who himself regarded emancipation as a mistake, asked Seward one evening "why the cabinet had done so monstrous a thing as to issue the proclamations." Seward, Lincoln-like, answered with a story. A revolutionary patriot in his section could not rest content, after the establishment of American independence, until he had raised a liberty pole. "What is liberty," he asked, "without a pole?" And so, Seward remarked, between puffs on his cigar, "What is war without a proclamation?"[5] Yet Seward did have his less flippant moods, as is shown in his letter to Charles Francis Adams, written after the final step had been taken. Will Britain and France, he asks, "interfere to strike down the arm that so reluctantly, but so effectively, is raised at last to break the fetters of the slave and seek to rivet anew the chains which he has sundered? Will they recognize the insurgents now and thus seek to commit themselves to maintain slavery among a people when slaves and masters alike agree that it shall no longer exist? Is this to be the climax to the world's progress in the nineteenth century?"

Seward's early caution sheds light upon that famous episode of the first reading – for details of which we are again under obligation to portrait painter Carpenter. Stanton's notes and Seward's own comments show that the Proclamation at this session impressed him unfavorably, and not impossibly his suggestion for postponement was only his way of accomplishing its demise. Seward, Lincoln told Carpenter, said, at the first discussion, that he approved the measure, but that he thought the time inopportune for issuing it. "The depression of the public mind, consequent upon our repeated reverses, is so great that I fear the effect

[5] Browning, *op. cit.* I, 609.

of so important a step. It may be viewed as the last measure of an exhausted government, a cry for help; the government stretching forth its hands to Ethiopia, instead of Ethiopia stretching forth her hands to the government." The President explained Seward's meaning in a pithy phrase of his own. "His idea was that it would be considered our last shriek on the retreat." Seward therefore recommended that its publication be put off until the North should obtain a military victory. Lincoln said that this objection had never occurred to him; he was much struck by its force, however, and he so told the artist. "I put the draft of the Proclamation aside, as you do your sketch for a picture, waiting for a victory." It seems a fair assumption, in view of Seward's evident hostility to emancipation, that he was seeking delay, hoping perhaps that time and events would cause the President to rescind his unhappy mistake.

Yet the history of Carpenter's painting illustrates again certain traits in Seward's mercurial character. In its original form that work of art set forth graphically the Seward assumption which he evidently wished to see ingrained in history, that he, not Lincoln, was the ruler of the United States during the Civil War. In the shape in which the picture left the White House for exhibition all over the United States, it greatly irritated Lincoln's admirers. Even Chase denounced it as a misrepresentation of history. "The Chief Justice," notes John Hay in his Diary for February 11, 1867, "showed me Carpenter's engraving of the Reading of the Proclamation. He objects to the whole picture being made subsidiary to Seward who is talking while everyone else listens or stares into vacancy." [6] Carpenter has himself described the principles on which he grouped his characters. The two elements in the cabinet, radical and conservative, were separated, with the figure of Lincoln between, acting as a kind of dividing wall, Stanton sitting and Chase standing at his right, the other five sitting or standing about the council table, on his left. "To the Secretary of State," writes Carpenter, "as the great expounder of the principles of the Republican party, the profound and sagacious statesman, would the attention of all at such a time be given. Entitled to precedence in discussion by his position, he would necessarily form one of the central figures in the group." Acting under this awesome belief the artist made Seward the dominating figure, even to the exclusion of Lincoln himself. The Secretary of State sat in profile in the foreground, a mass of papers resting on the table before him, inkwell and goose-quill pen convenient to his hand, as though to emphasize the remarks he is clearly directing at the President. Lincoln, with a paper in his left hand, which he has apparently just finished reading, is

[6] Hay, *op. cit.*, p. 272.

listening with a deferential regard, while the other members of the cabinet, so far as they are gazing at anything except empty space, have their eyes upon their colleague, absorbing his every word.

Engravings of the painting were widely distributed, and in a few years were hanging in thousands of American homes. But it afforded little pleasure to Lincoln's sincerest friends. The papers of Gideon Welles in the New York Public Library contain letters from Hiram Barney, Lincoln's appointee as Collector of the Port of New York, which echo this indignation. "The engraving," Mr. Barney wrote to Welles, December 4, 1873, "taken, I think, from Carpenter's painting of the Proclamation of Emancipation, represents Mr. Seward, with pen in hand, as if he had written that paper and had then submitted it to Mr. Lincoln and the cabinet. It is very probable that Mr. Seward chose for himself this attitude in the group, so as to produce the impression that he was the author of that great measure and of the instrument by which it was declared to the world. It was his fortune to appear to the world in a great many meritorious transactions as the moving, leading or controlling power, when in fact he often did not participate in the business or did oppose what was done during its performance. The foundation and early movements of the Republican party is an illustration of this statement. His attitude towards the party up to the time of Mr. Lincoln's inauguration was such that no proof could be found of his membership. It was a favorite saying of his during all that period: 'In religion I am an Episcopalian, in politics a Whig.' He was ready to advise that party and to accept its favors, but he was not a member and kept his record clear of responsibility for its measures and even for its existence." [7]

The Carpenter picture evidently preyed upon Mr. Barney's mind; the fact that Seward, contrary to the impression conveyed by Carpenter's work, was really opposed to the Proclamation was a particular reason for irritation. He returned to the matter in another letter to Welles, on September 27, 1877. "You were right in thinking that my interview with Mr. Lincoln after we left you was on the subject of the proclamation which was drafted in his own handwriting and in his pocket when we were together. When we reached what he thought was a place secure against interruption he read and showed it to me, and then, at my request, read it a second time for my suggestions. I made one which he adopted and advised him about the time and circumstances in which it should be issued. But we were interrupted three times by Mr. Seward, who came through closed doors and two empty

[7] This letter and the one that follows are in the Gideon Welles manuscripts in the New York Public Library.

rooms to find us and tried to hush up our conference, though he could have had no more than a suspicion, if he had that, of the subject of our conversation. Mr. Lincoln requested me not to talk about it, 'for,' said he, 'no human being has seen this or knows anything about it.' I think he wanted a witness to the fact that it was all his own work. Carpenter's picture groups the figures so that it would appear that Seward has just finished his draft and Mr. Lincoln was reading it for the first time. But the fact is Seward was not very well pleased with the measure."

When Carpenter's painting was hung in the Capitol – first on the landing stair wall of the House of Representatives, recently transferred to the old Supreme Court room – significant changes had been made. In 1878 Mrs. Elizabeth Thompson purchased the stodgy masterpiece from the artist for $25,000 and presented it to the United States Government. It was unveiled before the joint assemblage of the House and Senate with impressive ceremonies, James A. Garfield, subsequently the murdered twentieth President, and Alexander H. Stephens, Vice-President of the defunct Confederacy, providing the oratory. When the veil was drawn aside, it appeared that the criticisms which Lincoln's friends had lavished on what they regarded as a caricature of history had not been without effect. In the scene which thousands of visitors to the Capitol now look upon every year, Lincoln is indubitably the central figure. The quill pen which for several years had rested close to Seward's fingers had been transferred to Lincoln's right hand. The mass of papers lying on the table, which, to Mr. Barney and others, seemed intended to picture Seward as the author of the Proclamation, are clutched firmly by the President. Lincoln is no longer bending attentively towards Seward, as his first Secretary apparently explains the document, but is gazing straight ahead, while the other faces do not seem especially interested in the "Premier" of the cabinet, except perhaps Gideon Welles, who casts upon him a benevolent and slightly disapproving countenance. Many other alterations of less importance have been added to the first phase of the picture, which Lincoln had looked upon and, utterly oblivious of the undue importance placed upon his favorite adviser, had pronounced "as good as it could be made." It is the engraving of the original version, however, which still hangs in a multitude of old-fashioned American homes and still has the annoying habit of appearing in books devoted to the Emancipator.[8]

[8] The unrevised version even appears in so comprehensive a work as Sandburg's *Lincoln–The War Years*. III, 498.

[illegible] and used to hush up [illegible] Lincoln, he [illegible] [illegible] Lincoln [illegible] [illegible] of the [illegible] [illegible] [illegible] Lincoln [illegible] [illegible] talk [illegible] [illegible] [illegible] [illegible] [illegible] [illegible] [illegible] anything about it. I think he [illegible] [illegible] [illegible] [illegible] that it was all his own work. Carpenter's [illegible] [illegible] the figures so that it would appear that Seward had [illegible] [illegible] and Mr. Lincoln was reading it for the first time [illegible] Seward was not very well pleased with the [illegible]

[illegible] [illegible] [illegible] [illegible] in the Capitol [illegible] on the [illegible] [illegible] the House of Representatives, recently [illegible] [illegible] Supreme Court [illegible] [illegible] changes had been made [illegible] Mrs. Elizabeth Thompson purchased [illegible] [illegible] [illegible] [illegible] [illegible] [illegible] and presented it [illegible] [illegible] [illegible] [illegible] [illegible] before the [illegible] [illegible] of the House and [illegible] [illegible] [illegible] ceremonies. James A. Garfield, [illegible] [illegible] President, and Alexander H. Stephens, [illegible] [illegible] of the [illegible] Confederacy, [illegible] the [illegible]. When the [illegible] [illegible] [illegible] it appeared that the [illegible] which Lincoln's friends had [illegible] on what they regarded as a [illegible] of history had been [illegible] in the scene which thousands of [illegible] [illegible] [illegible] [illegible] every year. Lincoln's [illegible] [illegible] [illegible] [illegible] [illegible] [illegible] [illegible] [illegible] years and [illegible] [illegible] [illegible] had been [illegible] [illegible] Lincoln [illegible] had [illegible] [illegible] [illegible] [illegible] [illegible] [illegible] and [illegible] [illegible] [illegible] to [illegible] Seward [illegible] [illegible] [illegible] [illegible] [illegible] [illegible] by the President. Lincoln is no longer [illegible] [illegible] toward Seward, and his first Secretary [illegible] [illegible] the [illegible] [illegible] [illegible] [illegible] [illegible] [illegible] not [illegible] [illegible] in the "[illegible]" of the cabinet, except [illegible] [illegible] [illegible] [illegible] upon him [illegible] and [illegible] [illegible] [illegible]. Many other alterations of less importance [illegible] [illegible] the [illegible] [illegible] the picture, which Lincoln had [illegible] [illegible] [illegible] of the [illegible] importance [illegible] [illegible] [illegible] had pronounced "as good as it can [illegible] [illegible] [illegible] original version [illegible] [illegible] [illegible] [illegible] of old-fashioned American [illegible] and still [illegible] [illegible] [illegible] [illegible] [illegible] [illegible] [illegible] the [illegible]

[illegible] [illegible] [illegible] [illegible] [illegible] [illegible] [illegible] [illegible] [illegible]

BOOK SIX

Chase and "The Blairs"

I

THE YEAR 1864 proved to be a critical one in the history of the Lincoln cabinet. Before its end the reorganization which had been threatened so many times had become an accomplished fact. The change, however, represented no triumph for the Sumners, the Wades, the Chandlers, and the Greeleys who had struggled and intrigued so fiercely for a whole presidential term to gain control of affairs. The reconstruction was the work not of attacks from without, but of dissensions within. By December 1864, only two of the seven whom Lincoln had appointed on March 5, 1861, remained around his council table. William H. Seward and Gideon Welles still occupied their familiar, if somewhat uneasy, seats. But Salmon Portland Chase and Montgomery Blair had succumbed to the political complications of Lincoln's second presidential campaign, and Edward Bates, in his seventy-second year, had retired to a comfortable old age in St. Louis. The mere fact that Chase's was the most spectacular resignation indicates the extent to which the radical attempts to reorganize the cabinet to their advantage had miscarried.

That the cabinet disintegrated in 1864 was not surprising; the really astonishing thing was that it had held together so long. No such uncongenial or contentious group had ever assembled beneath the White House roof. Lincoln's conception of a coalition was politically sound, but on the personal side it inevitably led to trouble. For the most part Lincoln's councilors were forceful men, with their own programs, their own ambitions, their own vanities, jealousies, obstinacies, and defects of temper. Each had his set of ideas and his personal following, and on few matters had any two agreed. The criticism constantly made that the cabinet was not a "unit," that each of its members went his own way and lived by himself in a watertight compartment, was largely justified. An inner bloc – Blair, Welles, and Bates – did remain on approving personal terms, but that was the only element of harmony. Perhaps a qualification to this statement should be made in the case of Blair and Bates, who had little personal regard for each other, and who at times sharply disagreed in matters of politics and the conduct of the war. Still, these two positive characters generally held the same views on important questions – such, for example, as Reconstruction and the future of the Negro – belonged to the same wing of the party, and so may be linked with Welles as forming an anti-Chase, anti-Seward, and anti-Stanton entente. From the Diaries of Chase and Welles, and from the memoranda of Blair, could be culled an entertaining anthology of elegant extracts in which their fellow statesmen are described, over and over again, as deceitful, scheming, avaricious of power, and disloyal to the President. Both Welles and Bates esteemed Chase an ignoramus in matters of finance – a judgment that posterity does not accept; while Blair did not hesitate to denounce the Secretary of the Treasury as a "traitor" to Abraham Lincoln. The feelings all three entertained for Stanton were unutterable. The elder Blair's conviction that Stanton would "betray any man, no matter what his obligations to him, if he stood in the way of his selfish and ambitious schemes" was likewise that of his son. In the last year of their official association, Blair and Stanton were not on speaking terms. They would enter the cabinet room, take their seats without the usual greetings, and sit throughout the session oblivious of each other's presence. Relations between Blair and Seward were scarcely more cordial. The stories of wild altercations in cabinet that now and then reached the newspapers were usually exaggerated, but material in plenty existed for the reportorial talent to build upon. Maunsell B. Field once complained to Seward that he was keeping no diary, thereby depriving posterity of a most illuminating record. It would contain little, Seward replied, except a squalid account of quarrels within the cabinet, and would disgrace the nation if ever exposed to public view. Real patriotism demanded silence.

Long before the convention of 1864 Seward had become one of the strongest of Lincoln's supporters for re-election. "As they sat together by the fireside," relates Frederick W. Seward, "or in the carriage, the conversation between them, however it began, always drifted back to the same channel – the progress of the great national struggle. Both loved humor, and however trite the theme, Lincoln always found some quaint illustration from his frontier life, and Seward some case in point in his long public career, that gave it new light." Seward was probably not unacquainted with a talk that had recently taken place between Lincoln and Thurlow Weed. "Is there any man in the Democratic party," Lincoln had solemnly asked this New York politician, "who can push this war one day faster and one day further than I can?"

"Why?" "Because if there is such a man I want him to take my place." Lincoln was so serious that Weed took up the matter with the Democratic leaders and found that the "war Democrats" were prepared to support Lincoln in the approaching campaign, and that the other element in the opposing ranks, which desired a "negotiated peace" with the "South," was in such a state of confusion that it need not be regarded.

The same authority pictures a charming scene between President and Secretary of State in which the question of the succession was discussed. The conversation took place at one of those evening talks that had apparently become essential to the contentment of both men. Lincoln confided that he had hoped to see Seward his successor – thus compensating the Secretary and his friends for the disappointment of 1860. "No," Seward answered, "that is all past and settled. The logic of events requires you to be your own successor. You were elected in 1860 but the southern states refused to submit. They thought the decision made at the polls could be reversed in the field. They are still in arms and their hope now is that you and your party will be voted down at the next election. When that election is held and they find the people reaffirming their decision to have you President, I think the Rebellion will collapse." [1]

Another member of the cabinet, however, did not view his prospects with such philosophy. Chase had entered Lincoln's administration with the fixed determination of becoming his successor. Events had not discouraged, but rather incited this ambition. Not only had three years demonstrated, to Chase's satisfaction, Lincoln's utter inadequacy; they had provided a compelling issue on which he believed he could win. Chase had two distinct sides to his nature – he was a genuine idealist where the cause of the Negro was involved, but a practical aspirant where his political fortunes were at stake. His attitude on this question illustrates both phases of his character. Championship of the Negro, a noble cause in itself, offered a promising issue on which to ride into the Presidency. Chase's hesitation when Lincoln first read his decree giving freedom to 4,000,000 Negroes has already been noted; in a way he resented that document; it seemed a kind of impertinence, an encroachment on territory sacred to himself, an attempt to rob him of his presidential issue. The Negro and his future were Chase's property – let no man, not even the President, trespass upon that sacred soil! The extent to which extremists in the political, journalistic, and religious worlds reverenced Chase as the apostle of the black man inevitably made this conviction sink deeper in his mind. The man's vanity did the rest.

[1] Seward's *Seward*, III, 196, 197.

With him it was a matter of religious conviction. He devoutly believed that God had appointed him His chosen agent in this exalted mission. Now and then, in references to his chief, Chase would patronizingly approve his amiable nature, natural kindness, and "good intentions," but that the man was vastly superior to himself, in intellect and character, never crossed his mind. "I do not wonder," he wrote John Young, October 27, 1862, "that dissatisfaction prevails. The President, from the purest motives, committed the management of the war almost exclusively to his political opponents." As late as February 1, 1864, Chase was writing in the same key. "If to his kindness of spirit and good sense he joined strong will and energetic action there would be little left to wish for him. As it is, I think he is likely to close his first term with more honor than he will his second, should he be re-elected." Welles described Chase as complimenting the President "for honesty of intentions, good common-sense, more sagacity than he has credit for," but thought him "greatly wanting in will and decision, in comprehensiveness, in self-reliance, and clear, well-defined purpose." [2]

Perhaps the most annoying instance of this condescension – praise of Lincoln's minor qualities at a time when Chase was moving heaven and earth to undermine him – appears in a letter to the same correspondent of November 26, 1863: "I can never permit myself to be driven into any hostile or unfriendly position as to Mr. Lincoln. His course towards me has always been so fair and kind; his progress towards entire agreement with me as to the great question of slavery has been so constant, though rather slower than I wished for, and his general character is so marked by traits which command respect and affection that I can never consent to anything which he himself could or would consider incompatible with perfect honor and good faith, if I were capable – which I hope I am not – of a departure from either, even where an enemy might be concerned." [3] Here Chase draws his self-portrait as the man who was really the soul and the brains of the administration, and Lincoln as a good-natured underling whose increasing merit was measured by the extent to which "his progress" showed "entire agreement" with his Secretary of the Treasury. Perhaps Chase's attitude toward Lincoln and his estimate of his qualities come out best in a diary entry for October 11, 1862. He asked a certain Major Halpin, a dinner guest, his estimate of the President. The mere fact that the Secretary should have put such a question to a minor officer, and have seen no impropriety in recording the fact, indicates his lack of respect for the commander in chief. "A man irresolute," he quotes the Major's

[2] Welles, *Diary*. I, 413.
[3] Schuckers, *op. cit.*, p. 495.

answer, "but of honest intentions – born a poor white in a slave state, and, of course, among aristocrats – kind in spirit and not envious, but anxious for approval, especially of those to whom he has been accustomed to look up – hence solicitous of the support of slave holders in the border states and unwilling to offend them – without the large mind necessary to grasp great questions – uncertain of himself and in many things ready to lean too much on others." This was the kind of appraisement that tickled Chase's ears. "I found him well read and extremely intelligent" is his comment on this insolent understrapper.[4]

While Chase, with Christian forbearance, evidently strove to take as charitable a view as possible of Lincoln himself, he had nothing but contempt for the administration. His favorite criticism, set forth constantly in the letters that issued in a steady stream day after day from his pen, was that there was no administration. "I feel myself," he wrote William E. Dodge, March 31, 1864, "like one without a chart among forces of wind and currents which he cannot measure or manage. I can only do my best, and trusting Him with whom are the issues of all events."[5] In January 1864 Chase wrote Judge Dickinson of Ohio, sounding him on Ohio's preference for the candidate at the approaching Republican convention. The judge returned a frank but apparently most unsatisfactory opinion; the sentiment of Ohio strongly inclined to Lincoln. That is "most certainly erroneous," Chase replied; "the administration cannot be continued as it is, for properly speaking there is in fact no administration. There are departments and there is a President. The latter leaves administration substantially to the heads of the former, deciding himself comparatively few questions."[6] This was, of course, the familiar criticism – the one which had produced the crisis of late 1862, and almost accomplished the disruption of the cabinet. "Had there been an administration in the true sense of the word," Chase wrote the Reverend J. Leavitt, one of the editors of the *Independent*, a paper which, under Theodore Tilton, had been assailing Lincoln for a long time and proclaiming the virtues of Chase as a desirable successor, "a President conferring with his cabinet and taking their united judgments and with their aid enforcing activity, economy and energy in all departments of public service, we could have spoken boldly and defied the world."[7] The time came when Chase ceased to speak of the cabinet as a cabinet. "I am now going," he once informed Thurlow Weed, "to a meeting of the department heads." Dissatisfied

[4] Chase, *Diary*, p. 105.
[5] Schuckers, *op. cit.*, p. 400.
[6] Warden, *op. cit.*, p. 564.
[7] *Ibid.*, p. 562.

as he was with the cabinet as a working force, and with its members as individuals – except Stanton – the man's confidence in himself never weakened. "So far, I think I have made few mistakes. Indeed, in looking back over the whole ground, with an earnest desire to detect error and correct it, I am not able to see where, if I had to do my work all over again, I could in any matter do materially otherwise than I have." [8]

It is perhaps not strange that a statesman who entertained these ideas of his chief, and at the same time regarded so favorably his own qualifications, should have turned to himself as the most desirable candidate for the succession. The influence of aspiration for high office in warping the character of public men is one of the most fruitful lessons to be learned from American history. Probably none of the great men so disastrously affected by this ambition – such as Calhoun, Clay, or Webster – presented so melancholy a spectacle as Chase. In no instance has this desperate search for the unattainable attained such morbid proportions. "I shall ever strive to be first wherever I may be," he wrote in 1830, at the age of twenty-two, "let what success shall attend the effort," and from his earliest appearance in public life, the Presidency not only became his goal, in his belief it was his heaven-predestined right; any man who interfered with his quest, in his mind, was little less than sacrilegious. That support in this infatuation which Chase could not arouse in the outside world he found in his domestic circle. His long pursuit of the Presidency – for it did not end in 1864, but was resumed in 1868 and 1872 – introduced a new phenomenon into American politics. Up to this time, women had played little or no part in directing the course of parties. One or two had occasionally risen above the not too imposing state to which the standards of the time had assigned them. Martha Washington, Abigail Adams, Dolly Madison, Harriet Lane, Adele Cutts Douglas, Jessie Benton Frémont, were women who stood conspicuous in the American world of their day by virtue of character, social charm, and, at least in the case of Mrs. Adams and Mrs. Frémont, an apprehensive mind; but not one of them could be regarded as exercising a definite influence on history. One woman indeed, Peggy O'Neill, had caused the disruption of Jackson's cabinet and helped elect Van Buren President, but in this she was the victim, rather than the commander of events.

[8] Letter to J. W. Hartwell, February 2, 1864. Warden, *op. cit.*, p. 570.

Salmon Portland Chase (1808–1873)

Secretary of the Treasury (1861–1864) and Chief Justice of the United States (1864–1873)

Kate Chase Sprague (*1840–1899*)
Daughter of the Secretary of the Treasury and reigning hostess of the cabinet

From a painting by Thomas Sully

Francis Preston Blair, Sr. (*1791–1876*)

II

KATE CHASE had many of the qualities needed for activity of this kind. She was young, she was beautiful, she had an assertive, aggressive character, and, if a mind not well stocked with knowledge and culture, a quick wit, intelligent conversation, and a political sense which, in the judgment of most of her contemporaries, exceeded that of her father. In the spring of 1860, Carl Schurz, then thirty-one years old, passing through Columbus, Ohio, was invited to be a guest at the Chase home. Chase was then governor; the Chicago Convention, at which he hoped to be nominated, was only a few weeks ahead; naturally Schurz, leader of the Germans in Wisconsin, was a person worth cultivating at that particular time. Chase and his daughter impressed this keen observer as a remarkable pair. "More than anyone else Chase looked the great man. . . . His dignity of deportment never left him even in his unbending moods, for it was perfectly natural and unconscious. It really belonged to him like the majestic figure that nature had given him." Presently Kate entered the breakfast room. She "saluted me very kindly and then let herself down upon her chair with the graceful lightness of a bird that, folding its wings, perches upon the branch of a tree. She was then about eighteen years old, tall and slender and exceedingly well formed. Her features were not at all regularly beautiful according to the classic rule. Her little nose, somewhat audaciously tipped up, would perhaps not have passed muster with a severe critic, but it fitted pleasingly into her face with its large, languid, but at the same time vivacious hazel eyes, shaded by long dark lashes and arched over by proud eyebrows. The fine forehead was framed in waving, gold-brown hair. She had something imperial in the pose of the head, and all her movements possessed an exquisite natural charm. No wonder that she came to be admired as a great beauty and broke many hearts. After the usual polite commonplaces, the conversation at the breakfast table, in which Miss Kate took a lively and remarkably intelligent part, soon turned upon politics"[1] —

[1] Schurz, Carl, *Reminiscences*. McClure and Company, 1907–1908. II, 169–170.

and the imminent national convention, Chase making no secret of his anxiety for the support of Schurz and his German following.

A few years later, another young man, James A. Garfield, was a guest at the Chase home – this time in Washington, at E and Sixth Streets. Garfield passed many pleasant hours with Kate, playing chess, escorting her to army camps, occasionally taking a gallop in the country surrounding Washington – "she is a splendid rider," he notes. "Kate is quite a belle here from what I learn. They have a fine residence and live in splendid style. . . . She is a woman of good sense and pretty good culture – has a good form but not a pretty face, its beauty being marred by a nose slightly inclined to pug. She has probably more social influence and makes a better impression generally than any other cabinet lady."[2] Most observers did not use qualifications when describing Kate's beauty. The petulant nose that impressed these two romantic young men as a blemish seemed to others only to enhance the girl's provoking charm. "Kate Chase spent Tuesday night with us," Jay Cooke wrote his brother Henry, June 13, 1861. "She is a glorious girl." Her appearance at her first White House reception almost immediately lifted Kate to the social leadership of the new administration. Certainly the stately father and the brilliant, animated daughter made a handsome pair on entering the East Room. As Mrs. Seward, wife of the "Premier," was an invalid and seldom appeared in Washington, this left Kate, as hostess of the cabinet officer second in rank, virtually first lady of the cabinet and chief assistant to Mrs. Lincoln at state functions. But the post of second-in-command by no means satisfied her ambitions. At this first reception the girl of twenty-one, dressed in white silk with sprays of jasmine, made rather a pale figure of Mary Todd, in white satin and black lace, forty-three, mother of four children, who, if by no means the dowd that malicious gossip pictured her, could hardly compete with the tall, exquisitely framed figure – the brown eyes melting into blue, searching, demanding; the rust-gold hair; the small but willful mouth; the little, perfectly formed chin; the lively laughter and spirited talk of her youthful rival. For rival to the President's wife Kate became from the day she entered Washington. Just as Chase regarded himself as the man morally entitled to rule the administration, so his daughter believed that the position fate had intended for her was to be eventually mistress of the White House. That she sought to make herself the center of White House functions, generally with success – drawing to her circle the most distinguished, such as the French princes, with whom, thanks to a daily association

[2] Smith, T. C., *Life and Letters of James Abram Garfield*. Yale University Press, 1925. I, 238, 242.

for nine years with Mademoiselle Janon at Miss Haines's School in New York, she could easily converse in their own language – was perhaps natural enough, and it was also to be expected that Mrs. Lincoln would resent her pretensions and regard her soon as a presumptuous enemy. The fact that Lincoln, like all men, liked to bend over the lovely creature and bask in her entertaining talk did not improve Mary's fondness for the girl.

Yet Kate Chase, radiant as she seemed, had had a rather unhappy childhood and youth. Chase's entry in his Diary on the day of Kate's birth gives some indication of the time to come. A good part of the hours of the mother's travail Chase spent upon his knees praying "God to support and comfort my dear wife, to preserve the life of the child and to save both from sin. . . . The child is pronounced pretty," he subsequently notes. "I think otherwise. May God give the child a good understanding that she may keep His commandments." When the little girl first evinced positive traits – she was really a personality at three, self-centered, impatient of control, always exacting admiration and seeking to make the world revolve around herself – it was by religious admonition that the patient father strove to reform her ways. An outburst of temper was reproved by a repetition of the 119th Psalm; after a particularly outrageous escapade – such as misbehaving at morning prayers – Chase would read the tiny impenitent an extract from the Book of Job. "Was obliged to correct my dear little Katie – prayed with her" – Chase's Diary abounds with notations of this kind. It was not only the child's charm and imperiousness that brought adoring circles wherever she went; she had a quick, bright mind, and at five could read and write. "Heard little Katie read Bible as usual," was Chase's entry at the end of a most satisfactory day. The mother's invalidism – she, like so many women of that day, was a consumptive – and consequent movings from place to place in search of health, heightened the melancholy of Katie's early surroundings. She was only five when her mother died; fourteen months afterward Chase married again – for the third time; and Katie's domestic happiness, such as it had been, came to an end. She resented, with all her fiery little soul, this strange woman whom she was instructed to call "mother" and obey; by this time also what was unquestionably the most impelling emotion of her life, her worship of her father – beside whom, in her estimation, all other humans were dross – had taken deep root; she disliked this intruder intensely and was exceedingly jealous also of a little half-sister, Janette, who presently began to divide her father's attention.

At the age of seven, therefore, Chase carried the unhappy rebel to New York, and installed her in the fashionable school conducted by

Miss Henrietta Haines. Here she remained until her sixteenth year. That is to say, for most of Kate's childhood she was motherless and homeless. The Haines establishment ranked high socially; all the arts becoming a young lady of station were religiously cultivated; the instruction was of a more solid character than was usual in such places, for Miss Haines was a cultivated lady – tall, handsome, full of dignity and poise – and believed in something more than embroidery and a smattering of French as desirable for girls on the threshold of life. There was plenty, too, that appealed to Kate's vainer side. She was the belle of school cotillions, the most striking figure in the daily walks up Fifth Avenue, the most prominent performer at school exhibitions; and, in the horseback rides in the north part of Manhattan Island she easily outdistanced all her companions. But her life was still a solitary one. She did not go home for Christmas and Easter – traveling was too difficult in those primitive days; her father practically never came to New York; and, except for an occasional visit from Charles Sumner, who formed an attachment for "this very intelligent child," as he called her, that was to last a lifetime, school was unrelieved by domestic affections and influences. When Kate, at the age of sixteen, returned to Ohio to become the mistress of her father's household – for the third wife had died several years before – she had grown to be a stunning girl, vigorous in body and mind, better educated than most, but dominant in spirit and rather contemptuous of the local population, especially the masculine contingent – those who knew anything of Shakespeare began to refer to her as "Kate the Shrew," though their attempts at taming grotesquely failed – and defiant of convention. By this time, her father was a national figure; he had served in the Senate, was a powerful antislavery leader, had become governor of Ohio and, in the estimation of friends, was a likely presidential candidate. Barren as Kate found life in these rustic surroundings, one development in the governor's existence entranced her. From all over the nation shoals of letters came to Chase extolling his fitness for the presidential succession. Kate found these the most interesting literature she had ever read. She would pore over them days on end, and discuss them with her father at the dinner table and on buggy rides – for she used dutifully to drive the governor to and from his office morning and evening. Distinguished visitors gathered at the Chase board; slavery, the growth of the Republican Party, the critical presidential year of 1860, were the subjects of discussion; Carl Schurz, in the passage quoted above, says that Kate Chase entered into political discussion with "remarkable intelligence" and there is plenty of testimony from others to the same effect. This correspondence and these visitors only confirmed the belief already lodged in Kate's mind that her father was the greatest living American and stimulated an increasing contempt for all who presumed to dispute with him that eminence. Especially was the lanky backwoodsman from Illinois who had snatched the prize from its rightful heir at the Chicago Convention of 1860 an object of dislike. In Washington, the pleasure Lincoln displayed in her society naturally appealed to the girl's vanity, but at heart she never ceased to regard him as an enemy, the man who was standing between her idol and his destined goal.

Attempts to portray Kate Chase as an intellectual would not be warranted; she was a woman of strong mind and strong will, and in force of character superior to her father. Certain positive qualities derived from Scottish ancestors that had not been implanted in Salmon Portland had, by a strange but not unprecedented quirk of heredity, found lodgment in a fascinating girl. The softer feminine qualities, however, had passed her by. Love and tenderness were not Kate's dominating traits. She later did develop a maternal feeling for her little sister Nettie, whose arrival at first had aroused jealousy; but no man – except perhaps Roscoe Conkling, the dashing, handsome New York Senator, with whom Kate's name was afterward associated – ever held much sway over her emotions. For her there was only one man in the world and that was her father. Any attempt to encroach on her exclusive possession of this godlike figure aroused resentment. Today Salmon P. Chase and his daughter Kate are buried side by side in Spring Grove Cemetery in Cincinnati, with a grandiose monument erected in the statesman's honor; that would have seemed to her the appropriate resting place. Though Chase gave the child the name of his first wife, Catherine Garniss, there are anecdotes indicating that the grown woman was as jealous of this first of Chase's loves as of the stepmother who succeeded her own. Robert B. Warden, Chase's chosen biographer, charged that Kate had withheld essential documents because they would have revealed her father's great affection for this wife. In Washington the vigilant protection Kate maintained over her father, where aspiring women were concerned, had its humorous aspects. The Secretary was only fifty-six when he joined Lincoln's cabinet; his handsome exterior inevitably made him an appealing prospect to women; moreover he himself, scrupulously correct as was his life, had a strong liking for their society. He enjoyed nothing better, after a hard day in the office, than to drop in late for a cup of tea with the beautiful Adele Cutts, widow of Stephen A. Douglas; he would even take her driving in Rock Creek Park; and with at least two women, Mrs. Carlotta Eastman of Beverly, Massachusetts, and Miss Susan Walker of Cincinnati, he carried on a half-sentimental, half-platonic correspondence. That

Chase stood in awe of his daughter, indeed was afraid of her, is evident from the fact that this correspondence, so far as Kate was concerned, was clandestine. The ladies were instructed to send their letters to the Treasury office, not to the Chase home. It is not unlikely that Chase would have married Mrs. Eastman, but recoiled before the fear of his daughter's hostility. He did invite her to visit the home in E Street, but the coolness of Kate's reception caused the lady to cut the visit short. When Chase became President, as Kate unflinchingly believed he would, she intended to be the mistress of the White House. Thus ambition was the controlling incentive of her life. That she had many suitors was inevitable; she enjoyed their admiration, but marriage apparently did not enter her scheme of things. One of the men gossips reported her as having rebuffed was Lord Lyons, the bachelor minister from Great Britain. She was said to have remarked that she would never marry, but intended to devote all her interest to her father and his career. In a way her marriage to Senator William Sprague of Rhode Island did not violate this resolution. That her devotion to the Secretary of the Treasury had much to do with her acceptance of this cavalier, after keeping him dangling in uncertainty for more than two years, was the harsh judgment of the time.

For Sprague had the one thing needed to make the Chase existence complete – money. The lack of this essential had been a lifelong embarrassment to Chase and his daughter. He had never practiced law long enough to lay aside a nest egg; the legal services that had brought him fame, as "lawyer for runaway slaves," he had rendered without fee; the fifteen years before 1860 he had lived on the meager stipends paid governors and Senators in a parsimonious age. In ordinary times this had been hardship enough; but it took on fairly tragic proportions with Kate's attainment of womanhood. She had a passion for fine clothes and expensive living, and her extravagance, even as a child in Miss Haines's School, had given her father many anxious days. One morning Chase received a bill forwarded by Kate, then fifteen, for a summer outfit, consisting of a hundred separate items, "all for personal adornment," endorsed in this businesslike fashion: "I have examined this bill and find everything correct. C. G. Chase." The total sum, $305, would perhaps not seem so startling today, but for a poor Ohio governor, with a salary of $1800 a year – and not a very large income from other sources – it was staggering.

Chase's position as Secretary of the Treasury, with a brilliant daughter who soon became the rage of Washington, demanded at least a dignified background. His salary of $8000 could not supply it. Daily piling up debts for household expenses and a bank account that was frequently overdrawn hardly comported with that personal dignity which was Chase's most conspicuous asset. The stringency forced this most righteous of men to steps that approached impropriety. He borrowed money, for example, from Hiram Barney, to whom he had allotted the most powerful office in the Treasury Department, that of Collector of the Port of New York; he solicited loans, if not for himself, for relatives and friends, from Jay Cooke, the Philadelphia banker who was the fiscal agent of the Treasury Department. Whatever qualities young Sprague may have lacked, this hiatus in the Chase economy he could certainly bridge. He was a calico printer from Providence, Rhode Island, and was said to be the richest man in New England, the newspapers estimating and exaggerating his fortune at $25,000,000. All this and the business that produced it Sprague had inherited; that he lacked business ability the future showed – for his money slipped through Sprague's hands in the seventies, he himself dying unnoticed in Paris as recently as 1915. In 1861 in Washington, however, Sprague was the catch of the season, though it cannot be said that he had any other recommendation. In appearance, with slight frame and sallow face, he was not prepossessing. He had left school at fifteen with little education. He was a hard drinker – a failing that eventually became a vice, causing unseemly spectacles at social gatherings and on the Senate floor. Personal scandals, one involving an illegitimate child, had caused his exclusion from the best circles of Providence. He became governor of Rhode Island at the age of twenty-nine and Senator in 1862, by the corrupt use of money. His governorship alone was said to have cost him $100,000. John Hay, in his Diary,[3] curtly disposes of Sprague with the remark that he was "a small, insignificant youth who bought his place." It seems a little strange that a man so rigidly moral as Salmon P. Chase should have manifested, if not a cordial, at least an acquiescent attitude towards such a son-in-law. Perhaps could he have foreseen the day when Sprague would drag his wife's name in the mire, starting divorce proceedings against her on the most scandalous charges, and when the newspapers would be filled day after day with stories of their quarrels, he would have attempted to dissuade Kate from her dangerous experiment.

But the wedding took place in October 1863, in the presence of Lincoln – Mrs. Lincoln did not attend – the cabinet, and fashionable and political Washington, including a liberal representation of the diplomatic corps. The newspapers declared it to be the most pretentious function of the kind Washington had ever known, and Kate, in white velvet gown and long train, the most magnificent of Washington

[3] Hay, *op. cit.*, p. 12. April 26, 1861.

brides. For months afterward the doings of the Spragues – their parties, Kate's jewels and wardrobe, the $1,000,000 house, Canonchet, which she built near Point Judith, Narragansett Bay, the elaborate entertainments given there – occupied the newspaper reading public. The press treated the birth of her first baby almost like a royal event; the sad fate that pursued the marriage acted true to form in the matter of this boy, who, twenty-five years afterward, committed suicide. Public judgment on the alliance and the motives that had inspired it were accurately set forth by Henry Villard in his *Memoirs*. Sprague, he wrote, "had very limited mental capacity but had reached political distinction at an early age through the influence of real or reputed great wealth. It was at his headquarters that he became acquainted with Kate, the beautiful and gifted daughter of Secretary Chase. The acquaintance ripened into an engagement that was the social sensation of the day. She was far superior to him in every way and married him for the enjoyment and power of his money. It turned out one of the unhappiest marriages ever known in American society, ending in moral and material wretchedness for both parties."[4]

In marrying Sprague, Kate did not give up her father. The young millionaire purchased the fine mansion the Secretary had had such difficulty in maintaining, and Chase continued to live, as a paying guest, under his son-in-law's roof. With her husband's vast income at her disposal, Kate converted this handsome establishment into a headquarters for the promotion of the Chase presidential campaign. The more sordid pursuit of supporters, the angling for delegates, could be safely left to the politicians enlisted in the cause. Kate's activities were of a more subtle kind, the making of friends by the adroit exercise of social flattery. Her receptions and dinners were the great events of Washington; an invitation to the home the most desired. In that critical winter of 1863–1864, Mrs. Sprague distributed her favors mainly with one end in view. Any politician from the provinces, irrespective of his standing at home or his personal graces, became the object of her attention – provided he was likely to control delegates to the June convention. Her smaller dinner and supper parties were occasions for the discussions, plans, and even plots that formed the necessary prelude to the open contest. Even so strait-laced a Puritan as Lyman Trumbull, after having been admitted to Kate's inner circle on E Street, began to see value in her father as a presidential candidate.

[4] Villard, Henry, *Memoirs*. Houghton Mifflin Company, 1904. I, 175. The selections from this book are used by permission of the publishers, Houghton Mifflin Company.

III

IN ONE RESPECT the Chase aspiration was perhaps the most pathetic episode in American politics, for in the whole extent of the nation only two persons unreservedly and sincerely embraced the cause. These were Chase himself and his daughter Kate. Even after Gettysburg and Vicksburg, great hostility prevailed in many quarters against the Lincoln administration and loud cries were raised for a more competent conduct of the war. That Lincoln could not be reelected for a second term was the conviction of many competent observers – including, at times, Lincoln himself. In few cases, however, did the opponents of Lincoln turn with genuine eagerness to Chase. There were several groups to which the Secretary might have naturally looked for support. For two decades the professional abolitionists had regarded him as their political reliance. Yet not many of these, in 1863 and 1864, hailed him as their chosen candidate. Henry Wilson, Charles Sumner, Joshua Giddings, and Thaddeus Stevens were almost the only influential men in this company that seemed to favor – at times rather faintly – his nomination. Wendell Phillips and William Lloyd Garrison showed little interest in the proposal; indeed, in the earlier stages of the canvass, both these seasoned exhorters announced their preference for Lincoln. Certain antislavery editors and preachers – such as Horace Greeley, Charles A. Dana, Joseph Medill of the *Chicago Tribune*, Henry Ward Beecher, Theodore Tilton of the *Independent*, Whitelaw Reid of the *Cincinnati Gazette* – wrote approvingly of Chase though some changed their attitude as the discussion proceeded. Perhaps the Secretary's most devoted boomer was William Wales, editor of the *Baltimore American*, who frequently sent his editorials to Chase for emendation in advance of publication. An article in the *North American Review*, January 1864, by James Russell Lowell, one of the leaders of the Boston intellectual world and a strong antislavery man, eulogizing Lincoln's administration and eloquently advocating a second term, grieved Chase as a disheartening blow directly from the house of his friends.

The one heroic band which, above all the rest, might be depended upon to rush to his support was that radical group in Congress, the Jacobins, who for three years had found in him their main support in the cabinet, and whose views on Reconstruction and the future of the Negro were identical with his own. Yet little encouragement came to the Treasury head from this source. These leaders, for the most part, abhorred Lincoln as President, and would have gone to almost any extreme to dispossess him of the White House. Yet the alternative of Chase in Lincoln's seat did not appeal to them as a satisfactory solution of the problem. Thaddeus Stevens spoke a few approving words and John Covode offered the Secretary the support of Pennsylvania, provided his faction could secure immediate disposal of the Treasury patronage in the Keystone State – but these were the most friendly responses Chase received from his cherished allies in Congress. William Pitt Fessenden, his close associate in financing the war, and strident critic of Abraham Lincoln, made no favorable sign. Ben Wade, chairman of the Jacobin Committee on the Conduct of the War, maintained a flintlike silence. Zack Chandler kept belching forth his anathemas on "Honest Old Abe," but spoke no word of commendation for Chase as heir apparent. George W. Julian, the most idealistic of the extreme radicals, never lifted up his eloquent voice in Chase's favor. James A. Garfield, one of the younger of the firebrands and an unrestrained critic of Lincoln – even after Emancipation he described him as a "second rate Illinois lawyer" – regarded Chase's presidential hopes as a great mistake and tried to persuade the deluded man to drop them.

What was the explanation for this lukewarm attitude? Mere politics had much to do with it. Newspaper editors and other more or less detached makers of public opinion were not so restricted in their activities and utterances as Representatives and Senators. These latter patriots, eager, as legislators always have been, for re-election, could not too defiantly oppose public opinion in their districts, and, as 1863 drew to a close, no fact stood out more conspicuously than that the voting rank and file of the Republican Party, the war Democrats, and the soldiers in the field were demanding Father Abraham's renomination. The radicals might curse Lincoln under their breath – and even in the cloakrooms of Congress – and pray for another candidate, but they were not heroic enough to risk their political necks by doing so publicly. Nor had the Jacobins forgotten how Chase, in December 1862, had egged them on in their revolutionary attempt to destroy the cabinet, and then, at the critical moment, had turned against them. Their favorite candidate was Frémont, though Grant to many seemed the ideal man.

In the cabinet itself, in 1863 and 1864, Stanton alone encouraged the Chase aspirations. The Seward-Weed machine in New York opened all its batteries against them – and even Hiram Barney, Collector at New York and one of the leaders of the anti-Seward contingent, proved undependable where Chase's presidential claims were concerned. "Granny Bates," Attorney General, regarded Chase, because of his Negro policies, as one of the most evil influences in the nation. To Welles, whose great hero was Lincoln, Chase seemed little better than a renegade. But the man who above all, in cabinet and out, proved most vitriolic against this attempt to undermine his chief was Montgomery Blair.

The Soldiers' Home figures prominently in all accounts of Lincoln's days in Washington – that retreat on the outskirts of Washington to which a harassed President commonly sought sanctuary in the darkest times of the war. But another refuge provided even more comfortable relief from the torments of the National Capital. Silver Spring, a few miles across the Maryland border, in addition to pastoral quiet, gave human association of the most stimulating kind. The couple that presided over this suburban home, the elder Francis Preston Blair and his wife, Violet Gist, could offer all that personal charm, that sympathy, that understanding, that ever-ready advice and admonition so welcome to a man called every day to meet a hundred problems and beset on every hand by selfish intriguers. The very presence of these two experienced political and social leaders was a balm. Both had now passed their seventieth year and were basking in a life filled with beauty, culture, troops of friends, and all the other essentials of a contented old age. The sight of old man Blair, gray-headed, wrinkled, and stoop-shouldered, moving among his shrubberies, sipping his Madeira in the Acorn summerhouse, bending over his flower beds, lounging in his library with a favorite volume, or surrounded by a few companions at tea, formed perhaps the most soothing diversion in Lincoln's anxious days. Unforgettable was the remembrance of the old man, clad in silk dressing gown, in his beloved rose garden; he had the habit of picking his blooms by running his fingers up the stalks, a procedure that left nothing in his hands except the stemless flowers; he would thrust these into his large pocket, arranging them, after returning to the house, in a specially contrived silver dish.

This little ritual fairly symbolized the peace and delight of the Silver Spring estate. And there were more robust forms of pleasure. Both Blair and his wife were expert riders, and frequent gallopings about the Maryland countryside and even into Washington did their part in keeping them young and strong. Mrs. Blair never needed help in mounting or dismounting; a few mornings before her death, at the age of eighty-six, she had her favorite round of exercise, getting on and off the horse without assistance. Lincoln entered wholeheartedly into this existence. He especially liked the Blair grandchildren – there were always several at hand – and used to join in their games. The apparition of the long and lean President playing one o' cat with the younger Blair generation – running to first base, with arms outstretched and coattails billowing in the wind – was a sight not easily forgotten. There were more serious moments. Lincoln enjoyed not only the sylvan, but the intellectual aspects of the place. He was drawn to old man Blair for the same reason that he was attracted to Seward. He loved his comments on men and events, especially his reminiscences of a long political experience. Moreover, the present concerned Blair as much as the past; and, at least for the first two years of Lincoln's administration, he remained the President's closest adviser in times of crisis. "Between Francis P. Blair and Mr. Lincoln," wrote Ward Lamon in his *Recollections of Abraham Lincoln*, "there existed from first to last a confidential relationship as close as that maintained by Mr. Lincoln with any other man. To Mr. Blair he almost habitually revealed himself upon delicate and grave subjects more freely than to any other. When he had conceived an important but difficult plan, he was almost certain, before giving it practical form, to try it by the touchstone of Mr. Blair's fertile and acute mind."

But there was more to old man Blair than that gentleman himself; he was the head of a kind of dynasty, a family group that had long been in the center of public affairs. His son Montgomery was Postmaster General in Lincoln's cabinet; another son, Francis, Jr. – usually called Frank Blair to distinguish him from his sire – probably the most brilliant of the lot, was Lincoln's unfailing bulwark in Missouri and in Congress. His daughter Betty, herself a leading political hostess, had married Samuel Phillips Lee; this Lee was an admiral in the Federal navy when the war broke out, and unlike his cousin, Robert E. Lee, declined to go over to the Confederacy. He commanded the fleet that blockaded his own Virginia and North Carolina. Gustavus Vasa Fox, the able Assistant Secretary of the Navy, Welles's chief reliance, had married Virginia Woodbury, daughter of Levi Woodbury, governor of New Hampshire, United State Senator, and, in his latter years, Associate Justice of the United States Supreme Court, an alliance that brought him within the Blair family circle, for Montgomery had married another daughter of the same distinguished New Englander; the two brothers-in-law were, moreover, close intimates. Of this family corporation it was the three Blairs that played the strongest role as

Lincoln's supporters. Their ideas on the future of the slave marched side by side with Lincoln's. They favored, as did Lincoln, gradual emancipation. They believed, as did Lincoln also, in compensation to masters for slaves set free – at the rate of $300 and $400 a head. They endorsed immediate emancipation – with payment – in the District of Columbia and the territories; Frank Blair, as a member of Congress, had voted for both these bills when they were passed in the early days of the war.

It was commonly remarked that one could hardly enter Lincoln's sanctum without finding him cheek by jowl with one of this fraternal and paternal triumvirate. Montgomery's habit of lingering after adjournment of cabinet meetings for a private talk with Lincoln exasperated his cabinet colleagues – all except Welles, who, in a way, formed part of the Blair sodality. "On important questions Blair," noted the Secretary of the Navy, "is as potent with the President as either [Chase or Seward] and sometimes I think equal to both. With some egotism Blair has great good sense, a better knowledge and estimate of military men than either or both the others and, I think, is possessed of more solid, reliable administrative ability."[1] Welles's comparison of Chase and the Blairs might rank with one of Plutarch's parallels. "The Blairs are pugnacious, but their general views, especially those of Montgomery Blair, have seemed to me sound and judicious in the main. . . . Chase is deficient in magnanimity and generosity. The Blairs have both, but they have strong resentments. Warfare with them is open, bold and unsparing. With Chase it is silent, persistent, but regulated with discretion. Blairs make no false pretensions. Chase avows no enmities." Naturally all these evidences of intimacy with the head of the nation – Lincoln's frequent trips to Silver Spring, the access of the Blairs to his private rooms, the President's crossings of Pennsylvania Avenue for chats with Montgomery at the Blair "mansion," the sight of Montgomery's children playing on the White House lawn with the Lincoln boys – aroused to fury the anti-Blair element, the Abolitionists and radicals. Horace Greeley railed against them as "a dangerous family" that had got Lincoln completely under their thumb while the Chase following denounced them as "a family of Maryland serpents."

"When the Blairs go in for a fight," Montgomery used to say, "they go in for a funeral," and this war-to-the-death spirit was exemplified, above all, in the youngest of the trio. Frank, forty years old when war began, was the darling of his father's eye; the radicals were right when they accused the family of aiming at the Presidency, for both old man

[1] Welles, *Diary*. I, 205.

Blair and Montgomery confidently expected some day to see their favorite succeed to Lincoln's chair. If dash, magnetic control over men, supreme courage, both in the battlefield and in public life, a handsome person, immense capacity for work, and a fanatical love of country qualify a man for this post, Frank Blair would have made an ideal head of the nation. All these traits he possessed and more; if not a bookish man like Montgomery and his father, Frank was an extensive student of affairs and a speaker whose words were all fire and conviction. Since he was absolutely honest, the many efforts of the Jacobins to picture him as a grafter disastrously failed, as did practically all the other calumnies which, in an angry time, they hurled against him. That Frank was a hard drinker could not be denied; his tent during the war was too often the scene of conviviality; but he carried his liquor far more successfully than other martial gentlemen of his day. His wartime speeches were usually full of fighting arguments and soul-stirring epithets; those who disagreed with Frank were too likely to find themselves figuring in them as "cowards" and "traitors" and "damned whelps." His energetic temperament added force to these characterizations. In appearance Frank underwent some changes in the field, chiefly in the addition of a large reddish beard; but the wiry frame, thin and six feet high, the finely poised head, with large, rectangular brow, the sparkling gray eyes, aggressive nose, elongated horselike face, seemed to take on additional vitality from the stress of the times.

Frank came to Washington as Representative from Missouri in the first war Congress meeting on July 4, 1861, with enhanced prestige for his work in "saving Missouri for the Union" in the early part of the year, and from that time to nearly the end of hostilities he filled a dual role – that of legislator in the Capitol and of soldier in the field. The Copperheads, under Vallandigham, and the Abolitionists, led by Thad Stevens, might shout that this double life was unconstitutional and demand Blair's expulsion from the House; with Lincoln's encouragement and perhaps even with his connivance Frank kept the two dignities and rendered valuable service in both. In that disastrous summer of 1861, Blair, as chairman of the Committee on Military Affairs, piloted through the chamber the many bills needed to create an army, and also established his position as champion of Lincoln that was to make him a pre-eminent influence for the next three years. Even in 1861 the difficulties that were to burden Lincoln's existence scored their first innings. Frank Blair assumed the lead in expounding Lincoln's views and defending them. That his speeches on the Negro and Emancipation were read and revised by his father and brother Montgomery before delivery was the general belief. They aroused such animosity in the Chase, Stevens, and Sumner circles, and brought such fierce recriminations on the floor that perhaps Frank was relieved when the session came to an end and he was free to return to Missouri, organize seven regiments, and, as brigadier general, march off to join General Sherman. In this phase Frank succeeded so well that when the victorious Union Army paraded down Pennsylvania Avenue at the end of the war, he received, next to Grant and Sherman, the greatest popular acclaim. Both Grant and Sherman had great contempt for civilian officers, but both forgot their favorite abomination in the case of Frank Blair. His behavior at Vicksburg and Lookout Mountain won their hearts. They regarded him as the ablest of all the non-West Point generals, and it was on the recommendation of Sherman that Frank Blair was appointed to the command of an army corps.

But Sherman, greatly as he admired Frank Blair's fighting qualities, understood the other side of the family character. "Blair was a man of great courage," he said, "and talent, but was a politician by nature and experience. I regarded him as a volunteer that looked to personal fame and glory as an auxiliary, and secondary to his political ambition and not as a professional soldier." This same was true of old man Blair and Montgomery. In every question that arose they all saw, first of all, its political tendencies. The personal fortunes of the Blair family always claimed consideration. No one understood this failing so clearly as Lincoln himself. The assertion of the radical group that the Blairs controlled the President had no foundation in fact. Lincoln used the Blairs, as he used other men, where they could be most serviceable in the supreme purpose of preserving the Union. A typical exchange between Lincoln on one side and Halleck and Stanton on the other emphasized his attitude towards all who were seeking to dominate his administration. In July of 1864, Jubal Early, in his aborted raid on Washington, overran Silver Spring and burned Montgomery Blair's summer home. "Nothing better could be expected," commented the peppery Monty, "while poltroons and cowards run the War Department." This remark, reported to Stanton and Halleck, threw those gentlemen into a rage. They demanded Blair's dismissal from the cabinet. "Truth is generally the best vindication against slander," Lincoln wrote his angry subordinates. "I propose continuing to be myself the judge as to when a member of the cabinet shall be dismissed."[2] That represented his attitude towards Stanton and towards the Blairs themselves.

It was probably the Blair tendency to capitalize their importance for personal advancement, and, in a degree, their attempts to "control"

[2] Lincoln, *op. cit.* X, 157.

Lincoln, that led to an appreciable loss of influence. In December 1862, Lincoln and the Blairs had flatly disagreed on two important issues. The first concerned the formation of the new state of West Virginia. The question of its admission into the Union caused a cleavage in the cabinet. Chase and Stanton favored this radical move; Blair, Bates, and Welles opposed it. Montgomery Blair prepared, at Lincoln's request, a detailed constitutional argument against separating this western pro-Union part of the state from its parent – a learned paper which the President pigeonholed and ignored. The second serious disagreement involved General McClellan. Had the Blairs opposed that soldier's dismissal on military grounds their objections might have received more respectful consideration. Characteristically the matter seemed to them chiefly a political problem. Was not McClellan a presidential candidate? To cashier him summarily would be politically unwise, for it would make him a martyr and increase his popularity. The elder Blair spent the evening before McClellan's dismissal with Lincoln, beseeching him to give the man another chance, basing his argument on political expediency. The result proved to be a commentary on the Jacobin insistence that Lincoln was completely "run" by the Blairs. The President listened to the specious pleas, stretched his long legs, and ended the interview. "I said I would remove him if he let Lee's army get away from him and I must do so. He has got the slows, Mr. Blair." And then he added the familiar Lincolnian touch: "I have tried long enough to bore with an auger too dull to take hold." The President's knowledge that part of Francis Blair's plan was to elevate his son, the valiant Frank, to the post of McClellan's chief of staff, and in this way make him liaison officer between the army and the administration, probably did not increase Lincoln's respect for this advice.

As the year 1863 wore on, the relations became merely friendly and anecdotal; the signs that old man Blair's position as closest adviser to the President were less important began to prey upon the veteran's mind. Up to June 1860, there had been at least three attempts to obtain control of the Lincoln administration and to supplant that leader in the post to which he had been constitutionally elected. Seward's "Thoughts" of April 1, 1861; the insurrection of Chase and Stanton in August 1862; and, most formidable of all, the attempt of the Republican Senators, in December 1862, to dismiss the cabinet and appoint its successors, have already been described. Another more subtle effort in the same direction was evidently planned in June 1863 by Montgomery and the elder Blair. It is true that this *démarche* never became an uprising. The Blair proceeding, so far as the scanty records disclose, was an aspiration rather than a concerted movement. For details we are dependent upon that crusty chronicler, Edward Bates. One of Bates's most intimate confidants, and chief purveyor of inside Lincoln information, was a gentleman who bore the illustrious name of Isaac Newton. This hard-working Quaker and skilled horticulturist had one distinction, aside from his personal intimacy with Lincoln – he was the first head of the great Agricultural Department, though in that experimental period the office did not carry cabinet rank. Newton flits in and out of the crabbed pages of Bates's Diary, usually as the bearer of secret news – of plots and counterplots of the active gentlemen who were then pulling the strings of national politics. The fact that he held almost a cabinet post – Newton really laid the foundations of the present Department of Agriculture – and was known to be on friendly terms with the President, gave value to his revelations.

The most ambitious of these stratagems Bates discloses in his Diary entry of May 10, 1863. Montgomery Blair, Newton related, had set forth, in a long interview which he had sought, a plan which amounted to nothing less than the elevation of his venerable father to the post of exclusive private councilor – "dictator" is the word Bates used – to Abraham Lincoln. Montgomery bewailed the fact that his father's influence on Lincoln seemed to be nearing the vanishing point. "His father had not, of late, been admitted, as much as he desired, to private conferences with the President." Couldn't Newton, in some way, remedy this situation? Couldn't he "use his influence with the President to bring about more intimate relations?" Montgomery eulogized his father at length and extolled the services he could render Lincoln and the nation if placed quietly at the head of affairs. He said "that the old man was, beyond all question, the ablest and best informed politician in America – and was known to be such! That under his advice, the President would be saved a world of trouble and the nation far better served, than in any other way." (Upon this Bates comments: "I have abundant other proof that he is full in the faith that Wisdom will die with his father and him!") The first fruit of this Lincoln-Blair combination, Montgomery informed Newton, would be a complete reorganization of the cabinet. The only man worthy of being retained in his existing position was Gideon Welles. Bates himself was marked for decapitation. Seward and Stanton would be retired to private life. Chase might possibly be moved up to the Secretaryship of State, or perhaps Charles Sumner would succeed to that place. Joseph Holt would be a good man for Stanton's seat – he had been Secretary of War in the last two months of Buchanan's administration, after the departure of the "traitor" Floyd; Benjamin F. Butler and Nathaniel P. Banks also were worthy of consideration for the same office. Preston

King, Senator from New York, would make an excellent Secretary of the Treasury. Montgomery had expressed himself in the freest terms on certain of his colleagues in the cabinet. Stanton was a "great scoundrel – making all sorts of fraudulent contracts, to put money into his own pocket – that, in that way, 'Cameron was a fool to him.'"[3]

"I knew before," Bates says, evidently somewhat irked at the fact that, in Blair's new assize, he was himself marked for slaughter, "his very bad opinion of Seward and Stanton, and his jealousy of Chase. And as to me, I knew he was disappointed and dissatisfied because I declined from the start to be an agent of 'the Blairs.' In fact, that clique has mistaken cunning for wisdom and they believe fully in trick and connivance. They believe me a mere marplot – and that, as Cardinal Wouley said of Bishop Gardener, 'He was a fool, for he would needs be virtuous. I'll have none such near his Highness.'[4] True, I have no confidence in Seward and very little in Stanton; but that does not make me confide in tricky politicians, who have not the first conception of statesmanship."

[3] It is due to Stanton to repeat that no serious student of Stanton today believes this charge.

[4] Bates, as almost always, misspells and misquotes. "Cardinal Wouley" is evidently Cardinal Wolsey and "Bishop Gardener" should be Bishop Gardiner. For what Shakespeare really wrote, see *Henry VIII*, Act II, Scene 2.

IV

LINCOLN'S MESSAGE of December 8, 1863, and accompanying proclamation, came to Chase and his adherents almost like a declaration of war. These great state papers announced a scheme for readmitting the Southern states to the Union, which the radicals regarded as a betrayal of the cause and a surrender to the South. There was not a vestige of punishment or vengeance in the President's proposals. To forgive and forget, to gather together the shattered fragments and begin life anew on the basis of good will and fraternity – such was the general idea underlying Lincoln's plan for a regenerated Union. Full pardon was offered, with a few exceptions in the higher ranks, to all who had fought in the Southern armies, on condition that they take the oath of allegiance to the Federal government and agree to accept and support the presidential proclamations and Congressional acts on slavery. Whenever 10 per cent of the citizens of a Southern state, according to the census of 1860, had formed a government and applied for readmission to the Union, it would become once more one of the United States. In this Lincoln plan there was no provision for reprisals – no wholesale hanging of "traitors," no transformation of the South into a "desert," no rule by military governors sent from the North. It was a proposal for genuine reconciliation and permanent peace, not of retribution. It was a foreshadowing of the second inaugural: "With malice toward none; with charity for all."

The radicals, after preliminary murmurs of apparent approval, pounced upon this proposal as a negation of the high purpose of the war. The Blairs, in Congress and the hustings, came just as vigorously to Lincoln's support. They had their own explanation for the war, which was entitled to special consideration because of their Southern origin. Secession, they insisted, had never obtained wide popularity in the South. The masses, even in states like South Carolina and Georgia, still remained loyal to the Union. They were speaking, of course, of those known as the "people" – the middle and poorer elements who owned no slaves, or practically none, and who despised slavery, chiefly as an economic wrong to themselves. The independent farmers of the North and West, who worked their own fields, moved easily in all social strata, enjoyed free opportunity of education and the other blessings that comprise an independent existence, seemed, to the "mud-sills" and "poor whites" of Dixieland, to be the favored sons of fortune. The population of the Southern states, as a whole, Montgomery Blair pointed out, belonged to this slaveless, submerged majority. Political and financial power had for generations been centered in the hands of great plantation owners, who had used this power to form the Confederacy, "with slavery as its keystone," and to force their states into rebellion. Any plan of Reconstruction which did not make existence bearable for this inarticulate majority, urged Blair, would be the rankest kind of cruelty and injustice. Genuine statesmanship would link up the Federal government with the great mass of honest, sincere, and loyal Southerners for the purpose of reforming the Southern commonwealth in really democratic fashion. This was Lincoln's policy, and an identity of purpose on this question made the Blairs about his ablest co-operators in the work at hand.

But the Blairs were not only philosophers, they were also politicians and feudists, and with them great battles of statesmanship, however lofty the principles at stake, always involved personal conflict. And the "personality" who now crossed their path at every turn was the Secretary of the Treasury, Salmon Portland Chase. The dispute over Reconstruction involved also the presidential succession. The two issues aroused particular hostility in the two states which the Blairs regarded as more or less fiefs in their family, Missouri and Maryland. In both, the Republican Party was split into two factions. In Maryland the two wings of the party were known as radicals and conservatives; in Missouri, the Republicans were split into the same two divisions, popularly called "Charcoals" – a suggestion of their devotion to the dusky brethren – and "Claybanks." Henry Winter Davis, bitterly hostile to Lincoln since the day of his exclusion from the cabinet, championed the Maryland radicals, and Montgomery Blair, his successful rival in presidential preference, led the conservatives. In Missouri, B. Gratz Brown and Charles D. Drake managed the cause of the Charcoals, and Frank Blair that of the Claybanks. The Charcoal cohorts in Missouri were strong for Chase, the Claybanks for Lincoln, and in Maryland the same differences in presidential choices appeared and along the same lines.

The rivalries assumed a more turbulent character in rough-and-ready Missouri than in the more sedate commonwealth north of the Potomac. The Chase followers in Missouri were largely formed of those idealistic

Germans who had settled in the country following the great immigration of the late forties and fifties, whose antislavery zeal could be compared only with that of the most unrestrained abolitionists of New England. These two wings of the party, with their journalistic and platform supporters, kept the state in a turmoil throughout the Civil War. Their respective public meetings quickly developed into riots and the street parades usually degenerated into orgies of disorder. From the first Chase came to the support of the Drake-Gratz Brown Charcoals, endowed them liberally with patronage, and gave them, to the exclusion of the Blair conservative Claybank faction, liberal permits for trade in the Mississippi rebel region. Whenever members of the anti-Lincoln bloc came to Washington, Chase usually went out of his way to show them social attention. Receptions at the E Street house, graced by the enticing smiles of daughter Kate, warmed their hearts and at the same time enraged the less welcome followers of the Blairs. That Chase, with his offices, his indulgences to trade, and his receptions was cultivating this anti-Lincoln element with an eye to the Missouri delegation at the Republican National Convention was a natural suspicion. Certainly Frank Blair entertained no doubts on the question and girded himself for the fray.

In August of 1863 Frank returned from the front to find himself a popular hero; his exploits at Vicksburg had been heralded in the public press and the people turned out in force to welcome their soldier home. His entrance into St. Louis was a Roman triumph, with torchlight processions, public meetings, and other outbursts of public approval. That the Drake-Gratz Brown Charcoal pro-Chase elements did not participate in these rejoicings, and even circulated in their newspapers unfavorable reports of Frank's military conduct, argued ill for the future peace of the town. Far from behaving in a conciliatory manner towards these malcontents, Frank, in several appearances on the platform, gave additional reasons for hostility. One of his speeches, made to an audience of wildly cheering partisans, was so uncompromising that the Chase press attributed it to that indulgence in hard liquor for which the orator was so well known. The whole evening, said the *Missouri Democrat* — organ of the radicals, and constant assailant of "the Blairs" — was a "disgrace" to St. Louis. That Blair should set forth in detail his views on what he persisted in calling "the nigger question," that he should uphold the Lincoln policy of Reconstruction, eulogize the President and uphold him as the one public man to whom the nation could be safely entrusted, and disembowel the radicals and all they stood for, was to be expected; but it was the speaker's attack on Chase that caused the hubbub. The Secretary was accused of scheming for

Lincoln's seat, and with this end in view of creating a corrupt political machine in Missouri. That issue of which Frank was to make so much in the next few months – the abuse of trade regulations for political purposes – figured prominently in the indictment. While a friendly audience howled with delight and stamped its feet, Blair referred to the dignified Chase as a "rowdy" and "a blackguard," and declared that he was "no whit better than Jefferson Davis" – thus again resorting to that "traitor" thesis which the Blairs frequently fall back upon when analyzing the second member of the Lincoln cabinet.

With the hurrahs of his followers and the execrations of the partisans of Chase resounding in his ears, Frank returned to his military duties with the Army of the Tennessee to receive a major-generalship at the hands of William Tecumseh Sherman and to win fresh laurels at Lookout Mountain and Chattanooga. But the platform warfare of the Blairs on Chase still continued. The voice of Frank in Missouri had scarcely subsided before that of Montgomery was raised in Maryland. As an offset to the Henry Winter Davis anti-Lincoln campaign, the Maryland adherents of the President held what they called an "Unconditional Union Meeting" at Rockville on the evening of October 3. Montgomery Blair accepted an invitation to be chief speaker. There were other considerations than radical activity in Maryland firing Montgomery's zeal on this occasion. In particular Charles Sumner had recently published an article in the *Atlantic Monthly* on "Our Domestic Relations,"[1] a broadside that had been generally accepted as a setting forth of the plan of Reconstruction to which the radicals were committed.

In manner and matter it was a characteristic Sumnerian piece of literature. Arrogant, magisterial, interlarded with quotations from Plato, Grotius, Vattel, and other highly respected authors, it described the future of the Southern states in terms diametrically opposed to the plans that were known to be taking shape in Lincoln's mind. In contrast to Lincoln's hope for a peace on the basis of forgetfulness and compassion, the cultured New Englander proposed one of damnation. In a few well-turned sentences, he wiped off the map the eleven states that had formed the Confederacy. By secession every state in insurrection had "committed suicide"; by that act it had ceased to exist as a state; its constitution had become a historical parchment, and in place the Federal government found itself in possession of a large extent of territory, as much virgin soil, so far as its relation to the Union was concerned, as the Louisiana Purchase or the Mexican cession. These states had "vacated" their government, and had consequently become a clean slate – or, as Sumner preferred to put it, a *tabula rasa* – on

[1] *Atlantic Monthly*, XII, 507–529.

which the Federal authority could write whatever it chose. Just what their future should be was in the hands of the Federal government. In the new South which was taking form in Sumner's eyes, not even the old state names or the old state lines would necessarily be preserved. Virginia, North Carolina, South Carolina, Georgia, might very likely take their places beside Burgundy, Aragon, and the Saxon Heptarchy, which were once proud, independent sovereignties, but had long been extinct in the family of nations. In their stead, Uncle Sam would have a new stretch of dependent land, like Nebraska, Utah, and the Indian Territory, out of which, in due course, new states might be formed and admitted to the Union. Since all such territories, under the Constitution, would be subject to Congress, it followed that the reorganization of this new expanse would be the exclusive right and duty of that legislative body. The principle that was to work such havoc as the basis of Reconstruction after Lincoln's death was set forth in this article with all the elegant English and apt quotation of which Sumner was a master. No new state from the vanished old Southern regime was to be reinstated until it had adopted a constitution that met the approval of the Senate and House of Representatives. By this time, certain of the provisions that Congress would demand were well known. The onetime slaves would be elevated to complete equality with the whites, with all civic privileges, including the franchise. The pardons for rebels which Lincoln favored on such a liberal scale would be handed out most sparingly. But the all-emphatic fact was that Lincoln would have nothing to say about Reconstruction; that would rest exclusively – except, of course, as it was limited by the veto power – in the hands of Congress; in other words, in the hands of the Jacobins who held despotic influence in that body.

Montgomery Blair was on cordial personal relations with Sumner, whom, in many ways, he admired; but that did not prevent him from denouncing this program in words that rocked the Republican Party from one end of the nation to the other. The solicitude the Abolitionists evinced for the Negro, he declared, could have only one purpose. He raised high the most dangerous of issues in discussing the question: that of social equality, intermarriage, and a mulatto population. Frank Blair had already proclaimed that the essence of the racial problem in the United States was not slavery, but the Negro; Montgomery believed this also, as did Lincoln himself, and the only possible solution the three saw was the transportation of the colored population and its colonization in some tropical climate. "The Abolition party," Montgomery declared almost at the beginning of his Rockville exhortation, "whilst pronouncing philippics against slavery, seek to make a caste of another color by amalgamating the black element with the free white labor of our land and so to expand far beyond the present confines of slavery the evil which makes it obnoxious to republican statesmen. And now . . . they would make the manumission of the slaves the means of infusing their blood into our whole system by blending with it 'amalgamation, equality and fraternity.' . . . The cultivators of the evil," he continued, "must then become a hybrid race and our government a hybrid government, ending as all such unnatural civilizations have ever done: in degraded if not abortive generations and in making serfdom for an inferior caste – the unmixed blood of the conquering race inevitably asserting a despotism over it." This was the ambition, said Blair, that underlay the scheme of wiping out the Southern states and reorganizing the South as new territories. Recent articles in the *St. Louis Democrat* and the *Washington Chronicle* were clearly aimed at creating such a new American race, and "now comes the *Atlantic Monthly*, which lends to the present stock at Boston all it can boast of literary strength and elegance." The article in the *Atlantic* "may justly be quoted as the programme of the movement," and as "the Abolition manifesto." He then developed at length his favorite idea for the reconciliation of the seceded states. The Federal government should join hands, not with the ex-slaves, but with the loyal white non-slaveholding citizens who made up the bulk of the population. Any system of reconstruction which would punish them would constitute "most outrageous injustice." Only the "traitors" in the South – that is, the scheming politicians, agents of the slaveholding power – "have committed suicide. . . . Treason was not committed by any state, but by the individuals who made use of the states and attempted to dismember the national government."

To attack Charles Sumner and his reconstruction ideas was to attack Chase. The two men thought as one on this, and most other subjects. They had been intimate, daily co-workers for almost twenty years. Sumner was one of the few Republican leaders of prominence who regarded favorably – if not enthusiastically – Chase's presidential hopes. However, Blair assailed Chase not only by striking at Sumner; certain remarks in his speech hit directly at the Treasury head. When he ridiculed "these movements at Washington and Boston to annihilate the state governments," he had in mind, of course, the Chase-Sumner partnership for that purpose. And when Blair spoke of "the coadjutors of Presidential schemers in St. Louis and throughout Missouri," he might just as well have spoken Chase's name. "And do not all these efforts," said Blair, as a parting shot at his cabinet colleague, "indicate something of a design to command a great event in prospect of revolutionary means?" The great event, of course, was the forthcoming presidential election in 1864, for which both wings of the Republican Party were now forming their lines. The reference to "revolutionary means" appears to be merely a repetition of Thurlow Weed's cynical conclusion that Chase's real motive, in his Southern policy, was a desire to keep any Southern state from taking part in the contest of 1864.

V

IN ITS EARLIEST stage Chase's campaign was self-conducted, mainly in epistolary form. Long before anything resembling an organization had been created to push his candidacy, the industrious man was filling the mails with an endless stream of letters, discussing his fitness to succeed Mr. Lincoln in the White House. One wonders how Chase, occupying one of the most exacting offices in the government, at perhaps the most critical period in its history, could have found the leisure for labor of this kind. Men of all stations, lofty and obscure, of all trades and professions, were included among his correspondents. Chase's letters on the theme that was absorbing his thoughts all followed the same pattern. They began with a disavowal of aspiration for the presidency, and described the insistence of influential leaders that he was the one man fitted to deal with the crisis. The idea, he wrote, far from originating with him, was extremely distasteful; however, if the party really demanded his leadership, he had too great a sense of public duty to decline. The cause was the main thing, not personal ambition, and he was prepared, however unwelcome the presidency might be, to sacrifice his inclination for the good of the country.

A letter written November 26, 1863, to the millionaire politician who had recently become his son-in-law may be quoted as fairly typical of all. "If I were controlled by merely personal sentiments, I should prefer the re-election of Mr. Lincoln to that of any other man. But I doubt the expediency of re-electing anybody, and I think a man of different qualities from those the President has will be needed for the next four years. I am not anxious to be regarded as that man; and I am quite willing to leave that question to the decision of those who agree in thinking that some such man should be chosen." [1] "I have not the slightest wish to press my claims upon the consideration of friends or the public," he wrote to E. A. Spencer, December 4, 1863. "There is certainly a purpose, however, to use my name, and I do not feel bound to object to it. On the contrary, were the post to which these friends

[1] Schuckers, *op. cit.*, p. 494.

desire to place me as low as it is high, I should feel bound to render in it all the service possible to our common country." [2] This same delusion appears in all Chase's numerous letters of this period – that a nation, as a whole, was reaching out to him to replace the incompetent Lincoln, and that, as an unselfish patriot, he was reluctantly acceding to the prayer.

Presently more tangible evidences of a presidential boom appeared. That autumn of 1863 was the time of the famous Vallandigham governorship contest in Ohio. The "Peace Democrats" had nominated this most remorseless of Copperheads on a platform calling for the immediate end of the war, defiant of all the principles for which the administration stood. That Chase should return to Ohio to vote, and even make a speech or two against the enemy of the cause, would seem to be his duty as a good citizen; but his critics immediately saw a deeper meaning in his departure. His hardly concealed aspirations for the White House naturally made him the victim of the most unworthy suspicion. Blair declared that this stumping tour was an open declaration of war on the President. Edward Bates could express his contempt only by classical allusion. "The National Intelligence of today," he notes on October 20, "contains Mr. Chase's late speech at Cincinnati (and another at Indianapolis) in which he supposes that our successes are due to the Proclamation of Freedom. In other parts of these speeches Mr. C. attributes the success of the country to his own *admirable financial* system, quite as intelligibly, but in language not quite as plain as Cicero's – who swore 'By the immortal gods, I have saved my country!' That visit to the West is generally understood as Mr. Chase's opening campaign for the Presidency. At all events, the war is openly begun between Mr. Chase and the Blairs." [3] "Chase is understood to have special interest in this election," [4] Welles slyly comments on the Western tour. The de luxe pamphlet, *Going Home to Vote*, published by Chase in commemoration of his excursion, lends some color to these ungenerous inuendoes. The compiler of this brochure was Whitelaw Reid, who for a time had been closely identified with Chase's political prospects. "I have been in the habit of revising his [Chase's] speeches for publication," wrote Mr. Reid on September 30, 1864. "Perhaps you saw the pamphlet I made for him last year, *Going Home to Vote*, containing all his speeches on his western trip." [5] This comprised not only a reprint of Chase's speeches, but a somewhat jubilant day-by-day account

[2] *Ibid.*, p. 495.
[3] Bates, *op. cit.*, p. 311. Italics in the original.
[4] *Ibid.*, p. 469.
[5] The letter from which this extract is taken was published in the *New York Sun*, June 30, 1889.

of what is pictured as a triumphal tour. It really portrays Chase in a new aspect – that of a popular hero, a man who was hail-fellow with the crowd, ready at repartee, an object of familiar greeting by his fellow men. The portrait is not that of the statuesque statesman, but of the good-natured, almost rollicking favorite of the proletariat. From Columbus to Cincinnati the train stopped at way stations for brief speeches; there were blaring bands, military escorts, reception committees, immense congregations, and cannon salutes. Chase smiled delightedly when the rank and file hailed him as "Old Greenbacks," and joined in the roars when listeners interrupted his speech with complimentary familiarities. The "laughter" and "cheers" bracketed in this edition of the Ohio discourses indicated their popular response, even though certain generals, like Grant, Sherman, and Meade, and statesmen like Edward Bates, were not pleased by the emphasis laid on the sound financial policy of the government as responsible for recent military success.

Now all over the nation laudatory editorials began appearing in the papers as well as lengthy articles in magazines setting forth Chase's achievements. That familiar harbinger of a presidential boom, the "campaign biography," issued from more than one press. The most ambitious of these efforts, *The Ferry Boy and Financier*, followed a biographical pattern that has gained a considerable vogue in modern times. It was a "fictionized biography," a mixture of fact and invention, written by one of the most popular authors of the day, John T. Trowbridge. Chase himself supplied the material, in a series of letters addressed to Trowbridge amounting really to an autobiography. *The Ferry Boy* in the title fell in with the popular taste which demanded a humble origin for great men, but proved somewhat puzzling to Chase's admirers. It was "more to be commended," says Schuckers, Chase's secretary and one of his twin biographers, "for alliteration than description"; yet his dutiful research finally disclosed that, at the age of twelve, Chase did, for several days, "amuse himself during some portion of his time by ferrying passengers across the Cuyahoga." [6] Chase's letters would seem to imply that he felt a little shamefaced about this eulogy, which, largely because of the popularity of the author – and also because of the purchase of a large number of copies by Jay Cooke for free distribution – had quite a vogue, certain chapters even being printed in the *Atlantic Monthly*. "I have read *The Ferry Boy*," Chase wrote Trowbridge. "You have certainly thrown a great deal of attraction about what I remember as very dry facts. Indeed, from in-

[6] Schuckers, *op. cit.*, p. 11.

formation or fancy, you have collected some facts which are quite out of my recollection."[7]

He was even more embarrassed by an account of his life, illustrated by a steel engraving by John Sartain, which appeared in the *American Exchange & Review,* of Philadelphia – an article also inspired and financed by Jay Cooke. Evidently Lincoln had nudged Chase about this piece of publicity and received an answer that must have entertained him. "It was a matter in which I had no concern," Chase protested to his chief. "If any body wants my autograph, and I have time, I give it; if any body wants to take my daguerreotype – photograph – and I have time, I sit for it; if any body wants *to take my life,* in the way of a biographical sketch, *I let him take it;* and, if I have time, give such information as is wanted that he may take it more easily. Some friends wanted such a sketch prepared, and engaged a gentleman to prepare it. . . . How could I object? He asked for subscriptions and obtained them. How could I control or supervise that? I was very busy with the affairs of my department and had no time to look after such matters, even had I been aware of what was being done. If I had been consulted I should certainly have objected to any subscription by Mr. Jay Cooke or his brother, except such a moderate one as any friend might have made. Not that any wrong was intended to be done, but because the act was subject to misconstruction and there are so many to misconstrue."[8]

Clearly the ethical question of Chase's relations to the Philadelphia banker was pricking his conscience. The matter was, indeed, one that might well have raised qualms. Mr. Cooke was at this time the chief fiscal agent of the government, made so by appointment of Chase; his contract for the five twenty loan proved to be a valuable one, in both profit and prestige; it really established Cooke as one of America's greatest bankers – a lofty position he held until the failure of his firm in 1873 precipitated one of the worst financial panics in American history. Yet in 1864, Cooke and Chase's son-in-law, William Sprague, were the main financial backers of his presidential aspirations. Chase himself says in his apologia to Lincoln that all this was "subject to misconstruction," and the phrase will probably impress the present, more sensitive generation as rather mild. One can perhaps dismiss Chase as a guileless soul, made impervious to impropriety by an ambition that verged on mania, but Cooke knew what he was doing, and his ap-

[7] Warden, *op. cit.*, p. 589.

[8] Field, Maunsell B., *Memoirs of Many Men and Some Women.* Harper and Bros., 1874. P. 305.

proaches to Chase frequently betrayed the easiest of consciences. Thus, in May 1862, he purchased three hundred shares of stock in the Philadelphia & Erie Railroad and carried them in Chase's name; he subsequently sold the certificates at a profit, and sent a check amounting to $4200 to the Secretary of the Treasury.[9] Chase promptly returned the money, but he showed no indignation, kept Cooke as one of his friends, and even, six days afterward, requested the banker to make a loan to Mrs. Gamaliel Bailey, widow of the editor of the *New Era,* a paper most friendly to Chase and his presidential ambitions.

Nor did Chase apparently see anything improper in the undercover work which the two Cookes – Jay and his brother-partner Henry – now engaged in. Jay Cooke had one of the most far-reaching machines for inexpensive publicity the country has ever known. The Federal banking organization which was Chase's greatest achievement as Secretary of the Treasury was at his disposal. All the newly organized national banks became selling agents for government bonds. Cooke figured his army of salesmen at about 2500; they reached all the large cities and all the towns and rural districts. All these agents were utilized, under Cooke's supervision, as active workers in pressing Chase's claims for the Presidency. An essential part of Cooke's selling campaign was newspaper advertising. Country weeklies and city dailies eagerly contended for this well-paid business. Inevitably, in days of easy journalistic morals, this gave the Federal fiscal agent a powerful hold on the press and this he unblushingly manipulated in the interest of the Secretary. All newspaper owners knew that one of the best ways of obtaining this advertising was to display a friendly interest in Chase's candidacy. They were the frequent recipients of articles, for both the editorial and the news columns, setting forth the good points of Lincoln's Treasury head. "Mr. Cooke, through the created or maintained agencies," says Cooke's biographer, "was constantly voicing the praises of the Secretary of the Treasury and they were soon to be used almost openly to favor Mr. Chase's candidacy for the Presidency.[10]. . . Jay Cooke's loan agents and newspaper advertising system which he had created were cheerfully enlisted in Chase's behalf, but the movement was concealed under so much real patriotism and the hopes of the leaders were so short-lived that no particular harm came to the banker and his firms from his association with this rather unfortunate political experiment. . . . Mr. Chase not only favored but indeed rather expected the use of the five twenty advertising agencies for his personal

[9] Oberholtzer, Ellis Paxton, *Jay Cooke, Financier of the Civil War.* Macrae Smith Co. I, 274–275.

[10] *Ibid.,* I, 273.

political advantage."[11] The Cookes were also associated with Kate's husband, William Sprague, in several other plans which were expected to obtain the right kind of support for their favorite candidate.

That Chase should use the patronage of his office to advance the cause was not surprising; such was the universal practice of the time – it is not entirely unknown, indeed, to the present generation; but that he should indignantly deny the charge, in view of the evidence, comes as something of a shock. "I should despise myself," he wrote to Thomas Heaton, one of his supporters in Cincinnati, "if I felt capable of appointing or removing a man for the sake of the Presidency. . . . I have never sought to manage newspapers. I have never undertaken, and never shall undertake, to manipulate the press."[12] In May 1864, Weed's paper, the *Albany Evening Journal*, published an editorial calling Chase to account for converting the Treasury Department into a political machine. The Secretary wrote an indignant letter of protest to Seward, Weed's political partner. "The patronage of this department is not and never has been used with reference to that nomination."[13] The cynical Seward must have grinned as he read this disclaimer; no one knew better than Seward that Chase was as great a spoilsman as he was himself. Gideon Welles insisted that Seward and Chase had an understanding on patronage matters from the beginning. "These two men had political aspirations. . . . Chase thought he was fortifying himself by this arrangement, but he often was over-reached and the arrangement was one of the mistakes of his life."[14] Chase had in fact reduced the distribution of good things to a mathematical science; Ohio had one eighth of the nation's population, and so was entitled to one eighth of the offices in all the departments – with himself, of course, as the dispenser. At the height of the crisis over Sumter, Chase informed Seward that there were 269 vacancies in the State Department; of these, on this one-eighth basis, Ohio was entitled to thirty-three. When the Secretary of State balked over the appointment of one of Chase's strongest Ohio henchmen to the consulship at London, the Treasury head threatened to appeal to a higher court: "I have not thought it respectful," he wrote Seward, "to go to the President about appointments in your department, except through you; others do and it seems not unsuccessfully." Both Welles and Bates noted with disapproval Chase's use of the offices to promote his presidential schemes. "I think there are indications," wrote the Secretary of the Navy, as the campaign ad-

[11] *Ibid.*, p. 360.
[12] Warden, *op. cit.*, p. 565.
[13] *Ibid.*, p. 597.
[14] Welles, *Diary*. I, 138.

vanced, "that Chase intends to press his pretensions as a candidate, and much of the Treasury machinery and the Treasury agencies have that end in view." [15] "I am afraid Mr. Chase's head is turned by his eager pursuit of the Presidency," Bates observed on October 17, 1863. "For a long time past he has been filling all the offices in his own vast patronage with extreme partisans and continues also to fill many vacancies, properly belonging to other departments. In the judiciary his appointments seem to me particularly unfortunate, made without any reference to legal or judicial qualifications." [16] In another entry Bates accuses Stanton also of using his appointments to promote the prosperity of his friend. "If I were in his [Lincoln's] place I would never submit to have the influence of the two most powerful departments, Treasury and War, brought to bear upon the election – against the President and for the aspiring Secretary." [17] One of the most powerful politicians and journalists of the time was John W. Forney, Secretary of the United States Senate, editor of the *Philadelphia Press* and owner of a string of influential newspapers. "If Mr. Chase sanctions the unjust attacks upon the gentleman under whom he holds place," Forney wrote, about March 1864, "it will require little talent at figures to prove that the enormous catalogue of offices (almost a Blue Book in itself) attached to the Treasury Department is crowded with the personal adherents of the distinguished Secretary." [18]

To newspaper editors Chase showed the most friendly spirit. William Cullen Bryant, of the *New York Evening Post*, was bitterly hostile to Lincoln's renomination, and warmed up little to Chase as an alternative candidate. In February of 1864, Chase wrote Bryant, complaining of this inattention but offering to give one of Bryant's friends a good job. Greeley at this time was the Secretary's most important journalistic support. The eccentric editor evidently regarded his idol as qualified for any role; perhaps the wildest of the many crazy proposals that issued in the course of the Civil War from this "ink-slinger" (as he called himself) was that Chase be made commander of the Army of the Potomac. "If in 1864 I could make a President (not merely a candidate)," Greeley wrote Chase September 29, 1863, "you would be my first choice." The Secretary responded with a fulsome letter of thanks, remarking incidentally that there were two well-paying clerkships vacant in the Treasury, into which he was willing that Greeley put a couple of his friends.[19] Certain wiles, familiar to the present genera-

[15] *Ibid.*, I, 525.
[16] Bates, *op. cit.*, p. 310.
[17] *Ibid.*, p. 343.
[18] Carman and Luthin, *op. cit.*, p. 233.
[19] Schuckers, *op. cit.*, p. 394.

tion, such as the cultivation of religious and racial minorities, were not beneath the dignity of Chase. In 1864 the Catholics were a numerous and powerful group in Ohio, under the leadership of an extremely popular prelate, Archbishop Purcell, of Cincinnati. In November 1863, Chase wrote the Archbishop in glowing terms of General Rosecrans, then under a cloud because of his defeat at Chickamauga, adding that it was through his influence that Rosecrans had received his important command. The general was one of the nation's most distinguished lay Catholics. At another time Chase again took the Most Reverend Purcell into his confidence; he was attempting to persuade Seward to intercede at the Vatican, to have the Cincinnati churchman appointed successor to Archbishop Hughes of New York, who had recently died. Chase's agents were active with the Germans of Wisconsin and Missouri and he was also courting the Jews and Poles of New York, already a considerable element, with newspapers of their own. Senators and Representatives who showed any inclination to Chase were appropriately "recognized." Learning that Senator John Conness of California had shown an accommodating spirit, Chase wrote him broaching the subject of Treasury appointments on the Pacific Coast. Conness quickly saw the point and gave Chase assurances that no man appointed on Conness's recommendation would ever be permitted to work against the Secretary's interests. "From the moment I saw and heard of you," Chase replied, "I felt that Providence had sent us a bold, clear-headed and faithful man on the Pacific Coast. I feel sure I shall not be disappointed in the men I select in consultation with you."

In fact it was a matter of common talk in Washington that all the customhouses in the nation had been organized into a Chase machine. The attitude was well brought out in a letter to Chase from George S. Denison, Collector of the Port of New Orleans, now in possession of the Federals: "We are forming a Chase Club here and meet for organization next Monday. . . . I believe we can control the election of delegates to the National Convention." Ninety customhouse heads were removed when Chase became Secretary of the Treasury, practically all of the places being filled by his partisans. Politically these were the most powerful forces in their regions, for each collector of a port had a great subsidiary patronage. Hiram Barney, a Chase man who had been made Collector of New York, had the appointment of 1200 public servants at his disposal. Horace Greeley estimated that the Collector at New York could control the New York delegation to the national convention.

Naturally these familiar signs of an impending boom did not escape the attention of the master politician in the White House. But they do not seem to have caused much anxiety. To the protestations of his friends that he was nourishing a "traitor" in his official family Lincoln usually replied with a smile. Lincoln's secretaries, John Hay and John Nicolay, kept the President well informed of Chase's activities; other close associates insisted that he should dismiss the man who was seeking to displace him; bluff Tom Corwin, Minister to Mexico, told Lincoln that Chase was "embodied perfidy." But Lincoln, in a letter already quoted, had set forth the grounds on which he retained or dismissed his cabinet officers; their usefulness to the nation in the existing crisis was the one argument he deemed worthy of consideration. Lincoln, though he undoubtedly despised a man who sought the presidential nomination without first resigning from the cabinet, had a high regard for Chase's intellect and for his ability as a financier. He considered his management of the Treasury Department one of the most creditable achievements of the war. That was sufficient reason for ignoring an activity that was unquestionably disloyal to himself. Day after day commissions were placed on Lincoln's desk from the Treasury – men whom Chase had selected for public office. These were mostly extreme radical politicians whom Chase was appointing, Lincoln knew, in furtherance of his presidential campaign; yet Lincoln cheerfully signed them, seeming to take an almost humorous satisfaction in the act.

Perhaps one reason for the President's even temper was that he understood the utter folly of Chase's pretensions. "When the Presidential grub once gets in a man, it hides well," he remarked – this in reference to his own wish for renomination, which he made no effort to conceal; that Chase's aspirations were doomed to humiliating failure the experienced Lincoln knew from the first. While Lincoln good-naturedly kept appointing Chase presidential workers to office, Republican conventions were meeting in state after state, all of them passing resolutions demanding Lincoln's renomination and instructing the delegations to vote for him at the approaching national convention. That the three states from which Chase might have anticipated support – New Hampshire, in which he had been born, and Ohio, in which he had spent most of his life, and Rhode Island, of which son-in-law Sprague was supposed to be boss – ignored the Chase campaign and joined the Lincoln demonstration perhaps made the humorous gentleman even more indulgent. His secretaries have recorded the President's comment on these strange manipulations. " 'I have decided,' he said, 'to shut my eyes, as far as possible, to everything of the sort. Mr. Chase makes a good Secretary and I shall keep him where he is. If he becomes President, all right, I hope we may never have a worse man. I have observed with regret his plan of strengthening himself.

Whenever he perceives that an important matter is troubling me, if I am compelled to decide in a way to give offence to a man of some influence, he always ranges himself in opposition to me, and persuades the victim that he has been hardly dealt with, and that he would have arranged it very differently. It was so with General Frémont, when I annulled his hasty proclamation, with General Butler when he was recalled from New Orleans, with those Missouri people when they called the other day. I am entirely indifferent as to his success or failure in these schemes so long as he does his duty at the head of the Treasury department.' "[20]

Still personal relations between the two men became more embarrassed. They had never been on comfortable terms; one of the things Chase could never understand was why Lincoln so preferred Seward's society to his own. His selection of a house a mile distant from the White House he regarded as a mistake; it was so easy for Lincoln to drop in for a chatty afternoon visit with the Secretary of State, whose home was on the east side of Lafayette Square just across the street from the "Executive Mansion." Welles, too, lived on the north side of the same park, and Lincoln was very fond of "Father Neptune." Perhaps Chase's failure to understand what draws one human being to another was no more completely illustrated than in this belief that Lincoln's lack of warmth towards himself was merely a matter of geography. "Among men who called during the day," Chase notes in his Diary for June 30, 1864, "was Mr. Hooper, who related a conversation with the President some days ago, in which the President expressed regret that our relations were not more free from embarrassment, saying that when I came to see him he felt awkward and that I seemed constrained. At the same time he expressed his esteem for me." That rather completely expresses Lincoln's attitude towards his Treasury head. As Chase's campaign gained momentum, his reluctance to meet the President face to face became more manifest. He had always been one of the most punctilious in attending cabinet meetings, and most critical of his colleagues when they were absent. In late December of 1863, Welles quotes Senator Doolittle, of Wisconsin, "that there is an active, zealous and somewhat formidable movement for Chase and that Chase Clubs are being organized in all the cities to control the nominating Convention," and adds, as to cabinet meetings, "Chase avoids coming in these days."[21]

[20] Nicolay and Hay, *op. cit.* VIII, 316–317.
[21] Welles, *Diary*. I, 498.

VI

HOW MY heart sickens," wrote the garrulous Robert B. Warden, Chase's official biographer, "as I make up the long list of knaves and fools in whom the hero of this work confided!" Jacob Schuckers, Chase's other official biographer, selected by his daughters as a kind of antidote to Warden, similarly bewails the Secretary's poor judgment of men. In particular, he says, this presidential canvass "fell into bad hands; it was badly officered and badly managed." Both writers have in mind chiefly the two characters who had active charge of Chase's boom. These were Senator Samuel Clarke Pomeroy of Kansas, and James M. Winchell of New York.

They had been close associates in politics and business for several years, especially in Kansas during the Kansas-Missouri "border ruffian" days. Pomeroy, a William Lloyd Garrison abolitionist in early life, a professional antislavery agitator in the fifties, had arrived in Washington as first Senator from Kansas in the early part of 1861. A reputation for political corruption in attaining this seat had preceded him. That he had purchased it from the rough-and-ready legislature of a pioneer era was the prevailing belief. This suspicion could not then be established, but certain crises in Pomeroy's after career lend some color to the scandal. A committee of the Kansas legislature which investigated Pomeroy's re-election in 1867 reported unanimously that members of the legislature had been bribed. In 1873 Pomeroy failed of a third term because both the Kansas legislature and a committee of the Federal Senate proved to the satisfaction of his constituents that money had been used to purchase votes.

Pomeroy's public life in Washington accorded well with this character. He seemed to have had little interest in anything except the spoils of the senatorial office. The feuds that constantly raged between the onetime abolitionist and his colleague, the Huey-Long-like Jim Lane, afforded Washington a good deal of entertainment, but caused great distress to the occupant of the White House. "Lane knocks at my door every morning," Lincoln remarked, and the importunities of his rival were just as insistent. Perhaps Lane received more consideration than Pomeroy; at least that was Pomeroy's conviction, and, as a result, he declared war on Lincoln. Inevitably Pomeroy was drawn within the presidential orbit of Salmon P. Chase. His own private interest inclined him to the Secretary. Pomeroy was the owner of a considerable block of stock in the Hannibal & St. Joseph Railroad, which, under the Pacific Railroad Act, passed in 1862, was entitled to certain subsidies from Federal funds. The allotment of these grants lay in the discretion of the Secretary of the Treasury; at least it was Chase's duty to determine whether the conditions had been met which would make the claimant eligible to government largess. Thus the desire to stand well in Chase's estimation, combined with an intense animosity against the ruling executive, had combined by the latter part of 1863 to make Samuel Pomeroy leader of the forces that were working to secure a new dispensation in the election of 1864.

This same Pacific Railroad interest was close to the heart of two other men who presently assumed leading roles in the Chase campaign. James M. Winchell had also been a fiery abolitionist, newspaperman, Kansas correspondent of the *New York Times*, and presiding officer of the Wyandotte Convention, the body which had framed the constitution on which Kansas had been finally admitted to the Union. After this triumph, Winchell returned to New York, and became agent of the Pacific Railroad, a position that brought him into close relations with Pomeroy. A third member of the trio was a young man of a stamp entirely different from either of his seniors. Edmund Clarence Stedman was a cultured, educated man, a favorite in intellectual circles of both New York and Washington, a poet and literary critic whose writings had considerable vogue in their time, though they have fallen into neglect since his death. In 1862 Stedman, aged twenty-nine, having served a brief time as war correspondent for the *New York World*, came to Washington, and obtained a post as pardon clerk under Attorney General Bates. Bates evidently liked his assistant, and mentions him a few times in his Diary; however, he felt obliged to discourage Stedman's enthusiasm for General McClellan to which he was giving utterance on all occasions. The stirring verses, "Abraham Lincoln, give us a man!" – Bates presented Lincoln with a copy, which the President read to his assembled cabinet – sounded that note of criticism of the President which was to grow keener as the presidential year 1864 approached. In 1863 Stedman, tired of Washington routine, went to New York and entered the banking house of Samuel Hallett and Company, thus beginning that mingled career of Wall Street and literature which was to make him known as the "banker-poet." The Hallett firm was fiscal agent of the Pacific Railroad, and Winchell and Stedman necessarily saw much of each other. The friendship had political as well as financial consequences. Chase, as man and Secretary, had been Stedman's chief admiration in Washington. He soon joined the Pomeroy-Winchell forces, taking charge of the New York headquarters of the Chase presidential boom; for several months he led a varied life, speculating in stocks with Winchell as partner,[1] managing what he called a Chase "Bureau of Action" in New York, writing poetry and book reviews at night, visiting Kansas in the interest of the Pacific Railroad, and spending days in Washington seeking subsidies from Chase for that enterprise. His literary talents were pressed into service, though Stedman's Diary confesses that the labor was very "distasteful" and that he did not like the breed of politicians with whom he had to work. He spent much time, however, with Greeley, David Dudley Field, George Opdyke, Manton Marble, editor of the Copperhead *World*, and others who had actively enlisted in the campaign against Lincoln.

Many of the men prominent in the pro-Chase campaign, as appears from Stedman's companions in New York, bore names of light and leading in the nation. In December 1863 – soon after Lincoln had sent his message to Congress advocating moderation and commiseration in Reconstruction – another group, styling itself "an organization to make Samuel P. Chase President," began holding secret meetings in Washington. The list of best-known members had a decidedly Ohio flavor – Major General Robert C. Schenck, Rufus P. Spalding, John Conness, L. E. Chittenden, and Whitelaw Reid. General Schenck, five days before the first meeting, had resigned from the army to become Representative from Ohio. He had been a strong antislavery Whig, Congressman from 1843 to 1851, and minister to Brazil – he afterward served as minister to Great Britain by appointment of President Grant. Rufus P. Spalding was another Ohio Congressman, a war Democrat long personally and politically attached to Chase. John Conness was the Senator from California whom Chase, as already noted, had made dispenser of Treasury loaves and fishes in the far distant Pacific state. L. E. Chittenden, afterward one of the most laudatory writers of Lincoln memoirs, was at the time drawing a Federal salary as Register of the Treasury, by appointment of Chase. Whitelaw Reid, then only twenty-six years old, had already laid the foundations of a distinguished journalistic career. As war correspondent of the *Cincinnati Gazette*, he

[1] See Stedman, Laura, and Gould, George M., *Life and Letters of Edmund Clarence Stedman.* Moffet, Yard & Co., 1910. I, 327 ff. This contains many extracts from Stedman's Diary showing his work on the Chase committee.

had won national fame by his description of Shiloh and Gettysburg; as political reporter in Washington, he had sharply criticized the Lincoln policies and displayed a conspicuous leaning towards Chase. In 1860, Reid had championed Lincoln's rising star, thereby acquiring the resentment of his fellow Ohioan; the breach had since been healed and the brilliant young journalist had become one of the Secretary's closest friends, a relationship that lasted for the rest of the Secretary's life. Reid had accompanied Chase on the "going home to vote" excursion in October 1863, and by the time of the December meeting was in the confidence of Greeley – whom he subsequently succeeded as editor of the *New York Tribune* – Henry Winter Davis, Sumner, Garfield, Sherman, and other congressional antagonists of Lincoln.

How many of these eminent gentlemen approved of the most important achievement of this committee, the pamphlet *The Next Presidential Election*, which presently inundated the mails, cannot be known. Certainly John Sherman, Senator from Ohio, saw nothing objectionable in it, for it was broadcast, at government expense, under his frank – a favor for which he presently issued a confused explanation which deceived nobody, for his hostility to Lincoln had been no secret. Just who wrote this diatribe is not certain, though suspicion strongly pointed to James M. Winchell, co-worker with Stedman in the New York base of operations. This document of six closely printed pages did not advocate the Chase candidacy; it contented itself with exposing the futility of Abraham Lincoln and the utter absurdity of considering him as a presidential possibility in 1864. It was intended to afford politicians material for their arguments against his candidacy, and editors with inspiration for their anti-Lincoln editorials. According to the newspapers one hundred thousand copies were printed and placed where they would do the most good. The Lincoln that emerged from a reading of this paper was certainly a different character from the one now familiar to the world. This 1864 Lincoln was portrayed as an unscrupulous tyrant, ready to resort to all extremes to undermine the institutions of his country and settle himself in power for the rest of his days. The most elaborate objection urged against his renomination rather startles a reader of the mid-twentieth century. It is the one that runs through all of Chase's correspondence of the day. No President should ever serve for more than one term! The one-term precedent, Chase was accustomed to explain – and this brochure repeats his arguments – was so sanctified by custom that it had become practically a part of the Constitution. Since Andrew Jackson retired to the Hermitage in 1837, not one of his nine successors had occupied the presidential chair for more than four years. To violate that principle now would destroy the Republic and establish a dictator in the White House. In all parts of the country, the pamphlet insisted, Lincoln was appointing postmasters, customhouse officers, marshals, district attorneys, and the like – all of them Lincoln politicians, who, as delegates to the nominating convention, would present a unified phalanx for a second term. Nor was this army to be a purely temporary host; it was to be kept in constant preparedness, and would thus assure the President's renomination for as many successive terms as he might desire.

"If President Lincoln," the pamphlet said, "can now so wield his patronage as to secure his election for a second term, who so blind as not to see that four years hence he will have less difficulty in securing his election for a third term? For, with an army of more than half a million citizen soldiers under his command and an annual patronage of a thousand millions in money, he can, if he has half the brain attributed to him by his friends, have himself elected from term to term during his natural life." This picture of Lincoln as a military despot was constantly present in the author's mind. The President was deliberately letting the war drag on in order to keep himself in office. "If the 'military necessity' supplies a reason now for his nomination and the extraordinary patronage occasioned by the war furnishes the means of his election, as a matter of course, his interest is then to prolong the war as a means of perpetuating his power." Lincoln's one chance of re-election was by using "the military power in his hands, by suppressing the freedom of election in the loyal states. A victory won by the sword would be no victory but a lamentable defeat to the friends of liberty. . . . The temptation to a military candidate to use the sword to secure his own election is too great, the warnings of history too impressive for the American people ever voluntarily to submit to so hazardous an experiment." The rest of the document was devoted to Lincoln's failure as an executive. He was "weak," "vacillating," "incapable of settling upon any line of policy in regard to the rebellion. . . . The cant about 'honest Abe' was at first amusing, it then became ridiculous and now it is absolutely criminal." Perhaps the paragraph that most outraged Lincoln's admirers was a comparison to Jefferson Davis – much to the advantage of the Confederate leader. See what Davis, with only five million people behind him, with no money or resources, had accomplished, and then look upon the Lincoln picture: head of twenty million people, with all their wealth and industry at his command – and his failure, in nearly four years' blundering, to suppress the rebellion!

An avalanche of letters descended on John Sherman for using his congressional privilege to send great quantities of this literary masterpiece through the mails. One correspondent wrote him that "it was so mean and dastardly in character that it will brand with infamy your character as a statesman and your honor as a gentleman." It "was a stab in the dark, assassin style." This reference to anonymity could not be urged against another anti-Lincoln broadside that followed, about two weeks afterward. To this the name of Samuel G. Pomeroy was proudly appended; for the first time this leader appears in the light of day, though he had been actively at work behind the scenes for a considerable time. This is perhaps the reason why "the Pomeroy Circular," as it is always known in Lincoln literature, was less personally abusive than *The Next Presidential Election*, though practically all the charges and insinuations of its predecessor were repeated. In literary style and in matter the two articles were so much alike that they probably had the same author. Blair, in his usual peppery fashion, said that Chase himself had written the circular, but James W. Schuckers, who, as Chase's secretary and biographer, had better firsthand information, points to James M. Winchell as the ghoster for Pomeroy and it is reasonably safe to conclude that he was penman also of the earlier document. The same general contentions figured in both.

In only one respect did the Pomeroy Circular differ from the preceding theses, and this was important. It pointed out in emphatic terms the one American who did possess the necessary talents for the great task still confronting the nation. "We find unified in Salmon P. Chase more of the qualities needed in a Presidential candidate during the next four years than are combined in any other available candidate; his record, clear and unimpeachable, showing him to be a statesman of rare ability and an administrator of the very highest order, while his private character furnishes the surest guarantee of economy and purity in the management of public affairs. . . . The discussion of the Presidential question, already commenced by the friends of Mr. Lincoln, has developed a popularity and a strength in Mr. Chase unexpected even to his warmest admirers; and while we are aware that this strength is at present unorganized, and in no condition to manifest its real magnitude, we are satisfied that it only needs systematic and faithful effort to develop to an extent sufficient to overcome all opposing obstacles." Therefore the admirers of Mr. Chase were organizing on this platform: "The speedy restoration of the Union on the basis of universal freedom," and "an administration of the government during its first period of new life which shall to the fullest extent develop the capacity of free institutions, enlarge the resources of the country, diminish the burdens of taxation, advocate the standard of private and public morality, vindicate the honor of the Republic before the world and in all things make an American nationalist the fairest example for imitation which human progress has ever achieved."

This circular, though marked "strictly private," inevitably found its way into newspaper offices and was too sensational an item of news to escape publication. In giving it to its readers, the *Constitutional Union* of Washington ridiculed the injuction to secrecy. "We propose," it said, "to keep closely confidential all the unmentionable things contained in this 'strictly private document,' not by ourselves alone, but aided by our 30,000 subscribers." That fairly represents the spirit in which the Chase-Pomeroy manifesto was received. In hotel lobbies, dinner tables, the halls of Congress, and other places in which the matter was eagerly discussed, criticism centered on the utter folly of the thing. Chase might deny any knowledge of the circular but deceived nobody; his daughter Kate certainly must have known about it, for her husband, William Sprague, was one of the central group and the financial supporters of the enterprise. But that a member of Lincoln's cabinet should be engaged – or suffer his friends to be engaged – in these attacks upon his chief, that he should be openly seeking the nomination and at the same time not resigning as a member of the President's official family – here was something new even in the not too high-minded political scene.

Chase himself, when this letter became public, finally saw the point and wrote Lincoln offering to retire from the administration. He was utterly guiltless of this document, he informed the President, and had known nothing of its existence until it appeared in the newspapers. It was true that he had given his consent to the use of his name in the approaching canvass. He had been waited on some weeks before by a committee representing Senators, Congressmen, and "other distinguished citizens," and had reluctantly agreed to their request. But he had done this only from a sense of public duty. "I have never wished that my name should have a moment's thought in comparison with the common cause of enfranchisement and restoration, or be continued before the public a moment after the indication of a preference by the friends of that cause for another. I have thought this explanation due to you as well as to myself. If there is anything in my action or position which in your judgment will prejudice the public interests under my charge, I beg you to say so. I do not wish to administer the Treasury Department one day without your entire confidence. For yourself I cherish sincere respect and esteem, and, permit me to add, affection. Differences of opinion as to administrative action have not changed these sentiments nor have they been changed by assaults upon me by persons who profess themselves the special representatives of your views and policy. You are not responsible for acts not your own; nor will you hold me responsible, except for what I do or say myself. Great numbers now desire your re-election. Should your wishes be fulfilled by the suffrages of the people, I hope to carry with me into private life the sentiments I now cherish, whole and unimpaired."

Lincoln, of course, did not have the slightest intention of consenting to Chase's resignation – at this time. He was too able a party manager to make a mistake of that proportion. If there was any virtue in his plan for a coalition cabinet, it was especially needed at this moment. The dismissal of Chase, in February 1864, would have split the party in two and probably have led to its defeat in the coming election. For the fact could not be overlooked, and the practical Lincoln was the last man to overlook it, that more than a majority in both houses of Congress, and a great body of influential men in the country, supported the Chase view on Reconstruction rather than his own. To have repudiated Chase would undoubtedly have led to two Union parties and Chase's nomination by one of them in opposition to the regular candidate. That would have meant handing over the country to the Democrats and the end of the war, with the South as virtual winner. Lincoln therefore acknowledged Chase's letter in a brief note and said that he would reply to it in a few days. "On consideration," he wrote Chase on February 29, "I find there is really very little to say. My knowledge of Mr. Pomeroy's letter having been made public came to me only the day you wrote, but I had, in spite of myself, known of its existence several days before. I have not yet read it, and I think I shall not. I was not shocked or surprised by the appearance of the letter, because I had had knowledge of Mr. Pomeroy's committee, and of secret issues which I supposed came from it, and of secret agents who I supposed were sent out by it, for several weeks. I have known just as little of these things as my friends allowed me to know. They bring the documents to me, but I do not read them; they tell me what they think fit to tell me, and I do not enquire for more. I fully concur with you that neither of us can be justly held responsible for what our respective friends may do without our instigation or countenance; and I assure you, as you have assured me, that no assault has been made upon you by my instigation or with my countenance. Whether you shall remain at the head of the Treasury Department is a question which I shall not allow myself to consider from any standpoint other than my judgment of the public service, and, in that view, I do not perceive occasion for a change."

Chase himself rather ruefully noted the one conspicuous quality lacking in this letter. In a note to the always sympathetic Horace Greeley, he referred to this correspondence. To the Secretary's suggestion of resignation "the President had replied, closing with the statement that there was nothing in the condition of the public interests which called for a change in the Secretaryship of the Department; but there was no response in his letter to the sentiments of respect and esteem which mine contained."

BOOK SEVEN

End of the Coalition

I

THE *Next Presidential Election* and the Pomeroy Circular destroyed such slender chances as Chase may have had for popular support. Their one effect was to rally all Lincolnians to the President's side. Three days after Pomeroy's pamphlet appeared in type the Union Republicans in Ohio passed a resolution advocating Lincoln's nomination for a second term. Governor Tod of Ohio wrote the President, protesting against the unauthorized use Chase propagandists were making of his name. "The fact," he said, "that Mr. Chase has been laboring for the past year, at least, with an eye to promoting his own selfish purposes, totally regardless of the consequences to the government, as I believed to be the case, is also sufficient to induce me to oppose him." Thus the same misadventure which had defeated Chase's ambitions in 1860 had humiliated him again. He was a presidential candidate without the delegation of his home state. James A. Garfield, John Sherman, and other political intimates urged the Secretary to accept the inevitable and disentangle himself, as gracefully as possible, from his embarrassment.

Chase followed the advice of his friends, at least to outward appearances. In a letter to James C. Hall, written March 5, and generally published in the newspapers on the tenth, he went through the motion of withdrawing his name. But, maladroit as ever, he did this in a way that brought ridicule on his head. He had retired only from a sense of duty; his presence in the field seemed likely to endanger the sacred cause; his friends were still urgent that he remain a candidate. Hardened politicians, who knew that Chase had stepped aside only because he could obtain no delegates, laughed at this pretension. They also pointed out that this letter, and others addressed to personal friends, left the way open for Chase to resume his aspirations if things should take a more promising turn. "Mr. Chase will subside as a Presidential candidate," wrote Edwin D. Morgan, Senator from New York and chairman of the Republican National Committee, "after the nomination is made, not before." "The Salmon is a queer fish," commented the scurrilous Bennett in the *New York Herald*, "very wary, often appearing to avoid the bait just before gulping it down." The more sedate Edward Bates was similarly distrustful. "This forced declention [*sic*] of Mr. Chase is really not worth much," he wrote in his Diary for March 9, 1864. "It proves that the present prospects of Mr. Lincoln are too good to be openly resisted, at least, by men within the party. The extreme men, who urged Mr. Chase, afraid to array themselves in open opposition to Mr. L. will only act more guardedly – get up as many candidates as they can, privily with the hope of bringing Mr. C. in at last, as a compromise candidate." Lincoln's campaign manager of 1860, David Davis, now adorning the United States Supreme Court, diagnosed the situation in the same way. "Mr. Chase's declination," Justice Davis wrote Thurlow Weed March 21, "is a mere sham, and very ungraceful at that. The plan is to get up a great opposition to Lincoln, use Frémont and others, and represent, when the Convention meets, the necessity of united effort, that anybody can unite except Lincoln, etc., etc. and then to present Chase. There was a meeting of Chase's friends in the city [Washington] last night. They resolved not to support Lincoln, etc., etc. the greater part present were Treasury officials. How long can these things last?"

The unobtrusive author of the Pomeroy Circular, James M. Winchell, held similar views. He insisted several years afterward that Chase's real purpose in withdrawing his name was to spur the wavering spirits of his campaigners. Evidently Pomeroy and his co-worker, Kate's husband, had run to cover in face of the wave of indignation that greeted their literary efforts. "The movement in favor of the Secretary of the Treasury, Mr. Chase" – so wrote Winchell in a reminiscent article – "had culminated in disaster; that gentleman's chief supporters, including his senatorial son-in-law, having manifested a plentiful lack of nerve or zeal, when the critical question became public, of arraying him against his official chief, made haste to take him at his word of declination, diplomatically spoken, in order to rouse their flagging spirits." [1]

Another element in the Lincoln fellowship did not take too seriously this withdrawal. In all this fury the Blairs had not been quiescent. Chase's pretensions, indeed, afforded them the greatest opportunity of their career. In January 1864, Frank Blair returned from the battlefields of Chickamauga and Chattanooga to resume his secondary duties as Representative from Missouri. In a sense he came at the invitation of Lincoln himself. As the time drew near for the assembling of the Thirty-eighth Congress, Montgomery Blair candidly asked the President what were his wishes concerning Frank; should he resign his commission,

[1] *Galaxy Magazine*, July 1873. "Three Interviews with Lincoln."

give up the military life and devote himself exclusively to his career of lawmaker? Lincoln knew that the approaching legislative session was to be a difficult one. In the fierce lines being formed against his Reconstruction policy, he would need all the support that could be enrolled. There had been a good deal of talk, on the Lincolnian side, of Frank Blair as the next Speaker of the House. In such a post he would be a tower of strength to the Lincoln forces. On the other hand, as an ordinary member of the House, his services could have a doubtful value. His unrestrained oratory, his Blair habit of pursuing his foes, especially his favorite one, Chase, with heroic vituperation might do the administration more harm than good. Lincoln thought this decision concerning Frank Blair so important that he put his views in writing. Let Frank come to Washington, he decided, and place his resignation as major general in the President's hands; then let him enter the contest for the speakership. If he succeeded in attaining that distinction, Lincoln would accept the resignation and Frank could devote all his time in future to statesmanship. If he failed, Lincoln would replace his commission in his hands, and he could resume his duties with the army. By the time Frank reached Washington, in early January, Schuyler Colfax, openly anti-Lincoln, had been elected Speaker. Frank, however, lingered on; the Chase situation was getting critical, and he saw several ways in which he might spend a few weeks profitably to the Blair family and to the Lincoln administration.

The program of his new attack Frank had already outlined in newspaper articles and speeches in the summer of 1863. Chase, he insisted, was busily constructing his presidential machine, not only by the use of Treasury patronage, but by another device that was even more productive of results. The trading that had been going on between North and South for nearly three years had caused one of the most sordid scandals of the Civil War. The problem had become an acute one after the outbreak of hostilities. The cessation of commercial intercourse that inevitably followed Sumter had caused great inconvenience and even suffering to both sides. Since the beginning of the government the Southern states had been dependent on the North for most of the essentials of existence. Wearing apparel, shoes, tea, many kinds of food, and above all medicines, were articles of everyday need that could be obtained only from the region with which the Confederacy was now at war; the blockade had become so effective that they could not be obtained from Europe. On the other hand, the North was dependent on Southern states for certain staples such as cotton, tobacco, sugar, resin, tar, and other things without which its normal economy could not be sustained. The most important, of course, was cotton. The

Union needed this commodity not only to keep its own mills in operation, but to pacify the increasing demand from England and France. As the Northern armies began advancing into Southern states, especially those in the Mississippi Valley – Kentucky, Tennessee, Mississippi, Arkansas, Louisiana – great areas of formerly rebellious territory passed under Federal control. These sections contained accumulations of cotton and the other commodities sadly needed in the North. They contained also large populations, a considerable proportion loyal to the Union, which had been reduced to misery by the lack of necessaries of which the North possessed a large supply. Would there be any harm in re-establishing trade between these now redeemed areas – sections that had virtually become again parts of the Federal Union, and were under the administration of Federal armies – and their former customers in the North?

Formulated in this simple fashion, there seemed to be one reply possible to the question. From this situation rapidly developed several Acts of Congress which made legal certain trading operations with the onetime enemy. The whole difficult matter was placed under the jurisdiction of the Secretary of the Treasury. Chase was authorized to organize agencies and to grant special permits for this kind of intercourse. That such an arrangement gave opportunity for favoritism and corruption is evident; and, in fact, the depredations of the speculators who seized the chance of making quick fortunes forms one of the darkest stories of the time. Frank Blair claimed that Chase had used these prerogatives to strengthen his political machine. "Permits to trade" in rebel territory were valued higher than most political offices – they were likely to prove more profitable; and naturally the pressure from politicians and their friends for such privileges became ferocious. Blair asserted that Chase was distributing these favors in ways that would best promote his presidential prospects. In Missouri, he said, only radicals received the "permits" while the other wing – the Lincolnian wing – in the Republican Party was ignored. When Blair resumed his congressional seat in January, almost his first move was to rise and demand the appointment of a committee to investigate the granting of "trade permits" in the Mississippi Valley. The Chase forces in the House, under the leadership of James A. Garfield and the Speaker, Schuyler Colfax, who, if not openly supporting Chase's candidacy, were opposing Lincoln, succeeded in blocking this resolution. The popular revulsion caused by the Pomeroy Circular, however, gave Blair another opening, and on February 27 he came into the House with a prepared speech, which appeared in the *Congressional Globe* under the title, "The Jacobins of Missouri."[2]

[2] *Congressional Globe,* 38th Congress, I Session. Appendix 46–51.

It was devoted chiefly to Chase and his trade practices in the Southern states. It was also a spirited defense of Lincoln against his pamphleteering assailants. Pay no attention, Blair cried, to certain activities in Missouri and Maryland, states where a certain type of Republican was pledging support to Lincoln, but secretly working to undermine him. The vote of the recent Maryland state Republican convention at Baltimore endorsing the President was cited as a sample of the hypocrisy so prevalent in these doubtful regions. The radicals in that convocation openly had taken a stand for Lincoln's renomination, but secretly they were seeking his destruction. Henry Winter Davis and his pro-Chase organization had not dared to outrage the sentiment of the people so far as to vote against Lincoln, but had sought, "while thus putting the left arm around his neck, saying, 'How art thou, my brother?' to stab him under the fifth rib. . . . It is a matter of surprise that a man having the instincts of a gentleman should remain in the cabinet after the disclosure of such an intrigue against the one to whom he owes his position. I suppose the President is well content that he should stay; for every hour that he remains sinks him in the contempt of every honorable mind." Why did this Mr. Chase and his supporters in Congress oppose the investigation of his "trade permits"? Why did his friends in the House interpose when attempts were made to scrutinize these so-called favors to politicians "enlisted in the Chase campaign"? "I say here in my place and upon my responsibility as a Representative that a more profligate administration of the Treasury Department never existed under any government, that the whole Mississippi Valley is rank and fetid with the frauds and corruptions of its agents; that 'permits' to buy cotton are just as much a marketable commodity as the cotton itself; that these permits to buy cotton are brought to St. Louis and other western cities by politicians and favorites from all parts of the country and sold on 'change' to the highest bidder, whether he be a secessionist or not, and that too, at a time when the best Union men in these cities are denied permits." The same was true, continued Blair, of the "trade stores" which the Secretary had been authorized to establish in sections redeemed from the Confederacy. "These trade stores are given to political partisans and favorites, who share the profits with other men who furnish the capital, Mr. Chase furnishing capital to his friends and partisans in the shape of permits and privilege to monopolize the trade of a certain district or city; and furthermore it can be established that the practice of taking bribes on the part of these Treasury agents for permits to trade and for conniving at violations of law is so common that it has almost ceased to attract attention or excite comment." Such was the state of affairs, concluded Blair, that the Chase supporters refused to investigate!

"These dependents of the Secretary, these agents and missionaries of his presidential aspirations, are still extant and receive their salaries. Some of them, I suppose, employ themselves in distributing that 'strictly private' circular which came to life the other day which informs us that the friends of Mr. Chase have been secretly forming an organization in his favor all over the country and which charges the administration of Mr. Lincoln with corruption. None know better than the friends of Mr. Chase at whose door does that corruption lie as their efforts to stifle investigation here so plainly prove."

And now Garfield succeeded in "stifling" such an inquiry once more. His method was to offer a resolution providing for an investigation but stipulating that it should be held by the Committee on the Conduct of the War. Of course that put the whole matter in the hands of the Chase party. On this motion Blair demanded the "yeas" and "nays." "I want to see how many men there are in this house who wish to whitewash Mr. Chase." The Garfield proposal passed by a vote of seventy-five to sixty-three. Two months afterward, the irrepressible Blair again pressed his demand. This time the House granted his request, but the committee appointed by Speaker Colfax was headed by Garfield as chairman, and comprised a majority of Chase adherents. This committee never carried out the instructions of the House; it declined to call any witnesses, and after several weeks of inaction asked to be relieved of the duty of investigating the Blair indictment. As to the actual facts perhaps the nearest approach to an impartial verdict is that of Edward Bates, an admirer neither of the Blairs nor of Chase. "How the President will take it I know not," he wrote, "but if he'll just let me 'take the responsibility' I'll make short work of Mr. Chase's knot of ignorant and rapacious swindlers, from the Balise to Cairo." [3]

By this time the Blair-Chase contention had reached a stage of fever heat almost without parallel in the eighty years' history of Congress. The attack of February 27 proved to be a mild affair compared with the philippic that the younger Blair delivered two months afterward. Those who gathered in the upper house on April 23 understood, by a glance in the gallery, that the anticipated storm was not exclusively the affair of the younger Blair, but of the whole Blair family. There conspicuously sat the venerable head of the clan, freshly arrived from Silver Spring, and by his side his sprightly daughter Betty Lee, a handsome, smiling, valiant sister, all eager to cheer on one brother, while he engagingly vituperated the cabinet colleague of another. The remaining gallery seats were occupied, for news had leaked out of the forthcom-

[3] Bates, *op. cit.*, p. 382. Bates here includes as the area of irregularities the Mississippi Valley, from the Gulf to the Ohio.

ing performance; the Senate almost en masse abandoned its own quarters and crowded into the House, as it usually did on the promise of rough-and-tumble excitement in the lower chamber. Certain new developments had added fuel to Blair's sufficiently fiery temperament. The repeated refusals of the Garfield Committee to investigate Chase's "trade permits," even when directed to do so by the House, seemed partisanship of the most unscrupulous kind. The Jay Cooke newspapers – heavily endowed with Treasury advertising – had started a campaign of unrestrained mud-slinging against the Missouri soldier-statesman. The Chase cohorts in Missouri had sought to turn the tables on Frank by accusing him of grafting in government contracts and conducting an illicit trade in supplying whiskey and other drinkables to the army. The House did appoint, on Blair's demand, a committee to investigate these charges. The report dismissed them as calumnies and brought forth a fact that made Frank a popular hero once more, for it showed that the document on which his enemies had relied to support their statement was a forgery.

In his speech Frank placed this forgery directly at the door of Secretary Chase, for the crime, he said, if not instigated by the Secretary himself, was clearly the work of his agents. The scene was one of the most turbulent that the House had ever staged. Most of the members were on their feet the larger part of the time, Chase's friends yelling demands for order, Blair's adherents coming to his support with shouts of "good," "go ahead," "keep it up"; Speaker Colfax, completely losing control of the body, kept viciously pounding his gavel, declaring the speaker "out of order," ordering him to stop – in vain, for the House overruled his parliamentary decisions, perhaps because the show was too enjoyable a one to be shut off on technicalities. Who was responsible, asked Frank, for these "forgeries" against him published in certain newspapers? "These dogs have been set on me by their master, and since I have whipped them back into their kennels I mean to hold their master for this outrage and not the curs who have been set upon me." Many of the charges had been put in circulation by a newspaper "pensioned by the Secretary of the Treasury. . . . I am simply endeavoring to show the motives which caused me to oppose Mr. Chase and which opposition caused him to retort upon me by an assault upon my character and reputation by the forgeries committed and disseminated by his understrappers."

"The gentleman is out of order!" shouted Speaker Colfax, bringing down his gavel with a mighty bang. "You're all right!" responded the Blair supporters. "Go ahead," and Frank did, ignoring the presiding officer's interruption.

"I propose to show," he continued, "that the Secretary of the Treasury is using these abandoned plantations and grasping at all the powers and patronage for the purpose of providing a fund to carry out the operations of the Pomeroy committee against the administration which gave him place." Chase was rewarding supporters in every direction. He was giving his son-in-law, William Sprague, permits to buy cotton that would yield him millions of dollars. He was granting Ohio adherents the exclusive privilege of supplying the Southern regions with medicines. "All the southern people, in and out of our lines, loyal and disloyal, and even the contrabands, must get their pills from Cincinnati." Yet the committee refused to investigate these things! "Mr. Chase cannot escape. He is sure to answer, and however deeply the committee may lay the whitewash on, it cannot conceal the dark background. . . . The time will come when he will be held to strict accountability, when he will be called to the bar to answer for all he has done; and all the efforts made by his friends thus indirectly to shield him from the charges made against him will not serve their purpose." Then Blair passed to the chief promoters of Chase's candidacy. "Mr. Chase's banking agents, as well as his Treasury agents and special and supervising agents have all been brought into requisition to forge and counterfeit and tell lies to break me down for exposing and holding up to public contempt and scorn their employer and master. . . . A million and three quarters dollars realized by a banking firm in less than nine months is a comfortable competency for two or three private gentlemen and would aid in establishing a good many newspapers in the interest of Mr. Chase by these men, who are shown to be banking on political capital to a greater extent than upon their own money. Accordingly we find a great many newspapers in favor of Chase for President, and very few people." Blair's general conclusion was "that treasury officials, by means of outsiders, are now engaged in the most gigantic robberies of modern times, exceeding the famous operations of Clive in India."

Chase's withdrawal from the presidential contest should not be taken seriously. "Nobody is simple enough to believe that the distinguished Secretary has really retired from the canvass for nomination to the Presidency, though he has written a letter, declining to be a candidate. That letter was written because the 'strictly private' circular of the Pomeroy Committee unearthed his underground and underhanded intrigue against the President. It was such a disgraceful and disgusting sight to make use of patronage and power given him by the President against his chief, that even Chase got ashamed to occupy such a position publicly. For that reason his letter was written; he wanted to get down and work under the ground and work there in the dark, as he is now doing and running the Pomeroy machine on the public money as vigorously as ever. The work is now being done in Frémont's name and that poor creature is unconscious of being made a cat's paw to accomplish the objects of his intriguing rival. His program is to hold a convention of Jacobins and red Republican revolutionary Germans at Cleveland, Ohio, precisely as Calhoun used poor John Tyler to hold a side convention in 1844 to force the Democrats to drop Van Buren. The Cleveland convention is a whip convention which will say to the Union Convention to be held at Baltimore, 'if you insist on the nomination of Lincoln we will nominate Frémont against him as an independent candidate.' In this way, if the delegates who have been instructed to vote for Lincoln can be bought with greenbacks or frightened by the Jacobin hobgobblin, it is expected that Chase, who has so magnanimously declined to be a candidate will then be taken up as a compromise candidate. This is the program of the Secretary and the compromise candidate. It combines the tactics, the intrigues, the corruption and the frauds of Calhoun and Biddle combined." [4]

At this point the Speaker's "hammer fell" and definitely, for Blair's time was up. Frank left the House never to return; his next appearance in Congress was in 1871 when he came as United States Senator from Missouri. Leaving the Capitol after this farewell speech, Frank went up to the White House, received from Lincoln his commission as major general and the command of an army corps. He became part of Sherman's campaign in Tennessee and Georgia, and on the March to the Sea won new laurels for bravery and ability in the field.

The President's act in restoring Frank Blair to his command in the army and sending him to the front apparently with his blessing caused more perturbation than the speech itself. What could this mean except that Lincoln had approved Blair's attack on the Secretary of the Treasury? That Lincoln was the inspiring source behind the Missourian's anti-Chase campaign, that, indeed, Blair had been brought to Washington for this express purpose, the radicals had for some time been whispering; the presidential accolade, after Frank's most sensational outburst, seemed to confirm this suspicion. The fury and disgust of such vehement Chase men as Garfield were unrestrained. Lincoln's "creature," Garfield wrote a friend, "was sent here for a special purpose, which, when accomplished, he puts him back in his place, thus ratifying all he said and did when here. . . ." It was a "flagrant outrage against the rights of the Senate and the House, against the Constitution and the army, against the men who had put him in power and against

[4] *Congressional Globe*. 38th Congress, 1st session. Part 2, 1830–1832.

one of his own cabinet. . . . The President is bound hand and foot to the Blairs and they are dragging him and the country down the chasm." [5]

Salmon P. Chase, when he received news of the two acts – Frank Blair's oration and the apparent reward bestowed upon him by the President – became an entirely different person from the placid, dignified, philosophic Chase so familiar to history. Volcanic rage is not the characteristic usually associated with this man, but all who caught glimpses of Chase in the next few days picture him as unrestrained, violent, making both Blair and Lincoln the victims of his explosive temper. One observer in particular, A. G. Riddle, radical Congressman from Ohio, has left a picture of Chase in this unusual mood. The Secretary was at the railroad station, with his two daughters, Kate and Nettie, about to step on a train for Baltimore, when the news from Capitol Hill reached him. Riddle reports that his face was ashen, his voice hoarse, almost a croak; "his body so shaking with fury that the railroad car in which he was sitting fairly trembled under his feet. . . . I was shown to Mr. Chase's presence in the car set apart for his use. He was alone, and in a frightful rage and controlled himself with difficulty as he explained the cause. The recital seemed to kindle his anger and aggravate its intensity. . . . 'All this,'" Chase told Riddle, "'has been done with the cordial approval of the President, a view fully shared by some of my immediate friends.' . . . Mr. Chase thought of remaining in the city, at once tendering his resignation to the President. I implored him not to act hastily and said that next week – after a better ascertainment of the facts – he would be able to act in accordance with a dignified consideration of all the conditions, as was his usual rule." Then the train started, greatly to Riddle's relief.[6]

The lobbies of the Washington hotels and of Congress were naturally alive with rumors. That Chase would retire from the Lincoln administration was assumed as a matter of course. How could a self-respecting public man act otherwise? How could he continue to sit in the cabinet of a President who had shown such favor to a politician-soldier immediately after he had inflicted about the worst castigation any public man had been subjected to in the memory of the living generation? How could he keep on, facing across the cabinet table Montgomery Blair, brother of the outrageous Frank, and probably his co-worker in the preparation of the speech? Already gossip was busy fixing on Chase's successor. The complete disintegration of the Lincoln administration seemed unavoidable. That long anticipated final break between Lincoln and the radicals, so many times averted, now was

[5] Smith, *op. cit.* I, 376.
[6] Riddle, A. G., *Recollections of War Times*. G. P. Putnam's Sons, 1905. P. 267.

apparently at hand. Only some satisfactory explanation from Lincoln, even an apology to Chase, would avert the calamity. Blair's attack had been made on Saturday; on Sunday party leaders were busy with plans that might, at the last moment, save the situation. Chase, it was said, had even drafted a paper, to be signed by the President, denying all responsibility for Blair and expressing confidence in the Treasury Department. Finally the Ohio delegation in Congress appointed two of Chase's most earnest champions, A. G. Riddle and Rufus P. Spalding, a committee of two to wait upon the President and attempt to arrange some satisfactory compromise.

They were received by Lincoln in his executive office Monday morning. Both the emissaries were shocked by Lincoln's careworn appearance; "he looked like a man harassed by petty fault-finding and criticism, until he had turned at bay." Lincoln, after the usual salutations, withdrew to the end of the cabinet table and sat down, not, however, inviting his visitors to do likewise. "Mr. Lincoln received us politely but with no pretense of cordiality," Riddle subsequently recorded. Riddle began the session by stressing the need of harmony in the Republican ranks at this time; the salvation of the nation, he said, demanded Lincoln's re-election and recent events had endangered the harmony that was indispensable to success. He frankly told Lincoln that Blair's speech, followed by the President's apparent endorsement in renewing his military commission, "seemed as if planned for dramatic effect, as part of a conspiracy against a most important member of the cabinet and the administration. . . . The always alert, jealous and somewhat exacting abolitionists believe that Blair must have had at least your countenance in this wretched business and they demand the instant resignation of Mr. Chase. It is only by the strenuous exertion of one or two persons that this has been delayed. . . . Mr. President, Mr. Chase's abrupt resignation now would be equal in its effects to a severe set-back of the army under Grant. It would foretell the defections of his friends at Baltimore, equal in effect to the defeat of that army in a pitched battle. Their defection in November might be the destruction of our cause. I pray you to remember who these abolitionists are. They are the first, the oldest antislavery men – the abolitionists who conquered, first of all, the pro-slavery North, and who, with later allies, have conducted the great struggle to the issue of war, who made your accession to power possible. I know they have at times been over hasty. They were, however, the first to leap to your side and who have pressed most closely after you, nay, would push you forward."

At the end of these introductory remarks Lincoln's not too friendly countenance changed; he rose, came forward, shook the two Congressmen by the hand and, standing, spoke for nearly an hour. His remarks, so far as Riddle recorded them, were as follows: –

"Gentlemen, I am glad to meet you, glad for your mission, and especially glad for your way of executing it. It makes my statement easier than I expected. I nevertheless will say about what I intended. Your frankness and cordiality shall be fully responded to."

Then, taking up a batch of papers from the table, Lincoln asked: "Have you seen my letter to Mr. Chase of February 27, in reply to his of the twenty-second, concerning his candidacy and offering his resignation?"

"I have," replied Spalding.

"I have not," said Riddle.

Lincoln read the document. Then, placing it back on the table, he remarked, with a slight smile: "The Blairs are, as you know, strong, tenacious men, having some peculiarities, among them the energy with which their feuds are carried on." [7]

"Yes," interposed Riddle, "Montgomery says that when the Blairs go in for a fight they go in for a funeral."

"Exactly," said Lincoln, and then he referred to the Blairs' work in building an antislavery party in Missouri. "Frank has in some way permitted himself to be put in a false position. He is in danger of being kicked out of the house built by himself. You know that they contributed more than any twenty men to bring forward Frémont in 1856. I know that they mainly induced me to make him a major-general and send him to Missouri."

Lincoln gave what information he had on the recent disturbances in Congress. Frank had called on him and said that he wished to make a speech in the House on the Mississippi trade regulations. "I told him that if he did the subject justice he would be doing a public service. 'But if you intend to make it the occasion of pursuing a personal warfare, you had better remain silent.'" Lincoln said that the speech had greatly annoyed him. The trade regulations had been made by the cabinet. "When it assailed Mr. Chase for the working of the machinery it did him an injustice."

This reference, of course, was to Frank's first speech – that of February 27, on the "permit" system in the Mississippi. Lincoln then took up the latest explosion – that of the preceding Saturday, which formed the basis of the present protest. Before making his second speech, Lincoln explained, Frank had again called at the White House. He was leaving for the front that evening, and would like to resume his commission as major general. The President sent to the War Department

[7] See *supra*, p. 387.

and ordered Frank's resignation to be canceled. This, of course, automatically restored him to his old place in the army. In this interview Frank had said nothing to Lincoln about the farewell address he had been putting together for some time. "Within three hours," Lincoln said, "I heard that this speech had been made and I knew that another bee-hive was kicked over. My first thought was to have cancelled the order restoring him to the army and assigning him to command. Perhaps this would have been best. On such reflection as I was able to give the matter, however, I concluded to let them stand. If I was wrong in this, the injury to the service can be set right. And there you see how far I am responsible for Frank Blair's assaults on Mr. Chase."

The two envoys of Congress were delighted at the President's disclaimer. "Mr. President," said Spalding, "spare us all further details. We only ask your word." "Your word," Riddle chimed in, "is the highest human evidence."

Only one point remained. Did the President's letter of February 29, deprecating Chase's resignation, represent Mr. Lincoln's present feeling? "I can not see now," the President replied, "as I could not see then, how the public service could be advanced by his retirement." Thus the interview that had begun so unfavorably had a happy conclusion. Riddle, ending his account, said that Lincoln "was plain, sincere and most impressive." [8]

One man, however, was still dissatisfied. Chase insisted that the President's disavowal of responsibility for Blair's oratory, or foreknowledge of it, be put in writing. Unless the President should do this, he kept writing and telling his friends, he would not remain in the administration. Jay Cooke urged Chase to stand firm on this ultimatum. "If I were you," he wrote Chase May 4, "I would demand of Lincoln an open reprimand of Blair, and a disavowal of all sympathy with such base charges." "I hope my wrathiness," Chase replied May 5, "was not excessive. Indeed it was vexatious to think that all my labors to serve our country had found recompense, so far as Mr. Lincoln's special friends were concerned, and with his apparent (but as I hope, and believe, merely apparent) endorsement, only in outrageous calumny. I seldom consult personal considerations in my public conduct and so suppressed my personal inclination to resign my office, and denounce the conspiracy of which the Blairs are the most visible embodiments. After returning from Baltimore, I conferred with Governor Brough and other friends, who were earnest in advising against resignation, and I yielded to their judgment which, indeed, coincided with my own, though exceedingly contrary to my impulses." On Monday

[8] Riddle, *op. cit.*, pp. 270 ff.

Chase had learned "that the President disavowed in the most explicit terms all connection with, or all responsibility for Blair's assault, and expressed his decided disapproval of it." But this was merely "verbal" and Chase and his friends insisted on "a distinct statement in writing" which was "due to me, to Ohio and to the country." [9] A few days later he uttered the same complaint to Miss Susan Walker, one of the platonic friends whom he liked to take into his confidence. "I use as much philosophy as I can in relation to the Blairs, and really want to act in relation to them on Christian principles. But I cannot well command my equanimity when I reflect upon the unprovoked character of their assaults; the damage I see being done to our cause and country; and the apparent indifference to it all of Mr. Lincoln, who, though he disclaims all sympathy with them in their speech and action, does nothing to avert either." [10] What he called Lincoln's "endorsement" of Blair, Chase wrote another correspondent at about the same time, "must be disavowed by an act as public as that which made it apparently such. I presume it will be cheerfully conceded by Mr. Lincoln. This time I shall have no personal ground of complaint, though nothing can change the character of the Blair-Lincoln transaction so far as the public is concerned." [11]

However, Lincoln made no public disavowal. And Chase, despite his often-repeated threats of resignation if no such statement were forthcoming, did not resign.

[9] Warden, *op. cit.*, p. 584.
[10] *Ibid.*, p. 588.
[11] *Ibid.*, p. 587.

II

THAT DISGRUNTLED soldier-politician whom Lincoln's intimates regarded merely as a stalking horse for Chase now makes a brief appearance on this troubled scene. In his lurid speech in the House Frank Blair had made several references to John C. Frémont and also attacked a convention of the miscellaneous disaffected which was soon to be held in Cleveland, Ohio. In the Riddle and Spalding meeting with Lincoln there were guarded references to this same gathering. The movement had originated in Missouri, in that faction of the Republican Party known as Charcoals, which had been most outspoken in hostility to Lincoln and the Blairs, and most unbridled in admiration of Chase, though similar elements in other regions, especially New York and the New England states, had given it a somewhat guarded benediction. To what extent the Frémont come-outers represented a serious attempt to split the Republican Party in two, and to what extent it was merely a threat to create such a schism, is a matter of conjecture. However, in April a "call," signed by names that, for the most part, suggested a Teutonic background, was issued for a convention to be held in late May, to nominate a candidate for President who would more acceptably fulfill the needs of the hour than Abraham Lincoln. That this candidate would be John C. Frémont was the general expectation.

Frémont had been living for some time in retirement in New York City, nursing his grievances against Lincoln and enjoying his exaltation as a hero to the ultras in the Republican Party. That Frémont, though nominally a Republican, would eagerly respond to the demand that he stand as a third candidate in the coming fall election could be taken for granted. Yet there were those who saw a deeper plan in the demonstration than appeared on the surface. As practical politics, the Frémont movement was, of course, the last word in futility. Even the wild-eyed New England abolitionists and the German idealists who made up the larger part of its rank and file could not have expected to elect their candidate or to make any considerable showing at the polls. Another explanation – that by holding their convention a week before the regular party met in Baltimore the malcontents could induce it to accept Frémont in order to avoid a split that would spell disaster in November – seemed also unreasonable. In all attempts to disorganize the Republican Party Lincoln's friends were sure to detect the evil genius of Chase, and perhaps it was this now ingrained habit that led them to point to the Secretary as the real promoter of the Frémont secession. If not Chase directly, at least his supporters. Gideon Welles leaned to this explanation. Edward Bates wrote most disrespectfully in Biblical terms of his Missouri friends who were "going a-whoring after Frémont." That expert in political intrigue, David Davis, believed that Chase, or his advocates, were at the bottom of the Cleveland manifestation. Frank Blair had openly made the same charge in his famous diatribe. Montgomery Blair stigmatized the Frémont movement as a "Chase operation." The fact that the elements previously identified with the Chase boom were showing an oblique, but still friendly, disposition to Frémont lent some color to this suspicion. The *New York World*, always a champion of Chase, was now booming the insurgent. Twenty-six German-language newspapers, big and little, were doing the same. Schuyler Colfax, Speaker of the House, who had never forgiven Lincoln for his exclusion from the cabinet, was now regarded as most friendly to the Pathfinder; he had publicly proclaimed that he would not support Lincoln. Henry Winter Davis, the anti-Blair feudist of Maryland, would probably have favored any candidate who could have driven Lincoln from the field. "Davis," wrote Montgomery Blair, "was in full fellowship . . . in the Frémont movement." Governor Andrew of Massachusetts, Governor Curtin of Pennsylvania, David Dudley Field of New York, all onetime supporters of Chase, were now regarded as well disposed to Frémont, and there were many others of similar importance. The real strategy of the Frémonters Blair had explained in his explosive speech. It was to create such dissension in Republican ranks that the need of a compromise candidate, one who could heal all animosities and unite the party, would become imperative. Frémont would do as a temporary shadow candidate, but the man on whom all would unite would be Chase.

However, few of these undercover supporters appeared at the convention. Most of them, even the most fiery St. Louis Charcoals, were politicians; much as they might secretly sympathize with this anti-Lincoln proceeding, they had their future to look out for, and this departure from party regularity, in the all too probable event of Lincoln's election, might have most disastrous personal consequences. As a result, the much-heralded Frémont convention turned out to be really an assembly of political nobodies. The newspapers gave it little space, except the Democratic organs, which naturally rejoiced at any maneuver that promised to shatter the Republican Party. There were really no delegates; the convention kept open house, asking for no credentials from anybody; any person with nothing else to do could stray in, take a seat, air his opinions, and cast his vote. Certain ludicrous episodes lightened the otherwise dull proceedings. One perfectionist offered a resolution to the effect that every "delegate" should pledge himself not to accept office in the next administration, which was voted down amid roars of laughter. The German contingent, most of whom, besides being political philosophers, were freethinkers in religion, objected to any mention of God in the records. The presence of Elizabeth Cady Stanton exhilarated a disrespectful generation which had not yet learned to take seriously women in politics and led one humorist to describe the conglomeration as composed "of the gentler sex of both genders." The convention itself solemnly climaxed these absurdities by nominating Frémont, of New York, for President and John Cochrane, also of New York, for Vice-President – thus ignoring the constitutional provision that the candidates for these two offices could not be citizens of the same state. Lincoln, by one of his most famous pleasantries, added to the general ridicule. He asked a group of friends assembled in his office how many persons had gone to Cleveland. When told there were about four hundred, he reached for the Bible which he knew so well, quickly turned to the passage in Samuel I, and read: "And every one that was in distress, and every one that was in debt, and every one that was discontented, gathered themselves unto him; and he became a captain over them; and there were with him about four hundred men."[1]

If the object of the Cleveland Frémonters had been to entice the regular Republican Party with a candidate on whom both sides could agree, that purpose did not succeed, for when the Republican cohorts assembled in Baltimore on June 7, about a week after the rump assemblage had adjourned, they nominated Lincoln almost by acclamation. But this ostentatious unanimity did not really represent the sentiment of the delegates. In fact there was a good deal of hostility in the two days' proceedings both towards Lincoln and towards the cabinet. So far as Lincoln, the dutifully accepted candidate for a second term, was

[1] In 1866, John Bright made all England laugh and added a new word to the language – Adullamite – by quoting this same passage as descriptive of the secession of a group of dissenters from the Liberal to the Conservative Party. Lincoln had used the same comparison two years before. Charles Sumner was a regular correspondent of Bright, retailing all the news and much of the gossip of Washington. One wonders whether he could have told Bright this story in one of his letters.

concerned, this feeling was subterranean; in the matter of the cabinet, however, especially Blair, and in less degree Seward, the animosity was open and blatant. The convention showed its dissatisfaction with the President, in both speeches and platform, by taking a stand on pending issues directly opposed to his own; and it literally made the rafters ring with disapproval of Blair. Thus it would not be inaccurate to describe the Republican National Convention of 1864 as anti-Lincoln, anti-Blair, anti-Seward, and anti-cabinet. "How can we hope to live as a nation through the crisis before us," exclaimed Lucius Robinson, the most conspicuous sponsor in New York of the Frémont uprising, "with a weak executive and a cabinet in a state of discord and anarchy?" In the Baltimore convention these same manifestations – anti-Lincoln, anti-Blair, anti-cabinet – though not expressed in such extreme terms, were by no means silent. The assemblage had come together to nominate Lincoln for a second term; practically all the delegates, except those from Missouri, were under instructions for that purpose. The plan was executed with a noisy enthusiasm that seemingly proclaimed a hearty satisfaction. Yet the prevailing tone of speakers and platform was radical. The principles underlying the Reconstruction policy, as set forth in Lincoln's message and amnesty proclamation of the previous December, found no endorsement. One of the most incongruous spectacles was that of the Reverend Robert J. Breckinridge of Kentucky, an honored member of the Episcopal clergy, who, clothed in full canonicals, acted as temporary chairman. His speech almost sadistically demanded blood atonement by the South. "The fearful truth runs through the whole history of mankind," exclaimed the reverend gentleman, "that whatever else may be done to give stability to authority, whatever else may be done to give perpetuity to institutions, however wise, however glorious, practical and just may be the philosophy of it, it has been found that the only imperishable element of all free institutions has been the blood of traitors. No government has ever been built upon imperishable foundations, which foundations were not laid in the blood of traitors." This was something far different from the Christian charity that Lincoln was preparing to extend to the South, yet no references to Lincoln brought forth anything like the unrestrained applause that greeted these remarks. Henry J. Raymond's formal eulogy on Mr. Lincoln's administration, reported the *New York Tribune* correspondent, "fell heavily on hackneyed ears." The editorial on Lincoln's nomination, published in the *Tribune* on June 9, held forth scant hope for party harmony. The leading Republican organ in the nation frankly regretted that Lincoln had been nominated, though it accepted the result as inevitable, and as unquestionably representing the will of the party voter. "That the President has made grave mistakes in the prosecution of our great struggle," wrote Greeley, "all are aware; that he has *meant* to do wrong, nobody believes. We cannot but feel that it would have been wiser and safer to spike the most serviceable guns of our adversaries by nominating another for President and thus dispelling all motives, save that of naked disloyalty, for further warfare upon this administration. We believe that the rebellion should have lost something of its cohesion and venom from the hour in which it was known that a new President would surely be inaugurated on the 4th of March next. . . . All that is of the past. The will of a great majority of the Unionists has been heard and it says, 'Let us have Abraham Lincoln as our President for another term.' We bow to their decision, and ardently hope that the result may vindicate their sagacity and prove our apprehension unfounded." [2]

When Chase wrote complainingly to a friend that "the convention will not be regarded as a Union convention, but simply as a Blair-Lincoln convention" he showed his usual lack of judgment in appraising political portents. In only one respect could the assemblage at Baltimore have been regarded as a "Blair" proceeding. That was in its name. "National Union" had been the designation chosen by the Blairs for the new party as far back as 1860; the word "Republican" savored of abolitionism and sectionalism, and was disliked by the antislavery Democrats and the several other factions and wings of factions which it was desirable to bring into one organization. The fact is that the convention came with another duty in mind as important as, and probably much more pleasurable than, the nomination of Lincoln. The blood of the whole Blair family was as much its quarry as that of the "rebels and traitors" against whom the Reverend Mr. Breckinridge had declaimed. At that particular moment, indeed, the fortunes of "the Blairs" had reached their lowest stage. Delegations of radicals had sought audiences with Lincoln demanding that he dismiss Frank from the army and Montgomery from the cabinet – demands that the President had summarily rejected. The House of Representatives, almost at the time of the Republican convention in Baltimore, was expelling Frank from that body and giving his seat to one Samuel Knox, who had for some time been contesting the election. At the Baltimore convention, two delegations from Missouri had appeared, one representing the Blairs, the other their radical opponents. The ensuing struggle for recognition gave the gathering its most exciting episode. When the committee on credentials read its report, seating all the anti-Blair delegates and throwing the Blair adherents out of the convention, the whole

[2] *New York Tribune*, June 8, 1864.

body rocked and shrieked with approbation. "The roof of the theatre lifted," wrote one correspondent, when the Blair delegates walked out.

If the Blairs had suffered any illusions as to their standing in the Republican or National Union Party, the votes presently taken on this finding removed all doubts. Four hundred and forty delegates voted against the Blairs and only four cast ballots in their favor. But the convention was not satisfied with thus reading the unpopular trio out of the party; it sought to read them out of the administration. To the several attempts of Senators and politicians which have been set forth in these pages to dictate to Lincoln as to his cabinet must now be added that of this convention which nominated him for a second term. Henry J. Raymond, editor of the *New York Times* and national chairman of the party, made this almost the "keynote" of the occasion when, in a speech to the New York delegates he exclaimed, "Gentlemen, the necessities of the hour require the reconstruction of the cabinet." The Sumner cohorts had set apart not only Blair, but Seward and perhaps Welles and Bates, for "reconstruction." In this new campaign against Seward the Massachusetts delegation showed more Machiavellianism than is usually accredited to the downright Puritan character. As an offering for Vice-President they brought forward Daniel S. Dickinson, a war Democrat and high-ranking member of the bar. These abolitionists worked so zealously for this unexpected candidate that he received 108 votes on the first ballot. Their motives may have been obscure to the ordinary citizen, but seasoned politicians like Seward and Weed had no difficulty in explaining the maneuver. Mr. Dickinson was a New Yorker and, according to the political mores of that day, no state could have two representatives in the same administration. Mr. Dickinson's elevation to the Vice-Presidency would therefore have automatically exacted Mr. Seward's retirement from the cabinet. The nomination of Andrew Johnson made safe his political head.

But the real enemy whom the cabinet reconstructors had in view was Montgomery Blair. The first paragraph in the platform contained an attack not only on him but on Lincoln himself, for it declared in support of the radicals' plan, not the President's, for rebuilding the Southern states. The culminating clause demanding that the "rebels and traitors" arrayed against the Union should receive "the punishment due to their crimes" could not have made agreeable reading to the author of the Amnesty Proclamation. And never before had a political convention inserted in its party creed a condemnation of the cabinet of the President it was selecting for a second term, and whose administration and whose "practical wisdom" and "unselfish patriotism" and "unswerving fidelity" it had, in the previous section, commended to the nation. "Resolved, that we deem it essential to the general welfare that harmony should prevail in the general council and we regard as worthy of public confidence and official trust those only who cordially endorse the principles proclaimed in these resolutions and which should characterize the administration of the government." This "sixth resolution," wrote Alexander K. McClure many years afterward, "read in the light of the present, would seem to be a very harmless and proper expression on general principles, but every member of the convention voted for it, well understanding that it meant a demand from the supreme authority of the party that Montgomery Blair should retire from the position of Postmaster General." [3]

Blair himself quickly saw the point. A few days after the convention adjourned he called on Lincoln and offered his resignation. Lincoln refused to accept it. Blair told him, however, that it would be cheerfully placed at the President's disposal any time he thought the situation should demand it. In fact he gave the President his resignation, undated, so that it could go into effect any time that political exigencies required it. Blair was a man experienced enough to understand that the action of the national convention and the disharmonious state of the party had made inevitable his retirement, at an early date.

[3] McClure, Alexander K., *Our Presidents and How We Make Them.* Harper & Bros., 1900. Pp. 188–189.

III

HOWEVER, Blair's head was not the first to fall on the altar of party solidarity. That of his august opponent, Salmon P. Chase, preceded his by nearly three months.

When John J. Cisco, in the latter part of June, 1864, resigned his post as assistant treasurer at New York, he embarrassed Lincoln with both a financial and a political problem of serious proportions. The position that Mr. Cisco had so capably filled for more than a decade was, especially in Civil War times, a highly important one. Certain observers described it as the most influential post in the government next to the cabinet itself. Politically this assistant treasurer may not have possessed the power of the collectorship, but he ruled almost supreme over the financial concerns of the government. Not far from 90 per cent of the nation's revenues originated in the City of New York. The success or failure of the bond offerings which financed its military campaigns depended on the co-operation of New York's financial houses. The assistant treasurer of New York was the connecting link between the moneyed interests of the nation and the Treasury Department, a function that demanded personal tact, financial knowledge and skill, and unselfish devotion to the cause. Mr. Cisco had possessed these qualities in high degree. In an era of extreme office-jobbing, his experience stood out as a shining exception. Appointed by Franklin Pierce in 1853, Mr. Cisco had made himself so indispensable to the Treasury that, though a Democrat, a supporter of Buchanan in 1856 and of Douglas in 1860, he escaped the general proscription of 1861, and was kept in office. His record justified this clemency. Mr. Cisco served the Lincoln administration with the utmost loyalty, and was undoubtedly the largest single contributor to the success its financial measures achieved. When Secretary Chase visited New York, Mr. Cisco brought him into personal relations with the city's great men of money; his magnetic influence smoothed their differences, brought them together on essential questions, and really made the banking resources of the nation's financial capital available for the purposes of war. Obviously, good sense and good politics demanded a man of the same type as his successor. It seemed difficult to find one. The office was offered to three men in turn, all of them of the highest standing in banking and business circles. All three declined the post.

Now the politicians became active. For some time the Democratic atmosphere of the assistant treasurer's office had poignantly grieved the political leaders of New York. Mr. Cisco, appointed as a Democrat on nonpartisan grounds, had followed this excellent example in his treatment of his hundred or so subordinates. Most of these employees, on the advent of the Lincoln administration, were Democrats – something hardly surprising in that day, since most of them had been selected under Democratic Presidents Pierce and Buchanan. Mr. Cisco retained these men on the same enlightened principle of fitness and necessity that had led the Lincoln administration to retain himself. Such partiality naturally did not please the several factions then engaging in a cutthroat struggle for power in the Republican stronghold. The demand now arose that the assistant treasurer's office be "reformed." The reformation in question contemplated the immolation of all Democrats and their supercession by gentlemen who professed the true faith. One day at the height of the Cisco crisis, Senator Edwin D. Morgan of New York appeared in Chase's office with a formidable paper in his hand. This turned out to be a censored list of all the employees in the treasurer's New York office, and against most of the names had been inscribed the incriminating letter "D." This graphic exhibit, Mr. Morgan informed Chase, displayed the extent to which the hated Democratic enemy had obtained control of valuable patronage, and the need of a successor to Mr. Cisco, who would administer the appropriate remedy. Mr. Morgan, himself a successful financier and businessman, several times a millionaire, and ex-governor of the state, was speaking not only for himself, but for the Seward-Weed faction of New York Republicanism to which he belonged.

That element regarded itself as having been inadequately considered by the administration. The opposing group, pro-Chase and anti-Lincoln, had built itself up strongly in the Empire State, on the foundation of rich "patronage" from the Treasury Department. The trip of the three active leaders of the anti-Seward wing to Springfield in January 1861, to protest to the President-elect against the appointment of Seward as Secretary of State, has already been described. This trio, the very mention of whose names would act like an electric shock on the Seward-Weed cohorts, had enjoyed great favor at the hands of the Treasury. Mr. Hiram Barney, the leader, had been made Collector of the Port of New York – an office in which he had not proved to be a great success.

Judge Hogebloom, another of the famous anti-Seward pilgrims to Springfield, had been appointed appraiser of the port – a position only second to that of the collector in political power. The third member of the band, George Opdyke, had been elected mayor of New York, largely by virtue of the political strength his associates had obtained from the Federal government. All three, if not open supporters of the Chase presidential boom – something that would have been rather difficult in view of their official positions under Lincoln – were known to have been secretly sympathetic. The Cisco resignation gave Chase an opportunity to repair a great wrong. Would the Secretary of the Treasury place another of his henchmen in a place of such strategic importance? That he was still angling for a presidential nomination of some kind Weed and Seward and Senator Morgan devoutly believed. The mere fact that the Republican convention had met and named Lincoln for a second term did not still their apprehensions, for the underground movement had already been put in motion to force Lincoln to withdraw in the interest of some other candidate. Senator Morgan had already given Lincoln the names of three men, any one of whom would be satisfactory to him, as Senator from New York. All three were men of high character and ability, worthy successors to Mr. Cisco, but all had the disqualification, in Chase's eyes, of not belonging to his following in the Republican ranks, and of being conservatives on Reconstruction and intensely loyal to Lincoln. Between these two belligerent wings of his party there was little question where Lincoln's preference would incline, when it came to choosing a successor to Mr. Cisco. The President's personal feelings towards Chase had not increased in warmth as a result of the proceedings of the last few weeks, nor did he wish to widen the breach in the Republican ranks in the largest state of the Union by adding to the overwhelming emoluments Chase had already obtained at his hands. As for the public interest, there was little fear that any one of the three men proposed by Senator Morgan would be able to carry on the office with an efficiency and honesty comparable to that which Mr. Cisco had displayed.

Lincoln was rather astonished, therefore, when word came that Chase had fixed upon a gentleman by the name of Maunsell B. Field as his choice for the vacancy. That Mr. Field was a Democrat, probably a radical, since Chase had selected him, was known, but these qualities had little importance in this case, for he was a man without political influence or following of any kind, and, indeed, with no known interests or achievements in public life. For less than a year, he had been serving as Third Assistant Secretary of the Treasury, a position that

Chase had created for his particular benefit; but his relation to Chase had rather a personal than an official character. He was a man of ingratiating presence, good education, polished manners, and of some slight ability as a writer, but he had never figured in public life, even in a minor degree. Perhaps the most informing summation of Mr. Field's career and interests can be derived from the title of a book of reminiscences which he published in his later period: *Memories of Many Men and Some Women, being personal recollections of Emperors, Kings, Queens, Princes, Presidents, Statesmen, authors, and artists, at home and abroad, during the last thirty years.* That is, Field's attractions were flamboyantly social; he was endowed with the kind of talents that made him a favorite master of ceremonies and head of reception committees. When distinguished foreigners, such as Prince Jerome Bonaparte, Jenny Lind, the Prince of Wales, and other stars of this magnitude, paid occasional visits to democratic America, Mr. Field was usually at the forefront, escorting them from place to place and generally making their sojourn a pleasant experience. In Europe he had been attached, in minor capacity, to several diplomatic staffs, in this way acquiring – according to his own story – a really astonishing collection of intimates in the loftiest social station. Chase himself had a weakness for associating with highly placed ladies and gentlemen, and not unnaturally was drawn to so accomplished a person as Mr. Field. The two first met at Mr. Cisco's office in New York, for Mr. Field had been one of those obnoxious "D's" who, in the opinion of the politically minded Senator Morgan, were destined for "reformation." In business he had no more experience than in politics; indeed, he had had no career except a social one, knew nothing of banking or finance, and was totally lacking in that familiarity with the money kings which had made Mr. Cisco so valuable to the government.

Mr. Field had become a kind of social mentor to Chase on his visits to New York, and had charmed that susceptible official so completely that he was finally taken to Washington and installed in the Treasury Department. His associates there, perhaps from envy, spoke and wrote of him in disrespectful terms. According to Lucius E. Chittenden, register of the Department, Field had wormed himself into Chase's admiration by gross adulation. "Secretary Chase," wrote Chittenden, "was fond of those who recognized his eminence and were ready to serve him as their acknowledged superior." Field had "attached himself to his personal service . . . attended to his social engagements and became the authorized agent for communication with him. . . . His service was so attentive that the Secretary came to regard him as a kind of personal society representative." While paying due tribute to the man's cultivation and grace, Mr. Chittenden hints at unrevealed faults that detracted from his usefulness as a servant of his country. "There were facts, of which it is impossible that the Secretary long remained ignorant, which, though not reflecting upon his personal integrity, necessarily disqualified him for any position of trust or responsibility. . . . He was absent from the Treasury sometimes for weeks together, mysterious disappearances for which no one knew the reason. . . . It seemed impossible," concluded Mr. Chittenden, "to account for this nomination upon the ordinary motives which control human action."[1] Senator Morgan, in protesting the selection to President Lincoln, said that, if desired, he could procure a written protest against Mr. Field's promotion, signed by every Republican member of Congress.

By this time relations between Lincoln and his Finance Minister had reached a point where they were communicating with each other chiefly by written notes. Lincoln's son, young Robert Todd, described their association accurately as one of "armed neutrality." The President still retained his high opinion of Chase as a financier, but that feeling of constraint and awkwardness on personal contact which both men admitted to their friends had grown more acute. Chase's announcement of Maunsell Field as Cisco's successor strained this almost to the breaking point. Intentional rudeness was not one of Lincoln's characteristics, especially where members of his cabinet were concerned, but this obvious attempt of Chase to add the assistant treasurer's office in New York to his already large resources of Federal patronage proved too severe a test of Lincoln's perhaps most dominant quality – his infinite patience. By naming Field to this post Chase was simply naming himself, for the man, once installed, would become his automaton. The day after Field's selection had been forwarded to the White House, Lincoln wrote Chase declining to accept his candidate. "I cannot, without much embarrassment, make this appointment, principally because of Senator Morgan's very firm opposition to it. . . . Governor Morgan tells me he has mentioned the three names to you, to wit: R. M. Blatchford, Dudley S. Gregory, and Thomas Hillhouse. It will really oblige me if you will make choice among these three, or any other man that Senators Morgan and Harris will be satisfied with, and send me a nomination for him." This was really a peremptory command, but instead of obeying instructions, Chase asked for a personal interview. This the President refused – in itself an unprecedented snub from the head of the state to the second man in his cabinet, "because," he wrote

[1] Chittenden, Lucius E., *Recollections of President Lincoln and His Administration.* Harper and Bros., 1891. P. 371.

Chase, "the difficulty does not lie within the range of a personal conversation between you and me. As the proverb goes, no man knows so well where the shoe pinches as he who wears it. I do not think Mr. Field a very proper man for the place."

The disconsolate Mr. Chase went home, seeking comfort in the region that usually served as a refuge from the travail of his official life. "Oh for more faith and clearer light!" he wrote in his Diary that evening. "How stable is the city of God! How disordered is the city of man." However, he discovered, with more resourcefulness than he commonly evinced, a way out of his dilemma. That his efforts in the interest of Field had failed was evident. But Chase, in addition to other human weaknesses, had a strong vein of obstinacy and was determined not to yield to what today would be called a "directive" from the highest authority. There remained only one possible avenue of escape. The Secretary telegraphed Mr. Cisco, begging him, as a patriot, to withdraw his resignation and retain his office for at least another three months. To this appeal Mr. Cisco acceded, and the difficulty seemed to have been postponed at least until the following October. Between June and October many things could happen. By that time the country would know, for example, whether it was to have a new administration, or whether Mr. Lincoln was to remain in power for another quadrennium – for, in this period of history, the summer and October elections fairly indicated the outcome of the national contest in November.

Under ordinary circumstances, Mr. Cisco's act should have ended the impasse. There being now no vacancy in the assistant treasurer's office, no occasion existed for continuing the discussion about his successor. Chase, however, was still smarting from Lincoln's unwillingness to recognize Chase's supremacy over the Treasury patronage, an important matter in view of a complex presidential situation. Above all, Chase evidently thought that the Cisco business offered the opportunity of testing the supreme issue with Lincoln – of settling the question of who really was master. Chase profoundly believed himself indispensable to Lincoln. No other man, he thought, could maintain the credit of the government, without which the war could not be continued. He was also convinced that this was Lincoln's opinion. Up to June 1864 he had offered his resignation four times – perhaps five – and each time Lincoln had persuaded him to remain. On one of these occasions Lincoln had left the White House, called at Chase's home, and after a long discussion induced him to change his mind. "Here, Chase," he said, with the latest resignation in hand, "is a paper with which I want nothing to do. Take it back and be reasonable." Not strangely, perhaps, the Secretary had concluded that nothing could induce the

President to part with his services. The arrogant man now decided to put on the screws again. No cabinet officer in history had ever claimed the right to conduct his department independently of the Executive. Seward could be imperious, but he never presumed to make important appointments without consulting his chief. The letter which Chase now sent Lincoln gave the President one of two choices. The Treasury Department was to become a tightly sealed compartment, practically disconnected from the White House, its vast patronage to remain exclusively in Chase's hands, or he would no longer preside over its destiny. "The withdrawal of Mr. Cisco's resignation," Chase wrote Lincoln on June 29, "which I inclose, relieves the present difficulty; but I cannot help feeling that my position here is not altogether agreeable to you, and it is certainly too full of embarrassment and difficulty and painful responsibility to allow in me the least desire to retain it. I think it my duty, therefore, to inclose to you my resignation. I shall regard it as a real relief if you think proper to accept it, and will most cheerfully render to my successor any aid he may find useful in entering upon his duties."

Maunsell Field, the storm center of this episode, has left the most graphic account of Lincoln, when this missive reached the White House. The President, very busy with other matters, had placed Chase's letter aside, thinking that it dealt with routine concerns of minor consequence. "I went down to lunch" – so Field quotes the President – "and suddenly recalled that I hadn't answered it. As soon as I was back here, I took pen and paper and prepared to write, but then it occurred to me that I might as well read the letter before I answered it. I took it out of the envelope for that purpose, and, as I did, another inclosure fell from it to the floor. I picked it up, read it and said to myself, 'Halloa, this is a horse of different color.' It was his resignation. I put my pen into my mouth and grit my teeth upon it. I did not long reflect." [2] Nor did the words that presently flowed from the presidential pen deal in ambiguous phrases or superfluous compliments. "Your resignation of the office of Secretary of the Treasury, sent me yesterday, is accepted. Of all I have said in commendation of your ability and fidelity I have nothing to unsay and yet you and I have reached a point of mutual embarrassment in our official relation which it seems cannot be overcome or longer sustained consistently with the public service."

In view of all the attendant circumstances, especially the fact that Chase had not made this great refusal with any idea of retiring from the cabinet, but merely as a maneuver in that struggle for power which

[2] Field, *op. cit.*, pp. 296 ff.

had been waged for some time between himself and Lincoln, this letter amounted virtually to a curt dismissal. As always, Lincoln rested his decision on public grounds; he had declined his several precedent resignations because he believed Chase's conduct of the Treasury essential to the success of the war; he now relieved him from duty because the time had arrived when the man was no longer useful from that point of view. Naturally the news, which gained rapid circulation in Washington and the country, took everybody by surprise. After all, Chase was a great figure in national affairs, and represented in the cabinet the most numerous wing of the Republican or National Union Party. Of all Americans the one most astounded by Lincoln's act was Chase himself. His letters and Diary entries of the next few days betray the several emotions which stirred him. Astonishment, Christian fortitude, anger, vexation, complacent satisfaction with his own achievements, regret at his own temerity in thus challenging face to face the quiet man in the White House, now and then an outburst almost suggesting a snarl, are manifest in these self-communings. "I found a letter from the President," Chase wrote on June 30, "accepting my resignation, and putting the acceptance on the ground of the difference between us, indicating a degree of embarrassment in our official relations which could not be continued or sustained consistently with the public service. I had found a good deal of embarrassment from him; but what he had found from me I could not imagine, unless it has been caused by my unwillingness to have offices distributed as spoils or benefits, with more regard to the claims of divisions, factions, cliques, and individuals, than to fitness of selection. *He has never given me the active and earnest support I was entitled to;* and even now Congress was about to adjourn without passing sufficient tax bills, though making appropriations with lavish provision, *and he was, notwithstanding my appeals, taking no pains to insure a different result.*" [3]

Why had the President, Chase asked himself, not insisted on the withdrawal of his resignation? "I can see but one reason – that I am too earnest, too anti-slavery, and say, too radical, to make him willing to have me connected with his administration; just as my opinion that he is not earnest enough, not anti-slavery enough, not radical enough, but goes naturally with those hostile to me, rather than with me, makes me willing and glad to be disconnected from it." [4] An utterly unwarranted insinuation against Lincoln – that he was prepared to end the war and re-establish the Union without ending slavery – creeps more than once into Chase's meditations on his dethronement. But it is clear that he

[3] Warden, *op. cit.*, p. 619. Italics in original.
[4] *Ibid.*, p. 623.

was not so eager to be "disconnected" with the cabinet as his words would imply. He notes several times efforts made by his friends to induce the President to change his mind, and seemed to regret, half wistfully, that Lincoln had proved adamant. His Pittsburgh friend, Governor Morehead, who had been one of Jay Cooke's associates in Chase's presidential campaign, called at the White House the day following the resignation, in company with Congressman Williams, also from Pennsylvania, to urge Chase's restoration. "They attempted to induce him to send for me with a view to my return to the Department; but he would not consent to this. He thought we would not agree, and it was without use; and in this he was, I think, right." [5] On the same day Samuel Hooper, Congressman from Massachusetts, called upon Chase to report certain appreciative remarks Lincoln had made on his deposed Secretary. "I said that it was quite possible, had any such expression of good will reached me, I might, before the present difficulty arose, have gone to him and had a fresh understanding, which would have prevented it; but I did not see now how I could change my position. Indeed, if such were the real feelings of Mr. Lincoln, he would hardly have refused a personal interview with me when I asked it, or required me to consult local politicians in the choice of an officer whose character was so vitally important to the department." [6] Senator William P. Fessenden, whom Lincoln appointed Chase's successor, told his friend that the President had expressed a hope that the new Secretary "would not, without a real necessity, remove any friends of Governor Chase." "Had the President," Chase communes, "in reply to my note tendering my resignation, expressed himself as he did now to Mr. Fessenden, I should cheerfully have withdrawn it." There are plenty of other indications showing how little the unfortunate man had expected that Lincoln would grasp this opportunity of extruding him from the cabinet and how Chase really lamented the outcome.

Other manifestations added to his misery. There seemed to be no tendency, in press or private communications, to treat his departure as a public calamity. A few ultraradical organs bewailed the loss of so distinguished a public servant, and certain sympathizing friends, such as Sumner, Garfield, and Pomeroy, called to express their indignation, but for the most part a general feeling prevailed that Lincoln had acted with judgment and wisdom. His brother cabinet members, with the exception of Stanton, hailed Chase's ousting with what he himself described as "indecent rejoicing." That Thurlow Weed should exclaim in the *Albany Journal*, "Heaven be praised for this gleam of sunshine!"

[5] *Ibid.*, p. 620.
[6] *Ibid.*, p. 618.

was to be expected, but that solid citizens like his cabinet colleagues Gideon Welles and Edward Bates should exult almost as jubilantly was a different matter. "In coming to the conclusion that a separation must take place, the President was prompted by some and sustained by all his cabinet without exception," wrote Welles. "Chase's retirement has offended nobody and has gratified almost everybody."[7] And again: "The retirement of Chase, so far as I hear opinions expressed – and they are generally freely given – appears to give relief rather than otherwise. . . . I look upon it as a blessing. . . . I have little doubt that he was greatly surprised that it was accepted."[8]

"I have not conversed with many," observed Bates, "but as far as my information goes there seems to be a vague feeling of relief from a burden, and a hope of better things. I should not be a bit surprised if Stanton follows Chase. In that I see no public misfortune, for I think it hardly possible that the war office could be worse administered. I fancy that I see in this movement another effort of the radicals to bolt the Baltimore convention. If they could find a *feasible* candidate, I am sure they would do it. Mr. Lincoln, I hope, will find out, in time, the danger of leaning upon that broken reed." One explanation of Chase's resignation, according to Bates, "is that Mr. Chase hopes for the nomination for the Democratic convention to meet at Chicago and that Frémont and his friends will waive the nomination at Cleveland in his favor."[9] "We have a cabinet crisis," Seward contentedly wrote his wife July 2, "of which I might tell you much, but can write you nothing, except that from the first day of the administration the causes have been upheaving in the cabinet and in the country. It is well that the explosion produced no more severe shock than has occurred."[10] Naturally, this change in the cabinet was regarded as a personal triumph by the Blairs, whom Chase regarded as primarily responsible for his exit. "Chase, you see," the elder Blair wrote Frank, "hung on as long as possible, and dropped off at the last like a rotten pear, unexpectedly to himself and to everybody else. He supposed he could bully Lincoln by threatening to resign unless he was permitted to make the Treasury appointments without control."

In mid-July Chase left Washington, seeking rest and consolation in the New Hampshire hills among which he had been born. Only one member of the cabinet paid him the compliment of a farewell call. "Half of my fifty-seventh year is ended," he wrote. "Today I leave Washington a private citizen. Saw Stanton before leaving; he was warm and cordial as ever. No other head of a department has called."

[7] Welles, *Diary*. II, 94.
[8] *Ibid.* II, 63.
[9] Bates, *op. cit.*, p. 381.
[10] Seward's *Seward*, III, 230.

IV

EDWARD BATES'S suspicion that Chase, even after retiring from the cabinet, had not completely abandoned all hope of the Presidency is borne out by his behavior in this summer of 1864. For the exiled statesman that was a period of brooding and unconcealed resentment. The most critical election in the nation's history, one, indeed, on which the continued existence of that nation depended, elicited no word or action in the President's behalf. Instead, in letters to friends, in the daily self-communings of his Diary, in general conversation, Chase evinced an unappeased bitterness against his former chief. Samuel Bowles, editor of the *Springfield Republican*, notes this attitude of non-co-operation as late as September 4 – three months after Lincoln's nomination. "Do you notice," he wrote a friend, "that the 'Anti-Slavery Standard' and the 'Liberator,' the representatives of the old abolitionists, are both earnest for Lincoln? Yet a new crop of Radicals have sprung up, who are resisting the President and making mischief. Chase is going around, peddling his griefs in private ears, and sowing dissatisfaction about Lincoln. Oh how little great men can be!" [1]

Charles Sumner, in a letter to Richard Cobden, pictured again his friend's state of indecision, incidentally evoking a parallel hardly Plutarchian in discernment. "Chase for a long time hesitated in support of Mr. Lincoln; he did not think him competent. . . . The President made a great mistake in compelling him to resign. It was very much as when Louis XVI overthrew Necker; and, by the way, I have often observed that Mr. Lincoln resembles Louis XVI more than any other ruler in history. I once said to Chase that I should not be astonished if, like Necker, he was recalled! to which he replied that might be, if Mr. Lincoln were king and not politician!" [2] The redoubtable Senator Pomeroy – proponent of the "Circular" – breakfasted with Chase on July 6. "He cannot support Lincoln," Chase commented, "but won't

[1] Merriam, George S., *Life and Times of Samuel Bowles*. Century Co., 1885. I, 413.

[2] Pierce, *op. cit.* IV, 196–197.

desert his principles. I am much of the same sentiments, though not willing now to decide what duty may demand next fall." Pomeroy told Chase that he would avoid the issue by going on a buffalo hunt; not the Western prairie, however, but an ambition nearer home was keeping Chase close to the political field. Even in the time of his abortive presidential boom, Chase had had his eye upon the Democrats. The radical majority of the Republican Party, allied to the "War Democrats," with himself as the candidate of both, seemed, in Chase's eyes, the ideal combination. His letters of the summer of 1864 show that this combination still entranced him. He was so purblind to realities that he absurdly believed in the possibility of the Democrats dropping McClellan and the Clevelandites giving up Frémont and uniting on him as the man who could heal all differences. His little court of sycophants apparently stimulated this aspiration. "Pomeroy remarked that, on the news of my resignation reaching the Senate, several of the Democratic senators came to him and said, 'We'll go with you now for Chase.' This meant nothing but a vehement desire to overthrow the existing administration, but might mean much if the Democrats would only cut loose from slavery, and go for freedom and the protection of labor by a national currency. If they would do that, I would cheerfully go for any man they might nominate." [3]

The unprecedented political situation that summer of 1864 explains to a considerable extent the uncertainties and hesitations of Chase at this time. The Republicans, radical and regular, had held two conventions and nominated two sets of candidates, yet neither the decisions of the Lincoln convention nor those of the Cleveland bolters were generally accepted as settling the question. The two conventions had adjourned *sine die* but hardly had the crowds departed when irreconcilable elements in both demanded that they reassemble, rescind their decisions, and select new candidates. "The Baltimore convention," growled Edward Bates in his Diary of June 10, "(*National Union*, I believe it called itself) has surprised and mortified me greatly. It did indeed nominate Mr. Lincoln, but in a manner and with attendant circumstances, as if their object were to defeat their own nomination. They were all (nearly) instructed to vote for Mr. Lincoln, but many of them hated to do it, and only 'kept the word of promise to the ear,' doing their worst to break it to the hope." [4] Military disasters heightened the disaffection. Three days before Lincoln's nomination the battle of Cold Harbor had been fought, and this and other bloody reverses enshrouded the nation in gloom. Lincoln himself, as tragedy

[3] Warden, *op. cit.*, p. 627.
[4] Bates, *op. cit.*, p. 372.

followed tragedy, despaired of re-election. His famous sealed memorandum of August 23, recording his belief that the administration would be defeated, and pledging himself and his cabinet to co-operate with McClellan to save the Union before inauguration, merely reflected the pessimism that affected most loyal citizens.

With the possibility that both the regular and the bolting Republicans would drop their candidates in favor of another man, the hopes of Chase rose once more. News arrived in the middle of August, at probably the most despairing moment of the war, that a movement had been launched to persuade Lincoln voluntarily to abdicate his nomination, or, if he refused, to eject him forcibly from the contest. The insurrection had a far more formidable sponsorship than such an insane proceeding would seem to have deserved. Its leader was David Dudley Field of New York, whose brother, Stephen J. Field, Lincoln had a short time before appointed to the United States Supreme Court; and his most active co-worker was that same George Opdyke whose name has several times appeared in these pages as one of the chieftains of the anti-Seward-Weed contingent in New York. At a secret meeting in Mr. Field's New York home on August 14, eminent representatives of politics, journalism, and the professions prepared a "call" for a convention to be held in Cincinnati on September 18, "to consider the state of the nation, and to consecrate the Union strength on some one candidate, who commands the confidence of the country, even by a new nomination, if necessary." Horace Greeley, representing the *New York Tribune*, Parke Godwin, William Cullen Bryant's son-in-law, representing the *Evening Post*, Theodore Tilton, representing the *Independent*, the nation's most widely circulated religious weekly, were present. Whitelaw Reid, of the *Cincinnati Gazette*, did not attend, but was actively concerned in the demonstration. "That which I could do in the direction you indicate," Reid wrote, "has been done in inducing the *Gazette* to come out for Mr. Lincoln's withdrawal. The article has been telegraphed east and I hope has done some good." What Greeley thought of the situation was set forth in a letter to Mr. Opdyke, written some days after the session. "Mr. Lincoln is already beaten. He cannot be elected. And we must have another ticket to save us from utter overthrow. If we had such a ticket as could be made by naming Grant, Butler, or Sherman for President, and Farragut for Vice, we could make a fight yet. And such a ticket we ought to have anyhow, with or without a convention." Other participants in the discussion were Henry Winter Davis, William Curtis Noyes, and Francis Lieber, the idealistic German-American philosopher and scholar.

Greeley's inspired suggestion of Ben Butler as a candidate preferable to Lincoln gives some notion of the opinion entertained by these intellectuals of the man whom, even in 1864, they regarded as an ignorant, uncouth bungler. Chase himself was invited to an adjourned meeting at the home of George Opdyke on August 30, but refrained on the plea of previous engagements. His letter of regret, however, betrayed a guarded sympathy with the great cause at stake. "I sincerely hope that the deliberations of the gentlemen who will confer under your roof may be fruitful of benefit to our country, never more in need of wise counsel and fearless action by and among patriotic men. Mr. Noyes knows my views as well, perhaps, as anybody, and expects to be present at your meeting. But my views are by no means as clear as I could wish and I should be very glad to have the advantage of the clearer and better knowledge of other and better informed gentlemen." Honest old Jacob Collamer, of Vermont, replied in sharply contrasting strain; unlike Chase, his views were completely formed and needed no clarification from the confidential sessions being held in the drawing rooms of Mr. Opdyke and Mr. Field. In language as direct as courtesy would permit, he declined to have anything to do with the enterprise; instead he urged the malcontents to use all "their energies and efforts" in behalf of Lincoln's election, and said that any such plan as they were contemplating would "prove almost certainly disastrous." [5]

Chase's letter may be taken as a fairly complete revelation of his mental operations during this difficult summer. For him it was a period of indecision and of watchful waiting. Anything so dangerous as personal participation in the New York uprising was gently pushed aside. Yet he would not repudiate this attempt to force Lincoln from the contest; apparently he chose to stand in obscurity and await events.

And events now abruptly destroyed any chances which the anti-Lincolnian demonstration might have had for success. On August 29, the Democratic convention – Gideon Welles called it "a nest of foul birds" – met in Chicago and named its predestined candidate, George B. McClellan. The dominant personality at this gathering was Clement L. Vallandigham, the nation's most impassioned Copperhead, the man whom Lincoln, a year before, after his conviction of treason by a military court, had punished by exiling to the Confederate states. By blockade running and other valiant methods, Vallandigham had escaped to Canada, and campaigned for governor of Ohio while still sojourning outside the United States. Defiantly crossing the border, he started on a stumping tour, to the accompaniment of rioting mobs, preaching again

[5] On June 30, 1889, the *New York Sun* published a collection of letters dealing with the Field-Opdyke meetings. The quotations in the text are taken from these letters.

his favorite thesis – the secession of Western and Northwestern states from the Federal government and their adherence to Mr. Jefferson Davis's Confederacy; he wound up this campaign of education in Chicago, haranguing from street corners and finally appearing in the McClellan convention, where he was permitted to write the most critical plank in the platform. This consisted of a few lines that have passed into history as the most destructive blunder ever committed by a great party. It stigmatized the war as a "failure" and demanded "that immediate efforts be made for a cessation of hostilities." McClellan, indeed, in accepting a nomination for which he had been intriguing for three years, repudiated these defeatist words, but his rejection did not help matters much; especially as the war, which all summer had been going badly, almost magically upsurged on the path to victory.

The Democratic delegates, who had voted the war a failure, returned home with the frenzied cheers of the populace rising at every hand, and found the newspapers, which had paid scant attention to their own deliberations, filled with the triumphs of the Union arms. Bonfires were burning in every street, bells were ringing in all Northern towns and villages, cannon were pounding forth salutes, services of thanksgiving and prayer were filling all the churches. Sherman had captured Atlanta and had started on that march to the sea which was to leave the South a military ruin. Other victories, especially Sheridan's in the Shenandoah, added to the certainty of Confederate doom. Farragut, by seizing Mobile, had wrested from the Confederacy almost its last remaining port. The Democratic proposal to abandon the fight and yield to a Confederate triumph, combined with the abundant signs that the South, in a martial sense, was approaching annihilation, changed the political prospect in a twinkling. At the time of the first meeting of David Dudley Field's insurgents, on August 14, Lincoln seemed to be a losing cause; on the date scheduled for the final confabulation, August 30, no fact was more certain than his overwhelming success. No record has been preserved of this ultimate session, if indeed it was ever held. Most of its chosen spirits, after these almost simultaneous historical events, had precipitated themselves into the Lincoln ranks; Sumner and his companions began heralding the Union candidate from a hundred platforms. Greeley's *Tribune* at last decided that the nation could be safely entrusted to "old Abe" for another four years and Henry Ward Beecher presently waxed as fervent in praise as he had previously wailed in detraction. On September 27, a great meeting assembled in Cooper Union in New York over which Chase's accredited spokesman, William Curtis Noyes, presided and at which many of the leaders of the "Lincoln withdrawal movement" sat conspicuously on the platform, all in admiration of the candidate they had sought to displace. By September 17, Chase no longer hesitated as to his course. He returned to Washington and called upon the President. "His manner was cordial and so were his words; and I hear of nothing but good will from him. But he is not at all demonstrative, either in speech or manner. I feel that I do not know him, and I found no action on what he says or does. . . . It is my conviction that the cause I love and the general interests of the country will be best promoted by his election and I have resolved to join my efforts to those of almost the whole body of my friends in securing it."[6] In the short time that remained before the voting, Chase made several speeches in Lincoln's favor, the most ambitious in his home town, Cincinnati.

Chase's deposition had not solved all of Lincoln's cabinet problems. The difficult question of Blair still remained. Something would have to be done about him, for the retirement of the Treasury head certainly left the presidential council in an unbalanced state. The disenthronement of Chase had naturally elated the conservative elements, but the radicals, who made up the majority of the party, at least in Congress, were correspondingly enraged. The split which Lincoln had so dreaded had now opened wide. Blair, Bates, Seward, Welles – apparently the leading advocates of considerate treatment for the South, after its subjugation – had won the day in the party counsels. That left only Stanton and Chase's successor, Fessenden, as upholders of radical gospel, for Usher, who had succeeded Smith, counted for nothing in the cabinet either way. To cast Chase into outer darkness and to keep Blair was almost more than the party equilibrium could stand. Moreover, the final source of Republican authority, the national convention, had practically expelled Blair from the party – and this by a cataclysmic vote of 440 to 4 – and had asked for his removal from the cabinet. Lincoln could properly ignore such a demand when it was put forth by insurgent Senators, as he had shown in the case of Seward; but this manifesto by the party as a whole was a different matter. On September 23, therefore, Lincoln took advantage of Blair's offer, many times made, to withdraw from his official family, and appointed William Dennison, of Ohio, his successor.

Here, then, is the simple explanation for Blair's retirement; it is essentially the explanation that Lincoln himself gave Gideon Welles,[7] who was much upset by his friend's downfall and a little inclined, at first, to be critical of Lincoln. Blair himself said that he was a sacrifice to comfort the Frémonters – meaning those radicals and ultraradicals who

[6] Schuckers, *op. cit.*, p. 511.
[7] Welles, *Diary*. II, 153.

had taken stand, in open battle, against the President. In essence this was the case; Blair's diagnosis does not materially differ from the one Lincoln gave Welles in his confidential talk. The legend that has been evolved from these plain facts, however – that Blair's resignation was the result of a political "deal" by which the President immolated his Postmaster General as a price of Frémont's withdrawal from the presidential contest and his reluctant support of Lincoln – does not necessarily follow. Frémont did give up his preposterous candidacy the day before Blair's resignation in a snarling letter denouncing Lincoln in terms that do not suggest an amicable "bargain" with the President. Zack Chandler always claimed the credit for arranging the treaty by which Lincoln is supposed to have traded Blair for the Pathfinder's support. His anonymous biographer first brought the story to public notice, and, more recently, a collection of Chandler's letters to his wife, illiterate, boastful, excited and disjointed, give a self-portrait of the Senator as ambassador between the White House and Frémont's home in New York, seeking to patch up an arrangement that would ensure Lincoln, if not the support, at least not the vicious hostility of the Frémont enthusiasts. That Lincoln may have confided to Chandler his intention of reorganizing his cabinet is probable – for he had made the same statement to others; he was also politician enough to reap such capital as he could by taking the Senator into his confidence. It is not likely, however, that Chandler's arguments, or enticements, had anything to do with his decision. Soon after the Baltimore convention, Lincoln had told a committee of radicals, headed by George W. Boutwell, who had called to ask for Blair's resignation in accordance with the request of the national convention, that he intended, if elected, to make certain changes in his cabinet. Everyone understood, of course, that this referred to Montgomery Blair. Personally fond as Lincoln was of his Postmaster General, and highly as he esteemed his abilities and his worth, his presence in the cabinet had been an embarrassment for a considerable time. The biographer of the Blair family says that Blair had signed his death warrant when he made his miscegenation speech at Rockville in October 1863, almost a year before his retirement.[8]

Frank Blair's vituperation of Chase in the House had added to the President's discomfort. Montgomery's constant attacks on his colleagues, Chase, Seward, and Stanton, in themselves made his presence an incongruity in the cabinet. After his celebrated denunciation of Stanton as a "coward and poltroon," Lincoln had read his chosen in-

[8] Smith, William Ernest, *Francis Preston Blair Family in Politics*. Macmillan, 1933. II, 245.

timates a little allocution – which he regarded as of sufficient importance to put in writing – warning them against such explosions in the future, and plainly intimating that anyone who so indulged himself would lose his job. That had not restrained Montgomery in the least; he still kept up his pressure on Lincoln to get rid of Stanton and Seward.[9] Zachary Chandler's eloquence was not needed to persuade Lincoln to take a step upon which he had decided long before. Nor did his presidential prospects require it. By September 23, when Chandler claimed to have achieved his coup, everybody knew that his re-election was certain; none knew it better than Frémont and that is the reason why he abandoned his candidacy.

On Friday, September 23, Edward Bates and Gideon Welles had just left a cabinet meeting and were chatting for a few moments on the west side of the White House grounds. Blair came up to them, remarking, almost casually, "I suppose that you are both aware that my head has been decapitated – that I am no longer a member of the cabinet." Blair pulled a letter from his pocket. He had found it on his desk that morning on coming in from Silver Spring. He then read it to his former colleagues. "Executive Mansion, Washington, Sept. 23, 1864. Hon. Montgomery Blair. My dear sir: You have generously said to me more than once that, whenever your resignation would be a relief to me, it was at my disposal. That time has come. You very well know that this proceeds from no dissatisfaction of mine with you personally or officially. Your uniform kindness has been unsurpassed by that of any friend, and while it is true that the war does not seem greatly to add to the difficulties of your department as to those of some others, it is not too much to say, which I most truly can, that in the three years and a half during which you have administered the general post office I remember no single complaint against you in connection therewith. Yours as ever, Abraham Lincoln."

In parting with Blair, Welles notes, "the President parts with a true friend and he leaves no adviser so able, bold, sagacious. Honest, truthful and sincere, he has been wise, discriminating, and correct."[10] Blair expressed no resentment. "He thinks," says Welles, "it right and will eventuate well." All three Blairs accepted Lincoln's act in the same spirit. Montgomery's conduct and that of Chase after "decapitation" bring out into bold contrast the characters of the two men. Chase had retired to New England, cultivating his grievances, and watching the political outlook for any sign that might be turned to his personal account. From June to early September – which comprised the time

[9] Nicolay and Hay, *op. cit.* IX, 340.
[10] Welles, *Diary*. II, 156–157.

when Lincoln needed all the assistance he could get from his friends—he kept silence, showing no disposition to assist the cause. Montgomery Blair left the cabinet and immediately took the stump for the Lincolnian ticket. In a letter to his wife, written immediately after penning his resignation, he expresses a natural regret that the "President has given himself and me too an unnecessary mortification in this matter; but then I am not the best judge and I am sure he acts from the best motives" and "it is the best all around." The fiery Frank, recently wounded and on a thirty-day leave, wrote his father that "the failure to elect Mr. Lincoln would be the greatest disaster that could befall the country and the sacrifice made by the Judge [11] to avert this is so incomparably small that I felt it would not cost him a pang to make." One week after leaving the cabinet Montgomery appeared at a great Lincoln rally in Cooper Union, New York. His speech was an eloquent eulogy of Lincoln and a plea for his overwhelming election. Referring to his recent withdrawal Montgomery said: "I retired upon the recommendation of my father. My father has passed that period of life when its honors or its rewards or its glories have any charm for him. . . . He would not permit a son of his to stand in the way of the glorious and patriotic President who leads us on to success and to the final triumph that is in store for us." This continued to be Blair's attitude towards Lincoln the rest of his life. Up to the day of his death, in 1883, any man who attacked Lincoln's memory invariably found Montgomery Blair a most aggressive defender. On re-election, Lincoln offered Montgomery the choice of the ministership to Spain or Austria, but he declined, with the utmost good grace. After Lincoln's death the tide of Reconstruction, on the model of Thaddeus Stevens and Charles Sumner, drove him and Frank into the Democratic Party, but Lincoln never had a greater friend and admirer than the man whom political necessity had forced him to remove from his cabinet.

The venerable jurist who, in 1835, had succeeded John Marshall as Chief Justice of the United States, by conveniently dying on October 12, 1864, at the age of eighty-seven, ushered in the final episode in this Lincoln-Chase-Blair melodrama. Justice Taney's age and increasing feebleness had long riveted many anxious eyes on his probable successor. President Lincoln had already appointed three members of this highest court and that, in the natural course of mortality, he would be called upon to name its seventh presiding Justice had caused much apprehensive speculation. This anxiety was expressed in Ben Wade's indecent jest, that he had prayed God that Taney would sur-

[11] In the Blair family Montgomery was always called "the Judge."

vive the administration of James Buchanan but that the tenacious viability of the Chief Justice made it look as though he had overdone his invocations. Wade did not wish the proslavery Buchanan to appoint as Taney's successor another adherent of the principles which Taney had expounded in the Dred Scott case. General public opinion, well-based or not, that Jefferson Davis and the rebel cause had had, for more than three years, an ally in the Chief Justice of the United States did not cause that widespread regret over Taney's demise to which his great legal talents and high personal character would have entitled him. In the inevitable forecasts as to his successor, the name of Salmon Portland Chase had for some time held chief place. His views on slavery and Reconstruction made him the ideal candidate of the radicals. Those who believed in the soundness of his financial system regarded Chase as the man who could safely be entrusted with its defense and interpretation. Chase had not attained first eminence as a lawyer, for his practice had been constantly interrupted by his political career, and had, moreover, been most conspicuously identified with the defense of the black man; but most observers, including Lincoln, esteemed highly his intellectual powers, and had every confidence in his qualifications for the Supreme Bench. Chase had told Lincoln, more than once, that his real ambition was not the White House, but the Chief Justiceship. He had often remarked to intimates that he would like to spend the rest of his life on this court, but in no other capacity, he characteristically added, than as its head. Lincoln had said to several associates that, should a vacancy exist at any time during his presidential term, Chase would be the man. Not unnaturally, the Secretary had come to regard the appointment as already set apart for him. Hardly had Taney been laid to rest in his native Maryland when Charles Sumner and other radical leaders in the Senate and Fessenden and Stanton in the cabinet began besieging the President to fulfill general expectation and endow Mr. Chase with the property that had long been predestined to him.

That the elevation of Chase to what was generally regarded as the second place in the Federal system would rescue him from the embarrassments in which his foolish ambitions had enmeshed the man was one of the motives inciting his friends. But the more politically minded raised practical arguments against the choice. In the Seward-Thurlow Weed type of mind, Chase had lost all claim to consideration at Lincoln's hands. Seward's hostility toward Chase may be estimated from the man he urged Lincoln to appoint. He endorsed Montgomery Blair, a cabinet colleague with whom he was scarcely on speaking terms. Edward Bates also revolted from Chase as Chief Justice, in part perhaps because a hope was lurking in his breast that the President might look approvingly in his own direction. Bates had a national reputation as a jurist, and except for his seventy years might have been a favored candidate.

Welles, like Seward, favored Blair, but for different reasons; as always, Welles looked on the matter exclusively from public considerations; he had the highest respect for Blair's mentality, regarded the defender of Dred Scott as a great man of the law, and did not rank Chase highly for legal knowledge. Lincoln hesitated over Chase for one reason only. He did not accept at face value the Secretary's confession that his real ambition had always been John Marshall's seat and not the Presidency. Lincoln believed that, once in this exalted post, Chase would seek to use it as a steppingstone to the higher office. The President unfolded his mind freely to Charles Sumner, who was haunting his presence day and night in the interest of his friend. Would it not be a good idea, Lincoln asked Sumner, for him to send for Chase, and explain frankly the doubts that stood in the way of his preferment? He would tell Chase that if he would place behind him forever this impossible desire and devote his great powers exclusively to the bench, he would make one of the greatest Chief Justices in history. What Lincoln had in mind was to pledge Chase to lay aside all presidential hope in exchange for this appointment. Sumner pointed out a fact that had not occurred to him: that crass popular suspicion would charge that Lincoln had used his office as a means of getting rid of a troublesome political opponent. Lincoln agreed and abandoned the idea. If he could have followed his own personal inclinations, he would have selected Blair, whose father was pursuing him with almost the same assiduity as Sumner. But the idea was utterly impracticable. No man in the administration except Seward had been so unpopular with the Senate as Blair; there was no likelihood of his confirmation. The appointment would rip open again the party wounds that had been in large measure healed by his exit from the cabinet. To the pleas of Chase-hating politicians, who wrote and repeated to Lincoln all the hostile words and acts of which Chase had been guilty, he gave the same impatient reply. The President cared nothing, he said, for such arguments; the interests of the nation and the party were the only things to be considered. Personally he heartily disliked the man. Welles quotes William E. Chandler, Congressman from New Hampshire, to whom Lincoln confided that he would "rather swallow his buckthorn chair" than appoint Chase. One day, at the height of the excitement, one of Lincoln's secretaries placed on his desk a paper. "What is it?" asked Lincoln. It was a letter from Chase, couched in the most friendly terms. The President did not read it, but said, with a weary smile: "File it with his other recommendations." On December 6, Lincoln wrote out with his own hand and sent to the Senate the following document: "I nominate Salmon P. Chase of Ohio, to be Chief Justice of the Supreme Court of the United States, vice Roger B. Taney, deceased." [12]

Lincoln's fear was justified that Chase, after donning the Chief Justice's robe, would not drop his presidential yearning. Charles Sumner, after the nomination, rushed eagerly to the Chase home, to be the first man to congratulate him. He was met at the door by daughter Kate. The charming lady shook her forefinger, half mockingly, half in earnest, in Sumner's face. "And you, too, Mr. Sumner! You in this business of shelving papa? But never mind, I will defeat you all!" And almost at once father and daughter began laying plans for Chase's nomination in 1868. Despairing of any success from the Republicans, who would listen to no other candidate except Grant, father and daughter centered their hopes on the Democrats. As a result of their efforts, Chase received one half of one vote as the candidate of the convention that met in Tammany Hall, New York, and nominated Horatio Seymour. Yet at one time Chase's chances had seemed fairly good. "Competent judges have believed," wrote Albert Bushnell Hart, "that had Kate Chase been able to go into the convention and make her combinations on the spot she would have secured his nomination." [13]

Lincoln did not live long enough to witness the fulfillment of his belief that Chase would continue intriguing to become his successor. The last time the two men met face to face was on March 4, 1865, on the porch of the Capitol. On that occasion, Salmon P. Chase, Chief Justice of the United States, administered the oath of office to Abraham Lincoln, on his inauguration for his second term. One would like a record of the thoughts concealed in the minds of both men on this solemn occasion.

[12] Curiously, Lincoln does not give the appointee his correct title. The Constitution calls him simply "Chief Justice of the United States."

[13] *Life of Salmon Portland Chase*, in American Statesmen series. Ed. by J. T. Morse, Jr. Houghton Mifflin Co. p. 420.

INDEX